American Tragedy

**LAWRENCE SCHILLER
JAMES WILLWERTH**

AVON BOOKS
An Imprint of HarperCollins*Publishers*

AMERICAN TRAGEDY

"A BLOCKBUSTER."
New York Daily News

"THE JUICIEST JUICE BOOK YET! . . .
Schiller and Willwerth reconstruct, in stunning detail,
the events that followed the 1994 murders of
Nicole Brown and Ronald Goldman. . . . [Simpson]
emerges here as a calculating, tortured character who gives
this book the force of a great crime novel."
People

"A BOOK THAT IS IMPOSSIBLE TO PUT DOWN.
I haven't turned pages this quickly in years,
and the surprise of it for me is that I hated the
O. J. Simpson case while it was going on."
Norman Mailer

"GREAT NARRATIVE POWER. . . .
In the already vast Simpson literature, this book reaches
the furthest into the pith of the event, telling on an almost
day-to-day basis the way the defense team labored, plotted,
and squabbled its way toward rescuing Mr. Simpson from
what might very likely have been a conviction on charges
of murder. . . . *American Tragedy* will help us cope with
the deeper questions concerning racial morality
and justice raised by the Simpson affair."
New York Times

"I THOUGHT I KNEW EVERYTHING THERE WAS
TO KNOW ABOUT THE SIMPSON CASE,
UNTIL I READ *American Tragedy*.
I was riveted from beginning to end."
Dominick Dunne, author of *Another City, Not My Own*

To Suzanne, Marc, Howard, Anthony, and Cameron,
my wonderful children, and to Kathy Amerman,
my loving soul mate

—L.S.

You know, it was like a forest fire out of control
and you just had to watch it burn. There was nothing
you could do. I mean, we all felt helpless because it just
reached out and you can see more still growing.

FOREWORD

THIS BOOK IS A FACTUAL ACCOUNT OF THE DEFENSE OF O.J. Simpson in his criminal trial and the civil action that followed, and is directly based on personal interviews, documents, court transcripts, and other material I obtained while researching this work. More than three dozen people involved in the two trials were interviewed, nineteen face to face, in 240 separate conversations. Nine subjects sat with me for more than fourteen hours each. The transcripts of my interviews total more than 23,000 pages.

The information for this book comes from the collected memories of those interviewed and from my own observations since the early days of the case. As I have noted elsewhere in this book, I began my formal interviews in September 1995. In most cases the people I interviewed kept personal notes and diaries from the first days of their involvement in the case, and at their memories were supported by these notes and other written material.

Quotations from interviews have received limited editing merely to ensure a smooth transition from spoken to written form. Trial transcripts and other printed material have also been edited to a very limited degree, and I have tried to include the usual conventions of ellipses and brackets wherever possible. When any editing has been done, no material changes in meaning have been made. Quotation marks are sometimes used where conversations have been reconstructed from memory. In such instances, at least one of the participants has confirmed the substance of the conversation. On occasions when I have described conversations of which the memory of one participant may differ from others' in a material respect, the substance has been confirmed by a number of those present.

Since this is a book about the Simpson defense, I have not attempted to interview the prosecution team in the criminal trial, some of whom have published or will publish their own books and would have been understandably reluctant to share sensitive strategies with me.

—LAWRENCE SCHILLER

CONTENTS

Introduction

You've got to meet these guys, Joe Stellini told Bob and Tom Kardashian. Stellini was maître d' at the Luau, a singles hangout the brothers frequented. Born to wealth, yet restlessly earning their own first millions, Tom, the older brother, owned a Rolls-Royce; Bob didn't—yet. Devoutly religious but also bachelors-about-town, they were regulars at the La Scala in Beverly Hills, where Sinatra sometimes dropped in; they cruised the Factory, a flavor-of-the-moment disco. The guys Stellini wanted them to meet were celebrity athletes who made many of the same rounds: O.J. Simpson and Al Cowlings.

No small part of Stellini's introduction hinged on football. The brothers had played at Dorsey High School, one of the few integrated schools at the time. They lived and breathed football. At the University of Southern California, half a decade before Simpson and Cowlings arrived with athletic scholarships, they stayed close to the game as student managers, penciling in statistics and handing out towels when they might have been studying harder. You've got to meet these guys, Stellini insisted. He set up a Sunday tennis match in Beverly Hills. Harry and Pete Rothchild, two other Luau customers, had oil money and lived in a small castle with its own court on Summit Drive. Stellini arranged it.

The four met on a fine spring morning. At first Bob was intimidated. After all, Simpson had won a Heisman trophy. Though new to tennis, the athletes brought strength and superior speed to the court. Bob saw immediately that the famous running back with the big Afro was lightning at the net. His reflexes were amazing. You'd bang in a nice passing shot and he'd be right there. His teammate, Cowlings, owned a booming serve. Fortunately it missed sometimes. But it was Simpson's speed and agility, his awesome feet, that Bob remembered. The Kardashian brothers, skilled recreational players, ultimately triumphed in a close match lasting three sets.

After a few games, Bob relaxed. The professional jocks were friendly. At first, he felt that he was playing famous people. Then they were just a couple of guys who happened to be famous. The four went out to eat and everybody said, Hey, let's do it again next week.

Los Angeles in 1970, like those four men, was in its prime. An explosion in Watts five years earlier had shaken the city's smug assumption that everyone was equally happy in the City of the Angels. But where these men lived and socialized, there were fortunes to be made on movie lots, in recording studios, in aerospace, oil drilling, banking, and bread-and-butter farming.

Legend has it that fantasy has been the backbone of reality in California since the earliest days of the gold rush and the movie studios. If West Coast culture, as popular myth insists, can reinvent itself at whim, then the rich young men swatting tennis balls that morning in Beverly Hills were living examples of the self-transformations possible in California's chaotic scramble for riches and fame. Simpson and Cowlings were ghetto-born black men liberated by athletics from the culture of poverty. For millions of football fans, they were household names. The Kardashian brothers were the grandchildren of Russian-Armenian immigrants who made a fortune through their sweat and ingenuity. Aggressive and serious, Tom was learning what the family meat-packing business was all about. Bob, more of a maverick, loved music and had just opened his law practice. But that morning, all that mattered for these men in their mid-twenties was male bonding and a good forehand.

Something clicked for the four USC alumni. The game became a weekly ritual. The quartet began frequenting the city's best bars and restaurants, dining expensively, drinking, trolling for showcase women. Making the rounds together, they were always stars in the most exciting show in town.

Bob and O.J. got into a tight thing very fast. Tom, four years older, stayed more at the edge of the group. He'd already made one best-dressed list and was inclined to be a littly stuffy. They nicknamed him Mr. Mundane. The younger brother and Simpson shared a nasty sense of humor, a taste for practical jokes, an athletic flair, trash talk. One night they started talking to some woman in the Luau and Bob told her he was from the Armenian Mafia, an enforcer. He liked to break people's knees. She believed him; O.J. kept a poker face. Loved it. They started hanging out at night, going to dinner a lot. It seemed they talked about everything.

Simpson separated from his wife Marquerite for a year. Became interested in a young lady named Nicole Brown. He moved into the Kardashian brothers' plush home in Benedict Canyon complete with tennis court and swimming pool. The ultimate bachelor pad. He also rented space in Bob's law offices to oversee his off-the-gridiron businesses.

Life became even richer. Money followed by prestige.

Tom Kardashian had a Rolls Corniche. O.J. had a black '69 Rolls. Bob was still driving an old Pontiac Grand Prix, royal blue with black leather interior—maximum wheels by some standards. But in that crowd, the car to aspire to was a Rolls.

Then Bob finally bought his Rolls, also black. He even moved into the Summit Drive castle for a year. Priscilla Presley had bought it from the Rothchilds. Bob met Priscilla and before long Bob *hosted* those tennis matches. Cowlings, Simpson's childhood friend, stuck with his Cadillac. "I had a Corvette," Bob remembers. "My brother also kept a Lamborghini and a Jaguar XKE. We were living."

Charmed lives. They were living Everyman's—well, every twentieth-century American man's—fantasies.

American Tragedy

PART ONE

Five Days

1

Robert Kardashian, now a divorced, middle-aged millionaire, is in the bedroom of his spacious, cream-colored house in suburban Encino, California. He reads the Bible each morning. He begins his day with prayer. Every day. Today is June 13, 1994.

His faith is absolute. God had provided for his family's arrival in America and his life now. He'd heard the family stories so often. At the dawn of the century, an illiterate boy in a Russian-Armenian village is stricken with convulsions. The sick child cries out that he is God's messenger. For three days, as though God is guiding his hand, the frenzied boy writes a text prophesying apocalypse: Blood and slaughter will come. All Armenians will die. Leave this land. Go to Los Angeles, California.

Los Angeles?

No one in that village spoke English. No one had heard of Los Angeles. The City of Angels—the name might have come from a fairy tale. Yet the exodus began. Thousands of Armenians sold what they could, made their way across Europe, over the Atlantic, through Ellis Island, and across the whole continent to southern California. Only a few years later, Turkish soldiers swept through Armenia in murderous waves and slaughtered those who had failed to heed the boy's warning. Over one and one half million Armenians died in this century's first recorded genocide.

A government doctor at Ellis Island—Bob's grandfather loved to tell this story—made a smudged pencil mark at the bottom of his entry card. The twelve-year-old had failed the vision test: Entry denied. The card hung on a cord around

Grandfather's neck, and he tucked it under the top of his sweater. Other inspectors, farther along, were pushing the crowds through quickly. They let him pass. Another bit of help from the Lord to bring the Kardashian clan safely to America.

"I do not concern myself with great matters or things too wonderful for me. . . . O Israel, put your hope in the Lord both now and forevermore," the psalm concluded. Bob closed the Bible and knelt by the bed.

His prayers completed, Kardashian began his second morning ritual, twenty minutes on a StairMaster, the same on a treadmill. He liked routine. He showered, shaved, and breakfasted on nonfat yogurt, granola, and orange juice, then started work about eight A.M. His office was a large study in the middle of his house. He was two hours into his day when the phone rang; it was Shelli Azoff, a family friend married to Irving Azoff, who owned Giant Records and managed the superstar rock group the Eagles. Kardashian had made his first fortune in the music business and was now working on the second, but Shelli's call today was personal.

"I just heard about Nicole," she began.

"What do you mean?" The statement meant nothing to Kardashian.

"You don't know?"

"Know what?"

"I heard Nicole was shot and killed."

It didn't really register. Bob asked again: "What?"

"I just heard that."

"From whom?"

"From Alex."

Many of his friends, both men and women, went to Alex Roldan's salon on San Vicente Boulevard. This wasn't real. You don't hear from hairstylists about your friends dying.

"Shelli, that can't be. I'll call O.J., and I'll call you right back."

He felt a rush of unfamiliar emotions as he dialed his former secretary, Cathy Randa, who now worked for O.J. Simpson.

Cathy was in a meeting, couldn't be reached. Kardashian

dialed a private number at Simpson's home. A voice unknown to him answered.

"Who is this?" Bob asked.

"Who are you?"

"This is Robert Kardashian. I'm a friend of O.J.'s. Is he there?"

Kardashian didn't recognize the flat male voice. The man had said his name but it meant nothing to him. None of this was normal.

"Mr. Simpson isn't home," the voice said. He added he wasn't sure if the athlete was even in town. Kardashian wasn't sure, either. With Simpson's constant traveling, they caught up with each other when they could. Six months might pass between meetings, but when they did get together, it was as if they'd seen each other the day before.

"Well, uh, who are you?" Kardashian knew he had asked this before.

"I'm LAPD, Detective Fuhrman."

"Why are you there?" Kardashian asked.

"I can't say."

"Can you answer this? I heard that Nicole was shot and killed."

"She has been killed." The voice was flat, official.

"You mean, she wasn't shot?"

"All I can say is she was killed."

Bob was losing it. There must be more to ask, but he couldn't think of anything. He hung up feeling stupid. He dialed Shelli and repeated what he'd heard. He kept the conversation short. He didn't want to talk.

What had happened was beyond anything he could fathom. At parties buzzing with cocaine, he never indulged. Cruising the bars with O.J. and the gang, he sipped iced tea, went home at midnight. He drank the occasional glass of wine, nothing more. His steadfast religious faith was known and respected. But he was a hard businessman, a tough competitor, taking whatever advantage he could.

There was a side of him that was like O.J. Bob was a sports-loving jock. He partied hard. And if he had a weakness the church surely disapproved of, it was women. He kept that side of himself under strict control, but it was there. These things were all part of Kardashian's world. Murder was not.

Denice Halicki, a statuesque blonde who shared his house and life, came in. They had been together five years. A marriage was planned.

"I'm going over to O.J.'s," he told her. "Nicole was killed." He heard the words, but couldn't believe he was saying them.

That morning the 405 freeway was bumper-to-bumper. At the best of times Kardashian dreaded the 405, which passes Encino heading south toward West Los Angeles, then down to greater congestion near the airport. He took Mulholland Drive over to the on ramp at Sepulveda and found gridlock almost immediately. He spotted a pileup farther down and turned back on Sepulveda toward a longer route through the canyons.

Usually, driving the canyons was a pleasure in his two-seater Mercedes. Great houses on Mulholland Drive, hills still lush from the winter rains, mountains to the north, strange homes propped up on steep terrain by long stilts that somehow survive earthquakes. But today Bob noticed none of this. Winding down Beverly Glen, he called his ex-wife, Kris. She and Nicole were extremely close, and during his divorce the two wives' friendship made it hard for him to spend time with O.J. Awkward. But that was years in the past. Now Kris was married to Olympic decathlon gold medalist Bruce Jenner.

Kris was trying to phone Bob at his house when he got through.

"I just heard Nicole was killed," he said.

"I know, it's horrible. I can't believe it. Judy Brown called me." Judy was Nicole's mother. She said she'd talked to Nicole about eleven the previous night.

"She did?"

"I was supposed to have lunch with Nicole today at eleven-thirty."

Kris couldn't stay on the phone very long. She needed to call back Nicole's sister Denise.

"God," Kardashian blurted out to Kris, "I hope O.J. didn't do it."

Kris was silent. She knew what her ex-husband didn't: Simpson's relationship with Nicole had been turbulent, an emotional roller coaster. But neither said anything about Bob's wild comment. Marriages gone wrong and painful divorces were the stuff of everyday life—both of them could attest to that. Murder belonged to some alternate universe of tabloid headlines and bad movies. Bob's remark was just one of those crazy things that fall out of your mouth when reality blindsides you.

The homes became mansions as Beverly Glen neared Sunset Boulevard. Kardashian turned west on Sunset, drove past the vast UCLA campus and over the hated 405, and made a right turn on Rockingham. He pulled up in front of Simpson's house just after eleven o'clock. The press was gathering. The police were everywhere. He walked up to a tall African-American cop at the front gate.

"I'm a friend of O.J.'s. Can I see him?"

"You can't come in."

Normally he walked in without thinking. "I'm one of his closest friends," he insisted.

"I'm sorry, you can't come in. He's not even here."

"Where is he?" He couldn't believe he was asking that question.

"He'll be here soon."

Nobody would tell him anything. He stood around for about fifteen minutes. Fear and confusion mingled, then turned to annoyance. Finally he was thinking, to hell with it, and getting ready to leave, when Howard and Margaret Weitzman drove up.

Margaret was driving the family Range Rover. Bob and Margaret had dated for a while. After that, he gave a party in Benedict Canyon and Howard asked to meet her. He and Howard had been schoolmates at Dorsey High and USC.

Ten years ago Howard had been one of the country's most prominent criminal attorneys, the man who got John DeLorean acquitted after a jury watched the accused selling a stash of cocaine to an FBI undercover agent on videotape. Weitzman had moved over to entertainment law in recent years, but his instincts for criminal defense were still sharp. He'd helped Michael Jackson recently. And he represented Simpson in 1989 against charges of spousal abuse.

Now, today, arriving at O.J. Simpson's house, Howard wore a suit. Bob was amazed: Howard was dressed for battle.

They hugged each other, but when Kardashian asked what was going on inside, his friend turned all lawyer. He said he himself had to find out, and got back into the car just as the gate opened. The Range Rover disappeared inside; a few minutes later, Margaret drove away alone.

Standing among all the rubberneckers, Kardashian felt like a fool tourist. He had decided to leave when Skip Taft's black Cadillac pulled up about fifty feet down the street. Skip was a lawyer and O.J.'s business adviser. Cathy Randa sat in the backseat. The car stopped. O.J. Simpson, grim-faced, head down, carrying a black duffel bag over his shoulder, got out and walked through the Rockingham gate with Taft on his heels. Kardashian stood in the crowd. O.J. hadn't looked his way.

O.J. saw a cop standing next to the playhouse in the front yard and walked up to him. "What's this all about?" he asked the officer. For a second the cop, Brad Roberts, was caught off guard. "Don't you remember the phone call you got this morning telling you your wife, or ex-wife rather, was murdered last night?"

Simpson looked around. He said he knew that. Of course he knew. But he wanted to know why all the police were at his house.

"Well, O.J., I'm not the detective handing this case, but I'll tell you this. We're here because a blood trail led us here."

"A blood trail?" His voice carried a hint of a question.

Outside another gate to the house, another old friend of O.J.'s was feeling as stymied as Bob Kardashian. Wayne Hughes was a prominent USC alum who had known O.J.

since 1968. Simpson used to bring his first wife, Marquerite, and their kids for barbecues and swimming at his home. Their families had vacationed together. In recent years, they hadn't socialized as much: Hughes's second wife thought Simpson was too full of himself. Hughes didn't disagree—he'd never met anybody so concerned with his public image. But his friendship with O.J. was complex. The athlete had other redeeming qualities.

Now Hughes had come over to show solidarity, but the police wouldn't let him in. Hughes drove off to get on with his day; he'd get in touch later.

Detective Phil Vannatter, who looks like a tough guy and your kindly grandfather rolled into one, got back to Rockingham at noon with a search warrant. He has twenty-five years on the force, grandchildren now, and smokes too much.

Vannatter figures he has personally investigated at least two hundred murder cases and been involved with another five hundred.

The cop doesn't talk to the press much. When he does, he isn't necessarily polite. A year and half earlier, Culver City police sergeant Harvey Bailey told detectives he went roller blading alone at two A.M., then went home to pick up cookies his wife had baked and took them to the CC headquarters at four. She was in bed and he didn't wake her. It was Christmas morning. He came home at six to find her dead, strangled. Since the marriage was a mess, and Bailey had a girlfriend, Vannatter started looking at him. Bailey got a lawyer and went to the *Los Angeles Times*.

This annoyed the big cop. "We have not eliminated anybody as a suspect or settled on anyone as the prime suspect," Vannatter told the *Times* reporter. But he added: "If your spouse had been murdered and you didn't have anything to do with it, would you run and get an attorney?" Nobody expected warmth and fuzziness from Phil Vannatter. But by cop standards, he was considered straight.

Vannatter knew Simpson would be arriving soon. He told a uniformed officer at the gate to make sure Simpson didn't get inside the house.

Vannatter hadn't been there ten minutes when he heard Simpson was on the premises. A cop had put cuffs on him. Vannatter walked out to tell Simpson what was up. Howard Weitzman, an attorney he knew from many cases, approached O.J. Weitzman wanted the handcuffs off. Unless Vannatter was arresting Simpson.

Vannatter felt he had probable cause for an arrest, but he wouldn't have the scientific evidence until later in the week. The law requires you to file the case within forty-eight hours after taking a suspect into custody. Getting test results from the lab that fast wasn't possible. And the media were everywhere; it would be embarrassing if the blood evidence somehow ruled out Simpson.

Vannatter took out his key and released the cuffs. Simpson seemed very subdued. Then he invited Simpson and his attorney to Parker Center for a talk. That was downtown police headquarters.

Cathy Randa had emerged from Taft's car holding a Louis Vuitton garment bag. Kardashian walked over to her, thinking of a way to hustle himself inside the house.

"Robert, how horrible. Can you believe this?"

"Cathy, I don't even know what's going on. Let me take that bag." He was a gentleman.

"This is Mr. Simpson's luggage," Kardashian said to the cop at the gate. "May I bring it in?"

"You can't come in."

"But I've got his luggage here."

"I don't care. You can't come in."

Nice try. He and Cathy stepped aside, and he set the bag down. Hugging, talking again about how strange and frightening things seemed, a rush of words about "poor Nicole."

Kardashian and Randa watched Weitzman walk over to Vannatter and say something. Reporters and cameramen stood everywhere. Then Simpson walked toward an LAPD car parked in the driveway. He dropped his head and got in.

"We're going to Parker Center," Howard said to Bob as he walked out the gate. Skip Taft and Howard Weitzman got in Taft's car and drove away after them.

10

Kardashian offered to drive Cathy over to Simpson's offices on San Vicente Boulevard, two miles away. It seemed the only thing left to do right now. He picked up the Louis Vuitton bag and threw it in the trunk of his Mercedes. If nothing else, he could answer phones. That way he wouldn't have to think too deeply.

At Johnnie Cochran's Wilshire office ten miles east of the murder scene, everybody was talking. Cochran wasn't in, but his staff had one eye on the television news and wondered if he was already involved. Cochran is the city's most prominent black trial lawyer, a mesmerizing courtroom orator and cunning strategist as well as a sartorial peacock and social butterfly. But at the law firm he founded, his private office is centrally located and exactly the same size as the space given each of his attorneys. This encouraged easy hallway chat. If the boss had been in, everyone on staff would have dropped by sooner or later to hear the inside dope. And Johnnie would have it.

Of course, everyone from partner to secretary would want to know if they were getting the case, but no one would have asked Johnnie directly. If he wanted you to know, he'd mention it.

Today, as on most days, the office was busy. Cochran's lawyers had made millions over the years suing law enforcement agencies. Given the sorry state of American race relations, finding black victims of police abuse was about as difficult as getting wet in the rain. The firm's distinct African-American identity made it a pleasant place to work. Johnnie bought tables at most major social functions, black and white. Moving in the right circles and representing high-profile clients came with the territory. Johnnie was involved in Michael Jackson's problems. Two years earlier, he had convinced a jury to acquit Todd Bridges of murder despite witnesses who swore the young actor had shot his victim point-blank.

But the buzz that Monday morning was subdued. O.J.'s troubles might not bring the black community out in force. If Magic Johnson had been taken in for questioning about the death of his wife, African-Americans in Los Angeles would have been ready to riot. Johnson was not just a black superstar, but a local hero. He owned businesses in the community, involved himself in African-American issues, and contributed to local churches and charities. But many black athletes who found success ran across town with it. Often they married white women, glamorous "trophy wives" to replace the black wives they'd "outgrown." Black women took that very personally.

Many African-Americans in Los Angeles didn't think O.J. Simpson had the slightest sense of his roots. Even back in the days when he had a black wife, he lived in Bel Air with white neighbors. Then he dumped Marquerite for a hot blonde and never looked back. He didn't attend community events; he didn't put serious money into black businesses. When one of his few community ventures, a fast-food chicken place, was barbecued during the 1992 riots, everybody noticed that he didn't rebuild.

"I hope he did it," said a clear, distinct female voice. Shawn Chapman was a sassy former public defender, one of the firm's newest hires, a UCLA graduate who detested the star running back. Simpson was a classic black jock who chased white women. Years earlier, she had been on a student picket line protesting the pending execution of Robert Alton Harris when Simpson cruised by in his Bentley. He looked at the pretty black student holding up a sign—and stared right through her.

"And I hope he goes to prison!" Chapman sounded as if she meant it.

That was too much for Carl Douglas, the firm's managing attorney. Simpson was no hero, but he was still a black man about to get entangled with the white-run criminal justice system. "What's wrong with you?" Douglas barked. "He's a black man. How can you say that?"

Simpson had arrived at Parker Center and was about to be interviewed by Vannatter and his partner, Detective Tom Lange, when Weitzman and Taft walked in.

Vannatter didn't want Weitzman in the interview room. The only way we'll interview him is with you not here, the cop said. His lawyer doesn't have to be present. He isn't under arrest. As blunt as that.

Weitzman knew Vannatter was bluffing. But O.J. insisted he could handle this himself, no problem, nothing to hide. That was the trouble with superstars. Ego. Image. Hang with your lawyer and people are going to think bad things.

POLICE: This is Detective Philip Vannatter. I'm here with my partner, Detective Lange. We're in an interview room in Parker Center. The date is June the 13th, 1994; and the time is 13:35 hours, and we're here with O.J. Simpson. Is that Orenthal James Simpson?

SIMPSON: Orenthal James Simpson, yes.

The athlete is alone with them.

POLICE: Okay, Mr. Simpson, you have the right to remain silent. If you give up the right to remain silent, anything you say can and will be used against you in a court of law. You have the right to speak with an attorney and have an attorney present during questioning.

Simpson mouths an understanding.

They continue the *Miranda* warning. Simpson says okay to everything.

POLICE: Okay. And you give up your right to an attorney present while we talk?

SIMPSON: Yes.

Kardashian and Randa pulled into the underground parking garage serving the boxy white building at 11661 San Vicente. The Starbuck's where Nicole used to drink cappuccino with friends like Faye Resnick and Cora Fischman is just down the street. They walked into Orenthal Enterprises, Suite 632, as Kardashian had done hundreds of times, and O.J. was everywhere. Football pictures, moments with celebrities, award photos. He covered the walls of the small

13

reception area where Cathy sat. His image lined the hallways and filled his office. There he was standing with ex-president Gerald Ford. Over here he was scoring a touchdown. Now he's in the announcing booth. Big smiles, showbiz poses. The camera loves O.J., and he loves it back.

Kardashian sat down at Simpson's oak rolltop desk and started answering phones. He had a view of the Santa Monica mountains to the north but hardly noticed. A TV in a wooden cabinet could have provided news, but he didn't turn it on.

Cathy stayed outside at her desk. The calls never stopped. Whoever was free grabbed a ringing line. They told friends what little they knew. To the media they said nobody could make a statement now.

Half the world seemed to be calling to say how horrible it was, and Kardashian commiserated as well as he could. They asked how O.J. was feeling. Bad, he guessed. How are the kids doing? He didn't know. Buffalo Bills football people. Hertz people. Show business people. The press. And more press. Bob didn't attempt to keep count.

Kansas City Chiefs running back Marcus Allen called from a marlin-fishing competition in the Cayman Islands. He had been playing golf, and someone from the pro shop came out and said he had an emergency call. "Marcus," said his wife's sister, Debbie Cornell, "I have bad news. It's Nicole." Then Debbie said she was murdered, and the police thought O.J. did it. Allen was hungry for information now and had called people in Los Angeles, including Al Cowlings. A.C. said O.J. was okay, and little else. Marcus Allen told Kardashian he just couldn't believe what he was hearing. He called several times, saying it again and again.

All afternoon Kardashian wrestled only with acceptable thoughts. No room in his head for the idea that his friend had killed anybody. Cathy said O.J. had gone to Chicago. He had an alibi. Someone said they heard on TV that Nicole was killed with a knife; O.J. wouldn't use a knife. Juice owned nine guns, including an Uzi. A knife didn't fit into any scenario Kardashian could imagine.

So who could have done this horrible thing?

14

POLICE: Okay. . . . We're investigating, obviously, the death of your ex-wife and another man.

SIMPSON: Someone told me that.

POLICE: And we're going to need to talk to you about that. Are you divorced from her now?

SIMPSON: Yes.

POLICE: . . . What was your relationship with her?

SIMPSON: Well, we tried to get back together and it just didn't work, so we were going our separate ways.

POLICE: Recently you tried to get back together?

SIMPSON: We tried to get back together for about a year, you know, where we started . . . seeing each other . . . probably three weeks ago or so we said it just wasn't working.

POLICE: . . . How was your separation?

SIMPSON: The first separation?

POLICE: Yeah. Was there problems with that?

SIMPSON: For me it was big problems. I loved her, I didn't want us to separate.

POLICE: I understand that she had made a couple of crime reports, annoying crime reports or something?

SIMPSON: We had a big fight, uh, about six years ago on New Year's. . . . Then we had an altercation, about a year ago, maybe. It wasn't a physical—you know, I kicked her door or something.

POLICE: And then she made a police report on those two occasions?

SIMPSON: And I stayed—stayed right there until the police came and talked to them.

Weitzman was deeply frustrated that he couldn't get Simpson to follow the most basic defense procedure: Don't talk to the police without your lawyer, ever. But he and Simpson knew each other socially. It was all too casual, this.

With Simpson in the closed interview room, he and Taft had nothing to do. Parker Center's waiting areas aren't

15

designed for comfort. Weitzman particularly liked the cappuccino served at a nearby café. He and Taft headed over there.

POLICE: . . . When was the last time you saw Nicole, O.J.?

SIMPSON: We were leaving the dance recital, she took off and I was talking to her parents.

Simpson explains that the recital, at Paul Revere Junior High School, where his daughter Sydney danced, ended about 6:30 P.M., quarter to seven. Nicole drove away and returned a few minutes later in her black Cherokee van. Judy Brown climbed in, while the kids piled into Nicole's sister's car. Simpson got into his Bentley.

POLICE: . . . What time did you leave the recital?

SIMPSON: We were all leaving then. . . . Her mother said something about me joining them for dinner, and I said, no thanks.

POLICE: Where did you go from there, O.J.?

SIMPSON: Uh, home for a while. And got in my car for a while, tried to find my girlfriend for a while. Came back to the house.

POLICE: Who was home?

SIMPSON: Kato.

POLICE: So what time do you think you got back home, actually physically got home?

SIMPSON: 7:00 something.

POLICE: . . . Were you scheduled to play golf this morning someplace?

SIMPSON: In Chicago.

POLICE: . . . What time did you leave last night, leave the house?

SIMPSON: To go to the airport?

POLICE: Mmnh-mmnh.

SIMPSON: The limo was supposed to be there at 10:45. Normally they get there a little earlier. I was rushing

16

around, and somewhere between then and 11 o'clock.

POLICE: . . . Did you converse with the driver at all?

SIMPSON: He was a new driver.

POLICE: Remember his name?

SIMPSON: No. Just about rushing to the airport, about how I live my life on airplanes and in hotels. So that, that type of thing.

The American Airlines flight took off at 11:45 P.M.

About five miles from Parker Center, where Simpson is talking to the detectives, coroner's investigator Claudine Ratcliffe pulls on latex gloves, takes a pair of manicure scissors from a drawer, and clips Nicole Brown Simpson's nails closer than a living person could tolerate.

In the gloomy intake room of the Forensic Science Center, the rank odor of decaying flesh competes with the sharp smell of powerful disinfectants. This is where L.A. County coroner's office employees process freshly killed human beings. The atmosphere is toned down, quiet. On the examining table, Nicole remains in a semifetal position. Her hands are curled up in death. Ratcliffe slides the clippings from each hand into separate folded papers, and labels them. Next she pulls a thin birch stick from a sterile plastic package and scrapes under the remaining stumps of Nicole's fingernails. These scrapings are sealed separately. Finally, she clips samples of Nicole's head and limb hair and puts each sample into its own envelope.

POLICE: So yesterday, you did drive the white Bronco?

SIMPSON: Mmnh-mmnh.

POLICE: Where did you park it when you drove it home?

SIMPSON: The first time probably by the mailbox. Normally I will park it by the mailbox.

POLICE: Where did you park it yesterday for the last time, do you remember?

SIMPSON: Right where it is . . . on Rockingham.

17

POLICE: About what time was that?

SIMPSON: 8:00 something. Maybe 7, 8 o'clock. 8, 9 o'clock. I don't know. Right in that area. . . . Like I said, I came home, I got in my car, I was going to see my girlfriend. I was calling her and she wasn't around.

POLICE: . . . You got home in the Rolls. . . . And then you got in the Bronco?

SIMPSON: My phone was in the Bronco . . . the Bronco is what I drive. I'd rather drive it than any other car. And I was going over there and I called her a couple of times and she wasn't there . . . and I checked my messages, she had left me a message that she wasn't there, that she had to leave town. And then I came back and ended up sitting with Kato.

POLICE: And you weren't in a hurry when you came back with the white Bronco?

SIMPSON: No.

POLICE: The reason I ask you, the car is parked kind of at a funny angle, it's stuck out in the street.

SIMPSON: I don't know if it's a funny angle or what. . . . It's parked because when I was hustling at the end of the day to get all my stuff, and I was getting on the phone and everything, I forgot to pull—when I pulled it—bringing it out of the gate there . . . it's like, it's like it's a tight turn.

POLICE: So you had it inside the compound?

SIMPSON: Yeah . . . I brought it inside the compound to get my stuff out of it. . . . And I put it out and I run back in the gate before the gate closes.

POLICE: . . . Okay. How did you get the injury on your hand?

SIMPSON: I don't know. When I was in Chicago, I know how. But at the house I was just running around. . . .

POLICE: How did you do it in Chicago?

SIMPSON: I broke a glass. One of you guys called me and I was in the bathroom, and I just kind of went bonkers for a little bit.

POLICE: Is that how you cut it?

SIMPSON: It was cut before, but I think I just opened it again. I'm not sure. . . .

POLICE: Do you recall bleeding at all in your truck, in the Bronco?

SIMPSON: I recall bleeding at my house, and then I went to the Bronco.

POLICE: . . . So do you recall bleeding at all?

SIMPSON: Yeah. I mean, I knew I was bleeding, but it was no big deal. I bleed all the time. I mean, it's— I'm always—I play golf, and there's always something, nicks and stuff.

POLICE: So did you do anything? When did you put the Band-Aid on it?

SIMPSON: Actually, I asked a girl this morning for it.

POLICE: Yeah. And she got it.

SIMPSON: Yeah, 'cause last night when I was leaving, Kato was saying something to me and I was rushing to get my phone, and I put a little thing on it and it stopped.

Vannatter asks about the last time Simpson visited his ex-wife's house. The athlete explains that he is there constantly, "dropping the kids off, picking the kids up, kicking around with the dog." But he doesn't go in, especially since he began seeing Paula Barbieri. He says he doesn't know where Nicole and her parents went to dinner.

POLICE: You haven't had any problems with her lately, have you?

SIMPSON: I always have problems with her. You know, that's our relationship. It's been a problem relationship.

POLICE: . . . Did she have words with you last night?

SIMPSON: Pardon me?

POLICE: Did Nicole have words with you last night?

SIMPSON: No, not at all.

At the Forensic Science Center intake room, Ratcliffe concludes that the second victim's fingernails are too short to be clipped. He has been identified as Ronald Goldman. She skips the birch stick as well. There is nothing to scrape under. A hair sample, taken from his head, goes into a sealed envelope. She passes on chest hair: Goldman has none.

John Jacobo steps in next to take fingerprints. When he is finished, a technician follows to take blood samples. Goldman's and Nicole's hearts can no longer fill even a small vial. The technician has to harvest Goldman's blood from his lungs. Nicole's is taken from her calf and right thigh. The bodies are wheeled into cold storage to await autopsy next morning.

Johnnie Cochran returned in the afternoon. He worked with his jacket on and his expensive tie pulled tight. Style mattered in that office. They had no formal dress code, but attorneys guilty of sartorial misdemeanors, frayed collars, unimaginative ties, uncrisp suits, were talked about, even mocked. Cochran, a fountain of imagination, set the tone.

The office was angrily abuzz because it looked as if they weren't going to get the Simpson case. At first Cochran simply went into his office and said nothing. Everyone assumed he was furious. It was insulting that Simpson hadn't hired a black lawyer, and the black lawyer to hire in Los Angeles was Johnnie Cochran.

Lawyers crowded around Jan Thomas at the reception desk. She was a good source of information; all calls went through her. She was Johnnie's number one fan and very excitable. Johnnie was nowhere to be found, she said, and O.J. had called.

Of course Simpson hadn't called. But someone might have called and asked if he did. That was close enough. On TV, Simpson left Rockingham with Howard next to him, so everyone figured Weitzman had the case. They had to assume Johnnie was upset. But no one would ask, and he probably wouldn't show it. Anger wasn't Johnnie's style. When his ego was bruised, he toned down, sank into himself a bit. And he stayed out of the office.

But if Johnnie was upset today, he didn't show it. He called out to people who walked by, bringing them in, letting them know he was plugged in. He'd talked to Weitzman, he said. The two firms were working jointly on Michael Jackson's problems, after all. Cochran and Weitzman were old friends.

Johnnie had talked to other sources, too. He'd heard about incriminating material that the TV news didn't have. So much stuff that you had to assume the Juice did it. Simpson had a big collection of swords and exotic knives, Cochran said. O.J.'s car had blood in it. There was blood on the airplane. It sounded bad.

The lawyers were impressed that Johnnie was passing along news that wasn't on television. In time Johnnie would learn that half of it was wrong.

POLICE: O.J., we've got sort of a problem.

SIMPSON: Mmnh-mmnh.

POLICE: We've got some blood on and in your car. We've got some blood at your house. And it's sort of a problem.

SIMPSON: Well, we'll take my blood test and we'll see.

POLICE: Well, we'd like to do that. We've got, of course, the cut on your finger that you aren't real clear on.

SIMPSON: Can't be any clearer than I am, you know.

POLICE: Okay. Do you recall having that cut on your finger the last time you were at Nicole's house?

SIMPSON: A week ago?

POLICE: Yeah.

SIMPSON: No.

POLICE: Oh, so it's since then?

SIMPSON: Oh, I'm pretty sure, yeah. Just last night . . . when I was rushing to get out of my house.

POLICE: . . . What do you think happened? Do you have any idea?

SIMPSON: I have no idea, man. I—

POLICE: She didn't get any threatening phone calls?

21

SIMPSON: You guys haven't told me anything. I have no idea what happened. When you . . . said something to me today that somebody else might have been involved. . . . Everytime I ask, you guys say you're going to tell me in a bit.

POLICE: Well, we don't know a lot of the answers to those questions yet ourselves, O.J.

SIMPSON: Well, I've got a bunch of guns, I got guns all over the place, you know. You can take them, they're all there. I keep them in my car for an incident that happened a month ago that my in-laws, my wife and everybody knows about. . . . it was like 3:30 in the morning and I'm in a lane and all of a sudden the car in front of me is going real slow. . . . There's a car next to me and I can't change lanes . . . the car butts up to me, and I'm like caught between three cars, and they're Oriental guys and they weren't letting me go anywhere. And finally I went on the shoulder and sped up and then I held my phone up so they can see the light part of it, you know, 'cause I have tinted windows. And they kind of scattered.

POLICE: . . . You think they were trying to rip you off maybe?

SIMPSON: I thought definitely they were.

POLICE: Did Nicole mention she had been getting any threats lately . . . anything she was concerned about?

SIMPSON: . . . No, not at all.

Simpson talks again about trying unsuccessfully to reconcile with Nicole. He adds, "I don't think we had sex since I've been back from San Juan," where he'd been making a TV pilot. "And that was, what, two months ago."

POLICE: Did you ever hit her, O.J.?

SIMPSON: That one night, we had a fight. Hey, she hit me.

POLICE: Yeah.

SIMPSON: You know, and as I say, they never took my statement, they never wanted to hear my side, and they never wanted to hear, uh, the housekeeper's side. Nicole was drunk, she started tearing up my house, you know. And I didn't punch her or anything, but I—I—

POLICE: Slapped her a couple of times?

SIMPSON: No. No, I wrestled her is all I did. I mean, you know, I wrestled—Nicole is a strong girl, she's one of the most conditioned women. Since that period of time she's hit me a few times, but I've never touched her after that. And I'm telling you, this is five, six years ago.

He remembers giving Nicole "either the bracelet or the earrings" on her birthday, May 19. She returned them. "Take credit to her, she felt that it wasn't right that she had it and I said, good, because I want them back." Simpson tells Vannatter and Lange he's "in a funny place on this" because he then gave the jewelry to Paula Barbieri, never letting on where it came from.

POLICE: Did Mr. Weitzman talk to you anything about this polygraph we brought up before?

SIMPSON: No.

POLICE: What were your thoughts on that?

SIMPSON: Should I talk about my thoughts on that?

POLICE: Well, I mean, it's up to you.

SIMPSON: No, I mean, I'm sure eventually I'll do it. But it's like, hey, I've got some weird thoughts now. And I've had weird thoughts—you know, you've been with a person for seventeen years, you think everything.

POLICE: I understand.

SIMPSON: I've got to understand what this thing is, I don't—

POLICE: I understand.

SIMPSON: You know, if it's true blue I don't mind doing it.

POLICE: Well, you're not compelled at all to take this

thing, number one. And, number two, I don't know if Mr. Weitzman explained to you, this goes to exclusion of someone as much as to the inclusion.

SIMPSON: Yeah.

POLICE: Although, we do that to eliminate people. . . . You understand the reason we're talking to you is because you're the ex-husband.

SIMPSON: I know I'm the number one target. And now you're telling me I've got blood all over the place.

POLICE: Well, there's blood at your house, in the driveway, and that footstep. We've got a search warrant. . . . Is that your blood that's dripped there?

SIMPSON: If it's dripped, it's what I dripped running around trying to leave.

POLICE: Last night?

SIMPSON: Yeah . . . I was trying to get out of the house. I didn't pay any attention to it. . . .

POLICE: . . . So it was about five days ago you last saw Nicole. Was it at the house?

SIMPSON: Okay, the last time I saw Nicole, Jesus, physically saw Nicole—I saw her obviously last night. Uh, the time before, I'm trying to think. . . . Today is Monday, right? I went to Washington on maybe Wednesday. Thursday I think I was in Connecticut, then Long Island Thursday afternoon and all of Friday. I got home Friday afternoon. Paula picked me up at the airport. I played golf Saturday. And when I came home I think my son was there. So I did something with my son. I don't think I saw Nicole at all then. And then I went to a big affair with Paula Saturday night. And I got up and played golf Sunday, which pissed Paula off. So it was about a week before I saw her at the, uh, you know—

POLICE: Okay. And the last time you saw Nicole, was that at her house?

SIMPSON: Uhm, I don't remember. I wasn't in her house. . . . I don't physically remember the last time I saw her. . . .

Simpson seemed dazed when he walked into the Brentwood office suite about four P.M. Weitzman and Taft were with him. He hugged Kardashian and Cathy Randa, but when Kardashian asked what happened downtown, his answers were vague. Kardashian was curious and worried, but he wasn't going to push.

O.J. took a chair in the middle of the room. Someone turned on the television. Howard told them the police took a statement. This is what they normally do. Standard procedure. Kardashian realized that Howard was trying to make everyone comfortable. Weitzman added that he was sure everything would be fine. Kardashian wanted more: What did you say in the statement?

Simpson seemed disconnected from the conversation. "I told them what I knew," he said in a low voice. He added later that he gave blood and the police photographed the cut on his finger.

They watched television for about two hours, and nobody talked in detail about anything. The case was all over the TV. You could surf every channel and find little else. And here was the guy at the center of the mystery. But his lawyers weren't talking, and he wasn't talking. Kardashian wasn't asking.

Except for Cathy, it could have been a gathering of suburban men watching a sports event. Nobody talked about anything important or in any way personal. Kardashian wondered about the TV reports of a second victim, the man who hadn't been publicly identified. But he said nothing.

Simpson kept saying he couldn't believe this had happened. Sitting there in a golf shirt and slacks, he was quiet and subdued for the most part. He said he didn't believe it. Then his voice rose as the words cascaded out: You know, they're treating me like I'm a suspect! They're treating me as if I did it! For Kardashian time had stopped. A sense of unreality filled the room, choking off words. Nobody answered O.J. Kardashian stared at the television, said nothing. I can't believe this, Orenthal James Simpson said again and again. I can't believe this is happening.

2

TAKE ME HOME, SIMPSON ASKED KARDASHIAN WHEN THE small talk petered out and TV news had nothing new to say.

Bob looked over at O.J. as he drove. He seemed to be in a fog. Kardashian wondered if he was registering events outside the car. The only sound in the car was O.J. saying, again and again, I can't believe this is happening to me. I can't believe Nicole is dead.

When Kardashian turned off Sunset about 6:30 P.M., he saw the TV satellite trucks. Their antennae pushed skyward like wintry trees along Rockingham for several blocks. Crews sat by vans in folding chairs, camera people rushed around. Kardashian was appalled.

At the front gate, the media spotted Simpson and stampeded. Camera lenses filled every window, flashes went off, floodlights blinded them.

He crept along at five miles an hour, assuming the reporters would fall back before he ran them over. Before leaving the office, he had called to alert the house. Someone was opening the gate now.

Kardashian's relief that the clamoring mob was behind him lasted until he saw that police were searching O.J.'s place like a crime scene. Uniformed and plainclothes officers stalked around the compound. Detective Lange waited at the front door and fell in step behind them as Kardashian and Simpson trudged upstairs to the master bedroom. Skip Taft and Howard Weitzman followed.

The vast room they entered could have been a small apartment. Simpson's huge bed, with its off-white spread and matching half-moon headboard, faced a stone fireplace. Slightly to the left of the fireplace, glass doors opened onto a balcony overlooking the swimming pool and tennis court. Off to the right were the bathroom and large dressing area with stage lighting around the mirrors. An L-shaped couch sat in front of the left wall; a built-in TV behind it. All kinds of pleasant options: on cold days, a cheery fire or a view of lush trees, swimming, and tennis. Or you could click on the TV from bed.

Simpson suddenly became a concerned householder. He pulled Kardashian into the walk-in closet in the dressing area. "I want to see if these guys stole anything," he said. He said he kept at least eight thousand dollars in the closet, money he'd won playing golf. Golf bets? Kardashian didn't have time to be surprised.

The money's missing, O.J. growled. He started searching. Kardashian helped him go through drawers. In one they found a single leather glove: They took one of my gloves, Simpson muttered angrily. Kardashian didn't understand why it mattered. He and Simpson opened every drawer in the room. It's not here, Simpson kept saying. Kardashian was surprised to see O.J.'s guns, legal and illegal, still in the closet. The cops didn't care? An Uzi lay on the closet floor. Another gun was displayed in an open box. He knew O.J. had at least nine guns. One had a handle lock; the others could easily be fired if they were loaded. "I can't believe they left these," O.J. said.

Lange waited in the doorway. Simpson said, "You guys found my cash and took it?" Nothing is missing, the detective said, except what was booked as evidence. We'll give you a list. O.J. didn't ask about the glove.

Then it was Lange's turn. He asked O.J. what he'd worn Sunday night. "The pants and shirt are in the bathroom," Simpson said. Lange looked inside. Then he asked Simpson for his shoes. O.J. walked into the closet and brought out a pair of white Reeboks. The detective looked at the soles, then examined both shoes minutely. Would Simpson mind if he took them? No problem.

* * *

They walked the detective downstairs and out. Most of the LAPD had left.

Phones were ringing nonstop. People arrived. O.J.'s sister Shirley Baker and her husband, Benny, flew in from San Francisco bringing his mother, Eunice, frail and always in pain from arthritis. People crying, hugging, shocked, comforting each other. His sister Carmelita Durio was there. His children from his first marriage, Jason and Arnelle, arrived. Joe Stellini, who had stayed close all those years, came over. Joe Kolkowitz, a golf and tennis buddy, sat in the living room with hairstylist Neil Sloan. The housekeeper, Gigi, ordered some deli food.

The ground level of the mansion is heavy stone. Where masonry takes over farther up, lead-lined windows continue the Tudor style. The indoor atmosphere mixes warm clutter with elegance. Glass cases hold the Heisman trophy and smaller statues. A pool room is chockablock with special footballs, framed magazine covers, various awards. Photos of Ava Gardner, Richard Nixon, and O.J.'s July Fourth softball team.

Downstairs, life revolves around the den. One end of the room is taken over by a ceiling-high built-in wall with three television screens, videotape equipment, a sound system, and speakers. For a first-time visitor, the effect is like visiting the Starship *Enterprise*. You need lessons to turn on the various components. There are comfortable chairs around, a glass-topped coffee table.

The air in the large house tonight is both electric and subdued. Even among friends and family, shock, dismay, and sorrow have their limits. Nicole was loved. But she and O.J. hadn't been together. Things were awkward. Only the man in the den, fixated on the TV news, could set the tone.

Simpson talked back to the anchors and TV reporters as if they could hear him. Sunken-eyed, distant, withdrawn, this wasn't the man everybody knew. Not the Public Man, not even the private man. The drill became predictable. Silence for a while. Then: I can't believe she's gone. Why did this happen? What am I going to do? Then quiet again. Then "What are my kids going to do without a mother?"

Cathy Randa took the calls, saying whatever she could.

Most were routine, friends and businesspeople, curious, sympathetic. O.J. waved her away and kept talking to the television sets. But Cathy kept after him about Roger King. This guy keeps calling, she said, he's called three or four times. He keeps saying get Robert Shapiro, you have to have him. You have to get the best. He says he'll pay for it.

Pay for it? What was this? Simpson knew King a little through sports and TV work. Roger King and his brother, Michael, ran Kingworld Productions; they owned game shows and the tabloid show *Inside Edition*. But O.J. and King weren't friends, just acquaintances. King had a pretty good reputation. But what did he want? He said he'd pay for Shapiro?

The S.S. *Victoria* last sailed in 1866, and over a century later the mahogany paneling from its captain's smoking room adorns one of the most elegant dining rooms in Los Angeles. Raised to a rich burgundy glow by forty coats of lacquer, the antique wood is inlaid with mother-of-pearl. The walls are so striking that it's only fitting to call this place the Captain's Room.

The men and women at dinner tonight are investors in the upscale nightspot containing this lavish bit of antiquity. The House of Blues is a three-story club on Sunset Strip built to mimic a tin-roofed juke joint in deepest Mississippi. There is nothing, however, resembling a juke joint here in the third-floor Captain's Room. Downstairs, the house band is entertaining two floors of regular folks. The third floor is reached by invitation only, from a back elevator. Among those here tonight is the man Roger King is so concerned with, attorney Robert Shapiro.

A House of Blues employee approaches Shapiro to tell him he has an urgent phone call. Roger King isn't a man who gives up an idea just because someone won't talk to him. After failing to reach Simpson, he tracks down Shapiro.

Shapiro takes the call in a nearby room. He has barely said hello when King offers him a retainer to defend O.J. Simpson.

* * *

Kardashian noticed the kid who looked like a surfer, blond, wandering around the edges. Some people acknowledged him briefly, then went back to whatever they were doing. He entered the den and stood there. O.J. came to life. Thank God Kato saw me, Simpson said in a strong, clear voice. He can testify that I was in the house. Kato said nothing and eventually wandered off.

About 9:30 P.M., Simpson said he was drained. He'd slept about an hour flying to Chicago, got in at dawn, no sleep coming back. Then a grueling day here. He was going to bed.

Kardashian looked at Simpson. All afternoon and evening this hadn't been the friend he had known for twenty-four years. Something in O.J. always came alive when people were around, even in bad times. In this situation, anybody would be depressed, but the state Simpson was in now was too much. Even making every allowance for the bizarre circumstances, Kardashian knew O.J. had passed some critical boundary. His depression was abnormal, scary. Some part of his friend was in hiding.

Kardashian knew that Simpson held his public image close to his soul. Athletes are like that. Talent sustains them, but ego makes them champions. They may look and act like gods, but underneath they are often needy men and women who run faster, fight harder, and make that crucial extra effort for the applause. They get hooked on the cheers and acclaim. Image becomes everything.

Simpson's carefully nurtured celebrity persona was under siege. Instead of applauding, a hostile public, represented by shrill media hacks with cameras and notebooks, clamored at the gates. The tone of the television news made it clear that he was no hero.

Kardashian pulled O.J.'s sister Shirley aside. "Stay near your brother tonight," he cautioned. "Don't leave him." Shirley had seen what Bob had. She knew, too. She and her husband, Benny, had already planned to sleep on the couch in O.J.'s bedroom, staying awake in shifts.

Until three A.M., their suicide watch was uneventful. Simpson tossed and turned, stared at the ceiling, muttered, slept fitfully. Then he got up. Shirley was awake as he stumbled into the bathroom and failed to make the usual sounds. The nearby closet was full of guns. Shirley called out, "Don't do anything crazy, O.J." No response. She called out again, "Your kids need you." Another silence, but finally he answered her. If Shirley hadn't talked about the kids, Simpson told Kardashian the next day, that would have been the moment. Shirley knew he wanted to kill himself. He'd gotten up to do it.

3

KARDASHIAN HAD HARDLY SLEPT. HE'D GOTTEN HOME about 10:30 the night before. He had sat in the kitchen for a while with Denice drinking tea and eating a little. They watched the late news. He couldn't imagine going to bed. When he finally surrendered to his fatigue it was very late— and then he woke up at five A.M.

After praying, he got the morning paper and turned on the TV news. He sat there half awake, in a state of curiosity mixed with dread. He had wondered about the male victim. The paper filled things in a little: Ron Goldman was a waiter at Mezzaluna, an acting hopeful, a man-about-the-neighborhood, friend of Nicole.

At eight A.M. Bob told Denice he was off to O.J.'s and he would take her Rolls-Royce. He had a vague thought that O.J. might stay at their house to get away from the press; he'd need the bigger car for whatever luggage Simpson brought. Just as he was pulling out, Denice ran out. She reminded him not to forget to take the Louis Vuitton bag to O.J. It was still in the Mercedes's trunk. He'd completely forgotten about it.

Kardashian didn't bother to call ahead. Where else would O.J. be? He hoped the bigger car today would serve another purpose. The press didn't know his face yet, but they might remember his Mercedes from yesterday. He hoped he could stay in the shadows.

The 405 freeway was happily uncongested, and in half an hour he pulled up to the green gate and pushed the buzzer. Kardashian often walked in through the kitchen door, but he felt that greater formality was somehow needed now. He grabbed Simpson's garment bag from the trunk and said hello to Howard Weitzman, who seemed to be leaving. Inside the front door, Kardashian climbed the curving stairway past pictures of friends and family members and walked into O.J.'s bedroom.

Simpson was still in bed, sitting up, writing on a yellow legal pad. He hadn't touched a tray of oatmeal and fruit. Sunlight poured through the balcony doors, and the wall television was tuned to a news broadcast. Shirley and Benny sat on the couch beneath it. Did you sleep? Bob asked. The athlete talked about tossing and turning, but until they were alone he didn't mention thoughts of suicide. The phone rang and Kardashian answered. Frank Olson, the chairman of Hertz, was calling from London. How was O.J. doing? Simpson took the phone. He was fine, he told Olson. He couldn't believe what had happened. He was so shocked.

Kardashian was getting tired of hearing this, but he couldn't get beyond the same thought himself. He sat at the foot of the bed and O.J.'s verbal torrent started up again. Shock, disbelief, the same questions.

Now O.J. moved to something more specific: Howard Weitzman at the police station yesterday. The lawyer had been wearing a suit, after all. His role was obvious. The cops had asked some tough questions. They were looking hard at him. You go downtown with a lawyer, and people think something happened. That's how O.J. saw it. Howard kept saying things would work out: It's normal that they want to question you. But they searched the house all day long. They always look at ex-husbands. I've got to protect myself, Simpson said. Bob saw that he was getting depressed again.

How about getting up? Kardashian suggested gently. Let's go to your office and start the day. Almost obediently, the athlete left the bed and walked into the bathroom.

Kardashian heard the water running. A moment later O.J. was calling for him. Kardashian found him in his jockey shorts and bare feet, standing in a puddle of water. Simpson looked bewildered. He'd turned on the faucet, and water cascaded all over the floor. Opening up the cabinet enclosing the sink, O.J. saw that the elbow pipe underneath was loose. Cops had removed it. They were looking for blood. Kardashian was certain: They had been looking for blood.

Simpson understood this, too. Kardashian could see it in his horror-stricken face.

Kardashian had no idea that Detectives Vannatter and Lange had made it obvious to O.J. in their interrogation that he was the prime suspect. The TV news was certainly reporting it. Until this moment Simpson had managed to keep his distance from that fact. But as Kardashian watched, O.J. realized, as if he had seen a cosmic finger pointing in judgment, that he was *the* suspect. His friend had heard the words before, grasped it in a superficial way. But now, Kardashian could see, Simpson knew it right down in every cell.

Simpson bent down, grabbed the loose pipe in his large hands, and carried it to another sink, the one Nicole had used for years. He turned on that faucet and sluiced water into the bent pipe. Black sludge poured out, staining his hands. He washed and scrubbed and talked. I can't believe the cops went this far. I can't believe what they did. He poured more water in it, and more black gunk spewed out. I could have cut myself anytime in here, you know? They must have checked the shower, too. There could be blood there. Any cut, whenever.

Time seemed to stop. Cleaning out that pipe was becoming a ritual for O.J. Kardashian realized other things had happened here yesterday. He thought he saw fingerprint dust around the sink bowls and the shower. Police had searched the bathroom microscopically. O.J. seemed to be in a trance. He kept muttering, I can't believe this! The smell of sewage filled the room. At some point, O.J.'s brother-in-law came in. Kardashian and Benny watched in silence. Finally an Off switch clicked for O.J. The pipe was clean enough. Simpson turned away from the sink. He held out the elbow joint to his brother-in-law.

"Can you fix this?" O.J. asked. Benny allowed that he probably could.

As Simpson dressed, Kardashian mentioned why he'd brought the Rolls. He'd offered to take his friend home to Encino last night, but then the athlete had insisted he wanted to sleep in his own bed. Now Simpson liked the idea of staying in Encino. His own street was choked with press. Some of those telephoto lenses could even shoot through the windows from their distant positions outside the walls. "You're right. I'm trapped here," Simpson said. He hadn't seen Kardashian's new house; it had a guest suite off to one side, very private. Best of all, it was hard to find.

Simpson told Bob things would blow over after Nicole's funeral. He'd come back home after that.

But how to get out of the house? They talked about O.J. hunkering down on the floor of the Rolls so that the press would think Kardashian was leaving alone. But the TV crews were on stepladders peering over the wall. They'd see O.J. get in.

Kardashian had a better idea. For years, friends and neighbors allowed to use O.J.'s tennis court when he wasn't home had come in by a hidden path that connected to neighbor Eric Watts's property. That way they didn't have to ring at the front gate. The path was known to only a small circle.

Kardashian assumed the press wouldn't follow him. They might photograph him driving to the corner just in case they had no better visuals for the day. But they didn't know who he was. Once he turned off Ashford, he'd be free. Then he'd turn onto Bristol. O.J. Simpson would be standing on the corner.

Let's pack and leave, said Kardashian. He'd previously brought the garment bag upstairs from the Rolls's trunk. Simpson took it into the walk-in closet. Kardashian heard a familiar mild chaos as Simpson packed the bag with Bugle Boy shirts, slacks, jeans, and casual shoes.

34

"Bobby, can you go down to the Bentley and get me something?"

"Sure."

"Under the front seat. A little black case."

Kardashian found it easily enough. It looked like a small violin case, hard-shelled, black, with rounded corners and a little handle. He brought it upstairs and Simpson took it into the closet.

Bob loaded the garment bag into his trunk while Simpson left by the path through the Watts property. When the green gates opened for the Rolls, the waiting camera crews closed in briefly, then parted. They filmed Kardashian driving to the corner, then fell back as he'd predicted. Watching them recede in his rearview mirror, he drove down Ashford and turned right on Bristol.

O.J. stood on the corner like a hitchhiker with a black duffel bag slung over his shoulder. Bob pulled to the curb. They laughed like a couple of kids. Two hundred media people outside the gate, cameras, satellite trucks, the whole works. They're so stupid, Kardashian thought. All they understand is what's under their noses. Simpson's front gate was by now the most photographed portal in history, while O.J. himself stood alone on the next block.

Driving down Sunset Boulevard to Orenthal Enterprises, Simpson couldn't stop talking about the police search. Kardashian thought his friend was as thunderstruck as if the cops had smashed him in the face with that pipe from his bathroom sink. They'd spent eight or ten hours or whatever at the house, he said. They really went through things. They're watching me. Kardashian reminded him of Roger King's repeated calls the night before. Simpson barely remembered, but he knew Shapiro's name.

"I've met him," the athlete said. "I hear he's pretty good. Maybe we should call this guy. Just see if we are doing things right." Weitzman's name never came up. This was like getting a second opinion from a specialist, Kardashian figured. In recent years Howard had mostly done corporate and entertainment law. Both men knew that. He was certainly the right man for damage control and press problems. But now that the LAPD had made its intentions clear, maybe it was time for an expert in criminal law.

At Skip Taft's office, which adjoined O.J.'s, Simpson and Kardashian put the phone on speaker so everyone could hear. A few seconds later, Shapiro was on the line. "Bob, this is O.J.," Simpson began. He hardly ever used his last name when he introduced himself. "I'm sure you've heard about what's happened. I'd like to talk to you. You've been referred by Roger King."

Shapiro acknowledged that King had called him as well. His voice was reserved, silky. The lawyer invited Simpson to his office, but O.J. resisted: A visit might attract press attention. Shapiro said he'd come by.

There was some talk about questions for Shapiro. What happens when police are investigating you? What are the procedures?

Then Simpson remembered something: "I'd better find out what happened to my golf clubs." In a few quick phone calls, O.J. discovered his golf bag was at the L.A. airport. He decided to retrieve them after Shapiro left. Next he called Al Cowlings, who was supposed to drive Sydney and Justin—O.J.'s children by his marriage to Nicole—to Rockingham from their grandparents' home in Dana Point, where they had been taken after the death of their mother. He told A.C. to take them to Kardashian's house instead.

Cathy Randa brought Shapiro into the office.

Kardashian was immediately impressed by Shapiro's professionalism. He seemed to know exactly what to do; solid and confident, he took charge of the conversation immediately. He had a cool, polite, precise manner—like a therapist, Kardashian thought: He's here to help. You're the one who's excited, not him. He's the professional.

The room's comfort level rose fast, and Simpson seemed to emerge from his lethargy. Kardashian listened intently. You have to hire the best investigators, criminalists, forensics people right now, Shapiro said. You must bring them in immediately to get an independent review of the evidence. The longer you wait, the more the evidence will be disturbed.

Shapiro added that he always treated experts well. First-class travel, top hotels, the best restaurants. Some lawyers try to economize with tourist class and cheap hotels. That doesn't buy loyalty. Shapiro was talking as if he were already O.J. Simpson's defense lawyer. Kardashian asked if Howard should be brought into this conversation. Shapiro said no. Next he asked Kardashian to leave.

Kardashian was so surprised that he didn't mention he was also a lawyer. True, he ran businesses now and he'd let his license expire. But he was a lawyer nonetheless, and could properly be considered part of the defense team. But Bob didn't feel like being assertive. It didn't occur to him to challenge Shapiro.

He sat at a desk answering phone calls for two hours, feeling left out. Shapiro was the expert. Let him have his confidential meeting. Bob would find out what was happening, soon enough.

When Shapiro emerged from his private meeting with O.J., he was warning Simpson. Firmly. Your wife's just been murdered, and you're worried about golf clubs? It will look wrong, said the lawyer. Send someone else. Going there yourself would be stupid, out of character.

"But I don't know what to do with myself," Simpson had protested. "I can't go home. I can't do anything."

Shapiro was emphatic: Don't go.

Then Shapiro looked at Kardashian. "O.J. says you're an attorney. I want you on the case," he said. "I cannot do it without you." Bob said he was ready to help his friend.

Once Shapiro had said good-bye to everyone and left, Simpson and Kardashian got in the Rolls to go to Encino. "Let's go to the airport. I have to get my clubs," O.J. said.

Despite two days of unrelenting news coverage, nobody at Los Angeles International Airport made a fuss when Simpson stepped out of a Rolls-Royce at the American Airlines loading curb Tuesday afternoon. A few people glanced at him, but that was all Kardashian could see.

A woman at the ticket counter directed them to a customer service office near the baggage carousel. The distinctive golf bag with the Swiss Army Knife insignia was found immediately. Simpson slung it over his shoulder and put it in the trunk with the Louis Vuitton garment bag and the black duffel bag.

Forty minutes later, they pulled into Kardashian's garage. They took the golf bag from the trunk and left it in the garage. The other pieces of luggage Simpson carried to the foot of the stairs in the entryway.

Sometimes Sara Caplan thought she needed a map and compass as much as her law books and computer. The young attorney worked in the vast sea of offices belonging to the law firm Christiansen, White, Miller, Fink & Jacobs, but she was not part of it. Christiansen, White did civil work, and her boss, criminal defense attorney Robert Shapiro, rented space here. The Shapiro practice employed three lawyers. More than a dozen attorneys, plus their support staff, worked for Christiansen, White. But the big firm's office complex was so crowded that Shapiro worked two floors above Caplan. Her assistant was up there, as well. Ditto the law library. Naturally, she made the trip upstairs often.

When Caplan passed Shapiro's office, she knew he was into something serious. Today he had a hard, focused look in his eyes. She stuck her head in the door. "Is there anything I can help you with?"

"Yes, sit down." Shapiro's manner, as always, was an odd combination of warmth and formality. "We've just become involved in the Simpson matter. There's a lot to do."

Caplan left her boss's office with a list of people to call. Time to line up the team. She had always admired Shapiro's ability to keep track of parallel worlds when he worked on a case, to run dozens of simultaneous projects and subprojects without losing sight of the endgame, when the puzzle pieces of a case had to form one convincing picture. An astute strategist and stone-cold negotiator, Shapiro was noted for his ability to go head-to-head with prosecutors and hammer out advantageous deals for his clients.

* * *

The first thing a visitor notices about Kardashian's Encino house is its remarkable spaciousness. With fifteen rooms totaling nine thousand square feet, it is about three times the size of the average suburban dwelling. The high-ceilinged, open entrance hall leads to a grand staircase that divides at a landing halfway up, one stairway leading left to the master bedroom, the other to Kardashian's office, a billiards-media room, and a guest suite. The public rooms are cool and quietly expensive. Polished floors stretch through the living room to the formal dining room. The greatest warmth and softness in the decor come from the French Impressionist paintings Kardashian favors. A high-tech kitchen adjoins the breakfast room. Kardashian considers this a transitional house and has taken a lease. He's been here less than a month and it shows. There is no hint of a lived-in look on the first floor.

Sydney, eight, and Justin, six, were in the Jacuzzi in the guest bath, frothing bubble bath everywhere, when Kardashian and Simpson walked in. Adorable kids, Kardashian thought. Innocence and pain. As Bob watched from the doorway, O.J. stood silent for a moment and looked at his children. It was the first time he had seen them since the murders. They climbed out of the Jacuzzi and he knelt and put an arm around each child. I need to talk to you after you get dressed, he said.

Simpson left to unpack, then returned and took the children downstairs into the living room. They sat together on a green couch. Kardashian could see O.J. was looking out the window into the backyard as he talked. Kardashian stayed in another room, but Simpson's deep voice carried in the open house. Bob could hear him talking about Mommy being in heaven, Mommy loving them very much. The children began to whimper, and he thought he heard their father crying. One day Daddy's going to heaven to join Mommy, Simpson said. You have to love your Mommy and Daddy a lot. You have to be strong.

This will be conducted solely by us and for our purposes only, Robert Shapiro told Kardashian when he phoned Bob in Encino at 3:30 P.M. Shapiro directed Simpson and

Kardashian to an office in the mid-Wilshire area. Skip Taft would be coming, too. For our purposes only, he repeated in his best professional voice.

Privately Kardashian both feared and welcomed this idea. A polygraph would settle things. O.J. loved Nicole. He didn't kill her. The polygraph would be it. Settled. Finished. Every day was a new experience. This was just another one.

Kardashian drives Simpson to Wilshire in the Mercedes and parks in the building's basement. They take the elevator and locate the office of Edward Gelb. A receptionist hands them a sheet to fill out. The waiting room is grim. No art on the walls, no color, just the woman's desk and a credenza. If he didn't know better, Kardashian would guess no one worked here. It's a scene from a surreal spy movie.

Simpson starts filling in the form. Kardashian tells him this is no place to leave a paper trail. Shapiro enters with Skip Taft. Kardashian asks Shapiro about the form.

It's taken care of, Shapiro says quickly. Don't fill it out.

A middle-aged man, who Kardashian thinks is Gelb but is actually Dennis Nellany, opens a door from an inner office. (Gelb is in Spain.) Nothing personal will happen here, his face says. He's a pro. He's been through this a thousand times. He takes Simpson inside, and Kardashian and the others sit in the lifeless room and talk. The emptiest small talk. Shapiro wears a suit. Taft wears slacks and a golf shirt. Kardashian is in jeans.

Half an hour later, Simpson comes out alone. He's wound up, talking a blue streak: It was very emotional. Every time he heard Nicole's name, his heart started to pound. The test was very hard to get through. Difficult, very tough.

Kardashian assumes the examiner is scoring the test. The receptionist has left. Appearing at the office door, Nellany, Gelb's right-hand man, invites Shapiro, Kardashian, and Taft in. I'll give you the results, he says.

Simpson isn't invited.

Larger and better appointed, the examiner's office has framed diplomas and licenses on the walls, solid furniture, thick carpeting. Kardashian is surprised to see that the polygraph machine is fairly small. It ought to look sinister, or at least imposing. But it isn't.

Simpson scored a minus 22, Nellany says.

Kardashian has no idea what that might mean. Nellany speaks in a matter-of-fact voice. But Kardashian can feel the weight of the minus 22. He and Taft look to Shapiro. That is about as bad as you can do, Shapiro comments. His tone is crisp and factual, too.

Minus 22 means Simpson failed virtually all of the questions about the murders. Bob Kardashian can't believe he's hearing this.

Kardashian knows that polygraph tests contain reference questions about matters like your name, age, address. That way the examiner can identify your normal response when you tell the truth. He is vaguely aware that the reference questions are scattered among questions about the pertinent issues. The average test contains about thirty questions related to the crucial topic—in this case, the double murder.

There are some factors to consider here, Nellany adds. The test was administered close to the time of death, a very emotional time. The validity of the result . . . and now he lapses into professional jargon. Bob tries to make sense of the technical talk and concludes that O.J.'s intense emotional level might have affected the results.

Kardashian knows that doesn't settle it. He just doesn't know what to do. No way his friend could have done this.

O.J. is invited in now. Nellany tells him the same thing. Simpson's words explode from him: "What I said about Nicole, you know? Every time he said her name, my heart would beat like crazy! You guys have got to understand. I didn't do this!"

Kardashian watches his friend's face as if staring through an opaque window, desperate for the glass to become clear.

"I'm not surprised at what happened because I'm so distraught. I'm so upset. This test, you know, I'd like to take it again. I didn't do this!"

Kardashian and Shapiro watch Simpson, then look at each other. Wait a while, maybe a week, and do it again? Vaguely they agree. Taft nods. Shapiro slides the test results into a manila envelope and thanks Nellany. He carries the envelope as they leave. Outside, Shapiro turns to them. This is only between us. They walk to their cars in awkward silence.

"I was nervous," O.J. keeps saying on the ride back to Encino. "I was very nervous. They shouldn't have asked me some of those questions. Every time I heard Nicole's name, my heart would beat so fast. It would race, you know? And that thing would jump."

They got home about eight P.M. Denice made dinner, and they acted as if their lives were normal. Periodically Kardashian would look out a window just to be sure that no satellite vans had arrived. Simpson watched a cartoon video with his kids before they went off to bed.

Michael Baden, former New York City medical examiner, enjoyed the Hertz jokes. Those TV commercials were about his life—absurdly late for every plane he took, lumbering toward the departure gate laden with garment bags and high-tech carry-ons, forever puffing and panting through airports with seconds to spare. He was the O.J. Simpson of pathology. The only thing Dr. Michael Baden didn't do was vault over furniture.

Bob Shapiro called Baden at his East Eighty-sixth Street apartment in Manhattan. He was relaxing after a long day in court. Shapiro wasted no time. "Michael, I need you to come out here right away."

Baden had worked with Shapiro for the first time in 1990 when Marlon Brando's son, Christian, was tried for shooting his sister's lover. Imagine picking up the phone and finding Marlon Brando on the line. A week had passed since the killing, and police hadn't found the fatal bullet. Shapiro wanted another autopsy to see if the bullet was still in the body. Baden agreed to help.

After a painstaking postmortem, Baden found nothing. Then, with a nod to Sherlock Holmes, he asked to be taken to Brando's home. Police had closed out the crime scene days earlier and turned it back to the family. Baden found the bullet under the rug.

When news of the Simpson-Goldman murders broke earlier that week, Baden was in his office. He didn't hear about the crime until Monday night. Judging from the reports on TV, Simpson seemed to be in trouble. Shapiro explained that Simpson had retained him earlier in the day, and he needed Baden immediately for a second autopsy. Baden said he had to be in court Wednesday and couldn't travel until Thursday morning. Remember, he added, I can't just show up and do an autopsy. We'll need the family's consent.

Shapiro had another request: Whom did Baden consider the best criminalist in the world—the absolute best?

Baden didn't have to ponder. Henry Lee, he thought immediately. Dr. Lee ran the state police lab in Connecticut. His reading of crime scenes was legendary, nearly mythical. Not only were his scientific insights remarkable, but his courtroom persona was catnip to most juries.

Did Baden know him? Shapiro asked. It was nearly midnight on the East Coast. Did he have Lee's home number?

Let me call him first, Baden said. Lee worked late most nights, but the hour wasn't the issue. The real problem, which Baden didn't share with Shapiro, was that both Lee and Baden had professional conflicts. They worked for police agencies: Baden part-time for the New York State Police, while Lee was on staff full-time for the State of Connecticut. Police bureaucracies react badly when their experts work for the defense. Baden's potential problem was less acute because he worked for the state police only part-time. He needed no one's permission to work wherever he pleased. But he also knew that even his best friends in law enforcement resented his defense work. Their philosophy split the world into good guys and bad guys. So Henry Lee might wish to avoid Shapiro.

Baden's caution proved wise. Lee was noncommittal. He was aware of Simpson by reputation, but he had no immediate enthusiasm for the case. Shapiro wanted a second autopsy, Baden explained, but he also needed the best possible criminalist for crime-scene analysis. Finally Lee said, Okay, let him call me.

Fifteen minutes later, Lee called Baden to say he had agreed to fly to Los Angeles.

* * *

43

Hearing news of the killings, F. Lee Bailey thought, Poor guy. He's a nice guy, great athlete, this is outside his world. It must be terribly depressing. But it was only a passing reflection. In the subtropical West Palm Beach heat, 2,300 miles from the crime scene, barrel-chested Franklin Lee Bailey spent far more time contemplating the unthinkable: He might have outlived the public's attention span. After many glorious decades pulling rabbits out of courtroom hats, in recent years his magic show had become a disappearing act.

Bailey was suffering, in part, from his early success. Based in Boston for most of his career, he'd tried his first murder case at the tender age of twenty-seven. His stagecraft and basso-profundo oratory gave the impression of maturity. Yet he was only in his thirties when his most famous cases, the Sam Sheppard and Carl Coppolino trials, transfixed a scandal-hungry nation. Most lawyers that age are still serving their apprenticeships. Now, Bailey had remarked to more than one listener, I appear to have lived longer than I should have.

If a single case from a long career could define the moment when fame became a banana peel, consider the disaster twenty years ago which the public remembered as the Patty Hearst trial. He'd lost, thoroughly and embarrassingly. Then he'd unwittingly created a retiree image by moving to Florida in 1985. He took the Florida bar exam four years later, hoping the public would realize no sane lawyer endures a bar exam unless he plans to continue practicing.

It helped only minimally. Clients thought he ran a little retirement business which didn't include legal defense. They'd hire him if he were still practicing, some wistfully remarked. Bailey eventually concluded that his colleagues in the Miami criminal bar spread the word of his retirement and deliberately offered their services to clients who inquired about him.

Still, in the spring of 1994, Bailey would have described himself as a most happy fella. He and his third wife, Patti, had celebrated their ninth anniversary and his sixty-first birthday all on the same day, Friday, June 10. As it happened, he did have a second business, refurbishing used pleasure boats—distinctive craft, of course—and he enjoyed that. He and Patti lived in a modest condominium, about 2,500 square feet including the porch. They were both high-octane, Type A personalities. She attended college full-time, pursuing a biology degree. He traveled perhaps too much, but they found that the time they had together was well spent.

Bob Shapiro had come into Bailey's life in the late '70s when they worked on a case in Hawaii. He was now a dear friend, and they talked regularly. In 1983, Bailey was tried in San Francisco for driving under the influence. He asked Shapiro to be local counsel, and Shapiro could rightly take some credit for the acquittal. Bob called from time to time to seek advice on his cases. When Bailey visited Los Angeles, he stayed at Shapiro's home. In fact, Bailey was godfather to one of Bob's children.

Now Bob called. He had been retained to defend O.J. Simpson. Would Bailey help? Bob's speech was controlled as always, confident, even a bit snobbish, but Bailey could sense his excitement. He wanted Bailey's reaction to what he had already done.

Bailey congratulated Shapiro on his speed and decisiveness. He added that Shapiro needed a private investigator in Chicago. Simpson's demeanor on the trip to Chicago, during his stay, and on his flight home could have huge importance. Both men assumed the prosecution would produce expert witnesses to explain how a man who had just killed two people might behave. The defense needed to know every detail of Simpson's behavior. Bailey's lead investigator was a former New York City detective named John McNally, famous during his days on the force for tracking down a jewel thief named Murph the Surf. Since McNally was busy, he suggested Bailey call Pat McKenna in Miami—or, better yet, he'd call himself the next morning.

Years ago, McKenna had been a probation officer in Chicago, and he knew his way around. It made sense this time to call him first. Except that McNally had to do it.

McNally was Bailey's contact, and a wise lawyer never ignored the protocol of professional friendships.

When Shapiro called, Zvonko "Bill" Pavelic was in his basement office at home in Glendale, cut off from everything. Pavelic finished his investigations that way. He isolated himself with his computer and his tapes from mid-morning till midnight or later. He allowed himself only one break, for dinner with Maria and the kids.

He was proud of his tight, loyal family. That was one reason he worked at home in the big house that Maria kept so well. Sometimes he was late for dinner, but he never missed the hour afterward when he checked homework. The kids were doing well in school, and he intended to keep it that way.

Pavelic, a former L.A. cop, was now a private investigator. He preferred the term "consultant."

Robert Shapiro called just before eleven P.M. They'd worked together three years. Pavelic liked the lawyer's style—intellectual, highly organized, well prepared. Shapiro's particular genius, he thought, was laying a foundation so solid that the case was a winner no matter who presented it. They had won every case they'd worked on.

Would Pavelic like to join the defense team in the Simpson case? Shapiro asked. "Are you available?"

Naturally Pavelic said yes. He apologized because he couldn't make Shapiro's first meeting the next day.

But he shifted into gear mentally while he was still talking. He'd need Maria to clip newspapers. He knew he had to identify the documents already being generated in the case. The prosecution's discovery file would undoubtedly be voluminous.*

Bob Shapiro arrived at the Encino house at 11:30 P.M. All sorts of things had to be settled.

Howard Weitzman had called Rockingham, Orenthal

---

*A discovery file consists of lists of witnesses and their statements, police reports, statements and related paperwork, all test results, all photographs and tangible evidence, and any other results of all law enforcement investigations.

Enterprises, and Kardashian's house several times during the day. None of the calls were returned. It made Kardashian squirm. He'd known Howard nearly forty years, and he hated seeing a friend treated this way. But he said nothing. Something was happening here that took precedence over a valued friendship. Kardashian realized he had crossed some threshold, whether he had planned to or not. He was included in all the conversations now. He was beginning to understand that he was somehow at the center of things nearly as much as Simpson.

Shapiro went straight to it. "Did you do this? I have to know."

Simpson answered in the same blunt way. He didn't do it, wouldn't do it, couldn't believe all of this was happening.

Shapiro moved on, asking about the Pediatric AIDS Foundation fund-raiser Simpson attended with Paula Barbieri June 11, about Sunday afternoon and Sunday night, the flight to Chicago and the return. At last Kardashian was hearing talk about specifics.

Where was Simpson Sunday night between ten and eleven P.M.? He said he watched a Clint Eastwood movie in the den, then went upstairs to pack. Check the *TV Guide*. You'll see the listing. He heard the gate buzzer while he was in the shower. Didn't answer it. I'm used to Dale St. John knowing my pattern. He knows I'm late. He knows I rush everything to the last minute. But another driver had picked him up; his name was Allan Park.

Simpson cut his finger getting his cellular phone out of the Bronco, he said, cut it on a hook or something. Thought nothing of it. I don't know when I bleed. He showed them the cut. Kardashian didn't doubt him. He had seen his friend cut his hands and fingers before. They were usually nicked and scarred.

They talked more than two hours. Bob Shapiro was formally hired. Skip Taft would call Weitzman in the morning and explain. Dr. Saul Faerstein, a psychiatrist and friend of Shapiro, sent over a prescription to help the athlete get some rest. Everyone shook hands, and Bob Shapiro departed into the night. Simpson went off to the guest suite, hoping for a good night's sleep.

4

ON WEDNESDAY MORNING, JUNE 15, KARDASHIAN LEFT
his bed and washed up quickly. He didn't read *The One Year
Bible* and he skipped the treadmill. He walked down the
grand staircase to the landing and back up the opposite set of
stairs to O.J.'s room. He wondered if his friend was still
alive.

Simpson sat in bed watching a movie on cable, groggy
from the sleeping pills. "Man, I'm living a nightmare," he
said. "I don't know what's going on."

Denice made bacon and eggs, and they ate in the breakfast
nook with the kids. Shapiro had arranged a medical exam at
10:30 A.M. to check for bruises or cuts. Prosecutors, of
course, would try to say any injury linked Simpson to the
murder scene. The defense's own evaluation could prove
critical. Dr. Robert Huizenga, a professor at UCLA who had
been a team doctor for the Los Angeles Raiders, had agreed
to see O.J. Kardashian arranged for a photographer, Roger
Collins, to document everything.

Kardashian answered the phone shortly after eight A.M.
Howard Weitzman was furious. Skip Taft had called him.
O.J. wanted to make a change? He was hiring Robert
Shapiro? Why hadn't his old friend protected him from
embarrassment? Or at least warned him so he could protect
himself? He had experience in this kind of criminal defense.
Kardashian said O.J. didn't want Howard out completely.
Couldn't he work with Shapiro? He explained that Roger
King's calls led them to Shapiro. Howard argued that

48

Kardashian could have stopped all that. I don't have the power to say who's out and who's in, Kardashian protested. That was true enough. But he knew he should have kept Howard informed, and admitted that he was wrong about that.

It was very unpleasant. All Howard said at the end was that he would think it over. He didn't know if he wanted to be involved.

As they were leaving for the doctor's office, O.J. began to ask where Nicole's life had somehow gone wrong. Kardashian had no choice but to listen. What kind of life was she leading? he asked. Was she hanging with the wrong crowd? Did it lead to murder?

I want to move, O.J. said suddenly. I want to take my kids and just be alone somewhere. He seemed to wander in and out of the reality of his situation. He didn't mention jail.

They took the little Mercedes to Robert Huizenga's office. Nobody bothered them. The press is still waiting for you to come out the front gate at Rockingham, Kardashian said with a laugh. O.J. didn't react and Bob realized that he was still groggy.

Huizenga asked questions about Simpson's medical history. His family. A history of cancer, he mumbled. They went into another room for a physical. Huizenga noticed swollen lymph nodes. The photographer snapped Simpson in his undershorts from all angles to document the absence of marks or scratches. There were only the cuts police already knew about. Kardashian took the film.

Bob Shapiro walked in at one P.M. when the exam was over. As Simpson and Kardashian stood outside at the reception counter, Shapiro's cellular phone rang. The LAPD was calling.

"Mr. Shapiro," a cop said, "I'm sorry to have to inform you that Mr. Simpson has committed suicide. We have a confirmed report that he is dead."

Shapiro turned to Kardashian and Simpson with an odd gleam in his eye. He repeated the cop's words and turned back to the phone. "Really?"

"Yes, I'm very sorry."

"Well, let me ask him. Mr. Simpson is standing right here." Shapiro paused theatrically. "We're at his doctor's office. The doctor could check his pulse, but he looks fine to me."

Even O.J. laughed.

On Wednesday John McNally phoned Pat McKenna from New York to discuss the Simpson case. McKenna thought of the first O.J. joke he'd heard. He had to tell it: Hey, he's already pled guilty. They beat him to a pulp. The Juice—pulp—get it?

"Do you want to get involved?" McNally asked. "You want this or not?"

McKenna did. He always took new cases. Bad business not to.

A few minutes later Shapiro called. "As you know, I represent O.J. Simpson," he said. "I hear some good things about you from John McNally."

"That means I got to send him a check, right?"

Shapiro ignores the line. "No, I hear good things about you from Lee Bailey."

"I appreciate that."

"I want you to be my video camera. I want you to pick up O.J. Simpson from the minute he stepped off the plane in Chicago until the minute he got back on the plane. Tell me what happened."

"Should I take taped statements? I don't know your discovery rules out there."

"Don't worry about discovery. Just go do it."

Shapiro expected him to leave for Chicago immediately.

McKenna calculated that he had two hours to make the next flight. He called his ex-wife. Look, don't say anything to anybody. I might be getting into the O.J. case. Can you drive me to the airport and take the kids? His ex was the only person he knew who would keep the secret.

McKenna grew up in Chicago and in 1978 moved to Miami, where he took a job as a parole officer, then moved to the public defender's office in 1981 to run an alternative sentencing program for recovering drug addicts. McKenna's presentencing reports had such good detail and color that defense lawyers kept asking if he'd moonlight for them. He opened his own office in 1984.

Once he hung out his shingle, he did a lot of federal criminal defense work and hooked up with Bailey almost immediately. Lee did some consulting for Roy Black on the William Kennedy Smith case and gave them McKenna's name. His career was a wild ride.

McKenna caught his flight to Chicago within hours and checked into the O'Hare Plaza. Wasted effort. A new hotel manager was starting Monday: The temporary guy wouldn't let him talk to anybody. The Hertz people gave him a hard time. American Airlines wasn't much better.

McKenna hated to walk into a case blind, but here he was. He knew what he'd seen on TV, nothing else. He assumed Simpson had done it. The TV coverage was filled with stuff that sounded bad: an unexpected flight to Chicago, matching blood evidence at the crime scene and Simpson's home, bloody clothes in the washing machines, that knife somebody found in his yard.

I got a hell of a job here, he thought.

Wayne Hughes had left word for O.J. Monday night: to call if he needed anything. Now Simpson reached Hughes, the day before Nicole's funeral. It was a gloomy exchange. Hughes listened to a lot of woe-is-me material. Then O.J. got down to business. A man asks you to see that his kids are taken care of, to execute his will and trust, you have to assume he expects to die. It was a very tough telephone call.

By Wednesday afternoon Bob and O.J. were rushing. The Browns had scheduled the first viewing of Nicole's body at four P.M., and Laguna Beach was a ninety-minute drive. They had returned to Encino at two. Al Cowlings had taken Justin and Sydney to their grandparents' earlier that afternoon. Shapiro then arrived to pick them up in his black Mercedes.

Kardashian sat in back with Simpson, who started in again about Nicole running with the wrong crowd, then went

51

back to Theme One: He couldn't believe what had happened. Up front with his driver, Shapiro made calls on his cellular phone. They pulled up in front of the mortuary at five P.M. About fifty friends and relatives milled about, plus some cameramen. Ignore the press and go right in, Shapiro said.

Nicole was in the first viewing room. There were sprays of flowers near the casket and framed pictures resting on it. One showed Nicole in her Ferrari with Justin and Sydney. Judy Brown stood beside the casket, the rest of the Browns slightly apart. Kardashian saw Jason and Arnelle, Al Cowlings, and other family friends. Bob Shapiro stayed at the edge of the room. Several people hugged O.J. as he walked in, leaving Kardashian alone to keep walking toward Nicole.

He was stunned by her appearance in death. With all he knew, after all that had happened, he was still shocked. She had no color.

He hugged Judy Brown and the rest of the family and said how sorry he was. Judy thanked him for coming. Someone said Nicole looked so beautiful, and Nicole's mother agreed. She looks at peace, Judy said. It is a shame it was so violent, but now she looks at peace. Kardashian couldn't think of anything to say.

Behind him, O.J. approached the casket with Arnelle and Jason. He leaned down and kissed his former wife. He stood silently, looking down at Nicole. Arnelle began to cry. A wordless consensus formed in the room that he should have some time alone. People began leaving and someone shut the door. About twenty minutes later, Judy Brown walked in again. Kardashian heard Simpson's voice saying, I loved her too much. I loved her so much. Nic, he said, Nic. And more crying. Both of them.

About eight P.M., after Simpson and Kardashian had spent a little time at the Browns' house, Shapiro's driver took them back to Encino. Simpson cried during the long drive. Kardashian sat stoically, choked with feelings he couldn't express. What do you say to a man whose wife has been murdered? What do you say when the man is openly suspected of her murder? He and Shapiro broke the silence occasionally to talk about the tests that Baden and Lee would be doing. Then silence again until O.J. fought back tears and declared aloud how unbelievable it was. Again.

Paula Barbieri was waiting at Kardashian's home. She'd called Orenthal Enterprises from out of town the day before. It was agreed that she should come to Encino. Kardashian was pleased. His friend was sinking into an alarming depression. The medication Dr. Faerstein had prescribed seemed only to make him groggy. O.J. had no energy, and his moods were increasingly dark.

Cathy Randa sent Dale St. John's limousine service to pick Paula up at the airport. Kardashian was amazed to hear that Allan Park drove her in.

"I'm going for a walk," Simpson said. It was nine P.M.

"You're not going anywhere unless I go with you," Kardashian said.

"I want to be alone."

"No way." Bob was firm. "I'm walking with you."

"I'll tell you what. I'll walk twenty-five yards behind you. You just walk."

Kardashian felt the hair on the back of his neck rise.

"I told you," Simpson repeated, "I want to be alone."

"I'm going with you."

Simpson walked into the garage and reached in his golf bag. He took out a number 7 iron and walked into the street without another word. Kardashian signaled frantically to Al Cowlings and the two men followed him down Mandalay Drive at a respectful distance. Decent, but no twenty-five yards. Kardashian thanked God that he had Cowlings, a big powerful man, with him. His mind suddenly jumped to the two hundred reporters and cameramen still waiting outside the Rockingham gate. If they only knew what they were missing. It would have been worth a laugh if he hadn't been worried about a suicide attempt.

The stroll lasted nearly an hour under a moonlit sky. Simpson walked down the middle of the quiet street, chipping imaginary golf balls. Eventually, Cowlings caught up and walked with him. Kardashian joined them. They circled a long block and finally returned to Kardashian's front yard, where they sat on a wall and talked past each other.

What is going on? Simpson wondered aloud. Kardashian had no answer.

5

ON THURSDAY MORNING O.J. CAME DOWNSTAIRS, groggy again from the sleeping pills. He seemed to be sliding between dark and darker moods, morose, out of reach. He was barely tracking. Today was Nicole's funeral. An impossible day.

Simpson had given out Kardashian's number; the phone started ringing at 7:30 A.M. with calls from the East Coast. All before anyone had coffee.

Kardashian focused on security. He had to get Simpson to the funeral half an hour away in Brentwood, then to the cemetery a hundred miles south in Mission Viejo, and finally back to Encino tonight. He knew a swarm of press helicopters was inevitable, but he didn't want them picking up Simpson's presence at Encino. Limousines carrying the Brown family and O.J.'s children were driving up from Laguna Beach and the press would surround them like a wolf pack. He couldn't risk having a limo come to his house for the media to follow back afterward.

He decided to drive O.J. to Brentwood in the Rolls, and arranged for the Brown convoy to meet them in the parking lot of that strange Holiday Inn at the intersection of Sunset Boulevard and the 405 freeway that looks like a fat cigar planted butt-end in the ground. From there, it was only five minutes to St. Martin of Tours Church at Sunset and Saltair, where Nicole had attended mass.

Simpson fell into a drugged sleep during the drive. He was wearing a dark suit that A.C. had brought from Rockingham. It had taken him forever to get ready.

The Browns were more than half an hour late. Kardashian felt ready to burst. He and Denice watched the parking lot for satellite trucks and news vans. They were sitting ducks. O.J. slept peacefully.

Apart from this one glitch, Bob could hardly complain about the Browns' plans. They had made the church and cemetery arrangements—handled the funeral home, flowers, limousines, and catering—while O.J. was in hiding, depressed, barely functioning. He couldn't have managed any of this. Everybody knew it.

And of course he was suspected of murdering the woman whose funeral he was about to attend. Principal mourner, right next to the victim's parents. Kardashian didn't have time to contemplate how strange that was.

O.J.'s relationship with his former in-laws had never been ordinary. Friends occasionally joked that he was closer to Judy Brown than to her daughter. When he and Nicole fought, O.J. spent hours on the phone with his mother-in-law. He set up Lou Brown with a Hertz franchise at the Ritz-Carlton Hotel in Laguna Niguel. It seemed to be a good arrangement, but Lou said the business climate was wrong. Simpson sent two of Nicole's sisters to better colleges than the family could afford. He had helped her sister Denise financially many times.

When the limousines finally arrived, Bob woke O.J. In a fog, the athlete climbed into a white stretch and hugged Justin and Sydney. Kardashian heard him say something about Mommy in heaven as he and Denice Halicki sat down. Tanya Brown and her boyfriend were also in the limousine.

Kardashian was shocked to see five-year-old Justin without a tie. His mother was dead, and the child was wearing casual clothes. Kardashian's boyhood training equated respect with formal attire. At least Sydney looked right in a pretty flowered dress.

55

Two of Kardashian's kids were students at the St. Martin's school, so he knew the grounds well. You turn north off Sunset on Saltair and enter a long driveway. Today cameramen and reporters formed a solid wall of outstretched hands and big lenses, but it ended at the church gate. After they pulled inside, Kardashian looked for Ron Shipp, a former cop at the West L.A. station who sometimes did security work for Simpson. Shipp had put together a private bodyguard detail of off-duty policemen.

This is Dennis, Shipp said, introducing Kardashian to a tall, muscular man. He'll be with you everywhere you go. Kardashian liked that. He got Simpson out of the limousine and the three men walked into the church.

At that moment Robert Kardashian got a stiff dose of reality. Entering by the side door put him and Simpson squarely in front of hundreds of people who had all cared deeply about Nicole Brown. He felt their eyes immediately. And he understood instantly, perhaps for the first time, that his peers didn't share his feelings about his friend. These were close friends, acquaintances, business colleagues, people whose opinions and respect he valued. Now he saw hundreds of faces sculpted in sadness and anger. He felt the collective accusation—Murderer! Mourners whispered to each other. How brazen to come here, Kardashian imagined them saying.

TV news reports last night—leaks from the Los Angeles Police Department—had made it clear that Simpson would be arrested within twenty-four hours. But in the safe haven Kardashian provided for Simpson, the information was rain on an insulated window. Inside it was dry and warm. Nobody had consciously tried to ignore reality. The mind instinctively keeps bad news away as long as possible.

No longer. Kardashian could feel that cold rain now. O.J. Simpson was no hero in this room.

Meanwhile, Bill Pavelic met Robert Shapiro at his office in Century City. Elegantly appointed with original art, Baccarat and Lalique crystal. Polished and expensive, like its occupant. Then they moved to a conference room. Their forty-five-minute meeting ranged over the entire case. Nothing would be easy, Shapiro said. An arrest might be coming soon. He needed the investigator to do what he did best, run parallel with the police detectives and figure out how they saw things; then, as soon as possible, move their own investigation ahead of them. As always, the first days were the most important.

Pavelic felt that there was no private investigator in town better at living inside the collective mind of the LAPD than himself. He was an expert on the department's rules and procedures. He'd been on the force for eighteen years, won hundreds of medals, commendations, favorable incident reports.

His one experience with O.J. Simpson was part of his police history. When Simpson was one of the runners carrying the Olympic torch before the 1984 games in Los Angeles, Pavelic was assigned to protect VIPs. He and Simpson had talked briefly in the special seating section. Around that time, the International Olympic Committee's Life President, Lord Kellen, nearly died choking on his food. Pavelic had saved his life and he thought Simpson might remember the incident.

Bill Pavelic was especially proud of his street sense. He had been one of the few Caucasian cops, he liked to tell friends, who understood how things really worked in the black community. He got so deep into it that he saw things, he was certain, through nonwhite eyes. He discovered that African-Americans and dark-skinned immigrants of all backgrounds had a lot to fear from the LAPD. When the department couldn't prove something, some cops had no problem framing people who couldn't fight back. Pavelic complained loudly, and soon enough he was seen as disloyal. Before long, he was out.

That was how he saw it. The official records said Pavelic had left on a disability pension. He put his background to work as a private investigator and learned to make his computer think like a cop. That was why he was so concerned with early discovery material. If you took the documents, the crime reports, the logs, the affidavits and

57

connected them to each piece of evidence, then considered how each cop might view it, then you could make a pretty good guess where the department was going with the case. You could see who'd like one thing, who favored another. Sometimes you could see their destination and arrive there ahead of them.

Pavelic thought about what might be happening in the LAPD's lab, with both the police and civilian personnel. He would try to become the chief detective's alter ego, his counterpart on the defense team.

Silver-haired Gerald Uelmen was winding up his duties as dean of Santa Clara Law School on Tuesday. His kind-old-uncle looks relaxed his opponents into assuming he'd act like one in court—until he blindsided them. That's how he earned his nickname: the Cobra. He was due to begin a sabbatical from Santa Clara, when Bob Shapiro called. On June 30 he planned to begin at Stanford Law School, teaching one course and writing. Among other things, he hoped to finish a one-character play about William Jennings Bryan.

Uelmen knew Shapiro from the Marlon Brando case. He'd met Michael Baden then, as well. "Do you want to get in on it?" Shapiro asked.

"You bet. Your timing couldn't be better." Uelmen could delay his sabbatical by a semester. No big thing.

Simpson and Kardashian walked past Nicole's closed casket in the front of the center aisle and took reserved seats in the second row. Kardashian felt the eyes of Nicole's friends and family on them. O.J. sat next to Sydney, Justin, and Arnelle, behind the Browns. Kardashian noticed that Sydney sat quietly. She seemed to understand why she was there. Little Justin fidgeted.

Bob couldn't keep his mind on the sermon. He looked at the kids. He stared at the half-dozen pictures of Nicole and the children mounted on the casket. He lost track of time. At one point the congregation was asked to stand. Some mourners thought the service had ended and walked over to

58

the Browns to pay their respects. A long line formed, and some of it spilled over to O.J. Those eyes were friendly. Eventually people sat down again, and Judy Brown rose to give a short eulogy. The prayers and blessings continued awhile longer; then, finally, the ceremony ended.

Outside, Kardashian told Dennis that he wanted the ten-man detail to continue with them to the cemetery. He glanced up at the helicopters overhead, then at the gauntlet of press lining the drive leading out of the church grounds.

The metal birds stayed with them all the way to Mission Viejo, an hour away. Some three hundred mourners followed the limousines in private cars. They were followed in turn by a line of television vans. In Simpson's limousine the atmosphere was subdued. O.J. talked quietly to Justin and Sydney. Every now and then someone would look out the window and up. Kardashian counted nine choppers.

As they walked to the grave site, Bob noticed that news crews, barred from the cemetery, were filming from adjacent backyards. He should have been shockproof by now, but this crassness appalled him. Overhead, the helicopters made a terrible racket.

A priest stood by the grave as the mourners gathered. An awning and chairs had been set up for the family, and O.J. sat with the Browns without hesitating. After the brief service, he stood by Nicole's casket for a long time.

In New York City Dr. Baden drove his beloved antique Mercedes out to Kennedy Airport and parked in a short-term lot. He expected to be home by the weekend. It was obvious that O.J. Simpson had a lot of explaining to do. Ultimately, a client's guilt or innocence didn't really matter to Baden; it only minimally affected his role. His job, as he saw it, was to educate attorneys on the scientific strengths or weaknesses of the evidence.

Shapiro sent a car to pick him up at Los Angeles International. Baden had enjoyed traveling first class. Most lawyers flew him in steerage, but not Bob Shapiro. The driver took him to the Beverly Wilshire Hotel, where he checked into a mini-suite like the one provided for him during the Brando case. He called his cousins in Beverly Hills and left word he was in town for two or three days. That was all the time he could give Shapiro now. On Monday he was scheduled to testify in a homicide case in Ocean County, New Jersey.

Henry Lee was already there when Baden checked in. As they had previously arranged, they met for dinner. Lee, arriving at the hotel an hour earlier, had walked into a school of aggressive reporters. He felt harassed, but most of the journalists had left by the time Baden arrived. A few had asked questions. He knew that the bodies had been released from the coroner's office, so no secondary autopsy was likely. He didn't mention it, and beyond that, he actually knew little. But the media can get awfully creative even with a simple "No comment." He hated being on the spot like that.

A few hours later, Pavelic got a call from an officer on another matter. As they spoke, he realized that the cop was connected to the Simpson investigation. He said the department thought there was more than one killer. The wounds suggested each victim was murdered with a different weapon. Goldman's injuries indicated he had fought fiercely before he died.

Pavelic didn't ask how the department felt about Simpson. You never do that. No one discusses guilt or innocence at this stage. The talk sticks to what the cops have and what they are focusing on.

After the interment the procession moved off to the Brown family home in Dana Point. During the drive, as the car neared a Wendy's, Justin and Sydney said they were hungry. So Simpson ordered the chauffeur to turn in to the drive-in window. Every other car in line followed them: the white stretch limo, two cars filled with security men, two more limousines behind that, several private cars. The awestruck window clerk took orders for twenty hamburgers, french fries, and Cokes. His face made it plain he had never served

60

a funeral cortege before. Simpson paid him, and everybody laughed a little.

Kardashian was thinking about how to get back to Encino without being seen by the helicopters. The Browns' modest home sits at the end of a cul-de-sac so the choppers and cameramen had them trapped. Once there, Kardashian approached Al Cowlings: they began walking along the street to see where the helicopters were flying, where cameras were stationed outside the gated community. Simpson came out and joined them.

Kardashian's cell phone rang. It was Al Michaels, a good friend and an ABC-TV Monday night football announcer. He wanted an interview with Simpson. O.J. took the call and managed to say what was expected: He was feeling okay. He was trying to make sense of things. Then Bob had an idea and turned to Cowlings. The three men went inside. When it was time to leave, A.C. exchanged shirts and sunglasses with Simpson and got into O.J.'s suit jacket. Arnelle and Jason walked out to the limousine with Cowlings, staying close as if saying good-bye to their dad. Dennis, the security man, escorted Al to the limo and followed it out in the chase car.

It worked. The cloud of choppers took off after the stretch as it drove away. Kardashian, Simpson, and Denice waited about twenty minutes and left in A.C.'s Bronco. Nobody followed. They got back to the Brentwood Holiday Inn in rush hour traffic, unobserved. By now Simpson was asleep in the backseat. At the hotel, they split up. Kardashian and Simpson stayed in the Bronco for the ride to Encino. Denice followed in the Rolls.

Watching the late news, they laughed when footage taken by the choppers showed "O.J. Simpson" stepping out of the white limousine at Rockingham. Cowlings ducked his head at the right moment: The cameras didn't catch his face.

On the same broadcast they also heard that Simpson's arrest was imminent. The laughter died.

6

On Friday morning at 8:30, when everybody was still exhausted, Shapiro called and asked for Kardashian. Simpson was still in bed.

"I've got bad news," Shapiro began.

"What's that?"

"They've issued an arrest warrant for O.J. He has to surrender by eleven." Simpson would be charged with double homicide.

Kardashian's stomach began to churn. "Do you want me to tell him?"

"Why don't you wait until I get there. I'm on my way."

Kardashian felt ill. At least he didn't have to tell O.J. alone.

Denice reacted immediately. "You better call A.C."

"Right."

"He's O.J.'s best friend," Denice continued. "And he's bigger than O.J. If O.J. does something crazy, he can stop him."

Denice thought of something else: "Call someone to get the guns out of the house."

There were five guns in Bob's house: three rifles, a Smith & Wesson .38 that Kardashian had owned for years, and a pellet gun. Kardashian called his brother Tom, who now lived in Century City. Said that he needed him to take something out of the house. Okay, Tom said. Be there in thirty minutes. Too long, Bob said. By the time he got to Encino, it wouldn't matter. Randy Kolker, a friend living about five minutes away, agreed to come over.

Then he called A.C., who was still at Rockingham. "You better get over here right away. They're going to arrest O.J."

Cowlings said he was on his way. Then it hit Kardashian.

"How will you get here? Your Bronco is sitting in my driveway."

"Don't worry about it, man. I'll get there."

Randy Kolker pulled up. Kardashian waved him into the garage and closed the door in a sudden rush of paranoia: The police could be watching. Kolker asked what was up. Kardashian wasn't about to tell him, though he could see that Kolker was nervous. This cloak-and-dagger stuff wasn't Bob's style.

He brought the guns to the car wrapped in a towel.

"I just need you to get these out of here for a little while. I'll take them back later." That was all he said. He put the guns in Randy's trunk and opened the garage door before Kolker would ask anything more. They were good friends. Randy had to know Bob wouldn't put him in harm's way.

A while later, Kardashian looked out the window and saw someone in a black car drop off A.C.

Then Robert Shapiro arrives. "Is he awake?"

"I think so," Bob answers. "I haven't been up there yet."

"Well, we might as well get it over with."

They walk up the stairs and knock on the door. Simpson answers. They walk in. O.J. is still in the canopied bed, half under the covers, barechested, in undershorts, watching an old movie on cable. Kardashian sits down on the edge of the bed. Shapiro sits on the couch against the wall.

Shapiro speaks in a soft, kindly way. Almost gentle. Kardashian hasn't heard this voice before.

"O.J., the police have called. You have to turn yourself in today."

As Kardashian watches, Simpson hardly reacts. His face is blank. He seems to be staring off into space.

"They're going to charge you with double murder," Shapiro says, still gentle, "and you have to surrender yourself by eleven o'clock this morning."

Then Shapiro adds something that sounds ominous to Kardashian, something he's heard in the movies.

"If you have anything you want to tell us, O.J.," Shapiro says, "this is the time." His voice is professional and crisp again. "This is the last time you are going to be alone with your attorneys with no eavesdropping." Shapiro pauses, waiting for a reply. "This is the last chance you'll have to tell us anything you want to."

Still O.J. scarcely responds. "I've told you everything before," Simpson finally says in a weary voice. He turns on his side in the bed. "Basically, I've told you everything that transpired. I've got nothing to hide."

Then he adds that he can't believe it. "I can't understand why they aren't looking for other people. Two people had to do something like this. I don't understand why this is being blamed on me. I just can't believe this. It's like a setup."

Shapiro acknowledges the reply. But there's no time to linger. He's broken the news; it's over, he has other things to say. "I've got doctors and nurses on the way. We're going to take some blood samples and some hair samples, some photographs."

Suddenly O.J. comes to life. "I've got to take care of my kids," he says. "I have to make some calls."

Shapiro leaves, and Kardashian and Simpson are alone. Kardashian is startled to hear himself reminiscing about the fantastic life they had, the fun, the great times. He can hardly believe his awkward, valedictory air even as he speaks.

Simpson says he wants a little time to get dressed and think by himself. Kardashian leaves.

Alone now, O.J. reaches for a microcassette tape recorder belonging to Kardashian. Bending over it, still in bed, he punches the record button and tries to speak. Such a painful moan comes out that he clicks the STOP button. He tries again. A strangled groan, and he turns the tape off again.

Then, finally: "Oooh, boy! I don't know how I ended up here." The voice is haunting, raspy, almost sobbing. "I just don't know how I ended up here."

Simpson stops as if lost. There's a long silence. "I

64

thought I lived a great life. I thought I treated everybody well." He begins rushing his words. "I went out of my way to make everybody comfortable and happy." Now he slows down. His voice is breaking again. "I felt *very lonely* at times in recent years, and I don't know what it is. I mean, I had a loving girl in Paula. My kids loved me. Everybody loved me, but I don't know why I was feeling so alone all the time. And there was things that caught up with me. Uhhhhh, I don't even know what I'm saying here. . . ."

The entire recording takes less than ten minutes.

". . . Look where I am. I'm the Juice, whatever that means. But I felt at times like I was—ahhh!—I felt goodness in myself. I don't feel any goodness in myself right now. I feel emptiness . . . I don't even know what I'm saying here! I don't even know what this tape is for!"

Simpson winds down.

". . . Treat everybody the way you want to be treated and know your friends, share your pain with your friends; if I had made one mistake right now I'd realize that I didn't share my pain, and I think that's where I made my mistake." He exhales heavily. "Please remember me as the Juice. Please remember me as a good guy. I don't want you to remember me as whatever negative that might end here."

Simpson dresses in Bugle Boy jeans and a golf shirt, then walks barefoot into Kardashian's office.

Dr. Huizenga, psychiatrist Saul Faerstein, and two nurses are there. Denice brings in a huge breakfast tray. Paula wanders in and out of the room in tears. Simpson says he needs time to make some calls and write some things before the medical tests can begin.

Sitting at Kardashian's desk, he calls Louis Marks on the East Coast and Wayne Hughes locally. He asks these friends and business advisers money questions, and then tells them to be sure his children are provided for. He calls Skip Taft and begins to write his will on a yellow pad, talking and writing, faxing the will to Taft, waiting for it to come back with Taft's revisions, writing more, faxing again.

He calls Louis and Judy Brown in Dana Point, asks them to assume formal guardianship of his children. Skip will take care of the financial end. I want them raised in both cultures, he says. Don't raise them just white. Take them to black churches. He wants them to go to private schools. He asks to speak to Justin and Sydney. After that he calls Jason and Arnelle.

Simpson is now moving back and forth between the telephones and the impromptu medical station set up at the conference table, under an Impressionist painting.

Earlier that morning, Shapiro had called Baden at the Beverly Wilshire hotel. "There's been a change in plans," Shapiro said. "We may have an arrest this morning."

"If so," Baden argued quickly, "it's important that Dr. Lee and I examine Simpson. We'll need blood samples, hair, urine specimens now, before he's taken in."

Shapiro paused a moment. Then he agreed. "I'm on my way over to Simpson's location," he said. "I'm going to give you the address, a secret address. Can you take a hotel car and meet me there? Please don't communicate the address to anyone."

Baden quickly arranged to meet Lee downstairs. Then he called for a car. Both men stepped into the lobby carrying shoulder bags stuffed with cameras, film, and forensic and medical equipment. Baden fretted about being ambushed by media, but nobody was around.

Baden and Dr. Lee found Kardashian's house easily. The address meant nothing to the driver; it was a routine drop-off. As was his custom, Baden knocked on the front door to make sure he was in the right place while Henry stayed with the car.

For several long minutes, nobody answered. It was ten A.M. A housekeeper finally answered, said something in a language he thought was Korean. She looked Baden over, decided he belonged. Baden sent the hotel driver on his way.

Walking into the house with Dr. Lee, Dr. Baden felt as if he'd entered an exotic beehive. A tall teary brunette, fashion-model lovely, and a shapely blonde worthy of a centerfold walked past him and climbed a huge staircase in the center of the house. The housekeeper came and went. A short swarthy man with thick black hair appeared briefly.

66

From the TV news, Baden was vaguely aware that the tall brunette was O.J.'s girlfriend. The blonde seemed connected to the intense man. Baden spotted a powerful African-American who looked very upset hovering at the edge of things. Baden had no idea who Al Cowlings was.

Bob Shapiro came downstairs and said the police expected Simpson to turn himself in at eleven A.M. Please go to the second-floor office, he told Baden, and do your work as quickly as possible.

As he walked in, a young doctor and two nurses, none of whom he knew, were drawing Simpson's blood. Saul Faerstein, whom he knew from the Brando case, was nearby. Baden tried not to be obvious about it, but he stared at the superstar. What he saw surprised him. Not the hard-charging bigger-than-life athlete he'd expected. Not today, anyway. The man was quiet, polite, almost meek. He was even charming. But there was something in his eyes. Or rather, something missing. Something so subtle that Baden almost didn't catch it. Like a migratory bird, Simpson was gone.

Now Simpson is writing letters by hand, one to his children, another to his mother. He seals them and passes the envelopes to Kardashian. The longest letter follows, four handwritten pages on a yellow legal pad. He writes on the sealed envelope, "To Whom It May Concern, press or public."

The clock is rushing toward eleven. Kardashian prods Simpson to finish and get on with the tests.

"Why should I hurry? What can they do to me?"

Kardashian considers this. "You're right," he finally admits. "Take your time. What can they do?"

But Shapiro, who must live in the law enforcement world, can't accept that. "O.J., I gave them my word we'd be there at eleven," he argues. "I told them we were acting in good faith." Simpson ignores him and continues writing.

At the conference table, Baden introduced himself to both Simpson and Dr. Huizenga. As the nurse drew blood, he requested another tube for his own work.

I'm glad to have you here, O.J. said with extraordinary politeness. Baden acknowledged this and pulled out his camera, as did Henry Lee. Baden examined healing cuts on O.J.'s fingers. They were four days old by now. Dr. Lee, the criminalist, and Baden, the pathologist, started to discuss the knuckle cut.

Shapiro kept urging everyone to hurry. He explained that he wanted Simpson to arrive at Parker Center in his Mercedes, well dressed, calm, dignified. If an impatient police contingent found them in Encino, O.J. would be hustled away in handcuffs. Like a common criminal. No one was willing to say the words, but they hung in the air.

As Henry Lee took his pictures, Baden realized that the odd expression on Simpson's face, disguised at first by his considerable charm, was what clinicians call flat affect. O.J. was deeply depressed. His emotional self had fled. Baden serves on a board that reviews prison suicides. He turned to Dr. Faerstein. ''We have to notify the jail people to put him on a suicide watch.'' The psychiatrist agreed, and he briefed Shapiro.

It was now almost eleven, and Parker Center was at least half an hour away. Shapiro asked Faerstein to call and explain that they were trying to get O.J. down there, but that he was clinically depressed. There are three doctors here, Baden heard Faerstein explaining to someone, and we're trying to get him together to bring him down.

The detective told Faerstein they'd better do it very quickly. Otherwise the police would have to come get Simpson. Where are you? he asked.

Faerstein put his hand over the phone and turned to Shapiro. Don't give him the address, the lawyer said. Faerstein told the detective that he couldn't give it out: He was a psychiatrist and Simpson was his patient.

The testing dragged on. Skin samples, urine samples, hair and blood samples. Simpson sat at the table with a blank expression. Kardashian joked that Reebok had called and asked him not to wear their tennis shoes for the arrest. No one laughed. The clock was pushing noon. Shapiro asked someone to call Parker Center again. This time the police were not even polite. They demanded the address. Faerstein repeated that he couldn't give it out.

"We've issued an arrest warrant," the detective said.

When Shapiro heard this, his attitude shifted abruptly. Wait a minute, he said, that changes things. Baden understood. Now they were harboring a fugitive. Shapiro took the phone, and gave Kardashian's address. We'll wait for you, Shapiro said. Baden was riveted. Everything seemed very final now.

Simpson was still at the conference table when the tests ended a few minutes later. He motioned to Paula Barbieri and walked out. The police aren't going to wait any longer, Shapiro told Kardashian. Tell O.J. to get ready. Tell him to shower and wear a suit, something nice. This will be the public's image when he goes in. Kardashian left the room.

Baden found a window overlooking the street so he could see the police arrive.

Simpson and Paula Barbieri stood in the side yard, holding each other. "I want you to leave," Simpson said. She was teary and defiant. "I'm not leaving."

"I don't want you to see this. Look, I didn't do this thing. I love you, and I want you to stay strong. It'll be all right. A.C. has some money to get you back to Florida."

"I'm not going to leave."

Simpson was spent. His face emptied out. Cowlings held nearly $8,000 in cash and checks, the golf winnings that O.J. claimed had been stolen by the LAPD but that turned out to be under a sweater in the closet after all. Two thousand for Paula, the rest for Jason and Arnelle. O.J. told Paula to call her manager and go to the airport.

Paula's manager arrived quickly. Simpson and his girlfriend stood beside the house, embracing. Paula was crying, wouldn't get in the car. "A.C., give her the money and get her out of here," Simpson said almost angrily. Kardashian and Cowlings, half escorts, half bodyguards, got Paula into the car. It was embarrassing.

Everybody knew it was time. Simpson went to the guest suite. Cowlings went with him.

* * *

O.J. is sitting alone on the couch by the canopied bed when Kardashian enters. For a moment, he doesn't register what he sees. He takes in fragments: a green towel lying in his friend's lap, the pictures of Nicole and Justin and Sydney. Simpson's head is down as if he is praying. He stares wordlessly at the pictures.

Then Kardashian sees a pistol is wrapped in the towel on O.J.'s lap. He can hardly speak. "What are you doing!"

O.J.'s voice is a gravelly mix of anger and tears. Kardashian sees a tiger in a net.

"Man, I don't know. I just don't know what's happening."

Suddenly Kardashian remembers the small black hard-shelled case he pulled from under the front seat of Simpson's Bentley—the case O.J. told Bob to bring here to his house. It looked a bit like a toy violin case. But it wasn't.

Bob drops to his knees in front of the couch and holds out his hands. Simpson takes them. "Let's pray about it," Kardashian says. O.J. says nothing, but Kardashian begins by asking for strength, then for forgiveness, for the Lord to take pity on his friend and help him find his way, help him remember that people love him, that his children need him. He asks for understanding, for compassion. Help us, O Lord; thy will be done, thy kingdom come. Simpson's head stays down all the while.

"I'm gonna kill myself," he says in a rasping voice as soon as Kardashian finishes.

"You can't. You have your little children, and they need you."

Kardashian works hard to stay in touch. He has a feeling that a voice inside Simpson is talking now, not Simpson himself. He has to get past that and tries to get his friend to look at him. There's no spark, nothing for Kardashian to connect with.

"I just can't live with the pain. I just can't go on. Nicole is gone. I can't go on."

So many years of hard, unshakable faith, so many years of blind acceptance that God's plan will be evident—but now very little is evident, at least not to Bob. Kardashian suddenly knows he can share only part of his friend's journey. He can only hope that God will reveal Himself to O.J.

"Look, you know it's between you and God," he hears himself saying. "I think it's wrong. I don't think you should do this. But I can't do anything to stop you. You're facing prison. I don't know what I'd do in your position, so I'm not the one to say. Only you can make that decision. But God knows what's right."

As he talks, Kardashian wonders why he is so *accommodating*. Why isn't he stronger? Why doesn't he go after the gun? But something else is at work here, an iron sense of fatalism. O.J. is looking at two very bad choices. Either he kills himself, Kardashian assumes, or he goes to prison and endures unimaginable humiliation. To a superstar athlete who feeds off mass attention, public disgrace would be unbearable.

He offers another prayer. Take my friend to heaven if he kills himself, he asks. Bob had talked about the theological unlikelihood of getting there, but he prays now that God might relent. He's also buying time as a vague idea starts to take shape.

"I'm going to kill myself in this room," Simpson says.

"You can't. This is my daughter's bedroom." Kardashian is thinking fast. "I have my little girl in this room, and every time I come in here, I'll see your body lying there. You can't do that." His mind is whirling. "Why don't you go outside?"

Simpson rises from the couch slowly. The pistol is still wrapped in the green towel, which he cradles against his chest. The tall black athlete and the short dark-haired Kardashian climb down the stairs together and slip quietly through the door to the laundry room. Shapiro, Baden, and the others are in Kardashian's office, waiting for Simpson to reappear suitably dressed for surrender.

Standing by the window, Michael Baden can't believe that the police are taking so long. Later he would learn that they were lost. Kardashian, a private man by lifelong inclination, had purposely leased a house far off the main thoroughfares.

Shapiro, as usual, spends the time making calls. Dr. Huizenga and his nurses pack up their equipment.

"Well, maybe I'll just do it here."

O.J. and Bob are sitting on a four-foot-high retaining wall, rimmed by shrubbery, near the laundry room door. The gun and towel are in Simpson's lap. Kardashian says nothing. Simpson looks at the sun straight overhead, shades his eyes, and looks down.

"I can't kill myself in these bushes. It's too close to the house."

"Okay," Kardashian says. "Let's walk a little."

Simpson lifts the gun and towel to his chest again, and they walk almost casually into the backyard. Kardashian is skating boldly on the thin ice of O.J. Simpson's life. He has a sense that he is making good choices. This might, just might, come out okay. "Why don't you kill yourself in the yard out here?" he asks. "That way you'd be away from the house a little bit."

Simpson surveys the grounds and looks up at the sun again. "I'd be baking in the sun. I don't want to bake in the sun."

"What difference does it make?"

Kardashian can hardly believe he has said that. But it feels right. "You're not going to be here. You're going to be gone, and your spirit will be gone. What do you care if you're baking in the sun?" He is starting to believe that if he humors O.J. long enough, nothing will happen.

"I just don't want to be baking in the sun."

"Okay, let's walk over here." Kardashian motions to an area near his living room where an overhang provides shade. He glances up at the balcony that opens from his second-floor office. Fortunately, nobody is there.

Simpson stops by the first-floor living room window. "I'll do it there," he says.

"No, you can't do it there," Kardashian argues. "Every time I sit in the living room I'm going to see your body there."

Simpson examines the area where the driveway is extended to make room for cars parked beside the garage. "I'll do it there." As Simpson turns his head, he keeps the gun wrapped in the towel very tight against his chest. He doesn't really like that spot, either. "I can't do it in the driveway. Cars park there. They'd be parked over where I was. I don't want to do it there."

Al Cowlings walks out of the front door. Simpson is considering a spot near a side entrance where some empty cartons are stacked up. He rejects it. He doesn't want to be found in a pile of trash.

Cowlings looks at Kardashian, who rolls his eyes in a signal. Cowlings is silent. Kardashian decides to move his friend's suicide off the property altogether. He has no idea why he is doing this. "Why don't you just go down the street and do it? You could just walk down the street."

"I don't want to be found in the street."

"Then why don't you go to the Bel Air Church?" Bob says, "You were married there, and you lived across the street on Elville."

Simpson likes that. Cowlings can drive him, and he can take care of things right there. At the church where he married Nicole, near the street where he bought his first home in Brentwood.

But this is becoming too risky. Simpson will be somewhere else, out of his control. Kardashian loses his discipline for a moment. "A.C., we've got to stop him."

Simpson interrupts. "This is what I've got to do."

"A.C., you're bigger than me, you stop him."

"Come on, man," A.C. says. "What do you want to do this for? You can't do this."

"Hey, just leave me alone. This is something I've got to do."

Kardashian momentarily gives up. "You take care of him, A.C.," he says with deep sadness. "God knows I've tried."

They go inside to make final preparations. Kardashian has one last, strange card to play in this macabre game. He fetches his camera and brings out Denice and Cathy Randa, who are downstairs.

"You know what, if we're not going to see you again, I

want to get some pictures." At this surreal moment taking snapshots somehow makes sense. The camera is passed back and forth. Each friend poses, arms around Simpson. Kardashian adds a picture of O.J. standing alone. Weeks later, he discovers that all the shots were badly exposed. They all look terrible.

Now Kardashian turns his back on his friend of twenty-four years. A man should be allowed to kill himself if he wants to, he growls to himself.

Kardashian knows athletes are monstrous and magical beings for whom fame comes very early. Many have no life experience to prepare them for legions of worshipful fans and staggering wealth. They become dependent on praise and public attention. No street drug is as powerful, and Kardashian has understood his friend's addiction for decades. Few experiences in his life have been quite so sublime as hanging with O.J. The pleasure Simpson experiences when people focus on him is almost incandescent. O.J. so loves the attention you pay him that he makes *you* feel good.

Now his larger-than-life friend faces a fall so steep that Kardashian can't imagine it. Nicole is gone. And his other great love, the public, has turned on him. They will see him handcuffed. The humiliation and loneliness facing this man are beyond words. There is nothing left.

Kardashian walks upstairs to rejoin the doctors. The police should be here any minute. His last act as a friend is to leave the athlete alone to define his life as he wishes.

Kardashian shuts his office door behind him. Everybody turns to him. Shapiro asks about Simpson.

"He's getting ready, I left A.C. with him."

Kardashian sits down behind his desk. Everybody has packed his gear and is waiting. The room settles into hesitant small talk. Twenty minutes pass. The doorbell rings.

Kardashian and Shapiro walk downstairs first. The others follow and sit on the stairs. It is nearly two P.M. Kardashian opens the door, and two uniformed policemen in crisply pressed blues step inside as if this is all very routine.

"I'm here to get Mr. Simpson," one says.

"I think he's in his room," Kardashian answers with

Shapiro beside him. They turn to the foot of the tall staircase and Kardashian calls upstairs. The policemen stand behind him.

"The police are here, O.J. It's time to go."

Silence.

"O.J., it's time to go." Kardashian raises his voice slightly.

Nothing. Kardashian, his stomach churning, turns to the waiting cops. "Well, his room's up over there. He probably can't hear us. Come with me."

Kardashian and the officers climb the stairs. Bob calls out his friend's name several times. The three men turn right at the top of the stairs and walk into the hallway leading to the guest suite.

"This is his room." Kardashian knocks on the door. He has no idea whether he'll see his friend. No answer.

They open the door. The room is empty. The cops stiffen. He can see they've shifted gear.

"I don't know where he is," Bob says, trying to be calm. "Maybe he's downstairs."

One officer pulls his radio out of its leather holster and speaks into it. Other policemen are now downstairs. "He's not here," the cop says. "Is he down there?"

The first-floor police contingent quickly begins a house-wide search. Kardashian's office and den are in the same upstairs wing as the guest suite, so the two officers with Bob check those rooms. Kardashian shows them a hidden area behind a wall in the den. Nobody there. Cops search the garage and the areas outside the house where Simpson considered killing himself an hour earlier. One cop asks Kardashian who else is present on the property. He mentions Cowlings. His stomach hurts.

The cop tells him to find A.C. Kardashian asks generally around the front room. Nobody says anything. He pauses as if an idea just occurred to him and looks outside. His mind is whirling now.

"I don't see A.C.'s Bronco," he manages, hoping to sound helpful. "It's possible . . ." He stumbles. "It's possible that A.C. took O.J. in the Bronco with him."

* * *

Baden assumed that O.J. was saying good-bye to Paula in some private place. These things take time. But then the police started moving from room to room, talking into their radios. More time passed. Gradually the unthinkable occurred to everyone. The police were looking at him and the others on the stairs, too. Was he imagining this? Were they accusing him?

Next he and the others were herded to a room on the second floor and told not to leave. The house was sealed off. Professionally, he understood this. In their place, he would have done the same thing. He heard more police arriving and the clatter of a helicopter overhead. Shapiro, calm and thoughtful as always, offered a detective his thoughts on where Simpson might be. Kardashian had some ideas as well. Simpson might be headed for the USC campus or the Bel Air Church, Kardashian said. Both lawyers seemed genuinely surprised, Baden thought.

Nicole Pulvers, Kardashian's assistant, comes into the room and says quietly, "Telephone, Robert." Her voice has an edge.

"I can't talk now."

"It's your sister," Pulvers says firmly. She won't go away. It isn't like her to be pushy. Kardashian leaves the room and takes the call.

"I shot myself in the head," Simpson rasps into the phone, "but I didn't die." Kardashian surmises he's calling from A.C.'s Bronco.

Kardashian can't tell if this is a joke. Did the gun not fire—or is O.J. trying to be funny? A lot of strange humor has passed between the two friends over the years.

Simpson tells Kardashian that a minute earlier he had held the gun against his head and pulled the trigger. The pistol malfunctioned. Nothing happened. It isn't comedy.

"Where are you?" Bob asks.

"At the Bel Air Church."

As casually as he can manage, he asks, "Are you doing it there?"

"Nah, what a mess this is, right?" Simpson sounds oddly elated.

"The police are here." Kardashian looks over his shoulder to see if anyone is listening.

"All right. I'm going over to Nicole's now."

He has no idea what this means. To see the crime scene? To join her in death?

"Okay, I'll talk to you later." Kardashian adds desperately, "I love you."

Kardashian puts down the phone. As he walks back to the room where the police officers are he says to himself, If they ask who I was talking to, I have to tell them. But the cops never ask.

Louis Brown was at Nicole's condo sorting through his daughter's things when Simpson called. They exchanged pleasantries and O.J. said he was dropping by. When Simpson hung up Brown called the police. They converged on the Bundy-Dorothy corner within minutes. Cowlings and Simpson spotted them from a distance and didn't stop.

At Kardashian's home the LAPD issues an all-points bulletin. Detectives are asking Dr. Faerstein if he knows where Simpson might go. He tells them that his patient may be severely depressed. O.J. might try to visit his children.

Kardashian cautiously suggests the possibility of a suicide. Shapiro interrupts, "You have this letter he gave you. Maybe it will reveal where he went."

Kardashian would know *when* to read it, Simpson had told him—and this is a last request. He has to respect O.J.'s wishes. This isn't the time. But he has no choice, Shapiro says. He climbs the stairs to retrieve the letter from his coat pocket. A detective immediately asks him for it. He is furious with Shapiro.

"It isn't opened yet," Kardashian protests. "I want to read it first."

Read it aloud, the detective says. Huizenga, Lee, Baden, Shapiro, and two detectives listen.

"First, everyone understand I had nothing to do with Nicole's murder," begins the scratchy handwritten text. "I loved her, always have and always will. If we had a problem it's because I loved her so much." There are frequent

77

misspellings, and occasionally Bob must pause to puzzle out a phrase. "Recently we came to the understanding that for now we weren't right for each other at least for now. . . ."

Simpson thinks everyone should know how hard it was to separate from Nicole, how he hoped eventually for a "friendship or more." Kardashian reads each page and hands it to Shapiro, who scans it and passes it on to the police. Kardashian is amazed that Simpson would devote the entire first page to his marital history. He even mentions the 1989 beating, insisting that he "took the heat" to "protect our privacy." Does the world need to know this?

The letter rambles through paragraphs alleging that the press fabricated much of what is being said. It adds a "last wish" that reporters leave his children alone. A long section follows thanking financial advisers, social friends, golfing buddies, teammates, lawyers, his first wife, Marguerite; there's a love note to Paula Barbieri. One name in the laundry list of special friends is "Bobby Kardashian." About all his friends, Simpson says: "I wish we had spent more time together in recent years."

It becomes clear that this odd mix of farewells and self-defense will not provide clues to Simpson's whereabouts. The detective asks to have the original. Kardashian argues that it is a personal letter.

"It is evidence, Mr. Kardashian," the officer says.

Can he give them a copy? He looks to Shapiro for support. The law requires the original, Shapiro explains with mild irritation. Kardashian struggles to contain his anger and goes to his office to make copies.

"I've had a good life," Simpson adds. "I'm proud of how I lived, my mamma taught me to do unto others. I treated people the way I wanted to be treated. I always tried to be up and helpful. So why is this happening? I'm sorry for the Goldman family. I know how much it hurts."

There are six squad cars outside the house. Detectives now herd everyone to another room and post a guard. They search the house thoroughly. Kardashian assumes they are looking through Simpson's things, his Louis Vuitton garment bag, the black duffel bag, the golf clubs in the garage.

He can't be sure. He and Shapiro and the doctors cannot leave the second floor.

In the den, they speculate about where Simpson could have gone. Shapiro is on the phone, and suddenly he calls out to the cop at the door. He tells the uniform he has scheduled a five P.M. press conference. He and Kardashian must be interviewed now so they can go. Detectives take them to Bob's office. About halfway through the interview, Shapiro interrupts to say they must leave. The press conference must start exactly at five o'clock, he says, to make the dinnertime news programs. He and Kardashian will appeal to O.J. to turn himself in.

The detectives aren't finished, but let them go. Kardashian is amazed. Power of the media, he supposes. Shapiro had called his secretary and had her arrange the conference. He hadn't consulted anyone, including Kardashian.

He asks Kardashian to read the letter on television. My life isn't about this at all, Bob thinks. I'm not a public person. Speaking before three people in a sales meeting makes me nervous.

Shapiro sits in the back of the black Mercedes with him. On the way to Shapiro's office, Kardashian goes over the letter several times. The misspellings and awkward handwriting will make reading it aloud difficult.

". . . I think of my life and feel I've done most of the right things. So why do I end up like this? I can't go on. No matter what the outcome, people will look and point. I can't take that. I can't subject my children to that. This way they can move on and go on with their lives. . . ."

How can he read this in public? On television, no less! This is a suicide note. I'll break down, Kardashian thinks. I'll picture O.J. dead somewhere. I'll freeze up in front of the entire country.

He asks Shapiro for advice. Whatever you do, speak slowly, the lawyer says. Jack Nicholson made a fortune speaking slowly. You cannot look bad that way. Talk even more slowly than you are thinking.

He tells Shapiro about Simpson's gun. He has to assume

the worst by now. "I think he's dead. That's what he wanted."

They pull into an underground garage at 4:45, and walk to a conference room in Century City's Fox Tower where the press has gathered. The door is closed. When Shapiro opens it, Kardashian goes white. More than a hundred clamoring reporters and photographers face them. Every eye turns toward the two men in the doorway.

Shapiro glances at Bob Kardashian. "Let's go upstairs first," he says quickly.

He takes Kardashian to his office and invites him to sit down. Someone brings a glass of water. Before long, Bob is as ready as he'll ever be—which is to say, not ready at all. A few minutes later, they are in front of the media. Shapiro talks as cameramen maneuver for the best shots and reporters jostle one another. He appeals to Simpson to turn himself in. Kardashian stands beside him in a fog. He is deep inside himself mourning the death of his friend. Part of him surfaces enough to wonder how Shapiro can go through this charade when he knows the athlete is dead. But he has no time to analyze Shapiro's strategy. He hears the cultivated voice introducing him.

From the first moment, Kardashian feels separated from his body. Who is reading the letter? Where is that steady voice coming from? The man at the podium is confident, comfortable, serious, as befits the circumstances, but calm, as if he is explaining difficult matters to a friend—to millions of friends. He looks up from the text occasionally and makes eye contact with the cameras.

". . . Don't feel sorry for me. I've had a great life, made great friends. Please think of the real O.J. and not this lost person. Thank you for making my life special. I hope I help yours. Peace & Love, O.J."

Kardashian finishes and stares down at the remarkable signature. The "O" in "O.J." is a happy face. A big smile at the end of a suicide note.

Reporters crowd him, shouting questions, asking how to spell his name, asking to see the letter. Shapiro and some security men pull him away. As they sit in his office sipping soft drinks and watching the television coverage, Shapiro looks pleased. It was a perfect media event.

The media is butchering Kardashian's name. Bob never realized there were so many different ways to mispronounce it. My private life is over, he thinks absentmindedly. They can do what they want. It is six o'clock. Could Shapiro's driver drop him off at Rockingham? He'd promised to brief O.J.'s family. He has to tell Jason and Arnelle that their father is dead.

In Florida the tropical heat ranges from insufferable to merely unbearable as June inches toward July. As the week wore on, F. Lee Bailey in Miami stayed in touch with Los Angeles only professionally. He wasn't involved emotionally. McKenna was in Chicago. Bailey talked to Shapiro almost daily and watched the news every night, but his interest paralleled his location. He felt distant.

He was driving to meet a friend for dinner when Shapiro rang his cell phone. Minutes earlier, on the news, Bailey had heard that Simpson was a fugitive. Now Shapiro was in Century City about to begin his press conference and telling Bailey he was certain that Simpson had killed himself. He and Kardashian were about to go on television. The press was there, and as yet the police had no word of a suicide. So Shapiro was going ahead with the show.

Listening to Kardashian read Simpson's letter on his car radio, Bailey reacted emphatically. The letter *shrieked* innocence. Of course, he assumed most of the world would think otherwise. But he found it hard to imagine that a high-profile celebrity would murder his wife and a stranger in a densely populated area at a time when neighbors, dog walkers, and joggers could witness it. That did not add up, not by any measure the veteran criminal lawyer could imagine. And the savagery of the crimes—it was too much to stomach.

At Johnnie Cochran's law offices the Friday calendar meeting stopped when Kardashian began reading the letter. Every attorney in the room stared at the TV set as if the whole world had shrunk to one small rectangle. It was one thing that O.J. Simpson wasn't righteously black, but quite another that a famous black man was talking about killing himself. Even Shawn Chapman felt pity.

Almost everyone in the firm assumed from the outset he was guilty. When O.J. ran, they were convinced. Most of the lawyers were already riled after hearing Wednesday that Shapiro had the case. "Howard says he's out," Johnnie told people in the hallways. Shapiro doesn't have the experience. Why hadn't Johnnie been retained?

But now the mood was sadness, not anger. When Kardashian finished, they pushed through the calendar double-time so people could get home to watch the basketball playoffs. Top scorer Hakeem Olajuwon of the Houston Rockets was on the court that night.

Kathy Ferrigno, a San Diego State University student, looked out the window of her Camry on the Santa Ana Freeway in Orange County. "Chris! Chris! Chris! There's a white Bronco." Her friend Chris Thomas looked at the plate, then pulled beside the car. It was the white Bronco. Cowlings had the window down, his elbow hanging out. He looked calm, but he turned and gave them a stern look, a "dead" look. Kathy's mouth hung open.

Deputy Larry Pool was heading north on the same freeway when he caught a glimpse of a white Bronco emerging from the on ramp at Jamboree Road. Seconds later he was in the Bronco's blind spot, checking out the occupants. Knowing Simpson was a wanted man, he read the plate, 3DHY503. It came back a match. "Ten-four, I'm behind it," Pool radioed in. Everything stopped on the air. There was a long pause before he had acknowledgment from the dispatcher.

Noticing the black-and-white beside him, Cowlings turned and smiled nervously. Through the tinted windows it looked as if Simpson was in the back, Pool thought. Seconds later Sergeant Sewell joined the chase. Now there were two black-and-whites.

The Bronco stopped in heavy traffic at Grand Avenue in Orange County. Cowlings glanced to the side and saw two guns pointing at him. All he heard was the deputies ordering him to cut his engine. Cowlings started screaming, swearing, yelling "No!" and pounding his fists on the door. The blows were so violent the Bronco shook.

The traffic cleared at Grand Avenue and the officers found themselves behind Cowlings again, traveling down the freeway. The chase had begun.

This was trouble. Cowlings dialed 911. There was a bizarre logic in this: He needed police help, after all.

"This is A.C. I have O.J. in the car," Cowlings told the dispatcher. "Right now . . . we're okay. But you got to tell them, just back off." In his rearview mirror he could see the black-and-whites grouping behind him. "He's still alive, but he's got a gun to his head. . . . Let me get back to the house."

The cellular phone calls from the Bronco were being tracked by the police. O.J.'s phone signal was like a geolocation system. Even the media knew where he was. KCAL News was the first chopper to find the white Bronco and its flotilla of police cars.

In Chicago, McKenna had a drink at the East Bank Club downtown with an old friend who'd gotten pretty high-ranking in the police department. His friend gave up some general information, nothing big. The Chicago P.D. had taken photographs and drawn a floor plan of Room 915, where Simpson had stayed. It was actually a small suite. They'd lifted fingerprints from the telephone and a bathroom countertop. Broken glass was in the bathroom sink. The guy wouldn't say if the glass had blood on it. They did find blood on some pillowcases, a washcloth, and a towel. It was fresh. The department's opinion was that someone wouldn't be cleaning up fresh blood six hours after getting cut in Los Angeles.

McKenna's source had nothing good to say about the LAPD. They'd faxed a report to Los Angeles, and somebody leaked the *whole document* to the L.A. press. The Los Angeles media had taken things out of context and made Chicago look like amateurs.

Otherwise, it was a terrible day. The World Cup soccer matches started that afternoon in Chicago. President Clinton was there. The city was a zoo. Nothing he could do until Monday.

McKenna returns to his hotel and turns on the TV, and suddenly he sees Al Cowlings's Bronco on the freeway, being chased by the cops. McKenna watches the whole chase. He feels that for the rest of his life he will remember every detail of this day, the way he does the day Kennedy was shot.

On the freeway, Simpson listened as his friend Wayne Hughes recited the Forty-first Psalm. "I said, Lord, be merciful unto me: heal my soul; for I have sinned against thee. . . ."

Hughes was at a late lunch when his secretary sent word that O.J. was calling: some kind of emergency. He hurried back to his office and returned the call. It turned into a perfect last talk, if there can be such a thing. A rabbi had given him a special prayer from Psalm 41 when his son was ill. He knew it by heart and he recited it to O.J. "Mine enemies speak evil of me. . . . Against me do they devise my hurt."

Both men cried and expressed their love. O.J. talked about dying. Hughes thought, Well, if that's what he thinks is the right thing to do, maybe it is. O.J. cried out in such pain that Hughes assumed he was alone somewhere.

"But thou O Lord, be merciful unto me, and raise me up. . . ."

Simpson asked Hughes to look out for his kids' money, particularly Jason's. He wanted no advice for himself. His friend offered none. Simpson ended by saying he was on his way to see Nicole. Amid tears, they finally hung up.

Wayne Hughes couldn't focus on business anymore that day. Driving home, he heard the news that his friend was a fugitive and realized that his secretary had O.J.'s phone number. He called her from his car and told her to call the police: Give them the number. Tell them I talked to him.

The LAPD called him back quickly. Did Simpson have a gun? Hughes knew he owned guns, but there had been no mention of a gun this afternoon. Was Simpson alone?

84

Hughes couldn't imagine anyone talking like that unless he was.

Uniformed officers stop Kardashian when he pulls up at Rockingham.

"I'm Mr. Simpson's doctor."

He wasn't thinking about how to talk his way inside. Medical credentials appear out of the blue when he opens his mouth.

The police let him enter since the family knows him. Cops are everywhere downstairs with their walkie-talkies. He decides that O.J.'s bedroom is the most private place to talk and asks everyone to come up. About ten people follow— sisters, cousins, a niece's boyfriend. He focuses on Jason and Arnelle.

Compared to this, reading the letter on national TV was easy. He stands next to the bedside table and stares out the glass doors. His friend's son and daughter sit nearby on the edge of the bed. Other relatives take the couch. The room is painfully still. Incongruously, he feels like an entertainer. He has complete control of the room.

O.J. loved them, he begins.

Kardashian can't say it yet.

O.J. loved them so much he wanted to safeguard their future. He wanted them to have the money they needed. Kardashian takes a deep breath. A long trial would have depleted it. And he couldn't bear to have them humiliated in the press. Terrible things would be written.

"I feel your father will kill himself." Nobody says anything. "He doesn't want to go to jail. I think he's probably already killed himself by now. He loved you very much."

Silence follows. It's as if no one is breathing.

Jason, big and burly, jumps off the bed as if someone has set him on fire. He bangs on a mirror, then a door, in his fury and pain. Oh my God! Oh my God! He hits the door so hard it cracks, runs into the bathroom, and starts to cry. A cousin rushes in to calm him.

Arnelle stares at Bob, tears falling from her eyes. He tries to say more, but can't. Your father loved you so much. He wanted to leave you money. He got caught in something that kept snowballing. He felt he had to do this.

On the couch, someone grabs the remote and turns on the TV to see if there is news. Kardashian looks at the screen. He sees a white Bronco on the freeway with police cars following.

"What are you talking about?" someone shouts. "O.J. and A.C. are in the Bronco. They're on television!"

Kardashian doesn't know whether to laugh or cry. He is ecstatic and profoundly embarrassed all in the same instant. But nobody notices. Everyone in the room is hypnotized by the image of the Bronco. A TV anchor says Simpson is riding in the backseat with a gun to his head. Al Cowlings is driving.

Jason races out of the bathroom, yelling, "Come on, Dad! Come on!" Arnelle is praying; her face is streaked with tears, her hands clasped. The room fills with cheers.

"You upstaged me again, you son of a bitch," Kardashian says ruefully.

The phone rings. Tom Kardashian is calling from the house in Encino. "A.C. just called. They're going to come in. He's looking for you." His wife, Joan, had answered A.C.'s call. Cowlings kept saying, Where's Bob? Where's Bob? And Tom didn't know. He tried Rockingham on a hunch.

Bob wants the telephone number in the car. Tom had forgotten to find out.

He hangs up and asks around the bedroom. No one knows. It's a new phone, Arnelle says.

A uniformed cop appears in the doorway. He'd climbed the stairs while Kardashian was shouting over the television. Does anyone have the number?

Then Bob remembers: 613-3232. He's called it once or twice at most, but now it comes to him. God's will, he says to himself.

He dials the phone by the bed. Simpson answers. Everyone in the room turns from the television set to Bob. "O.J., it's Bob."

"Hey, man."

86

The athlete's voice is oddly mellow, but also out of control. Kardashian hears highway noises and police sirens.

"I tried to see her, but they wouldn't let me. I was going to do it at the cemetery."

"What do you mean they wouldn't let you?"

"There was a police car blocking the way." Simpson's voice trembles slightly. Kardashian feels the edge. "We drove around the back and looked over the fence. I wanted to climb the fence, but there were people around."

He hears Cowlings talking: Put that thing down. Come on, O.J., put it down.

"We drove to some orange field and sat there for a while," Simpson continues. "I was going to do it there, but I couldn't see myself lying in some field. I can't be remembered that way."

The cop is standing two feet away, motioning for the phone. Kardashian waves him away. He knows he can't hand the phone over. Everything Bob's ever heard about suicidal people says you stay on the line.

The tension is tearing holes in him. Kardashian was raised to respect authority. He went to military school; he goes to church. The police officer again asks for the phone. Bob doesn't respond. He is going to save his friend's life if he can.

Now the cop reaches out. Kardashian continues to ignore him, stiffening slightly, waiting to see if he'll try to pull it out of his hand. But the cop knows the rules of suicide prevention, too. He moves back.

"If I can't do it with Nicole, I want to do it at home." O.J. is talking in a low half-crying voice. "But first I want to see Mamma."

Eunice went back to San Francisco, Kardashian tells him. But he can call her. He doesn't say she's been hospitalized because of the stress. "Come on in, O.J."

The phone cuts out. He redials frantically. Nothing. Then he connects.

Simpson wails, "Why wouldn't they let me do it, man?"

Kardashian gently moves the subject to better times, women they knew, parties, trips, kids. The phone cuts out again. He redials. Gets the taped voice saying Your-party-isn't-available. He dials again. Arnelle and Jason sit transfixed. The room is deathly quiet except for the voices of TV commentators and highway sounds.

Two other policemen come to the bedroom door. Kardashian doesn't know it, but the SWAT team is on its way. The house is flooded with police. Let me talk to him, a detective says. Kardashian shakes his head. The cop insists.

"No." He shakes his head again.

On the other end, Simpson is muddled. He doesn't ask who Kardashian is talking to. But the conversation is becoming ominous again. "I've got this gun to my head. What a mess, huh? I just want to be with Nicole. That's all I want. How did I get into this, Bobby?"

"Come on in, O.J." Kardashian tries to sound calm. "You can do what you need to do here."

It is in God's hands now. If Simpson gets home and still wants to kill himself, so be it.

"What a life we had, Bobby, you know? We really had some great times. I love you so much, Bobby. You know what our life was together. How great it was when we lived in that house. We had fun. How could it come to this, Bobby? I just don't know what's happening."

"Come on, Juice, put the gun down," he hears A.C. saying over the traffic noise. "Put it in your lap, man. Put it down."

Cowlings now has the phone. He and Kardashian talk strategy frantically, trying to stay calm.

"You've got to bring him in, A.C. Come on." Kardashian doesn't know if he is pleading with Cowlings or trying to pump him up. ·

The phone dies. Redialing doesn't work. Kardashian looks at Jason and Arnelle: Your dad's on his way back. The room melts into obvious relief. It is time to go downstairs and wait for him. The police start moving them, Jason and Arnelle first. Kardashian dials again. A detective asks, Can you come downstairs, Doc? The cop promises he can use the phone downstairs.

The ground floor is a war room. Police everywhere, both

uniformed and plainclothes. But the new players are SWAT team cops, unlike any cops Kardashian has ever seen. They are an occupying force, a military unit, with combat boots, helmets, bulletproof vests, automatic weapons. Men stand in the shrubbery with leafy branches protruding from their helmets. A gunman perches in a tree. Combat cops walk by with stern expressions and high-tech weapons slung over their shoulders.

Kardashian punches buttons on the desk phone in the kitchen. He gets Simpson again. The Bronco is close now. O.J. seems anxious to tell Kardashian again what a good friend he is, what good times they've had. The Bronco approaches Sunset Boulevard.

Police move everyone out. Into the backyard. The street. They have to force some of the family to leave. Arnelle and Jason are escorted away.

"I want to kill myself at home," O.J. says. "All I want to do is come home and do that."

Kardashian lowers his voice.

"There's a lot of police here, O.J. I don't think you'll be able to do everything you want to do."

He has no time to consider the wisdom of saying this. Should he have warned his friend? O.J. needs to come in, but an army of sharpshooters is waiting. Should he bring him in? Maybe shoulds don't matter now. He only knows he must keep talking. Besides, he doubts how much his friend understands clearly.

Someone grabs his shoulder roughly. A combat cop orders him out. The man's voice is hard, military. Kardashian stares at him, clutches the phone for dear life, puts his hand over it.

"I absolutely will not leave this house! Get your hands off me. I am his doctor!"

"You're leaving right now!"

"I will not leave!" Kardashian roars back. He is out of body again. He can hear his own voice. "I am talking to O.J. on the telephone. I am trying to bring him in. I will not leave this house!"

The cop looks at him. "Okay, Doc." And walks away.

* * *

The real doctors, Baden, Lee, and Huizenga, were returning to homes and hotels after their bizarre house arrest. Back in Encino, on Kardashian's TV, they had watched the LAPD announce Simpson's flight. Then the news switched to Shapiro, who urged O.J. to come in. And Kardashian read the letter, which they'd first heard on the grand staircase.

Back at the Beverly Wilshire, the hotel desk handed Baden at least thirty phone messages from journalists. He ignored them all. His son lived in Santa Ana. They were on the phone when the hotel operator cut in: CNN talk show host Larry King was waiting. Baden knew him from earlier cases, so he took the call. Usually King phones while he's on the air. He asked Baden about the Bronco chase.

Bronco chase? Baden's TV was on, but the sound was off. He hadn't been paying attention. He'd noticed a car on the screen with a police escort, but the connection to the Simpson case hadn't registered.

Suddenly he was doing a live Q & A on national television. His talk with King became a voice-over while the Bronco led a posse of squad cars north toward Brentwood.

Simpson might kill himself, Baden told King and the CNN audience. The gun in the car was no empty gesture. The athlete had been severely depressed when Baden examined him earlier in the day. His farewell note seemed genuine.

Kardashian and Simpson are still talking when several policemen walk into the kitchen. Kardashian assumes they will try again to throw him out, and he braces himself. But hostage negotiator Pete Weireter holds out his hand. He is easy, approachable. The man with him is Michael Albaneze, the SWAT team commander. Albaneze is hard and very tense.

"Doc, he's turned off Sunset," Weireter says. The Bronco is on Rockingham now. The negotiator motions to the front door. "We're going to need you up front here with us."

Eight or ten SWAT team members stand inside the doorway carrying automatic weapons.

"He's going to want to see me," Kardashian says in his

best psychiatrist's voice. "I've been talking to him for the last hour and a half. The only way he'll feel comfortable is if he sees me. Make sure I'm standing where he can see me."

"No problem, Doc."

"But we have an obligation," he adds. "We can't let you get out front because he may shoot you."

Kardashian almost laughs but remembers he is a shrink today. He chooses his words carefully. "He's not going to kill me."

Still, he has to respect them. They are concerned about his safety, but they don't know what he knows.

He spots a SWAT team member with branches on his head running across the lawn, like a tree running from a forest fire. He sees another gunman in the dollhouse.

The troops near him talk back and forth on their radios: He's turning; he's coming up the street. Kardashian can follow the Bronco's progress easily. A dozen news helicopters move in a rotating formation above it. Between the wail of police sirens and the *whup*-ing of the choppers, the noise is deafening.

Kardashian realizes he is drenched in sweat, his heart pumping wildly. Weireter says he'll talk to O.J. first, try to get him to put down his gun. He says, "I want you to know we'll try to do this without force. That's our first and primary objective."

"Just make sure he sees me at all times." Kardashian is all therapist. "If you take me away, he could perceive that as a threat. He'll feel comfortable seeing that I'm standing here."

"Doc, you'll be up front the whole time."

The Bronco's hazard lights flash as Cowlings pulls through the gate. A black-and-white tailgates him in. The Bronco's windows are tinted dark, but Cowlings opens the door slightly, turning on the dome light. Kardashian can see O.J. in the backseat, facing the house, a shadowy figure cradling pictures of Nicole, Justin, and Sydney against his chest with one hand, holding a gun to his head with the other.

Someone runs in from the street. Police yell and rush forward. Who is that? Get him out of here! Everything is confusion, and for several long seconds, Kardashian has no idea what has happened.

Then he yells, "Wait, wait! That's his son. That's Jason!"

"Get away from here, Jason!" Cowlings yells savagely. "Get the fuck out of here!"

But the young man is as big as a pro football fullback, and he's made it through the defensive line. He won't be denied his moment. "I just want to talk to my dad!" He throws himself against the window. "Dad, you can't do this! Dad, put the gun down. You can't do this. We love you!"

Two cops drag back Jason, who flails and screams. "Leave me alone! It's my dad!" The police pull him through the front door and into the house.

Kardashian is close behind Mike Weireter. Too close. He instinctively pushes forward, but feels a hand grab his belt and pull him back. He is standing with Commander Albaneze and a black SWAT team officer he doesn't know. One or the other pulls him back by his pants more than once.

Weireter's first words are swamped by the unholy racket overhead. Kardashian sees maybe a dozen helicopters. Worse, Cowlings will not leave the car, and he and Weireter aren't getting along. Kardashian can't tell if they are shouting at each other out of anger, or simply to be heard. Cowlings keeps yelling, Leave us alone! We'll be okay! As if he plans to sit in the Bronco all evening. Simpson just wants to come home, Cowlings yells. He wants to talk to his mamma. Let him! Leave us alone!

Weireter tries to talk around Cowlings. He attempts to introduce himself to the man he cannot see. He gently asks the shadowy figure to put down the gun. His manner is easy, soothing.

Simpson is behind the passenger side, facing the window Weireter is talking into. But the negotiator must talk through Cowlings. He cannot make eye contact.

A.C. spots a heavily armed sharpshooter. Get that fucking guy out of here! Get him out! Cowlings is an active volcano. If a stranger saw this, Kardashian thinks, he'd assume A.C. is the desperate fugitive, not the guy in the backseat.

Weireter continues talking to Simpson through Cowlings, who continues to smoke like a hot frying pan. The negotiator retreats to a phone just inside the door. He calls Simpson. Weireter and Simpson have been talking only a few minutes when the phone's battery, so faithful for so many hours on the freeway, dies. Weireter has an LAPD phone, which Kardashian offers to take to the Bronco.

"We can't risk you," the negotiator says.

"I'm not worried about it."

Cowlings calls out that he'll come get it. The cops discuss this. Despite their fear of Cowlings, they agree. The big man gets out and throws his arms around Kardashian.

"Get him out, A.C."

"He goes in and out, you know? He's not the same guy."

"Give him the phone. These guys aren't going to do anything. He'll be fine," Kardashian says.

Weireter hands him the phone for Cowlings. "Here you go, Doc."

Cowlings starts to laugh. Doc?

Kardashian grins and rolls his eyes. A.C. walks back to the Bronco.

Weireter realizes he doesn't know the new phone's area code. He can't tell whether he has to make a local or long-distance call. He tries several local codes. Nothing works.

Simpson has the cell phone in the Bronco twenty feet away, but they can't call him. Nobody on the SWAT team knows the number. Kardashian watches in amazement. Suddenly it's a sitcom. A wanted man is sitting in the car with a gun to his head, holding a phone, and they don't know his telephone number. Finally they yell to Cowlings to call *them*.

The new phone's battery dies. It lasts less than a minute.

Watching the Bronco, Kardashian is horrified to see Simpson lean back slightly and position the pictures of his wife and kids on his chest so they won't slip down. Then he takes the pistol with both hands, opens his mouth, and slides the barrel inside.

The athlete holds the gun in his mouth for a while. Kardashian involuntarily holds his breath. Then O.J. pulls the gun out—Kardashian exhales—and positions it against the side of his head. He sits up and clutches the pictures to his chest with his free hand.

Cowlings provides a running commentary. Turning to Weireter, he yells: He's got the gun, he's going to shoot himself. He's got it to his head. Cowlings sits with his arm on the back of the passenger seat. He turns to Simpson. "O.J., don't do it. Your kids need you. Your mother needs you."

"Don't do it," Cowlings says again. And Simpson doesn't.

The LAPD gets another cell phone. Simpson asks for Kardashian.

"Juice, you know we love you. Put the gun down, come on in."

Bob senses a slight softening in Simpson's position. A.C. is loosening up a bit. Weireter feels it, too.

"They mean what they say. They won't hurt you. Just come on in."

But how to get Cowlings out of the front seat? It helped that he came out to get the cell phone. Simpson didn't seem to be upset. Weireter and Cowlings work out a scenario. Cowlings won't raise his hands. He won't be handcuffed in front of Simpson.

The big man emerges slowly from the car and walks almost casually into the house. Combat cops handcuff him inside the house and take him out the back way.

All day Simpson's voice has been soft, raspy, and low. He is making demands now almost in a whisper.

"I'm not coming out unless I have three things."

He wants to call his mother. He wants time with Kardashian. The police must arrest him inside the house where the cameras can't record it.

On his side, Weireter says the gun must stay inside the car. Deal. It appears to be settled.

As Kardashian watches, Simpson pulls himself over the divider, feet first, and drops into the driver's seat. All Kardashian can see is a white tennis shoe coming over the top of the seat, then a leg in Bugle Boy jeans.

"Let's see more of you. Come on, O.J. Show us more," Kardashian says quietly. The police are struggling to stay calm.

As Simpson slides into place, a glint of metal flashes. The combat cops erupt in words and quick movements. "He's got something metal," one yells. "There's something shiny!" Everybody moves. The noise from the helicopters drowns out their words.

"No, no!" Kardashian screams. "It's not a gun. He's got pictures." Worse, the framed photos are wrapped in the green towel that held the pistol all day. "It's a metal picture frame!" Kardashian yells in terror.

Everybody goes back to watching the car. Simpson's leg gives way to his upper trunk and head. His whole body flops into the driver's seat, half sitting, half standing. He looks at no one. He stares straight ahead over the wheel, his face like glass, clinging to the framed pictures. Kardashian guesses he is steeling himself for his new life.

Move slowly, O.J., the negotiator says in a soothing, comfortable voice. Take your time. Move your feet, O.J. Simpson starts to swing out of the seat. Turn them. Simpson is stepping into his new life. Put them on the ground, O.J.

And then he is staggering twenty feet toward Kardashian as if he is ankle deep in mud, hugging the pictures of his wife and children. O.J.'s legs buckle. Kardashian sees that his face is ashen, almost dead. Simpson collapses into his arms, and Kardashian is nearly knocked down. The cops move in and grab Simpson just as his knees touch the pavement. Kardashian, bent over, hugging him, talks breathlessly in his ear.

"Juice, thank God you're alive. It's going to be okay. It's going to be okay."

"I'm sorry, man. I'm sorry." O.J.'s head is buried in Kardashian's arms. He seems oddly embarrassed. "I just couldn't do it."

Kardashian says it's going to be okay, it's going to be okay. Kardashian and the small crowd of cops stagger down a front hallway to some chairs just inside the television room. O.J. collapses into one.

"I'm sorry to put you all through this."

Simpson says it again to all the policemen standing around. "I'm sorry. I'm sorry what I put you through."

The SWAT team pulls back now. Weireter will ride downtown next to Simpson, but the combat-equipped cops move out fast. It is quiet, even sad. To Kardashian, nobody here seems elated at this trophy collar. Cops from West L.A. station regularly visited Rockingham. They brought footballs; O.J. signed autographs.

Now Kardashian sits on a low coffee table in front of Simpson and looks up at him. He reaches across and takes his hands. He turns to the police. "Can you give us a minute?"

Simpson bows his head, and Kardashian leans forward. They pray.

"God will take care of you," Kardashian promises. "Everything will be okay. And remember, I love you."

Minutes pass. Finally Simpson raises his head. He asks for a glass of orange juice. Can he go to the bathroom? A policeman brings the glass. Four cops escort him to a nearby toilet. He asks about his mother, and the detectives are ready. Kardashian has told them she is in a hospital in San Francisco. He didn't know which one, but they found her. A detective dials a number and gives the phone to Simpson.

The athlete talks to Eunice in the low, haunted voice Kardashian has been hearing all day. He begins to cry. Kardashian guesses that Eunice is telling him to stay strong. He apologizes several times, crying and talking. And she says it again, Stay strong.

As he talks, detectives speak into their walkie-talkies: Get the car ready. He's here. We're going to bring him down. When O.J. and his mother are done, it is time to go.

"I'll see you down there," Kardashian says.

Simpson stands up with a blank face as the detectives turn him and cuff his hands behind his back. He is like a limp noodle, Kardashian thinks. He can hardly stand to watch it. Kardashian is not allowed to speak to him again. Don't waste your time coming downtown, the detectives tell him. We're going to book him, and he goes right in. There's nothing more you can do tonight.

The storm of helicopter noise at the door jars Kardashian

back to reality. An unmarked car is waiting. Simpson is lowered into the backseat. A cop puts his hand on the athlete's head and shoves him gently down so he won't bump the door frame. Just like in the movies.

Bob Shapiro had gone to Rockingham to be with his client, but the police wouldn't let him in. He stood in a nearby yard with the other spectators. Then he called Michael Baden and asked to meet him so they could talk about the next steps.

In the lobby of the hotel, Baden was approached by a television crew. He was pleasantly surprised when they agreed to drive him to Rockingham, despite his unwillingness to talk on camera. Rubberneckers and other TV trucks jammed the streets. By the time Baden's friendly TV crew turned onto Rockingham, Shapiro was driving away.

Baden waved and the lawyer pulled over. Thanking his temporary hosts, Baden got into the Mercedes. Shapiro took him to a restaurant. He wanted Baden to look at the autopsy reports before Monday.

It was about nine P.M.

Most Americans thought they were seeing a modern-day version of Greek tragedy. Bill Pavelic had a different view. Watching wearily at home after a long day of talking to potential defense witnesses, he saw an LAPD militia invading Simpson's house. In his mind, they were poking around and making things disappear. Potential evidence could be vanishing. It's all about tactics, Pavelic muttered to himself. This was a free ride for the other side. They could snoop everywhere on the pretext of saving a man's life.

Watching television in his bedroom with his wife, Lee Bailey was puzzled. When a depression deepens, he reasoned, suicide is bottom of the pit. How did Simpson climb out? Why did he go home? He was inclined to think of the athlete's extraordinary homecoming as an act of redemption, a statement of hope.

He knew the public would disagree, just as they would scoff at the televised suicide note as a sign of innocence. Bailey knew Simpson's ego was shattered. Simpson had rushed back from Chicago only to be caught up in a maelstrom of accusations. Gone from hero to monster in a few hours, he was tumbling down the mountain of success. Simpson had borne it for a few days; then he gave up. The public would infer guilt, Bailey concluded. But we in the business know better. Bailey broke with conventional wisdom in one more way: He preferred to think of the Bronco journey as an escort home rather than a chase.

As the most difficult day of his life winds down, Robert Kardashian realizes he has no way to get home. He also understands the symbolism of being stranded here. He could have gone to Rockingham last Monday and wished his friend the best, said, Call if you need anything—and gone back to his office and his life. He could have assumed that O.J.'s future lay with lawyers and experts. He could have kept his distance. No longer.

You can't save a man's life, save it more than once, and not be bound. If not to him, then to your sense of righteousness. Or God's will. When he chose to help Cathy answer phones, when he finds himself now in his friend's home–turned–war zone: All of that must be God's will.

Finally Kardashian asked the police still there if they could help him. A SWAT team commander who lived in Agoura Hills, just past Bob's home, said he'd drop him off. Tom and Joan Kardashian had waited for him. Denice and her family were there, too. Other friends came by. He was drained but somehow on edge as he shared the torturous mix of his joy and sorrow.

"At times I've felt like a battered husband or boyfriend." That sentence from Simpson's letter bothered Alan Dershowitz, the noted Boston attorney, as he appeared on CNN just after Simpson was taken into custody. "The language of the day is that you defend by saying you were abused," he told the interviewer. "And it's an epidemic: It's very dangerous, and it goes to the core of our sense of responsibility."

PART TWO

The Grand
Marshal

1

SIMPSON HELD AFTER WILD CHASE

—<u>Los Angeles Times</u>, June 18, 1994

ALL NIGHT AL COWLINGS HAD HARDLY BEEN ABLE TO sleep. Now it was the morning after Simpson's arrest. He was trying to sort out his emotions. He knew only that when O.J. needed him, he had to show up.

When it all got crazy, when Juice was wandering around Kardashian's place with a gun, he'd done what he could. Years before he'd lost someone he loved, O.J.'s baby girl Erin. A.C. was like a second father to all of O.J.'s kids. Maybe they were his closest friends. When Erin drowned in the Rockingham pool, part of Cowlings's world died forever. Even now, it was hard to think about.

Thank God he'd been there yesterday when O.J. was in mortal danger. He couldn't stand losing another friend.

When it was finally over, A.C.'s own arrest, his booking, all the police stuff went by in a blur. Wayne Hughes was there for him. He posted bond and bailed him out.

Now, as the sun rose, he was coming down. Hughes had told him last night: There'd probably be charges. None of that mattered. The happiest moment of A.C.'s life was when his friend left the gun behind and climbed out of the Bronco. Out into life again.

Kardashian has also had a rough night. At eight A.M. his phone pulls him out of a fitful sleep. An operator asks if he'll accept a collect call.

"Hey, I'm going crazy down here." The voice is raspy, quiet.

How did O.J. get to a phone? Kardashian has no idea how jail works. "How'd you sleep?" he asks.

"I didn't sleep at all. They gave me some medication. But I didn't sleep."

Kardashian can't think of anything intelligent to say. He only knows his friend can't stand solitude. "How's your cell?" he finally asks. "Is anybody in with you?"

"Nah, I'm by myself. The only other guy in the cell block is Eric Menendez. Can you believe my luck?"

"Listen, I'm coming down with Shapiro and Skip later this morning."

"I've got to talk to people. I've got to see somebody."

Kardashian could hear the pleading. Simpson would have hated that. He had always bestowed attention. Now he was begging for it.

Bob dialed Shapiro and told him that Simpson was going nuts. Shapiro asked him to stop by his house. Skip Taft would meet them at the jail.

Kardashian left without reading his *One Year Bible*. At ten o'clock he punched the buzzer on a security gate fronting an enclave of expensive houses in the hills off Benedict Canyon Drive. Shapiro's place was a quarter-mile in. Kardashian was surprised to see that the lawyer lived in the same canyon development Bob and Tom had bought into twenty years earlier. The lawyer's house was tasteful and elegant, but Kardashian had assumed a high-powered attorney would have something big. Shapiro had a Rolls in the garage and a Mercedes out front.

Riding downtown in Kardashian's two-seater Mercedes, Shapiro might have been a stalwart colonel briefing his lieutenant as their jeep raced to a critical mission in World War II. As Kardashian drove, Shapiro explained his view of the previous night's action and talked of tactical moves for Monday's arraignment. He wanted Simpson in civilian clothes.

You've been here every step of the way, Shapiro told Kardashian. I can't do this without you. He asked if Kardashian had activated his lawyer's license: It would mean

102

more, he explained, than jailhouse access or attorney-client privilege.

"I got it going the day you asked me to assist you," Kardashian replied.

Shapiro wanted him as a *player* on the defense team. That was the message Kardashian got.

At the L.A. County Jail, they pulled into an empty upper section of the parking garage, in an area reserved for county employees. Shapiro had permission. Reporters swarmed toward them, but Shapiro was ready. Never say "No comment," he told Kardashian. Speak slowly, walk slowly. Be pleasant and say something they can use.

But Kardashian had no stomach for this. "You're the man," he told Shapiro. "You do it."

"We're just here to visit our client," Shapiro said. Crews followed them right up to the door.

At a window in an empty hallway, Kardashian and Shapiro identified themselves and answered questions about guns and recording devices. On weekdays, lawyers see their clients in a large room filled with long rows of tables divided by glass partitions. A deputy is always on duty at an observation post. The room also has glassed-in visiting areas for notorious or celebrity defendants.

The first sally port door guarding the corridor into the attorneys' room opened. Shapiro and Kardashian stepped into a bare chamber facing another door leading out. Behind them the first door clanged shut, echoing like a dreadful bell. Kardashian had seen too many James Cagney movies, he thought. This was the real thing. If he wanted to leave, they could stop him.

Skip Taft and the psychiatrist, Saul Faerstein, waited inside. The greetings were gloomy. Can you believe we're here? What a way to spend a Saturday. The room with stools where inmates sit behind a three-foot-high glass partition was empty. Today the area was watched by a deputy on a raised observation platform. The visitors walked to one side of the glass and sat down.

Kardashian nearly lost it when Simpson came into the room between two deputies. O.J. moved slowly in prison blues and Reeboks without shoelaces. Bob saw dark eyes, a drawn face, stubble, chains around the waist, handcuffs. The sadness in Simpson's eyes made him want to cry. This is what our lives have come to, he thought morosely. He knew that Simpson was on suicide watch, wasn't allowed a razor. But he hadn't been ready for this.

Kardashian tried to reach over the glass and shake hands. A deputy stopped him: No physical contact allowed. Shapiro took the center stool. Kardashian sat on one side, Skip Taft and Saul Faerstein on the other.

Simpson spoke his usual lines: He couldn't believe what had happened. Why was he here? How could Nicole have gotten in with the wrong crowd? Then: "I should have pulled the trigger yesterday."

Kardashian, too, lapsed into a familiar role. "God has a plan for your life. You weren't supposed to die."

Exhausted but unable to sleep, Bob had gone to his library last night to look for a particular Bible; a gift from his sister, it was a modern translation, called *The Living Bible*. He wrote an inscription to O.J.: "These are the vitamins for your soul. I love you, please read this every day." This would keep O.J. going, keep him sane.

Walking in, Kardashian had handed the Bible to a deputy who had checked it for contraband. Now he gave it to Simpson.

"This is my Bible," Bob said softly. "Make sure you read it every day."

Simpson almost smiled. "Thanks, Bobby, I appreciate it. I'll read it. I'll need it."

Kardashian's emotions got the better of him and he began to preach. "God has put you in this place," he said in the strongest voice he could muster. "You had every intention of killing yourself. You pulled the trigger, and it didn't go off. There's a reason."

"Yeah, you're right. I just couldn't do it." Simpson was passive, head down.

"I believe God has better plans for you than spending the rest of your life in jail. There's no reason to be here unless you did it," Kardashian said.

Simpson's face was empty. He launched into his usual

denials. The lawyers and psychiatrist sat patiently for an hour until the monologue lost momentum. When his client finally seemed ready to listen, Shapiro talked about the Monday arraignment, how deputies would transport Simpson to a holding cell in the courthouse. How Kardashian would bring him a suit. Shapiro asked if he was comfortable.

Not really, Simpson said. His neck hurt. At home he slept on two pillows because of old football injuries. In the cell, he had none. He hated having no windows. His only view of the outside was through a food delivery slot, a foot wide, six inches high. He could watch a TV set through the slot. He had a toilet with no seat; a sink; and the cot. Otherwise, yeah, things were fine. He'd talked a little to Eric Menendez.

Shapiro interrupted. Don't talk to anyone about the case. He was adamant. Inmates will snitch on you just to get a better pillow. They're looking for any bit of information they can use. You're monitored twenty-four hours a day. That includes your phone calls. Everything you say is recorded. O.J., life is different here. Be aware of that.

O.J. asked about Justin and Sydney. Kardashian said they were in Dana Point with the Browns. O.J. began to cry. "You know I've never had a chance to grieve," he said, choking. "I haven't had the chance to grieve for Nicole."

Dr. Faerstein spent twenty minutes alone with Simpson while the others stood back. Then Howard Weitzman arrived and stayed about an hour. He and Shapiro hardly spoke. Each visitor had some private time with Simpson. More than four hours passed.

"Do you have to leave now? Can't you guys stay? Please don't leave me here, guys." He said it every time someone stirred in his seat.

"I'm here," Kardashian kept saying. "I'm here, and I'm going to stick by you. This is a horrible mess, but I'll be here until the end."

"You've got to come and see me tomorrow. I'm going crazy in here." O.J. Simpson had been in jail less than twenty-four hours.

They left at five P.M. exhausted, pleading a meeting.

Outside, the press converged again. Shapiro told them that his client was saddened and depressed by the tragedy.

While Kardashian and Shapiro visited their client, LAPD lieutenant Earl Paysinger was having a bad day. An internal affairs investigator wanted to know why the blue steel .357 Magnum O.J. Simpson had held against his head in the Bronco was registered to a ranking LAPD uniform.

Paysinger referred him to Mike Ornstein, an executive at the National Football League. Paysinger sometimes did security work on the side for the Los Angeles Raiders. Six years ago Ornstein had asked him to help find Christmas gifts "for guys who have everything."

The defense would later learn that Paysinger took Ornstein to the LAPD Academy store. In his official capacity, the lieutenant bought four Magnums, three stainless steel and one blue steel, all with little violin cases, and registered them to himself. Ornstein gave him the cash for the purchases. No waiting, no fuss.

Ornstein was playing Santa Claus to famous football players, including O.J. Simpson. As they parted, the lieutenant reminded him to tell the football players to reregister the guns under their own names.

Simpson hadn't bothered.

Mike Ornstein told the internal affairs investigator who called that he had expected no special treatment from Paysinger at the Academy store. Not at all. He hadn't known about any fifteen-day waiting period. He had just been in a rush to get the Christmas gifts out.

That evening, June 18, friends were waiting when Kardashian got home. He planned an ordinary evening out. They went down the hill to Emilio's on Ventura Boulevard.

As Kardashian and the others walked into the restaurant, people whispered and pointed. He was startled at first. Then he began to enjoy it. He was amazed at how many people made no attempt to be discreet. He was public property.

Later, they were sitting on his patio having yogurt. Bob's friends wanted to hear his account of the previous week. He understood, at least a little. The media had been calling nonstop. Connie Chung had called. Barbara Walters had called five times that day. He hadn't spoken to any of them. About 10:30 P.M., the phone rang again. Kardashian's friend Todd Kraines answered it. Barbara Walters was on the line again. Tell Barbara I'll call back, he said. He never did.

2

It's not going to shock me if we see an O.J. Simpson sometime down the road . . . say, "OK, I did do it, but I'm not responsible." We've seen it in Menendez. It's going to be a likely defense here, I believe, once the evidence is reviewed by the lawyers. . . . We'll be waiting.

—Los Angeles County D.A. Gil Garcetti
on ABC's This Week with David Brinkley,
Sunday, June 19, 1994

ON SUNDAY MORNING, THE NINETEENTH, THE PHONE woke Kardashian again. Again, a collect call. Then Simpson in a hushed voice: "Happy Father's Day."

"I wish I could say the same to you." Bob propped himself up on his elbow. "It's going to be a horrible Father's Day, isn't it?"

"Yeah."

The voice was heavy, slow, down. Kardashian had to push the conversation to get more than one-word responses. "Are the kids coming in?"

"No."

"Are you going to call them?"

"I've got it set up."

Simpson had worked out a story for Sydney and Justin: Daddy is with the police. He's helping them find the people who did this to Mommy.

Was Bob coming down? Kardashian said he and Shapiro would be there around one.

When Kardashian hung up he returned to his morning readings. He went back to June 14 and started with the recommended passages in I Kings, Acts, Psalm 132, and Proverbs 17. When he finally reached June 20, he found that the verse from Proverbs seemed particularly apt: "A friend loveth at all times, and a brother is born for adversity."

Just before lunch Shelli Azoff, Bob's sister-in-law Joan, and several other friends came by to help Denice with the phone calls. Kardashian turned on the TV and discovered he couldn't get away from Gil Garcetti. On every channel, the district attorney discussed homicide and domestic violence and predicted an insanity or diminished-capacity defense.

On *Nightline,* two days earlier, Garcetti had told Ted Koppel: "We have a man who was fleeing, and that fact alone in our mind establishes guilt." On CBS, he linked the case with the plague of spousal abuse, charging that a local judge had "kissed off" the 1989 incident when Simpson beat Nicole.

Kardashian didn't know about O.J.'s alleged abuse. He'd never seen it himself. Whenever he was around, things seemed fine.

On NBC this Sunday, Garcetti was explaining that his office filed one murder case linked to domestic violence every nine days. The connection was obvious. Big cases were political, no escaping that. The Bronco chase and the suicide talk had led to signs of public sympathy for Simpson. People stood along the freeways, holding up placards supporting O.J. They were saying good things on call-in shows. Kardashian knew that celebrities always did well with juries, and O.J. was a sports hero who treated his fans well. He signed autographs. He was gracious, a charmer. People loved him.

Soon enough Shapiro was on TV. Garcetti's premature

talk was unconscionable, the attorney said. To comment on a case before the arraignment violates the rights of the defendant.

On Sunday, Alan Dershowitz arrived in Israel to attend a conference. He expected his comments about Simpson on CNN the previous Friday to irritate some old friends: Howard Weitzman, whom he'd helped win an acquittal for John DeLorean; Bob Shapiro, with whom he'd worked on the Christian Brando case. Now Shapiro rang him in Tel Aviv.

"I need your constitutional input," Shapiro began. "I'd like to talk to you about becoming involved on the Simpson case."

"I need to review what I've said on CNN and PBS. I might have accidentally barred myself from joining."

"Don't even think about that," Shapiro replied. "O.J. said he's totally innocent. That is the only defense which will be raised." There was no hesitation in Shapiro's voice. "I want the three greatest lawyers I know on this case: Lee Bailey for trial strategy, Gerry Uelmen for California procedure, and you for your genius on constitutional law."

Shapiro's appeal to Dershowitz's scholarly vanity settled it. You're a teacher, Shapiro argued. This case will be widely publicized and perhaps show our legal system as it hasn't been seen before. You'll be able to talk about the lessons of the Simpson case. From the inside.

Dershowitz signed on. He would use TV, the phone, and fax to monitor the trial from his Harvard University office. Now and then, he would fly to California for the weekend.

After visiting Simpson, Kardashian went to pick up his four kids for a Father's Day dinner. He didn't like to enter his ex-wife's house: He still felt awkward about seeing her with her husband, Bruce Jenner. He and the children had a ritual. Robert Junior and Khloe waited outside. When he honked the horn, Kourtney and Kimberly came out.

He hadn't seen the kids since the previous weekend. They'd seen him on television, of course. Robert, the youngest, had no real sense of things, but the others clamored to hear the details during their dinner at Chin Chin's. Kardashian talked in general terms: how sad Uncle O.J. was, what a tragedy about Nicole. His kids had known Simpson all their lives—gone to parties at Rockingham, taken trips to resorts in Mexico. Kardashian was touched that they wanted to write him. He promised to take the letters down to the jail.

"Mommy says he's guilty," one of the girls added. "Mommy and Bruce both say it."

For a moment, he thought he would explode. Kris was entitled to her opinion, no problem. But he didn't want his kids in the middle of it.

"In America we believe a person is innocent until proven guilty," he said carefully. "I don't believe Uncle O.J. could do something like this. Wait until the end of things before you make up your mind."

He turned the conversation toward school projects and summer plans. The kids looked great in fresh summery outfits on the hot night. He mentioned that Barbara Walters had called him and got another zinger:

"Barbara Walters called Mommy, too."

3

THE COURTROOM WAS CROWDED ON MONDAY, THE TWENtieth of June.

"Orenthal James Simpson. Is that your name?"

The athlete seemed asleep on his feet, rocking a little, drugged. His skin was drawn almost skeletally over his face, painfully tight around sunken eyes. Municipal Court Judge

Patti Jo McKay, a black woman with a splash of silver in her hair, asked the questions.

Simpson closed his eyes for a second, rocking forward as if he might fall. He almost missed his cue. "Yes," he finally said.

"Mr. Simpson, do you understand the charges as I read them to you?"

"Yes."

Shapiro placed his right hand on Simpson's left shoulder, squeezing and directing. The athlete seemed to sink into himself, but when Shapiro squeezed his shoulder, he surfaced long enough to do what was required. Simpson wore the same dark blue suit he had worn to Nicole's funeral. Because of the suicide watch, deputies kept the tie, belt, and shoelaces. The crisply starched white collar was buttoned, and his pants sagged slightly. As he sat at his counsel's table, a television microphone picked up a sad grumble: "I'll do anything to stay out of that cell."

Someone handed a message to Judge McKay, and she ordered the camera out.

"Have you discussed these charges with your lawyer, sir?"

"Yes."

Earlier, Shapiro, Skip Taft, and Kardashian had met Simpson in the holding cell, a large cage enclosed in wire mesh. Simpson seemed distorted and shadowy.

Shapiro talked to Simpson in a soft, fatherly voice. It will last only three or four minutes, he said. I'll take care of things. Just stand there. Don't worry about anything.

Judge McKay then asked, "Do you wish to enter a plea, guilty or not guilty?"

"Not guilty."

Afterward, they drove to Shapiro's office for a press conference, at which Shapiro told the media that he and his client looked forward to hearing the evidence against him in the preliminary hearing. Shapiro was tipping his strategic hand just slightly. A grand jury had been impaneled and had begun hearing testimony the day of the Bronco chase. Witnesses were scheduled to appear all this week. If the grand jury handed down an indictment, there would be no preliminary hearing. Though the defense would eventually see the grand jury transcripts, "eventually" wasn't good enough. Shapiro wanted the information now. A preliminary hearing was vital to Shapiro's blitzkrieg strategy: The defense would see immediately what the other side had and could cross-examine prosecution witnesses. Shapiro knew that fighting for that preliminary hearing would be his first major battle.

When he'd accepted a collect call from O.J. on the previous day, Sunday, Wayne Hughes assumed Simpson would be tearful and sad. He'd heard the keening cries of disbelief before. He would listen again. He would offer prayer and reaffirm friendship. He would listen. One last time.

Now, after the arraignment, Hughes's longtime friend called again, filling the telephone wires with cosmic blues. Hughes cut him short. "If you're calling up for sympathy, O.J., don't call anymore."

Simpson barely heard him. But Wayne persisted. "I don't have the emotional energy to feel sorry about the past. If you want to fight this thing, then let's get on with it. But I don't want any more of these poor-me conversations."

Hughes hadn't built a business out of nothing and made millions by wringing his hands when there was trouble. It was time to focus. He had bailed out A.C. after the Bronco chase. He had guaranteed a $275,000 bond. He was there.

Simpson complained, again, that the police weren't looking at anybody else. Hughes was exasperated.

"You've got two black guys in a white car hiding out in Orange County," he shot back, referring to the Bronco chase. "If stupid was a defense, you've got the best defense."

Later that afternoon a female deputy, a lieutenant, told Simpson, "We've got too many letters for you." O.J. Simpson was not the first celebrity to spend time in the L.A.

County Jail, but his mail amazed the staff. During his first weekend behind bars, he received more letters than all the other inmates combined.

For Simpson, who couldn't bear solitude, these letters became his life raft. All his life, O.J. had hardly been able to breathe if he had to be alone. Something in him died without the admiration of others. Now here were hundreds of letters tied up in bundles and stacked in his cell. People cared; people believed in him. They were offering prayers, condolences, the warmest support and confidence. He wasn't alone.

On Tuesday, June 21, Kardashian went to lunch at The Grill in Beverly Hills. The food rarely disappointed, and it was a great place to be seen.

Bob Shapiro lunched there regularly. Kardashian liked the restaurant, but over the years he'd felt snubbed. When he wanted a reservation, they were usually full. If he did get a table, it was in Siberia.

Today he was in a hurry, and The Grill had a nice cobb salad. Kardashian decided to test his new status. What's the point of being in a public mess if you can't get a good table in a restaurant?

The maître d' greeted him like an old friend.

"I'm alone, Alan," Bob said. "I just want a quick salad." He tried to imagine how bad a table his solitude would merit.

"No problem, Bob. Right this way."

Kardashian found himself in one of the restaurant's best spots, a back booth on the right. If I'd brought in Elizabeth Taylor and given Alan a hundred bucks, he thought, I wouldn't get this table.

He'd been there less than two minutes when Howard Weitzman walked up. "You're a bigger media star than I am," Weitzman said, smiling.

Lawyer-agent Ed Hookstratten came over. He moved in A-list circles, representing newscasters and sports figures. "Bob, I see you're alone. Do you mind if Pat O'Brien and I join you for lunch?"

In Kardashian's previous life, Hookstratten would barely have said hello. Pat O'Brien was a nationally prominent sportscaster. Kardashian was afraid he might start laughing.

They ate with him and moved on. He asked the maître d' for his check.

"No way, Bob. It's on the house, my pleasure."

Kardashian walked out of The Grill grinning like a Cheshire cat.

Later that afternoon Bob took Jason to see his father. On the way down to the jail, Jason wanted to know how to behave. "Can I touch him? Can I hug him?"

The glass wall and the rules against physical contact made this impossible, Kardashian explained. Your father is still very depressed. He won't be the guy you remember.

Jason was a quiet, private young man, not unlike Kardashian. Bob asked him what had happened after the police pulled him off the Bronco Friday night. Jason talked in a low, somber voice. They took him into the backyard. They said a few things, tried to calm him down. Jason kept telling them he couldn't believe his dad did it. Finally the cops let him go.

When they met the press outside the jail, Kardashian assumed Shapiro's role. Let me talk, he said. Jason is here to see his father, he told the reporters. They kept walking.

They weren't allowed to use the attorneys' room, and Kardashian had to search for the visitors' area. About twenty minutes after they'd stepped up to a window, Simpson sat down on the other side of the glass. He smiled when he saw his son. Kardashian thought he looked almost happy. Jason stared at the numbers on his father's jail blues. Simpson pointed to a telephone handset. Jason picked it up.

"Hi, Jason. Can you hear me?"

"I love you, Dad. I'm sorry you're in this situation."

"Don't worry about me. You go see Sydney and Justin. Tell them I'm working with the police. Tell them I'm looking for the man who hurt Mommy."

Jason cried and again declared his love, sobbing how horrible all this was. Kardashian was amazed that Simpson didn't add his cosmic regrets. Instead, O.J. became fatherly. He asked for a status report on the Rockingham house and offered Jason advice on public behavior. They talked for half an hour, until Kardashian said it was time to go.

Kardashian got home at seven o'clock, exhausted. He took Denice and her father to Jerry's Deli on Ventura Boulevard. They sat in a booth by the window.

Michael Levy, an old friend, came over and asked to join them. Levy was a film producer and had done a long stretch as an agent for Swifty Lazar. Don't use Bob Shapiro, he said immediately. He's never tried a murder case.

This was the first of many similar conversations with friends and even total strangers. Get rid of Bob Shapiro, people told Kardashian. He's a deal maker. He can't try the case.

That same evening, June 22, every news program in America led with a dead woman's fear-choked voice and the roar of O.J. Simpson's rage.

"Could you get somebody over here now to . . . Gretna Green? He's back. Please!"

It was her second 911 call in less than a minute. Nicole Brown's voice was raw with fear. Her ex-husband had broken into her house and now he stood screaming in the yard, she said in her first call. The dispatcher answering the October 25, 1993, emergency call reacted with trained calm.

DISPATCHER: What does he look like?
BROWN: He's O.J. Simpson. I think you know his record! Could you just send somebody over here?
DISPATCHER: What is he doing there?
BROWN: . . . He broke the back door to get in. . . .
DISPATCHER: Wait a minute, we're sending police. What is he doing? Is he threatening you?
BROWN: He's going fucking nuts. . . .

Kardashian thought the district attorney had started the public relations war. If Simpson seemed less than a monster after riding in the Bronco with a gun to his head, then appearing crestfallen at his arraignment yesterday, this tape would fix everything.

Bob Kardashian didn't have a word for his reaction to the 911 tape. Thunderstruck, baffled, shocked—all of that, plus something else he couldn't name.

In Kardashian's opinion, O.J. Simpson wasn't a violent man. Bob had seen him scream and yell when he missed an easy shot in a tennis game, but it stopped there. No throwing his racket to the ground, no tantrums. Certainly there was never any violence toward Nicole. Kardashian had vacationed with them in Mexico, been skiing with them many times, and had never seen a hint of abuse. Once, in New York, he'd seen Mr. and Mrs. Simpson argue—and it was *Nicole* who'd gotten physical, a little pushing and shoving. Even that was mild, truly minor. No way could you call it domestic violence.

The out-of-control man on those tapes who broke down a door and bellowed his rage was someone Bob Kardashian had never met. Until that moment, Bob would have said he knew O.J. about as well as anyone knew Simpson. Now he had to question everything. Was he really O.J.'s friend, or just the admirer of a mask the athlete always wore for him?

The question, and the taped voices that prompted it, were so unsettling that Bob blocked it out. For the moment, there was nothing else to do.

Wayne Hughes was hardly pleased to hear the 911 tapes, but he was not entirely surprised. He'd known Nicole since the Buffalo Bills days, when he sometimes flew east to hang out with O.J. Nicole often made the same trip. They considered themselves friends. One night in 1982, she had turned up at his house, angry and frightened. She showed him a red welt on her side; Simpson had hit her. Would Wayne help calm O.J. down? Hughes had gone over to their house, but there was no sign of Simpson. Evidently he'd driven off by himself to cool down.

Then, on New Year's Day 1989, Hughes went with Simpson to the Rose Bowl game. USC, Simpson's alma mater, was playing Michigan. It was only hours after another beating incident that had made both the papers and the police blotter.

No, these tapes weren't a complete shock to Wayne Hughes. His friend was a complex man.

That Tuesday night and all day Wednesday the twenty-third, Bob Shapiro cried foul: O.J.'s right to a fair trial had been jeopardized; no judge had ruled yet on whether the tapes were or were not evidence.

Meanwhile, Gil Garcetti insisted he had no knowledge of the 911 release. "Frankly, I almost called Chief [Willie] Williams last night to ask what is going on with these tapes," he told reporters. The LAPD, in turn, said they'd given up the tapes only when media representatives cited the California Public Records Act and the city attorney's office approved the release. But city attorney staffers claimed they were told that the LAPD had talked to the D.A.'s office, which said it *wasn't* using the tapes as trial evidence. The LAPD said it had opposed releasing the tapes all along.

Whatever the truth, every potential juror in southern California had now heard possible trial evidence. Shapiro and his constitutional law specialist Gerald Uelmen had a battering ram to knock down the closed grand jury door.

It was not a moment too soon.

By late Wednesday, June 22, at least fifteen prosecution witnesses had testified before the grand jury. The defense already had the names of most of them. Kato Kaelin, Simpson's houseguest, talked about hearing thumps on his wall. Nicole's neighbors Sukru Boztepe and Bettina Rasmussen described being led to the bodies by a stray dog. Officer Robert Riske detailed the bloody crime scene. Detectives Phil Vannatter and Tom Lange told the jury about the bloody glove found at Simpson's Rockingham house, about blood inside the Bronco parked outside, about blood drops leading toward the back alley at Nicole's condo, about a blood trail from the Bronco at Rockingham up to Simpson's front door. Criminalist Dennis Fung described the evidence he had collected.

Jill Shively offered particularly damning testimony. She told of nearly colliding with O.J. Simpson's Bronco at the corner of Bundy and San Vicente, three blocks from the murder scene, on her way to the market. It was 10:50 P.M., and the Bronco was speeding north on Bundy with its lights out—on a direct route from the crime scene, one could assume. She saw it run a red light. She swerved one way, the Bronco the other. The car nearly crashed into her.

Then a Nissan driven by a young man screeched to a stop, blocking the Bronco's path. The Bronco driver leaned out of his window and screamed angrily, "Get out of the way! Move!" Shively recognized Simpson immediately. She'd seen him around the neighborhood. He turned and glared at her. The Nissan backed up, and Simpson roared off.

Unfortunately, the prosecution learned only after Ms. Shively's testimony on Tuesday that they were her second audience. She'd sold the story to *Hard Copy* for $5,000. Worse, she didn't tell prosecutors Marcia Clark and David Conn about that before entering the grand jury room on June 21. They asked if she'd told her story to anyone else. Only my mother, she said. *Hard Copy* aired the next evening.

On June 23, the same morning that Bob Shapiro and Gerald Uelmen cried foul over the 911 leaks, Marcia Clark recalled Shively to the stand and exposed her as a liar.

Q: And then you were interviewed by a television news program called *Hard Copy* concerning this subject matter . . . during which you showed your subpoena on camera?

A: That's correct, I did.

Q: . . . When you appeared to testify before this grand jury, you met with myself and Mr. Conn for the very first time. Is that correct?

A: That's true.

Q: During the course of that interview, you were asked by Mr. Conn whether you had discussed the subject matter of your involvement in this case or the statement that you had given to the police with anyone else.

A: That's true.

Q: And you told him at that time, you told myself
also, that you had only spoken to your mother?
A: That's true. . . .

Clark now turned to the twenty-three grand jury members
and made clear her contempt for Shively's dishonesty:

"Ladies and gentlemen of this jury, because it is our duty
as prosecutors to present only that evidence in which we are
110 percent confident as to its truthfulness and reliability, I
must ask you to completely disregard the statements given
and the testimony given by Jill Shively in this case. . . ."

The moment was vintage Marcia Clark. She stood tall,
with the straight-up posture she learned as a dancer in a folk
ballet troupe: Her intensity was obvious. She would win an
indictment against a celebrity murderer or an ordinary street
thug if she had the evidence. She was known as an
impassioned champion of crime victims. But she would not
cut corners. Shively had been a dream witness. She alone
put O.J. Simpson near the crime scene at the time of the
murders. But now it was obvious Shively was shady.
Unreliable. Marcia Clark would not tolerate that.

Still, with blood trails, a bloody Bronco interior, and an
incriminating glove at Rockingham, what grand jury
wouldn't decide that the prosecution's case merited an
indictment? A vote was scheduled for Friday afternoon.

Meanwhile, Shapiro and Uelmen, arguing that the grand
jurors might well have listened to Nicole's terror along with
the rest of America, worked on an emergency motion
demanding that each of the twenty-three be questioned "to
ascertain the nature and extent of their exposure to improperly released evidence in this case." The 911 tapes, which
had been a shocking blow when first released, became a gift
to the defense. The motion demanded that if the court
agreed the panel had been tainted, the grand jury be
dismissed at once.

F. Lee Bailey was in Nassau on business when Shapiro
phoned and asked if his office had any briefs on this topic.
They did, and faxed them to Shapiro.

Three decades earlier, Bailey had argued before the U.S.

Supreme Court that Dr. Sam Sheppard's right to a fair trial had been violated by widespread publication of inadmissible evidence. Newspapers had reported Sheppard's refusal to take a lie detector test; also, they said that witnesses would talk of his hair-trigger temper. The high court set aside Sheppard's conviction. In the retrial, Bailey won an acquittal and became internationally famous.

Uelmen's brief was based in part on Bailey's material—which, Uelmen wrote, might "induce a sense of déjà vu for those now engaged in the proceedings against O.J. Simpson." Sheppard was "a prominent and well-known person," accused of bludgeoning his wife to death. A juggernaut of hostile publicity arose from prosecution and police leaks.

A hearing on Uelmen's motion was scheduled for the afternoon of Friday, June 24.

On Friday morning Shapiro and Uelmen found themselves before Superior Court Presiding Judge Cecil Mills, who didn't mention the defense motion scheduled for that afternoon. He simply read a statement saying that he had conducted a *personal* inquiry into the matter, in response to the concerns of District Attorney Gil Garcetti. The grand jurors, he concluded, might have heard potential evidence not "officially" offered by Garcetti's office. To protect Mr. Simpson's due process rights and "the integrity of the grand jury process," Judge Mills was recusing the grand jury.

The preliminary hearing Shapiro wanted was scheduled for June 30. A big win for the defense.

CNN began blanket coverage of everything that had any bearing on the Simpson case.

On Thursday, June 23, the topic on CNN was knives and wife-beating, opening with a sound bite from the 911 tapes. CNN's Mary Tillotson then introduced attorney Lisa Kemler, whose spousal abuse defense of Lorena Bobbitt had made legal history. Kemler waited in a Washington, D.C., studio while feminist attorney Gloria Allred and noted defense attorney Johnnie Cochran, considered a Simpson "friend," stood by in Los Angeles.

Cochran took the first question. He was outraged by the tapes' release. They would prejudice Simpson's right to a fair trial, no question. Domestic violence, of course, was disturbing to everyone. But so were law enforcement leaks: The bloody glove. The ski mask. Something new every day. A man could be guilty of domestic violence, Cochran said, without being a murderer.

"Are you thinking of joining his defense team? I've heard that's a possibility," Tillotson asked.

"Well, I've heard that also. I think that's a rumor. I consider him a friend and this is a very, very, *very* serious case. It's difficult to defend someone whom you feel close to, one you have a relationship with as a friend. So the jury's out. I would certainly rather not at this point."

To the audience at Cochran's Wilshire Avenue law offices, that sounded about right. Johnnie was now on the air every day. Local TV, networks, CNN. He was making good money and getting the firm's name around.

In Cochran's firm, opinion about O.J. Simpson had shifted since the Bronco chase. The lawyers still argued over guilt and innocence, but they all felt a connection to Simpson's pain. The gun to the head. The desperate talk.

The lawyers had been riveted on Friday the seventeenth, when Kardashian read Simpson's farewell letter. Now O.J. was a constant topic of conversation. He'd left his community behind. But his suicidal behavior made him human.

By June 20, Monday, real sorrow was palpable in Johnnie's office. Cochran was visibly upset. Chapman realized that the contempt she felt for Simpson just a week ago had vanished. She no longer wished him guilty; she felt sorry for him.

Johnnie wasn't saying much except that he was excited about the TV work. It's a dead-bang loser case, he told his colleagues, and I get all this money to be a commentator. What a wonderful world.

Cochran had good reason to like his life. He drove a Rolls with custom plates—"JC JR"—lived in a big house in upscale Los Feliz, had connections all over town, and kept solid roots in the black community. He stayed in touch with his old neighborhood, getting his hair cut and his dry cleaning done there, worshiping at Second Baptist Church. Add the lavender suits, the designer ties, a personal trainer, and friends in high places. Denzel Washington had asked for Johnnie's input when he was researching his role as the black lawyer in *Philadelphia*. Cochran was flying.

But what about O.J.? They weren't intimate friends; their relationship was social and business both. Johnnie had helped host a party when Arnelle graduated from Howard University. He and O.J. crossed paths regularly and always enjoyed meeting. But they came from vastly different backgrounds. Simpson had grown up in a broken family in an inner-city ghetto; he became a football star, then an actor and pitchman, and never looked back. To the community, he didn't even seem black.

Johnnie's family was from Shreveport, Louisiana, and stayed together after settling in Los Angeles. One of the first black students at Los Angeles High School, he suffered through that and went on to UCLA, then Loyola Law School. Everybody said he was slick. Maybe. But he was definitely smart about what mattered. Blackness, for Cochran, was a public thing. A useful tool. He financed a UCLA scholarship for African-American students and a low-income apartment complex dedicated to his parents. He involved himself in Democratic party politics and got close to former mayor Tom Bradley, Bill Cosby, and just about every other powerful African-American in the city.

But most of all, he made his money in a way that mattered. He represented the victims of cops who abused and killed African-Americans. Police brutality was hardly a new problem, but having the police establishment attacked by a razor-sharp black lawyer in a thousand-dollar suit who talked to juries in cadences that reminded even white people of their favorite preacher—that was brand new.

Cochran's tie was always perfectly knotted, in court, at the office. He scribbled notes on scrap paper and on envelopes—but in front of the jury, it was showtime. No long yellow pad. No three-by-five cards. The man just told the story, laid it out straight and plain.

Cochran made a fortune: $45 million in civil judgments in

the last ten years, millions before that. All of it by fighting on the side of the angels.

In Cochran's office, there were a few whites. A distinct minority, they came and went. There was a camaraderie among the entire staff that transcended racial politics. For the most part, the white world stayed outside. Inside the firm you were family. Words that shocked and offended white society were coin of the realm. "Nigger" and "motherfucker" were terms of affection.

Johnnie's reputation soared after Leonard Deadwyler was shot and killed by cops in 1966 as he rushed to the hospital with his pregnant wife. The young lawyer's impassioned voice resonated throughout the city during the televised coroner's inquest. Even though Cochran lost, his caseload snowballed. He was a natural for the Simpson case.

But for the moment he was a natural on television.

Forensics experts, private investigators, and top-drawer lawyers weren't cheap. No problem. O.J. was a millionaire.

On Thursday, the twenty-third, Skip Taft explained to Kardashian and Shapiro that his client's money was not, as bankers say, liquid. The money was there, but it was tied up in the Rockingham house, a Manhattan condominium, and business investments. Simpson had only half a million dollars available in certificates of deposit, stocks, and bank accounts. Rockingham was worth three or four million in today's market; at least three million of that was clear. The New York condo might sell for a million.

Kardashian had assumed the issue was settled after Roger King's calls on June 13. King would sponsor the defense; he'd said so half a dozen times. But in the surreal week that followed, Kardashian, a seasoned businessman who should have known better, didn't follow up.

Now King's silence was deafening. Kardashian and Taft pondered their next move. Hit him up for a million? Maybe a hundred thousand? They estimated that the defense would cost $2.5 million. Taft said O.J. could cover that—eventually. But he couldn't write checks that size. Kardashian and Taft still assumed it wasn't a problem. O.J. had rich friends; they'd lend him the money, with Rockingham as collateral.

Shapiro seemed comfortable with this plan. On the Saturday morning after O.J.'s arrest, Taft told Cathy Randa to organize a six P.M. meeting at Shapiro's office. All week friends had been asking how they could help. So Cathy said they were getting together to meet Shapiro, hear a bit of strategy, and talk about how to deal with the press. She hadn't been able to get everybody together on such short notice. Kardashian hadn't worried about it. The meeting could wait.

This week it worked out. Today's meeting was set for late afternoon in Shapiro's large conference room. About twenty people were there. Wayne Hughes, whose firm, Public Storage, was one of the biggest in the industry, had the deepest pockets. Also present were old friends and golfing buddies without personal fortunes: Joe Stellini, Alan Austin, Joe Kolkowitz, Marvin Goodfriend, and L.A. Raiders quarterback Vince Evans. Financier Louis Marks remained in New York, but Kardashian assumed he would help. The 1981 Heisman winner, Marcus Allen, brought his wife, Kathryn.

At first, the show belonged to Shapiro. The lawyer talked briefly about his move-fast strategy. His blitzkrieg. They would press for a speedy trial to get Simpson home. Shapiro warned everyone that the media coverage would be relentless.

As if on cue, Simpson called from jail. His voice on the speakerphone was electrifying: "I want all of you guys to know that I'm innocent. I didn't kill Nicole. I didn't do the things they said I did."

Three days earlier at his arraignment O.J. had been a sadly diminished version of his former self. Now the public man was starting to reappear. Simpson's voice was strong. He asked who was there, then went around the table thanking each person, making small talk, working the room like a pro.

Marcus Allen was the first to cry. Soon everyone present was in tears. I miss you, one friend said. I love you, said others. How can I help? I'm with you. Then O.J., too, started to cry. "Thanks, your support is all I need, I'll be okay."

The meeting ended with lots of raw feelings. This wasn't a moment to ask for money. Kardashian and Taft still had to see what Wayne Hughes would do.

Earlier in the week Drs. Michael Baden and Barbara Wolf had spent two hours at the LAPD crime lab examining evidence. Detective Phil Vannatter, Lieutenant John Rogers, and criminalists Erin Riley and Collin Yamauchi stood by as lab chief Michele Kestler supervised.

Baden, the longtime New York City medical examiner, was well known to the LAPD lab staff. Dr. Barbara Wolf, tall, attractively bookish, and red-haired in middle age, rarely passed through Los Angeles. She had spent much of her career in Boston; then, in 1991, she'd become director of anatomic pathology at the Albany (New York) Medical Center. Her résumé was impressive. In 1991, for instance, she had helped exhume the body of civil rights leader Medgar Evers so that decades after the fact his murderer could finally be convicted.

Baden was surprised that no one had done a rape kit on Nicole. New York law enforcement labs always test for recent sexual activity of any kind. A woman's killer may not have raped her, but semen or saliva can yield identifying information about its depositor. Staffers said that rape testing wasn't standard L.A. County procedure. We just don't do that, coroner Lakshmanan Sathyavagiswaran said. Baden said gently that he should have.

Looking at pictures, Baden noticed evidence of a bruise on Nicole's brain which the coroner had missed. Altogether, Baden found sixteen separate objectionable items; a young administrator graciously listed them for future reference.

Barbara Wolf knew she would eventually have to design a computer program to track the prosecution's medical evidence. Ultimately there would be more than four hundred exhibits.

Later that same day, Baden passed through the sally port of the L.A. County Jail. He didn't expect to accomplish much by questioning Simpson. He assumed the client was another jock who'd sailed through college untouched by higher learning.

When the deputies brought Simpson to the visiting room Baden again saw the obvious symptoms of clinical depression. Simpson's face showed little emotion, and his body sagged, devoid of energy. He began by apologizing for the trouble he'd caused.

But then Dr. Baden was startled as O.J. asked sharp, thoughtful questions. Shapiro had explained things, Simpson said, but he wanted to hear about scientific evidence from the scientists.

Baden, worried that Simpson might react badly to the gore, summarized the autopsy results carefully. He wondered why so much food remained in Nicole's stomach. Simpson said she often nibbled at restaurants, then stuffed herself later in the evening at home.

Baden said that one autopsy finding suggested cocaine use, a subject that interested Simpson so much that he provided the doctor with a complete history of Nicole's recreational cocaine use. Finally, Baden asked about Simpson's habits.

O.J. swore angrily that *he* didn't use cocaine. False reports of drug bingeing had followed him for years. He'd heard that Jim Brown, the social activist, actor, and former star running back for the Cleveland Browns, had said on a talk show that he knew for a fact Simpson used cocaine. Why, Simpson demanded, would Brown say that? Baden couldn't comment.

Simpson was most impressive on the subject of his son Jason. Baden had assumed that Jason had risked triggering Simpson's suicidal impulse the night of O.J.'s arrest, when he dashed out and pounded on the car window. That frenzy might have pushed O.J. over the edge.

Just the opposite, Simpson said. Something quite different had happened. Confronted by the obvious love of a son he had fought with so often and so bitterly during the boy's adolescence, he suddenly considered staying alive. Jason had somehow cut through his narcissistic fog and stirred a sense of obligation, perhaps pride. "It sort of woke me up,"

Simpson said. "I heard Jason's voice, and I came out of things. I came back."

He wasn't all back, Baden thought, but he was on the way.

4

By now the defense had received the LAPD "murder books" and some discovery from the prosecution, which contained the preliminary facts of the police investigation. From this material plus newspaper clippings, TV reports, and the defense's initial interviews with Arnelle, Kato Kaelin, Allan Park, Cathy Randa, and Simpson himself, defense investigator Bill Pavelic started to piece together what had happened the night of the murders and the following morning. As an ex-cop, he drew on his knowledge of what the police do at a crime scene. They don't always go by the book. They cut corners—some officers more than others—but their reports make them sound like Boy Scouts. Pavelic knew how to read between the lines of police verbiage and find the hidden stories in the photographs the D.A. had turned over.

He loved his job.

On Sunday night, June 12, Patrolmen Robert Riske and Miguel Terrazas responded to a report of possible intruders at the home of an elderly woman. As the officers arrived at the address, a typical Brentwood couple complete with an impressive Akita flagged them down.

They told the officers: There's a body in the walled courtyard over there. A dead lady. This stray dog, clearly someone's pet, was found wandering, agitated, uninjured but bloodstained. The Akita led them to the dead lady.

Riske aimed his flashlight at the lawn and saw so much blood that he and Terrazas knew they had to stay off the walkway. He radioed for an ambulance and backup and moved through some flowers toward the open gate while Terrazas approached on the grass, both men staying to the left of the walkway. The woman was on her left side in the blood, not quite in a fetal position, hair covering some of her face, a leg tucked under the fence.

About two feet short of the woman, they saw a second body. A man was jammed against a small tree stump and iron fence, slumped on his right side, half sitting in the dirt. His sweater was pushed up and revealed a lot of bloody skin. There were cuts on his neck, back, head, and hands. The plants around him were bloody, branches broken, pushed askew. Riske got inside by pulling himself around the edge of the gate, walking tightrope between the fence and the woman.

He stepped over her to get to the stairs and saw more blood. The door at the top of the stairs was three-quarters open. The woman was wearing a black dress, bare shoulders, no shoes. Blood everywhere.

Moving his beam around, Riske saw partial shoe prints on the stairs. More shoe prints down a side walkway toward the back. He went inside. A framed lithograph of O.J. Simpson hung in the hallway. Further inside, he spotted an envelope on a kitchen counter with Simpson's name on the return address. The victim must be the famous athlete's wife or girlfriend, he concluded. He reached for the phone on the counter and called his watch commander.

Riske moved up the property line to the right of the walkway for a better look at the man. From the neighbor's side of the fence, he could examine him without disturbing the bloody crime scene. Bending down to get his beam under the shrubs, he saw an envelope. Then he noticed a leather glove and what looked like a knit cap half hidden under a plant.

Riske then shone his light into the one open eye of the

male victim to check for involuntary movement. The man might be alive. The pupil didn't dilate. He touched the man's eyeball. The lid didn't twitch. It was a double homicide. Police backup arrived. Patrolman Terrazas guarded the back of the house while other cops wrapped the entire end of the block, from Dorothy to Bundy, in yellow tape.

Riske went inside the apartment to do a thorough search. The most obvious thing was that nobody had ransacked or burglarized the house. He checked the closets for anyone hiding. Nothing. All the lights were on. The stereo in the living room was playing light jazz. Riske noticed a cup of Ben & Jerry's ice cream on a banister above some steps leading to the garage. The ice cream was half melted. The spoon was lying on the steps. He checked the garage and found a Ferrari inside. Nothing looked out of place.

Moving upstairs, they saw that a TV set was on in the master bedroom, bedcovers piled up in the middle of the mattress. The lights were on in the hall and above a balcony with exercise equipment. In the master bathroom, a sunken tub was filled. Three candles burned on a counter behind it.

Then two smaller bedrooms. The stunned cops found a child in each, a boy and a girl soundly sleeping and seemingly unaware that anything had happened. Their doors must have been open the whole time. Riske went outside to tell the sergeant, who called for a car. The confused, sleepy kids, anxious at being wakened by policemen, were asked to get dressed, then taken out through the garage. Patrol officers Bill Heider and Joan Vasquez arrived in a black-and-white. They would baby-sit and try to locate relatives. It was 1:10 A.M.

"Where's my mommy?" Sydney was crying, or close to it.

A reasonable enough question, but Officer Heider had no answer that would help. "I don't know," he said gently. "Do you want anything?" It was the darkest of nights.

As the officers drove toward West L.A. station, Vasquez heard the fear in the girl's voice, as if something in the backseat were shaking her. "I'm just tired, and I want my

129

mommy,'' Sydney whimpered. The little girl might be nine or ten.

Pavelic studied the LAPD's crime-scene logs. He called friends at LAPD to see what else he could learn. He put in twenty-hour days, and finally what happened in the early hours of June 13 started to come together.

Detective Mark Fuhrman was in bed in Redondo Beach when Ron Phillips called at 1:05 A.M. Phillips was West L.A.'s homicide coordinator; Fuhrman's name was on the duty roster. Fuhrman was told the basic facts of a double homicide; 875 South Bundy; the female victim might be the ex-wife of O.J. Simpson. Fuhrman dressed quickly and drove north on the 405 freeway. He met Phillips half an hour later at the station at 1663 South Butler Street.

Phillips was waiting with a vehicle and a homicide kit. When they arrived at Bundy at 2:10 A.M., watch commander Sergeant David Rossi put Fuhrman and Phillips together with the uniform who discovered the bodies.

First, Riske pointed at things through the gate with his four-cell flashlight. Fuhrman saw that the woman's blood was still draining along the tile grouting. Riske moved the light to the dead man. He cast the beam at a plant with long bladelike leaves near his feet. Fuhrman followed the light down to a knit cap and a glove.

Because of the sight lines from outside the gate, the detectives couldn't easily examine what Riske was pointing at. Riske took them around to the back, where Terrazas stood perimeter guard. They went in through the garage. Riske showed them the melting ice cream, and Fuhrman noticed the framed lithograph of Simpson in the hall. They had a better view from this vantage point. Riske moved his beam around the bodies and pointed out shoe prints, heel prints, and blood drops.

Riske showed Fuhrman and Phillips how the shoe prints led down the side walkway, toward the back of the house. Then he illuminated drops of blood to the left of the shoe prints. Fuhrman saw immediately that someone had walked out the back way dripping blood. Riske led them down the side walkway, aiming his beam on the partial prints and the blood drops so they could step around them.

At a back gate by the garbage cans, Riske showed Fuhrman and Phillips more blood. He pointed to a smudge on the latch and to drops on the lower rung and the middle of the gate's center mesh. Finally, he showed them loose change—pennies, dimes, and a nickel—on the driveway.

Riske took them back through the house. While details were fresh in his mind, Fuhrman made notes, listing some seventeen items.

Afterward, he stood around with Lieutenant Spangler, who commanded West L.A.'s detectives, and with other cops like Phillips, Roberts, Nolan, and some of the uniforms. Crime-scene tape was now up; the block to the north was sealed to traffic. The time was three A.M.

During the graveyard shift, the police station house was half empty and dark. The two officers took the kids to an office next to the conference room. While Officer Heider tried to locate the next of kin, Officer Vasquez stayed with the children.

"What are all the police doing in front of our house?" Justin asked.

Vasquez didn't answer.

"Where's my mommy?" Sydney demanded. "What happened to my mommy?" Getting no answer, she asked again.

Vasquez said she didn't know. She asked what TV shows they liked, what they enjoyed doing.

The Power Rangers, Justin volunteered. He was a green belt in karate. "My mom is going to start going with me again," he said.

"I go to dance class," Sydney added. "Today Mom and Dad and everybody went to see me dance, but I didn't like it because it was cowboy stuff. I like doing jazz better." But the small talk didn't last long. "Where is my mommy?" Sydney asked. The tears started again. She repeated the question. Every time she asked about her mother, she cried.

Vasquez found some paper plates, cups, and straws, Scotch tape, and rubber bands. Showed them how to make paper hats, let them draw on the plates. That kept them occupied about forty-five minutes.

"Justin, you know something happened to Mommy," Sydney said, turning to her brother. "She would have come for us by now." Justin didn't have an opinion about that.

"Justin, I heard Mommy's best friend's voice and I heard Mommy crying. Did you hear her, Justin?"

The little boy shrugged his shoulders. Vasquez checked herself, didn't ask who the friend was. Hard enough to keep these kids calm.

"I'm so tired," Sydney said at four A.M. "No way I'm going to school today."

Her brother added he was just tired, that was all. "Why can't Mommy just come and pick us up?"

Then Vasquez asked if they wanted to learn to spell their names in sign language. The kids caught on quickly. Sydney actually giggled briefly.

Half an hour later, the children were hungry. Heider stayed with them in the vending machine room while Vasquez went to an Asian fast-food place.

They decided to play Hangman. They were good at the game and were absorbed for a while. At 5:30 A.M. Heider asked if they knew any telephone numbers of relatives. They gave him Arnelle Simpson's number.

"Why can't Dad just come for us?" Justin asked suddenly.

His sister answered, "Because he doesn't stay with us sometimes."

Pavelic knew that Robbery-Homicide, the elite corps of detectives from LAPD, would be assigned the case when it became known that Simpson's ex-wife was involved. Phil Vannatter and his partner, Tom Lange, were named lead detectives. Vannatter arrived first, and Phillips walked him through.

Pavelic knew that the cops would obey their unwritten rule that you stick to one route in and out of a crime scene. The responding officer sets it up; everybody follows. So Phillips took Vannatter around the same way Riske had shown Fuhrman. The grand tour, cops call it.

They followed the bloody shoe prints on the side walkway to the drops and smudges on the gate and finally out to the loose change and the blood drop on the driveway. Someone had tracked the victims' blood, and that someone was also dripping his own blood. Vannatter stood on the landing a second time to think about what he had—and the potential problems. Simpson's name, of course, meant a media mess. Tom Lange arrived from his home in Simi Valley at 4:25 A.M. and Phillips walked him through too.

Everybody knew that Nicole's children, Sydney and Justin, eventually had to go somewhere besides the police station. O.J. Simpson, the children's father and the victim's ex-husband, was the obvious person to see. They had to interview Simpson sooner or later, and sooner made sense. It was almost five A.M. and still dark.

Pavelic figured that Vannatter must have driven from Bundy to Simpson's house at Rockingham.

But the police reports didn't say who went or who climbed Simpson's wall to release the gate's hydraulic arm and gain access to the estate. No mention of how many officers or detectives were at Rockingham. No names. No radio logs. Nothing.

Pavelic knew from Arnelle that nobody answered Simpson's front door when the police first rang. In the back of Simpson's house are two guest apartments. Pavelic assumed that Lange and Phillips looked through a glass door to one of the rooms. Someone was sleeping. Phillips knocked.

Kato Kaelin, a kid with wild hair and bloodshot eyes, came to the door. He seemed friendly, but disoriented. He told the detectives to talk to Arnelle, and pointed to her bungalow. The detective asked him if he'd been drinking. He said he didn't drink. Then a test for drugs. The officer pulled out a penlight and checked his eyes. Kaelin didn't object. He passed the test.

The detective asked if he could look around the apartment. Again Kato didn't object. The cop checked his closet and bathroom to make sure they were alone, then looked at his shoes and clothes. He asked whom the Bronco belonged to, and the kid said O.J. Kato was asked if anything unusual had happened that night. Pavelic found out from a police source that Kaelin said he had heard a crash and a thump on his wall at 10:45 P.M.

Phillips knocked on Arnelle's door while Vannatter and Lange stood behind him. She answered quickly. "Do you know where your father is? We've got to get in touch with him. There's a police emergency."

"Isn't he here?" Arnelle gestured toward the house. Vannatter needed to go inside. She rummaged around in the room and emerged with a key, then led them into the house.

Vannatter asked where the maid slept. Arnelle took him around the bar, into the kitchen, and to a utility area. She opened a door and he saw an empty room. Maid's day off. Arnelle said she could call her father's secretary, Cathy Randa. She'd know Simpson's schedule.

Phillips's call woke up Cathy Randa. She told him her boss had taken the red-eye to Chicago and was staying at the O'Hare Plaza.

Phillips called the hotel and the operator said Simpson had left a message not to be disturbed. The detective said it was an emergency. A minute passed. Then she put him through.

"Hello."

"Is this O.J. Simpson?"

"Yes, who is this?"

"This is Detective Phillips from the Los Angeles Police Department. I have some bad news for you."

Phillips told him.

"Oh, my God! Nicole is killed? Oh, my God, is she dead?"

The athlete howled in pain. Phillips let him cry and finally cut in.

"Mr. Simpson, please try to get ahold of yourself. I have your children at the West Los Angeles police station. I need to talk to you about that."

Simpson did not calm down.

"What do you mean, you have my children at the police station?"

"We had no place else to take them. They're only there for safekeeping. I need to know what to do with your children."

"Well, I'm going to leave Chicago on the first available flight. I'll come back to Los Angeles. Is Arnelle there?" Simpson asked to talk to his daughter.

Arnelle had learned the news from Tom Lange minutes earlier. She was hysterical, too. She didn't stop crying while talking to her father. When she hung up, she asked to call Al Cowlings. Simpson had asked her and A.C. to pick up Sydney and Justin from the police station and take them to their grandparents' home in Dana Point.

Vannatter was eyeballing things around the house when a detective walked in with Kato and suggested Phil talk to the kid. Then the detective walked away.

Pavelic suspected the glove was found sometime after the phone call to Simpson. Nothing in the reports about finding it, only the photographs taken hours later. They said a lot to a trained cop like Pavelic. The photographs told part of the story. On a narrow pathway inside Simpson's estate and about three feet away from an air conditioner, a glove was pictured. Pavelic figured Vannatter must have thought hard upon seeing it. He also knew someone had to go back to Bundy and look at the other glove. Cops would want to know if the glove they were seeing at Rockingham matched the glove at Bundy. Any detective would want to check that.

Ron Phillips made the first phone call to the coroner's office at 6:49 A.M. The medical examiner's office is run by L.A. County, not the LAPD, so it's not automatically in the investigative loop.

Phillips told the dispatcher he had a double homicide.

"The press is going to be crawling on us like ants when they find out what's going on. This is the first call and we got a lot of work to do yet. But we need you guys rolling so that we can get these bodies out of here as soon as possible. But not just yet.

"We're kind of not following procedure," he continued, "but we are kind of asking a favor. You know, kind of work [with us] a little bit on this one. The problem is, when this thing breaks, we are going to have news from everywhere here. It is going to be a high-profile type deal. It is the ex-wife of a very prominent sportscaster or sports celebrity."

The dispatcher wanted to know who.

Phillips hesitated only a moment. "Okay, I'm going to have to trust you on this. It is O.J. Simpson's ex-wife."

Phillips said he'd call again when they wanted them there.

At Bundy, police photographer Rolf Rokahr had been taking the evidence photos Pavelic was looking at. An officer kneeling down and pointing to a glove. Lots of photographs, all out of order. Some taken at Bundy, others at Rockingham. Some at night, some in daylight.

Discovery reports and logs indicated that criminalist Andrea Mazzola had weekend duty. When Homicide called, she woke up Dennis Fung, her senior at LAPD's Scientific Investigation Division. He would supervise. That was procedure.

Fung and Mazzola arrived at Rockingham at 7:10 A.M. Vannatter briefed them and showed them a red stain by the door handle of the Bronco. Then the blood trail up the driveway. The early-morning air was cool.

Fung and Mazzola started on the Bronco door. They used tweezers to lift sterile gauze swatches from plastic packaging. Each blood drop or stain required a substrate control sample to determine what was present on the unstained surface. This meant dampening a swatch with distilled water and swabbing an area near the blood spot, being careful to touch nothing but the unstained surface of the car. The swatch was put in a plastic Baggie, which in turn was inserted into a coin envelope. Before collecting the next sample, you had to clean the tweezers with distilled water. Then, for the blood drop itself, a new wet swatch was rubbed against the tiny stain, then put in its own Baggie and coin envelope. Each stain yielded at least two swatches: one from the bloodstain itself, and the control to document and preserve the area the blood was taken from. That way a lab worker could determine or rule out contamination of the bloodstain. The Bronco door samples were taken at 8:15 A.M.

Vannatter left sometime thereafter to get a search warrant for Rockingham.

Fung then looked through the window of the Bronco and noticed the stains inside, but didn't attempt to collect them. That would be done after the car was towed to the impound yard. He and Mazzola took samples from the driveway drops after that, finishing at 9:15. Fung began his notes; before the day was over, they would be eighty pages long.

At 9:30 A.M., they were led to the back walkway to collect the glove. Kneeling to scoop it into a paper bag, Fung noticed a sheen on the leather. He concluded that whatever was on the glove was dry by now.

At ten A.M. the criminalists left for Bundy. So far, they had collected samples from ten blood drops or stains, plus the glove from the back walkway.

At 8:08 in the morning Phillips made the second call to the coroner's office, and an hour later coroner's investigator Claudine Ratcliffe logged in at the crime scene. Her primary job was to identify and remove trace evidence from the bodies. Mortuary attendant John Jacobo pulled up in the L.A. County van ten minutes later. Detectives briefed them; then Ratcliffe took two Polaroids of each body. Next, she lifted the arms of both victims to determine the degree of rigor mortis. Both bodies were stiff, she concluded.

At 10:40 A.M. Ratcliffe lifted the shroudlike blanket covering the female victim, poked a hole in her dress, and inserted a thermometer under the right rib cage. The coroner's thermometer is needle-nosed so it can penetrate the flesh and register the temperature of the liver. The male victim's sweater had been pushed up in the death struggle, so she did not have to maneuver the thermometer through his clothing. His body registered 82 degrees Fahrenheit. The environmental temperature was 70. The readings would help determine the approximate time of death.

She and Jacobo lifted the corpses onto plastic sheets, then into body bags and onto gurneys. The two bodies left the crime scene in the van Jacobo drove at 11:35 A.M.

Vannatter returned to Rockingham with a search warrant before noon. Simpson arrived at his estate and was taken to Parker Center by Vannatter and Tom Lange for an interview.

Fung and Mazzola worked at Bundy for five hours in the growing heat of the day. Pavelic knew the criminalists labored under the media glare, in close quarters with a crowd of detectives and other lab personnel. They harvested bloodstains and substrate controls from the steps, the courtyard, the back gate. They took blood drops and substrate controls from the walkway.

Fung started numbering items at 100 for the Bundy evidence. They collected the knit cap, the glove, an envelope carrying eyeglasses, a banana sticker that said "Bonita Ecuador." They also collected Goldman's pager, a set of keys, and a ring nobody could place.

Fung and Mazzola drove back to Rockingham at three P.M. and took samples from more blood spots in the foyer at 3:30. Fung also collected a pair of socks from the master bedroom, and took a stain in the bathroom at 4:40 P.M.

Vannatter came back to Rockingham from Parker Center at 5:15.

That was what they had so far. Pavelic sat down to write his report. Shapiro needed it ASAP.

5

On Friday afternoon, June 24, Kardashian visited
the confined space where Ron Goldman had struggled and
died. The patch of grass, shrubs, and one small tree was no
bigger than a walk-in closet. He looked at the plowed-up dirt
by the fence and shrank from imagining the desperation that
created such havoc. The place where Nicole fell was no
easier to contemplate. No room to move; just enough space
to crumple at the foot of the stairs.

Dr. Henry Lee, who'd left L.A. after Simpson's arrest,
returned as early as he could, but when Shapiro, Baden,
Pavelic, and Kardashian got to the Bundy yard just after 6:30
P.M., the police said they had to leave by seven. The light
was fading, anyway. Dr. Lee took more pictures than anyone
could count, and everybody else stood around and tried to
imagine things. Or, in Kardashian's case, *not* to imagine
them.

On Saturday afternoon they returned to the crime scene
and spent several hours walking, talking among themselves,
reconstructing. Tom Lange and Ron Phillips watched, along
with at least one local commander. Bill Pavelic carried a
video camera, and Baden and Henry Lee took even more
still photos.

Kardashian canvassed the entire condo. The master bedroom seemed oddly small to him. In a back room, someone
found a knit cap that looked identical to the one found at the
crime scene.

"They didn't book this? They didn't tell us she had caps
like this over here?" Kardashian said.

But mostly he and the others stood by the front porch, looked at the tiles, and wondered how the murders had happened. Did the killer just walk in? Did the buzzer ring? Did Nicole come to the front door? Did she let her murderer in? How did Ron Goldman figure in this? The garage was the other gathering spot. They looked out at the back alley for a long time.

On Saturday afternoon, the twenty-fifth, the defense team assembled in Shapiro's office to look at the discovery material the D.A. had provided the defense, as required by law. Pavelic had been reading the various reports and was up on the written material. It was obvious the pictures and evidence sheets had been thrown together with no concern for chronology or topic. Exhibits were dumped in boxes in no discernible order, labeled illegibly, unlabeled, or cryptically labeled.

The defense could only guess whether all the relevant information was there. Prosecutors were required to provide the defense the names and addresses of every likely witness, all written and recorded witness statements, all police and scientific reports and notes, test results, incidentals like crime-scene logs and telephone records, plus such tangible evidence as photos of bloody clothing, shoe prints, weapons, fingerprint lifts, and records of blood swatches or pictures thereof. The whole conglomeration was referred to as "discovery." These untidy cartons could more accurately be called obfuscation.

Unfortunately, the law says nothing about passing on the discovery in an orderly way. State legislators had apparently assumed professional courtesy would cover that.

Bob Shapiro's associate Sara Caplan, who had the task of organizing the discovery material, had never anticipated this problem. Her contact at the D.A.'s office was Bill Hodgman, a gangly soft-spoken fellow who ran the elite unit for high-profile trials. He was always a gentleman. Three years earlier, Hodgman had slogged his way through the long, numbingly complex securities-fraud trial of Charles Keating without once losing his temper. Some thought him saintly.

Caplan called him often to complain that the discovery was arriving in tangled piles. Hodgman was conciliatory, endlessly polite. But nothing changed.

Now, today, the air was blue with comments about the ancestry and personal habits of the people who had sent the defense team this mess. The game had barely started but the other side was already playing dirty.

Then Henry Lee began talking. He picked up pictures and discussed what he saw in a stream-of-consciousness narrative. The room fell silent. Lee seemed to be thinking out loud:

Difficult to see human shoe prints at the crime scene, he said. So much blood. The topography runs downhill; blood flows that way. Lots of smears. Something must be present to produce the smear. Blood patterns show two different shoe prints. Maybe one Goldman's, maybe second person at crime scene.

Lee held up the pictures with the shoe prints and examined them with his magnifying glass.

Blood appears on Nicole's leg and arm. Something had to smear it. She was slit with the killer's right hand, left to right. The murderer was right-handed. Blood spurts are also from left to right. She flipped around and fell. Eight to eleven blood drops on her back. Can't be hers. Blood smears on her back. Must be someone else's. Twelve to fourteen drops on the right leg. Must be from a different person.

Kardashian realized his mouth was open. Lee wasn't looking at blowups, just ordinary pictures. Not even original photographs, just copies. How could anyone see these things?

Nicole was barefoot. The police hadn't taken pictures of the soles of her feet. We don't know if she stepped in blood or not, said Lee. That's important. The killer or killers may have been let in the front gate. She turned to walk back inside. He grabbed her. It happened quickly. Nicole was on her knees when her throat was slit. White dog hairs on Nicole's back. The bushes are crushed. A dog didn't do that. Someone was waiting there.

* * *

O.J. Simpson was not on Henry Lee's mind until the night Bob Shapiro phoned him. I don't watch football, he explained. His instinct was to stay away. His Connecticut State Police workload was heavy. He averaged 350 additional consulting requests each year. If anyone but Michael Baden had called, he would have said no immediately. But he talked to Dr. Baden almost daily. Baden's open-mindedness always impressed him.

He made his conditions clear to Shapiro. His bosses had to approve; his fee would be divided between the University of Connecticut and a Department of Public Safety scholarship fund. Most important, he wasn't in or out of the case until he'd examined the evidence. He wouldn't talk to anyone beforehand. It had to be Henry Lee, his magnifying glass, and the evidence. In a room, alone. And then he might opt out.

That was where he stood going into this meeting.

At this moment he was still undecided. His supervisors were amenable, but he had to use vacation and personal time. He'd arrived in Los Angeles a week earlier, expecting to examine photos and evidence reports immediately. Instead, the press at the airport annoyed him. Then the next day he was at Kardashian's under house arrest in the middle of a national soap opera.

On first entering Kardashian's house last week, he'd thought Al Cowlings was O.J. Simpson. That was worth a private chuckle.

Upstairs, he and Baden were introduced to the real O.J., who apologized for taking him from his family on a weekend. Very odd, that. Lee let Baden do the talking while he took pictures and collected blood, hair, and saliva samples. Baden advised him that Simpson had a cut on his knuckle requiring documentation. Lee saw several superficial cuts on other parts of Simpson's hand. Each one had to be documented, he said.

Then, of course, the Bronco chase began. When finally allowed to leave Kardashian's house, Lee checked out of the hotel and took a red-eye flight back to Connecticut. He had not seen one iota of evidence. He didn't like this.

But he had agreed to come back and he prided himself on his word. Years earlier, friends in Maine had asked him to sit on an interview panel to hire a chief criminalist. There was a blizzard in New England that day, but Lee drove north as promised. It was a harrowing trip. He arrived in Maine to find that none of the job candidates had shown up.

The discovery material here today reminded him of that snowstorm. Hundreds of crime-scene pictures taken by the LAPD. Nothing was in sequence. He grouped the photos into "scenes" without knowing what he was seeing. He began to notice inconsistencies. Now things were getting interesting. He saw evidence positioned one way, then another. He found pictures of several pieces of evidence in different spatial relationships. Sometimes he found four arrangements of the same objects. He explained that he saw the Bundy glove and knit cap, for example, in three different ways. "Something is fucked up here," he told his breathless audience.

In 1965, Henry Lee had emigrated to the United States with a young wife, $50 in his pocket, and five years' experience as a police captain in Taiwan. Born in a village near Shanghai, Lee was one of thirteen children of a successful businessman who fled with his family to Taiwan when Henry was six. Lee's mother pressured her children to work harder, produce more. Typical Chinese mother. He never forgot the lesson. His wife, Margaret, found a teaching job in New York while he discovered Taiwanese college credits weren't accepted by U.S. schools.

While studying at City College of New York, Lee worked as a waiter in a Chinese restaurant, a stockboy, and a groundskeeper. Then he won a scholarship to John Jay College of Criminal Justice. He eventually completed a doctorate in biochemistry at the N.Y.U. School of Medicine and taught forensic science at the University of New Haven. Then the Connecticut State Police offered him the directorship of their forensics lab.

The cops noticed immediately that Lee read crime scenes like Sherlock Holmes. In one early case a fifteen-year-old girl was bludgeoned to death near a stream. Lee pulled several hairs from the water. He told nearby police officers they probably belonged to someone of Native American extraction. Police eventually identified a young boy as a suspect. They were chatting with his family when someone mentioned in passing that the boy's father was a full-blooded Canadian Indian.

Within a few years, Dr. Lee had turned a primitive forensics department into a nationally recognized laboratory. Then the Helle Craft case brought him national fame. Craft was a Danish-born flight attendant who disappeared one winter night in Newtown, Connecticut. Her husband was suspected of foul play, but no one could find the body until someone reported seeing a man operating a wood-chipping machine during a snowstorm. Lee managed to prove that a grisly residue of minute bone fragments, a piece of a finger, other tissue, and hair found nearby were the mortal remains of Helle Craft. The husband was convicted of her murder.

As the meeting progressed, Dr. Lee moved on to Ron Goldman.

Most wounds are on the left side, done from the right, he said to the defense team. He was trapped in the corner, which accounts for some of the wounds. One close-up photo of Ron with multiple smears; therefore he put up a fight. Perpetrator should have bruises and scratches. Soles of Ron's shoes are bloodstained. He had stepped in someone's blood. Was it Nicole's? His own? The murderer's? Had the police ever checked this?

The eyeglasses envelope shows lines that look like a partial shoe print. Another one in the dirt. Berries were present on the back walkway along with the blood. Why no berries on his shoes? Here's a double-loop fingerprint. Whose is it? We don't know.

Lee turned to the Rockingham pictures: one drop outside the gate, four inside. What's the distance between the drops? Should be equally spaced—not equally spaced. Here's a cigarette. One at O.J.'s house, three at Nicole's. Who smoked it? O.J. doesn't smoke. Did they take DNA? Who opened the front door? If he had blood on him, why no blood on the doorknob? Bed is unmade. O.J. said he was sleeping.

The police went through Simpson's clothes searching for bloodstains. They looked in his bathroom and closet, picked up his shoes. The shoe size wasn't that far off.

Then to Kato's room and the window to the back walkway—could you climb in and out of it? Could you throw a glove out and hit the spot where the LAPD found it?

Lee held the room as if he were a sorcerer explaining how real magic is accomplished.

On Sunday afternoon, June 26, Shapiro, Kardashian, Pavelic, and Drs. Baden and Lee played sleuth during their official visit to Rockingham. Kato Kaelin was someone they thought long and hard about.

Kato, after all, had volunteered the strange story about crashes and thumps in the night that made the picture on his wall shake. Would police have searched the back alley if he hadn't said that?

And who, after all, was this strange man living rent-free on Simpson's estate? He looked unstable. They knew he had some kind of relationship with Nicole. Was he her lover?

Equally important, Kardashian told them about the path through the tennis court gate to neighbor Eric Watts's backyard. O.J. wouldn't come around to this side of the house, Kardashian explained. When it's dark, O.J. gets scared. He would never climb that fence. He had an easier route.

Inside Kato's apartment, they banged hard on the wall. The picture didn't move. Kardashian led half the team to the back walkway. He and others rammed into the wall like football players. Again, the picture stayed motionless.

The inside team removed the window screen and Pavelic leaned out. Then Kardashian. The spot where the glove was found was fifteen feet to the right of someone leaning out of the window. Could Kato, or the cop who came into his room, have tossed it there from the window? Possible, but the angle was bad. Baden looked at dozens of pairs of shoes in Kato's closet. Most lacked the kind of heel that the footprints at Bundy suggested. They took three pairs for Henry Lee to test.

Inside the Rockingham foyer, Dr. Lee found three drops of blood not listed in the evidence sheets. Kardashian was amazed again. The drops were tiny but in plain view. They were right there as you walked through the door. The LAPD had missed them.

Checking the driveway, Kardashian saw that the other drops had a washed-out, sun-dried look. Without knowing about them ahead of time, he wouldn't have guessed they were blood. They looked ancient. "Blood has no time," Henry Lee had said earlier. Whether it fell to the ground three minutes or three years ago, a bloodstain could provide information.

Far more important, the doctors were genuinely perplexed by the Rockingham glove. Michael Baden had never worked a case where the primary evidence was so conveniently laid out. Neither had the other forensics specialists. Their collective experience straddled thousands of homicides. They were used to tracking down hairs, fibers, semen, and fingernails. Bits of fabric might be left behind. Ballistics might match a bullet to a gun.

Bill Pavelic was the first to say it: "How often do you see a case where something so obvious as a glove is taken from one place to another?"

When Kardashian visited O.J. on Monday, June 27, he brought up theories about Kato.

"No, he's a good guy. Leave him alone. No way Kato would be involved in something like that." O.J. was adamant.

Like Kardashian, Baden knew that Simpson constantly wondered aloud why the police weren't looking for someone else. On their first visit, Baden had mentioned Kato to O.J. as well. He assumed the client would be fascinated. Instead,

Simpson said it was impossible. Kato Kaelin could never be a suspect. This isn't the way a guilty man talks, Baden thought. He figured Simpson would jump at the opportunity to implicate someone else.

Simpson did point to another possible villain. Nobody got more of his angry attention than Nicole's friend Faye Resnick. Kardashian and Simpson started chewing on a drug-deal-gone-bad scenario. Had the murderers thought they were killing Faye? Resnick was taking drugs while living with Nicole, O.J. said. Was someone after Resnick for drug debts? Ron Goldman also surfaced. What do we know about him? Was he doing drugs? Did the killers follow him to Nicole's? Kardashian and Simpson methodically laid out the questions for Shapiro.

Automatically, the defense team wondered about Jason and, just as often, about Al Cowlings. Shapiro brought up Jason's name frequently. But both had airtight alibis. Jason was a chef, on duty at Jackson's on Beverly Drive. The restaurant kitchen is open; patrons can watch the cooks at work. Hundreds of people saw Jason the night of June 12. As for Cowlings, since his days at USC, he had known Bubba Scott. He was at Scott's daughter's birthday party the night of the murders.

By the last week of June, only O.J.'s woeful denials spoke of his innocence. As those first weeks passed, his defenders found further reassurance in his almost surreal absence of calculated behavior. How many murderers would sit alone with the police and give a tape-recorded interview while their lawyers went for coffee?

Holding a .357 Magnum to his head in the Bronco could be seen either way. The general public read guilt into such dramatic despair. Simpson's defenders withheld judgment.

It was Pavelic who gave them their first real hope, however elusive: He saw corruption in the police casework.

Under any circumstances, Pavelic would have looked for it. His career with the LAPD had ended in angry protest. In 1984, Pavelic had testified against fellow officers who killed a fleeing suspect. One cop was fired, another suspended for six months. Pavelic assumed he was stigmatized forever. But by 1990, he'd made it to supervising detective in the Southwest Division. Then he got in trouble again.

His men were investigating a date rape at USC when their bosses began showing a heavy-handed interest. Pavelic, his partner, and their immediate supervisor eventually concluded that then-chief Daryl Gates and a deputy chief were listening to the suspect's father, a prominent lawyer with influence inside the department.

Pavelic and his men protested publicly. And Bill raised similar charges again before a "people's tribunal" when activist groups held hearings on the LAPD after the Rodney King beating. Pavelic told the crowd that lying and covering up were the norm in the department.

That earned him a desk job. In 1992, he and the brass reached an accommodation. He took a disability pension for asthma and chest pains. He told one doctor he'd rather spend time in a gulag than go back to work. His pension was set at $29,316 a year.

As a private investigator, Pavelic was particularly good at following law enforcement paper trails. He was immediately suspicious of the lack of specifics in the Bundy and Rockingham reports. Pavelic's red alert signals flashed as he studied Phil Vannatter's affidavit for the Rockingham search warrant.

No indication who found the bloody glove. Nothing about going into Kato Kaelin's room. Very little information about the murders at Bundy. Nothing about climbing the wall. Vannatter's affidavit said they learned, after talking to Arnelle and Kato, that Simpson had left on an *"unexpected"* trip to Chicago. More important, the information about Arnelle and Kato was a handwritten addition to the typed affidavit. Had the judge or someone else asked a question during the hearing that prompted Vannatter's addendum? Bill knew they'd called Cathy Randa and learned from her that Simpson's trip was a planned business trip. The detective had misrepresented the facts about the departure in order to obtain the search warrant. O.J.'s departure was not "unexpected." Vannatter knew that. Pavelic knew then that Vannatter had been forced into a further material omission, the omission of the fact that they had scaled the wall at Rockingham before obtaining the search warrant.

He also noticed that the affidavit said that Simpson took the flight "in the early morning hours of June 13, 1994." That expanded the window available for the killings. The cops further "observed" the glove on the back walkway "during the securing of the residence." Whether intentional or not, the language suggested that the LAPD investigators had assumed at once they had a crime scene.

Vannatter wrote that "scientific investigation" confirmed that human blood was found on the Bronco. Pavelic knew that at the time he wrote the affidavit, only a routine presumptive test had been done.*

Detective Vannatter had more than twenty years on the force, but his affidavit was amateurish. Why had he omitted so many damaging details? Pavelic suspected that the LAPD was rearranging things and embellishing information. Vannatter and Lange, for example, had failed to log themselves out of Bundy when they went to Rockingham. The police logs showed them signing out at ten A.M. as if they'd never left Nicole's condo.

He also noticed that the criminalists didn't list how many samples of each bloodstain were taken. A deliberate omission? No doubt in Pavelic's mind.

A few days before the preliminary hearing, Shapiro received a twenty-nine-page memo outlining every mistake Pavelic saw.

On Monday, June 27, Pavelic saw photographs of the Bronco taken by LAPD photographers at 7:30 on the morning of June 13. To his eyes, the car was parked normally. Pavelic knew there was talk of the car jutting out from the curb. He assumed immediately that the cops had been inside the car and moved it.

When he mentioned this to Shapiro that afternoon, the lawyer thought he was overreacting. Human error, he said.

---

*A presumptive test determines whether a substance is blood. The test does not distinguish between human and animal blood.

The omissions mean *something*, Pavelic insisted. "I've worked with these guys," he argued. "I know Robbery-Homicide Division. I've actually seen them frame innocent people. You can't take anything for granted."

The week before, only two days after the Bronco chase, Pavelic had put together a memo for Shapiro asking for sixty-eight pieces of LAPD paperwork, ranging from communication tapes and follow-up investigative reports to the watch commander's daily reports. He also requested the table of contents for the murder books, which contained virtually everything the detectives had.

On the same day, June 27, Pavelic spoke to Simpson on the telephone for the first time. "If you don't know this case inside out," he said, "don't expect your lawyers to know it."

As Pavelic saw it, an investigative consultant does case management. Gumshoes work for lawyers. Consultants work for the client. Getting the client involved was part of his job. Don't be intimidated by your lawyers, he told O.J.

Within a week, he was telling Simpson that *he himself* had to become an investigator. "You've got to read. You've got to ask questions. It will be like a football game, momentum swinging back and forth. Don't be scared. There's a reasonable explanation for everything."

Simpson hardly reacted at first.

"We're dealing with a frame-up," Pavelic insisted.

Within days of the double murders the first messages from O.J. reached Cochran at home. Jim Hill, a former pro football player and now a Los Angeles sports commentator, said Simpson wanted to see him. Simpson had to be out by Halloween to go trick-or-treating with his kids, he said. Cochran waffled. He told Hill that the Juice should wait for the preliminary hearing. See what evidence they've got. Maybe he won't need my help.

Cochran's office was family, and Johnnie kept everyone informed. "I talked to O.J.," he announced. Morale soared. This case needed Johnnie. "He wants me to meet with him, but I told him he had to talk to Shapiro first. Otherwise it would be improper. And I needed to talk to Shapiro, too.''

A week later Cochran called Shapiro and explained that O.J. had asked to see him. But he wasn't going to visit Simpson; he preferred to keep things discreet for now.

By the last days in June, Simpson was repeatedly telling Kardashian, ''Get me Cochran.'' Everyone understood that the jury pool would be predominantly black. He and Taft talked of bringing in an African-American woman with trial experience to ''assist'' Shapiro. The constant talk of Shapiro as a deal maker rather than a trial attorney couldn't be ignored.

A MATTER OF JUSTICE; PREPARING THE DEFENSE

For more than a week, the case of the People of the State of California vs. O.J. Simpson has been hijacked by the media's helicopters, mobile units and klieg lights. Restoring law and order to the proceedings is now a must. Toward that end, Simpson's attorney, Robert L. Shapiro, must now assemble a strong legal team. . . . In legal circles, Shapiro is considered a consummate diplomat, an exceptional negotiator and a mensch. . . . He is also a good trial lawyer who has never tried a potential death-penalty case. . . . Dist. Atty. Gil Garcetti . . . has chosen the "right" attorney for the job. . . . [Marcia] Clark "made her bones" last year when she obtained a death sentence against Albert Lewis and Anthony Oliver for murdering two worshipers in a South-Central church. Before that, she successfully prosecuted Robert Bardo who stalked and killed actress Rebecca Schaeffer.

—Charles L. Lindner, <u>Los Angeles Times,</u> June 26, 1994

6

THE PRELIMINARY HEARING BEGAN ON THURSDAY, JUNE 30. Kardashian rose at 5:30 A.M. and once again skipped his Bible reading. He drove half an hour to Century City with Denice, and met the rest of the defense team. They'd hired a Lincoln Town Car for the investigators, Denice, and others. Shapiro's driver, Keno Jenkens, took Kardashian, Shapiro, and Uelmen in the Mercedes.

Pulling into the parking lot behind the criminal courts building, Kardashian was reminded of the day after the murders when he drove O.J. home: satellite trucks on the side streets, cops and rubberneckers everywhere, a gauntlet of reporters and cameramen. He noticed one addition today: vendors. They hawked T-shirts reading "Don't Squeeze the Juice" or "Pray for O.J." The press was jammed into the stairway that led down to the courthouse.

In the holding cell adjacent to the courtroom, Simpson was nervous, pacing. But Kardashian realized he was ready. The suicide watch had been lifted. O.J. wore a burgundy tie with tiny white polka dots. It added restrained color to O.J.'s dark blue suit.

The others had noticed an awakening too. O.J. was asking hard questions, revealing a sharper edge. Part of him remained hidden, but something healthy was surfacing. In a steady, fatherly voice, Shapiro explained that the prosecution would lay out its case in these hearings. The defense would have a chance to cross-examine each witness.

Outside, he asked Kardashian and Taft if they wanted to

sit at the counsel table. Both men held back, choosing seats just inside the railing.

By now Shapiro was planning a high-risk start-up. Gerry Uelmen felt the defense had a shot at excluding virtually everything the LAPD had gathered inside the Rockingham compound, thirty-four pieces of evidence. The erudite law professor, a former federal prosecutor and expert on Bill of Rights issues, wanted to make trouble for the prosecutors.

In fact, he urged something more radical. Motions to suppress evidence are normally filed in Superior Court during a trial when the prosecution's case is fully visible. Uelmen preferred to make a preemptive strike. He wanted to hit the LAPD before they could put a reasonable story together explaining why detectives climbed a wall to intrude on a private home on the strength of a minuscule drop of blood on a car.

Shapiro liked the idea. He knew, however, that trial lawyers all over the country and TV experts would say that his team was jumpy and that he was amateurish in filing the motion now. He'd undoubtedly hear it from the TV commentators, who now included Johnnie Cochran. But Shapiro's strategy was to move so quickly that the prosecution felt rushed. The faster we go, he told everyone, the more we'll force them to make mistakes. Keep them off balance.

He was already pressuring the scientists. Could they complete their work by early fall? His daring plan was to go to trial within sixty days. The law gave him that right.

Uelmen's ideas fit into that strategy perfectly. Shapiro even thought Uelmen might prevail. His arguments were based on classic search-and-seizure law. "The residence is fully enclosed by walls and fences," the motion said, "and is entered through two electronically controlled gates."

The defense motion charged that the search warrant obtained six hours later failed to describe what the cops were looking for. The detectives said they'd gone to Rockingham to make a death notification. But they climbed the wall after spotting something that looked like a drop of blood on a car outside. They woke Kato Kaelin and searched his apartment without bothering to ask him if he knew about anybody getting hurt. They woke up Arnelle Simpson without telling her about the murder. They finally called O.J. Simpson and notified him, and Simpson said he'd return immediately. According to the letter of the law, they should have left after their telephone conversation with O.J.

Instead, they found evidence and declared the premises a crime scene. Arnelle Simpson was told to leave her father's home at 7:30 A.M. The area was now under LAPD jurisdiction.

The motion went on to explain that Detective Vannatter waited until 10:45 A.M. before obtaining a formal search warrant. That was six hours after someone went over the wall. The affidavit claimed Simpson "left on an unexpected flight to Chicago during the early morning hours of June 13, 1994," when Vannatter already knew otherwise.

Shapiro had high hopes. He had asked that the motion be argued at 8:30 A.M., before the preliminary hearing actually started. But now, on June 30, prosecutors said they'd just received the paperwork. The oral arguments on the motion were postponed until July 5.

Little else was accomplished that Thursday morning. The defense objected to the LAPD lab's demand for one hundred hairs from Simpson's head. Judge Kathleen Kennedy-Powell allowed forty. Shapiro was signaling the prosecutors that he intended to fight *everything*. Kennedy-Powell called an early lunch break at 11:30; Bob Shapiro had to attend a funeral.

That same day, F. Lee Bailey came to town. Shapiro invited Kardashian to join them for dinner—just a social thing. Shapiro said that he might be asking Bailey for advice. But, Kardashian thought, Bailey's not on the team.

Kardashian anticipated a great evening and wasn't disappointed. He and Denice were charmed by the legendary attorney. They went to Eclipse, a hot new restaurant just across the street from Morton's.

Halfway through dinner, the maître d' came over. "Mr. Kardashian, Roger Moore is here and he would like you to stop by his table." Great, Kardashian thought. We can always use James Bond's help. "Come on," he said to everybody, "I'll introduce you to Roger Moore."

Next Elaine Young, a prominent Beverly Hills realtor, invited them to sit with her. Bob often saw her around town, but she had never spoken to him. Rod Steiger sent over a bottle of wine. After that, Fred DeCordova, Johnny Carson's old producer, stopped by their table.

If Lee Bailey was part of the defense team, nobody mentioned it to Kardashian that night.

On Friday, July 1, the media were asking if the prosecution had the murder weapon. Someone in the D.A.'s office thought so.

Recently, while Simpson was on location filming a new TV series, a clerk at a downtown cutlery store had sold him a folding knife. The clerk had given the police a duplicate of O.J.'s knife, and the coroner's office was checking to see if the blade matched Nicole's and Ron's wounds.

When court convened, Allan Wattenberg, the owner of Ross Cutlery, testified for the prosecution that Simpson bought a bone-handled knife with a six-inch blade for $74.98.

His clerk, Jose Camacho, added that Simpson wanted the knife sharpened. Camacho said he had sold his story to the *National Enquirer* for $12,000. He told less forthcoming tales to nonpaying news media, he explained. Wattenberg admitted he was getting part of the money.

"This is silly," Simpson said. "They're making a big deal out of nothing. That knife is sitting at home."

That morning Kardashian was showing Uelmen and Pavelic through the Rockingham house. Simpson phoned them from the jail. "That knife I bought downtown, is it still there?"

"I don't know," Bob replied. "Where is it?"

O.J. told him to unlock his bedroom and look on the hidden shelf behind the vanity mirror on the right of his dressing table. Kardashian found the knife. The oiled blade had never been used. The price tag was still there.

155

Nobody touched the knife. They didn't want to end up as trial witnesses. Kardashian couldn't believe the police had missed it.

That Friday, Judge Lance Ito was sitting briefly as the Superior Court's presiding judge over criminal matters. After Simpson's call to Kardashian, Shapiro asked for an *ex parte* meeting—that is, a private meeting that excluded the prosecutors because privileged information would be discussed. Shapiro explained that the knife their client had purchased from Ross Cutlery was in his home.

Ito agreed to appoint a special court officer to retrieve the knife. He named retired judge Delbert Wong. That afternoon Kardashian met Wong at the same Holiday Inn where he'd met the Browns' limousine the day of Nicole's funeral. Judge Wong drove with Kardashian to Simpson's home.

Kardashian had a sense of ritual as he took Judge Wong upstairs and unlocked the bedroom door. The item we've discussed is here, he said. They stood before the vanity mirror. Would you like me to open it? Kardashian asked. Wong said yes.

He handed Wong a tissue so the judge could handle the knife without touching it.

I want you to notice the price tag, Kardashian said.

Kardashian asked Wong to open the knife to observe its mechanism and blade size. I'd like you to observe that the knife is brand-new, Kardashian said. Wong looked at the blade and shut it.

I'd like you to identify where this knife was found and what shelf it was on, Kardashian continued. They locked the bedroom door and left.

The defense team couldn't believe its luck. They now knew the prosecution had no solid evidence connecting Simpson to a possible murder weapon. If the Ross Cutlery clerk was an important prosecution witness, the other side must be convinced that the knife Simpson bought was the murder weapon. The defense knew otherwise.

They'd asked for the special court officer so that Ito could hold the unused knife as rebuttal evidence, evidence held in reserve to refute whatever the prosecution might introduce. It need not be presented for discovery by the other side. Let the prosecution build up this knife as the murder weapon. The defense could show it to the jury with a dramatic flourish— brand-new, factory oil still on the blade, price tag intact, location and condition attested to by a court-appointed neutral party of unimpeachable credentials. The defense team smiled like Cheshire cats.

On Friday afternoon, July 1, Judge Kennedy-Powell held up a manila envelope. The defense was stunned. Ito had gone on vacation. Another judge who knew nothing about the arrangement had sent the sealed envelope down to Municipal Court with instructions to enter it into evidence. Shapiro and Uelmen rushed to the bench and explained. They convinced Kennedy-Powell to keep the manila envelope closed and return it to the Superior Court. But the strategic value had been destroyed. Marcia Clark and Bill Hodgman had to realize that the envelope contained the knife. The defense had lost the opportunity to blindside the prosecutors.

They wear these robes, Kardashian said to himself, but they really aren't very smart.

Hostile and obscene phone calls rained down on Ross Cutlery that afternoon. "You rotten bastards! I'm going to blow up your store for what you did to O.J.!"

"I'm going to kill you assholes for what you did to O.J.!"

By the time Judge Kennedy-Powell sent the envelope back to Superior Court late on Friday, Wattenberg and Camacho had received at least twenty threatening calls.

That same afternoon Sukru Boztepe and Bettina Rasmussen testified about being led to the crime scene by the Akita. Kardashian noticed that Simpson's shoulders shook when Mrs. Rasmussen described the river of blood. O.J. took several fast deep breaths, raised his eyes to the ceiling, then stared at the floor. Then he became calm.

* * *

Cochran seemed to be ignoring the preliminary hearing as he worked in his office. His TV set was off. But the other lawyers watched, surprised that everything had begun so fast. They were amazed when Shapiro and Uelmen moved to suppress the Rockingham evidence.

You only get one bite at the apple, one attorney declared. If they lose here, they can't raise the same issue during the trial. No municipal judge will go that far out on a limb and throw out the evidence. Why didn't they wait for the trial? The hallway talk turned hostile to Shapiro. Does O.J. have the right people? Is Shapiro up to the job?

Johnnie didn't criticize Shapiro. He threw out reasons why *they* shouldn't be involved. The evidence is overwhelming. The case looks terrible. O.J. was his friend. It's impossible to do your best work for a friend.

But Johnnie saved his best oratory for the talk shows. On the first day of the hearing, he and local criminal defender Roger Cossack appeared on ABC's *Nightline*.

Why was the defense fighting so hard now? moderator Forrest Sawyer asked.

"Two things are at stake here," Cochran explained. "There's the court of law and also the court of public opinion. Clearly, Mr. Shapiro wants to indicate he's going to litigate and contest every point. On the other hand, Marcia Clark and William Hodgman are doing the same thing. This is a real battle, Forrest." But in the long run it was the court of public opinion that would matter to Simpson.

Cossack ventured: "They don't have a particularly powerful case. There's no confession, there's no murder weapon, and there's no eyewitness. We all know in a circumstantial evidence case, anything can happen, particularly when you have a well-loved defendant."

"I share Roger's view," Cochran added quickly. "I think lawyers tend to puff a little bit about their cases. We haven't seen all of the prosecution case yet, but I think they may have puffed a little bit at this point."

Johnnie was moving fast that evening. A little later in the CNN studio, anchor Jim Moret asked him if he expected Simpson to be defended "affirmatively."

"There are certain things he wants to get out before the public." Johnnie sounded authoritative. "Clearly, O.J. Simpson will not testify. But if he's got certain evidence he wants to bring out before the public, now's the time."

7

ON SATURDAY MORNING, JULY 2, AT SEVEN A.M., KARdashian bit the bullet and called Roger King on the East Coast. He reminded him of his numerous calls offering to pay Shapiro's fee. Bob asked for a million dollars.

Talk to my brother Michael and his lawyer in California, King said.

King's lawyer, Bob Madden, wanted to meet immediately with the defense team. He insisted they had something big to discuss. Kardashian wondered what could be so urgent.

The middle of the preliminary hearing was hardly the moment to waste time with a media entrepreneur. So said Shapiro. Madden pushed. Kardashian arranged for a luncheon meeting that afternoon.

King and Madden arrived with a huge deli platter. Bob was nonplussed. Did they think this was a wedding, a wake, a church supper? Nothing to do but take everybody out to the patio.

Michael King began by describing how successful and cash-rich King World was. Their properties included *Oprah*, *American Journal*, and *Inside Edition*. Kardashian squirmed as precious time passed.

"With that much money you can make a solid contribution to O.J.'s defense fund," Kardashian finally said.

They were a public company, King replied. They couldn't make contributions or loans. But there was another way: He offered up to $5 million in return for providing *Inside Edition* and *American Journal* exclusive access to the defense camp and exclusive interviews with Simpson.

Shapiro rose from his chair. "You have wasted my day, gentlemen. I've got to go."

Shapiro walked out.

Kardashian thought of King's insistent calls and found it hard to look either King or Madden in the eye. Showing them to the door, he thought how amazing this was. Without the King brothers, Bob Shapiro wouldn't be O.J.'s lawyer. And all they had been doing the night they called was trying to set up a media deal.

Wayne Hughes had been watching the televised preliminary hearing closely that week. He listened to the commentators and heard the press conferences and hallway posturing. He was getting uncomfortable.

The *style* was wrong. Attacking the LAPD made no sense to him. He hated the innuendoes. He hadn't liked Shapiro since he believed the lawyer had let Simpson and Cowlings run off in the Bronco. The June 23 meeting in Shapiro's office, with its soap opera emotionalism and implicit sales pitch, upset him further. Too much theater, no substance.

He couldn't figure out why Skip Taft and Bob Kardashian were in the courtroom. One was a money lawyer, the other a businessman. Kardashian hadn't practiced law in years. Wayne had never really gotten along with Bob.

He had called Skip Taft at the end of the first day of the preliminary hearing to arrange a private visit with O.J. Taft could be present, nobody else. Hughes planned to break some crockery. Maybe O.J. wouldn't welcome that right now, but somebody had to talk straight to him.

The day Kardashian met Michael King, Simpson came into the attorney visiting room and Hughes launched right into it: I don't think this is the way to conduct your defense. There is too much television posturing. Attacking the police is stupid. The people you've got are wrong.

Hughes turned to Taft. "I don't want to criticize you to

O.J. unless you're here, Skip. The others, I don't really care about. But if you asked me would I want you as my lawyer sitting there in the courtroom, if I were on trial for murder, I'm going to tell you, no. You'd be one of the last guys I would hire. And if you're charging O.J. for sitting there, it's improper.''

Hughes had brought a few notes along and consulted them now. "And Kardashian. If you can tell me that you'd hire Bob Kardashian if you were arrested for murder, then I'm going to listen to you. If you can't tell me that, then what in the hell is he doing there? If he's there as a friend, that's fine. But if he's getting paid—''

"Well, he's hired,'' Taft interrupted.

"How much is he getting?''

Taft didn't answer. Now Simpson wanted to know: "Well, how much *is* he getting?''

Hughes thought he heard Taft say something he couldn't believe. Was Kardashian getting $3,000 a day?

"It's sickening,'' Hughes declared. "That's a million dollars a year for Bob Kardashian. He probably can't get hired anywhere else.''

He then turned to Taft. "Skip, you're the wrong guy sitting in the courtroom. You're the right guy taking care of his business.''

And then Shapiro: "You've got the main lawyer running all this flashy stuff. He wants to be on TV.''

Simpson asked Hughes if he could straighten things out.

Hughes hesitated. His young son, David, had leukemia and needed him right now. He agreed to spend two or three days talking to people who might recommend new faces. He'd made a few calls already and was hearing names. He liked Gerry Spence out of Wyoming, but several confidants felt that a Los Angeles attorney would be better. He knew some names.

"Johnnie Cochran?'' O.J. asked.

"Yes, Johnnie Cochran.''

"I think he and I should talk,'' Simpson said. "Would you contact him?''

Hughes agreed. He left the jail with a sense of purpose.

* * *

That same Saturday afternoon, July 2, Kardashian was wondering how so many big egos would fit in Shapiro's conference room. The attorney had invited twenty-two top lawyers, primarily criminal defense specialists, to an early-evening meeting. He wanted to know how he was doing. Larry Feldman and Roger Cossack were there. So were Michael Nasitir and Skip Miller. Jay Jaffee, Dick Sherman, Richard Hirsch, and Patricia Glasier were among the other bright lights.

Shapiro asked the assembled legal talent how they felt the team was perceived in the media, what they thought of the motions filed so far, their opinions of his strategy.

Everybody was very positive and Shapiro treated the group to dinner at Nicky Blair's. It was a feel-good meeting, Kardashian thought. But then, those willing to show up were probably kindly disposed toward Shapiro anyway. He wasn't sure what the defense had learned.

Then Shapiro invited Kardashian to a screening at producer Robert Evans's sprawling home in Beverly Hills. Evans's estate is actually several buildings wrapped around a yard and pool. Warren Beatty, Annette Bening, Victoria Principal, Dr. Harry Glassman, and superagent Sue Mengers were waiting when he, Shapiro, and Denice walked into the screening room.

Sue Mengers sat with Kardashian and explained breathlessly that she and record-industry mogul David Geffen met at Geffen's house every morning and hovered over the TV set. They took no telephone calls until Judge Kennedy-Powell called a courtroom break.

Maybe Geffen will get on the phone with me now, Kardashian joked.

Mengers speculated that Kardashian's book rights would be worth more than Shapiro's. He was, after all, both lawyer and friend. In the movie, Al Pacino or Robert De Niro should play him. They both laughed.

Kardashian was flavor of the month. He loved it. Denice sat with Annette Bening for a long time. They never did see the movie.

* * *

All through the last week, Kardashian had lived with the early-morning collect calls from O.J., not to mention the late-night collect calls, and now the weekend calls. On Sunday morning, July 3, Simpson had called five times. Kardashian had enjoyed a good laugh the day before when his mother refused O.J.'s call. Mr. Kardashian isn't here, she told the operator. It made perfect sense to her. O.J. was calling Bob; Bob was out. Simpson called again. Again Mrs. Kardashian told the operator she wouldn't accept the charges.

O.J. demanded constant companionship. Visiting hours for family and friends were limited. But Simpson knew his lawyers could drop in anytime. He complained. He begged. He wanted visits every day after court. He wanted them there on weekends.

In short, he was driving everyone crazy. After a long court day, the lawyers, experts, and investigators needed to prepare for the next day's session. They needed to sleep. An occasional meal was helpful, too. O.J. could talk for two or three hours without pausing for breath. Nobody had that kind of time.

The solution was one of Bob's assistants, Nicole Pulvers, fresh, eager, and, by happy accident, just out of law school. She'd passed the bar a year earlier and wanted to do entertainment law. Her mother, Joni, an old friend, had asked Kardashian to advise her. When they met, Nicole offered to work for Bob, unsalaried. An internship. She wanted to learn about the music industry. Kardashian agreed. He was soon so impressed with her work that he put her on salary. Now he had the perfect assignment for her.

Nicole would be O.J.'s jailhouse companion, or, as defense team members occasionally joked, baby-sitter—or Jewish mother. Her job was to visit him when he wasn't in court. She was formally listed as a defense lawyer and paid $25 an hour. No shortage of hours. Now Simpson had someone who would listen to him ad nauseam. He could stay in the lawyers' room all day and visit with friends and family, now called material witnesses, as long as there was an attorney present. Her given name was no small irony. But O.J. had a new listener.

By the first of July, Pat McKenna had filed his reports on Simpson's stay in Chicago June 13.

McKenna found that the trail of witnesses started in Chicago with Jim Merrill, a twenty-seven-year-old Hertz sales representative, and dispatcher Bharat "Bombay" Shah, both of whom who arrived at Terminal 3 at 5:20 A.M. Simpson was the second passenger off the plane.

He wore blue jeans and a long-sleeved denim shirt, sleeves rolled up. Merrill noticed that he carried a Louis Vuitton garment bag slung over his shoulder and a smaller black duffel utility bag in his left hand.

Simpson shook hands with Merrill and both men walked to the baggage claim area. O.J. then sat near the carousel with his elbows on his knees, smiling and answering questions when people came up.

Bombay said he stowed Simpson's bags in the backseat and put the golf clubs in the trunk. Merrill and O.J. then drove to the O'Hare Plaza Hotel. Merrill helped Simpson check in with his luggage, but, he said, he kept the golf clubs. Merrill was scheduled to take Simpson to the course later, in the same car. Merrill said he gave his home and cell phone numbers to Simpson.

McKenna then interviewed Anthony Corkran, the O'Hare Plaza night manager who had been on duty when Simpson arrived at 6:08. Simpson had a lightbulb smile, he said. Another clerk said he asked Simpson to sign a 1977 Buffalo Bills trading card for a friend. Simpson did. Corkran said he watched Simpson turn toward the elevator. He said he was really tired.

Corkran added that O.J. turned back. He'd forgotten his room number. Another guest in the lobby called out that it was 915. Everybody enjoyed this. Corkran remembered looking at his watch. It was 6:16 A.M.

McKenna couldn't report everything about the time Simpson spent in his hotel room. He did find local people who spoke to O.J. on the phone in those hours, people from American Airlines and Hertz. Bill Pavelic said he'd take care of the long-distance calls McKenna found listed in Simpson's hotel bill.

Then Pat talked to Caroline Gobern, who was on duty at the hotel checkout counter the morning of June 13. Gobern said she was confronted by an incredibly rude Simpson pounding on her counter. She had a customer ahead of him and Simpson interrupted: "I need a cab."

Gobern said she maintained a polite mask—you do that in hotel work—but she was annoyed. McKenna dug into this. Weren't departing guests usually in a rush—you know, planes to catch, appointments to keep? Absolutely, Gobern said. But Simpson's behavior was far beyond normal rushing. Just incredibly rude. Later, she even complained to her boss about it.

"I need a cab right now!" Simpson was boiling.

Gobern called the Park Ridge Cab Company for him, but she knew it would be some time before a taxi arrived. She explained this and asked Simpson if he wanted the airport shuttle. No. He wanted the cab. Then he demanded a Band-Aid for his hand. Gobern found one for him in the office medicine cabinet.

Simpson went outside and started talking on a cell phone. Gobern said Simpson then got a call at the desk, and she sent someone to bring him in. He took the call and then left the lobby. Gobern could see him waiting outside. He was very agitated. Abrupt and demanding.

Turns out O.J. had been calling Jim Merrill. The Hertz representative said he got O.J.'s frantic call at home just before eight A.M. "Jim, I need you to pick me up. Please come quickly!" Merrill said he'd be there as soon as he could. Minutes later Simpson called again on Merrill's cell phone, demanding to know where he was. Jim explained he was driving as fast as he could.

Minutes later Simpson called again: "Where are you, Jim?" Merrill told Simpson he was halfway there. He told Pat it sounded like the athlete was crying. "What's wrong?"

"Jim, I can't talk about it, but please hurry."

When Merrill pulled up in front of the hotel, Simpson was gone.

McKenna picked up O.J.'s trail with Dave Kilduff, VP,

Sales, at Hertz's corporate offices in Des Plaines, who had been driving several Hertz people from the airport to the O'Hare Plaza that morning. He saw Simpson sitting outside on a bench when he pulled up. They had met once or twice at other Hertz events. Now, he told McKenna, something seemed odd.

Kilduff walked over to Simpson, held out his hand. "Remember me? Dave Kilduff of Hertz."

Simpson looked up and said, "You've got to get me to the airport."

Simpson got in the car with Kilduff. He held his hands over his face. "Oh my God! Oh my God!" he kept saying. He seemed on the verge of tears. Kilduff saw Simpson fishing in his black leather bag for his airline ticket. He told Kilduff his flight was at 9:15 A.M.

Kilduff said he then noticed a cut on Simpson's left hand for the first time. It was bandaged but still bleeding a little. "Oh my God, this is bad! You're going to hear about this on the news," Simpson said to Kilduff.

Kilduff said he called American Airlines on his cell phone to get the gate number. Simpson remembered his golf bag in Merrill's car. He told Kilduff, "Tell them to just send my clubs on another flight." As Simpson got out of Kilduff's car, a fan ran up to him, but O.J. dashed past him into the airport.

Merrill told McKenna he found out what was happening from the guys Kilduff had dropped at the hotel. Jim took the golf clubs out to O'Hare, hoping to catch up with Simpson. The clerk called baggage handling: Forget it. The clubs would go on the next flight. McKenna had also located Anna Pumo, the American Airlines clerk who tagged the clubs, lifted them over the counter, and put them on the conveyer belt. The golf bag was enclosed in a black cloth travel bag. Pumo said the whole package was fairly light. She thought there were just a few clubs and some clothes inside.

On Sunday, July 3, F. Lee Bailey met O.J. for the first time. "I'm awfully happy to see you, and I want you to know I had nothing to do with killing my wife or this other guy."

166

It was O.J.'s standard monologue, but it was new to Bailey. "O.J., tell me what happened," he said.

The old lawyer thought the heavens had dumped a monsoon on him. He heard about the athlete's love for Nicole, about the cops not looking for anyone else, about how unbelievable everything was.

This gave Bailey a chance to observe. Just sit back and pay careful attention. This man is either Laurence Olivier in the best performance of his life, or he's telling the truth, he thought.

Kardashian had driven Bailey over for a Sunday afternoon visit. Walking in, Bailey was inclined to be easy on Simpson. He had just read Pat McKenna's reports, which described a man acting remarkably naturally. A murderer would have been playing a role. One could still assume a monster in the closet who had finally gone berserk, but Bailey felt that was alien to this man's character. Now he had time to focus on Simpson and make a serious judgment. He had no interest in involving himself in a losing case so far from home. He watched Simpson closely, alert to his own reactions.

Bailey was not without pride in his judgment. He had interviewed hundreds of murderers over the years. His decisions about clients, he felt, were seasoned and calculated. Truthfully or otherwise, the majority claimed to be innocent. He'd taken cases on both sides of that wretched line. He knew the difference.

This man's demeanor was not staged, he decided. Bailey couldn't recall a more impressive first encounter. He said, "I believe you are innocent."

The two superstars seemed to reach through the prison glass and form a relationship. They talked for three hours. They spoke as if Bailey had already joined the team.

Walking out, Bailey turned to Kardashian. "There is no way this man could have committed those murders. He is innocent."

Kardashian could have wept with relief. So much evidence. So much doubt. Now here was an expert who believed what Bob hoped for.

"How do you know?" he asked.

"I've looked into the eyes of many murderers. Most of them will say they didn't do it. You get so you know if they're telling the truth."

Then the media descended. Bailey announced his decision publicly: He was on the Simpson case.

Dr. Baden was pleased when his daughter, Sarah, agreed to visit him in L.A. during her summer break. She was a bright Princeton prelaw student, and he enjoyed her company enormously. To keep her close, he put her to work.

The doctor was studying forensic reports on Tuesday, July 5, when Detective Mark Fuhrman climbed into the witness chair. Sarah was opening mail and called out to her father. Something about this guy. Check it out. She didn't like him.

Baden realized his daughter was right. Fuhrman's testimony was flawless, sharp, composed. He was too slick. This man isn't telling the truth, Baden thought.

The Badens weren't alone in their opinion. F. Lee Bailey, like the rest of the defense team, had known nothing of Fuhrman until that moment. Watching the same testimony on TV, he realized immediately that the detective's account meant that either Simpson had left the glove on the walk, or that the killer dropped the glove off at Rockingham to implicate him. A possibility for a very clever killer who also knew Nicole's personal history. But not a likely scenario.

Bailey was staying with Shapiro's friend Michael Klein, and listened to Fuhrman very carefully. He didn't like what he saw. Here is a man outside in the dark, Bailey thought, and he tells us he doesn't have his vest on. He's apprehensive, but he's not afraid. He's at risk. He's dramatizing things. He has a bad flashlight, but it's not so dark he misses the glove on the walkway. He's a junior officer, but he finds everything. He goes to the Bronco. He persuades Vannatter that they have to jump the wall. He's obviously full of himself. He's quite an actor. I'm getting a vibration, Bailey thinks. And he pages Shapiro in the courtroom.

"Something is wrong with this witness, Bob."

It doesn't make any difference, Shapiro tells Bailey, the judge will suppress the glove.

Bailey seethes while Gerry Uelmen cross-examines Fuhrman. The cop is so wrong! He'd alerted Bob. Uelmen is a brilliant constitutional scholar but he lacks any instincts about homicide cops. He doesn't understand how they'll hammer down reality into another shape if that's what a conviction requires. They will lie. They'll perjure themselves without a qualm. Now here's this slick, scary cop who went over the wall, who found the glove, the blood, and Kato Kaelin. And Shapiro let Uelmen do the cross!

Earlier in the week, when Mark Fuhrman said he had found the glove, Pavelic was stunned. *This* was the guy who found the glove? That night Pavelic went to his computer. By now he had a program in place that tracked every individual involved in the case: what evidence each person looked at, what reports each one filed.

He couldn't find a single LAPD report identifying Fuhrman as the cop who found the glove. Not even the search warrant affidavit. As far as you could see in the paperwork, Fuhrman hadn't noticed the blood on and in the Bronco. He hadn't gone over the wall, hadn't interrogated Kato Kaelin. In fact, he hadn't been at Rockingham that morning.

The Bundy crime-scene log listed Fuhrman arriving at 2:10 A.M., leaving at ten A.M. Period. At Rockingham, he was logged in at 5:15 the following afternoon and left at 7:10 P.M.

If the logs were to be believed, Fuhrman had never left Bundy to go to Rockingham with Vannatter, Lange, and Phillips. He hadn't returned to point at the Bundy glove while a police photographer snapped a picture. He didn't take a Polaroid of the Bundy glove to Rockingham so Vannatter could make a comparison. The man who wasn't there.

Pavelic started to put the facts together.

Robert Deutsch, a lawyer Pavelic knew, called him that night. "Bill, do you realize who this Fuhrman is?"

"I guess I don't."

Fuhrman had been part of the Britton case, which Deutsch and Pavelic had worked together. A black man armed with a knife had robbed and brutally beaten people at automatic teller machines on L.A.'s West Side in 1988. Fuhrman was part of a CRASH Unit stakeout team that spotted Joseph Britton threatening someone with a knife at an ATM. Britton ran. He claimed he tossed the knife over a hedge before the cops chased him down. The CRASH team said Britton waved the knife at them.

They shot him six times. Most of the bullets came from Mark Fuhrman's gun. Britton claimed that Fuhrman walked back to the hedge to get the knife and dropped it beside him. "Are you still alive, nigger?" he sneered at the wounded man. Britton went to prison and sued the LAPD for using excessive force.

Fuhrman was *that* cop. Once reminded of the connection, Pavelic remembered that the Britton incident was just one item in a hefty dossier.

Years earlier, Pavelic had checked out everyone on the CRASH team and found pure gold under Fuhrman's name. The detective had filed for a disability pension in September 1981. He wanted out because of stress. The records said that a department psychiatrist had given him a temporary medical leave a month before he filed. The detective complained that he was getting angrier and angrier at "low-class" people, notably Latino and black gang members—angry enough to kill someone. In one of the interview summaries, a doctor reported that Fuhrman used the word "nigger."

Pavelic knew that in April 1992 the Workers Compensation Appeals Board had judged Fuhrman temporarily disabled and given him time off. But a year later the Board of Pension Commissioners looked at a thick stack of contradictory psychiatric reports and concluded Fuhrman should go back to work.

"I'm going to need the pension reports and Fuhrman's psychological profiles," Bill told his friend. Deutsch was happy to send them to Shapiro.

Some therapists wrote that Fuhrman shouldn't carry a gun. Others felt he was exaggerating the street trouble he saw in hopes of bailing out of a job he didn't like with a golden parachute. The LAPD had an unusually large number of officers applying for stress pensions in those days. It was getting expensive. The force wasn't about to let anyone out easily.

Fuhrman appealed the Pension Board judgment to Superior Court. That put his psychiatric evaluations on the public record.

Bill also began hearing from LAPD friends who had watched the preliminary hearings. "Please be advised that several LAPD police officers and detectives have contacted me and are eager to help O.J.," he wrote in a memo to Shapiro. "If there is one common denominator in these phone calls, it is that Mark Fuhrman is a pathological liar."

Of course, nothing is ever simple in an investigator's life. Pavelic began to suspect that the LAPD was sending him disinformation. Anything to make the defense waste time and money.

"Anita," for example, called to pass along the details of a woman's death in the San Fernando Valley. An ex-boyfriend found her hanged in her home. The boyfriend supposedly told cops that the dead woman had found Nicole's and Ron's bodies on the night of June 12.

Startling information. Anita talked like a cop. She referred to the homicide investigation's incident number. She called again with more information. But the death turned out to be a routine suicide. No connection at all to the Simpson case.

Then a woman called to say that Ron Goldman was bisexual, with a male lover in West Hollywood. The lover found out Ron was dating Nicole, so he murdered them.

Pavelic talked next to Christine Kornides, who called Shapiro's office. She wanted the defense to know she often saw Nicole and Kato jogging and kissing.

Bryan Clark, an actor, called after seeing Jill Shively on *Hard Copy*. Clark had sued Shively successfully in small claims court for $6,000. Shively was a liar, he said.

Pavelic spoke to Frank Chiuchiolo, in town from San Francisco on the night of the murders to burglarize homes. Hiding in some bushes across the street from Nicole's condo, Chiuchiolo saw two well-dressed white men. He heard a thumping noise and a woman's faint scream. A dog barked eerily. He heard a man curse, "Slit the nigger-fuckin'-lovin' bitch!" He saw the two men run out through the back alley.

Pavelic walked around Bundy and identified the house where Chiuchiolo said he was hiding. He sent Shapiro a memo saying they should fly Chiuchiolo to L.A. for an interview. Within weeks reporters discovered that the man regularly "witnessed" high-profile crimes. He liked the publicity.

A man named Brian McMorron called to say he was driving through the intersection of Bundy and Wilshire between ten and eleven the night of June 12 and nearly hit a man running across the street in a ski mask. Pavelic went to the location with McMorron, who said the guy was white, potbellied, and had a ponytail. Pavelic videotaped the intersection.

A letter signed "Blue" from a writer claiming to be a black LAPD lieutenant advised O.J. to hire Johnnie Cochran, and concluded: "All stops are being pulled in your case. Strings are being pulled across the country. The L.A.P.D. and the D.A. do not want to lose your case, so beware. I know for a fact that lies are being blended into your case."

An LAPD source told Pavelic that they had interviewed a beauty salon attendant who said that Ron was straight and dating an older woman with two kids, presumably Nicole.

Bob Kardashian called Pavelic to say he'd gotten a call from a man who said he was a regular at Mezzaluna. A week before the murders he had seen somebody with a ponytail who looked Latino walk up to Goldman and threaten him about money. I'll get *her* to put up the money, Goldman said. Said the ponytailed guy: If you don't, we'll take care of her. Pavelic followed up, but the source refused to speak to him.

On Thursday, July 7, Robert Shapiro begins cross-examining deputy coroner Irwin Golden, who performed the autopsies on Nicole and Ron Goldman.

Bailey's frustration grows as the hearing continues. Then he goes wild when Shapiro cuts up poor Irwin Golden. It's worse butchery than any deputy medical examiner ever perpetrated on a cadaver. He knows Michael Baden is helping Shapiro. Bob is only doing what any kid out of law school could do, asking the questions.

SHAPIRO: The detective who is in charge of a homicide comes in with a knife and he tells you, "this may be similar to the murder weapon"; is that correct?

GOLDEN: Yes.

SHAPIRO: He asks you to check to see and you're telling us that you didn't think it was indicated for you to perform a proper evaluation?

GOLDEN: Well, I said it could be . . . I didn't think it indicated to go through each wound, wound by wound, to try to exclude that weapon. That can be done at some other time.

SHAPIRO: You understand a man is sitting in jail faced with charges of double homicide, do you not?

GOLDEN: Yes.

SHAPIRO: Well, when could that be done to protect his rights? . . . When would you suggest doing these tests?

GOLDEN: Now?

SHAPIRO: I have nothing further.

For Shapiro, his cross-examination of Golden was a triumph. For Baden it was quite another story. Michael Baden knew that Golden had done a very good autopsy, better than John F. Kennedy's. The coroner didn't deserve this. Of course, it helped the defense to make Golden look foolish. And by coaching Shapiro, Baden had participated in the humiliation of a colleague. He told the lawyer to ask about comparing the knife to the wound, which he knew Golden hadn't done. Baden had compared the knife; he knew it didn't match.

"It's because of me this happened. No lawyer would think of asking such a question," Baden said out loud. He was supposed to be a scientist. An impartial expert. Provide information and let the attorneys figure out how to use it. That was how he saw his proper role. He vowed not to cross the line into advocacy again.

> . . . Golden, as he left the courthouse after giving testimony, was seen pounding the walls of an elevator with his fists and cursing Shapiro. A Newsday reporter [Mitch Gelman] who boarded the elevator with Golden overheard him muttering, "Why did he have to ask me that question? Why did he have to ask me that question?"

> —Newsday, July 8, 1994

On the opening day of the preliminary hearing, Judge Kathleen Kennedy-Powell had made a point of mentioning that she had attended Gerald Uelmen's classes at Loyola. On July 8, though, she ruled against her former professor. The evidence collected at Rockingham when Fuhrman went over the wall, including the bloody glove, was admissible. The press called it "a major blow" to the defense.

Pat McKenna was still waiting in Chicago for further instructions as he watched the preliminary hearing on TV. He hadn't heard a word about his report and nobody would take his phone calls. Finally he got Bill Pavelic on the line.

I'm in charge of investigations, Pavelic tells him. I'm a consultant. I'm coordinating everything. Here's my wife's name, my phone numbers. You should bill at $100 an hour.

McKenna thought that sounded fine. He had connected with the guy in charge.

Only maybe not. He hears from Lee Bailey, who wants him and John McNally in California. Pavelic isn't doing anything, Bailey complains. He never leaves his computer. There are some other guys on the case who might as well be sitting with Pavelic for all the good they're doing. Maybe stuff is happening, he tells Pat, but Bailey can't see it. Nobody is working the streets.

So McNally and McKenna, the M&M twins, are hitting the West Coast.

8

By Saturday, July 9, the feeling was growing that Bob Shapiro might not lead the remarkable team he'd assembled into trial.

Bailey had considered this possibility from the outset.

His friend never presented himself as a legal pugilist. Shapiro coordinated things, then moved in to cut the deal. In this assessment Bailey meant no disrespect: You never get a chance to deal unless you convince an eager-beaver prosecutor his case is weak. That's hard. Bob had already assembled the forensic experts and Gerald Uelmen, who might make a deal possible.

But Shapiro never decided what deal to make. He'd hinted to Bailey before Simpson's arrest that he had doubts about O.J.'s story. He flirted with the insanity plea that Boston attorney Alan Dershowitz mentioned on the *Charlie Rose Show*. A week later Shapiro was saying, the D.A. hasn't got enough evidence to convict this guy of anything. They've got the glove, but it will be suppressed.

Moreover, Shapiro was off again, on again, on the issue of Simpson's guilt. After visiting O.J., Bailey tried to pull rank. This is your big brother talking, Bob. This is your Dutch uncle. I've done a lot of time with murder cases. I can read clients. If he did it, I'd be out of here.

The toughest thing for an old publicity hound like Bailey was staying out of sight. Shapiro insisted on it. Shapiro's friend investment banker Michael Klein offered the guest quarters in his elegant Mediterranean-style mansion in the flatlands of Beverly Hills. Klein's estate quickly became a greenroom for aspiring lead attorneys. Even F. Lee Bailey. Gerry Spence, the Wyoming miracle worker who flaunted fringed buckskin coats and cowboy boots, came to town to consult and settled in at Klein's. Comfortable rooms, great food, swimming pool. But to Bailey it felt like a jail. Shapiro would not let him attend the preliminary hearing.

Gerry Spence felt he was being courted when he arrived in L.A. on July 9. Simpson had called his home in Jackson Hole several times and asked him to help. Spence knew that Shapiro was under pressure to recruit a trial warhorse. Wayne Hughes also called. He sounded like a take-charge fellow.

But Spence was quirky about his cases. He worked for free, often as not, but he required philosophical weight. He worried that this one was only celebrity-driven. He was sixty-five years old. He had no time for sound and fury signifying nothing.

If he came to L.A., Spence said, he'd have to be in charge. I can't be involved in a case I don't control, he told Shapiro. After that, their conversations became lifeless. Shapiro talked of his problems with the defense team, but he asked no advice. He kept saying Spence was his mentor. But he didn't ask Spence to join the team. Spence understood the ritual.

In one of those conversations, Shapiro mentioned that he was considering Johnnie Cochran. The Wyoming lawyer knew from his talks with Simpson that Cochran might be retained no matter what Shapiro wanted. Spence thought Cochran an excellent choice, but he sensed that Shapiro didn't want Johnnie as lead trial counsel. He got the impression that Robert Shapiro had great confidence in himself for that role.

JUDGE CITES "AMPLE EVIDENCE,"
ORDERS SIMPSON TO STAND TRIAL

—Los Angeles Times, July 9, 1994

176

On Saturday, July 9, Wayne Hughes was driving home when his car phone rang: Bob Shapiro wanted a meeting. Small world, Hughes thought. The lawyer agreed to come to Hughes's house in Malibu on Sunday morning.

When they met, Hughes spoke of his friendship with Simpson. He was in a position to help financially, he said, but he wanted a clear picture of the defense. Bob Shapiro offended Hughes immediately. This has to be a confidential meeting, he said, and asked Hughes to send his young son David out of the room. Hughes refused. The conversation went downhill from there.

Cochran was in Chicago at the NAACP convention on the ninth when things began to heat up. O.J. called Johnnie's answering service six times that day. On the seventh try, the operator put them together.

"You've got to come see me," O.J. began. Simpson pushed hard. Johnnie said he would have to call Shapiro first. Cochran flew back to Los Angeles the next day and met Shapiro on neutral ground, a tennis club in Beverly Hills.

Shapiro began as he had with Spence. These are the problems we face. It's a team effort. I'm talking to Gerry Spence about joining the team.

Cochran had no patience for posturing. Cochran never solicited clients. Clients approached him. He'd gone back and forth on the O.J. thing a hundred times, and one thing was certain: He had to be asked.

And O.J. had *asked*. Now it was Shapiro's turn.

Cochran responded, as usual, that the client wanted him in on the case. That's why he was there.

Shapiro didn't take the hint. I think you'd be an asset, he suggested. But he'd have to talk to Spence.

What are the fees? Cochran asked.

The money is limited, Shapiro replied.

That Sunday afternoon Shapiro walked into the strategy meeting in casual clothes and a baseball cap. He had just come from seeing Hughes and Cochran. The entire team was assembled. "I just had the most horrible meeting with

Wayne Hughes," he began. "We met to talk about funds for this case, but I ended up walking out on him. I have never met anybody so self-centered and egotistical as Wayne Hughes." Shapiro came as close to a tirade as he was able, but he was too disciplined to blow. "Hughes does not want Skip Taft involved in the defense because he thinks Skip is in over his head. He does not want Bob Kardashian. He feels it is foolish for Bob to be involved because he's not a criminal lawyer. If they're out, I am resigning from this case."

Bob Shapiro resigning?

"Wayne Hughes wants total control," he said. "He wants to run the case as if it were his own. He was so insulting that I'm taking myself off the case."

Was Shapiro bluffing?

"I have a cruise to go on, a cruise to Europe, and I put it off. It leaves in a week. I'm going to take my cruise. I'm going down to see O.J. today and tell him that I am off the case."

Baden and Lee looked at each other.

"I want all of you to continue. You've done excellent work, and you shouldn't leave just because I am." In the same measured tones, Shapiro explained he wouldn't be responsible for financial arrangements hereafter. If the forensic experts decided to stay, their fees would not be his business.

Nearly everyone said they would leave if Shapiro did. You brought me into the case, Henry Lee said to Shapiro. If you leave, I will do the same. Michael Baden wasn't sure what to do. He couldn't imagine deserting a client. But he couldn't have imagined Shapiro resigning, either.

Taft and Kardashian were horrified. Kardashian spoke first. "Wait a minute, Bob: You don't want to resign. If Wayne Hughes isn't the guy, then we'll get somebody else. We'll work it out."

"We've got to think of the best interests of O.J. Simpson," Taft added.

"I'm going to see O.J.," Shapiro announced. "Alone." Kardashian knew that if O.J. would listen to anyone, it was

Shapiro. Hughes couldn't get O.J. out of jail; Bob Shapiro could.

Henry Lee wished he were back in Connecticut. Every case had its bad moments, but this infighting was absurd. First, he'd been astonished by the treatment he received at the LAPD lab. They made him work with useless equipment. They put ridiculous limits on what he could see. These people were colleagues who knew his work. They had been unbelievably rude. He wasn't getting the information he needed. The discovery material looked as if it had been stored in the path of a typhoon. There was simply too much material to digest.

And now the lawyers were fighting. He'd never seen anything like this. Without this man Wayne Hughes, they had no money? He made no personal profit from these cases, so he cared nothing about the fee. But he did care about his own sense of professional dignity.

Shapiro's departure was a perfect excuse to quit.

Besides, with each passing day, the case was becoming more difficult for Dr. Lee.

LAPD criminalist Greg Matheson's testimony at the preliminary hearing was devastating. The blood at Bundy and Rockingham, said Matheson, was determined by PGM subtype serology tests to be consistent with Mr. Simpson's blood.* Lee knew that PGM subtyping was primitive compared to DNA testing, but the results pointed in an ominous direction. The PGM tests organized blood and other bodily fluids by combinations of enzymes. Matheson testified that less than one-half of one percent of the population had the combination of enzymes shared by O.J. Simpson and the killer. One in two hundred people. In the past, defendants had been routinely convicted on such evidence.

And DNA results would follow. Some preliminary tests were already in.

*These tests type the phosphoglucomutase (PGM) enzyme in human blood and semen.

179

Lee believed without reservation in the validity of DNA testing. He detected vague antiscientific attitudes among his teammates, wishful thinking. He confronted Shapiro very early. Don't ask me to go against DNA, he warned. I will never testify that it is inadmissible or unreliable. Retain others if you want such opinions presented.

He felt a terrible conflict between his certainty that DNA testing was valid and his strong sense that something was wrong with the discovery photos. He told Shapiro he needed to speak directly to the client. If Simpson didn't convince him of his innocence, he would quit.

Johnnie was back in his office on Monday, July 11.

Details of O.J.'s calls and Shapiro's meeting with Johnnie hit the hallways immediately. Everybody scrambled to hear the latest.

Shawn Chapman's office wall adjoined Johnnie's. Cameron Stewart worked on the other side of Cochran. The two young lawyers were bookends with big ears. Sound drifted through from the boss's office. When Jan at the switchboard let it be known that Simpson was calling, people dropped in on Shawn and Cameron as if they'd been sent engraved invitations.

Cameron had the best sound. The lawyers joked that sitting in her office was like putting your ear against a stereo speaker. One particular call got everyone excited. You could hear Jan telling Johnnie that O.J. was on the line. Then Johnnie started talking.

"Yeah, man. Okay. I talked to Shapiro. Whatever you need, you know? I'm there for you."

O.J. was giving his version. Johnnie was listening. It went on for twenty minutes.

"Oh, man," Cochran then said, "I know what you're saying is right. Okay, what I've been hearing is wrong. I'm there for you. Whatever you want, no problem."

When the conversation ended, Johnnie got back on the phone as fast as he could punch the buttons—probably to tell somebody that O.J. wanted him. He might take a pass, of course. But O.J. was calling him. The man wanted his advice. He was relying on him. The TV shows were exciting, but O.J. topped all that.

Everybody was grinning. They were getting the case!

"I want to speak to Bill Cosby. I need to talk to Michael Jackson. After I do that, I'll make a decision."

Johnnie was still at it. Would he get the case? Everyone knew he would, but the drama had to play out. He'd been helping Jackson with his long-running media circus concerning the singer's relationships with little boys.

"I've spoken to Michael. I assured him that he would always come first. He wanted O.J. to have the best help he could get."

The firm's lawyers can feel it getting closer. A few days later, Johnnie said: "I'm going down to see O.J."

Shawn Chapman was so excited she hugged Cochran. She smiled: Bring it back. Bring that case back here.

Finally Cochran called Chapman and Carl Douglas into his office. He leaned back in his chair, rainbow tie tight, resplendent in a lavender suit. "O.J. wants me to handle his case. What do you think?"

Chapman jumped up and down, shouting "Yes, yes, yes!" She knew she'd get a piece of it. She was one of the few lawyers in the firm with criminal trial experience.

Douglas held back. He was the firm's managing attorney, after all. His job was to think about personnel and money. Trials like this are really stacked against you, he warned. There's a lot of work here. Maybe more work than money. But Carl knew they had to take it. Who could resist?

9

On Tuesday, July 12, McNally meets Pat McKenna at Los Angeles International Airport. "It's crazy out here," he tells McKenna. "Television crews everywhere."

They go straight to Rockingham. Pavelic is waiting for them with Jason and Arnelle. Right from the get-go, Pavelic gives them a fine welcome: "I don't know why you guys are out here," he says.

McNally plays diplomat. "Look, Bill, just so you understand: I didn't come out here to step on anyone's toes or take control of anything."

McKenna can't believe this. "I'm just a grunt," McNally says. "I'll do what I'm told."

Arnelle shows them around the house. Pavelic briefs McKenna and McNally on his theories. McKenna immediately wonders why everybody's talking about fucked-up police reports, conspiracies, drug hit men. Who cares? He wants to knock on doors in the neighborhood where the murders happened and find out if anybody saw or heard anything. Pavelic is saying, No, we already did that. Nobody's talking. You're wasting your time if you go over to Bundy.

Well, maybe he's right, McKenna thinks. The media and the kooks and the tourists have probably overrun it by now. But John and I have to do it. That's what we do. We knock on doors.

McKenna liked to joke that working with John McNally was always Christmas. Chubby guy, white beard. McNally was organized like a Marine Corps general, while McKenna was always slipping and sliding like a buck private. McNally was a knock-down street guy, with connections on the other side that pissed off the FBI. But he could turn around and give a lecture that made the Feds sit up.

McNally had left the NYPD after sixteen years. Everybody knew him as the man who caught the guy who snatched the Star of India sapphire out of New York's American Museum of Natural History. Then McNally turned up as Lee Bailey's private investigator on the Patty Hearst case. Next, Claus von Bülow. Along the way, the FBI's mob wiretaps. But the government had a different version. *That* McNally ran security checks for the Gotti mob.

McKenna didn't care. The only thing that mattered was the case at hand. He liked the way McNally picked up on little things. For instance, McNally heard about the shoe prints and said: We have to find every receipt for every pair of shoes that O.J. ever bought in his life and make sure they don't match up with those prints at the scene. He figured Skip Taft would have all that. He was pissed when Taft didn't.

The investigators go over to Mezzaluna just to look. They drop by Ben & Jerry's. McKenna asks if the cops have come by. The clerk says no. McKenna thinks, Wait a minute, the police haven't been here? The clerk doesn't know what flavor Nicole bought the night she was killed, but the clerk who sold the ice cream to Nicole will be in later. So they come back. She remembers Nicole bought Rain Forest Crunch.

They buy some and check out the ingredients: French vanilla ice cream and jungle nuts and other stuff. Bailey will want to know if it melts faster because it's got so much sugar. Bailey is a detail man. You can never have too much information for him.

Hot assignment the next day: The twins are sent to Benedict Canyon to hook up a computer for Bailey's godson. Shapiro's son. McKenna doesn't mind; it's a chance to meet the big guy, Shapiro, at his home. The only time they'd talked was that first day on the phone in Florida. He kept hearing that Shapiro really liked his reports. Now he could finally meet him.

They walk up to the front of the house, and Bob Shapiro is

in the garage boxing. He's in trunks, wearing gloves with his wrists wrapped, hitting the tall bag. McKenna had heard that this was how Shapiro stayed in shape.

"Hi, I'm Pat McKenna."

Shapiro stops and looks at him. "The kids are in the house," he says. And he holds up a glove to show he can't shake hands, goes back to boxing.

McKenna can't believe it. You do a case with Lee Bailey or Roy Black, it means sitting down and talking about it. He'd also worked for a few lawyers who treated you like the lowest hired help. You want to speak to me, do it through the chain of command.

Bottom line: The kid liked the computer.

FROM: William G. Pavelic
TO: Robert Shapiro
DATE: July 13, 1994

Please be informed that on July 12, 1994, Barry Hostetler and I interviewed a witness who stated that on June 12, 1994, at approximately 1055 hours, she observed three [later the story would change to four] Hispanics in their late 20's running from Nicole Simpson's courtyard area.

The witness further stated that she is positive that two of the three suspects held something in their hands. All three entered an "undercover type police car," silver in color, and quickly departed northbound on Bundy.

This witness called the LAPD and was told by detectives that the investigation was completed. She also contacted the District Attorney's office and was "kissed off."

The witness owns a jewelry shop in the West Side Pavilion and is very credible. She took down names and documented everything.

FROM: William G. Pavelic
TO: Robert Shapiro
DATE: July 13, 1994

Please be informed that on July 13, 1994, I telephonically interviewed Mr. Carlos Martinez. Mr. Martinez works for Phoenix Towing Co. in Montebello.

Mr. Martinez stated that one of their two truck drivers knows for a fact that O.J. Simpson's vehicle (Ford Bronco) was ransacked by John Meraz when he was transporting the vehicle from Rheuban Motors to Parker Center. Since this incident, Mr. Meraz was fired from Viertels Tow. . . . Mr. Martinez further stated that Hard Copy is already working on this matter.

A week later Pavelic sent Shapiro the following fax:

FROM: William G. Pavelic
TO: Robert Shapiro
DATE: July 20, 1994

NOTE: THE FOLLOWING INTERVIEW IS VERY SIG-NIFICANT BECAUSE THE FEMALE PERSON WHO IS BEING DESCRIBED IN THIS INTERVIEW RESEMBLES NICOLE'S FRIEND CORA [FISCHMAN].

On July 20, 1994, I received a call from Mr. Thomas Talerino.

Mr. Talerino stated that on June 12, 1994, at approximately 2055 hours he and his roommate were roller skating in the 800 block of Bundy St. When Talerino reached 877 So. Bundy he observed a woman with shoulder length black hair wearing black tights. The woman was standing next to a mountain bike near a wall separating the two properties. Mr. Talerino felt that the woman was deliberately hiding her face.

As soon as he passed the woman, Mr. Talerino observed a male white squatted in the shrubbery near the front wall of 875 S. Bundy. Mr. Talenino [sic] described the person as a male white "with dark slicked back hair."

Mr. Talerino asked his roommate if he observed the woman and he described her as being Oriental.

The first week McKenna was in L.A. he and McNally got up each day at 5:30 A.M. and read discovery material in their hotel rooms over coffee. They were staying near Shapiro's office, so they walked over about seven and followed Shapiro into his office when he arrived. Things didn't shut down until at least eight P.M. Then they had dinner and a few drinks.

They couldn't get in sync with Pavelic. It wasn't working. He was always at his office in Glendale thirty miles away. Cochran brought in another investigator. McKenna wanted to bring the guy up to date, get him copies of everything. Pavelic nixed that: Don't give him anything. The new man didn't last long.

A newspaper article quoted Skip Taft as saying John McNally was hired to head up the investigation of who really murdered Nicole and Ron. Pavelic didn't like that.

To McKenna, Pavelic looked all wrong. "John, he's got four different fucking eyewitnesses who say four different things."

McNally had heard it before.

"He has this Mary Anne Gerchas who sees four Hispanic men running towards her. He has someone named Brian McMorron who sees a fat white guy in a ski mask. There's a burglar seeing two white guys in suits running out the alley. Tom Talerino sees a white guy with slicked-back hair crouching by the wall and an Oriental woman who won't look at him."

McNally is tired of Pavelic and his witnesses. It isn't moving the case forward.

"Three out of these four people have to be full of shit. Maybe all four, unless ninety guys committed this murder. You got Mexicans running one way, white guys the other."

When McKenna wasn't griping about Pavelic, he thought about him: Bill Pavelic has these *theories*. Kato's got a girlfriend in the porno business who dated Goldman or something. If we can show a *casual relationship* between Goldman and Kato—what is he talking about, a casual relationship? You don't say things like that unless you can nail them down.

* * *

Shapiro considered himself an expert on handling the media. His articles on the subject had appeared in law journals. He knew how to use off-the-record comments to the right journalist. As soon as Shapiro heard from Pavelic about Fuhrman's background, he put his skills to work during an interview with *New Yorker* writer Jeffrey Toobin. Shapiro suggested that Mark Fuhrman was a "racist cop," and Toobin found the material to support Shapiro's statements. When the magazine hit the stands on July 18, the defense had dealt its first race card. Selected items from courthouse files on Fuhrman popped up throughout the article. Toobin cited an unnamed defense attorney as his source. At the time, Shapiro, of course, denied that he was that source.

Denice's father chaired a worldwide evangelical group called the Full Gospel Businessmen's Convention. He asked Kardashian to address one of their meetings at the Anaheim Convention Center the Saturday after Toobin's article appeared. Bob was reluctant.

He was expected to talk briefly, for maybe fifteen minutes. He simply stood up on the stage and spoke from his heart. He told his audience how he brought Simpson the Bible in jail and prayed with him.

"God has a plan for everyone," Kardashian concluded. "I hope you will keep O.J. Simpson in your prayers."

"What about Ron Goldman?" someone in the crowd yelled. "What about the victims?"

Kardashian realized how very isolated he'd become in three short weeks.

"You're right," he replied, deeply embarrassed. "We should pray for the victims."

By the end of the second week in July, McNally and McKenna are drinking with people close to Shapiro, and they pass a message to Lee Bailey: You will never set foot in that courtroom. Their source tells them the trial will be Bob Shapiro doing a drop-dead closing argument, with Gerry Uelmen handling law. Shapiro sees Bailey as his cover, to be kept in the background. He can tell everybody he already has a hot trial lawyer, doesn't have to recruit anybody else.

Comes the trial, Bailey sits down while Shapiro steps out in front.

Pat McKenna wants a look at the guy whose trail he followed around Chicago. He and Dr. Lee know each other from the Kennedy rape case in Florida. The rumpled investigator and the scientist in the suit drive to the jail together.

McKenna has another reason for buddying up: He wants Henry Lee's take on the client. Did Simpson do it or not? He knows Henry wouldn't say it right out. Henry's a scientist. He tells you what the evidence shows him; he doesn't offer an opinion on guilt or innocence. At least not out loud. But McKenna knows he'll learn something from Lee.

The ride downtown scares McKenna. Henry says the DNA evidence will put O.J. at Bundy. He needs an explanation from Simpson.

They do the hands-on-the-glass routine, and the next thing you know tears are welling up. Talking to O.J. face to face is like a conversation with Niagara Falls. He starts the woe-is-me and I-would-never-hurt-Nicole routine. So what? McKenna has seen crocodile tears in jails from Miami to Chicago.

Now Lee tells Simpson about possible DNA tests and other things that show his blood in all the wrong places. Suddenly it gets interesting: McKenna sees O.J. doesn't have that look on his face he knows so well, that geez-I'm-gonna-get-caught look. This is different. Like: How could this be? What does this mean?

Then he hears Lee say there must be an explanation. Could be that the blood was already there. Could be contamination.

On the way home, McKenna is dying to know what Lee thinks, but doesn't want to ask point-blank. McKenna tells Lee what he learned in Chicago. How absolutely regular Simpson seemed. Witness after witness described somebody who sounded like no actor.

Lee talks about evidence: You must take a lot of evidence in, and a lot away. McKenna isn't sure what that means, but he has a strong feeling that Lee is leaning toward Simpson's innocence.

While he chats with McKenna, Henry Lee has two things on his mind. While Simpson talked and cried, he watched the man's hands. They are very big. We need to find a glove like the gloves in evidence. We must measure his hand and measure the glove.

And Henry Lee's mind struggles with his heart. The DNA will say Simpson is involved. But his demeanor cries out something else. Is he such a good actor, or is he telling the truth? That's why I quit police work thirty-six years ago, Lee thinks. So difficult to deal with human beings. You don't know whether they tell the truth or lie. I want to be totally objective. That's why I became a scientist. I look at that place behind the Rockingham house where the glove is found. Common sense tells you the glove belongs to Mr. Simpson. I look at the fence. Vegetation is growing there. Nothing disturbs it. Common sense tells you nobody climbed over that fence.

Though Kardashian had no formal authorization, throughout July, he played the role of O.J.'s negotiator and fund-raiser.

Money was the last thing he and Skip Taft had time to focus on that month. Earlier, when Taft had approached Shapiro to discuss his fee, the lawyer said that Larry Feldman, a lawyer everybody knew from the Michael Jackson case, would negotiate for him.

Taft estimated that $2.5 million was the likely total cost. He spoke to Feldman over several weeks, and they eventually settled on $100,000 a month plus expenses, with a $1.2 million cap, for Shapiro. They assumed that the trial would last six months.

Now, with Cochran on board, Kardashian assumed Shapiro would reduce his fee so he and Taft could offer Cochran some kind of parity.

Shapiro had a different view. "No, no. I have a contract. I'm staying with it."

This is business, Kardashian reminded himself. If we have cash-flow problems, then Bob Shapiro may have to wait.

Kardashian soon discovered that Cochran had the impression from Shapiro that the total defense budget was about a million dollars. Cochran was looking for $30,000 to $50,000 a month. Considering the overall budget, that was fine. Cochran settled on $50,000 a month plus expenses, with a $500,000 cap, and he threw in Carl Douglas and Shawn Chapman.

The rest of the negotiations were easy. Lee Bailey came in free, expenses only. Shapiro would take care of Bailey; they were friends. Bailey asked just one favor: I'm first in line as trial counsel if any civil lawsuits develop. No problem, said Kardashian.

Gerry Uelmen signed on for about $350,000. So did Alan Dershowitz. The experts and the private eyes were being paid weekly rates.

That left Kardashian. He hadn't negotiated anything for himself. He'd never heard about $3,000 per week, or per day, or per any period, until Taft mentioned it to Wayne Hughes. Kardashian remembered Shapiro saying, "I can't do this case without you. You've got to be involved." But when Kardashian mentioned a fee for himself, Shapiro answered, "Get it from O.J.; I'm not giving up a dime." After listening to Hughes, O.J. had said Kardashian's money should come from Shapiro's side. Now Shapiro wasn't cooperating.

Shawn Chapman was already at work on Thursday, July 14, when she learned they were scheduled to visit Shapiro's Century City offices to start the case. Johnnie and Carl would drive her over. Nothing was public yet.

She went home and changed into a better dress.

Sara Caplan met them in an eyebrow-raising miniskirt that briefly stopped Cochran and Douglas. Even Chapman was startled. Shapiro was at a meeting, Sara said. The African-American lawyers looked at one another. They felt that Robert Shapiro had sent his first message.

Caplan took them into the lawyer's ornate office. It was no bigger than the offices they occupied individually on Wilshire Boulevard, which softened the sting of the snub. Caplan helped further by telling Cochran breathlessly how much she admired his work, how she'd looked forward to meeting him. Johnnie was pleased.

The office floor was stacked with row upon row of boxes jammed with manila folders, each carefully labeled "Bronco, blood," "Rockingham, glove," and so on. Chapman was impressed with the organization. Caplan passed her hand over the huge cache of material. "We need to get you copies of all this."

She suggested they look at crime-scene and autopsy pictures. Chapman had seen thousands of autopsy photos. Her suave boss had no such experience.

"Oh my God," he exclaimed, "this is terrible!" He was shaken and upset. Douglas said little.

Oddly, the autopsy photos made their client more sympathetic. Cochran had come back from his jail visit a convert. The man he talked to couldn't have done something like this. In the hallways, he preached of his conversion. "I've talked to him. He absolutely didn't do this. I believe him."

Cochran persuaded the others. To her own amazement, Shawn Chapman believed in Simpson now. They looked at the ghastly pictures and agreed that O.J. Simpson couldn't have done *this*.

After less than an hour they left carrying a single box of discovery materials that Caplan gave them. Shapiro still hadn't returned.

Kardashian's first moment in the media spotlight on June 17 had been scary but also sublime. Stand up before the lights and read your suicidal friend's letter. Afterward, everybody cheers.

Now he'd gotten the tabloid treatment. *Premiere Story* did a show about the Louis Vuitton bag O.J. took with him to Chicago. They showed footage of Bob carrying it after Simpson returned to L.A. The breathless question was: What was inside? Did Kardashian hide the contents? Could it have contained the murderer's bloody clothes?

Enter Kardashian in a black hat. *Premiere Story* portrayed him as a dark and sinister character. He'd helped Simpson sneak away to Encino with the bag. And then Simpson had left Kardashian's house with another bag.

The show taught Bob another lesson about the distorting mirror of public life. He was great copy. His hard, chiseled face, slightly flattened nose, and dark hair with a silver wedge combed back tough-guy style made him the perfect accomplice, the shadowy manipulator advising the rogue prince. At the preliminary hearing, a reporter joked that Kardashian was the guy Central Casting sent when you needed someone to play the thug hanger-on. His connections to the music business, with its well-known dark side, added flavor.

Kardashian felt violated. The tabloids had a piece of him now.

The Friday calendar meeting, the day after Johnnie, Carl, and Shawn looked at autopsy photos in Bob Shapiro's office, was somebody's birthday. Johnnie always brought cake, sometimes champagne. It didn't matter whether you were Jan the receptionist or Carl Douglas the managing attorney. Birthdays were celebrated.

Today, July 15, was a champagne day. But the birthday took second chair.

"As many of you know, I've been having discussions with O.J. Simpson." Johnnie beamed at the head of the conference room. "He wanted me from day one, but I couldn't meet with him until after the preliminary hearing."

Everybody had heard it, one way or another. Nobody minded hearing it again.

"You may know I've met with him," Johnnie said, "and I must tell you that he's absolutely innocent. He didn't commit these crimes. It's an outrageous travesty of justice.

"Shawn and Carl will be working on the case. That will mean handing off their cases to the rest of you."

Nobody smiled. Shawn had forty active cases. She was bound for glory while everyone else took on her ordinary workload.

On July 19 Gil Garcetti met with black community leaders on the issue of fairness in the Simpson case. The meeting was held at the city's Crenshaw district Urban League headquarters, and the *Los Angeles Times* gave it the front page. Representatives of the NAACP and Dr. Martin Luther King's Southern Christian Leadership Conference attended. The Reverend Cecil Murray of the high-profile First African Methodist Episcopal Church was on hand. Urban League president John Mack chaired the gathering.

When a black hero is charged with murdering his white ex-wife, African-Americans can hardly ignore American history. The community leaders knew that white Americans had lynched black men for fooling around with white women in California as well as in the Deep South. We'll have no legal lynching now, the leaders implied. Recall those terrible riots when a white suburban jury acquitted four white policemen of beating Rodney King.

They asked Garcetti for his word that the Simpson jury panel would be racially mixed, and closely interrogated beforehand. We cannot have jurors, John Mack told reporters afterward, "who are blinded by any hang-ups they may have about an African-American man married to a white woman."

The other voice that day was that of Johnnie Cochran, identified only as a prominent African-American attorney. He attended the meeting as a community representative. In the hypnotic cadences that made such great TV sound bites, he spoke of the need for fairness. He told television crews that Garcetti had promised fairness. The community would be watching, Cochran said.

Three days later, he appeared at Simpson's second arraignment as a member of the defense team.

Carl Douglas and Shawn Chapman were now on the defense team in the hottest trial in America. A huge media circus, talk of the town. But on July 22 they had to watch it on TV.

Johnnie, who hated to bring bad news, said, "I'm going to court tomorrow. You'll be coming at the right time. For now, I need you to stay in the office." Shawn and Carl just nodded.

Cochran and Bailey had prepped Simpson for his second arraignment. O.J. emerged from the holding cell with a thumbs-up sign, dressed in a dark pin-striped suit, white shirt, and tie. He appeared remarkably confident. The public man had returned.

Criminal procedure requires two arraignments before a trial in Superior Court: one after the arrest, a second after the preliminary hearing.

Today they appeared before Judge Cecil Mills, the presiding judge of L.A. County Superior Court. He announced that Judge Lance Ito was assigned the trial unless the defense team or prosecutors wished to object. Shapiro and Cochran talked quietly for a few seconds. Ito was known as tough, fair, and smart. They could do worse. "Judge Ito is a choice that is acceptable to us, Your Honor," Shapiro said.

It was time. Simpson stood.

"Are you ready to enter a plea at this time?" Mills asked.

"Yes, Your Honor."

"How do you plead to counts one and two?"

"Absolutely one hundred percent not guilty, Your Honor." Johnnie Cochran had given O.J. the line that would become a trial watchword.

That evening, when Johnnie returned to the office, Chapman and Douglas saw that he was flying. The grand marshal leading the parade. He loved the cameras, the crowds, the fanfare, but what he loved most was the applause from his office as he walked in. This is a whole new day, he told them. O.J. was pumped. I made sure of that. He was ready.

Douglas and Chapman glumly wondered if they would get to court at all.

The next day Lee Bailey faxed Shapiro a memo. "Like it or not, one of the most troublesome areas of this entire case is O.J.'s letter read by Kardashian on TV coupled to the gun-at-head 'chase.' Serious people—many of whom want to believe that O.J. is innocent—have told me that they simply cannot get by these two events as anything other than solid evidence of guilt." Bailey's fax pointed out that the farewell letter sought sympathy for O.J. but expressed no indignation about Nicole's "slaughter" or sorrow over her death. "We need to face these problems squarely."

The Athlete Syndrome and O.J.'s demeanor were also on Bailey's mind. Even more important were the timeline and O.J.'s recorded statement to the police. Bailey considered Simpson's interview with the police "coherent, exculpatory, and consistent with the talk of an *innocent* man in bewildering circumstances." It might be one of the strongest weapons in the defense arsenal.

10

On Tuesday, July 26, almost the entire defense team sat around the oval table in Shapiro's eighteenth-floor conference room. The agenda was crowded and so was the room. Documents, binders, notebooks, folders, cluttered the table. Some fast-food chicken was ordered in. Three sets of jury consultants were auditioning. Johnnie Cochran and his staff would be introduced.

Bob Shapiro stood up, very much in command. He looked around the room. "How many people here believe O.J. Simpson is guilty? Raise your hands."

Shapiro's face betrayed nothing. Everyone in the room stared blankly, watching him. Waiting. Howard Harris, a computer expert brought in by Bailey, wondered if this was a joke. He searched Shapiro's face. It gave nothing away. Around him, people seemed embarrassed.

The silence dragged on. No hands were raised.

As if nothing unusual had happened, Shapiro moved on. He introduced Cochran, Douglas, and Chapman. The African-American lawyers felt out of place in sharp business clothes while Shapiro wore slacks and an open shirt and Kardashian wore his uniform, jeans and a golf shirt.

For Cochran's people, the unspoken issue was power. When a trial lawyer comes in, he becomes team leader. That wasn't happening here. Cochran talked often enough, but his signals said he was taking it easy, feeling things out. Carl and Shawn expected Johnnie to push a little.

If two of the jury consultant teams had read the room as well as they claimed to read juries, they might have suspected the fix was in. Tall, blond Jo-Ellan Dimitrius was local. She had experience in criminal trials and was known for her work helping black defendants. She talked authoritatively of focus groups, shadow juries, and mock trials. She showed slides summarizing a preliminary telephone survey she'd done on potential jurors' attitudes about Simpson. The other teams were from out of town and worked mainly in civil trials.

Dimitrius made it clear that she'd match her fees to their budget. She wanted in. There was no contest.

The big secret, known only to the newest members of the defense, was that Dimitrius had already met with Cochran about this case. He knew her work from the Reginald Denny trial: Several black gang members were accused of nearly killing Denny during the Los Angeles riots. News cameras videotaped the incident. The beating was vicious; the nation was outraged. And the defendants got wrist slaps. Dimitrius's other credits included picking the Simi Valley jury that acquitted four white police officers accused of beating Rodney King.

Shawn Chapman liked the fact that Johnnie, Carl, and she were the hands-on trial lawyers in the room. Johnnie's experience was known. She'd been a public defender, and Douglas had worked as a federal public defender for five years. Except for Bailey, they were the only ones present who dealt regularly with juries. She loved it when people around the table asked the consultants useless questions. Her team was *bad*. The good kind of bad, as the black community understands the term.

Bad or good, she noticed that Shapiro never missed a chance to drop Simpson's name. You know: Let me talk to O.J. about this. Or: Well, O.J. won't want to do that. He had O.J.'s ear. Remember that. Team members might debate issues, but whenever Shapiro ran with O.J.'s name, it settled things.

In the car afterward, Carl practically screeched at Johnnie. Why didn't you take over? You can't run this team if you sit back.

As always, Johnnie showed no strain. "It's the man's office, Carl. It's the first meeting. Give it time. Everything will work out."

During the past week Shapiro had been showing signs of stress. Kardashian felt he was bearing the brunt of it. At a morning hearing, Shapiro had turned to him and said, "Don't walk out of court with me." He asked why. Shapiro said he was annoyed that Kardashian had aggrandized himself at Shapiro's expense while talking to a *New York Times* reporter.

Kardashian was baffled. He almost never talked to reporters.

The day before Simpson's July 22 Superior Court arraignment, Shapiro called Bob at home. He said that Johnnie Cochran would be at the defense table. Then he ordered Kardashian to stay away. Bob was shocked: "I talked to O.J. He expects me to be there."

Shapiro repeated it: Stay away.

Kardashian called Skip Taft. Simpson needs your support, Taft said. Go.

I don't want you there, Shapiro said when Bob called back. It will divert attention from what I have to do.

Bob didn't sleep. Who the hell is he to tell me not to support my friend? The next day, Kardashian was in court.

On July 27 Shapiro invited Kardashian to lunch at The Grill as if nothing had happened. Kardashian accepted, assuming the invitation was a conciliatory gesture. He thought it odd when Shapiro lowered his car's convertible top and drove achingly slowly through Beverly Hills. The direct route would have taken less than five minutes.

Shapiro made no mention of the arraignment incident. As they finished lunch, he told Kardashian he had to run an errand. Would Bob mind taking a cab back to his office?

Kardashian walked to the Beverly Wilshire Hotel and hailed one, no problem. As the cab dropped him off, Kardashian saw Shapiro pulling up to the Century City building. He felt as much mystified as slighted.

On August 3 Johnnie took Carl and Shawn to meet Simpson for the first time. They were startled when O.J. walked toward them in shackles, jail blues, deputies everywhere. Shawn had visited this jail many times and thought herself beyond surprise. But she'd never seen a man like *this* in blues.

"This is the first day that I woke up feeling really mad at Nicole. I dreamed about her. I woke up feeling really mad at her," Simpson said after the introductions. Then he laughed in relief.

The laughter sailed like a summer kite. When Simpson took them on the Bronco chase, the kite crashed. He made them feel the choking embrace of his death wish. They felt the .357 Magnum against *their* heads.

Shawn Chapman began to cry.

Simpson pulled the trigger. He curled up against the glass that separated them and sobbed uncontrollably. "Why didn't it go off?" His voice rose to an anguished keening. "Why didn't it go off!"

Johnnie Cochran's face was wet. Carl, however, remained calm.

Simpson talked about Nicole, their history, where he had been on the night of the murders. He insisted that he'd talked to Vannatter and Lange for the most obvious reason: He hadn't done anything wrong.

The attorneys stayed several hours. On the way home, all three were exhausted. But happy. Carl fumed at Shawn for losing her composure, but Johnnie defended his young colleague. He seemed proud that they had both cried. Even the stoic Douglas was riding the wave of positive feeling. He saw that O.J. was *ethnic,* more black than he'd expected. "He has sort of a street edge," Carl said. He was "a brother."

They liked him enormously.

PART THREE

Territories

1

"I KNOW PEOPLE IN THE TV INDUSTRY," SHAPIRO TOLD the defense team on August 8. "I'll talk to them about playing movies that show people being framed by the police. Perhaps *Twelve Angry Men*."

Shawn Chapman is amazed by this attempt to influence potential jurors. She can't decide if it is brilliant or off the wall. For now, Cochran says nothing. The rest of the team is also noncommittal.

It is ten A.M. Monday and they're meeting in Shapiro's small conference room. He sits at one end of the table. Kardashian is next to him wearing a baseball cap. Cochran is in an olive suit; Carl's double-breasted suit is gray.

The room is acquiring an unprofessional, lived-in look. Somebody's slacks are draped over a hanger against the wall. A shirt hangs from the hook next to an abstract painting. Lee Bailey, Sara Caplan, then Pat McKenna sit at the right side of the table. Skip Taft has the chair next to Johnnie. Jo-Ellan Dimitrius after that. Shawn Chapman and Howard Harris sit farthest from Shapiro.

Today there is no agenda. Only an endless free-form meeting in the room off the kitchen.

Cochran mentions a letter from Mark Fuhrman's lawyer threatening to sue for slander over Toobin's article in *The New Yorker*. Johnnie says he has mailed a response explaining that he wasn't on the case yet.

"Don't send out letters without notifying me first," Shapiro says. Then he reads his own letter to Fuhrman's lawyer. Shapiro sees an advantage in the lawsuit and doesn't want Fuhrman backing away. If the detective has a financial interest in the case, the defense can exploit that on cross-examination, Shapiro says. Cochran agrees. The team sits idle as Shapiro and Cochran jockey for position.

For two weeks, Kardashian has watched the two lawyers circle each other, competing for O.J.'s attention. Shapiro spends a lot of his time making sure O.J. thinks he's running the show. He has become as much PR agent as attorney.

Cochran is also no shrinking violet. He's lobbying hard for Simpson's attention. But Kardashian sees a profound difference between the two men. Johnnie has connected with Simpson more deeply than Shapiro has. He cares about O.J.'s needs and feelings. And there's a passion in Cochran: He has believed in O.J.'s innocence from the day he signed on.

Shapiro, however, asks the team if they think O.J. is guilty. He appears to believe that O.J. *could* have done it. Of course, he's not *sure*. A showdown can't be far off.

To make matters worse, Kardashian can't get Bailey off the phone. He, too, is trying to position himself. In late July the cover page of Bailey's faxes from Florida was headed "Robert Shapiro & The Good Guys versus Gil Garcetti & The Bad Guys." Next to Shapiro's name was a drawing of a knight. By Garcetti's, a dragon. The way Bob sees it, Bailey is trying to ensure that *he* will be the lead attorney.

But O.J. knows Bailey can't relate to a black jury day after day. That's why Johnnie's on the team. Shapiro announces that Bailey will handle the science. Bailey insists he's the only one to take on Fuhrman. Marine to Marine. Now it's Shapiro and Bailey versus Cochran. McKenna and McNally can be counted on to side with Bailey, of course. Today Cochran is sitting on the sidelines.

Shapiro tells everyone to clear all media contacts with him. No unauthorized quotes. The team must speak with one voice. Shapiro's voice, Kardashian thinks. Johnnie clearly doesn't like it. Lee Bailey starts harrumphing. Shapiro's on TV so often, Kardashian thinks, that people expect him to give the weather report. Now he wants everyone else to shut up?

Shapiro brings up Bill Hodgman, their liaison for discovery material at the D.A.'s office. "I don't trust him," Shapiro says. "Stay away from him. He's an asshole."

"I have a lot of respect for Bill," Cochran replies. "He'll do right by us."

"He's hiding things," Shapiro insists. "He's lying to us."

Nothing is resolved. Johnnie says he'll call Hodgman at home.

Now the subject moves to O.J.'s younger daughter, Sydney. Did A.C. ever ask her about "Mommy's best friend" who made Nicole cry? Kardashian explains that the Browns won't let A.C. talk to Sydney. They're becoming very uncooperative. Why help O.J.? The Browns are saying he did it.

Later in the day Shapiro's speakerphone clicks on. O.J.'s defense depends not only on the dueling egos in this room, but also on a small army of long-distance experts. Before the preliminary hearing, Shapiro recruited the famous Harvard law professor Alan Dershowitz, who now consults from Boston. Shapiro had also taken the advice of Dershowitz and Uelmen and retained two world-class lawyers on DNA legal issues, Barry Scheck and Peter Neufeld.* Kardashian wonders how all these egos, agendas, and loyalties will figure into the mix.

Now Barry Scheck and Peter Neufeld are checking in from New York. Scheck had been out in late July to meet all the players. All the 'toons, as he called them. Those characters on TV. It wouldn't be long before Barry became a 'toon himself.

Scheck and Neufeld run something called the Innocence Project, which uses DNA testing to defend its clients. Shapiro has made it clear the two will be working backstage, coaching Bailey and the others on how to handle scientific issues. On the phone today Scheck and Neufeld have one

---

*DNA is the abbreviation for deoxyribonucleic acid, the genetic material that is the "blueprint" for the development of every living thing. Except in the case of identical twins, every individual's DNA is unique.

message: Take the DNA findings seriously. The first test results will be in soon.

Kardashian has an item for the agenda. When A.C. was bailed out of jail after the Bronco chase, he gave Wayne Hughes some scraps of yellow paper, something O.J. had torn up and given to him in the Bronco. Kardashian has just received them from Hughes.

They spread them on the floor and get into the task like kids around a jigsaw puzzle. Soon O.J.'s words come together. Simpson insists he is innocent and says he wants to go to heaven. There are actually two notes, they discover: one, written at Kardashian's desk, to O.J.'s kids; the other written to A.C. during the chase.

Simpson writes about how he got into this situation, how things went further and further downhill—so that now he's sitting with a gun to his head.

Kardashian reasons that Simpson would never compound the sin of suicide by lying. Bob can't believe O.J. would say anything but the truth at that moment.

The next day, Tuesday, August 9, Kardashian meets Johnnie Cochran for lunch at the Checkers Hotel. Bob has invited Johnnie. This is their first opportunity to talk privately. He wants to tell Cochran he is not Shapiro's boy; all he wants is a good defense for Simpson.

Kardashian says Shapiro has been keeping him at a distance recently, so when Simpson asks Bob questions about the case, he can't answer knowledgeably. This upsets O.J.

"It looks bad for everybody," he tells Cochran. "I *must* know what is going on."

Cochran is receptive, even gracious. He understands what O.J. needs. Bob has the impression that Johnnie will go against Shapiro, Bailey, or anyone else if necessary.

"I'm available at all times for anything you want to do," Kardashian says. "I expect to be in the courtroom every day."

Then Bob tells Johnnie about O.J.—how Simpson will

204

probably react in various situations; Cochran seems to understand that Kardashian is offering him the real O.J.

Searching through the mountains of discovery material the previous week, Pavelic came across a police interview with one of Nicole's neighbors, Robert Heidstra. The interview was typed on plain white paper edged with scribbles summarizing its main points. According to the introductory note, Detective D.L. Payne and Officer B. Parker interviewed Heidstra at six P.M. on June 21, 1994.

> Mr. Heidstra stated that he walks his two dogs on a nightly basis at approximately 2200 hours. He takes the same route every night. On the night in question, Sunday evening, June 14, 1994 [the "14" was circled to note a typo], he left his apartment with the dogs at about 2215 hours.

A note in the margin read: "20 min. later, 10:40 P.M."

> Shortly after turning south on Bundy drive, Mr. Heidstra heard the sound of the Akita dog owned by Nicole Brown Simpson begin to bark furiously. The barking was non-stop and the dog appeared agitated. Mr. Heidstra is familiar with the sound . . . it barks frequently whenever Mr. Heidstra passes the location with his two dogs.

Thinking the Akita might be loose, Heidstra changed his route, using the alley across the street from Nicole's condo which would take him back to Dorothy Street and home. The margin note says, "10:45 P.M., through front gate."

> As he reached the alley, he heard a male voice loudly cry, "Hey, Hey," then the sound of a large metal gate closing. It was his opinion that the sounds came from the Brown estate. . . . He then heard the sounds of two men loudly arguing, but he was unable to discern what they were saying specifically. All the while, the Akita continued to bark non-stop and in fact continued to bark until about 2300 hours.

As Mr. Heidstra reached Dorothy Street, he looked west and observed a large white vehicle. . . . The white vehicle turned left ["left" was circled and "right" was scribbled below it] south on Bundy Drive and drove from the location at a high rate of speed.

Pavelic also noticed the following letter from Simpson to Nicole, dated June 8, just four days before the murders. It was found by Mark Fuhrman during the search on the afternoon of June 13.

O.J. SIMPSON ENTERPRISES
11661 San Vicente Blvd.
Los Angeles, California 90049

June 8, 1994

Dear Nicole:

To set the record straight, when Arnelle, Jason or myself are at home to watch the kids, especially around the pool, they are welcome here at any time. I would love to have them 24 hours a day, as it is their home too.

However, Gigi is not an emergency cook, baby-sitter or errand runner for you! She is an employee of mine and I expect you to respect that—now, and in the future.

O.J. Simpson

VIA MESSENGER

Early in August, Dr. Saul Faerstein sent Skip Taft a bill for $25,000—for one month's visits. Simpson had seen the psychiatrist at odd hours and at great length, no question. But the bill enraged him. He insisted that he didn't want to see Faerstein ever again. Ever. He ordered him fired. Skip Taft admitted to Bob he was a little surprised at O.J.'s extreme reaction.

Faerstein called Kardashian. He felt Simpson should still see him. Therapists and their deadly professional calm always made Kardashian edgy: O.J. is in jail for murder, and this guy wants $25,000, but on the telephone everything is cerebral and cool. So Bob adopted the same tone. "Saul, at that price, I don't think it's necessary."

Faerstein was conciliatory but firm. They could work something out about the bill, he said, but therapy should continue. Simpson was still fragile.

Kardashian didn't need a psychiatrist to figure that out. O.J. was enraged by each week's tabloid stories. The latest crisis involved the grand jury testimony of a guy named Keith Zlomsowitch, who had dated Nicole for a while. Now, weeks afterward, it had surfaced. The story made Simpson look like a stalker. Kardashian took Pavelic down to see O.J. the morning after the tabloid hit the stands. Simpson ranted for nearly forty-five minutes.

A week earlier, Kardashian had read the transcript of Zlomsowitch's testimony. Marcia Clark had asked the questions. O.J. and Nicole had agreed to separate on January 6, 1992. Nicole then moved to a rented house on Gretna Green Way with Justin and Sydney. Later that month, Zlomsowitch, who managed Mezzaluna restaurants in Brentwood, Beverly Hills, and Aspen, met Nicole at the Colorado restaurant.

He came to town in April and invited Nicole to bring a few friends down to Mezzaluna. It was a busy night, and Zlomsowitch alternated between running the restaurant and chatting with Nicole and her friends. Then Simpson came in.

> ZLOMSOWITCH: He leaned over our table, rested his hands on the table and sort of stared at myself and the other male individual. . . . "I'm O.J. Simpson and she's still my wife."
> CLARK: How would you describe his tone of voice?
> ZLOMSOWITCH: Serious, if not scary. . . . I was for sure intimidated. . . . He left the restaurant, and [Nicole] followed him out. . . .
> CLARK: . . . Can you describe her appearance or demeanor when she returned?
> ZLOMSOWITCH: She was visibly shaken. . . .

Another occasion was more sinister.

> ZLOMSOWITCH: . . . We decided we were going to go to a restaurant called Tryst. . . . Mr. Simpson walked into the restaurant, walked directly by our table, looked at everybody at the table as he walked by, made it very clear that his presence was there, walked over to a table approximately ten feet away from ours, pulled the chair sideways as if to face our table directly, sat down and just stared at our table.
>
> CLARK: . . . Did Mr. Simpson make any further contact with you?
>
> ZLOMSOWITCH: He came over to the table at one point, sat down in the booth next to Nicole . . . I don't recall exactly what was said at that point. I was scared. I was shaken.

O.J. told Bob he went to Tryst that night and saw Nicole with Keith and about ten other friends. He absolutely did not pull up a chair and stare at them. He absolutely did not threaten them. He was meeting a party of his own friends and he was late. When he walked in, he saw Nicole's friend Cora Fischman at the bar. He said hello to everybody, gave Nic a kiss, then went to his table. The press took everything out of context.

Keith also told the grand jury about a night when he and Nicole were dancing at a club. Simpson showed up there, too. They left quickly and returned to Gretna Green.

> ZLOMSOWITCH: We lit a few candles, put on a little music, poured a glass of wine and we sat on the couch in the downstairs living room. We began to become intimate. . . . The next day I came back to the house. The kids were swimming in the swimming pool, me and Nicole were sitting alongside. . . .
>
> She made a comment that her neck was stiff. . . . We went into the bedroom off of the swimming

pool, very close to where the children were so we could see the children swimming, and I began to give her a neck message.

CLARK:: Did she remain dressed?

ZLOMSOWITCH: Yes, she did. . . . I looked up and Mr. Simpson came in through the back door which was adjacent to the pool . . . right up on top of us, physically within two feet. . . .

CLARK: What happened next?

ZLOMSOWITCH: Mr. Simpson . . . said, "I can't believe it. Look what you are doing! The kids are right out here by the pool. . . . I watched you last night. I can't believe you would do that in the house. . . . I saw everything that you did."

Simpson demanded to talk to Nicole alone, but Zlomsowitch refused to leave.

ZLOMSOWITCH: . . . He said, is this what it's come to? I can't even talk to you alone? . . . After a few minutes of going back and forth, Nicole said to me, it's okay, Keith, just wait in the kitchen. . . . I waited for approximately 15 minutes, at which time Mr. Simpson came out of the room and approached me in the kitchen. He stuck out his hand . . . and he said, "No hard feelings, right?" And I looked up at him and I said, it's okay, or something to that effect. And he said, "You understand, I'm a very proud man. I'm very visible in this community."

Kardashian was surprised that Zlomsowitch feared for his life. This is just O.J. being O.J., Bob thought. Simpson didn't lead a clean life, who does? But he wasn't mean or evil. He always knew how to act in public. All Bob could get from Keith's long tale was that O.J. had been a little upset about Nicole's behavior. Bob wondered if O.J. had actually spied on Nicole and her date.

Bob knew the media were always ready to hurt you. Even now Simpson couldn't understand the animosity toward him. The press had always treated him well. Except for a tabloid story or two, the media had barely noticed the 1989 beating incident. Now he was stuck in jail with no way to defend himself.

By August the media onslaught was endless. Mary Anne Gerchas, who claimed to have seen four men running from the murder scene, was featured on the tabloid TV show *Hard Copy*. As a witness she could have been crucial to the defense. They had not even had a chance to interview her. Now that she'd sold her story, her credibility was gone.

2

PAT MCKENNA COULDN'T GET USED TO THE ENDLESS mountain of discovery. Read a hundred pages, five hundred more arrive. This is a street case, he'd lament to Bailey. Where are these thousands of pages coming from? I must have read the equivalent of *War and Peace* ten times.

The defense had to scrutinize every one of these documents. McNally and Pavelic were good at it. You have three guys trying to figure out what this little number up here means, what that time there means, McKenna said. It's all about attacking this slipshod police investigation.

These cops rolled in and thought they'd solved the crime the first day, McKenna decided. On the second day they figure Shapiro's a plea-bargain type of guy. The fourth day Garcetti goes on TV saying O.J. will plead out.

So these bozos sit on their duffs while people in the neighborhood, eyewitnesses and earwitnesses, are being blocked, shoved off, deflected, McKenna tells Bailey.

Everybody knows you find hot leads in the first twenty-four to forty-eight hours. It's like tuna fishing. You're reeling them in. The action is hot. But you sit on your ass like these cops did, the leads get cold. Now you're ice fishing. Waiting days for a nibble.

The police didn't see it that way. They had O.J.

TO: File
FROM: JEM/PJM [McNally and McKenna]
RE: Marcus and Kathryn Allen

On July 31, 1994 at 10:15 A.M., I interviewed Marcus and Kathryn Allen by telephone. They are currently at their home in Kansas City.

The Allens were on vacation in the Cayman Islands. . . . There was a message from O.J. She [Mrs. Allen] described O.J.'s voice as very distraught. He was wailing, crying and bellowing, "Oh my God. Oh my God! Where are you guys? I really need you. . . ."

Kathryn said, "O.J. we love you. We'll do anything for you."

During the first week of August it was becoming obvious to Kardashian that most of O.J.'s friends were staying away. They were all on the county jail visiting list as material witnesses. It was a long list. They could see O.J. anytime. But the stream of visitors was slowing to a trickle. Maybe the novelty had worn off. Wayne Hughes was out of the picture. Marcus Allen had cried big tears in that meeting a week after the arrest, but lately he hadn't shown up.

TO: Mr. Shapiro
FROM: McKenna
RE: Marcus Allen—Phone calls
DATE: August 8, 1994

Ed Hookstratten, Marcus Allen's agent, is reluctant to provide me with copies of Marcus Allen's home phone bill and a copy of his hotel folio from the Cayman Islands.

As you know, Allen's sister-in-law, Deborah Cornell, was house sitting for Marcus and Kathryn when they went on vacation to the Caymans. Deborah made numerous phone calls from that residence to the Cayman Islands when notified of the murders. Marcus then made numerous phone calls from the Caymans to Cathy Randa, A.C., O.J. and others during the week. If Mr. Hookstratten would provide these records to us on an informal basis it would expedite the completion of our timeline.

On Wednesday, August 10, Johnnie Cochran told O.J. that Garcetti's office was soon to decide whether or not to ask for the death penalty. Johnnie needed information that might influence prosecutors to ask for life imprisonment instead. The defense needed to know about Simpson's charities, the various causes he supported, and any influential friends who might write letters.

Cochran expected Simpson to be helpful. Instead he was indifferent. "I don't care about the death penalty." There were other matters more pressing. He told Johnnie he couldn't believe that Nicole's friends weren't coming forward to say he hadn't beaten her. Johnnie tried to get back to the death penalty. Simpson dismissed it again.

"If I'm convicted, I'll kill myself. I don't care what they do. They can go for it."

Late on the night of August 12, Kardashian's doorbell rings. He and Denice are in the backyard with friends, eating lasagna and a Caesar salad.

As Kardashian opens the door, Detective Carr, whose name he knows from the discovery documents, hands him a grand jury subpoena. A deputy district attorney stands next to Carr with another subpoena for Denice and a third for Bob's housekeeper. The grand jury is hearing testimony about A.C.

Kardashian sees them out, and notices that his hands are shaking. He's never had trouble with the law. He remembers Simpson's gun case, that little black toy violin case. His fingerprints are on it. Denice is scared, too. All she did was support her fiancé and his friend.

They both have trouble sleeping that night.

The next day Kardashian tells Denice, ''The body is weary, and the mind just keeps going.''

Before the murders, he went to bed every night at ten and woke up at six. Now he goes upstairs at midnight, wakes up at two, then three, then five. He can't focus on his Bible. He drags through the days, even though it seems he's always rushing. He's scrambling to keep his business afloat. When record-company people return his calls, he's either in court or at Shapiro's office.

You don't need an MBA to know what happens to a sales business if you can't connect with your customers.

Thursday night, August 11, Bob goes to get his .38 Smith & Wesson from his closet shelf. This has become a twice-daily ritual since he started getting threatening phone calls. Each night he puts the gun beside his bed. Each morning he returns it to the closet. Tonight the gun is missing.

He asks Denice whether she moved it. She didn't. He asks who was in the house today. Just the housekeeper, Cruz, and a mover who helped move them in. He'd repaired a few items broken during the move back in May. Today he delivered them. Kardashian left a message on the guy's pager. He called Cruz at home and asked if she'd borrowed the gun. No, sir. No way. She's afraid of guns.

''All I need,'' he says to Denice, ''is to have it found with a bullet missing after a robbery at some 7-Eleven.''

He decides to call the police. The desk sergeant says they can't send someone until morning. No problem. Bob goes to bed. The phone rings at midnight: The sergeant can send someone now. It can wait until morning, Kardashian tells him.

He can't get back to sleep. At three o'clock he hears noises outside. Is somebody going through his trash cans?

A single detective arrived at seven A.M. He wrote down a description of the pistol. Kardashian said the gun was worth $250. The cop left without looking in the closet.

Ten minutes later, more police arrived: the lieutenant in charge the day O.J. and A.C. took off in the Bronco; and Kardashian counted two plainclothes detectives, some uniforms, a fingerprint expert, and a photographer. A small army. They stayed an hour and a half. The photographer took pictures throughout the house. The fingerprint officer dusted the closet as well as the guest room where Simpson had stayed. He asked for Kardashian's and Denice's fingerprints. Bob thought of O.J.'s gun case.

All this for a stolen .38? Bob wondered. Why do I have the feeling I'm being set up for something?

3

ON MONDAY, AUGUST 15, ALAN DERSHOWITZ IS IN California. He predicts: "Marcia Clark will try this as a domestic abuse case." The defense team has gathered in a massive conference room in Century City. Through the tinted windows of the seventeenth floor, you look across prosperous Westside Los Angeles to the Pacific Ocean.

Dershowitz is standing. The conference table is so wide that the lawyers, experts, and investigators sitting in leather rocking chairs can't pass notes across it. Twenty in all are present today, too many for their usual cramped room near Shapiro's office.

Dershowitz's presence is unusual. Most of the time he's in Boston, "attending" by speakerphone. He worked on the Brando case without once actually attending a meeting in California. But this case has lured him to the West Coast.

"She won't do the usual thing of starting with the bodies

and working backwards,'' Dershowitz explains. ''She'll build the client's profile as a batterer first.''

Shapiro leans forward, looking puzzled. Cochran stops scribbling. McKenna and McNally, usually impassive in these meetings, look up. The collective body language is skeptical.

Form follows function, Dershowitz says. He explains: Leading with domestic violence is to Marcia's political advantage. Also Garcetti's. The D.A. has a tough reelection campaign coming. Female voters will reward him. ''I smell an abuse case coming,'' he insists.

Marcia will use some of the battered woman syndrome theory, Dershowitz says, to explain why Nicole stayed so close to an allegedly terrifying man: Battered women often seem devoted to their tormentors. Years of abuse leave them psychologically paralyzed.

He says he knows Dr. Lenore Walker, the psychologist who pioneered the subject. But the defense could use a different element of Dr. Walker's work. O.J. doesn't fit her profile of a batterer. So let's consider Walker as an expert witness.

Most of the team is caught off guard by Dershowitz's input. They are unwilling to shift gears. Today everyone is focused on jury selection, the time line McNally and Bailey have been working on, the first reports of the DNA testing, and Henry Lee's perception that something is screwy with the physical evidence. Cochran tells the group he sees a straight-forward prosecution and a solid defense. The D.A. will show physical evidence. The defense will show how it was corrupted. Maybe Marcia Clark will introduce spousal abuse. They'll grant Dershowitz that. But it's stupid, it won't work in a case like this. The prosecution probably sees that too.

Bob Shapiro reminds the group of what they already know: Simpson is obsessed with the abuse allegations. Whenever he visits O.J. he hears, ''Clear my name.'' Shapiro sees O.J. as more concerned about the damage to his public image than about a possible death penalty. You'd almost think the murder trial is a minor annoyance. Simpson's told everyone he wants to be home by Halloween. Shapiro is humoring his client, but barely.

Two hours into the meeting Dershowitz makes another surprising prediction: Detective Mark Fuhrman will never again take the witness stand for the prosecution. Marcia Clark is too smart to let him be cross-examined. She won't use a witness with such explosive racist baggage even if it's inconvenient to omit him. Clark doesn't need the man who found the glove, Dershowitz says, only the person who collected it as evidence.

Dershowitz says that Toobin's article is the reason for Fuhrman's demise as a witness. A few people shift uncomfortably in their chairs. Small wonder: Rumor has it that Shapiro was behind the leak.

Time for lunch. They are tired to death of the chicken from Koo Koo Roo, Shapiro's favorite fast-food place.

That afternoon Edward Blake spoke up. "This is incredible!" The DNA expert, a researcher at Forensic Science Associates in Richmond, California, was normally calm and confident. Now he was so startled he practically shouted. Had he really heard just now, in casual chatter no less, that Phil Vannatter had taken a reference sample of Simpson's blood *back* to Rockingham? Vannatter having the blood for an extended period of time, plus taking it back to the crime scene, was unorthodox at best. He was amazed that no one else was astonished.

Evidence contamination was already a defense issue. Now they *really* had something. "This is unprecedented," Blake continued. "This is totally improper."

The lawyers around the table were starting to form an intriguing question: Can we prove that Simpson's reference blood contaminated the blood evidence? Or, perhaps, in some cases, could the reference blood have been used to *create* evidence? The scientists knew that Simpson's blood sample contained EDTA from the special test tube used to store such samples.* How much EDTA would be in one tube? How could one demonstrate the chemical's presence in the evidence being used against Simpson? Laboratory technicians don't normally test for EDTA. The research literature in this area would be perilously thin.

Someone suggested tracing the sodium in the EDTA. Preposterous, Blake thought. Sodium is everywhere. Then someone had a truly mad notion: Weigh all the blood swatches taken from the reference sample. Does the blood in them equal the amount of blood taken from the tube? Impossible, Blake decided. The cloth weighed far more than the dried blood. They'd have to extrapolate in a way that is absurdly difficult. Maybe Dr. Lee can solve the problem, Scheck says. They'd talk.

Barry Scheck hadn't known that Vannatter had driven to Rockingham with Simpson's reference sample. But if Scheck assumed Simpson's innocence, logic suggested that the blood at Bundy and Rockingham had been planted. How? Scheck focused on Simpson's reference blood as an obvious possibility. Was any missing? Scheck found the laboratory logs in the discovery material and added up the amounts of Simpson's blood taken from O.J.'s reference sample for testing, comparing them with the amount remaining in the reference sample. The numbers startled him.

When it came his turn, Barry spoke to the team from notes. "We have blood unaccounted for in Simpson's sample. That shouldn't happen."

Almost everyone in the room had seen the logs. But only Scheck carefully checked the numbers. Back in July, Bill Pavelic had complained that something about the tubes was wrong. Simpson's tube was labeled Item 17 for the grand jury investigation, then changed to number 18. Pavelic also found a picture of the tube holding Simpson's blood. It was messy, as if the contents had leaked or spilled.

The key, Scheck knew, wasn't realizing there was missing blood, but proving it. That would be difficult.

* EDTA is a preservative also used in foods and household products. In blood, it acts as an anticoagulant.

"I want to remind you that we still have serious problems," Scheck said somberly. "We know that there is blood in the Bronco. The police say it's Nicole's. There was more blood at Bundy and at Rockingham. The preliminary DNA reports are very strong. These are things we still can't explain."

Scheck, short and pushy, with a shock of uncontrollable hair, had joined the team at the end of July. He and his colleague, Peter Neufeld, had helped free at least seventeen men wrongly convicted of rape or murder, often using DNA testing to overturn the convictions. They were pioneers in such cases.

Unlike most of the defense team, Scheck hadn't watched the Bronco chase on June 17. He was in the audience at Madison Square Garden for the Knicks-Rockets game and knew nothing about Simpson's flight until he walked into the Garden snack bar during a break and saw the chase on TV.

Scheck guessed immediately that he might become involved. The press was saying that blood evidence would be a big part of the case. He later learned that just about everyone Shapiro called in the first few days suggested hiring him.

Nobody, however, asked Scheck about his second area of expertise. Nearly a decade earlier, he'd convinced Manhattan prosecutors not to press charges against Hedda Nussbaum for failing to intervene when her lover, Joel Steinberg, beat their adopted daughter to death. The case transfixed the nation for months. Scheck's defense of Hedda Nussbaum, of course, was a version of battered woman syndrome. Steinberg had abused Nussbaum so badly and for so long that she was emotionally disabled, incapable of helping herself or anyone else. By the time Scheck joined the Simpson team, the cases in which he'd defended battering victims outnumbered his DNA cases.

In the weeks after the murders, Ed Blake assumed he would hear from the prosecution, perhaps from the defense as well.

A year usually passed before any murder case went to trial. A high-profile case might not reach court for two years. So he was surprised to hear from Barry Scheck in late July that this case was on a fast track.

When Scheck called him, Blake had one foot out the door, en route to a vacation house in New Jersey. Bob Shapiro was exploring a lot of directions, Scheck said. Blake thought working on the defense sounded fine, but made no commitment. Then Lisa Kahn from the Los Angeles D.A.'s office offered him a retainer: The prosecution wanted him. Right away. Blake told Kahn that Scheck and Neufeld had been in touch; he might already be spoken for. He phoned Scheck immediately. "I need to know about you guys. Am I compromised because we've had discussions? Are you going to retain me?"

At that point, the New York lawyers hadn't been *formally* hired themselves. But Scheck replied, "Consider yourself retained." By the end of the week Scheck and Neufeld were fully aboard as consultants.

Depriving the prosecution of Ed Blake was a masterstroke, everybody later agreed.

Ed Blake had a towering reputation as a DNA expert and criminalist. His other skill was reading L.A. County prosecutors. He had worked with Garcetti's people often.

Those prosecutors cover up problems. Count on it, Blake told Scheck. It's a reflex. "There is an absence of candor in that office," he said: What you saw in the Rockingham search affidavit will happen again. And you can build a strategy on it. Wait for their mistakes, then attack the lies and misrepresentations. The mishandling of evidence Henry Lee has identified will lead somewhere. Vannatter going to Rockingham with the blood vial provided another opportunity for the police to plant evidence. If you push these prosecutors, they will open doors for you in their haste to close others.

Blake knew that L.A. County would bring in Rockne Harmon and Woody Clarke, the state's two best-trained DNA prosecutors. DNA evidence was a new field and immensely complicated. The local people lacked the expertise required by a high-profile trial. Harmon worked in Alameda County, practically next door to the Berkeley campus, and Clarke worked in San Diego. Blake had taught them forensic serology and genetics and worked with them on their early DNA cases. He knew how Clarke and Harmon would approach the blood evidence.

Simpson had always impressed Blake. They were about the same age, and as an undergraduate Blake had watched the USC star break through UC-Berkeley's defensive line as if they were high school second-stringers. But what impressed him most was the athlete's effortless transition to pitchman and movie actor. Simpson was a contemporary American hero, Blake thought. A superstar who had reinvented himself.

Blake felt that the blood evidence, and the possibility of missing blood from Simpson's sample, might ultimately be the key to the defense.

Then the defense's jury consultant, Jo-Ellan Dimitrius, presented some remarkable results from a San Diego State University poll. The university's Social Research Laboratory had asked its subjects thirty-nine questions. First, routine queries: Are you a registered voter? Have you ever been convicted of a felony?

Then, specifics: "Last June, Los Angeles police arrested a well-known black celebrity and former football star after a freeway pursuit. He has been charged with the stabbing murders of his former wife and her male friend. Can you tell me the name of the defendant in this case?" Just about everybody could. Further questions revealed that most people knew the case well.

Then Jo-Ellan delivered the big news: Twenty percent of the sample believed O.J. Simpson innocent. The number is high, she explained, for a case that hasn't gone to court. And 50 percent don't *want* to believe Simpson is guilty. Smiles everywhere. Carl Douglas, usually so serious, grinned broadly. F. Lee Bailey trumpeted that the client *must* take the stand. Kardashian leaned back in his chair and clenched his fist below the table. Incredible, he thought. The press paints a hideous picture of Simpson, and people still respect him. They *want* to believe in him.

4

THE NEXT MORNING, AUGUST 16, THE MEETING CONTINUES. In ten days the defense team has a hearing on its latest motion, and this morning it's on everybody's mind.

Under the law, the defense may test evidence independently once the prosecution has finished its own tests. But prosecution tests sometimes consume all the samples, particularly blood evidence. It's to the prosecution's advantage to leave nothing for the defense. And defense lawyers aren't required to return the samples after testing or reveal their results unless they use them in the trial. Blood swatches given these defense lawyers, Marcia Clark has said, will vanish down a black hole.

The week before, the defense had filed a brief demanding the prosecution split its samples with them now. They would argue their case at a so-called Griffin hearing, named after the first challenge on this issue. Barry Scheck and Ed Blake aim to send the prosecution a Trojan horse.

Not everyone understands the strategy. We'll give the appearance we want a slice of every blood swatch, Scheck explains. Which we don't: The tests take too long and cost too much. We might get a result that hurts the client. It isn't discoverable, but it will leak for sure, Barry said. So forget testing. But we'll pretend we want to; it's good public relations. We will argue: Let *our* experts have a look. That way, Marcia can never say we passed up the opportunity to check their results.

Actually, Scheck and Neufeld want this hearing so the team can catalog all the blood evidence and scrutinize the collection and processing of that evidence. The prosecution can't say there's not enough to share unless they detail every bit of what they found and what they have. Dennis Fung, Andrea Mazzola, and the LAPD lab technicians will have to testify, and the defense lawyers can cross-examine them.

As of this date, Scheck explains, we don't know what the other side actually has, what it's testing *for,* and where. If we're going to attack the LAPD procedures, we need to know who handled the evidence and who had access to it. The hearing will give us the information we need to attack the prosecution's blood evidence.

In the Griffin motion the defense will ask Judge Ito for a sample from each bloodstain the prosecution plans to test. Gerry Uelmen's brief will say that this case hinges on DNA evidence, and that if nothing is left after the prosecution finishes, Simpson's right to a fair trial will be violated. The plan is for Bob Shapiro, coached by Barry Scheck, to argue the motion.

After a short break, John McNally reports on the potential time-line witnesses he and McKenna are interviewing. The dog walker, Heidstra, is promising. What makes it work for their time line is that one of Heidstra's dogs is elderly and arthritic. "Can't make it for ten steps without resting," McNally explains.

"Speed it up," Shapiro says impatiently. "We're not interested in the age of the dogs."

McNally turns scarlet. Shapiro understands nothing! He and McKenna canvassed house-to-house to find the guy—as usual with reports turned over to the defense prosecutors, Heidstra's address and phone number were blacked out on the police report. They learned that Heidstra left his apartment with his dogs at 10:15, took a long way around, and finally got to the alley across the street from Nicole's condo, where Heidstra heard somebody yelling. If his dogs were walking slowly enough, it pushed the murder back to later that night, when Simpson couldn't have done it.

McNally had told Bailey that Heidstra might have been listening to murder sounds as late as 10:55 P.M., when O.J. was seen at Rockingham. McNally and McKenna plan to ask the guy and his dogs to walk that route with the detectives timing it.

"Let's move on," says Shapiro.

Right, McKenna muses. Heidstra and his geriatric mutt may exonerate O.J., and the lead attorney doesn't seem interested. Is he a stone-face who never visibly reacts to anything, or does he really miss the point?

McNally remembers an occasion when they were looking at autopsy pictures. One close-up of Nicole showed her wristwatch at ten o'clock. Shapiro got excited and exclaimed, "Now we know the time of death!" The lawyer sounded *pleased*.

McNally was appalled: This guy doesn't have a clue. We have fifty-two minutes during which the crimes could have occurred. We're trying to narrow that period down, not expand it. If the victims were killed at ten, O.J. had nearly a whole goddamn hour to clean up and get home. But does Shapiro realize that the close-ups of the bodies weren't taken until the next day? There's nothing to indicate that the watch was stopped. The problem was that there was only one photo showing Nicole's watch, and the picture could have been taken at ten the next morning. Unlike Shapiro, McNally had not focused on the fact that Simpson was on his cellular phone at 10:02 P.M., trying to reach Paula Barbieri.

On the second day of the meeting, Henry Lee presents newly enlarged photos of the crime scene. Some are copy prints from the discovery; some are his. He points to tiny striations on the cement tile at Bundy, and similar patterns in the blood on Ron Goldman's clothing, and one on the bloody envelope containing Judy Brown's glasses. They could indicate a second set of footprints, he says.

Lee had said the same in a July meeting. The team liked the idea then, but they couldn't see anything. Today the patterns are obvious in the blowups of the photos. Shawn Chapman is excited. He's showing us proof that somebody else committed the crime, she thinks. He's saying O.J. may have been framed!

Lee then shows blowups of the Bundy blood drops. "The drops are too neat," he says. "Too perfect. Much too similar." That kind of drop comes only from blood falling down straight, Lee explains. Someone would have to be standing still for blood to drip from him in that pattern.

TO: Sara Caplan
FROM: RLS
DATE: August 12, 1994

Please go see O.J. tomorrow; take thorough notes re the following:

First date of separation after the divorce; what happened during that time?

Who was present at the alleged incident at Tryst restaurant?

When he was with Stellini at Mezzaluna, who was with Nicole?

What other witnesses may have been present at both places?

Chronology of first reconciliation and breakup; second reconciliation and breakup. (We need as detailed a report on this as O.J. is willing to provide.)

During the same week, that of August 14, Johnnie Cochran told Shawn Chapman to look into the domestic violence issue. Visit O.J. often, he said. Find out what all this means to the case. Chapman sat through many conversations and eventually wrote a lengthy report covering the same subjects that Shapiro assigned to Caplan.

Chapman found the assignment pleasant at first. She had no doubt of Simpson's sincerity. Her tearful first visit to O.J. with Johnnie and Carl had settled that. She enjoyed O.J.'s routines, his stories, even the woe-is-me monologue. As a woman she took battering very seriously, but as a lawyer she knew that the wife beating in this case related only to motive. The D.A. would try to make a jury link Simpson's supposedly violent temper with a willingness to kill.

Shawn concluded that Simpson did not talk like a man with a motive. He was in love with Paula Barbieri when Nicole was killed. He insisted on that. At length. Of course, when Shawn, Johnnie, and Carl first met O.J., he said he was "really mad" at Nicole. She took that to mean he was convinced that Nicole had let her life degenerate to a level that put her in harm's way. Now he was charged with her murder, and his children had no mother. He was alone in jail to mourn their shared past, the future they'd never have. If O.J. was "mad" at Nicole, it made sense to Chapman.

Sara Caplan turned in her report to Shapiro on Saturday, August 13. She had asked Simpson about the incident at Tryst.

> When O.J. walked in, Nicole's friends were at the bar. . . . Nicole and O.J. spoke and both agreed to try to stay. . . . O.J. sat with a model he had worked with on a commercial and her boyfriend. . . .
>
> O.J. went by Nicole's house on his way home after the Tryst meeting. He thought she might be alone, but he saw her with Keith. This was when he was still trying to mend the friendship in early 92. Two weeks after, when O.J. confronted them, he was not angry or hurt. O.J. shook Keith's hand. The kids were not home when he talked to them. [Zlomsowich testified before the grand jury that O.J. shook his hand the next day after admitting seeing them "become intimate" the night before.]

During August and the first days of September, Shawn Chapman and Simpson were having long, long talks. He suggested nannies and housekeepers the defense should interview. Then he warned Shawn he'd gotten a very cool response when he'd called Kardashian's ex-wife, Kris jenner, asking why she and others weren't coming forward to say he wasn't a batterer.

Soon Chapman realized he was telling her his life story. His mother had worked in San Francisco General Hospital's psychiatric wing for thirty years, raising O.J., his brother, and his two sisters alone. His father, Jimmy, never lived with the family. When O.J. was sixteen and his father tried to discipline him, they fought and didn't speak for a decade. They reconciled when Simpson's first marriage foundered.

Ten years after marrying Marguerite in 1967, Simpson wanted to divorce. He'd already separated from her once, moving in with the Kardashian brothers, then going home a year later. The marriage wasn't really working, but Marguerite announced she was pregnant. O.J. found the news depressing. Marguerite's religious upbringing precluded abortion, and O.J. wouldn't leave a pregnant wife. He decided to spend some time alone in the mountains with his dog.

"Before embarking upon this trek," Chapman wrote, "O.J. went to breakfast with Joe Stellini, where he saw NBS [Nicole Brown Simpson] for the first time. He began dating her about a week later."

Soon after, O.J.'s job required him to live in New York. Marguerite stayed in California, and Simpson flew Nicole east regularly. Nicole's sisters, Denise and Dominique, lived in New York, and he saw them occasionally. Simpson had already met Judy Brown, Nicole's mother, though a few years would pass before he met Nicole's father, Lou. "He considers them a close family," Chapman wrote, "but thinks they are 'dysfunctional.'"

As to drugs and alcohol,

> O.J. hung out with his teammates on the Buffalo Bills. . . . Scotch was his favorite drink, although he didn't drink very much or very often. He sometimes smoked marijuana, but he didn't like that it made him tired. He experimented with cocaine, but didn't like the "speeded up" way it made him feel. He had sex with many women, but his only relationship was with NBS.

226

By mid-August, Henry Lee was losing patience with the defense management. His job was to deal with scientific facts, not to support the client's innocence or guilt. He was increasingly frustrated by the subtle pressures Shapiro and other lawyers directed his way. The lawyers were not crude. They did not ask for advocacy. But they clearly hoped his speculation would support Simpson's innocence.

The pesky media made the problem worse. The lawyers somehow expected him to put on a good face, say helpful things if reporters cornered him.

He'd already had one heated argument with Shapiro. "Not my role to prove somebody guilty or innocent!" he barked at the lawyer. Lee told Shapiro he had far too much work in Connecticut to waste time out here arguing legal philosophy: I call it like it is. If I see something you don't like, fine. Once again, Lee thought of quitting.

His working conditions were also difficult. That old story about the blind men and the elephant applied to this case. Sifting through piles of disorganized evidence, he wondered what was here. The trunk? The tail? Lee had no idea how much more discovery was still to arrive, until it arrived. He needed to see the whole beast. And his defense colleagues asked him to do the most routine lab work, chores any technician could have handled.

At the least, Lee wanted the lawyers to define his role. Ed Blake was handling DNA. A retired FBI agent who specialized in hair was coming in. Shapiro had also retained an expert on shoe prints. Baden and Shapiro each phoned Lee to insist that they valued his independence. Please bear with the case, Shapiro asked. Perhaps, Lee told them. He said he would see.

5

HOWARD HARRIS HAD WORKED WITH F. LEE BAILEY IN Florida for seven years and thought of himself as a quiet man. He'd worked with defense teams, but these legal divas made him feel exceptionally invisible.

Harris designed defense-team computer systems and managed case information. But Bailey brought him to California for a somewhat different task. By now 300,000 letters for O.J. had arrived at the L.A. County Jail, and Harris's job was to set up a system for sorting and tracking them. He assumed he'd need only minimal computer support, then discovered that Shapiro lacked even that. The lawyer's secretary, Bonnie Barron, worked with an old computer and neither she nor Shapiro was computer-literate beyond the simplest workaday level.

Meanwhile, Sara Caplan was sorting the discovery paper storm into cardboard boxes. To Harris, the case management here was primitive. He began making suggestions, and within a week Simpson's mail was forgotten. Harris brought in more than $15,000 worth of equipment, including document scanners and programs that would make it easier and quicker for everyone to share information.

McKenna and McNally came in early every day and hung out with Harris before meeting with Shapiro. Harris, the invisible man, worked in the office all day. Hunched over his keyboard, he watched the show.

Harris had expected to like Shapiro. Lee Bailey was godfather to Bob Shapiro's son and had spoken highly of him. But Harris could see their relationship starting to deteriorate. It was a subtle thing: In defense-team meetings,

228

Bailey would give his opinions, which were based on decades of experience. Shapiro would appear distracted or bored. His indifference bordered on disrespect. Shapiro had asked Bailey in, and now he didn't seem to value Lee's contributions.

By mid-August, Harris noticed that Bonnie was making arrangements for her boss's sparring partners, lunches, dinners, a trip to Las Vegas to see a fight, a Rolling Stones concert, even a massage. Harris had watched dozens of attorneys prepare for trial. Each had his own rituals. But he'd never seen a lawyer put in so little office time.

Howard was particularly amazed that Sara Caplan, hardly an experienced criminal trial lawyer, seemed to be the only attorney working with the discovery material. Shapiro was never on hand when incoming discovery had to be sorted or when defense paperwork was shipped to the prosecutors. Caplan, aided by McNally and McKenna and sometimes even Harris, spent long hours deciding which documents should go to the D.A.'s office, which shouldn't. Harris could hardly believe he was making judgment calls on what was discoverable in this case and what wasn't.*

John McNally, who could be one stone-faced cop, was visibly upset about working on the discovery material. I'm not supposed to be doing this, he grumbled. This isn't my job. But he did it anyway. Harris knew that on many days Shapiro wasn't scheduled to be in court. So where was he? Shapiro was supposed to be the lead attorney. As far as Harris was concerned, he wasn't acting like one.

In one defense meeting, Shapiro asked McKenna and McNally to clock the time it took Ron Goldman to walk from Mezzaluna to Nicole's condo. Only one small problem: Goldman drove. Presumably everyone knew it.

---

*In criminal cases, the requirement is that the defense and the prosecution provide each other with their discovery material. However, in California the defense is required to provide the prosecution only with discovery of evidence it will present at trial, while the prosecution must provide the defense with all of its discovery.

McNally was fed up. He'd never seen a lawyer on a major case behave like this. This lead attorney had Marlon Brando's daughter, Pietro, who was about to enter law school, pasting his newspaper clippings in an album that looked like a model's portfolio. Another young woman was grabbing the pieces of cardboard from the tons of mail coming in and cutting them to fit photos of Shapiro, who was autographing them with a gold pen and sending them out. Everyone else was breaking his back on this chaotic case while Shapiro dealt with his fans.

On the third and final day of the August meeting, Shapiro said, "Sara, Carl, Shawn, Jo-Ellan: All of you please leave."

The three women and Carl were stunned. They looked at Shapiro, then at each other; then they picked up their papers and walked out. Cochran, Kardashian, and Uelmen remained in the conference room. McKenna and McNally stayed. Why was Shapiro excluding them?

By the time Douglas and Chapman sat down in the reception room, mortification, then rage, had replaced astonishment. Douglas was livid. He began to pace. "Fuck this motherfucker!" he hissed. "Fuck him! He's asking me to leave with the investigators still in there? We are being totally dissed. Fuck that!"

Shawn was just as angry: We're in the office till nine every night, then working at home until one A.M., seven days a week! And Shapiro treats us like this? This is serious. A major insult.

Jo-Ellan Dimitrius told Shawn that in all her years as a jury consultant she'd never been asked to leave a lawyers' meeting. Never.

Real bitterness was solidifying around Robert Shapiro. His rudeness, though galling, was incidental. The core issue was his ambivalence toward their client. Periodically he expressed doubts about Simpson's innocence. At first people had assumed he was playing devil's advocate. Not anymore.

Shapiro's management style was another problem. His

moods were wildly unpredictable. He could be charming, then turn cold and imperious. He was harsh with anyone he didn't like. Didn't try to hide his disdain. He appeared in the newspapers more often than in the office.

Now he'd deeply offended Douglas and the three women on the team. And they had no idea why. Eventually the investigators came out and ushered them back in. Douglas glared at Shapiro, who continued the meeting as if ordering fellow attorneys around like gofers was normal professional conduct.

As Cochran's group rode downstairs afterward, Johnnie said that Shapiro had passed on some information from his interview with Nicole's friend Cora Fischman. It seems Faye Resnick had told Cora about her, Faye's, sexual involvement with Nicole. "I don't want this to get out," Shapiro had said.

Douglas's fury rocked the elevator. Why had Johnnie tolerated this disrespect? It's one thing if he wanted to speak to you alone, Carl fumed. But leaving the investigators in and kicking lawyers out? Forget it!

"You're absolutely right," Johnnie said quietly. "I'll say something to Shapiro."

A few days later Shapiro apologized. "Sometimes I don't do things exactly right," he said. "I'm really sorry." He seemed sincere, but the damage was done. Even Jo-Ellan Dimitrius, who criticized no one publicly, greeted Shawn and Carl on several of her faxes as "fellow empathizers."

From the beginning Harris had been troubled by the fact that the four detectives left the crime scene to go to Rockingham to notify the next of kin. They should have contacted the Browns and the Goldman family. But Harris was also concerned that O.J. couldn't really piece together what he was doing when the killings took place. Still, the prosecution's time line gave Simpson no chance to clean up after what had to be a gory mess.

Then Harris met the client. Simpson's eyes held him through the glass wall. The way O.J. talked about his life, his feelings about Nicole—it was so strong. After that, Harris could no longer imagine that Simpson had done it. Harris had no interest in evidence pointing to Simpson's guilt.

6

On Monday, August 15, at 8:30 p.m., Kardashian's moving man said he needed to talk, but not on the phone. Kardashian and Denice met him at the Twin Dragon restaurant with his three-year-old son. Bob thought the child was a prop, a bid for sympathy.

The burly mover explained he'd embezzled over $400,000 in 1985 and done nineteen months. Then later, he was convicted of a second felony. Two strikes.

Now he was scared. He'd taken Bob's gun: the third strike, automatic life without parole. He'd done it because his best friend was sleeping with his wife. He wanted to scare them. He figured he'd make an excuse to come back to the house, return the gun, no one ever the wiser. He'd totally forgotten Bob and Denice were involved in the O.J. thing.

The mover started to cry as the little boy looked curiously at him. Kardashian had no interest in sending the guy to prison for life. The mover said he had the gun outside in his truck.

"People are probably watching us here," Kardashian said.

He and Denice drove to a supermarket to buy orange juice and left the car unlocked. When they came out, Kardashian put the juice in the trunk. He saw the gun wrapped in a white washcloth.

Next morning, he called the detective. A woman had called without giving her name, he explained, said: Look in your mailbox. He had the gun now. He wouldn't file charges if they caught anybody. Lucky for Bob's mover: The detective had run his name through the computer. He found the man was a convicted felon and had planned to talk to him.

On Thursday, August 18, McNally and Pavelic visit the house adjoining the south edge of Simpson's property. The maid there saw something the night of the murders. Pavelic had interviewed her in July. Today she tells them again that Detective Mark Fuhrman interviewed her on June 13, the day after the murders. Why was there no report from Fuhrman in the discovery?

The woman is a Salvadoran named Rosa Lopez.

> Ms. Lopez stated that on June 12, 1994, at approximately 2000/2030 hours, she observed O.J. Simpson's Bronco parked near the Rockingham gate, and that the Bronco remained parked there until the following day.

Lopez said she saw Simpson and another man leave the Rockingham estate at nine P.M. in O.J.'s black Bentley. At about 9:30 she thought she heard a prowler walking inside Simpson's fence "in close proximity to O.J. Simpson's air conditioning unit." Simpson's dog started to bark, which frightened her. When O.J. returned around 9:45, she felt better. Then she walked her employer's dog, about 10:15 or 10:20 P.M. Once again she saw the Bronco sitting by the curb.

> Shortly after midnight she heard two or three men talking outside O.J. Simpson's Rockingham residence. . . . Ms. Lopez is absolutely positive that O.J. was not part of this group of men.
>
> On June 13, 1994, at approximately 0800 hours, an LAPD detective, subsequently identified as Mark Fuhrman, knocked on her door and informed her that "something horrible happened.". . . She was not given a business card

and Det. Fuhrman did not write down any information that she related to him. He asked her for permission to check out the fence separating the two properties. . . .

Ms. Lopez stated that she first observed the Bronco parked near the Rockingham gate at approximately 2030 hours and is adamant that the Bronco was not moved until the following day.

The investigators are pleased. Lopez will be an important time-line witness. The fact that the LAPD is apparently burying Fuhrman's interview with her suggests a police cover-up.

The Griffin hearing, which had started on Monday, August 22, worked exactly as the defense had hoped. They lost—as they had expected. No one had believed that Judge Lance Ito would force the prosecution to give away its evidence. But winning had never been the point. A detailed probe into the prosecution's blood evidence was what the defenders wanted from the Griffin hearing, and they got it.

As they cross-examined each witness during the hearing, they were able for the first time to inventory the blood evidence. They discovered that the LAPD had no standard system of record-keeping in the critical area of evidence collection. LAPD criminalists Fung and Mazzola had collected stains without recording the number of gauze swatches they used for each. Some bloodstains merited seven swatches, others three. The swatches were not of uniform size or shape. They weren't tagged. Only the coin envelopes holding them were marked. Once at the lab, they were dried and placed in a folded paper, called a bindle.

Scheck and the others were delighted. The physical handling of the evidence was sloppy; the records were incomplete and there were no notes of who collected each stain. Without records of how many gauze swatches belonged to each stain, without tags on every swatch, there were endless possibilities for mixing the evidence. There was no way for the prosecution to guarantee that a specific test result belonged to a specific blood swatch. Sophisticated testing showing that a given bloodstain matched the defendant's blood sample would be made less significant by the LAPD's sloppy collection and cataloging methods. If someone accidentally slipped an untagged swatch into the wrong envelope, a stain supposedly from one place at the crime scene could actually have been collected from somewhere else.

It also appeared that the criminalists didn't know how to preserve blood evidence properly. Peter Neufeld discovered that Andrea Mazzola was only a trainee. Then her supervisor, Dennis Fung, let the plastic-wrapped samples sit in a hot truck for an entire muggy June day. Blood is a complex organic compound. When exposed to air and heat it will undergo changes that can eventually make it useless for testing. In forensic jargon, the term is "degradation." How much had the blood samples degraded by the time Fung got them into the refrigerated case in the lab? Plenty, Neufeld suspected. Certainly he would investigate the issue.

One of the biggest police departments in the world, one of the biggest cases ever, and these criminalists were making fundamental mistakes. It was a dream come true for the defense. The Griffin hearing had more than paid off. Now Scheck could envision a defense strategy based on attacking the LAPD's handling of the evidence.

SIMPSON DEFENSE LOSES BID FOR SHARE
OF BLOOD SAMPLES; COURT'S RULING CLEARS
WAY FOR PROSECUTION TO CONDUCT DNA TEST,
BUT DEFENSE MUST BE GIVEN
ACCESS TO LEFTOVERS

—Los Angeles Times, August 27, 1994

The Griffin hearing helped the defense, but by the third week in August, the preliminary reports about the DNA tests did not. The labs were saying that test results would show O.J.'s blood was everywhere: at the crime scene, on the glove, and at Rockingham.

*   *   *

During defense meetings through August and September, Scheck, Neufeld, Baden, Ed Blake, Henry Lee, and Barbara Wolf found themselves on the same side of the DNA issue. This is explosive information, they all agreed. This is important. We must take into account the damage this can do.

Bailey and Cochran weren't convinced. Shapiro waffled but finally used reports of the test results to support his doubts about Simpson's innocence.

Shapiro, like Cochran, clearly knew little about DNA; he appeared to have no grasp of the issues involved. "You mean," he asked Baden one day, "you can't see the DNA in a bloodstain?"

Baden was momentarily startled. "That's right. Not even with a microscope." Not everyone is a scientist, he had to remind himself.

Then it occurred to him that the lawyer might be transforming a layman's ignorance into legal strategy: This complex, almost incomprehensible DNA test says this blood came from Mr. Simpson. But if you can't see DNA, not even under a microscope, how much can you trust the test results? Ladies and gentlemen of the jury, how can you base life-and-death decisions on some academic abstraction?

Cochran and Bailey were cavalier about the DNA testing. Bailey saw no problem, period. Scheck and Neufeld are nervous Nellies, he thought. They're afraid you can't prove a big enough police conspiracy to explain away all the evidence. "They don't see how you can try a case admitting this is O.J.'s blood, this is Nicole's," Bailey complained to Cochran. The strategy was simple: You don't fight DNA. You leave it alone. If the evidence tested for DNA was improperly collected, improperly handled, maybe even planted, the results mean nothing.

Cochran was even more relaxed; time and again, he brushed aside the blood evidence. It doesn't matter what the DNA results are. We have Vannatter carrying around O.J.'s blood. That opens the door to it being planted. That takes us most of the distance. The other part is: Nobody understands this DNA stuff anyway. *Nobody cares.* "If we can't under-

236

stand it, this jury won't understand it either," Cochran said often. He knew what a downtown jury would believe.

O.J. agreed. He didn't do it. And he didn't care about the blood evidence: These neurotic Jewish guys from New York worry about everything. New Yorkers are like that. Always fretting about something.

Scheck and Neufeld kept pushing: It's dangerous to underestimate DNA evidence. We've seen prosecutors present this material to devastating effect. Juries *can* understand it. Prosecutors use charts. Pictures. They make it easy to follow. How we present our attack on these test results will be crucial.

Ed Blake pointed out that Lisa Kahn had already signaled the prosecution's intent by sending two swatches from the blood trail at Bundy to Cellmark for RFLP testing.* Cellmark was a leading forensics DNA lab, and RFLP testing was a lengthy process. If RFLP testing showed that blood at Bundy matched O.J. Simpson's reference blood, then only he among *millions* could have left that blood at Nicole's condo. By means of the RFLP tests the prosecutors were hoping to exclude just about every other person in California from the crime scene.

Blake explained that RFLP tests are more sophisticated than PCR-based typing, which the LAPD's science lab did soon after the murders.** PCR typing requires roughly the

---

*An RFLP (restriction fragment length polymorphism) test is a sophisticated DNA test measuring varying lengths of DNA strands produced by their reaction to a specific enzyme. The results can yield ratios demonstrating that the likelihood of two people having the same genetic patterns is hundreds of millions to one.

**PCR (polymerase chain reaction) typing (also known as molecular Xeroxing) is a process in which tiny bits of DNA are replicated thousands of times to allow analysis and comparison. Once the DNA is amplified, it can be typed through genetic probes. While hundreds of genes can be examined, not all are suitable for forensic analysis. In the Simpson case, the DQ-alpha and D1S80 genes were among those compared. The genes analyzed through PCR are not the same as those examined through RFLP testing. PCR results can yield ratios demonstrating that the likelihood of two people having the same combination of genetic markers is in the tens of thousands to one.

amount of blood you'd find on the head of a pin and involves replicating tiny bits of DNA as much as a million times so it can be compared with reference samples. The "exclusion factor" for PCR is one in 500 to 2,000—that is, the donor of the sample is the only one in 500 to 2,000 persons with that PCR typing. PCR results are not as impressive as those from RFLP analysis, but in most cases they are enough to get a conviction.

Dr. Lee confirmed his colleagues' assessment: "If DNA testing is done properly, it's reliable. Almost impossible to fight."

Cochran and Bailey grew increasingly displeased as Ed Blake kept reminding the team that prosecutors would make this a classic "double transfer" case based on an essential principle of forensic science: When two people or two entities come into contact, they exchanged physical material, no matter how tiny the amount.

Blake laid it out for them: Let's say we have Ron's and Nicole's blood, from the crime scene, in Simpson's home and car. And we have Simpson's blood on the Bundy walkway. The forensic task is to identify what was exchanged and explain how it was exchanged. The prosecutors will do this, Blake repeated. The key element of proof will be blood, he explained. "It is absolutely essential that you understand how all this can be put together by a competent prosecution."

By late August, Scheck suggests that the defense drop any thought of attacking the reliability of the testing labs. The samples were being tested in multiple labs and each lab was producing the same results. Given that reality, the possibility of laboratory error would never fly as a credible defense theory.

Scheck and Neufeld were rigorously ethical. No one would try to bamboozle the jury with bogus scientific arguments. There would be no overload of irrelevant theory. The defense should attack and neutralize the blood evidence some other way. Scheck and Neufeld's working assumption was Simpson's innocence. They would do the research needed to find unassailable explanations for all the blood evidence that might stack up against the client. Blake explained how the PCR typing done by the LAPD was susceptible to cross-contamination. The defense would have to scrutinize LAPD lab procedures. There may also be a serious tampering issue. Everyone likes that, but lots of work will be needed to prove it. Scheck was ready to put in the hours. He knew there'd be more to report as his work proceeded.

In late August, Kardashian is still worried about his grand jury subpoena. He has visions of the Spanish Inquisition, the Star Chamber. He's hired Alvin Michaelson to advise him, and their first meeting is at Bob's home. The conversation isn't reassuring.

"You may have to testify," Michaelson says.

"I will not testify under any circumstances! I have lawyer-client privilege whether they want to believe it or not."

Michaelson shrugs.

Kardashian is annoyed: He needs an attorney who sees things his way. "O.J. always knew I was an attorney. Shapiro knew I was an attorney from the day he met me. It is unconscionable that they would put pressure on me to testify. Whatever I saw can obviously be used in the Simpson trial," Bob continues. "They say this grand jury applies only to A.C. But the cases are intertwined. Anybody can see that."

Michaelson says he'll look into it. Bob wonders if he should get another lawyer.

On August 24 Shawn Chapman took Victoria King to visit O.J. King sat through Simpson's one-man drama, and she wasn't impressed. Shawn was floored.

King was the best writer in Cochran's firm. Johnnie hinted that she might be asked to help their client write a book. But for now, he wanted her to help Simpson write a letter to *Newsweek*. A recent cover story had been headlined, "He Lived Two Lives: An Inside Look at O.J. Simpson's World."

The magazine had written about Simpson's lifelong

balancing act between the white and black worlds. The article quoted O.J.'s friends on the subject of his fetish for blondes, on his lack of ties to the black community. Simpson told everyone who visited him that he thought the piece was racist.

Simpson always loved a fresh audience. Victoria asked what he wanted to say in the letter, and he produced his standard monologue. Why had Nicole led such an awful life—the usual.

Even Shawn was getting bored by now, particularly with the detailed accounts of his sexual adventuring: I had no motive to kill Nicole. I had all the women I wanted. Still, Shawn thought O.J. was compelling that day. She expected King to be swept away.

But: "He's in denial about a lot of things," Victoria said afterward. "I think he has real problems. He didn't convince me at all that he was innocent."

They argued on the way back to the office. He goes on and on and on about Nicole, King said. It's bizarre.

Shawn had heard O.J.'s speech so often that she was comfortable with it. She was angry that King had not been convinced.

He's so inconsistent, the older lawyer replied. How can he say he didn't have feelings for Nicole when he talks about her endlessly? He's so sexist! The way he brags about his conquests is awful.

Shawn knew that King was a feminist. Strike one. I am too, Shawn thought, but not like her. Victoria was prim and unforgiving, inflexible. Strike two.

King called Simpson a sexist obsessed with a woman who kept leaving him, which gave him a motive for murder.

Shawn told Johnnie immediately. King was one of Cochran's favorite lawyers—the most wonderful thing on earth, he said. Everyone else in the firm wanted to knock her down a peg.

"What? She said *that?*"

Strike three. Johnnie was incredulous. He was one hundred percent with O.J. now, and he couldn't understand anyone who didn't see things his way. King visited Simpson again and continued to help with his writing, but she had nothing else to do with the defense.

Before the trial was over, she left the firm.

That same day, August 24, Kardashian drove downtown to meet Alvin Michaelson and his partner, Janet Levine, to file a motion to nullify his subpoena.

Michaelson filed the motion; the prosecutors asked for time to file a response. Then Bob went to Ito's courtroom and sat through a DNA hearing.

By the next morning his throat was sore and he knew he was coming down with something. He'd never felt this kind of tension. All he wanted to do was sleep, but between the pain and the tension, it was impossible.

Then Janet Levine called Bob at home.

"Who is this guy who hates you so much?" she asked.

"What do you mean?"

"Wayne Hughes," she said. "He told the district attorney you're a liar and a cheat. He said you're charging O.J. three thousand dollars a day in legal fees."

Bob's headache was blinding.

"Hughes talked to the D.A.? Doesn't he know that can hurt O.J.?" What was Wayne telling the prosecutors? Kardashian wondered. Was he discussing the Bronco chase? What accusations was he throwing at Bob?

Kardashian was furious: If Hughes says I'm dishonest, then the D.A. will assume I was part of a plot to help O.J. escape. If I'm forced to testify before the grand jury, they might make me testify at O.J.'s trial! Kardashian's rage blotted out his headache. I can't believe Hughes would do this! I'm going to sue his ass!

On August 26, Janet and Bob met again at the courthouse. She handed him a two-inch stack of papers, including Wayne's declaration. Kardashian read some of it, and cooled down. Hughes hadn't accused him of lying and cheating. Just of incompetence and greed. No problem there. He already knew Wayne didn't like him. The $3,000 a day annoyed him, since it wasn't true. But on the other hand, it did support his argument that he was one of O.J.'s attorneys.

That same day, Kardashian listened as Janet argued his motion before Judge Stephen Czuleger: Kardashian was counsel, she said. Whatever happened between him and O.J. was privileged. O.J.'s right to a fair trial would be jeopardized if Bob testified. In Judge Ito's courtroom, at the very same time, Ito ruled that Simpson would have to take the stand and say under oath that he believed in those early days that Kardashian was his attorney.

Kardashian knew that would never happen. The defense would never put O.J. on the stand at this point. The other side could cross-examine him, a guaranteed third-degree about his state of mind, plus anything else they might try to drag in.

But Ito had also ruled that the grand jury couldn't ask Kardashian about his conversations with Simpson or with his assistant, Nicole Pulvers. Bob began to think he should testify. Maybe it was better that way. If he didn't, the press would invent all kinds of sinister implications.

7

LATER THAT WEEK KARDASHIAN SAT IN A VIEWING ROOM at the Playboy mansion and wept. He hoped the others wouldn't notice.

Skip Taft, Bob Shapiro, Sara Caplan, O.J.'s trainer, and others were there. The prosecutors had subpoenaed this workout video, which O.J. had made for Playboy a month before the murders. They wanted to show that Simpson was hardly so arthritic that he couldn't kill two people with a knife. But O.J. had told Kardashian he had been forced to stop the taping several times. His knees wouldn't bend. He couldn't move in certain ways without grimacing. Now they were watching the unedited taping.

On the screen, he saw the old Juice. Memories flooded him: the good times, the parties, tennis, hanging out. Simpson sang along with the music as the trainer led the workout. He seemed happy, joking, having fun. The tape had been made only a few months ago. It was all ancient history.

On the tape, O.J. kept talking about his bad knees. But when he started the exercise routine again, he was the friend Kardashian used to know, jovial, enjoying himself. Kardashian kept wiping tears from his cheeks. Afterward he and Skip walked around the grounds. Reminiscing. Trying to digest what was happening.

On Saturday, August 27, Jo-Ellan Dimitrius met the defense team at the Murray Hill Focus Group Center in Santa Monica at 9:15 A.M. Watching from behind the one-way glass, the defense team was amazed. Jo-Ellan worked with about seventy-five people divided equally among three rooms. In each room she showed slides and asked questions, with an assistant. The groups were splitting along ethnic lines almost without exception—but even more surprising was this: Black middle-aged women were Simpson's most aggressive champions.

Kardashian watched spellbound through the viewing glass as Jo-Ellan asked her questions. Was there enough time for the murders? What would you need to hear to vote guilty? To vote not guilty? What about Simpson's letter? The 911 tapes? What do you know about DNA? What are your impressions of Mark Fuhrman? Should Mr. Simpson testify? What are your impressions of him? The session lasted nearly three hours.

Jo-Ellan's questions encouraged in-depth answers. The feelings and prejudices of the group emerged as if in a therapy session. Johnnie, Carl, and Shawn were startled. They'd assumed African-American women would dislike Simpson for marrying white.

Instead, black women hated *her*.

They resented Nicole's lifestyle. The big house, the servants, the travel, the jewelry—all from a black man's money. Shawn felt the envy. They didn't criticize Simpson for living an upscale white lifestyle, leaving his community behind. That wasn't important. He'd left them long ago.

The gut issue was Nicole. This white woman had lived *their* fantasy. She had things they should have had. The team was stunned. The women came close to calling Nicole a whore. They came right to the edge of suggesting she got what she deserved. Everybody had assumed that black women would be risky jurors. They might easily turn against O.J. Clearly, the lawyers had been wrong. Virtually every middle-aged African-American woman in the focus group supported Simpson and resented the murder victim.

What they learned that day influenced the defense's thinking throughout the trial—including, of course, their plans for jury selection.

Black men under twenty-five were the second-best group. But their support for Simpson wasn't nearly as strong. Whites were ready to convict Simpson. Latinos were mixed, hard to predict. Asians were no help.

If Nicole were black, Shawn knew, this would be an entirely different case. The black community was convinced that white society didn't care about black-on-black murders. No, the general outrage was all about a black man sexually involved with a white woman. Now the woman was dead. The white community knew what to do about *that*.

For Cochran, the day went well. He'd always picked juries with his gut and planned to do the same this time. He'd never worked with a consultant before. Of course he knew Jo-Ellan and respected her talents. He'd brought her in, after all. But he wanted as black a jury as possible. If Jo-Ellan's statistics and science had gotten in the way of his professional instincts, he'd have been frustrated. But they were in harmony. Cochran walked out smiling.

Of course, he'd have to fight for that jury. Jo-Ellan knew that Marcia Clark and Bill Hodgman were also talking to jury consultants. They would probably learn the same things. The people the defense now wanted were exactly the ones the prosecution would fight to keep off the jury.

That same afternoon, Kardashian took Johnnie, Carl, and Shawn over to Nicole's condo accompanied by the defense investigators. Tom Lange and Ron Phillips met them there on behalf of the LAPD. A crowd of reporters waited. Even now, their presence amazed Kardashian.

Like everyone else, Shawn was shocked by the claustrophobic murder scene. We have to get the jury out here, she thought. They have to see for themselves that the killer couldn't have escaped injury struggling in this space.

Helicopters were overhead; rubberneckers and TV crews crowded the sidewalk. People were packed shoulder-to-shoulder outside. There wasn't room to open the gate. The walkway had become a tourist attraction.

Inside, Johnnie went upstairs and found a dark blue knit cap. Kardashian couldn't believe it. The same cap he'd seen a month earlier and asked the police about? Cochran took it to Tom Lange, who said it was a child's hat. McNally pulled it over his own head. It came all the way down to his chin. We know she had ski caps in the condo, Kardashian thought. But the police don't care.

LAPD STATEMENT FORM

Name	Date/Time of Interview	Location
EYESTER, Cretia	8–31–94 1030	150 N. Los Angeles

Witness is the area sales account representative in Southern California and Arizona for Aris-Isotoner. . . . Witness viewed several enlarged photographs of evidence, Items #9 and #37 (brown leather gloves) . . . she determined that Item #9 and Item #37 were both brown leather Aris gloves.

Witness also viewed a VHS tape (NFL live—Thanksgiving—11-25-93 in Dallas, Texas) in which O.J. Simpson was filmed wearing brown gloves. She determined the gloves to be Aris. . . .

8

WEDNESDAY, AUGUST 31, IS GRAND JURY DAY. KARDA-shian wakes up alert and calm. But as he drives downtown his confidence begins to fade.

At the courthouse, Kardashian is mobbed by the press. Microphones in his face, reporters shouting questions about his testimony that he can't answer. Janet Levine waits for him on the thirteenth floor, where there are more cameras. He walks toward the waiting room.

He sees Wayne Hughes there and nearly falls over. Time to have it out, Bob decides.

"I read your statement to Marcia Clark," he begins. "You said that I'm making three thousand dollars a day. That's absolutely false."

"Well, somebody told me that."

"So you told the district attorneys that you heard I was earning this? I agree with you on one thing: I'm not a criminal lawyer. And so I'm definitely not worth a million dollars a year. But I took great offense at what you said about me. I want you to know that."

Hughes concedes that he didn't really know what Kardashian was making. To Kardashian that sounds like an apology—at least, an acknowledgment of error. Now he was ready for the grand jury.

* * *

The room looked like a college lecture hall. The grand jurors sat in tiers. They wore name tags and took notes.

Kardashian was sworn in and read a statement saying that by court order his testimony would be limited to the Thursday and Friday of the first week after the murders, and the events leading up to the Bronco chase.

The experience was much like that of reading O.J.'s letter on television. Kardashian was remarkably calm. Someone else was testifying. That person wasn't nervous. He wasn't the same guy who woke up at night in a cold sweat.

Then Christopher Darden, a respected deputy D.A. who prosecuted cops, asked who answered the phone at Kardashian's home office. Bob assumed Darden hoped he'd say, "One of my secretaries." Then Darden could subpoena Nicole Pulvers as a secretary. Darden knew she was a lawyer with attorney-client privilege, but the question was: What capacity was she working in?

So Kardashian replied, "One of my assistants."

Darden laughed at Bob's maneuver and let a moment pass. "Assistant, huh?" He laughed again.

If Simpson was suicidal, Darden asked, why hadn't Kardashian removed the kitchen knives from his house as well as the guns?

"Why would I do that?"

"So Mr. Simpson wouldn't slash his throat."

"Mr. Simpson hates the sight of blood. It wouldn't have entered his mind."

Then it was over. He'd been on the stand about two hours. He'd expected to be there two days.

Moments later, Bob took the elevator down to the ninth floor, where O.J.'s hearing was still in progress. The attorneys were in Ito's chambers. Simpson was depressed, and Kardashian sat with him.

"The mornings are the worst," O.J. mumbled. "They wake me up at five. They just turn on the damn lights. They shove in some food on a tray. I didn't eat it today. Sometimes I do, sometimes I don't. Then I've got nothing to do for five shitty hours. They don't turn on the TV until ten o'clock. Sometimes I read. But sometimes I can't. I sit in this goddamn tiny little place with nothing to do. It's killing me.''

Kardashian listened.

''We do the courtroom thing, and I sit in this stupid holding cell while you guys go to lunch. They serve me crap from the jail kitchen, hamburger and soggy vegetables or some shit. You guys come back from some French restaurant. I just can't figure out why this is happening to me.''

Simpson started to cry.

''You've had forty-seven good years,'' Kardashian told him. ''Now you're having a few bad months. Look at it that way. It puts things in perspective.''

When the lawyers returned from Ito's chambers, Bob moved back to the rail and sat in his usual place. His mind returned to the hearing on the thirteenth floor. It wasn't Cowlings the prosecutors were after. They were using the grand jury as a front to find out what went on in *Kardashian's* house that day, what the defense experts had been doing.

PROSECUTORS ASK FULL SEQUESTERING OF SIMPSON JURY

To protect jurors from intense media coverage of the O.J. Simpson double murder trial, prosecutors Friday asked Judge Lance A. Ito to sequester jury members from the time they are selected until their discharge. . . . "If ever there was a jury in the history of the world that needed protection from publicity, this jury is the one," they wrote in their motion.

—Los Angeles Times, September 3, 1994

Around the first of September, McKenna starts looking into Nicole's friend Faye Resnick. He loves these drug investigations. So many complex networks, like a jigsaw puzzle. He gets pulled into working way past the hours he can bill. But it balances out. He's spent so much time with people in the drug business that he has sources everywhere.

Now he hears a new story, the weirdest so far: that O.J. was financing major drug deals through the Mafia. Simpson reneged on a deal. The wiseguys kill Nicole. The lead was anonymous, of course. But the guy talks about a killing in Florida that's supposed to be related. He knows the right names. Got to check it out.

Nothing comes of it. You need hidden money to finance drug deals. Simpson makes his money in plain sight. Corporations and movie studios pay him. He has a business lawyer, Skip Taft. He has accountants. Every move he makes is documented.

But the possibility of a drug connection nags. Simpson keeps talking about Faye Resnick's drug problems, which somehow got everybody killed. So McKenna asks a friend to go to Colombia and mention a few names. Very quietly. McKenna can't do it himself: Too many people on both sides of the law are watching his connections. His friend comes back from South America with new names. The people McKenna knows say, Whoa, where did you get this? These names are hot! But they don't lead to Resnick.

On Wednesday, September 7, Shapiro, Cochran, and Kardashian visit O.J. "Let me show you what it will be like," Shapiro says as Simpson leans back in his chair—his posture when he feels in control.

The attorneys sit on one side of the glass partition, elbow-to-elbow in three chairs. On his side of the glass, Simpson has more room, but his movements are limited by belly chains shackled to the floor.

Simpson wants to testify. He's been saying it for weeks. The trial is now scheduled to start in a month. Kardashian knows O.J. wants to do his own public relations.

Simpson is confident he will do the job well. "I have a life after this. The only way I can live it is to tell everybody what happened."

All right, Shapiro says. He starts in a steady, silky voice. "I'm going to ask you a few questions."

Kardashian looks at his friend. O.J. is ready. Ask away.

"Have you ever hit your wife?"

Simpson stiffens. He glares at Shapiro and leans forward. Kardashian knows his friend's mannerisms well. O.J. does not like this.

"Have you ever cussed at your wife? Have you ever yelled at your wife?"

Simpson launches into long-winded, aggressive answers, a life history every time. Shapiro offers no pleasantries, just more questions.

"Have you ever lost your temper at your wife?"

Simpson's voice rises. He dances away from topics, talks about what Nicole did to him.

"That's not good enough, O.J.," Shapiro says quietly. "The more you explain, the more trouble you get into."

Cochran has come to the jail thinking O.J. will do well. Nobody's perfect the first time, and everybody knows Simpson wasn't prepared. In the end, he will make his own decision about testifying, and Cochran will support it. But today it is obvious that Simpson could be a disaster on the stand.

"Marcia Clark is going to be a lot tougher on you than I am," Shapiro says.

Simpson is far from beaten. But he's taken a hit. "Maybe it's harder than I think," he admits.

9

That afternoon, September 7, the entire team gathered in the big conference room. Jo-Ellan was about to describe their ideal juror: a black, middle-aged, divorced woman. Her presentation was the opening act in a meeting that would drag on for nearly three days. She held up the inch-thick survey. Her University of San Diego researchers had talked with two hundred L.A. County African-Americans: men and women, young and old, rich and poor. The results were striking.

Dimitrius pointed to brightly colored pie charts and graphs. The team members followed along, using their own copies. One thing was obvious: A black jury would give Simpson room to defend himself. Only 3 percent of the two hundred African-Americans her team talked to assumed that he was guilty. Thirty-seven percent thought he was innocent. When the question was approached indirectly, 66 percent felt he didn't have enough time to commit the murders.

Black jurors, Jo-Ellan said, would be receptive to a defense based on police incompetence and corruption. Forty-four percent said Los Angeles cops had treated them unfairly at least once. Twenty-nine percent believed that blacks were "rarely" treated well in the local legal system. Fifty percent were only slightly more positive: "Sometimes" blacks got good treatment, they said. Without question, the LAPD incompetence unearthed at the Griffin hearing would impress a black jury.

Other charts broke down opinions by age and sex. Divorced or widowed females continued strong. Nearly half the divorced or widowed people thought the DNA evidence unimportant. Only 6 percent of the women (versus 17 percent of the men) would send Simpson to jail based on DNA evidence alone. Forty-nine percent of divorced black women wanted to see O.J. acquitted. They *really* hated Nicole. Only 32 percent of the men felt the same. Sixty-three percent of the young people wanted him acquitted, but they also believed in DNA. Fifty-one percent of the divorced and widowed women thought O.J. was innocent. For married women the number was 54 percent.

Jo-Ellan's analysis identified the ideal juror, and the research showed that stories of battering wouldn't impress her. Dimitrius's focus-group findings, combined with survey results, now framed the defense's approach to jury selection.

* * *

That same day Shawn Chapman distributed her report on the alleged incidents of spousal abuse.

Nicole's diaries and friends would tell one story. O.J. offered a more colorful response. For instance, Shawn had asked about a San Francisco incident in the late 1970s. Had O.J. thrown Nicole's clothes out the window after slamming her against the walls of their apartment?

My daughter Erin was on life support, Simpson told her. She came out of the Rockingham pool unconscious, and the doctor said, "We have to pull the plug." O.J. left the hospital and drove with a friend to San Francisco, where he had an apartment. He was drinking. Nicole joined him, but they started fighting about another woman. He yelled, "Get out of my house!" and threw her clothes out of the third-floor window.

Then Shawn discussed the time when Simpson took a baseball bat to the windshield of Nicole's Ferrari. Nicole and O.J. were living together, but she wanted to marry. "He was in the backyard when NBS pulled into the driveway. They immediately started arguing about his failure to commit to marriage. He sat on the hood of the car and had a baseball bat in his hands. (He wasn't sure why, but he thinks he'd been practicing swinging before she arrived.) He was tapping the hood of the car with the bat. . . . NBS started screaming about his chipping the paint on the car. He then deliberately banged on the hood and said, 'Now it really *is* dented. So what!!!' [She] called the police."

Simpson and Nicole were married on February 2, 1985. Sydney arrived on October 17. O.J. told Chapman that Nicole began to pull away from him when their daughter was born.

He began a relationship with some actress. . . . NBS did not have any suspicions about O.J. and other women at all. She had suspicions before they were married, but not afterwards. . . . At the end of 1987, NBS got pregnant for the second time. She and O.J. did not have sex for six months. . . . Justin was born on August 6, 1989. O.J. had a second extramarital relationship. . . . (It should be noted

252

that O.J.'s relationships with these women are to be distinguished from the many sexual flings that he had over the years during his marriage to NBS.)

Chapman asked about New Year's Eve, 1988, when O.J. and Nicole had both been drinking. He remembered an argument about another woman; it started while they were making love. "She scratched him, and he grabbed her. She ran out of the bedroom, and he locked the door. He heard NBS breaking things downstairs. He locked her out of the house and went back upstairs. . . . NBS had called the police from Michelle's [a housekeeper's] room at the guest house."

Simpson said nothing about hitting Nicole.

When O.J. told the police that they had been to his house eight or nine times before (as indicated in the police report), he was referring to the number of times the West L.A. police had been to his house to chit chat about football. . . . The following day [January 1, 1989], A.C. took NBS to St. John's Hospital because she was complaining of a headache. O.J. attributed this headache to a hangover, but thought she should go to the hospital just to be safe. O.J. admits that NBS had bruises on her neck and near her eye. He says that he had scratches the next day, too.

In Chapman's twenty-two-page single-spaced report, Kardashian finds the incident in 1992 when Simpson looked in the window of his ex-wife's house and saw her having oral sex with Keith Zlomsowitch. "O.J. explains that any person his height would have seen them upon walking up to the front door. . . . Once he saw NBS with Keith, O.J. was hurt, but in a way relieved . . . he realized that the thing he had worked so hard to prevent had already happened."

Kardashian had spent a good deal of time with O.J. and Nicole at their parties and on vacations together. She was a tough lady. She got physical with O.J. He got physical with her. Minor stuff. Bob never saw it get out of hand. He almost laughed at one detail from 1993: "NBS wrote O.J. a letter in which she admitted that most of their problems had been

253

her fault.'' I never get letters like that from my ex-wife, Bob thought. What am I doing wrong? He had to admit, though, that O.J.'s recollections were one-sided.

He noticed that O.J. minimized the incident in 1993 when Nicole called 911.

> O.J. had seen a photo of NBS, Faye and two guys at NBS's house. Faye wondered if the photo bothered O.J. O.J. admitted that it did. . . . NBS agreed to remove the picture. Soon thereafter, NBS found pictures of Paula at O.J.'s house and she got very upset. They started arguing. As usual, NBS would say what she wanted to say and then walk out. . . . He followed her [home], where she had closed and locked the door. He kicked in the door. She called 911 and told O.J. that the police were coming. The police came and took a report. . . . Later, NBS apologized [to the police] for calling [them] but said that O.J. "makes her crazy.''

For the defense team, Chapman's report was bad news. The prosecution was sure to portray O.J. as a stalker. But perhaps he was just approaching the front door of Nicole's home and happened to look through the window. McKenna checked it out and found that O.J. was telling the truth: When you walked up to the front door you could easily see the living room couch.

Shawn Chapman had heard O.J.'s unedited memoirs. She had questioned him about every horrible incident she found in the prosecution's discovery material. The D.A. had dozens of spousal abuse witnesses. If O.J. took the stand, she concluded, the cross would be brutal. The 911 incident wasn't as bad as many other things she'd heard as a public defender. But given O.J.'s wholesome image, the tape was shocking. Shawn talked to a friend in the public defender's office who had represented Robert Bardo, the stalker convicted of killing actress Rebecca Schaeffer. Marcia Clark had handled the stalking issue as if it were a loaded gun in Bardo's hand. She'd exploit the stalking issue here. The prosecution might work to establish a Jekyll-and-Hyde scenario.

Listening to Chapman give her report, Michael Baden suddenly remembered a Joyce Carol Oates monologue called ''Lethal.'' Bits and pieces of it were coming back to him: ''I just want to touch you a little,'' the voice begins tenderly. ''That delicate blue vein at your temple . . .''

Baden had come to believe long ago that Simpson didn't talk like a murderer. The LAPD match of gloves at Bundy and Rockingham troubled him deeply, but his belief in the client's innocence was sustained by the glove being so oddly out of place in the photos. And there was no motive: O.J. loved someone else. But what if things got out of hand the night of June 12, 1994?

Oates's monologue was haunting Baden.

''Don't giggle! Don't squirm! This is serious! This is the real thing! I just want to suck a little. I just want to press into you a little. . . . It won't hurt if you don't scream but you'll be hurt if you keep straining away like that, if you exaggerate. . . .''

Could it have happened that way at Bundy? Baden had been impressed when Simpson rejected the team's suspicions about Kato Kaelin. A guilty man would be eager to blame another. Now a new thought intruded. Wouldn't a man who'd committed a crime of passion, an otherwise decent man, *also* refuse to blame someone else? Baden felt chilled.

He couldn't block out Oates's monologue: ''I just want to bite a little. I just want a taste of it. Your saliva, your blood. Just a taste. A little. You've got plenty to spare. You're being selfish. . . . You're provoking me. . . . You want to castrate me. You want to make me fight for my life, is that it?''

That was how it went: lover to rapist to murderer who sees himself as the put-upon victim.

* * *

Baden was hardly naive about homicides. He knew where he stood on this case. By coaching Shapiro on his questions to deputy coroner Golden, he had even crossed the line to advocacy, an error he'd promised himself not to repeat. He believed what the client said. But the Oates monologue rang in his mind like a tiny, insistent bell.

In the first week of September, Scheck and Neufeld started documenting their difficulties in getting discovery material from the prosecution.

September 7, 1994

RE: Progress Report on DNA Discovery and Request for Teleconferencing Hearing

Dear Judge Ito, Ms. Clark and Mr. Hodgman:

. . . Ms. Kahn "hoped" to be able to talk on September 7. Instead of calling us today, we learned this afternoon that last night a carton of discovery documents, including approximately 700 pages identified only as DNA documents, were turned over to Mr. Shapiro. We are informed that the documents were provided without any index nor table of contents and that no effort was made to assist defense counsel to discern which of the 700 pages refer to which discovery requests. . . .

"This is the backbone of the defense effort," Lee Bailey began in his full baritone during the second day of the meeting. He showed the defense a working draft of the time line. His presentation held the team's attention for nearly four hours with computer graphics and minute-by-minute calculations.

"We know that the client was psychologically incapable of these crimes," Bailey intoned. "But if we show that he was *physically* incapable of committing them, it will be overwhelming." Bailey strutted as he talked. "Such a showing is one sure way of driving prejudice and speculation out of the case. Out of the courtroom. Out of the jury's collective deliberation.''

Howard Harris had created a time-line computer program. Bailey had aerial photos of the Bundy-to-Rockingham area to match action, time, and location. Shawn Chapman felt as if she were at a law school lecture. Vast, complex issues were now reduced to single sentences. What a showman, she thought. The only problem was that a show like this, with all those bells and whistles, would be as expensive to mount as a rock concert.

By the afternoon of the second day, the sobering effect of Shapiro's practice interrogation with O.J. had worn off. The client told everyone he wanted to testify. Definitely.

Cochran prudently sat on the fence. F. Lee Bailey declared himself "one hundred percent" in favor: O.J. Simpson had magnificent stage-craft. His innocence would fill the courtroom.

"I quizzed him in the lawyers' room," Shapiro reminded them. "He flunked."

Moreover, Shapiro had massive legal lore on his side. The oft-consulted Gerry Spence made it a matter of dogma: *Never* put the client on the stand. Almost all criminal defenders agreed that the testimony of the accused was seldom worth the serious risks. But Simpson had worked his magic on so many of the team that they believed he could seduce the jury as well.

Even O.J.'s most starstruck admirers, however, knew that Marcia's cross would be punishing. O.J. needed a tough coach, and Carl Douglas got the assignment. Show him what a cross-examination is *really like*, they said. Hit him hard.

Then Johnnie Cochran brought up jury sequestration. It was almost certainly on the horizon.

"We'll lose a lot of good people!" he said. Only bizarre old white folks would be willing to spend months cut off from real life. Jo-Ellan used softer language, but she agreed that people willing to be sequestered on a lengthy trial are usually retirees. People living alone. Those who won't miss their families. In other words, oddballs and loners. The defense was looking for family people rooted in the community.

The defense developed a strategy to keep the jurors' goodwill. Let the jury pool think the *prosecutors* want them locked up, Johnnie argued. The defense team? We're your friends. We trust you. Let all the requests come from the other side. Better still, let them know that the massive inconvenience of sequestration is caused by media leaks from the prosecution.

Alan Dershowitz attended most strategy sessions by speakerphone. Sometimes he was at his desk, sometimes on his treadmill. On the third day of this meeting, he was in Los Angeles. He told the team that stalking doesn't always lead to murder. We'll file a motion on that, he said, plus one on the word "stalking." Stalking is now an established crime; the word has legal meaning and thus is prejudicial. The same is true of "domestic violence." We prefer "domestic discord."

Above all, Dershowitz advised, the defense had to neutralize the prosecution's "bad man" ploy: By releasing the 911 tapes, Garcetti's office has turned a hero into a bully, a wife beater. The public no longer wishes our client to be innocent. The jury pool comes from that public.

Some public relations repair is possible, Dershowitz said, but our basic strategy is to separate murder from domestic violence. Some 4 million women are beaten each year in the United States. But how many are murdered? Fewer than 2,000. Anticipate the argument that most of those murdered women were killed by abusive husbands and boyfriends. Point out that a high percentage of those 2,000 victims were not previously battered. The relationship between battery and murder is complex. It is fair and accurate to say that spousal abuse is not an independent predictor of murder.

After the meeting Shapiro motions Kardashian into his office. "Shut the door. I've figured it out."

"What do you mean?"

"O.J. got mad because she didn't invite him to dinner at Mezzaluna. He took a knife over there to slash her tires."

Kardashian can't believe this. Shapiro has Simpson sneaking into Nicole's garage. She hears a noise, puts down her ice cream, and goes out to investigate. "She caught him," Shapiro says. Then Nicole storms back into the house. O.J. follows her. She orders him out the front. "He got mad and slashed her throat. Then Ron Goldman came. He killed him, too."

"It didn't happen like that. No way!" Kardashian hates what Shapiro keeps doing, and he storms out of his office.

After everyone left, Cochran and Shapiro spoke alone. This happened often. Johnny usually passed on whatever he learned to Shawn and Carl. On the drive back to their offices today, Johnnie said nothing.

Then Johnnie says, "Shapiro said that O.J. took this lie detector test and failed it."

The car is so silent you can hear three people breathing. After a pause, Johnnie says, "I don't believe it."

Carl and Shawn are silent. They rarely listen to Shapiro anymore; he smiles I-told-you-so at damaging evidence.

The polygraph was done two days after the murders, Johnnie says; Shapiro took O.J. to a guy who does private tests. O.J. said the wrong thing on almost every question.

The silence continues briefly. Then the lawyers start thinking like lawyers again.

How could he do this? they ask. Polygraphs aren't reliable! You can't expect any client to go through a lie detector test two days after two gruesome murders. Any client's nerves would be shot. There are so many other factors to consider.

Simpson didn't do it. Nothing will stand in the way of winning this case. The polygraph is a closed book.

PROSECUTION WON'T SEEK DEATH PENALTY
AGAINST SIMPSON; DISTRICT ATTORNEY WILL
ASK FOR LIFE IN PRISON WITHOUT PAROLE

—Los Angeles Times, September 10, 1994

McKenna has to grin when Lee Bailey gets the best piece of the D.A.'s announcement. The news hits the street as Bailey is leaving the jail. The camera crews surround him. He's blasé. Says it means nothing. Our client is innocent; we'll prove it in court.

10

By the second week in September, word was everywhere that Faye Resnick's book would say she and Nicole had been lovers. At least briefly. The rumors started surfacing a few weeks before. The subject came up during Shawn's visits to O.J. He brushed it aside.

"I've heard this," he said. "Nic would never do it. It's not true."

But the rumors didn't stop. Shapiro let it be known that he had solid information but wouldn't say if he'd seen the manuscript. Meanwhile, he didn't visit O.J. to discuss it.

On Wednesday, September 14, Simpson calls Shapiro, who suddenly tells O.J. it's all true. Faye's book isn't due out until mid-October, a month from now, but Shapiro says he knows the lesbian stories are true. O.J. says he knew about Nicole's use of drugs, but not this.

Later, in a defense meeting, Shapiro mentions his conversation with O.J. Remembering what Simpson said to her, Shawn is certain O.J.'s upset. Then she wonders why Shapiro couldn't have found time to visit him.

This is wrong, Kardashian thinks. Why did Shapiro leave O.J. on the phone with nobody to talk to? Sure enough, that night Simpson calls Kardashian and complains. He's angry. Shapiro provided only brief, cryptic information, mindful that sheriff's deputies listen in, but Simpson got the message. He is confused, angry, and clueless all at once. "Bob should have come down," he says.

Then, suddenly, Simpson is calm. He already knew many of the details, he tells Bob. "Nic and I had a really honest conversation during the time we got back together."

Kardashian doesn't believe it. This is O.J.'s way of dealing with embarrassment: He's not ruffled, not surprised; he knew about it all along. Bob has heard the routine fairly often over the years.

Shapiro asked Kardashian to talk to his ex-wife, Kris, about Faye's relationship with Nicole. She introduced them, after all. The next day Bob met Kris in front of her house.

"Did you know about it?" Bob asked.

"No," she said, then asked him where he heard it. Bob said he had to keep that confidential.

"Faye is probably lying," Kris said. "I heard the rumors for the first time last week. But some of the dates in the book don't make sense to me. And I haven't talked to Faye in three weeks."

Then she changed the subject abruptly. "Don't get in too deep here," Kris warned. "You haven't been around O.J. for two or three years. You don't know what he does. You don't really know what you're talking about."

Bob asked what she meant.

"It doesn't look good, you know. How do you explain blood all over the entry . . . and blood in the bathroom?"

Kardashian fumed. "You're allowed to bleed in your own house," he said.

"Oh, I see. Then how do you explain O.J.'s blood at the crime scene?"

"It was old blood," Kardashian says, remembering what Henry Lee had told him. "He could have bled there three weeks ago. Or three months."

"And Nicole's blood in the Bronco?" Kris asked.

"Nicole's been in that Bronco before."

"Robert, he's guilty. Why is the defense trying to cover it up?"

Kardashian controls himself. It would be too easy to start an argument. "Why don't you just wait to see what happens?"

"Got to go," Kris says, and turns to enter her house.

On Thursday, September 15, Gerry Uelmen quietly reads the troubling results of hair and fiber comparisons to the defense team in the small conference room. Hairs found on the Rockingham glove match Nicole's and Ron's. Even the Akita's fur is on the glove. Hair on the knit cap found at Bundy is consistent with Simpson's. Even worse, hair like O.J.'s was on Goldman's shirt.

There's one piece of good news: There are no hairs like O.J.'s on the Bundy or Rockingham gloves. But, Uelmen says, now we have to figure out how the other hairs got there. We've got some distance to go, Kardashian concludes.

TO:	Robert Shapiro, Johnnie Cochran
FROM:	William G. Pavelic
SUBJECT:	Discovery Material
DATE:	September 16, 1994

As we near the trial date, I must inform you that the district attorney's office has not provided us with the most important discovery material that we have requested for weeks, to wit: Radio communication tapes—transcripts for June 13, 1994, MDT [Mobil Digital Terminal] teletypes for June 13, 1994, W.L.A. [West Los Angeles] Sgt. logs for all of June 13, 1994, W.L.A. Watch Commander logs for all of June 13, 1994 and W.L.A. Monthly Activity Reports that pertain to Mr. Simpson.

. . . they have consciously and deliberately impeded, retarded and obstructed the defense from obtaining this rudimentary material. . . .

I firmly believe that the requested material will reveal

that . . . uniform officers assisted the detectives at the Rockingham location before Mark Fuhrman scaled the wall, that the detectives made O.J. Simpson a suspect from the very beginning, that the detectives ignored other possible suspects, that W.L.A. Day Watch Patrol officers assisted in the search of Mr. Simpson's residence before DA Marcia Clark arrived and before the search warrant was obtained.

SIMPSON TO TAKE THE STAND . . .

". . . He is going to testify," declared Johnnie L. Cochran Jr., a longtime Simpson friend who said he has spoken with him almost daily since joining the high-profile defense team two months ago. "He has absolutely nothing to hide," Cochran said in a telephone interview. "He wants to testify. He wants to keep the record straight. . . ."

—The Washington Post, September 17, 1994

"I think what you said in *The Washington Post* was inappropriate," Shapiro told Johnnie at the Saturday, September 17 meeting.

We need a unified position on whether or not O.J. is testifying, Shapiro insisted. The team had finally agreed to say that Simpson wants to testify but that the decision hasn't been made yet. Shapiro still wanted all press contacts cleared through him. *That* again, Kardashian thought.

A few days before, Shapiro had invited the whole team to a party at his friend Bob Evan's house for a screening of the new movie *Forrest Gump*. No one from Johnnie's firm had shown up.

Now Shapiro told those assembled, "I wanted to clear the air. Look, I was trying to show some appreciation to all the workers," he said to Johnnie. "This would have meant something to them. All my secretaries were there. All the other people behind the scenes. I felt you should have come."

"There's no air to be cleared," Cochran answered sharply. "We didn't come to this case to party. We didn't feel it was appropriate. We're working. We're getting ready for trial. We don't go to Hollywood parties.''

Today Gerry Uelmen is on the speakerphone, while Alan Dershowitz is in L.A. for the weekend again. The lawyers discuss resubmitting their motion to suppress the evidence collected at Rockingham. Then they turn to the latest DNA results, from the tests concluded on September 8. The blood samples collected at Bundy match Simpson's. Johnnie's camp considers this irrelevant: The blood was planted, or else it was old blood.

Alan Dershowitz feels differently: "It's not that the LAPD's errors prevent the prosecutors from proving their case," he begins. "Our theme should be that police errors have caused an innocent man to appear guilty. *That* idea should frame our defense efforts.''

Johnnie beams at Dershowitz. Shawn Chapman feels as if a window has now opened, letting in sunlight. They all understand the case in those terms. But until now, nobody has said it so clearly.

The LAPD focused on O.J. at once and then stopped looking, on the assumption that O.J. was guilty, Dershowitz adds. Such sloppy police work, slipshod evidence gathering, and poorly supervised procedures done by trainees have had the cumulative effect of making an innocent man look guilty.

During a break, Cochran takes Dershowitz aside, compliments him, shakes his hand.

Next on the agenda are the upcoming TV appearances. Johnnie says he knows Connie Chung well. "I can make those arrangements,'' he says. "And I'll call her at home.''

Shapiro interrupts him: "I had dinner with Connie last night.''

Shawn Chapman's assignment is to shepherd the Simpson family—Jason and Arnelle in L.A., O.J.'s mother and sisters in San Francisco—through the network interviews. The Brown and Goldman families have been doing national television. Now O.J. has decided it's time to fight back. Everyone knows these appearances influence potential jurors.

But today Chapman is getting tired of watching two so-called adults fight over who'd make one lousy phone call. The childish bickering persists to the point of silliness. She almost laughs out loud as imaginary dialogue pops into her head:

"I had drinks with Connie after you had dinner."

"I had dessert with her after you had drinks."

"I'll call. I have her cell phone number."

"The public one. I have the *private* cell phone number."

Shawn no longer needs to hide her mirth. The others are chuckling openly.

Two days later Chapman is in a limo with Jason and Arnelle on the way to meet Katie Couric of the *Today* show. Jason is nervous. And so is Shawn. They don't teach Media 101 in law school, she thinks. If these kids get in trouble, it's my head.

They pull into the Beverly Wilshire Hotel's rear driveway. A minute later they are in Katie Couric's suite. She has coffee waiting, which she serves herself. Katie is so sweet, the kids' new best friend. Shawn remains wary.

Cochran and Couric's producers have worked out the ground rules: No questions about the evidence, because one or perhaps both kids will testify at the trial.

"Jason, is your father a wife-beater?" Couric asks on camera.

"What do you mean by 'wife-beater'?" Jason asks.

A man who continually beats and hurts his wife, Couric says. Shawn takes a deep breath. "Stop," she says.

"Well, then, no," Jason is saying.

"Okay, *stop!*" Shawn has to wave her arms to get their attention. She pulls Jason and Arnelle off to the side. "That cannot be your answer," she tells Jason.

Then she turns to Couric. "You have to ask those questions again." The ground rules were clear, Shawn insists. Couric agrees to cut the last exchange. They'll reshoot. If this goes wrong, Shawn knows she'll never get another worthwhile assignment on the case.

Couric asks again, "Is your father a wife-beater?"

"Absolutely not," Jason says.

Two hours later Connie Chung meets Shawn at San Francisco International Airport. Chung is carrying a little pizza: "I didn't think you'd have time to eat, so here's lunch."

As they drive over to O.J.'s sister's house, Connie's CBS crew is already there setting up. "I feel like I already know you from TV," Connie tells Shawn. "If you want to talk to them alone for a while," she adds, "I'll drive around for an hour and come back."

These people know how to play you, Shawn thinks. Most likely the crew needs another hour anyway.

Shawn sees at once that O.J.'s family had no idea of the chaos a TV crew could inflict. Shirley and Benny Baker's small bungalow is now a junkyard of cables, wiring, duct tape, lighting stands, cameras. O.J.'s mother, Eunice, has arrived from the nursing home. She and Shirley are appalled, nearly hysterical. Eunice, a frail lady in her eighties, wants her favorite chair. It's been put in the backyard.

Shawn tries to brief Eunice. The older woman seems disoriented; she isn't listening. Shawn is frightened.

Connie walks in, all smiles, so reassuring.

She starts gently with Eunice, asking about O.J.'s childhood. Then: "How do you feel, your son always being a ladies' man? He could get whatever woman he wanted, couldn't he?"

Eunice smiles at the memory. "Women didn't care if he was Jack the Ripper."

Shawn's heart stops. "Stop everything! You cannot use that!"

Chung turns to her, cool, easy. "I won't."

Shirley approaches Shawn. "O.J.'s on the phone."

Shawn passes the message to Eunice. The entire CBS crew lights up. Can they film the conversation?

"I don't think that's appropriate."

Connie's sweetness evaporates. She pushes hard. "Could you just ask him? Could you please?"

All her life Chapman's admired Connie Chung: a minority champion, a feminist hero. Now she is ugly. Only one

way to end this shabby drama: "I'll ask O.J." After a few
words with Simpson, she returns to Connie. "He says
'No!' "

"Can we re-create it, then?"

"No."

"Can we ask her what she talked to her son about?"

Shawn checks her watch, nearly ten P.M. "It's over. Time
for you to go."

As the crew packs up, the field producer asks Shawn if
they can come back tomorrow to film Eunice returning to the
nursing home. Eunice says no. Shawn seconds her.

In the morning, Shirley calls Shawn. The CBS crew is
there again, uninvited. The family is furious. Suddenly
nobody likes Connie Chung.

11

SEARCH IN SIMPSON CASE UPHELD

The detective in charge of the O.J. Simpson double-
murder investigation recklessly misstated facts to get a
search warrant, but the situation at Simpson's estate
was suspicious enough to justify a search anyway, a
judge ruled Wednesday.

"I cannot make a finding that this was merely negligent," Superior Court Judge Lance A. Ito said of the
statements made by Detective Philip L. Vannatter in a
search warrant affidavit. "I have to make a finding that
this was at least reckless."

—Linda Deutsch, AP, September 22, 1994

It was Thursday, September 22. Kardashian's day started badly. The freeways were jammed. Again he was carrying O.J.'s courtroom suit. He got on and off the freeway—tense, cursing—and he pulled into the courthouse parking lot at five minutes to nine. Too late for O.J. to change. He'd wear the suit another day.

As Bob walked into the building, a photographer mispronounced his name. "Mr. Kar-day-zan, Mr. Kar-day-zan." He asked about the Louis Vuitton bag. Mr. Kar-day-zan, what about the bag?

Today Bob had had enough. "When you learn how to pronounce my name," he growled, "I will tell you where the bag is."

Things went downhill from there. During the breaks Kardashian was frantically trying to line up O.J.'s friends as guests for Larry King's CNN show. Part of the defense media strategy. Every night on TV there's been a different friend or Simpson family member talking to the jury pool. Marcus Allen kept throwing it back to his agent: "I'd love to if Ed says it's okay." The agent said no. Bad career move.

O.J. is fighting for his freedom, Kardashian said to himself, and one of his best friends is worried about career moves?

At the last minute King's people got one of O.J.'s golfing buddies.

> Sources have confirmed [that] results from RFLP testing—the most definitive type of DNA test—reveal that the blood on Simpson's socks is a genetic match with Nicole Brown Simpson's blood.
>
> —Tracie Savage, KNBC, Los Angeles

Last night, September 21, a local NBC-TV newswoman, Tracie Savage, reported test results that, Simpson's lawyers know, don't exist. Today Judge Ito is furious: He was so determined to stop press leaks that he'd ordered all DNA results sent to him sealed. The prosecution and defense teams are both in an uproar, too.

None of Savage's story about the DNA testing is true. In court, Marcia Clark tells Ito that Cellmark hasn't even been sent the sock from O.J.'s bedroom. No DNA test has been done on it. Ito announces in court that the Savage report is false and threatens to ban Channel 4 from the trial. In fact, maybe he'll ban all the media. For the whole trial. The LAPD starts damage control, leaking to the press that the first serology tests from *their* lab suggest Nicole's blood was indeed on that sock.

No question the jury pool is being influenced, days before the trial is to start. Everyone suspects the LAPD and the D.A.'s office are responsible for the leaks.

That evening, in Robert Shapiro's small conference room, Johnnie tells the team what the press corps already knows: Tracie Savage has a confidential source in the LAPD who has provided truthful information in the past. The consensus is to demand a special inquiry into the leak and announce that Savage's report proves a police conspiracy. How could the LAPD know that DNA testing would show Nicole's blood on the sock *unless they planted it there?*

One of the lawyers suggests they expose the source who started all this. That idea gets an enthusiastic reception.

They soon realize the ramifications go deeper. They can call for a dozen special inquiries and throw subpoenas at everyone. One way or another, Cochran says, Judge Ito will protect the police. He's an ex-D.A., and his wife is the highest-ranking woman officer at the LAPD.

Nonetheless, they can still turn the incident to their advantage. The evidence logs from the discovery show that Dennis Fung noted no blood on the socks when he collected them from O.J.'s bedroom. He didn't put them in a special container for bloody clothing. A police lab inventory sheet shows that the LAPD lab head, Michele Kestler, and Greg Matheson saw the sock when it came to them. They wrote on the sheet: "No blood found." But now the LAPD says there's blood on the sock! The defense should send champagne to Tracie Savage. Her story strongly supports the defense theory of a police conspiracy to plant evidence. The defense team decides to use this incident as a major part of their case when the time comes.

Next day, the defense request for a hearing investigating the leak is turned down. The earlier announcement that the reports were wrong erased any prejudice against Simpson, Judge Ito says.

On Friday, September 22, Benny Baker and his wife, Shirley, O.J.'s oldest sister, flew to L.A. with Eunice Simpson. It would be the first time she'd seen her son since his arrest. Shawn met them at the airport.

Sheriff's deputies were waiting for them at a side door of the jail. The press mobbed the front entrance. Eunice was wheeled through the sally port. Staring straight ahead, silent, the elderly woman maintained a regal posture as she approached the attorneys' room.

O.J. was waiting for them. He beamed when he saw his mother. It was the biggest smile Chapman had ever seen on his face. Eunice didn't say a word. She just looked at her son.

Simpson started talking directly to Eunice, asking about her health, the flight. His mother never looked away from him. Hardly said a word. Shirley and O.J. did most of the talking. She brought him up to date on family matters.

You could see that Mrs. Simpson wasn't saying much. O.J. didn't have to say he was innocent.

Afterward Chapman took them to Rockingham. The formal trial and jury selection would start Monday. Simpson's family would be there.

That night Ed Blake is working late in his office when the phone rings. "Professor Blake, would you hold for O.J. Simpson?" Already this sounds wrong. A guy in jail has a secretary?

"Professor, this is O.J."

The voice sounds right. Simpson, if this is Simpson, wants to know what is going on with the blood on the socks. But Blake has never met the client; he doesn't really know his voice.

270

"Mr. Simpson, please stop for a second. From my perspective, I don't know who you are."

The man protests that he *is* O.J. Everybody knows him. No problem.

"I don't know that woman who set up the conference call," Blake insists. "I don't know that you're not somebody from the media with a voice that sounds like O.J. Simpson's."

"Well, uh, I understand that."

"I can't discuss any of this without permission from one of your lawyers."

"But I really need to talk to you about this stuff."

Blake considers a moment, then says, "Why don't you call Bob Shapiro. Have the connection made through him."

Blake can't recall being directly approached by a client before. He explains blood evidence to counsel; the lawyers deal with the client.

In less than an hour, Shapiro calls with Simpson on the line. "I *really* need to talk to you," O.J. repeats. "I have to know about this blood on the sock." Blake gets the message: Simpson is anxious, impatient. Can't even wait to discuss it with his attorneys. Now Blake talks freely, for about thirty minutes.

THE REAL BATTLE BEHIND THE SEQUESTER
DEBATE: WHO'S ON SIMPSON'S JURY?

. . . There are no reported cases of a prosecutor ever requesting a judge to sequester a jury. . . . What Clark seeks to achieve through a sequestered jury is to eliminate certain groups of prospective jurors whom the defense wants: blue-collar workers, people with children in the home, professionals and students, among others. What she wants are jurors who fit this profile: authoritarian personality, older than 50, white or Latino from a demographically conservative area, first- or second-generation Asians, "go-alonger's" rather than "show-me's," women who hate sports, women who have been abused, police supporters and conformists. . . .

—Charles Lindner, Los Angeles Times,
op-ed page, September 25, 1994

12

SIMPSON TRIAL BEGINS TODAY
WITH JURY QUESTIONING

Well, three months of anticipation are ending with the most widely publicized murder trial now beginning. Jury selection—that is—for O.J. Simpson. Simpson's trial is said to be beginning at this hour in Los Angeles.

—Reid Collins, CNN Live, September 26, 1994

MONDAY MORNING, SEPTEMBER 26, IS HOT AND MUGGY under gray skies. Kardashian counts sixty satellite trucks in the back parking lot of the courthouse. The streets are mobbed. Helicopters. Makeshift TV platforms teetering in the empty lot across the street. The arraignment, the preliminary hearing, now jury selection—at each stage, a bigger media circus.

The VIP elevator deposits the attorneys in a back hallway near Department 103, Judge Ito's courtroom. They walk through security into the courtroom. Kardashian nods to a sheriff's deputy and enters a corridor fronting the holding cell where O.J. waits alone. Today Bob hands the deputy a clean shirt and a dark blue suit. O.J. changes in the small attorney's room next to the holding cell. Simpson is nervous, fussing with his clothes, pacing, complaining about the lousy breakfast they'd served at sunrise.

272

It is 9:15 A.M. The deputy says it's time. Bob returns to the courtroom and takes his seat next to the railing. A moment later, O.J. comes through the same door and sits next to Shapiro and Cochran. Jo-Ellan Dimitrius is a few feet away. Nobody looks at Marcia Clark and Bill Hodgman some ten feet to the right.

"Back on the record in the Simpson matter."

Ito had requested a thousand potential jurors. Today 219 people were on hand. The judge called a recess so that both sides could study the hardship forms of people otherwise able to serve. He ordered them to reconvene in the eleventh-floor jury selection room at 1:15 P.M.

Johnnie approached the bench and motioned to his client. "Your Honor, can he sit out here? We've got to go over this with him."

Ito allowed it.

"What do you want for lunch?" Kardashian asked Simpson. "We're ordering. Do you want a steak? You can have anything you want."

"I want a tuna sandwich with pickles."

"Your first meal outside, this is all you want?"

"I'm losing weight. Get some chocolate cake, too." He rubbed his hands together.

The defense team's order arrived, including O.J.'s tuna sandwich, two pieces of chocolate cake, and a Dr. Brown's soda. Simpson was clearly excited. He was eating "real food."

The jury room on the eleventh floor looks like an overfurnished movie house. Judge Ito sits where the screen would be. People in theater seats fill most of the space. A few find the couches against the back wall, while others sit in the aisles, on the floor. The group is racially mixed, not weighted toward blacks. Everyone wears a white badge with red and black lettering in a plastic sheath with a bar code and JUROR on it.

The room falls silent as Simpson enters. Obviously aware of his impact on the jury pool, he takes a moment to stand still before being seated.

The judge begins with greetings and has the prosecutors introduce themselves. Robert Shapiro introduces Simpson; then Shapiro and Cochran introduce themselves, along with Jo-Ellan Dimitrius. Ito asks his clerk, Deirdre Robertson, to stand and wave. "She's the most important person here," Ito says, smiling. "We don't operate unless she's here with us."

Very homey, Kardashian thinks.

Ito divides the jurors into two groups—the first is those able to stay through the anticipated end of the trial in 1995. He tells them they will have to fill out a seventy-five-page questionnaire. They groan.

"The good news is that I have cut it down significantly. What was submitted to me by the lawyers was over a hundred and twenty pages."

While prosecutors, defense lawyers, and Simpson watch, Deirdre Robertson draws the first number from the iffy group of jurors. Three reporters, led by the Associated Press's veteran trial reporter Linda Deutsch, take notes. Robertson pulls out 0032.

Simpson's football jersey bore the number 32.

This smaller room for juror interviews has an intimate atmosphere. A small conference table, so small you could reach across the table and touch the opposition. "It was like being in the room with a movie star," Deutsch writes in her notebook. "They saw Simpson closer than they would ever again."

Number 0032, the first potential juror, comes in to meet the group.

"I don't know if this is an omen," Ito jokes, referring to her number.

She's nervous and doesn't answer.

She works for a small company and gets a base salary plus commission. Her boss will pay the base. She is willing to do without commissions. Ito keeps her for the larger pool.

Ito instructs surviving pool members to avoid media coverage of the case. "When you see a newspaper article, move on to the next article. Go to the funny pages. Go to the sports section. When you see it on TV, zap the remote and watch *The Simpsons* instead, meaning the cartoons.''

That got Ito a laugh.

''When the talk shows come on, and they start to talk about it, switch to Howard Stern.'' Ito catches himself. ''On second thought, don't do that. He has talked about this case as well.''

More laughter.

On the second day of jury selection, September 27, Simpson is dressed in a golf sweater over a shirt. He is confident, impassive. He never says a word when a juror is present. He just takes notes on his yellow pad.

During a lull, Simpson tells Linda Deutsch what he was singing under his breath yesterday. Andrea Ford of the *Los Angeles Times* had heard the words ''A new day has begun. . . .''

''It's from *Cats,*'' says Simpson. The tune is called ''Memory.'' ''That song really gets to me because it says 'Touch me,' and I can't touch my kids.''

At a break Deutsch calls her office: Look up the lyrics. Eventually she adds to her story more of the melancholy verse about abandonment and lost days of glory.

Marcia Clark and Bill Hodgman are also working with a jury consultant, Don Vinson. He is considered the grandfather of modern jury selection techniques. Vinson and Dimitrius worked together in the past, even though he does mostly civil cases now. His experience, though, is a gift to the prosecution. But Jo-Ellan has heard gossip that Marcia and Bill aren't taking Vinson seriously.

Back in the large jury room, Kardashian can see that most of the would-be jurors are unhappy with the fat questionnaires. The final document includes 302 questions. Answering them is so tedious that people are playing games, cursing, laughing. Despite the grumbling, most struggle through gamely.

''The process of jury selection,'' Jo-Ellan has told the defense, ''is actually one of deselection.''

Her job is to identify the wrong people as well as the right ones. One of Dimitrius's secrets, kept even from the defense team, is to salt the questionnaire with trick questions subtly tied to the belief that Simpson is wrongfully accused. Answer those key questions the right or wrong way, and Dimitrius's computer flags you.

13

On Friday, September 29, Kardashian met Skip Taft over lunch to talk about budget problems. Taft said they were running out of money. Everything had to be cut back.

Kardashian knew expenses were running at least $50,000 a month above the lawyers' fees. Shapiro was still getting $100,000 a month.

Kardashian had one way to help. "Don't worry about paying me," he told Skip. "If there's money left at the end, pay me then. If there isn't, I'll live with it."

In the afternoon, Kardashian went back to court. Bob and O.J. locked eyes when Simpson and his lawyers emerged from the small jury room. Kardashian could see he was tense. All the defense motions were being denied. But Bob suspected that O.J.'s tension also had a deeper source. Simpson had watched hundreds of strangers file into the jury selection room. Bob could see it register: A few of these people will decide the rest of my life. He had controlled his own life for so long. People around O.J. did things his way. No more. Maybe never again. Kardashian was sure that knowledge was getting under O.J.'s skin.

FIRST PHASE OF JURY SELECTION
ENDS AHEAD OF SCHEDULE

The first phase of jury selection in O.J. Simpson's murder trial ended ahead of schedule Thursday when lawyers and the judge agreed their pool of 304 potential jurors was enough to move on to personal questioning.

The court is looking for 12 jurors and 8 alternates to hear the two murder charges against Simpson.

—Linda Deutsch, AP, September 29, 1994

During the first week of October a lawyer calls Pat McKenna. He says, I've got this client who told a police detective she heard a woman screaming the night of the murders. McKenna calls her. She's an investment banker, a credible witness. Detective's name is Ito—no connection to the judge—and he never followed up. McKenna can't reach the detective by phone.

Anyway, the banker said she heard this bloodcurdling scream at 10:30 P.M. But her home's pretty far from the crime scene.

So McKenna hires a woman to let out a big scream near the crime scene while he waits at the banker's place. He hears it. So do others.

Then he canvasses the neighborhood for people who might have heard the scream and discovers that one of them, Denise Pilnak, even called 911. So McKenna wonders: If Denise Pilnak heard his staged scream, why didn't she hear something during the night of the murders, when she was sitting out on her porch, which fronted Bundy? That doesn't look good for their banker witness.

Besides, Johnnie doesn't want the banker. He has Heidstra hearing Hey, hey, hey! at 10:35 or 10:40 P.M. Let's not move the time line back toward 10:30.

TO:	All Attorneys, Investigators, Support Staff, Expert Witnesses
FROM:	Robert Shapiro
DATE:	October 4, 1994
RE:	Statements to the Press

It is agreed that, until further notice, there will be *no* interviews given in this case. The only exception will be to Alan Dershowitz for previous commitments regarding promotion of his book.

As we continue the process of jury selection, it is imperative there be no exceptions.

By October 4 a power struggle has emerged over who sits next to the client. Each day Simpson walks out of lockup and takes the closest chair. Bob Shapiro immediately takes the chair next to him, on O.J.'s right. No way will Shapiro let Johnnie have that seat next to O.J.

So far the order is Simpson on the far left, then Shapiro, then Cochran. The fourth seat goes to whoever argues the day's motion, usually Uelmen or Scheck. It hasn't dawned on Cochran yet to sit at O.J.'s other side.

"You've got to sit next to him," Carl says angrily after court. Then an old theme: "You've got to take charge in the meetings!"

"We don't have to force it," Johnnie says with a sigh. They've had this conversation before. "We'll be in charge. It will happen by default."

Ito seemed to be handing down a new denial every day. On October 4 the defense lost two motions to suppress the evidence collected at Rockingham. The defense had moved to exclude the LAPD lab's test results on property seized there. "The court finds that there is no case law to support the defense arguments. The items seized . . . were reasonable. . . ."

For weeks Simpson has been worried about these dismal results. He tells Kardashian, "I'm not getting a fair trial. This judge doesn't give us any kind of break."

For the first time Simpson has turned the holding cell into a mock courtroom. As Kardashian watches, he walks in circles, one finger raised as if making points before the court. "Your Honor, this evidence was obtained illegally. It ought to be suppressed." O.J. switches identities and

278

becomes a second lawyer: "Now, why didn't he suppress this?"

When Simpson feels he has the argument properly polished, he turns to Kardashian. "Get Johnnie and Bob in here."

Kardashian fetches them. Simpson has them watch while he makes his case in his imaginary courtroom. This is how he wants things done.

When they leave, he keeps on practicing. Maybe there is comfort in the illusion of control. At least, Bob thinks, it helps pass the time.

When Kardashian arrives at the courthouse with Simpson's clean clothes the next day, O.J. is already pacing in the holding cell. This time he's talking aloud to Nicole. He has a distant look, as if he's talking to, well, God. Bob finds this stranger than the mock lawyering the day before. Simpson doesn't seem to hear Nicole answer. He just talks to her.

"Nic, what were you doing? Why were you involved with those people?"

These imaginary conversations grow longer day by day. Kardashian hopes nobody else overhears them.

"What kind of guys were you into? What were you involved in?"

Kardashian knows O.J.'s theory: Nicole met her murderers through Faye Resnick and her addict friends.

"That was a drug crowd, a drinking crowd. Why were you with them?"

As usual, Kardashian listens quietly. He doesn't know what else to do. O.J. says he has vivid dreams every night and tries to make sense of them the next morning. He rarely talks about specifics, just feelings. "You know I'm really mad at Nicole."

Kardashian says gently: "Why are you angry at her?"

"She was with the wrong crowd. Why did she do it?" Bob has heard all this before: Had she chosen her friends more wisely, O.J. wouldn't be in jail now.

Kardashian lets Simpson play out the drama and pull

himself together. Never mind that he's heard it a hundred times. It seems to help.

The deputy appears. Time for court. Simpson slips behind his public face. Kardashian walks down the corridor and into the courtroom.

By now Cathy Randa had organized a group of volunteers to read and sort the 300,000 letters Simpson had received. Many correspondents repeated the same themes; they offered encouragement, prayers, support. There was a smaller amount of racist and hate mail.

On October 6, 1994, a woman in northern California wrote to Simpson. The letter was placed in a stack for him to read.

Dear Mr. Simpson,

I am not sure why I am writing . . . but the circumstances you are now in I have dealt with most of my life. . . .

My mother was murdered by my father when I was 8 years old. I am now 37. My father pled insanity, since there were witnesses. . . . I have never gotten over losing my mother nor will I ever.

I can only feel for your children and hope that you did not do this. If you did, I hope you stay with your plea of not guilty. There will always be your word that you did not do this. Your children will have a chance at life and a father.

I know for myself this tragedy has made me feel different, as if I am not as good as everyone else in this world. I pray for a different outcome for your children. . . .

Only God will have to judge your reasons and you have to live with yourself.

All your fans, I am sure, feel for you and yours, and the pain you must be going through.

I don't think we have the right to impose our thoughts or beliefs on you, so forgive me.

Thank you.

14

THREE FULL DAYS OF DEFENSE MEETINGS BEGIN ON OCTO-
ber 8 in Shapiro's big conference room. Gerry Uelmen's
seven-page single-spaced memo "Strategizing Reasonable
Doubt" starts the first session.

"Reasonable doubt should be presented in this case like
the leitmotifs of a Wagnerian opera with each item of
evidence, each objection, each argument, reinforcing our
major themes."

Kardashian checks his dictionary to see what "leitmotif"
means. Nice image, he thinks.

Uelmen states three general themes. "The police and
prosecution rushed to a judgment in this case that was rash,
premature, and inconsistent with much of the evidence.

"Rather than suggesting a deliberate effort to 'frame'
O.J., we should portray their errors as a misguided zeal and
a reckless disregard for the truth."

Uelmen goes on: "O.J. Simpson is a tragic victim of
circumstances. We must present him as a gentle and kind
person who experienced great anguish in losing his former
wife and being falsely accused of her murder."

And finally: "The marital breakup of Nicole and O.J.
Simpson was no different from the failures of hundreds of
thousands of marriages. If the prosecution overcomes our
objection to the admission of evidence of 'stalking' or
spousal abuse, we must present a careful analysis that places
all of this evidence in the context of the true relationship
between Nicole and O.J., showing the accommodation they

had achieved, the lack of any motive on his part at the time of her death, and his concern for the welfare of his children. Our primary source of this evidence cannot be O.J. himself.''

That afternoon Barbara Wolf again tells the team that the prosecutors are still sending blood evidence to more than one laboratory; this testing is expensive. The D.A.s have sent dozens of swatches to three different labs for slightly different kinds of DNA testing. Wolf concludes they are going to compare the various test results and thus substantiate the astronomical statistics that come with RFLP testing. They'll bring in population geneticists. The blood in *this* stain, she predicts they will say, can only belong to one man in millions.

This isn't the only unusual aspect of the case. Wolf was amazed to discover that a coroner's photographer partially shaved the victims' heads and removed clothing for pictures before the pathologist ever saw the bodies. Indeed, she has never seen a case like this before. In her experience, pathologists check the body *before* technicians start clipping nails and taking samples.

But in this case, a pathologist didn't even go to the crime scene. In the East, pathologists are routinely present at crime scenes to ensure proper handling of the bodies. As a rule, the police never touch a body until a pathologist arrives.

So many things about this case trouble Wolf. If the prosecution had solid evidence, why are they obstructing discovery? Blood swatches were sent out for testing with one set of numbers. They came back with different numbers. Are the D.A.s absurdly disorganized, or are they trying to confuse the defense? It amazes her that the material itself was simply thrown into boxes without even an attempt at orderly arrangement.

She wonders too about the indications that Henry Lee found a second footprint, and about the coroner's testimony admitting the remote possibility that two knives were used. Then consider the important questions Dr. Lee raised about the evidence collection and handling. You just don't make mistakes like those the LAPD had made here.

Barbara Wolf is the quiet member of her team. In August, Shapiro asked her to organize the evidence. Until then, team meetings were chaotic because the various lawyers were referring to several different evidence lists.

The work has become her second shift every night. Today Dr. Wolf distributes a twenty-six-page update on the status of 327 pieces of evidence they've seen so far.

Ed Blake then reports that the lab working on DNA testing appears to be doing everything properly. "The results seem to be accurate. And bad for Simpson."

Blake has been monitoring the DNA testing at the California Department of Justice lab in Berkeley, near San Francisco. Gary Sims, the analyst doing the work, is one of the best. Blake knows these attorneys are desperate to hear the DNA results are wrong. Maybe they are. But not through any mistakes at the DOJ lab.

This is O.J. Simpson's blood, Blake says more than once. Accept it. Go on from there. The statistical probabilities are beyond argument. Maybe it's old blood. Maybe something went wrong in the LAPD lab. But DNA testing is solid science and there's no question whose blood this is. Scheck and Neufeld agree.

Then Blake turns to the most recent preliminary results, which will become official in the coming week. The Bronco's console shows a mixture of O.J.'s, Nicole's, and Ron Goldman's blood. The D.A. has been hinting at this but now the results are in. Soon it will be final. No question possible anymore. All the lawyers exchange glances.

Goldman's blood is the real problem, Blake says. There are innocent explanations, however tenuous, for finding Simpson's and Nicole's blood in the vehicle. But Goldman never had reason to be in the Bronco. He and Simpson never met.

Nearly all the DNA tests are completed and final. Only the socks found in O.J.'s bedroom are still being tested.

Everything so far, especially Goldman's blood in the Bronco, points to the client. Today no one manages to bring up police conspiracies. The lawyers are silent, trying to assess this latest barrage of bad news. It's depressing.

"You're saying that the likelihood that it's O.J.'s blood is almost certain?" Shapiro asked Blake.

"Right."

"And Ron Goldman's blood. That's certain?"

"Right."

"The likelihood that it's O.J.'s blood is almost certain." Shapiro then let the silence drag on. He rocked in his chair and nodded slowly.

Kardashian had a different view. All along, Shapiro thought O.J. might have done it. Now Goldman's blood has convinced Shapiro O.J. is guilty. Has Shapiro been right all along?

The DNA results also dismayed Michael Baden. Simpson told me the truth, he thought. I've believed that all along. But if he is truthful, why do these findings point in the opposite direction? Yes, Baden thought, we have our doubts about the evidence collection, but the DNA findings are powerful. The most optimistic thing I can imagine is that we don't have the whole truth yet.

The meeting finally ended. Everyone went home discouraged.

The next day, October 9, Kardashian arrived early to see Shapiro before the Sunday meeting. He knew that Shapiro and Ed Blake were going to call O.J. after yesterday's meeting to give him the DNA results and discuss worst-case options.

"I think I've got the right scenario now," Shapiro tells Kardashian immediately. "Suppose O.J. went over there with an ice pick, and he was just going to flatten her tires."

An ice pick? Kardashian is too numb to summon his usual outrage.

"He goes over there with the ice pick, and things just escalate," Shapiro continues. "Maybe he should plead. You know he could have done this. We can get him voluntary manslaughter.''

As Kardashian talks to Shapiro, Simpson calls the office. ''I didn't do this thing!'' O.J. is distraught at the DNA results. ''Where are you guys getting this?'' He is nearly crying. At first Shapiro alone talks to O.J. while Kardashian stands next to him.

''I want to talk to everybody,'' Simpson now demands.

Shapiro switches on the speakerphone. O.J.'s desperation fills the room and the adjacent hall. By now most of the team has arrived; they crowd into Shapiro's office. No one speaks.

To Shawn Chapman, the weight of yesterday's DNA results is enormous. Ron Goldman's blood in the Bronco is impossible to explain. Ed Blake says the DOJ testing is solid. Is this it? Shawn wonders. Will the case really end like this?

''I didn't do this!'' Simpson seems very far away. ''I know you guys are getting these results. I know it looks bad. I can't explain these things, this DNA stuff. But I didn't do it. *I just didn't!*''

The silence is heartbreaking. Chapman believes that everyone in this room thinks Simpson did it. Except Cochran. She can't read Johnnie's face. He seems unmoved. Even now, Cochran's faith is unshakable. The science says one thing, the heart says another.

Finally Shapiro speaks. ''We've heard you now, O.J.,'' he says gently. ''We've got to get to work.''

Kardashian thinks, Who wants a lawyer who's sure you're guilty? Why doesn't O.J. fire Shapiro? He sees the answer immediately: Simpson doesn't have the guts. He can't fire his own attorney. He's certainly not capable of committing these crimes: He doesn't have the guts. That's been Lee Bailey's point for weeks.

Shapiro repeated to the entire team what he said to Kardashian. ''He could have done this. Maybe he should plead.'' By now, still in shock from Simpson's desperate phone call, they had all moved into the conference room. Standing at the head of the huge table, Shapiro repeated his proposal:

Maybe we should get the best deal we can. "We can get him voluntary manslaughter. He could do five to twelve years."

Kardashian wanted to start yelling at Shapiro: You see the damn blood evidence and you fold. You're a pleader. Have you talked to the D.A. already? How do you know how many years he'll get? You don't want this to go to trial, because you know Johnnie will take over.

But Kardashian said nothing aloud. Others started to express cautious skepticism, reservations about a plea bargain. But when the team took a break, several members of the defense came up to Kardashian angrily: He's supposed to be leading this case, and he's saying O.J.'s guilty?

The next day, Dr. Lee reviews the evidence suggesting a second shoe imprint. Clear, if fragmented, patterns are evident. Some are on the concrete. He found the imprint during his first visit to Bundy and he took pictures. Today he displays the LAPD's crime-scene photos, which somehow missed all the areas he photographed. He doesn't speculate why. Of course, by the time Lee first visited Bundy, many others had walked on the concrete. But Lee is convinced that the fragmentary patterns seen there are consistent with a partial shoe imprint he found on the envelope containing Judy Brown's glasses, which Goldman had been returning to Nicole. The envelope was on the ground not far from Goldman's body, possibly dropped and stepped on during Goldman's death struggle. The pattern does not match Ron's boot. The second killer comes back into everyone's mind.

Dr. Lee also reminds them that blood drops leading to the back gate at Bundy look to him as if the blood fell from someone standing still. Further, the blood is so degraded that it lacks enough DNA for RFLP testing. It could be old blood. Lee offers no further speculation. But he also reminds the group that the blood on the back gate was collected in July, not June. That drop appears in July and yet it contains more DNA than the blood taken from the walkway in June— enough DNA for the highly incriminating RFLP test! But again, Lee doesn't draw conclusions.

Larry Ragle, a retired lab chief and criminalist from

Orange County, now on the team, tells them that it is possible to test the blood from the back gate for the preservative EDTA. EDTA should not be present in the blood left at the crime scene. On the other hand, Simpson's reference blood sample was mixed with EDTA, because it was drawn into a special syringe prepackaged with a standard amount of EDTA. He suggests they test for EDTA on the gate swatch and then test to see if its strength is similar to the EDTA in Simpson's reference blood. Nobody has done that yet.

Henry Lee's analysis has brought the team back from the brink.

Then Barry Scheck updates them on the missing blood from O.J.'s reference sample. It's simple arithmetic, he says.

Parker Center nurse Thano Peratis testified that he drew 8 milliliters of blood from Simpson. Next Barry reviews the numbers he's compiled on Simpson's blood: Collin Yamauchi used 1 milliliter on June 14. Technician Lisa Flaherty withdrew 1.5 milliliters on June 21, then returned 0.8 milliliter. Net use, 0.7 milliliter. Yamauchi took another .05 milliliter on June 25. Greg Matheson extracted .75 milliliter on June 27. The defense was given 1 milliliter for its tests. Throw in another 0.8 milliliter for spillage.

Scheck's voice is rising. That totals 4.3 milliliters. There should be 3.7 milliliters of blood left in the tube. But the log shows that only 2.6 milliliters remain.

What happened to 1.8 milliliters of O.J. Simpson's blood? "Why is blood missing from Simpson's vial?"

Scheck is flushed. His hair bounces as he talks.

Ed Blake then tells the group that when Gary Sims at the state lab opened a bindle—a paper wrapped around the original blood swatch—he discovered a "wet transfer." The wrapping paper bore an imprint of blood from the gauze swatch.

That shouldn't have happened, Blake explains. The LAPD lab people had testified they'd dried the swatches overnight before placing them in paper bindles. The dried swatches shouldn't have imprinted on anything.

Does this raise the possibility of police tampering? The original bindles were initialed by LAPD criminalist trainee Andrea Mazzola. She testified to that at the Griffin hearing when she listed the blood evidence. The bindles received at DOJ were not initialed.

But Lee explains that the wet transfer could mean nothing: This paper packet might have been accidentally put in the refrigerator overnight. Someone could have left a window open. In either case, the swatch might not have dried completely.

Lee's and Blake's obvious openness unnerves the more gung-ho team members. Henry talks to the prosecution routinely about their work, not his findings. "They should know about mistakes," he explains. "Nothing to hide. I give both sides exactly the same thing." Such evenhandedness is contrary to a defense counselor's adversarial instincts. Barry Scheck thinks strategically: Never let the prosecution know what's on your mind until the discovery rules make you disclose information.

As the meeting ends, Ed Blake again points out that the blood reports, soon to be official, will point to O.J.

15

ON TUESDAY, OCTOBER 11, IN ITO'S COURTROOM, SHA-piro turns to O.J. during a break and urges a plea bargain. The lawyer whispers, but the sound carries.

"Bob, why would I plead guilty to something I didn't do?" O.J. replies, his eyes wide with disbelief.

Barry Scheck has just argued a motion demanding sanctions against the prosecutors for producing DNA test results so slowly. Ito calls Scheck, Cochran, and the prosecutors into chambers. Shapiro stays behind with Simpson; Kardashian sits next to O.J.

Kardashian listens incredulously. Lee Bailey sits quietly three chairs away, overhearing everything. John McNally, who walked into court moments earlier, stands near Shapiro.

"O.J., I'm not saying 'You do this.' Just hear me out. I'm giving you an alternative. Let's just talk about it for a moment."

"I don't want to talk about it! I didn't do it. I'm not going to plead. Period." Simpson's voice is rising. His eyes turn hard with anger. "How could you bring this up? You're my lead attorney."

As Shapiro explains what he believes is the state's theory, Bailey listens, wondering whether it isn't Bob Shapiro's theory, too. "You were offended when the family refused to allow you to go to dinner with them at Mezzaluna. You decided to punish Nicole by slashing her tires. You went to her home with a knife and were about to slash them when she caught you."

Bailey wonders if Shapiro has any idea how extraordinary this proposal is. Especially the setting of the conversation! In the annals of homicide, he thinks, I've never seen the like.

"She caught you, and you were so embarrassed. You didn't want her to tell anybody. So in a rage, you cut her throat. Goldman came by, and you thought he was her lover. You were so enraged you killed him."

McNally doesn't dare move.

"The bloody clothes and the knife go in the golf bag to Chicago. You have an early golf date, so the golf bag stays in the limousine. The L.A. detectives call, and you rush back to the airport without the bag. It follows you back on a later flight. A day later, after we meet, you and Kardashian go out to the airport and recover the bag. You take the bloody clothes and the knife out. Kardashian disposes of them."

Bailey looks over at Bob Kardashian, whose jaw has dropped to the floor. Simpson is deeply upset.

"You've got to be crazy!" O.J. finally explodes. "I never wanted to go to Mezzaluna! Why are you wasting your time on theories that aren't going anywhere?'' Simpson's voice nearly breaks. "I don't *ever* want to hear you talk about this again.''

Shapiro gets up without a word and walks into Ito's chambers to join the other lawyers.

McNally sees Kardashian is still shaking. Beside him, the client is also trembling.

"John, sit down here,'' Simpson calls out. "I've gotta talk to you. I'm so upset I can't even remember what I want to say. Bobby, tell John what just happened.''

McNally says, "I overheard it.''

Lee Bailey takes Kardashian's arm, leads him to the anteroom. "You realize this is insanity. It's now being suggested that you are an accessory after the fact to murder.''

"I know. I can't believe what I'm hearing. Is this a joke? I'm not an accessory to anything!''

Bailey's loyalties were shifting. He, like Skip Taft and Kardashian, now believed Shapiro was trying to persuade O.J. to plead because it was his only way of staying in control of the case.

McNally walked up to Lee and Bob. "He's putting you right in the middle of a double homicide. Maybe now you'll get rid of him.''

Except for the timing, others among O.J.'s attorneys looked upon the incident as Shapiro presenting an alternative to his client.

As Cochran and Shapiro returned from chambers, the bailiff came to take O.J. back to the holding cell. "Don't listen to Shapiro,'' O.J. called out to Johnnie.

Cochran replied calmly, "This is crazy.'' He turned to Shapiro: "Bob, leave it alone. We're not going to talk about this now.'' Then he joined the others.

"You've got to take over the case,'' Kardashian told Cochran. "Bob should take a backseat. You should run the case.''

"I'll do whatever it takes to get O.J. out,'' Johnnie said, coolly. "But O.J. is going to have to step up to the plate and

290

tell everybody what he wants done. Maybe you can talk to him.''

Kardashian was afraid that his friend wouldn't—or, more accurately, couldn't—do that. Not even after what had happened today.

On Friday, October 14, voir dire has begun. Each attorney can now ask individual jurors whatever he wishes. "You see a lot of people on our side of the podium, don't you?" Bob Shapiro asks prospective juror number 458. "You don't see nearly that many people over here on the prosecution side, do you?"

"No," the juror answers.

"Why do you think that is?"

"Apparently Mr. O.J. Simpson has engaged more people."

"The fact that we have Mr. Dershowitz that I've hired who is a professor at Harvard, does that cause you to feel, 'They must be in trouble if they went to this guy'?"

"Not necessarily" was the answer.

Shawn and Carl, who had so despised Shapiro a few days earlier for urging O.J. to plead, were impressed in spite of themselves.

"If you were sick or injured, would you want to go to the best doctor you could afford?"

"Yes."

"If you were wrongfully accused of a crime, would you want to go to the best lawyers you could afford?"

"Yes."

Carl Douglas scribbled a note to Shapiro: "Outstanding." Shapiro does this so well, Shawn Chapman thought. No notes, hands in his pockets, thoroughly engaging. This guy, who infuriates everyone routinely, can also perform brilliantly. He puts a whole new face on everything. Maybe Shapiro *was* right for this jury. Douglas was willing to consider the possibility.

Johnnie, however, sat there impassive. He didn't like Shapiro's approach. Perhaps, Shawn thought, Johnnie considers it too theatrical. Maybe even hammy.

Later, on the way home with his colleagues, Johnnie asked Shawn's opinion.

Urged on by Douglas, Chapman didn't spare Cochran's feelings. Both lawyers hoped their boss would borrow a bit of Shapiro's stagecraft.

"Johnnie, I thought Shapiro was really, *really* good."

Then Johnnie firmly rendered his verdict to Shawn and Carl: Shapiro's performance was bizarre.

TO: Robert Shapiro
                Johnnie Cochran
FROM: William G. Pavelic
SUBJECT: Interview of Mr. Phil Coleman re: Mark
                Fuhrman

Mr. Coleman, a Vietnam Veteran and an African-American businessman, stated that he met Mark Fuhrman in the latter part of calendar year 1984 or early 1985. At that time, he co-owned a retail clothing store in Redondo Beach with Mary Flint, a 34 year old Caucasian woman. Their retail store was located next to the U.S. Marine Recruiting Station.

. . . Mr. Fuhrman and his partner visited the recruiting center several times and observed Mr. Coleman with Ms. Flint and other Caucasian customers. . . .

Mr. Coleman was told that Mark Fuhrman was seeking a position as a Marine Reserve. Sgt. Ron Rohrer confided to Mr. Coleman that Mark Fuhrman didn't like him because he (Phil Coleman) was "Hanging out with white women."

When Sgt. Rohrer introduced Mark Fuhrman to Phil Coleman, Mr. Fuhrman refused to shake Mr. Coleman's hand.

The recruiting personnel became so embarrassed by Mark Fuhrman's open racist conduct that they deliberately avoided him. . . .

Even in mid-October, F. Lee Bailey found the letter the defense received from Kathleen Bell in July downright inspiring. He reread it often:

Dear Mr. Cochran:

. . . Between 1985 and 1986 I worked as a Real Estate Agent in Redondo Beach for Century 21 Bob Maher Realty, (Now out of business). At the time, my office was located above a Marine Recruiting Center off of Pacific Coast Highway. On occasion I would stop in to say hello to the two Marines working there. I saw Mr. Ferman [*sic*] there a couple of times. I remember him distinctly because of his height and build.

. . . Officer Ferman said that when he sees a "nigger" (as he calls it) driving with a white woman, he would pull them over. I asked would he if he didn't have a reason, and he said that he would find one. I looked at the two Marines to see if they knew he was joking, but it became obvious to me that he was very serious.

Bailey was in London in July when Bob Shapiro first called him about the *New Yorker* article and Fuhrman's civil suit. He remembered Shapiro's call precisely. Fuhrman found the glove, the lawyer said. He's a racist. He's confronted O.J. before. Our motion to suppress will eliminate the glove as evidence. The case will go away.

He may be my good friend, Bailey thought at the time, but Robert is in La-La Land on this one. The indictment will never be dismissed. And, of course, it wasn't.

However, Bailey had taken advantage of the moment. "Bob, that's wonderful if it happens. But I won't believe it until it does. You're a guy who depends a lot on plea bargaining. If the cops have to be jumped on, there might be a need for a hit man from the outside. That way, you don't have any lingering resentment with the police."

"That's a good idea," Shapiro agreed.

Officer Ferman went on to say that he would like nothing more than to see all "niggers" gathered together and killed. He said something about burning them or bombing them, I was too shaken to remember the exact words he used. However, I do remember that what he said was probably the most horrible thing I had ever heard someone say. What frightened me even more was that he was a police officer.

Now, of course, Bailey was trying to change the dynamics of his role. After Shapiro tried to convince Simpson to plea-bargain, and attempted to implicate Bob Kardashian, Bailey could no longer support him in good conscience. If you don't believe in the client, you quit.

"This is a case about a glove," Bailey gloated privately.

. . . I am certainly not a fan of Mr. Simpson, but I would hate to see anyone harmed by officer Ferman's extreme hatred. If you have further questions, you may contact me at work or at home.

Sincerely,
Kathleen Bell

Bob Shapiro's recent actions had opened a door for Bailey. Kathleen Bell had rolled out a red carpet. Bailey could take center stage in the courtroom performance of his life, presiding over Mark Fuhrman's demise. A task, Lee Bailey felt, for which he was ideally qualified.

16

KARDASHIAN LOOKED AT HIS WATCH WHEN THE PHONE rang. It was after eleven P.M. on October 15.

"I've just finished Faye Resnick's book. It is very damaging," Shapiro began.

"What do you mean?"

"She's telling many of the same stories O.J. told us. Many of the details match. But it's all told from her point of view. And it's very damaging."

Shapiro said the book described numerous episodes of harassment and battering that made Simpson look obsessed and violent, a man who had to control everyone around him. Kardashian wondered again why he'd never heard any of these stories. None of this was the O.J. he knew. Was he naive? Stupid? Had he hung around O.J. like some star-struck innocent who never saw what was happening under his nose? He couldn't believe that.

If O.J. was a wife-beater and perhaps a murderer, why was Bob sticking with him?

Kardashian thought of his life, of the price he had paid so far for his involvement in this trial: the public harassment, the threats, his business trouble. Would Simpson have gone through this much for *him?* Probably not, he thought. So Bob needed to know why he was taking this journey.

During the worst of these days, he thought often of a dear friend from college, someone he had gone through adolescence with. Maybe even a closer friend than Simpson.

One day this college friend called. He was on trial for bribery. In his industry everyone paid off someone, but he'd gotten caught. His friend had assumed his colleagues would stand by him. But they all disappeared. His wife left him. His son never called.

Kardashian, younger then, had felt rage at this desertion. He flew to New York and prayed with his friend. The trial was brief. The man was convicted but avoided jail. Bob didn't condone what his friend had done, but his religion taught him to love the sinner, though not the sin. Kardashian hoped he would always live up to that.

If Simpson had murdered Nicole and Goldman, Kardashian would never condone that act. He still sometimes wondered if he was doing the right thing. He thought he was. He didn't care how it looked to anyone else. He had to be clear in his own mind. By standing next to Simpson, he was living up to the principle "Hate the sin, not the sinner." Perhaps at this point that was all he was still sure of.

Prospective juror No. 32 bowed out of the O.J. Simpson case Monday, saying the pressure of bearing the number Simpson wore on his football jersey was too much.

The woman complained of "undue attention to my jury number" and said "the public wanted to know everything about me."

—Linda Deutsch, AP, October 17, 1994

On Tuesday, October 18, Shapiro, Cochran, and the others arrived early and argued in chambers that Resnick's book would affect jury selection. Judge Ito decided that everyone, defense, prosecution, and the court, should read the published book immediately.

"Something has been brought to my attention regarding this case that is of significant import to the court," Ito told the jury pool. He then excused the potential jurors and sent a clerk out to buy copies of *Nicole Brown Simpson: The Private Diary of a Life Interrupted*.

The prosecution retreated to its offices on the eighteenth floor. The ninth-floor courtroom became the defense team's study hall. Lawyers lounged on chairs inside the railing or reclined on the back benches. Some entered the jury box. They tried to concentrate.

"She is such a liar! No way this happened!" O.J. shouted as he turned the pages. "It didn't happen! *This did not happen!*" Resnick's book read like an R-rated movie, occasionally an X. Drugs, sex, violence. Simpson was incensed.

At first the lawyers tried to quiet him. But soon they became annoyed. O.J. wouldn't let anyone read. "It wasn't like this! No way!" he kept shouting. Simpson loudly recounted his versions of Resnick's stories, the same tortured anecdotes that every defense team member now knew by heart.

"Can we send him back to the holding cell?" one of the lawyers joked. The laughter was hollow. There was work to do, and a deadline to meet.

When the jury pool returned at 1:30 P.M., nobody had finished reading.

"Ladies and gentlemen, I wish I could tell you a funny story about why it is we find ourselves in this situation," Judge Ito said with obvious embarrassment.

One more thing: "I'm going to order you not to read any newspaper, any magazine, to watch any television or listen to any radio programs, because the coverage in this case is unavoidable."

The panel groaned audibly.

"I do not ask you this lightly," Ito continued. "And I realize that to some of you there is nothing more enjoyable than sitting down with a cup of coffee and reading the morning newspaper. Unfortunately, I can't allow you to do that."

Marcia Clark asked for a quick bench conference.

"The attorneys have brought to my attention that I forgot one thing. . . . You are to stay out of bookstores."

Then he sent them home for two days.

NEW BOOK SAID TO THREATEN SIMPSON'S RIGHT TO FAIR TRIAL

An explosive new book threatens O.J. Simpson's right to a fair trial, a trial judge said Tuesday as he abruptly suspended jury selection and ordered prospective jurors to avoid newspapers and TV and to stay out of bookstores.

Ito dismissed prospective jurors for four hours while he and lawyers reviewed the book, "Nicole Brown Simpson: The Private Diary of a Life Interrupted," which was released Monday and co-written by Faye Resnick, a friend of Ms. Simpson's. Afterward, he sent them home until Thursday.

—Linda Deutsch, AP, October 18, 1994

The next morning the team meets Simpson in the holding cell. Shapiro explains that the book will create a storm of bad publicity. We need continuance to deal with the ramifications of its publication, he insists.

O.J. has conditions. "If you're saying there's no way we can get a fair trial, okay. But we can't delay the trial unless I get out of here."

That's a tall order, but Shapiro says he will try.

When court convenes, Shapiro addresses Ito. "Your Honor, we have hurriedly, late last night, even into the early-morning hours, put together a motion for dismissal of this case with prejudice. It is firmly our contention and belief that Mr. Simpson cannot under any set of circumstances . . . receive a fair trial in this matter. . . . If Mr. Simpson is afforded the right to have bail," Shapiro argues, "and be placed under house arrest during this period of time so that he does not suffer punitive incarceration prior to conviction, we believe we have a chance to get a fair trial."

He's absolutely eloquent today, Kardashian thinks. There are days I can't stand him. But this is the best I've ever seen him.

Resnick's book is on tape, Shapiro continues. Excerpts were broadcast on every national and local news show last night. "Portions of those tapes I heard myself. They are extremely prejudiced, beyond prejudicial. I mean, they just come out and say Mr. Simpson is guilty, that he virtually told the writer that he was going to commit these crimes.

"Mr. Garcetti, three days after the filing of these charges, pronounced that Mr. Simpson was guilty. . . . That is followed by the grossly negligent release of 911 tapes that were played ad nauseam . . . followed by at least three significant news leaks of false information. . . ."

Then Marcia Clark has her turn.

"The defense has also leaked. . . . They have attempted to speak of Mark Fuhrman with the most vicious of allegations concerning racism, one of the most inflammatory charges that could possibly be made. . . ."

Shapiro denies that he was the source of the leaks on Mark Fuhrman. "The allegations of racism that may come up as it affects credibility would only be from Detective

Fuhrman's own words. . . . Either he said it and it was true, or he made it up and it was a lie. Both affect credibility. And that's all we have said. . . . The issue here is one of a fair trial.''

Cochran doesn't like Shapiro's remarks and addresses the court on the same issue. ''I just want to say something about this race card. . . . There are racial issues. These jurors know it. Everybody knows it. . . . We as lawyers would be derelict in our duties if we did not ask people about these things. . . . Race plays a part in everything in America. We don't make it an issue, but society makes it an issue.''

Then Johnnie surprises everyone. ''Your Honor, Mr. Simpson would like to address the court briefly on this issue.''

Ito invites Simpson to stay seated if he likes. ''How do you feel?'' he asks.

Simpson stands up. ''Well, I feel I've been attacked here today. I'm an innocent man. I want to get a jury. I want to get it over with as soon as I can.''

Kardashian sees his friend about to launch into a long story.

O.J. explains his dilemma in rambling fashion: He needs a delay to ensure a fair trial, but he also needs a speedy resolution. His biggest concern is being away from his two young children.

He's working the room well, Bob knows.

''Miss Clark said that I was trying to run,'' Simpson continues. ''Everyone knows that I called my father-in-law. I was not in a frame of mind—I admit that I was not in the right frame of mind at the time I was trying to get to my wife—''

''Your Honor, excuse me,'' Shapiro interrupts.

Simpson ignores him. ''. . . I was headed back home. . . .''

Shapiro's voice rises to a drill-sergeant bark.

''Mr. Simpson, I am telling you that I will not allow you to speak and I will resign as your lawyer if you continue to do so.''

Simpson suddenly sits down. ''Thank you.''

"Thank you, sir," Judge Ito adds.

Ito denies the defense request for a continuance. However, he writes the electronic media requesting they delay broadcasting interviews with Resnick "until after the jury in this case has been selected and sequestered." Only Larry King acknowledges the request.

Back in the holding cell, O.J. is complaining. "Bob, you didn't let me finish. I was just getting to my point." Shapiro is still angry.

Shapiro made a good move; O.J. was headed for trouble. But Kardashian has to smile ruefully. If O.J. had talked only a little longer, Shapiro might have quit.

After Shapiro leaves, Simpson admits that some parts of Resnick's book are true. She's right about this, he says more than once. But mostly it's, This didn't happen, that didn't happen. Kardashian doesn't know what to believe.

That night, October 19, A.C. called Bob and asked if he could come over.

They'd stayed friends since that day all those years ago on the tennis court. Bob was never as close to Cowlings as to O.J., but he was close enough. A.C. had been the ring bearer at Kardashian's wedding. A six-foot four-inch black man, tough and muscular, carrying the ring at Bob's very white wedding. To Kardashian, he was a teddy bear, a guy who'd do anything for you. He could be very tough if need be. But that wasn't part of their relationship.

Since the murders they'd been seeing each other twice a week, more often than most people realized, and they talked on the phone almost daily. A.C. was the only one Bob could really talk to now. The Bronco chase, and the struggle to save O.J.'s life, bound them forever. Sometimes Bob talked to Skip Taft. Sometimes to Denice. But it was with A.C. he shared the deepest things. Especially the question that haunted them both: Did O.J. do it?

Each time they mulled it over, they groped toward the truth. They debated the time line and the blood evidence. They analyzed the marriage. They compared notes about

O.J.'s moods. Stalking? They knew he followed her once in a while. They didn't know how often.

Could he have done it?

The blood evidence weighed heavy on Kardashian. Bob trusted Ed Blake's expertise. If he said the DNA testing was okay, it was. To others, Kardashian could pretend that nothing bothered him. He could tell his ex-wife it was old blood. He could listen to Henry Lee discuss a second set of shoe prints and wonder whether the cops had planted something. But the sheer volume of evidence was affecting him. Why was O.J.'s blood in *so many places?*

Worst of all, why was Ron Goldman's blood in the Bronco? That question got down into his bones. The reports said the Bronco had been locked, and when the cops opened it for testing, they found blood inside. Now it turned out to be Ron Goldman's blood. Kardashian exhausted himself trying to find an innocent explanation for how it got there, something that didn't implicate O.J. He could find nothing.

There was more on Kardashian's mind that night in October when he took A.C. into his office and shut the door. He was starting to remember little things O.J. had said over the years that betrayed a coldness. Hints of anger. Cruel jokes. Like the moment in the unedited training video he had watched in the Playboy mansion. O.J. had commented that a certain move was a good way to beat up the wife: It left no marks. He'd said this with a smile, just a casual aside.

O.J. hardly ever talked that way in front of Bob. But sometimes he slipped. When he did, Bob ignored it. Everybody, after all, has a dark side. Men of his generation never discussed such things. You just controlled that dark side.

A.C. seemed to have something on his mind, too. But although tonight he talked a good deal, he didn't reveal much. Tonight A.C. was talking about O.J.'s "thing" about Nicole, but Kardashian wasn't sure exactly what he meant. Was it O.J.'s obsession? His following her around? Something was happening before the murders, A.C. told Kardashian, something was happening and it bothered him. Maybe O.J. did act the way they were saying, A.C. admitted. He didn't explain further. Kardashian knew better than to press him. When A.C. felt pushed, he clammed up. Besides, Bob wasn't sure he wanted to know.

Tonight they go back and forth. All the way to guilty, to innocent, and back to guilty again. Marcus Allen comes up. Faye's book says Marcus and Nicole were having an affair. If that's true, Kardashian thinks, A.C. probably knew about it.

Bob remembers Marcus Allen's frantic phone calls in the week after the murders. Was there more behind them than an old friend's concern?

A.C. starts to weep over Nicole. When things got bad with O.J., she called him and he'd fix things. He can never do that for her again.

Finally A.C. and Bob agree: We know this guy. He's a chicken when it comes to certain things. This isn't something he could do. He doesn't have it in him.

If O.J. is eventually convicted, Kardashian thinks, that only means the law says he's guilty. An acquittal only means the prosecutors couldn't prove their case. Neither one will satisfy Bob.

The blood evidence will remain. Why was O.J.'s blood in so many places? Why was Goldman's blood in the Bronco? Kardashian can't bear to take the question to its logical conclusion. If O.J. did it, he knows a part of him will always refuse to recognize it. But only a part. The inner conflict tears him apart. He knows A.C. feels much the same.

A.C. leaves for home about midnight, fatigue and gloom in every line of his body.

The next night Kardashian read the transcript of Marcus Allen's September 22 interview with the LAPD. "Mr. Allen described this relationship as warm and congenial, but not to the level of being best friends. They would see each other once in a while." Bob knew this was not true.

At least he understood Marcus Allen's agenda now. The guy who called from the Caymans, all upset and caring; the guy who cried at the meeting right after O.J.'s arrest: All along, he had more on his mind than O.J.'s welfare.

Now Bob knew why Allen hid behind his agent when they asked him to go on TV. Bad for his career, the agent always said, which might be true. But maybe Marcus was carrying heavier baggage. Maybe Faye Resnick was right; he was sleeping with Nicole. Then he pretended to be O.J.'s dear friend while telling the cops otherwise.

Marcus Allen got *married* at O.J.'s house! They weren't close friends?

> He added that he would play golf with Mr. Simpson from time to time. Generally, if one of Mr. Simpson's regular partners failed to show, he would fill in. He admitted that prior to his marriage in 1993 to Kathryn Allen, he would be invited to Mr. Simpson's estate to parties.

That was all? Bob read this passage with disgust.

> Mr. Allen described his relationship with Nicole as that of acquaintances. . . . He stated his wife's relationship with Nicole was that of acquaintances.

Trouble comes, and you learn about your friends. Sometimes more than you want to know.

> He was also asked about the alleged problems between him and OJ as a result of the alleged affair. He stated emphatically that there had been no affair between Nicole and himself nor had anything like that come between his friendship with Mr. Simpson. He denied having dinner with Mr. Simpson just prior to the murders of Ms. Brown and Mr. Goldman, where they discussed the alleged affair between Nicole and himself. Mr. Allen was asked this several times during the interview. Each time it was asked, detectives received the same answer.

What was Allen hiding? From this report you'd think he hardly knew Simpson. The worst part of this, Bob thought, is that I've got to tell O.J.

17

Faye Resnick's memoir is filled with potential witnesses for the prosecution. She outlines the pattern of abuse which the D.A. assumes led to the murders.

Yet Marcia Clark and her colleagues would first have to extract Resnick's invaluable account of O.J.'s violent behavior from her overwrought narrative. On October 20, at the criminal courts building, Marcia Clark, Bill Hodgman, Christopher Darden, and Phil Vannatter started a series of interviews with those named in the book. Naturally, Faye Resnick was first.

The prosecutors tried to zero in on O.J.'s abusive behavior. Resnick explained she knew little about the abuse until fairly late in her relationship with Nicole.

RESNICK: I'd bring things up to her and she would just say it was a bad time. . . . But she didn't elaborate on anything until really the last part of her life.
CLARK: Up until that point, what had she told you?
RESNICK: She had admitted to the 911 incident one time.

The two women attended the same therapy group. Nicole fled one of the sessions when questions about domestic violence came her way. Resnick found her outside crying.

RESNICK: She told me that's why she had to leave O.J. Because when the world found out about the beatings, she could no longer live with herself. She

also told me something really distressing that I
would like off the record.

CLARK: Let's not go off the record, Faye.

RESNICK: This is the time when she told me about her
family. That doesn't have to be in there, does it?

CLARK: Yes, it does. It does. That doesn't mean it'll
come out in evidence, but it really wouldn't be a
good idea to go off the record.

RESNICK: . . . the only reason she stayed with O.J.
after that was because of her family. They needed
her support financially. And when she told them
that she wanted to leave him, they made her feel so
bad about it.

Clark probed each incident methodically. "There was a time
that she was pregnant with Justin that he beat her?"

RESNICK: There was one time that she talked about
where he broke her rib and she went to the hospital.
She told them she had fallen off a bike. But I'm not
sure if this is the time where he broke her rib, hit her
with a wine bottle in the wine cellar. . . . I know
she said he beat her during her pregnancy. He made
her feel fat: he made her feel ugly: there was verbal
abuse: there was manipulation. He was always out
womanizing when she was pregnant. . . . He
wanted her to be just like she always was, the perfect
Barbie Doll.

But the beatings, the psychological abuse, the time Simpson
allegedly pushed his wife out of a moving car—these were
merely background. The prosecutors needed a moment when
Simpson's domestic violence could be linked to murderous
intent. Resnick said there were many.

CLARK: When was the first time O.J. threatened to
kill Nicole?

RESNICK: . . . It was right after Chris's birthday
party.

305

In April 1994, Simpson and his ex-wife had vacationed near Cabo San Lucas with several friends, among them Resnick and her fiancé, chiropractor Christian Reichardt. Like all the previous attempts at reconciliation, this one went badly. Nicole withdrew into herself, but said little to Simpson about breaking up. Back home, after O.J. flew off to Puerto Rico to film his new TV series, Nicole told Faye she was now determined to end the relationship. But she was afraid to confront Simpson directly. She ignored his phone messages from Puerto Rico. She kept the conversations short when he caught her at home. After each call to Nicole, O.J. phoned Resnick. He wanted to know why Nicole wasn't talking to him, who she was having an affair with. "Like I'm really going to tell him," Faye told the prosecutors.

> RESNICK: . . . When I say in the book that it was déjà vu every time he would call, I'm very serious. The man was like a broken record. He would go over and over the same things. . . . He said to me, if you don't tell me why she's not calling me and what is on her mind, I don't know what I'm going to do.

But for the moment, no death threats. Simpson returned to Los Angeles. On April 30, Faye gave a birthday party for Christian. Simpson had asked her to delay it so he could be there and he'd also asked her to persuade Nicole to pretend to be his loving companion for that one evening. To ensure a pleasant occasion, she agreed. Soon after, the athlete seemed to realize that the deep freeze was unlikely to change.

> RESNICK: I'd say there were at least ten conversations between those two days, Monday and Tuesday. Nicole alluded to the fact that she didn't want to have anything to do with him again. Then she'd back down because she saw how aggressive he was becoming.

Simpson kept phoning Resnick angrily. He insisted he didn't

understand these on-again, off-again signals, complained that Resnick hadn't warned him this was coming, accused her of lying to him.

Simpson finally decided to see a therapist. After his first session he called Faye in high spirits.

RESNICK: He said, "Oh, I feel so much better. You know, the shrink gave me a lot of hope. You know, he feels that I just have to be cool and Nicole will come back to me." . . . [O.J.] called Nicole right after that, and Nicole said, "Did you talk to him about why I don't want to be with you?"

He said, "What are you talking about?"

She said, "Because of the abuse, because I'm afraid of you, O.J., because I'm afraid you're going to kill me."

And he said, "Why would I say that? That was in the past. I haven't touched you recently. Why would I tell him I ever touched you?"

CLARK: Now, she's the one who told you this part, right?

RESNICK: Yes, but he also corroborated it.

CLARK: What did he say?

RESNICK: . . . He called me and said, "It's over, she said she's never coming back to me." It was screaming, yelling, violent behavior. I mean, I felt sorry for the phone.

And I said to him, "O.J., she thinks you're going to kill her. She thinks you're going to hurt her like you've done in the past. You didn't tell your shrink about any of that, so you're not working on your issues. So how is she supposed to feel that you'll ever change? She's afraid of you."

And O.J.—he went off. Because, you see, you're not supposed to talk to O.J. about anything he's ever done. You're not supposed to confront O.J. about any fault that he has.

And when he heard that I knew about all of the abuse . . . that's when he said, "Damn right, I'll

kill her if I find her with another man. I know she's
been seen with another man and I'll kill her . . .
she'd better stay monogamous to me until August
when I leave and keep up the image."

[CLARK: What did you do?]

RESNICK: . . . This was too real to me. I tried to calm
him down. "O.J., look, you've got children, you
know. Nicole, you know. You don't kill people, you
know, it's not something you do." . . . He told me
twice he was going to kill her. I was amazed. . . .
He also told Nicole that day he was going to kill her.
Nicole and I had conversations about the fact that he
had told us both.

Resnick's credibility would be far stronger if her account
could be corroborated. Chris Darden and D.A. investigator
Dana Thompson interviewed her now ex-fiancé, Christian
Reichardt, at his lawyer's office. Reichardt was no longer any
friend of Faye Resnick. He hated her book and had said as
much on national television.

DARDEN: What was it about Miss Resnick's book that
caused you to appear on the Barbara Walters show?

REICHARDT: A lot of inaccuracies.

DARDEN: . . . Is it your view that the book is substantially inaccurate?

REICHARDT: The situations occurred, but how they
are described, how they supposedly transpired, I
have a very different point of view in those.

Darden asked him for examples. Reichardt recalled a moment in the book when, at a restaurant, in front of Simpson,
Nicole mentioned a former lover.

"In that split second, O.J.'s charming face turned into a
profile of rage," Resnick wrote. "O.J.'s face twitched
uncontrollably. His body language was extremely aggressive.
Horrified, I watched as sweat poured down his face. The
veins in his neck bulged. His cheekbones bunched up,
twitching beneath his skin. He ground his teeth in rage and

308

hissed at me. 'Goddamned bitch! Why the fuck does she do this?' "

Then, as Faye's memoir had it, Simpson followed Resnick into the women's bathroom, smashing the door lock, ranting all the while. Back at the table, he was so out of control that she insisted on leaving. O.J. followed them outside, yelling at Nicole, "Get in the car, you fucking bitch, I'm taking you home!" Nicole refused, fearing personal harm. The argument attracted a passing police cruiser, and Simpson magically reverted to his friendly superstar persona.

> DARDEN: Now in the book, Faye describes Simpson forcing the door or kicking the door in to the women's room. Did you see that?
> REICHARDT: . . . I never heard about it until I read about it in the book.

Darden turned to O.J.'s murder threats. Reichardt had been an annoyed observer of the odd triangle of angry telephone calls.

> REICHARDT: Faye and O.J. would talk on the phone for hours. . . . It was a situation where Faye being on drugs, those conversations didn't make any sense. . . . after the conversation [Faye] said, well, he said this and this and this and this, and he said he's going to kill her. I tried to say, look, you know, people say that.
> DARDEN: Well, how were they talking?
> REICHARDT: They were not screaming, yelling, arguing. They were talking.
> DARDEN: So Faye didn't seem excited or upset during the telephone conversation?
> REICHARDT: Yeah . . . it wasn't so much that she sat down and grabbed me and said, "He's going to kill her! He said he's going to kill her." It was more like, "Oh, he said he's going to kill her." And I said, "Look, Faye, people say that." . . . It's got her concerned, but not upset.

DARDEN: . . . You told Barbara Walters the conversation was heated.

REICHARDT: Have you ever been around a drug addict that's high, a free-base person?

DARDEN: Well, I'm just asking you, was the conversation in a normal tone?

REICHARDT: It was a normal tone for Faye being high.

To TV audiences in conservative middle America, Christian Reichardt, with his shoulder-length blond hair and wire-rimmed glasses, might have looked more like a surfer than a chiropractor. To the prosecutors, he was easier to read: a disgruntled ex-boyfriend with an obvious allegiance to O.J. Simpson. But lengthy interviews with Nicole's friends had yielded other stories of abuse. In rough outline, Resnick's account checked out.

D.A.'s investigator Stephen Oppler learned from Kris Jenner that Faye Resnick might indeed have special insight into Nicole. Jenner had introduced them.

JENNER: O.J. had a tendency to have that wandering, roving eye. He was cheating on her a lot and she was always finding out. And so Nicole, as I saw her, was always saddened and sort of depressed. . . . She always had this cloud over her. . . . And a lot of people would assume, especially when they met Nicole, that she was aloof or snotty or stuck up or something. . . . And I think Faye was one of the few people that I introduced to Nicole who pegged it right off. She just said, "This girl's really sad." And I said, "Yes, she is."

And Jenner, while knowing few details, saw that the cloud contained real fear.

JENNER: In early '90 . . . I said, "Why don't you just leave him then? If you're not happy, leave." And she said, "If I left he'd kill me."

310

Maria Baur, married to Nicole's cousin Rolf, had worked at Rockingham as a housekeeper for four years in the mid-1980s. She told Darden she did not witness displays of Simpson's temper. She never saw bruises on Nicole. But she arrived at work one day to find Nicole walking outside, arms crossed as though she were cold, crying.

> BAUR: I asked her, "What's going on, Nicole? Can I help you with anything?" She said, "Oh, no, Maria, please don't ask. I don't want to get you involved."

Inside, Baur saw that family photographs had fallen down from the walls along the staircase. Broken glass was everywhere.

> DARDEN: Did she ever tell you that he had been hitting her?
> BAUR: She did tell me one time when she lived on Gretna Green. She was crying that morning, all upset because she was talking to her family. . . . And she told me that they were on O.J.'s side. They didn't believe all the stuff that he did to her.
> DARDEN: She told you what he had done to her?
> BAUR: Yes. . . . That day when he put her in the closet, in the wine closet there.
> DARDEN: What else did she tell you?
> BAUR: . . . He did pull her by the hair, he put her in the closet, you know.

Rolf Baur, Judy Brown's nephew, was also interviewed. After immigrating to the United States in 1964, he worked in an airplane parts factory. In 1980, Nicole offered him part-time work as a Rockingham groundskeeper. He stayed for three years, then ran one of Simpson's Pioneer Chicken franchises until it was torched during the 1992 riots. Like his wife the week before, he added a few pieces to the growing mosaic when he met with D.A. investigators Dana Thompson and Michael Stevens.

THOMPSON: Did you ever see Simpson use any drugs?

BAUR: Yeah.

THOMPSON: What kind of drugs?

BAUR: Cocaine.

THOMPSON: How did you know it was cocaine?

BAUR: I was taking it myself. . . . I got hooked at the factory that I worked in. I was on it for about three years . . . I just happened to be cleaning up in the yard in the back and a friend of his [Simpson's] came over. And he knew I was taking it and he wanted to know if I wanted some. So all three of us went down to the guest house. We sat down, and we did quite a few lines there.

THOMPSON: Did he ever mention it, or did it appear that Nicole knew about this?

BAUR: Yes, she knew about it. . . . I just stumbled into the office and I asked her if she had some stuff for me. . . .

THOMPSON: Stuff, meaning?

BAUR: Coke, if she can get ahold of some coke for me, because I was pretty strung out on that stuff.

THOMPSON: And what did she say?

BAUR: . . . She opened the drawer up and there was a rock of coke.

THOMPSON: What size?

BAUR: He [Simpson] screamed at her for giving me some because it was two thousand dollars' worth.

THOMPSON: . . . Were you there when he screamed at her about it?

BAUR: Yeah.

THOMPSON: . . . Did Nicole ever make comments to you about cocaine use?

BAUR: Yeah. . . . She didn't like it. He always goes berserk. . . .

THOMPSON: When was this?

BAUR: . . . You know, '83, '84, '85, somewhere around there.

THOMPSON: . . . Do you know if she was using cocaine at all?

BAUR: She used to, many years ago. . . . I'd say at
   least ten years ago.

Baur saw the knocked-down pictures and broken glass the
same day his wife did. But he saw no bruises, no beatings.
He saw something else:

BAUR: . . . She got beat up one time, and he [Lou
   Brown] took pictures. . . . It's stuck in my mind.
   But that's years and years ago.
THOMPSON: . . . Did you have a conversation with
   Nicole where she mentioned to you about her fear of
   knives?
BAUR: . . . Over the years there was many things that
   we always talked about. You know, my fear for
   snakes and her fear for knives.
THOMPSON: She'd always been afraid of knives?
BAUR: . . . Always been afraid of them. . . .
   Anybody with a knife, that just tears her up.
THOMPSON: Did O.J. know that was her big fear?
BAUR: Oh, yeah . . . because we were sitting in
   conversations many times.
THOMPSON: . . . Did he say anything?
BAUR: No, never made any comments about it.
STEVENS: Did you ever see him tease her about it, as
   far as actually pulling out a knife or anything like
   that?
BAUR: No, never.

Nicole was particularly incensed, Resnick wrote, when
Simpson, angry at apparently being rejected, wrote to her on
June 6 that she could no longer claim Rockingham as her
legal residence. This meant that Nicole couldn't claim the
Bundy condominium as tax-deductible investment property.
At the June 12 recital, according to Resnick, Nicole was so
angry that she refused to let Simpson sit with her family. His
crude economic pressure showed he had no interest in his
children's welfare, she said.

Resnick was at Exodus, a residential drug rehab, on June

12. That evening, she talked to Nicole on the phone. She wrote, "After the recital, Nicole told me O.J. again tried to approach her while she was standing with the family as they congratulated Sydney on her special day.

" 'What did he say, Nic?'

" 'I don't know. Before he could say much of anything, I told him, Fuck off! Get away from us! Get out of my life. You're not welcome with this family anymore.' "

Prosecutors noticed that Resnick didn't mention this exchange during their interview with her.

CLARK: When was the last time you spoke to her?
RESNICK: At 9 o'clock that night.
CLARK: And what did she tell you?
RESNICK:. . . She said that he wanted to sit with her or go to dinner and she told him absolutely no.

That was all Resnick said.

In their search for other accounts confirming Resnick's, the prosecutors interviewed Nicole's friend Candace Garvey, who had been standing next to Nicole right after the recital. Stephen Oppler asked her about the confrontation:

OPPLER: I remember somewhere in the book it says that Nicole told O.J., was it that night, that it was definitely over. . . . I can't find the exact passage I was talking about, but you mentioned something off tape, that there was a conversation in there where Nicole basically told O.J. after the recital to get lost.
GARVEY: Mmnh-mmnh.
OPPLER: She says F-off?
GARVEY: Mmnh-mmnh.
OPPLER: And you said you saw her right after that conversation?
GARVEY: Mmnh-mmnh.
OPPLER: And you said that she was . . . ?
GARVEY: As happy as I've ever seen her.
OPPLER: Did you know that she had left him then?

314

GARVEY: No, because . . . . my husband said, let's go,
we're leaving.
OPPLER: So you didn't know that conversation took
place until afterwards?
GARVEY: No, I didn't. I didn't know until I just read it.
OPPLER: Until you just read it?
GARVEY: Last night.

All Oppler can do is move on.

OPPLER: Were they [Faye and Nicole] pretty close?
They were best friends then at the end, as far as you
know.
GARVEY: You know what? I never saw them together
really. I don't know their relationship. I'm sure they
were very close. Faye is a very warm and infectious
person. . . . I'm sure she can be a very good
friend. . . . And I think she had a lot to say for this
case, but she's mixed some non-truths with the
truth. . . . I think most of it is true. But I think they're
going to have a problem with this non-truth stuff.

18

ON OCTOBER 23 MORE DNA TEST RESULTS CAME IN. THE
DOJ had now done a D1S80 test, which showed that the
Rockingham glove possessed a mixture of O.J.'s, Nicole's,
and Ron Goldman's blood.* The discouraging results of-

---

*A D1S80 test is a PCR-based test that measures the genetic marker
known as D1S80 on the DNA strand.

fered a new strategic possibility. The scientific validity of DNA testing could be challenged in a so-called Kelly-Frye hearing.* In California, scientific evidence is admissible only when the science is widely recognized by the scientific community. DNA testing was still somewhat new to criminal courts in the western United States. Gerry Uelmen's research, in fact, had turned up cases from this year, 1994, in which a few California judges rejected some DNA results.

Some of the team thought a Kelly-Frye hearing might be their best next step; however Ed Blake Henry Lee, and Michael Baden thought the idea was ridiculous. They accepted DNA testing fully and they assumed California courts would, too. But Alan Dershowitz and Gerry Uelmen argued that the challenge might be crucial if they ever had to appeal this jury's verdict. They could raise the issue on appeal only if it became part of the record now. Barry Scheck told Shapiro and Cochran to plan on an extended hearing, perhaps as long as four weeks. They gave him the go-ahead.

By then, a jury would probably be seated. Would Ito let the jury wait it out while they argued this complex issue? The target date for the hearing was late December.

In the last week of October, Kardashian drives Shapiro home a few times. It usually means he'll hear the latest theories of guilt.

"They found Nicole's blood on the heel print," Shapiro announces. To Bob this is awful news. DNA tests now show Nicole's blood in the partial heel impression on the Bronco carpet. And her blood is on the Rockingham glove.

Shapiro asks Kardashian, "How would that get there?" Planting drops of blood is one thing. Manufacturing a heel print is vastly more complex, he says.

---

*The name comes from two court cases. In *Frye v. The United States*, the court ruled against admitting lie detector tests because of widespread scientific mistrust. Afterward, in federal courts, the scientific credibility of any technical procedure became known as the Frye test. *People v. Kelly* was the California precedent on the same issue.

"You've been driving this car for a year," Shapiro continues. "Your daughter drives it. Your dog rides in this car. And I bet if we went through your car carefully, we would not find blood on your carpet. So how did that blood get in the Bronco?"

Once these conversations had infuriated Kardashian. Now they simply depress him. He's so exhausted he doesn't bother to object when Shapiro asks him to relay this information to O.J., to convince him to plea-bargain. For a moment Bob thinks Shapiro must know what he's talking about. After all, he has experience in these things. Then he snaps back abruptly. Whatever his private worries, he believes O.J. is entitled to his day in court. Simpson has made it clear he wants *defense* attorneys, not deal-making attorneys.

On Thursday, October 27, deputies found a yellow high-lighting marker in O.J.'s cell. The deputies called it contraband. Now O.J. will endure three days without telephone or television, starting this weekend. Losing the TV is bad enough. Taking O.J.'s telephone privileges away is worse, Kardashian thinks. The athlete calls team members, friends, and family nonstop, right up to the jail's cutoff hour every night.

But nothing hurts O.J. as much as not being able to call Justin and Sydney. It is Halloween weekend. Get me out by Halloween so I can trick-or-treat with my kids, Simpson has clamored for months. Weekly he calls his kids at the Browns' home in Dana Point.

Justin tells him he'll be a Power Ranger. Simpson explains that he can't come along.

"Daddy, why can't you come home and do your police work here? Why are you gone so much?"

"I'm looking for whoever did this horrible thing to Mommy," he repeats.

"But why do you have to do it there?" the boy asks again.

Simpson knows that kids at school have told Sydney, perhaps even Justin, that he is a murderer. He is deeply depressed when Kardashian visits.

317

"A few years ago, who wouldn't have traded their life to be O.J. Simpson?" he laments. Kardashian can see the monologue starting. "Who'd think that someday I'd be known by everyone at this jail?"

Kardashian can't think of a comforting answer. Easier to go along with the day's script. "Yeah, me, too. Who'd think I'd even know my way here, let alone have all sorts of jailers and inmates call me by name?"

Simpson warms to the old theme. "It's so mind-boggling. When you think how much my life has changed in such a short time. . . ." He's in gear now. "There is no way I did this. I can't believe they aren't looking for anybody else."

On Thursday, October 27, Kardashian said to Shawn Chapman: "Put this guy on the material witness list. He has to see O.J. in the next couple of days."

"Who's Lawrence Schiller? I've never heard of him."

"He lived across the street from O.J. for years. But this is about something else. He's going to make some money for us."

Kardashian was having no luck getting loans on Rockingham or the New York condo. Simpson's cash was dwindling fast. After consulting with Simpson, Kardashian and Taft cut everybody's salary by half. Not permanently; the other half was "deferred." Shapiro took the biggest cut, agreeing to drop from $100,000 a month to $50,000.

At the end of October, Shapiro called McKenna and McNally into his office, where Skip Taft was waiting. He asked if they could take a pay cut. McNally asked how much. Taft was vague, but McNally thought he was hearing as much as 80 percent. McKenna said he'd be willing.

"I can't," McNally said.

He was committed to other cases and already behind schedule. Better to bow out of this one. They asked how long it would take to finish the time-line chart. He figured about a week.

Something else: The defense needed an affidavit from

McNally supporting the interview he and Pavelic did with Rosa Lopez. They wanted that right away.

"You owe me money," McNally reminded them. He was tempted to offer a blunt quid pro quo: You want your affidavit? Pay me. In the end, he didn't. You can't get blood out of a stone, he decided. Pavelic, Harris, and others took their cuts and stayed. McNally would be gone by November 1.

On Sunday, October 30, Shapiro threw a Halloween party at Chasens for one of his wife's charities. He seemed to enjoy the spotlight. Earlier he'd let the financier Marvin Davis list him as an item to be raffled off at Davis's annual Carousel Ball. "Win a Lunch with Robert Shapiro," the program said. That Friday morning at court, some inventive cameramen passed out rubber masks of Shapiro's face, and a dozen "Shapiros" lined the courthouse steps as he walked in. Novelty stores were doing a brisk business in masks of all the major players in the case.

The multiple Shapiros got a nice sound bite. "This, I think, is fabulous," the real Shapiro smilingly told the cameras. "Fabulous!" He donned one of the masks himself as he walked through a metal detector.

"He'll have lots to say," Kardashian tells Larry Schiller on Halloween as they drive downtown to see O.J. Skip Taft is at the wheel.

"The problem will be getting him to stop," Bob continues. That would be perfect, Schiller thinks, that's where the story is.

Kardashian assumes major issues will be settled tonight. Simpson has to decide if a book should be published based on the more than 300,000 letters he's received. If so, what kind of book? What would Simpson say? How good a book could be done quickly? How would publishing now affect the trial?

When he met Simpson, Schiller tried to list his credentials, the books published, prizes won. He needn't have bothered. Simpson started his tale of woe immediately.

The two men connected easily. O.J. had a new audience; Schiller had Simpson. Their book would be Simpson's first substantial statement since his arrest. Schiller knew within minutes that it would achieve its purpose for the defense: It would sell.

Kardashian and Schiller knew each other through their ex-wives. Bob had once asked Larry to help him make a staggeringly expensive birthday video for Kris's friends: Kris and some of her friends singing "I love my friends" to the melody of Randy Newman's "I Love L.A." from locations all over the city. Schiller had dropped by Simpson's office to tape him singing part of the song. Before it was done, the video cost $18,000. Kardashian never blinked. No problem to spend that much on a whimsical gift.

Simpson didn't remember Schiller. That didn't matter. They talked for two hours without pause.

"I need ten more hours with him to do this book," Schiller told Bob afterward.

"No problem," Bob assured him. "You're a material witness now."

TO:	Robert Shapiro, Johnnie Cochran
FROM:	William G. Pavelic
SUBJECT:	Identification of Bloody Shoeprints
DATE:	November 2, 1994

I am sending you a copy of a recent N.Y. article that quotes a high ranking source in the Los Angeles Police Department as saying that until recently, investigators thought that the bloody shoeprints leading from the bodies of Nicole Brown Simpson and Ronald Goldman were made by sneakers. . . . These would have been virtually impossible to identify, given the numbers of sneakers in circulation.

However, a crime-lab breakthrough in Los Angeles has identified the shoe prints as coming from a brand of loafers selling for more than $300.00 a pair.

Detectives are interviewing sales staff in the hundred or so L.A. area stores that carry the brand. They are also searching the sales records of such stores nationwide.

19

By November 2 the jury pool had been narrowed down to forty-two people. The peremptory-challenge round began that day with opening statements from each side and the questioning of individual jurors. The next day prosecution and defense could each dismiss as many as twenty jurors without explanation.

Johnnie Cochran began for the defense. "I want all of you to look at Mr. Simpson as he sits there. Mr. Simpson is cloaked in the presumption of innocence."

Johnnie scanned the dwindling group of potential jurors, keeping in mind Jo-Ellan Dimitrius's perfect black female juror.

"It is not because he is O.J. Simpson," he continued. "It is because every accused in every case since the Magna Carta is cloaked with that presumption of innocence."

In Shapiro's conference room the day before, the team's mood was almost triumphant. There was a solid core of middle-aged black women in the pool. Cochran had fought Shapiro's insistence on a year's delay. "Look at these jurors," Johnnie had protested. "This is the best group we're ever going to get. We need to take these people right now."

Jo-Ellan agreed: an excellent group. She had ranked them from 1 to 42. Team members had studied the list, arguing tactics and strategy, most of the previous day. For starters, they agreed to convince the jury: We don't want sequestration. We trust you.

"The decision hasn't been made yet, I hope, with regard to sequestration," Cochran told them now. "Some of us are opposed to that. But if in fact some of you are sequestered . . . I won't tell you who to be mad at, but it won't be us. I want to make it clear: We don't want you sequestered.''

Johnnie insisted on discussing the racial issues with the jury. "Our position is nobody wants to introduce race into anything," he said. "But if you live in America one would be foolhardy not to mention that there are times that race plays a role. . . . Can you, a diverse group, come together, get along, and go about this task not along racial lines, and, based upon the evidence, render a decision? Can you do that?''

Cochran waits. The pool answers yes. Nods. Spoken words.

"And so that the defendant's race will not count for him or against him. Do I have your assurance on that?''

Another collective yes. This time more quickly.

"So that the fact that Mr. Simpson, who is an African-American, is married to a Caucasian will not be held against him? Because anybody who has such a view shouldn't be on this jury.''

Kardashian recalled Jo-Ellan's discovery: The black women hated Nicole, not O.J.

"The prosecutors always say 'the defendant,' " he continued. "They never refer to Mr. O.J. Simpson. That is Mr. O.J. Simpson over there, and we are going to remind you, a human being. He is part of the people. . . . On the other hand, they always refer to the victims as Nicole and Ron, attempting to personalize them. So we understand that. It is not subliminal. We didn't fall off a truck and neither did you.''

Johnnie tells the jury how to think about prosecution witnesses.

"Will you all be willing to listen to the evidence and look at the people who knew and who know O.J. Simpson? Would you agree with me that the people who know O.J. Simpson will be in a much better position to tell you about him than the prosecutors here who never met him before this case? Would you agree with me on that?''

The jurors don't answer.

Then Bob Shapiro questions the jurors individually.

"Twelve of you," he started, "will have the awesome responsibility of sitting on perhaps the most intensely watched case in the history of criminal justice."

Boilerplate. The usual rhetoric. But Shapiro unearthed a wrong-headed juror.

"What do you expect of Mr. O.J. Simpson in this case?" he asked a man on the panel.

"His attorneys would be the one [*sic*] to, you know, prove his innocence."

"Is there anyone else who agrees with that statement?"

No one agreed. Point made.

Shapiro then moved to a black woman very high on Jo-Ellan's list, juror number 230. She is divorced, fifty years old, and works for Los Angeles County administering vendor and collection agency contracts. Juror 230 is small and smartly dressed. She has an obvious presence. He asks her solid but easy questions:

"Are you able to come to the conclusion that a police officer is held to the same standard as other witnesses?"

"Yes."

"Would you have any problem concluding that a witness that happened to be a police officer could in fact not be telling the truth?"

"No, I have no problem."

He moves on quickly so the prosecution won't notice his interest.

Juror 19 is a less obvious possibility. The thirty-two-year-old Latino man drives a Pepsi-Cola truck. He's divorced, with a three-year-old son. Not black and, of course, not female. But he teaches martial arts. In fact, he was a member of the U.S. tae kwon do Olympic team.

"Juror Number 19, we are all governed by the same canons of ethics and the same rules of court, you understand that?"

"Yes."

"And therefore, you would not think that a lawyer for the

prosecution knows more than a lawyer for the defense in this case?''

"No, sir.''

Juror 98, a fifty-two-year-old black female postal worker with a hard, serious face, is also near the top of Jo-Ellan's ranking. Her answers on the questionnaire are subtly pro-O.J. Now he asks: Is she willing to make the sacrifices sequestration might involve? "It is not something that I would like to do, but it is something that I will do.''

"And why will you do it?''

"I know in my heart I'm fair and I would like to listen to the evidence and do the best I can.''

"Is it also something that you would consider of being a good citizen and putting something back into the community?''

She hesitates a moment. "Well, I could think of a lot of ways to put things back into the community?''

"Other than this?''

"Other than this.''

Then it was Marcia Clark's turn: "All of us, every single one of us, I think, here have very good impressions of the defendant. We've all seen *Naked Gun*. He made us laugh. Good guy on TV, sports commentator. We've had him referred to as the All-American Hero, the clean-cut image of the American Man. . . .

"This is not a popular case for the prosecution to bring. Wouldn't you agree? Wouldn't you *all* agree? This is not a fun place for me to be. . . . Do you think that the people in this case are going to have a pretty rough time proving to you that such a fine person committed such a terrible crime? Juror 98, what do you think?''

Clark has zeroed in on the postal clerk.

"I'll say it like this. You might say it's tough, but I would say it would be tough in any case, whether it be him or anyone else, to say that someone had committed a crime, to present that case.''

Clark moves on to her broad theme: "The rules don't

change if it's Mr. O.J. Simpson, if it's Mr. Jones, if it's Mr. Gonzalez. . . . Fair is fair for everyone.''

Clark mentions one of her office's high-profile defeats: the mostly white Simi Valley jury's acquittal of four white policemen accused of beating African-American Rodney King.

"Do you think that had something to do with the fact that they were being tried in a community and by a jury that was all white, that it was tried in a community where a lot of police officers lived? Juror 1040?''

"I think it probably did, probably.''

"Juror 305, what do you think?''

"Yes, I do.''

"More proof we cannot go on these kinds of issues,'' Clark says. "Race is not a reason to convict. Race is not a reason to acquit.''

Then a slap at the defense theories: "Dope dealers did it. A Colombian cartel did it. The Mafia did it. Three white burglars did it. I've even heard one that said Ron and Nicole are not dead.''

Clark was on a roll.

"Yeah. Yeah. That's out there. It's all out there. The next thing is going to be space aliens did it.''

After lunch, Bob Shapiro serves notice again that the defense will grant the prosecution no leeway.

"We want to voice an objection to the unprofessional conduct before the jury in saying, 'We all saw the tape at Simi Valley and we know how unjust the verdict was.' It is against the canons of ethics for a prosecutor or any [other] person to comment to a potential juror on the outcome of another case. And to do it in this way was beyond professional and warrants severe sanctions.''

"What do you suggest?'' Ito asks.

"Additional peremptories for the defense.''

The judge tables the issue. He'll think about it. The team has sent a message that the defense will seek out any advantage, small or large. The privilege of excusing more jurors than the prosecution can is serious business.

* * *

Bill Hodgman, tall and calm, takes over the questioning. He starts with Juror 230, the L.A. County office worker. She's a defense favorite who also sounds good to prosecutors.

"We have talked quite a bit about how you as a juror are to deal with information which comes from outside this courtroom. . . . How would you resolve that conflict?"

"I wouldn't look outside. I'd stay with the evidence. I'm to deal with whatever is presented to me in this courtroom from that witness stand, period. Point-blank."

A perfect juror. The defense attorneys hide their enthusiasm.

November 3, 1994. Twelve jurors will be picked today.

"The prosecution will exercise the first peremptory challenge," Ito explains. "I will allow any reasonable amount of time in between challenges that you wish to take to consult."

Marcia Clark starts. "The people thank and excuse Juror number 51."

The defense team huddles. They have two major options. They can match the prosecutors challenge for challenge. If Clark and Hodgman excuse too many black jurors, they can mount a Wheeler challenge charging that the state is purging the jury of African-Americans.* Or they can sit tight. Right now, the defense has a solid number of people they like. They sit tight.

Shapiro rises. "Your Honor, we believe we have a fair and impartial jury and we will accept the jury as presently constituted."

Without hesitation, Hodgman sends another juror home.

Another defense huddle. Cochran, Douglas, and Chapman already have a grudging respect for Clark and Hodgman. Prosecutors usually worry about getting slammed with a Wheeler challenge. If the challenge succeeds, it means the prosecution made obvious blunders. That can damage careers.

For a week the defense has tried to scare the prosecution,

---

*A Wheeler challenge is named after the precedent-setting 1978 case *People v. Wheeler*, where the state singled out and removed potential jurors based on race.

protesting to the press that Clark and Hodgman were interrogating blacks differently. "An insidious effort to try to get black jurors removed for cause because they are black," Shapiro said, "because they have black heroes and O.J. Simpson is one of them."

Clark and Hodgman weren't fazed then and they aren't now. They are excusing plenty of black jurors. The team decides again to take what they have.

Johnnie rises. "Your Honor, the defense will again accept the jury as presently constituted."

Hodgman takes no notice. He excuses Juror 1217.

The defense then excuses Juror 352.

The prosecutors ask for a moment. Carl Douglas is dumbfounded when he sees they are consulting with David Wooden, their black law clerk. Until this morning, Wooden sat by the railing and ran errands for them. Shawn Chapman is also astonished. The D.A.'s official jury consultant, Don Vinson, hasn't been seen in weeks. Wooden is only a clerk, but suddenly he's their expert on African-American jurors.

The prosecutors bounce Juror 1055.

Shawn Chapman can feel the tension rising as the team decides to settle again. Shapiro stands. "Thank you, Your Honor. We'll accept the jury as presently constituted."

Kardashian notes that Simpson is watching closely. O.J. has his favorites on the jury. He's a changed man. For months he had told Kardashian the jury's color didn't matter. "I don't see race," he insisted. "Race is not an issue."

Then O.J. finally listened to Johnnie and Jo-Ellan, read her computer printouts, saw that whites and blacks reacted very differently to him. Now he watched the jury panel closely.

"I need black jurors," he said to Kardashian before court that morning. "I came into this color-blind. I thought everybody was the same. I realize I need them. It's sad."

Hodgman quickly removes another juror. Then Johnnie excuses one. After lunch, Hodgman removes one more. After a short huddle, Shapiro sends yet another juror home.

Bill Hodgman rises. "The people will accept the jury as presently constituted."

Everything stops. Now the prosecution is settling.

The defense team huddles for real now. Shawn feels the beginning of a headache. Team members kneel on the floor to get closer to the table, whispering so they can't be overheard. Reporters watch, their pens motionless over notebooks. Even the jury pool stares. Chapman can hear the clock ticking.

"We'll be in great shape if we can get four blacks," Johnnie had always said. Now they have six. More black jurors than we ever dreamed of, Shawn says. Jo-Ellan agrees.

But Cochran isn't satisfied. "We've got to kick off this one," he says, pointing at Jo-Ellan's chart. Nobody can believe he wants to take the risk. If Cochran excuses a juror, that will give the prosecutors another shot. They could lose a black juror over it. But Cochran is leading now.

He rises. "Defense will ask the court to thank and excuse juror number 1187."

Sure enough, Marcia Clark takes out Juror 1164. Quickly, Shapiro excuses another.

Again, the prosecution accepts the jury.

This last exchange has kept things reasonably even. Time to quit? Cochran raises his head and checks the group waiting outside the jury box. Throughout the day, deputies have been bringing potential jurors into the courtroom well before their turn to be questioned. That way, as jurors are dismissed, the next is seated quickly. Now Cochran sees that the jurors-in-waiting are mostly black.

The defense already has jurors they never expected to keep. Women from the top of Jo-Ellan's list. To lose them now would be devastating. But Johnnie wants to roll the dice again.

"Defense will ask the court to thank and excuse juror number 1040." This was the person who agreed with Clark that the Rodney King verdict was racially influenced. Some team members liked her; Johnnie didn't.

Clark and Hodgman huddle awhile, then accept the new panel.

The team can hardly contain itself. The prosecutors have now accepted four juries, the latest with seven blacks. "We have seven!'' Shawn is jubilant. But Cochran won't stop. He points to a female juror on the computer sheet. ''Fuck it,'' he growls, ''I'm getting that lady off!''

''Johnnie, we have to accept,'' Carl urges. ''This is better than we ever imagined!''

Everyone is scared now.

''Just calm down,'' Shapiro commands. ''We are not in a rush.'' He turns to the judge. ''May we have a few moments, Your Honor?'' He asks Jo-Ellan for her opinion. She is noncommittal. Cochran wins. Luck, be a lady tonight. Preferably an African-American lady.

Cochran sends juror number 209 home.

Marcia Clark excuses another juror. Lawyers on both sides are rubbing their necks now, massaging aching temples.

Shapiro rises and knocks out number 799. The prosecutors excuse another.

Bill Hodgman rises. ''Your Honor, the people accept the panel as presently constituted.''

But Shapiro takes out one more, number 1179. He does this one ''reluctantly, based on correspondence.'' The juror had asked to be excused for hardship.

''All right, 1179, thanks a lot.'' Judge Ito's smile is wearing thin. ''We were glad to have you.''

A black woman steps in to take the empty seat.

Marcia Clark rises. ''Your Honor, the people accept the jury as presently constituted.''

Now it's time to stop. Eight black jurors. Time to pocket the dice. They look at the men and women in the jury box. Is this it? Johnnie asks the team, ''Do you guys all agree that this is who we should accept?'' They agree.

Shapiro and Cochran both stand, vying for the moment. ''Your Honor,'' Shapiro says, ''we jointly accept the jury.'' Cochran smiles, ''We jointly do it, too, Your Honor.''

Judge Ito beams. ''The O.J. Simpson jury,'' he announces. Then he swears them in.

Cochran turns to Douglas and Chapman with a wide grin. ''You guys wanted me to give up when we had six.'' He pokes them again. ''You guys were scared.''

Today Johnnie Cochran has taken control of the case.

Even the feisty Douglas agrees. "You're right, Johnnie. We were ready to wimp out with six. You kept going. And we got eight." Now the challenge was to keep them. Carl knew that would not be easy.

Walking back to the holding cell, Simpson, too, was excited. "If this jury convicts me," he joked to Douglas, "maybe I did do it."

20

THAT EVENING, NOVEMBER 3, DR. BERNARD YUDOWITZ, who held several distinguished positions in forensic psychiatry, sat in the attorneys' room at the L.A. County Jail while O.J. described his father's last hours.

Simpson's face was wet with tears; his voice broke. The psychiatrist listened as O.J. told of impulsively traveling to San Francisco to see his father one day in 1986, somehow knowing he had to. They'd never had an easy relationship. His father had separated from his mother when O.J. was a child. Unable that day to find his dad at home, he called Nicole in Los Angeles to learn that the older man, ill with cancer, had been hospitalized again. O.J. found him talkative and comfortable. They joked about the son's showing up just in time, as in those Hertz commercials where he was forever almost late. They chatted for ten minutes or so.

Then, knowing that Nicole was worried, Simpson left to telephone her. His sister found him in the hospital hallway. "Come quickly!" she called. "I ran back into the room, and my dad was dead." Simpson had been gone only a minute.

Dr. Yudowitz's professional alarm systems were quiet. It

was hardly unusual for a man to cry over the death of his father. Throughout their visit, he was listening for Simpson's capacity for empathy. How deeply, at unconscious levels, is he involved with others?

Yudowitz, hired by the defense to evaluate Simpson, asked questions, considered O.J.'s reactions, and tried to form a clinical portrait. In his considerable experience, every murderer fit one of several psychological categories. Some were icy psychopaths devoid of all feeling for others; others were jealous husbands or inept stickup men who killed in moments of rage or confusion. Yudowitz had evaluated more than five hundred people convicted of capital offenses in his career as director of psychiatry for the Department of Corrections in Massachusetts and medical director at Bridgewater State Hospital for the criminally insane, also in Massachusetts.

If Simpson was a killer, he expected to see it.

But now O.J. said something that utterly baffled him.

"I don't understand why God gave me those five minutes with my dad," Simpson sobbed, "and didn't give me a second with Nicole."

Without missing a beat, Simpson had moved from his father's deathbed to his absence from Nicole's last moments.

"It hurts so much about Nicole! I don't know why God didn't give me any time with her! There was so much we needed to resolve. If I only had a few minutes."

Yudowitz was perplexed. Innocent or guilty, the man evaded the usual categories as adroitly as he'd once ducked tacklers. Simpson had no obvious mental illness. Showed no sign of the constant, inappropriate aggression that marks criminal insanity. Yudowitz knew of no clinical history of sadism, voyeurism, or loss of control. On the contrary, Simpson's careers in football and sportscasting required that he have his wits about him at all times.

He did not appear to be a psychopath, uninvolved with other human beings. To the psychopath, people are insects, objects. Swat them. Step on them. Dispose of them if they're irritating. Yudowitz knew that Simpson supported charitable causes, had a wide network of friendships, loved women. Psychopaths were almost always misfits. Healthy people usually found them frightening. But even in jail, even through a glass partition, Simpson's personality radiated warmth, intensity, involvement.

Of course, there were so-called "secondary" killers. Yudowitz knew that about 80 percent of all murders are spontaneous, dictated by circumstances. An alarm goes off, and a bank robber shoots someone. A husband, discovering his wife in bed with her lover, lashes out and kills.

If Simpson fit any category, it was that of the good citizen living a sensible life who murders in momentary rage or passion. Unconsciously, he commits an act of violent desperation against himself. By killing, he's given up, ended the life he lived up to that moment.

The puzzle for Yudowitz was that O.J. Simpson didn't act like a man who had written himself off. His compulsion to plead his innocence was intense. At first, the psychiatrist couldn't stop him long enough to interject questions. Simpson groped desperately for an understanding of what had happened to him. The doctor was surprised that the client wasn't accused of a crime of passion, second-degree murder. The charge here was murder in the first degree, premeditated murder.

Yudowitz sat before the glass with the text of Simpson's recorded statement to police. It was especially important for him to reconstruct O.J.'s frame of mind before the murders.

When Simpson moved so quickly from his father's death to Nicole's, sobbing that he had not had a minute, even a second, with her before the end, Yudowitz had no doubt that he felt an extraordinarily intense connection to his ex-wife. The relationship had been deeply passionate, he decided. He was struck by O.J.'s repeated praise for Nicole as the mother of their children. Simpson insisted he loved his kids, but knew she was the better parent. If his children mattered so much to him, Yudowitz wondered, how could he destroy the most important person in their lives?

He had, of course, reviewed Simpson's history of battering, but it did not measure up to that of the killers he knew. In seventeen years of stormy marriage, O.J. and Nicole had resolved any number of conflicts peacefully. Yes, there were incidents of violence, but there was not, by the doctor's standards, a pattern. The theory that domestic violence led to murder in this case made no sense to him. Simpson talked constantly of his frustration when conflicts weren't resolved. As he did, Yudowitz was reminded once again of his sorrow that he lacked those final moments with Nicole. No killer he'd ever met regretted not having the chance to set things straight with his victim.

Alone in the taxicab riding back to his hotel after his final visit, Yudowitz concluded that Simpson fit none of the profiles—with one possible exception.

Fewer than 1 percent of murderers are psychologically classified as atypical. In these cases, circumstances trigger an out-of-character response in a normal person. The tragedy happens in a flash. Until the actual moment, the killer assumes himself incapable of murder. Ever. Then, for reasons the murderer himself never understands, he kills.

Once the victim is dead, the situation is so horrifying to the killer, so inconsistent with his entire personality and history, that he refuses—unconsciously—to admit it occurred.

The killer enters a deep state of denial. In reality he has done something antithetical to his personality and his values. This *could not* happen, says the unconscious. Ergo, it *did not* happen.

Yudowitz was convinced that Simpson was no murderer, at least psychologically. But the slender possibility that Simpson was atypical troubled him. He knew that these killers are so horrified by their act that they meticulously clean up evidence of the crime. Quite unconsciously, they scrub away blood, clean their fingernails, shampoo their hair. They do everything possible to remove evidence from their person. "Why is this on my hands? How could—this isn't—let's get rid of it." They want nothing around to trigger memories of what they have done. Not because they are trying to evade the police; such consequences never enter their minds. They simply cannot bear any reminder of the evil they believe they could not possibly have committed.

In this trancelike state they sometimes destroyed evidence so effectively they left police no trail to follow. He knew of cases where killers had run from the scene in a frenzy, throwing away weapons and incriminating clothing helter-skelter. The objects were never found. The killer himself had no idea of their location. Detectives were lucky to solve such cases.

But Yudowitz knew of the blood evidence already in hand. He considered Ron Goldman's blood in the Bronco particularly incriminating. He knew that Lee Bailey, who had called him, felt the blood evidence raised questions. That was why Yudowitz was here. If given the opportunity, he had to concentrate on the possibility that they had an atypical murder here. Three sessions with Mr. Simpson were only a beginning. If the defense wanted him to continue, it would be a complex inquiry.

PART FOUR

TFC

1

COWLINGS WON'T BE PROSECUTED, D.A. DECIDES

Al Cowlings, O.J. Simpson's best friend who was at the wheel during the famous low-speed pursuit preceding the football great's arrest, will not be prosecuted for his role in the flight, the Los Angeles County district attorney's office announced Monday.

. . . One of the prosecutors handling [the Cowlings case], Christopher A. Darden, will shift to the Simpson case. . . . Darden, 38, is considered one of the office's most highly regarded prosecutors: He has taken 19 homicide cases to juries and has handled a number of delicate police investigations.

—Jim Newton, Los Angeles Times, November 8, 1994

THE PRESSROOM FOR THE COURTHOUSE IS ON THE EIGHteenth floor, near Gil Garcetti's office. Chris Darden dropped in regularly.

Most reporters thought him slightly odd. You never quite knew why he talked to you, or what he was driving at. He had a disconcerting habit of lapsing into silence in the middle of a conversation. He wasn't angry or upset; he was letting the wheels turn, just thinking. The peculiar thing was that he slipped into these silences while maintaining eye contact.

Though Darden was a bit odd, he was no flake. He had specialized for years in prosecuting corrupt cops and this had earned him a lot of respect. No one questioned his integrity.

Some reporters felt Darden complained too much. When things didn't go his way, he pouted. No other word for it. But, on balance, most reporters on the eighteenth floor liked him.

Darden's arrival in the Simpson case surprised the press. His involvement with the Al Cowlings grand jury argued against his joining the team. Cowlings was a separate prosecution. But reporters had wondered aloud from the beginning whether A.C. had a role in the double murder, perhaps as cleanup man. They assumed he would be charged with something—perhaps harboring a fugitive or aiding flight. Darden couldn't be involved in both cases.

Equally important, the Cowlings grand jury was clearly a fishing expedition for the Simpson prosecutors. Gil Garcetti had virtually admitted that when he said that the grand jury was meeting "for investigatory purposes" rather than to seek an indictment. Garcetti insisted that Darden's addition to the Simpson team didn't breach the so-called wall of separation between the two cases. "That wall is inviolate," he stated at a press conference.

On Tuesday morning, November 8, Darden was sitting quietly at the prosecution table for the first time. The Associated Press reported that Darden's race was now obviously a factor in the case.

From the defense table, Carl Douglas had a view of Darden at the prosecutors' table backed by the mostly black jury. We have black jurors, he told himself. So we get a black D.A. Publicly, Darden sat quietly. Privately, when only the defense could hear, he indulged in courtroom trash talk: I'm gonna kick O.J.'s ass. He's guilty as hell, Darden said on his first day in court.

Johnnie Cochran was shocked. His staff had expected to work comfortably with Darden. Johnnie's firm made much of its money filing civil suits against the same corrupt cops whom Darden prosecuted. More than once, Darden had referred cases to them. As a D.A., Darden was limited because the system fought him hard when a bad cop turned up. But everyone in Cochran's firm respected him for his work. Besides, there was an unspoken kinship among

338

African-American lawyers. Johnnie was a kind of father figure to young black attorneys all over town and had been a prosecutor himself. He took mutual respect between Darden and his team for granted.

Within days, Darden's trash talk disillusioned Cochran and Douglas and hardened them. Why was he doing this? Okay, it's bravado. A black thing. But this was extreme.

No one in the press knew the contents of the sealed motion filed on November 14. But they assumed that Johnnie Cochran wanted Chris Darden off the case.

Darden's involvement with the Cowlings grand jury was the stated reason. But the day before, Cochran had telegraphed that race was the real issue. "All of a sudden he shows up here," Cochran said in a press conference. "Why is that, now that we've got eight African-Americans as jurors? Why now?" Johnnie kept it diplomatic. "Christopher Darden is a fine lawyer," he added, "but I don't think he should be on this case."

A black lawyer moving to recuse a black prosecutor? No one had seen *that* before!

With the press, Johnnie raised questions about Darden's access to privileged information from the Cowlings grand jury. But no one doubted that this was really about skin color. The defense team wasn't about to let a black prosecutor divide the jurors' loyalties. To black jurors, Cochran was a hero. His carriage, his manner, his oratory, his expensive suits—all inspired pride. Chris Darden, impressive in his own way, might steal Johnnie's thunder.

A.C. had been talking to O.J. on the phone for all these months, but he couldn't watch the trial on TV. It was too painful. The newspapers and the nightly news confused him. All those experts, so much talk. When A.C. didn't understand what was happening in court he talked to his own attorney, Don Re, and soon they became friends. A.C. had his own case to worry about, so he started learning the law. Don Re explained the court procedures to Cowlings. Showed him that Simpson would get a fair shake, a fair trial.

The first time he visited O.J. in jail, A.C. knew it would create a media circus. The press would ask him what had happened in the Bronco.

Cowlings had wanted to see Simpson for months, but, having been arrested himself after the Bronco chase, he had been in danger of being charged with aiding and abetting Simpson's flight. Keep a low profile, his lawyer advised. Let this blow over. Now it had, and he couldn't wait to see O.J. A.C. was excited as he walked the gauntlet of cameras and microphones outside the jail.

Inside the visiting room, A.C. sat waiting for his friend. When O.J. came in with shackles on his ankles and wrists, a chill went through Cowlings's body.

Juice sat down and smiled. A.C. was on the edge of falling apart, but kept it together for as long as he could. They didn't say much, just small talk, smiles on their faces, tears in their eyes. This was a nightmare. And neither of them could say when it would end.

TO:	Robert Shapiro
	Johnnie Cochran
FROM:	William G. Pavelic
SUBJECT:	Judge Ito's wife, Peggy York
DATE:	November 17, 1994

I was just informed that Peggy York was assigned to West Los Angeles Police Station from February 1985 to May 1986.

I was further told that Lt. [now Captain] York had several run-ins with Mark Fuhrman.

Douglas knew as he read Pavelic's fax that any officer who had supervised Mark Fuhrman might know about his bigotry. As a defense witness, Peggy York could help establish Fuhrman as a racist or worse.

But it was complex. Captain Margaret York was Judge Lance Ito's wife. If she testified, her husband might have to give up the "Trial of the Century."

Four days after Pavelic sent his memo, Captain York made her position clear in a sworn declaration to the city attorney.

I, MARGARET A. YORK, HEREBY DECLARE AS FOLLOWS:

If called as a witness I could and would testify competently to the following:

. . . I do not recall being assigned, instructed, or charged to investigate the existence or behavior of a group referred to as "MAW" or "Men Against Women." I believe that if I had been given such an assignment, instruction, or charge that I would recall it.

. . . I recall that Mark Fuhrman was among the officers assigned to patrol at West Los Angeles during the period that I was a watch commander there. . . . I have no recollection of the nature of any interactions between then-Officer Fuhrman and me, or of any other contacts I may have had with him.

Chapman and Douglas had to smile. This was one *very* carefully worded declaration. Okay, Captain York, you don't want to talk. They also assumed her statement was truthful.

Harvey Levin, an investigative reporter at the local CBS outlet, Channel 2, had heard otherwise. According to an LAPD source, someone in the West L.A. station in 1986 had scrawled "KKK" over Martin Luther King's birthday on the squad room calendar. Fuhrman was enjoying the joke so much that watch commander York took him into her office. She must have cut him a new asshole, said the source, because Fuhrman came out shaking. Word was, he hated uppity women as much as he hated uppity blacks. Hard to imagine that Captain York didn't remember Mark Fuhrman. Levin went back to his source and geared up to break the story.

Over the next three weeks Bill Pavelic also checked the veracity of York's declaration.

TO: Robert Shapiro
          Johnnie Cochran
FROM: William G. Pavelic
DATE: November 25, 1994

On September 28, 1986, the Los Angeles Times reported: "At the West Los Angeles Police station, black and women officers complained (1985) to their supervisor that white policemen belonged to a clique that was harassing them, the Times learned. The clique was known to some as 'White Anglo Saxon Police (WASP)' and to others as 'Men Against Women.' ''

One black woman rookie—the first ever assigned to the West Los Angeles station—alleged that she was maliciously soaked with gasoline at the station's fuel pump by a white policeman.

A police source has informed me that . . . Mark Fuhrman was one of her training officers. The source further stated that Peggy York was well aware of this and other acts of misconduct.

TO: Robert Shapiro
Johnnie Cochran
FROM: William G. Pavelic
DATE: November 26, 1994

Earlier this week CBS—Channel 2 investigative reporter Harvey Levin confirmed and reported that on December 31, 1985, Peggy York admonished the W.L.A. officers because someone defaced the station's 1986 calendar by inserting the letters ''KKK'' on the . . . Martin Luther King Holiday.

During the admonishment Mark Fuhrman was openly snickering causing Peggy York to meet with him one on one. . . . Since the aforementioned report was aired, Peggy York has acknowledged and recalled the incident.

We need to subpoena her watch commander log and ascertain from her if she documented this incident in Fuhrman's divisional personnel package.

Judge Ito's wife seemed to have a selective memory, Douglas thought. He was furious. The defense now could upset the trial if need be. Somewhere down the line Captain York's declaration would be a valuable weapon.

* * *

"This is outrageous," Ed Blake complained to Barry Scheck.

Earlier in the month the prosecution had subpoenaed him as *their* expert witness for the Kelly-Frye hearing. Never mind that he was already working for the defense. Of course, Blake was routinely hired by various D.A.s when defense lawyers challenged DNA science. But that wasn't the situation now.

He knew somebody in Garcetti's office would probably ask him the big question: Is there any difference between using DNA testing to exonerate an innocent man and using it to convict a guilty one?

None, he'd have answered. Does the evidence have the same weight one way or the other? Yes, he would say.

That would settle a lot of this bickering over DNA validity once and for all. But in this case he happened to be on the wrong side to say it.

Blake knew that his friends in Garcetti's office had ignored the obvious: Trials are adversarial proceedings. He was O.J. Simpson's hired gun, like it or not. When Gerry Uelmen filed a motion to nullify the subpoena, the scientist added a personal declaration: "If you don't quash this subpoena, I'll refuse to come." The message was: If you call this reluctant witness you will force litigation and have to decide whether or not to throw him in jail. That would stop the case dead—which neither side wanted.

In the last week of November, John McNally, no longer working for the defense, meets some friends for dinner at Peter Luger's, one of New York's old-line steak houses.

One of the group is Mike McAlary, a columnist for the New York *Daily News*. Naturally, the Simpson case comes up. McNally is still angry with Shapiro. He tells a few stories. All off the record, of course. But it isn't long before McAlary has reason to run the story.

2

ROBERT KARDASHIAN'S PHONE RANG LATE ONE NIGHT toward the end of November.

The caller, a man, said he was from the *National Enquirer*. We know you have access to a transcript of Mr. Simpson's interview with the Los Angeles Police Department, he said. "We'd like some excerpts from it. We'll pay you $150,000."

Kardashian didn't recognize the man's name. He wondered if he was being set up.

"Absolutely not," he said.

The man spent a few more minutes trying to persuade him. Kardashian hung up.

Then the transcript appeared in the *Star,* another tabloid. Kardashian assumed the leak came from inside the defense team. He asked Pavelic to help find the rat.

"At least I would have given the $150,000 to the defense fund," he told Pavelic.

A few days later rumors reached Kardashian that Bob Shapiro had leaked the transcript. A middleman had been paid $5,000. Kardashian looked no further. He couldn't figure out why Shapiro would do it, but the lawyer was being blamed for everything, right? Accusations were flying in every direction, but nothing sounded as convincing to Kardashian as the Shapiro scenario. He had been seen, so the story went, at a restaurant with Tony Frost, a senior editor with the *Star,* who sent a bottle of champagne to his table. But the *Star* insisted it had had no contact with Shapiro.

Pat McKenna told Carl Douglas that Shapiro had asked

him weeks ago to take the interview tape to Simpson. Shapiro had the only copy. Tell Bonnie to get the tape from my safe, Shapiro said. The interview was on a tiny microcassette, so on the way to jail McKenna bought a tape recorder. He let Simpson hear the tape—not that O.J. seemed very interested, the investigator noted—then returned it.

Shapiro contended that Bailey got the tape from McKenna and leaked it to the *Star*. In this scenario, of course, Pat was the middleman. McKenna maintained that he'd been given the tape so that he and Bailey could be set up.

By evening Kardashian is enraged. He is normally circumspect, but today he can't contain himself. O.J. needs to hear a few things.

"O.J., you know my only motive is to help with your defense. I have nothing to gain by this. I'm not getting paid."

Simpson says nothing. Bob is unsure how far to go.

"Let me tell you exactly how I see things," Kardashian says. "If you're not interested, say so."

"I want to hear you, Bobby."

Kardashian feels spring-loaded. For five months he has sat through monster egos, petty bickering—and even some brilliant lawyering, when the infighting left time for it. Seeing the LAPD transcript in a tabloid rocked him. He had to speak out.

"First of all, Johnnie Cochran believes one hundred percent that you're innocent. F. Lee Bailey believes one hundred percent that you're innocent. But Bob Shapiro doesn't believe it—at least, not one hundred percent. That's why I think Johnnie should give the opening and closing statements. I think he should run things."

Simpson was silent.

"Your innermost feelings come out when you're arguing something. How can you be passionate in the opening and closing when your feelings are different from your words?"

He knew Simpson didn't like the racial issue, but at least now he understood that it was important.

"The jury has eight black members. Who can address them better than Johnnie Cochran? In the beginning, we had

345

Shapiro set up as the coach. We said that either Gerry Spence or Johnnie Cochran would do the trial. I think we're at the point where we have to make decisions."

Bob couldn't tell if O.J. was taking him seriously. He seemed interested. He nodded. He agreed. But would he act? Simpson always agreed with everyone face to face. That didn't mean he'd follow through.

"Bob *should* be the coach," Kardashian went on. "He should be in the courtroom overseeing everything. He's there for all the strategy. But coaches don't play in the game. That's Johnnie's role. He should be the quarterback. He should take the lead in the courtroom."

Was he getting through to Simpson? Kardashian still didn't know, but he pressed on.

"At least Johnnie should give the closing argument. If you want, he and Shapiro can share the opener. Lee Bailey could do the DNA. He's great at cross-examination. He doesn't live here, so he can get away with hammering the LAPD. Johnnie and Bob will have a harder time with that. Johnnie's ready to take the lead, but you have to say the word."

That was it. He looked at Simpson. Waiting.

"I like your analysis, Bobby. I agree with it. Maybe you could start the ball rolling."

Kardashian felt a weight lift off him. "With this team," he smiled, "we're going to have you home by June."

He'd been pleading his case for nearly two hours. One of his best, if unofficial, pieces of lawyering.

I, JEFF STUART, declare:

On November 13, 1994, I was supervising the visiting area at a time Mr. Simpson and Mr. Roosevelt Greer [*sic*] were visiting in the area adjacent to the control booth.

At one point during the conversation, both Mr. Simpson and Mr. Greer spoke in raised voices which were discernible from within the control booth. I did not try to overhear the conversation. However, I was able to discern a portion of the conversation.

. . . This memorandum submitted under seal reflects a true and correct account of the statements made by Mr.

Kardashian expected a quiet day in court on November 29.
But suddenly TV and radio newspeople were saying that O.J.
had confessed. Prosecutors were filing a motion to get some
deputy's statement about Rosey Grier, the football player-
turned-preacher who ministered to Simpson regularly, admitted as evidence.

Kardashian was dumbfounded. O.J. tells me he's innocent a few hundred times, he thought. He tells A.C. the
same thing. He tells the lawyers fifty times, the scientists
another fifty. Then he shouts through the glass to Rosey that
he killed Nicole and Ron Goldman. With a deputy a few feet
away.

Johnnie and Carl had a catchphrase: TFC. This Fucking
Case. This was a classic TFC moment. Things just came at
you from nowhere. This one was scary. You never knew with
Ito. He might let it in. Johnnie was already calling him ''the
third prosecutor.'' Carl and Johnnie got to Rosey as fast as
they could. Grier said it didn't happen.

Since the statement was sealed, no one, neither defense
nor prosecution, knew exactly what Deputy Stuart thought
he had heard. Rosey figured he overheard something when
Juice got all emotional about not having time to straighten
things out with Nicole. O.J. wanted to tell Nicole he was
sorry for some of the things he had done. Grier remembered
something like ''I want God to know that I'm sorry.''

Was this the same story that had impressed Dr. Yudowitz?

Douglas asked Simpson. O.J. thought he might have said,
''I wish Nicole was here for me to tell her I'm sorry.''
Everybody on the team had heard it before.

But Grier thought something else might be involved. He
worked with poor people through a church group and
inevitably tangled with the police from time to time. Being
an ex-football player about the size of a grizzly bear, he
didn't always turn the other cheek. Being black, of course,
meant automatic trouble with some of the sheriff's deputies.

On this last visit he'd called ahead to the watch commander's office to say he'd be seeing Simpson at five P.M.

He arrived on time. But an hour later, the deputies still hadn't brought Simpson out. Grier was getting upset. He noticed the two deputies in the control booth laughing, pointing at him.

He stood up. "Man, if you have something to say, get down here. Be a man and say it to my face!" Grier said.

The deputies didn't move. They just got angry. But they brought O.J. out.

Amazingly enough, it was during this visit that O.J. Simpson supposedly confessed.

The prosecution argued that Simpson lost his clergy-penitent privilege when he raised his voice. A tenuous argument; California law on clergy privilege was strong. In theory, the team had no problem. But Douglas worried about Ito. He was admitting all sorts of evidence. Johnnie was worried; Shapiro was nervous. Lawyers like to say they are "concerned." That's code for "scared to death." Carl knew that everybody, right down to the investigators, was "concerned."

Alternate jurors were being selected. The seated jurors hadn't been sequestered yet. They must have heard all about this.

Lance Ito decided to visit the jail and investigate personally.

He asked Kardashian and Carl Douglas to sit where Simpson and Grier sat and talk as Grier said they did. Shapiro and Cochran followed the judge into the deputies' booth. Judge Ito listened.

"We're going to have to soundproof this room better," Ito said after a few minutes.

Then he surprised the lawyers.

"Would you like to see Mr. Simpson's cell? I'm going to allow two of you."

He chose Cochran and Kardashian. They took the elevator down to the cell-block levels and found Simpson alone in his cell in a largely deserted corridor. He was in an old chair, feet up through the bars of the closed cell door, peering at a small color TV on a wheeled cart just outside.

"Home, sweet home." Simpson smiled.

Kardashian was depressed by the tiny cell. The tight little

348

space held a sink and an open toilet. Simpson's bed was an inch-thick mattress on a cement slab. He barely had room to stand.

"I can see why you're not doing your push-ups," Bob said.

"Yeah, the only thing I can do is walk up and down this hallway."

The TV cart also held a boxy pay phone whose cord stretched only a short distance. Simpson could just reach the handset through the cell door. Kardashian imagined O.J. straining against the door with the receiver to his ear during defense meetings.

Green walls, guards, a pay telephone on a cart. You look up and see the surveillance camera pointed at you. No room to move. Kardashian got more sorrowful.

Just four days into December the team gathered around the conference table in Shapiro's office. It was Sunday morning and Bob Shapiro was in an excellent mood. "Everyone was so cordial last night," he marveled. "I had the feeling black people love me just as much as they love Johnnie. Black women, too."

Shawn Chapman was incredulous. The night before, an organization called the Brotherhood Crusade had honored Johnnie as Man of the Year. He'd filled two $500-dollar-a-plate tables with the defense team, including Shapiro. African-Americans in formal dress had welcomed Cochran's guests with open arms. Of course, they knew Shapiro's face from the media coverage and embraced him as Simpson's champion. "Black women love me as much as Johnnie," Shapiro had told Kardashian. Now he was saying it again. Shawn could hardly believe it. Didn't he realize he was riding Johnnie's coattails?

But Chapman knew the grandstanding contained a message: I can relate to that jury, too. I'm as popular in that community as Johnnie. I can lead the defense team.

Much of the meeting that morning focused on the Kelly-Frye hearing. Barry and Peter's constant theme was: Take DNA seriously. Don't assume the jury will ignore it. This was aimed right at Johnnie, now so content with his jury. They won't care about DNA, he kept saying.

Today Barry and Peter had something new to report. Ed Blake and Gary Sims had noticed something odd about the swatch that had transferred blood to its paper wrapper. The imprint on the paper didn't match the shape of the swatch inside. This indicated the possibility of further tampering. They had already considered that new blood might have been added to a swatch and might not have dried when it was wrapped. But the mismatched imprint suggested that a different swatch could have been substituted for the original.

"Something is wrong," Scheck said, echoing Dr. Lee.

Then Barry explained that Ito was assembling his own panel of experts for the Kelly-Frye hearing. Scheck and the others had heard that Ito had asked another Superior Court judge, Dino Fulgoni, to help him recruit their DNA experts. Fulgoni had been an L.A. County prosecutor for twenty years and headed the medical-legal section of the D.A.'s office. In that capacity, he and Lisa Kahn, the prosecution's DNA expert, had litigated a key DNA case involving the Cellmark laboratory which was still being appealed.

Now Fulgoni was asking DNA experts all over the country, some considered pro-prosecution, to join the court's panel. Scheck knew that Fulgoni told one of them, a Harvard scientist named Dan Hartl, "I'm authorized by Judge Ito to make this call."

Scheck noted that Fulgoni's role now fell into a legal gray area. California law clearly forbade Fulgoni from *presiding* over Simpson's Kelly-Frye hearing. Since Fulgoni had worked with Kahn on a case that raised the same issues now before the court, it was clear Fulgoni could be recused for cause. But his current role as a representative wasn't clearly covered by existing laws. Scheck argued that it was improper and urged an attack.

The situation was sticky. Cochran and Shapiro were convinced that Ito was the fairest judge they were likely to get. Attacking him on the Fulgoni issue would, at best, offend him, and, at worst, recuse the judge. The best strategy was far from obvious. Maybe they should pass on the Kelly-Frye hearing.

Simpson was on the speakerphone and said he didn't want

350

a Kelly-Frye, period. He understood the issues as well as any of the nonexperts in the room. Challenging the DNA science didn't matter. Public relations was the real problem.

"It will look as if I'm trying to get rid of the DNA evidence against me," Simpson said. "That's not the way I want to be seen. Anyway, it's a waste of my money."

The lawyers said they'd consider it. Waiving a Kelly-Frye hearing was dangerous. You gave up all chance to challenge the science, during the trial and on appeal.

3

U.S. JUDGE REFUSES TO INTERVENE FOR
SIMPSON LAWYER. SCHEDULING CONFLICT
WITH A NEW YORK CASE MAY FORCE
POSTPONEMENT OF KEY HEARING.

Throwing yet another wrench into the timing of the O.J. Simpson murder trial, a federal judge on Friday declined to intervene in a squabble between two jurists by refusing to overturn an order that requires one of Simpson's lawyers to begin a New York trial next week.

In a sharply worded ruling, U.S. District Judge Kevin Thomas Duffy accused lawyer Peter J. Neufeld, a DNA expert, of putting off work for his New York client once he was presented with the more glamorous Simpson case.

Los Angeles Times, December 3, 1994

PETER NEUFELD'S AGGRESSIVE STYLE HAD OFFENDED ITO in pretrial hearings. During jury selection, Cochran and

351

Douglas found themselves sharing an elevator with the judge. Ito asked, "You're not going to bring back that Neufeld, are you?"

Johnnie said he assumed Neufeld would return.

"I regret that," Ito said bluntly. "I don't like him."

There was nothing to do but laugh. But Douglas was stunned. This was no joke. He knew that Ito didn't like Scheck's abrasiveness, either.

Since Neufeld was now stuck at the New York trial, Carl and the others sensed that Scheck was increasingly edgy. He had no one who spoke his special language. The scientists knew DNA, but Scheck couldn't plot legal strategy with them. Barry mentioned Bob Blasier, a defense lawyer up in Sacramento who knew a lot about computers and DNA. Douglas knew that Scheck had been talking to him since September. Soon he'd arrive.

The defense team crowds into Judge Ito's chambers at the end of the first week in December. Ito sits behind a messy desk piled high with legal texts and papers. The lead lawyers from both sides—Cochran and Shapiro, Marcia Clark, Bill Hodgman, Chris Darden—take the long couch in front of Ito's desk. Douglas and Chapman for the defense, and the prosecution support staff, stand or take chairs behind the couch.

Today Ito hopes to set a hearing date to decide which allegations of abuse and battering he'll allow as evidence. But Clark and Darden seem preoccupied, almost giddy.

Ito suggests a date.

"We can't decide yet, Judge," Clark answers. She is coy. "We're working on something. It's going to have an impact on how this domestic thing transpires."

"Marcia, what are you working on?" Johnnie asks.

Clark looks at Darden and giggles. "We can't say, can we?" Darden agrees, laughs quietly, and whispers to Clark.

"Can you give us a hint?" Judge Ito asks.

Clark whispers to Hodgman, then turns to Darden. "Can we say anything?" She is flushed, seems ready to laugh again. Finally: "We really can't say what it is, Judge. But you guys will know soon enough."

Everyone is on edge. "Marcia, what does it have to do with?" Johnnie asks in his polished preacher's voice. "Is it new discovery?"

More whispers. "We really can't say anything."

Ito asks, "When will you be able to let us know?"

Another whispered conference. "A few days."

Ito then schedules the Kelly-Frye hearing for December 12.

A few days before the hearing, the defense meets for a briefing on DNA. When terms like "poly markers" and "RFLP" start flying around the table, Carl Douglas notices that those uncomfortable with the subject leave the room. Barry Scheck says, Anyone who's going to present our position has to learn the material. Douglas knows there's no way Johnnie Cochran or Bob Shapiro will master DNA issues. Maybe it's time for Scheck to come forward.

Bailey offers to do the Kelly-Frye hearing: *He* will present the DNA issue. Johnnie says nothing. Carl voices his concerns privately. "Don't worry about it," Cochran says. "The DNA guys will come up with something." Followed by a Johnnie-ism: "The Lord will work it out." Which brings the team back to Bailey. Lee's self-assurance is breathtaking, even greater than Johnnie's. Douglas remembers hearing Dershowitz talk about Bailey. You never sense he's uncomfortable, Alan said. His motto is "Never let them see you sweat." Dr. Baden said much the same: "What a quick learner Lee is. He really picks up on things." The team decides Bailey will do the courtroom work while Barry suggests questions.

Will they succeed? Douglas remembers Baden's reservations. "Lee can pick up a lot," the scientist said, "but he'll never have what Barry has acquired over the years."

By the end of the day the defense decides to advance the hearing to January.

4

THAT MONDAY, DECEMBER 5, BILL PAVELIC WATCHED
sadly as Bob Shapiro once again pressed his theory that the
time possibly frozen on Nicole's Swiss Army wristwatch
would free O.J. Simpson.

"That photo shows Nicole Simpson's watch stopped at
two minutes after ten o'clock. We can argue that was the
actual time of death," Shapiro said.

The crime-scene photo showed the watch at just after ten
o'clock. McKenna assumed the picture was taken the
morning of June 13. Nicole's watch was probably still
running, and this frame happened to be shot on the hour.
Besides, why do we want to give O.J. *more* time to kill
Nicole?

Shapiro had discussed his watch theory through September and October. He kept asking how long it would have
taken Ron Goldman to walk to Nicole's condo, when
everybody knew that Goldman drove there. John McNally
got red in the face every time Shapiro brought it up. In
September, Shapiro asked McKenna to time the walk.
McKenna laughed—a job's a job—and did it. Shapiro had
also asked Pavelic to check it out. He estimated that
Goldman, walking, would have reached the Bundy gate at
10:15 P.M.

Finally, Pavelic asked Shapiro what this was all about.
Having worked with him for years, Pavelic knew that
Shapiro's mind was like a catacomb. Ideas took shape in the
darkness, but were never revealed until completed. If they
didn't pan out, they stayed buried. Unlike Bailey, who

grandly announced his theories, Shapiro was profoundly uncomfortable sharing the early stages of his thinking. He made assignments without explanation. He thought aloud and out of context, in front of others. Depending on your point of view, he sounded enigmatic or just out of touch. He wanted his experts and investigators to bring him puzzle pieces. He would put them together.

With this remarkably open and combative team, these traits hurt Shapiro badly. He was supposedly the leader, yet he often mystified his colleagues. Pavelic knew Shapiro's mind was complex and could juggle parallel scenarios effortlessly. Pavelic always assumed that Shapiro had some good strategic reason for wondering aloud about Simpson's guilt. But Shapiro never explained himself. Pavelic watched the bafflement and exasperation on the faces around the room. If you threw an idea at this team, they expected you to justify it. If you didn't, they were puzzled, then eventually offended.

Now, at this December 5 meeting, he was still pushing the watch idea. A few weeks earlier, Pavelic had pulled him aside after the others had once again dismissed Shapiro's musings.

"Where are we going with this?"

Shapiro finally explained: If Nicole's watch stopped when she fell, she died at 10:02 P.M. O.J.'s cell phone records show that he called Paula Barbieri at 10:03. Not very likely that he dialed Paula while standing over Nicole's body. But also, who said her watch was accurately set?

Now add Ron Goldman. Witnesses say he left Mezzaluna with Judy Brown's glasses no later than 9:50 that night. Presumably, he went to his nearby apartment, changed clothes, and drove a friend's car to Bundy, parking on Dorothy. If he changed quickly, knowing Nicole was waiting for him, he probably would have arrived about 10:05 P.M.

But earlier Pavelic had reminded Shapiro that they couldn't rule out the possibility Goldman walked, despite having a car parked nearby. You must consider everything. So Shapiro kept asking how long it would take Goldman to walk from his apartment to Nicole's.

If he had changed quickly first, the answer would be about 10:15 P.M. But the prosecution said he drove, arriving at 10:15. If Nicole died at 10:02 P.M., would O.J. have pulled out his phone, called Paula Barbieri at 10:03 P.M., and still be standing there when Ron Goldman rang the gate buzzer eight to twelve minutes later? Shapiro felt certain that Goldman must have driven to Nicole's and arrived at 10:05, not 10:15 as the prosecution believed. Shapiro had also asked Pavelic to find out if the watch was indeed broken. So far, Pavelic hadn't been able to confirm it.

"I refuse to develop tunnel vision in this case," Shapiro insisted. "We can't lock ourselves into one time line. I want to avoid the mistake the prosecutors are making. They have a barking dog and one time of death. I want to see all the possibilities."

Watching Shapiro talk to the skeptical defense team, Pavelic saw a great irony. In trying to avoid painting himself into a corner with a single time line, Shapiro had cornered himself. He was so angry at Lee Bailey's grandstanding, so threatened by Johnnie Cochran's blackness and courtroom presence, that he was explaining himself even less than usual. Shapiro's remarkable mind was as active as ever, but he wouldn't—or couldn't—communicate with his peers. He was burying himself.

DATE: December 8, 1994
TO: Robert L. Shapiro
           Johnnie L. Cochran, Jr.
FROM: William G. Pavelic
SUBJECT: Interview of Bethy Vaquerano
           (Nicole's maid from June 1985 to April
           1988)

Ms. Vaquerano stated the following: O.J. Simpson was very generous and kind toward her and her 12 year old son Erick. Nicole was a very nasty and mean person. Nicole assaulted O.J. on many occasions. She observed Nicole throw a crystal vase at O.J. Nicole struck O.J. with a baseball bat missing his head by a couple of inches. . . .

Nicole used profanities and referred to Ms. Vaquerano as "fucking bitch." Nicole referred to her gardener as a "dumb Mexican." Nicole referred to Jews and African-Americans in the most demeaning terms.

Nicole was very confrontational and always started the fights with O.J. O.J. would argue with Nicole and eventually leave the house. Nicole told Bethy that the media made a big deal out of the 1989 incident. Nicole laughed at the 1989 incident.

When O.J.'s family was visiting him, Nicole referred to them as niggers. . . .

JURY SELECTION IN SIMPSON TRIAL
ENDS AFTER 11 WEEKS

A lengthy string of setbacks, sidetracks and postponements came to an end in the O.J. Simpson murder trial Thursday as both sides accepted a racially mixed panel of alternate jurors. . . .

When the process concluded, the nine-woman, three-man alternate panel included seven blacks, four whites and one Latino. . . .

—Los Angeles Times, December 9, 1994

Sequestration had not been the problem the defense anticipated in getting the jury they wanted. Just about everybody was willing to serve, black, white, Hispanic, or other. Including lots of middle-aged African-American women, Jo-Ellan's perfect jurors.

Now it was time for the defense team to play out the second part of their jury strategy: Next week they would file a sealed motion in favor of sequestration. They wanted the jury shielded from the media.

However, Carl and Johnnie knew four, maybe five, jurors would probably be dismissed in the coming months. One man worked for Hertz and waffled on whether he'd ever met O.J. He was someone the defense wanted. The prosecution would be scrutinizing him. Carl was certain a black woman

with domestic trouble in her past wouldn't last. Too bad—
she liked Simpson a lot. Then there was the black FedEx
driver who made the prosecution nervous. And a black
woman with big eyes and a hard-set jaw was probably a
prosecution target. Johnnie was surprised that she and the
black woman with domestic trouble hadn't been knocked out
in the peremptories.

SIMPSON PROSECUTOR GETS OK

The judge in the O.J. Simpson trial Monday refused to
remove a member of the prosecution team, rejecting
defense arguments that a prosecutor unfairly had access
to grand jury information.

In a written ruling, Superior Court Judge Lance Ito
said ". . . there appears to be no conflict of interest"
with Deputy District Attorney Chris Darden, who
headed the grand jury probe of Simpson friend Al "A.C."
Cowlings.

—Associated Press, December 12, 1994

PHOTOS OF BRUISED NICOLE BROWN SIMPSON
SEIZED FROM SAFE DEPOSIT BOX

Prosecutors in the O.J. Simpson case drilled out the
lock on Nicole Brown Simpson's safe deposit box and
seized photographs of her with a bruised forehead and
injured left eye, defense sources said Wednesday.

The pictures found in the safe deposit box purportedly
show injuries Ms. Simpson had after police were sum-
moned to the Simpson home in 1989. . . .

In a TV interview, Ms. Simpson's father wept when he
recalled seeing the pictures. Lou Brown said his daughter showed the photos to him two or three days after the
New Year's Eve 1989 incident.

"She never thought I got the significance of it, and I
didn't at the time," Brown said.

—Linda Deutsch, AP, December 14, 1994

Carl Douglas sat in his office that evening and tried to assess this latest news. This was obviously the secret Clark and Darden had laughed about in Judge Ito's office a few weeks back.

It was definitely a problem. Pictures of a battered and bruised Nicole could do O.J. no good. Not to mention Simpson's handwritten letters the D.A. found with the photos—letters in which O.J. told Nicole how sorry he was for hitting her.

> If I ever willfully inflict physical injury on you hereafter, I hereby agree that the Pre Nuptual [*sic*] Agreement between you and me shall be null and void, from this date hereof forward. Dated Feb. 3, 1989.

The letter was signed. Nicole had preserved it in her safe-deposit box.

That afternoon, Simpson told Douglas that Nicole had written him an impassioned letter in 1993 in hopes of reconciling. She had contributed to the domestic strife, the letter said. O.J. said it made him look like a battered husband. Arnelle retrieved it from her father's New York condominium.

> I'm the one who was controlling. . . . I know New Year's eve started it. I sank into a depression that I couldn't control. I also agree with you now—that I went through some sort of mid life crisis—"that 30's thing." . . .
>
> . . . O.J., you'll be my one and only "true love." I'm sorry for the pain I've caused you and I'm sorry we let it die. Please let us be a family again, and let me love you—better than I ever have before.
>
> I'll love you forever and always. . . .
>
> Me
> [Drawing of smiling face]

The hearing on the admissibility of "domestic discord" incidents was now scheduled for January 4. If Ito let in

359

O.J.'s letter to Nicole, the defense now had an ace in the hole.

In early December, Bob Blasier was getting a lot of phone calls from Barry Scheck. The world of defense lawyers who understood DNA was a small one; Bob and Barry already knew each other. Blasier, a thin bald man with sad eyes, was pleased to hear from Scheck. Months earlier he'd sent a letter to Bob Shapiro offering to join the team gratis. Working on the trial of the century, win or lose, was an excellent career move. But Shapiro never answered.

Blasier had more courtroom experience with PCR testing than Barry. Many tests pointing to Simpson relied on PCR-based DNA technology. Blasier had argued the first extended and successful Kelly-Frye challenge to PCR. A few California courts had recently rejected DNA testing, particularly PCR-based work. Scheck had worked primarily with the older, more accepted RFLP testing. Now Blasier became Scheck's unofficial adviser for the Kelly-Frye hearing. Bob knew the issues in depth.

"They're just not giving the DNA issues the attention they deserve," Scheck said today. "They still think Peter and I were nuts for doing that Griffin hearing in August. But the hearing gave us a look at all the blood evidence. We learned so much," Scheck said. "And they still don't get it."

Scheck liked to play devil's advocate. A week later he was on the phone again. "Bob, sit down." Blasier was already sitting.

"What would you think if we waived the Kelly-Frye challenge?"

"You're crazy, Barry. He has a defense there. Why would you want to give it up?"

"Hear me out. Look, our challenge to the blood evidence isn't going to be against technology. We've researched Ito's past rulings. We won't be able to win that one. He won't exclude this evidence on those grounds."

Blasier felt that a Kelly-Frye challenge was important for Simpson's appeal record.

But Scheck was reasoning in a different direction. "The jury is probably going to be sequestered," he continued. "We don't want them locked up a couple of months while we have this long pretrial hearing."

Judge Ito, Blasier knew, was saying publicly that the hearing would take three weeks. But Ito didn't know Barry Scheck. He was one lawyer in love with detail. Blasier knew a sequestered jury would be dying in a hotel—or would be at home watching the whole show, if Ito allowed them out. "We lose any way you look at it," Scheck concluded.

Barry's idea contradicted everything Blasier knew as a defense lawyer. You protect your client every possible way. "If you need to appeal," he argued, "you've given up all those issues."

"We can't try this case for appeal. There's no appellate court in the world that will let O.J. go with all this evidence. Our only chance is to challenge the technology during the trial itself, in front of the jury. If Ito lets us."

Scheck talked again about the LAPD's sloppy lab work, the wet swatch transfers, the blood missing from Simpson's reference sample. In particular, he told Blasier of odd DNA differences in the Bundy blood drops trailing east to west toward the back gate. The drop nearest the bodies, he said, contained 33.6 nanograms of DNA. Moving west, the next drop had barely 5 nanograms, the drop after that, 1.8. The fourth drop had 12.1 nanograms. And the final one, just before the gate, had 31.6. Why such differences? He was reading every LAPD lab note. Somewhere in the notes there'll be an answer, he told Blasier.

"Henry Lee says that a single drop of blood should contain about fourteen hundred nanograms," Scheck explained. "We have stunning proof that a severe bacterial degradation took place in these samples. The blood was collected twelve hours after the murders. How did they lose ninety percent of their DNA in twelve hours? How can one drop have thirty-three nanograms, another barely two? If they all fell at the time of the murders, they should be about equal. And Lee tells us that these drops don't have big enough tails to come from a man walking away in a hurry.

Their shape suggests the blood was dropped from somebody almost standing still.

"We have better ways to attack *this* DNA than a Kelly-Frye hearing," Scheck concluded.

Reluctantly, Blasier began to agree. He knew that the highly conservative California Supreme Court had recently agreed to rule on the validity of DNA science. Their ruling might undermine future defense challenges. Blasier swallowed hard. "Let's waive it," he said. He felt like part of the team.

Scheck now explained his strategy to Blasier: We'll go through the holidays *saying* we're doing this Kelly-Frye hearing. I'll provide witness lists. Let the prosecutors think they're getting a look at our case. We'll file another sealed motion for sequestration. We'll say we want to protect the jury from the Kelly-Frye hearing. Hide our true intent all through the process. Let the prosecution spend time preparing for it. Time when they should be doing other things. Let them think the trial won't start until late February. During the Christmas break, *we* work on our overall case. In mid-January, we'll be ready for trial. *They'll* be ready for a Kelly-Frye hearing. They'll be off balance and two months behind.

"Would you be willing to come down here?" Scheck then asked.

Blasier was pleased. He'd been ready a long time.

"I want you to meet some members of the team before the holidays," Scheck explained. "Bring your computer. You can show them some of the things you've done." Barry had just one caution: "Stick close to me. We're dealing with some fairly significant egos."

5

ON SATURDAY, DECEMBER 17, KARDASHIAN AND SKIP Taft invited Johnnie Cochran to breakfast at the Pacific Dining Car in downtown L.A. In the restaurant's ornate dining room, they started what they hoped would be a smooth transfer of power.

"We have to put you in charge," Kardashian said. "Shapiro has to take a secondary position. We have to do this now and tell O.J. right away. Do you want to do it? Are you up to it?"

Comfortably regal as always, Cochran smiled and reassured them. "I agree. I'm all for it."

Kardashian and Taft said they envisioned Johnnie taking over the trial work with Bailey's help. Shapiro would sit at the defense table and consult, nothing more.

"I assumed I'd be doing this," Cochran said. "This jury can relate to me." He smiled again. "I can win this case."

Driving to the jail with Taft, Kardashian felt as if his Mercedes had wings. It was settled. Johnnie was ready and willing.

Kardashian wished he could send Shapiro packing altogether. It wasn't possible. He and Skip had to keep the team together. Shapiro had assembled the team, run the preliminary hearing, questioned the jury pool in voir dire. He had to be at the defense table. They couldn't let the jurors think the defense was squabbling and disorganized.

Kardashian found Shapiro's black Mercedes in the county jail parking lot. He had wanted to tell O.J. on Thursday, but saw Shapiro's car and drove away. Same thing Friday. Now on a *Saturday!* He assumed Shapiro was monopolizing the visiting room so no one else could get to the malleable client. This was the same guy who couldn't visit O.J. to break the news about Nicole's bisexuality. Now he visited all day, every day. Bob and Skip drove away.

Bob was also incensed that Shapiro was taking his family to Maui until after the New Year. Everybody's working their butts off, gearing up for trial next month. He's going on vacation just before the trial starts!

Shawn Chapman couldn't believe that Shapiro was going away. "This can't be true," she'd said. Carl was also angry. Kardashian asked her what Johnnie would do. She shrugged, gave him a knowing smile. They both knew what Johnnie would do: He'd just watch. Johnnie would wait for the right moment. He would wait for Shapiro to go to Hawaii. Then he'd move.

As Bill Pavelic saw it, his boss was taking a well-deserved rest after working himself to the bone for six months. A solid defense apparatus was in place; everybody had an assignment. Now most of the team were leaving town. Lee Bailey and Pat McKenna would be in Florida with their families. Barry Scheck was off to Mexico. Gerry Uelmen planned to be in northern California. Alan Dershowitz was in Boston. Michael Baden and Henry Lee were also back East. Shapiro said that Johnnie had mentioned a trip to New York, possibly to South Africa. Simpson faced a lonely holiday in jail.

It also made sense to Pavelic that Shapiro would want to spend long hours with his client. With his lead lawyer going away for two weeks, O.J. needed comforting. Pavelic listened as Shapiro spent Thursday telling Simpson what had been accomplished to date. The experts were in place. The arguments were polished. They had Lee's two shoe prints, Blake's wet transfers, Scheck's work on O.J.'s missing blood, and Gerry Uelmen and Alan Dershowitz ready to attack constitutional issues. Simpson needed these assurances that his lead attorney had things in good shape.

During the Thursday visit, Shapiro encouraged Simpson

to air his ideas for the opening statements. Then he offered his own. He suggested that both he and Johnnie present statements.

On Saturday, the day Kardashian and Skip had breakfast with Cochran, Shapiro reviewed the team hierarchy. He worked his way toward the subject of Johnnie Cochran. Shapiro admitted that Johnnie should lead in the courtroom. He was the more experienced trial lawyer. He was black. The jury would be more comfortable with him. Simpson agreed. He let Shapiro take the conversation wherever it was going. The lead attorney never addressed the larger issue of team control.

Finally, Shapiro told O.J. he was off to Hawaii for two weeks. He was exhausted. He'd been double-timing for six straight months. Weekdays, weekends, nights. This was his only chance to spend time with his family before the trial began. He was taking work with him, of course. He'd be in close touch by phone and fax. He hoped Simpson understood.

No problem, O.J. said.

Kardashian had driven downtown five times and found Shapiro's Mercedes parked at the jail every time. Now, on the following Monday morning, it was there again. He seemed to arrive at ten A.M., when the jail opened, and leave at 7:45 P.M., when it closed. Kardashian called a deputy he talked to occasionally.

"I need to see O.J. when Shapiro isn't around," he said. "Could I ask a favor? Would you call me if Shapiro leaves before closing time?"

The deputy phoned about five o'clock. "Elvis has left the building," he said.

Bob called Skip Taft, and together they drove to the jail. Simpson, as usual, had said nothing to Shapiro directly, but now he was furious. "Can you believe this guy? I'm sitting here in this crappy place. He's off to the beach!"

"We've talked to Johnnie." Kardashian was grinning. "He's taking over."

Simpson broke into a smile.

"Johnnie will become more aggressive at team meetings," Bob explained. "Things will be run out of his offices. That means no office rent or staff to pay. At Shapiro's almost everything cost extra. You'll save money. It ensures you'll get out of this jail. Johnnie will head up the strategy. In that role, Bob is gone."

"That's great, Bobby. That's what I need," Simpson said.

But Kardashian knew that Simpson would waffle again. He had to prevent that.

"O.J., when you talk to Bob the next time, you've got to be tough. You have to tell him he's still the quarterback. But Johnnie and Lee Bailey are the running backs and this is a *running* team. There will *be* no passing."

"Bobby, I need to talk to people. I have to have a conversation with each guy and see how people feel."

Kardashian wanted to kick something, possibly O.J.

"O.J., this *has* to be done if you want to get out of here. Johnnie is the guy who believes in you. He's the one who'll impress the jury. Remember what you told me during the voir dire? You said you could see *why* Shapiro pleads his cases. You have to be tough now. This *must* be done."

They stayed until the jail closed. They were getting there—but had they brought O.J. along?

ITO ORDERS DNA HEARING, DISALLOWS JAIL
REMARKS; ARGUMENT OVER USE OF
SCIENTIFIC EVIDENCE COULD DELAY OPENING
STATEMENTS UNTIL FEBRUARY

Prosecutors will not get to ask what O.J. Simpson told Rosey Grier during an emotional jailhouse outburst last month, but they have prevailed in their efforts to win a full-scale hearing on the admissibility of DNA evidence, Superior Court Judge Lance A. Ito ruled Monday. . . .

—Los Angeles Times, December 20, 1994

On Tuesday, December 20, Bob Blasier packed up three days' worth of clothing, his laptop, and his overhead projector, and flew to L.A. His plane was delayed and he took a cab directly to Shapiro's Century City office. As he wrestled his luggage and equipment out of the elevator, he thought he saw Barry Scheck. They hadn't been in the same room for at least four years. It took Barry a moment to recognize him.

"Bob! I'm sure glad you're here."

Scheck ushered him into the small conference room where Howard Harris asked him for a quick show-and-tell. Blasier was ready.

While most defense attorneys dragged document-stuffed briefcases to court, Bob carried a laptop. He scanned discovery material and other casework into it. He could call up any document he needed in the courtroom. He created his own computer graphics and used his overhead projector to display them on courtroom screens.

His computer's hard drive stored a set of law books. He could research briefs at the defense table and write them immediately on the laptop's word processor. Thanks to a sophisticated program already installed, he could index the court reporter's transcripts as the trial progressed, retrieving anything he needed from the trial record on a moment's notice. In a paper-heavy case like this one, Blasier was gold.

Scheck loved it. Howard Harris was less delighted: Blasier might easily replace him.

Scheck ran to get Bob Shapiro, who was leaving for Hawaii. He was very gracious. After watching some of Blasier's computer wizardry, he mentioned that he had seen a profile of Bob and his DNA work in *The Daily Journal,* a legal newspaper. The article was headlined "Litigator Gains National Fame."

Blasier was surprised at Shapiro's easygoing charm. He had seen so much of the man on television that he expected a pompous egomaniac. Shapiro said he didn't recall receiving Blasier's earlier fax, the one he never answered. He apologized now.

With Christmas just days away, Lee Bailey suggested that his Florida contingent of Pat McKenna, Howard Harris, and even John McNally spend time preparing for trial. Though McNally was off the case, he agreed to meet them in Miami over the holidays.

The discovery was still a mess. But now they had time to ship copies of everything to Miami and have it scanned into Howard's computer over the holidays. Nobody would miss the papers. Every lawyer, scientist, and investigator had his own set of relevant discovery material.

With Bonnie's help, McKenna and Harris packed up the files. The shipment totaled twenty boxes.

On Thursday, December 22, Douglas, Cochran, and Kardashian sat in Johnnie's office, connected to distant team members by speakerphones. The conference call was scheduled to complete the strategy for waiving the Kelly-Frye hearing. Dershowitz, Scheck, Neufeld, Uelmen, Skip Taft, Bailey, and Shapiro talked on land-line phones. Bailey was over the Atlantic en route from London, his connection fading in and out. Shapiro had been in Hawaii only a day.

The Kelly-Frye discussion had barely started when Shapiro interrupted. "I've been thinking that O.J.'s Bronco was stolen by the two killers.

"I've analyzed all the evidence," the lawyer went on. "It's possible the killers broke into the Bronco, drove it to Bundy, and committed the murders. They smeared the victims' blood around the inside of the vehicle, drove back, parked it, and dropped the glove off—"

Laughter was erupting from the other speakerphones.

"Bob, don't waste our time with this bullshit!" Johnnie interrupted angrily. "Let's move on. We've got work to do."

Everything froze. No one said a word. Carl Douglas waited. Johnnie had made his move! The silence from Hawaii was deafening.

"This is an open line, Bob," Johnnie continued testily. "We can't be discussing things like that on an open line. Let's move on."

Douglas knew the team routinely discussed theories and

strategy on open lines. But he wasn't about to defend Shapiro. This was too good. Everybody could feel the command structure had shifted.

"We've always talked about delicate matters on the telephone," Shapiro protested.

"Let's move on, Bob."

Barry Scheck took the floor as the conversation returned to Kelly-Frye issues.

Scheck said he needed to talk through some strategic concerns. Though some members of the team were ready to cancel the Kelly-Frye hearing, he couldn't shake the uneasy feeling that some of the tradition-minded lawyers might reinstate it at the last minute. Someone suggested they could save time and money by staging a token hearing challenging just PCR testing—so-called molecular Xeroxing—which wasn't fully accepted in the minds of some California judges.

Scheck knew this was foolishness. A hearing on the PCR issues alone in a case of this complexity, he pointed out, couldn't be done without a thorough review of all the DNA science. He had researched the case law and could present strong arguments on laboratory error rates. That issue alone might well settle the future of DNA testing in this case. But a hearing of these issues itself would take courtroom time and O.J.'s money. "This will be the mother of all Kelly-Frye hearings," Scheck told his colleagues. "It will take ages." He understood that giving up the right to raise the DNA issues on appeal defied conventional legal wisdom, but felt compelled to remind his colleagues that the alternatives were worse.

Scheck aimed his arguments at Johnnie's infatuation with the jury they'd so carefully shepherded through selection. No doubt the prosecutors were hoping for a lengthy hearing, which might force Judge Ito to sequester the jury for months. The panel would be exhausted and resentful before they even heard opening statements. Or Ito could let the jurors stay home to be exposed to the media coverage of incriminating DNA evidence. In either case, the prosecution benefited. Ito might even have to excuse some of the defense's "dream jurors." They could not take that gamble.

Finally, Scheck felt his colleagues were listening to him. But he wasn't completely sure. He was working long nights in his room at the Century City Marriott, and worrying more than usual.

When the agenda was completed, Cochran scheduled another telephone meeting for the following Tuesday, December 27. Shapiro said he wouldn't be in Los Angeles until January 1. He suggested meeting on the second.

"Waiting that long would be a travesty," Peter Neufeld said.

Cochran agreed with Neufeld. "Bob, we have to move ahead."

Shapiro said he'd fly back early.

"Don't worry about it," Johnnie said. "Don't cut your trip short."

Carl Douglas felt a warm glow. The power shift was within reach. Almost everyone was now behind Johnnie.

When the meeting ended, Taft and Kardashian took Cochran to see O.J. for more talk about quarterbacks and running backs. Johnnie was showing some muscle now. The problem was Simpson. He liked the football analogy well enough, but still didn't have the nerve to face Shapiro.

"I can't be involved in this infighting," O.J. said. "You guys have to work it out. I'm on trial for my life. I've got other things to think about."

PERSONAL AND CONFIDENTIAL

TO: All Experts and Attorneys
FROM: Robert L. Shapiro
DATE: 12/22/94 [faxed on 12/23/94 from Hawaii]
RE: Information Request

Please fax to me as soon as possible a list of errors, omissions or mistakes that the police and laboratories have made during this case. Further, it would be helpful if you would point out improper proceedings or questionable practices that you are aware of.

I have a private and secure fax for your response. If you have any questions call me directly and ask for "Tony De Milo" in room 3018.

Tony De Milo? The memo sent ripples of laughter through the defense. How will the press find him? How will the guy survive without media coverage?

The anti-Shapiro movement was in full cry. He was faxing off orders from poolside. Let's get the worker ants on the mainland working harder, someone joked. Help Bob Shapiro look good.

6

OVER THE HOLIDAYS, CARL DOUGLAS REMEMBERED THE day Bob Shapiro ordered him and the three women out of a defense meeting while the others discussed Faye Resnick's sexual relationship with Nicole. Afterward, McNally had come out to the hallway and commiserated with him. Douglas had realized even then that people were lining up against Shapiro.

A quiet alliance formed between McNally and Douglas. McNally needed a lawyer with whom he could discuss details. Shapiro was no help. Lee Bailey was in and out. Johnnie Cochran was up to date, but he was no reader. Carl was actually learning the files. He even read McNally's memos.

"I've found my guy," McNally told McKenna. "I'm going to hook onto him."

They got along well. Douglas, cautious and precise, needed McNally's street sense. The detective, all rough edges and aggressive intelligence, profited from Douglas's lawyerly perspective. When McNally left the case in November, McKenna picked up the connection, sidestepping Shapiro completely. One day McKenna pulled Douglas aside.

"Is Shapiro sending you everything?" he said.

"What do you mean?"

"You know how everything is supposed to go to everybody? You may have the impression that Shapiro's people are sending you copies of everything. I'd check into it."

Douglas wasn't happy at what he was hearing. Later he raised the issue with Johnnie, who responded in his usual way: Don't get overwrought. Things will come to us.

Carl Douglas was at home on Christmas Eve. At ten o'clock the phone rang. "Season's greetings!" Bob Shapiro said cordially.

Shapiro had never called him at home. Douglas was so startled he barely replied.

The lawyer wished Douglas and his family a happy holiday and asked about his plans. Carl mumbled something. "I'm feeling rather alone out here," Shapiro confessed, "somewhat out of touch."

Douglas couldn't think of anything to say.

After a moment, Shapiro said, "Oh, I'm sorry. Did I wake you?" In Hawaii it was three hours earlier.

Douglas decided not to correct that impression. He remained silent, and Shapiro said good-bye. He's trying to feel me out, Douglas thought. He knows something is happening.

"Shawn, this is Robert Shapiro. Please call me as soon as you get this message."

Returning from a Christmas Eve party, Chapman was amazed to hear the voice on her answering machine. Shapiro never called her at home. She listened to the message with growing annoyance.

"I am learning that people think I've been doing under-handed things. It's not true. But I do want to apologize for anything that may have offended you. I'd really like to talk to you.

"Please call me. I'm under the name Tony De Milo. I really need to talk to you."

Chapman returned the call. She was furious with Shapiro for many reasons, but, well, it *was* Christmas. She got his hotel voice mail. I appreciate that you called, she said. Merry Christmas.

SIMPSON SUMMARY TRIAL OVERVIEW

TO: Defense Trial Team
FROM: FLB

. . . At the end of opening statements we need to have the jurors thinking to themselves: if these people can prove half of what they've just told us, O.J. is outta here!

None of the above will have much value unless and until it is translated into "downtown" dialect by our able colleague, Cochran; given the makeup of the jury, he would probably be very effective at delivering his translation himself.

Bailey faxed his thirteen-page memo to defense-team members wherever they happened to be on Christmas Day; adopting Hollywood-speak, he advised them that it was a "first cut." Bob Shapiro called Bailey immediately.

"I hope you haven't sent anything to Johnnie Cochran."

"I sent it to everyone," Bailey told him.

"You're endorsing him for the opening statement."

"Of course. It's understood he'll play that role."

Shapiro understood nothing of the kind. Bailey listened with a certain detachment as his friend argued—rather belatedly, Bailey thought—for his own lead role. Shapiro felt he was the right lawyer to lead in the courtroom. The overall strategy was his.

In Bailey's mind, the issue had long been settled. But mischief was afoot, he knew, and he had made his own move. A few days earlier he had spoken to O.J. in jail and gotten the distinct impression that he himself would now be number two in the courtroom. Indeed, he was convinced Simpson wanted *him* to inform Bob, his old friend, that the back bench beckoned. Bailey resisted that; if the news came from him, he would seem to be feathering his own nest. Simpson himself had to inform Shapiro. Or Johnnie.

But Bailey did feel it appropriate to meet with Cochran to ensure his place in the new order. He now had a sense of professional gravity, of history in the making.

"I've got an obligation to O.J. whether I get money or not," he told Cochran. "It's up to you. If you want me to go out there and be with you during the trial, I'll do it."

Bailey was ready to sign a lease on a condominium in order to stay in L.A. He needed confirmation of his status immediately, he said.

"Lee, if you feel you can handle it, and you certainly are very confident, you have my blessing," Cochran replied. "You just have to explain it to O.J. You don't need me there for that."

"I want you to know I'm satisfied the guy's innocent, and my heart goes out to him. I'll abide by your decision."

"I want you there."

Which led Bailey, now on the phone with Shapiro, to raise another sore point. Their friendship was becoming increasingly brittle, but Bailey felt they couldn't postpone discussing money any longer. He told his friend that he *had* signed a lease on a condo and expected to be in the courtroom for the duration. Shapiro mentioned budget problems: There was no money for Bailey.

"Bob, I'm a little disappointed at the arrangements you've made for me."

"How much money do you want? I'll buy you out," Shapiro said.

"It's not that simple. The client wants me there."

"I've always viewed you as a volunteer. You were here to help me," Shapiro added.

"What?"

"You're a volunteer here. You're a consultant."

For Bailey, their friendship ended at that moment. Conversations thereafter, he said to himself, would not be meaningful. On December 27 Lee Bailey prepared to fly to Los Angeles to take his rightful place.

With his friend and partner Peter Neufeld in New York and the other team members disappearing for Christmas, Barry Scheck wasn't in a holiday mood. He was working sixteen-hour days in a closed loop between his room at the Marriott and a desk in Bob Shapiro's office a block away.

So far, he had not seen the kind of trial preparation he thought necessary. The team's casual disorganization had shocked him when he arrived. Now it depressed him. Shapiro had put the case on a fast track. But the lawyers weren't educating themselves quickly enough. *No one knew the whole case*. No one had a fully integrated view of strategy. So Scheck decided, quietly, unilaterally, to acquire the necessary overview.

Barry missed his family, and he felt lonelier as Christmas approached. He was run-down. He had developed a hacking cough. He walked daily from his sterile hotel room to Shapiro's empty offices, propelled only by his sense of professional obligation: No one had asked him to work this hard. He spent hours reading the discovery. He was also writing a long strategy memo on blood evidence, faxing drafts here and there for comment.

The late nights were the worst. Barry couldn't shake off his terror that the team might go with the Kelly-Frye hearing at the last minute. Johnnie's people might realize how unprepared for trial they were, and decide to use the hearing to buy two extra months. Scheck had to be ready for that eventuality. Sometimes he found himself in Shapiro's office at four A.M. copying or collating, chilled because the building's heat had been off for hours.

"How did I get here?" he asked aloud late one night.

Of course, the infighting made things worse. Barry didn't want to take sides. He understood Shapiro's strengths and weaknesses. He knew that Lee Bailey was both a brilliant trial lawyer and a windbag. Bailey, he knew, couldn't *really*

375

handle the DNA evidence. Perhaps he could master two or three levels of complexity—but this case demanded ten. Scheck still had no real sense of Cochran, so far a silent presence at most team meetings. He had been impressed when Johnnie cut off Shapiro earlier that week, but Johnnie remained a mystery. On the other hand, Scheck was impressed by Carl Douglas's ideas and ability to focus.

Under it all, he despaired over this high-priced game of King of the Mountain. The whole country is poised for the so-called trial of the century, he thought. If they could see all these A-list lawyers and experts trying to one-up each other, no one would believe it.

Finally, between Christmas and New Year's, he took a week off in the Mexican resort town of Puerto Vallarta, where his wife and children joined him. This was *almost* a vacation. Attorneys Allan Karlan and Harold Rosenthal came down to work on the case with Scheck while their families enjoyed the beaches. It was a great time—with one flaw: The Mexican telephone lines constantly interrupted Scheck's fax transmissions.

During Christmas week, Kardashian pondered his job description. Best Friend. Pseudo-Criminal Lawyer. Unpaid Volunteer. Now a new one: Team Therapist. During the holidays his phone rang off the hook. People faxed him constantly. Every lawyer on the team had something to say about the infighting. Kardashian didn't kid himself. They didn't want his opinion; they wanted a pipeline to O.J.

Bob got daily faxes and calls from Shapiro. The poor guy has no time to work on his tan, Kardashian thought. Bailey called with his usual complaints about Shapiro. Johnnie wanted to discuss his plans for taking over.

The day after Christmas, Bob and Johnnie visited Simpson to brief him once again on the changing power structure.

"Shapiro is a one-man office," Kardashian explained. "He hires extra staff for his cases, which you pay for. He charges you a huge rent for the conference room. He owns one computer. He isn't well organized. Johnnie has plenty of space, lots of staff and computers for us at no extra cost. Carl will organize things. It makes sense to move everything to his firm."

"That sounds okay," O.J. said. "Do you think we should talk to anybody?"

"Let us take care of it," Cochran told him.

Kardashian arrived at Johnnie's offices at eleven A.M. on Tuesday, December 27, for the scheduled meeting. Skip, Johnnie, Carl, Shawn, Bill Pavelic, and Jo-Ellan Dimitrius were waiting. Bailey and Shapiro were on the phone from Miami and Maui. Johnnie greeted Bailey with special warmth.

On the surface, the meeting was a general review of the case, but Johnnie's changing role was the real agenda. He was confident, selecting topics, leading discussions, calling on people. The tension between him and Shapiro was obvious, but Johnnie was able to keep the disembodied voice from Hawaii at bay while the meeting lasted. Johnnie was taking over. Bob was fighting. Hard to do from a distance of several thousand miles.

7

TWO DAYS AFTER CHRISTMAS, CARL DOUGLAS TOOK HIS ringing phone into the laundry room because his baby boy was sleeping nearby. He was startled to hear Simpson's voice. "Carl, I want you to be my coordinator."

Douglas already knew about his new role from Johnnie. Hearing it now from Simpson was another matter. Douglas was flattered, nervous. He stood throughout the conversation.

"I want you to keep me informed," Simpson continued. "I want you to be my point person so that whenever things are done it all goes through you. You manage everything."

Flanked by the washer and dryer and baskets of laundry, Carl Douglas felt like a very important lawyer.

Simpson said, "You know, Johnnie's going to be taking the lead now."

O.J. was pulling it together. Douglas remembered how pleasantly surprised he had been on first meeting Simpson. O.J. was *down*. Douglas had expected to meet a Bryant Gumbel, a white man with dark skin. Instead, here was this larger-than-life African-American, strong, emotional, with an awesome bass voice. Douglas hadn't expected O.J. to be so sharp. He was a jock, after all. Clever maybe, but not deeply intelligent. Yet he was.

"I want you to do it," Simpson said now. "I want you to coordinate my case."

When they hung up, Douglas woke up his wife. He had to share the moment.

The next day he drafted a memo advising everyone that all discovery, records, and casework should be transferred to his office before the next meeting.

Extra chairs were needed. And even the most stoic team members had complained about Shapiro's menu: takeout chicken, deli sandwiches—or nothing. At one meeting only crackers were served. Douglas vowed there would never be a food problem again.

Moreover, Johnnie's firm always worked from prepared agendas. Every meeting. No exceptions.

MEMORANDUM
AGENDA FOR JANUARY 2, 1995

1. Overview of today's meeting with the client.
2. Media contacts/leaks to the press.
3. Attorney assignments for the upcoming week's hearings.
4. Concise summary reports/updates from each of our experts.

5. Overall view of up-to-date scientific findings from L.A.P.D., D.O.J., Cellmark, and F.B.I. lab, presented by Dr. Blake and Dr. Wolf.
6. Discussion of which experts we will call at trial.
7. Update on status of proposed graphics and animation, particularly as it concerns opening statement and cross exam.
8. Discussion by our experts of areas of impeachment for prosecution experts based on [their] prior testimony and published materials.
9. Discussion of trial strategy, opening statements, review of key witnesses, direct examination and cross, as well as discussion of attorney roles during the trial.
10. Discussion of agenda for January 3rd meeting.

During the last days of December the word around Johnnie's office was that Shapiro had been billing O.J. close to a thousand dollars every time the team used his large conference room. Infuriating, if true. Now the investigators would work in Johnnie's offices: no charge. No need to hire extra secretaries. Pat McKenna and Howard Harris would move into an apartment to save hotel costs. So many ways to save money. Shapiro had used very few of them.

Tension was building along more personal lines. McKenna told them that during his long pre-Christmas visits with O.J., Shapiro had criticized Cochran's people. Johnnie's firm was inefficient, the lawyers lazy. Shawn and Carl didn't work hard, Shapiro told O.J.

The next meeting, scheduled for January 2, would be a hot one.

On Friday, December 30, McKenna was still in Miami. He got a strange call from Bailey: Shapiro's going crazy because Johnnie's becoming the main guy. You and Howard get back to L.A. Ship the files back faster. Ship them to Cochran's office. Make sure you get everything.

McKenna had known something might happen over Christmas. But he didn't expect this hysteria. Returning the newly organized files to Johnnie's office instead of Shapiro's was a big move, obviously. But Shapiro couldn't complain,

McKenna figured. They weren't even *his* files. These sets were Howard's and McKenna's. Everyone else, including Shapiro, still has his own set.

Then the fax war erupted. Johnnie had sent out his agenda for the January 2 meeting. Shapiro replied two days later with one of his own.

TO: All Attorneys and Experts
           cc: O.J. Simpson (via Bill Pavelic)
FROM: Robert L. Shapiro
DATE: December 30, 1994
RE: Agenda for January 2nd meeting

       VIA FAX

1.) Review of key witnesses, examination and cross-examination, and discussion of what attorneys' actual roles should be during the trial. . . .

Kardashian nearly laughed out loud. "Attorneys' roles" had been item 9 on Carl's agenda. Shapiro put it in the first paragraph.

The rest of Bob's memo was a virtual rewrite of Carl's. Different style, same stuff.

The next day Pavelic tells Douglas and then Bailey that Shapiro's murder books, containing LAPD reports and witness interviews and crime-scene photos, are missing from his office. All the crucial photographs are gone.

Come out here tomorrow, Bailey tells McKenna. It's getting ugly. McKenna and Harris caught a plane the next morning.

TO: O.J. Simpson, Skip Taft, Johnnie Cochran,
           Michael Baden, Barbara Wolf, Henry Lee.
FROM: Robert Shapiro
DATE: December 30, 1994
RE: Expenses

O.J.,

    I was shocked to learn that you have been misinformed that my office space is costing between $7,000–8,000 a month. The truth is that I have rented an additional office/-conference/war room for $980 and a computer room for $471. Additional secretarial space for the staff and telephones are at no cost to you.

As for the experts' travel arrangements, it is very important for me to maintain *my* good will with these world-renowned experts that I have employed on your behalf. I treat them the way I would friends or other visitors of importance—with admiration, dignity and respect.

Dr. Baden has complained—and rightfully so—about staying at the Hyatt on Sunset, a second-rate hotel for rock 'n rollers. . . . therefore, I will personally pay for all the experts' rooms, food and transportation to maintain stability and basic good will.

O.J., unless you personally object, let's put this ridiculous scenario to rest.

RLS

The buzz around the New York *Daily News* that weekend was that Shapiro was being fired. And if you call a certain hotel on Maui, and ask for Tony De Milo, you'll get Robert Shapiro.

To the media it was old news that the defense team was seething with conflict. But now the *News* heard that the lead lawyer was hiding in Hawaii under an assumed name. They had a hook for a good story. *News* reporter Michelle Caruso worked the phones all afternoon to verify the facts.

NEW SIMPSON GAME PLAN—
BENCH SHAPIRO; SOURCES SAY COCHRAN
WILL HANDLE MAJOR ARGUMENTS,
OFFER DIFFERENT STRATEGY

O.J. Simpson is expected to demote his lead attorney, Robert Shapiro, to a second-string role, the New York Daily News has learned.

Shapiro, who has been running the show since soon

after Simpson's June 17 arrest, will take a back seat to co-counsel Johnnie Cochran.

And legal legend F. Lee Bailey, who has served as a behind-the-scenes strategist, is expected to assume an expanded role.

The revised lineup, sources said, is the work of Simpson himself, who wants veteran trial lawyer Cochran to handle most of the courtroom duties.

Using football lingo, Simpson recently told Shapiro that he could still be the quarterback, but that Cochran would be the halfback, and Bailey would be the fullback, "and there's gonna be no passing," one source said.

The source said the financially squeezed Simpson had recently considered going so far as canning the high-rolling Shapiro, who has irked some defense team members with his penchant for headline grabbing.

But other sources said Simpson still valued the flashy attorney as a vital strategist.

After initial grumbling, Shapiro indicated that he would grudgingly accept the reduced role, sources said.

Shapiro, who sent bottles of DNA cologne to the media and others as Christmas gifts, was vacationing in Maui at the Grand Wailea hotel with his family under the alias Tony De Milo.

—New York <u>Daily News</u>, January 2, 1995

8

On January 2 reporters at the jail were waiting when Cochran arrived to see Simpson. "Are you in charge now?" TV people yelled. "Is Shapiro getting the boot?" Then Bailey arrived. "What's going on between you and Shapiro?" someone asked.

When Shapiro arrived the questions turned ugly. "Are you *out?*" reporters shouted. "Has F. Lee Bailey taken your place?"

In the visiting room, Cochran, Bailey, and Shapiro sat down with Simpson. The tension could have cracked the glass between them. Shapiro started by arguing against letting Johnnie take over the courtroom.

"Bob, just a minute," O.J. interrupted. "You told me months ago how great a lawyer this guy is. Why don't you want him to take a bigger part?"

"Perhaps I should resign," Shapiro said evenly. "Perhaps I should leave the case."

"Bob, I don't want you to resign," Simpson answered.

Bailey saw the bargaining chip at once. Shapiro had brought the experts in; now he could threaten to take them out.

Bailey glanced at Johnnie Cochran. Almost as benign as O.J., Bailey thought. He doesn't confront. He observes. Shapiro's threat was left hanging in the air.

Bailey and Cochran left the jail together for the scheduled meeting at Cochran's office. They assumed everything was settled: Shapiro wouldn't resign, but would move to third position.

Bailey now became gracious. "I sympathize with Bob," he said to Johnnie in the car. "I hate to see him look left out. Why don't we assign him to the airline witnesses? They're bulletproof."

Cochran nodded. Bailey took this to mean "I'm listening," not "I agree."

"He can't screw them up," Bailey continued. "They won't be hurt in cross-examination in any important way because what they say is so obviously true. Why don't we give Bob that segment of the trial?"

As the lawyers filed into Cochran's tiny conference room before noon, Shawn Chapman motioned Sara Caplan into a private office.

"Pat McKenna said that you and Bob were at the jail before Christmas telling O.J. that Carl and I weren't doing any work." Chapman tried to keep her voice even.

Caplan began to cry.

"That isn't true," she said, pulling herself together. "I can't say much here. You know that. I can say that I didn't agree with any of the things Bob said."

Shawn couldn't contain herself. "We were friends!"

"I should have spoken up. I apologize. I know how hard you and Carl have been working. I'm so sorry."

They both ended up crying.

Finally, there's some logic in dealing with the issues, Barry Scheck thinks while scanning the document in front of him.

Everyone is reading Carl's printed agendas. Two rows of team members surround the table. Lawyers and first-rank experts up front. Investigators, lesser lawyers, and others in chairs behind them. Johnnie Cochran has set the tone with dark slacks and a black button-down shirt. Everyone is dressed casually. Shapiro has not yet arrived.

"Welcome back, Merry Christmas, Happy New Year." Cochran smiles. "As you'll see, there's an agenda in front of you. Everyone take a look at it. Lunch will be here in the next half hour."

Then Bob Shapiro walks in, his face hard, angry, a stark contrast to his laid-back jeans and baseball cap. He shakes hands all around, then takes a seat at the opposite end of the table from Cochran.

"Let's get this straight," Shapiro says firmly. "I am in charge. I've had a meeting with the client. He wants me to be in control of the case. I will be involved in giving opening remarks." The air is suddenly crackling with tension.

Cochran makes no move to stop Shapiro.

"I have assignments to make today." Shapiro continued. "One involves Lee. I expected that Lee would handle the DNA work, but now that we are waiving the Kelly-Frye hearing, he won't have time to become familiar with another topic. So now I'm not sure where he has a role in this case."

"Bob, tell the truth," Cochran interrupts. "Tell the truth. The client said just the opposite."

"That's your *problem*, Johnnie," Shapiro snapped. "You never let anybody talk."

"Bob, after you left the jail, O.J. called me, very upset. You frightened him by threatening to resign. He may have said words that caused you to think you were still in charge, but he didn't mean it."

Shapiro refuses to yield the floor, but Johnnie is not about to be quiet. Not yet.

"As a matter of fact," Cochran added, "O.J. will be calling here in a few minutes. We'll get all this straightened out."

Bailey cut in. "No less than the client himself asked me, your friend of twenty years, to advise you that he wished Johnnie to take the lead. He couldn't bring himself to tell you. How ironic that an accused murderer can't even bring himself to tell his lawyer that he has to take second place."

Bailey hasn't finished with Shapiro.

"You know, I think it was reprehensible—badgering the client, threatening to resign. Then you come back here and say you are in control. I don't think that's right at all."

Now it's out in the open: Bailey has switched sides. Some members of the defense don't know what to say or do.

Then the phone rings. Simpson's voice emerges from a speaker positioned mid-table. He keeps his greetings short. "First and foremost, the plan is that Johnnie and Lee Bailey are taking a much more active role," Simpson says.

Everyone stares at Bob Shapiro.

"Johnnie and Lee will carry the ball in the courtroom," O.J. continues. "They'll be like running backs. Bob is the quarterback. But this won't be a passing game. He'll be doing strategy."

Shapiro sits silently.

"O.J.," Kardashian interrupts, "if Johnnie is in charge of the trial but we have to clarify an issue, who's in charge? Who's the CEO?"

"You've all been working hard, and I appreciate that," Simpson answers, dodging the question. "We have a job to do, and we have to work together to do it."

It's a pep talk, Kardashian thinks in wonderment. We're all sitting here wanting to get things settled, and O.J. is giving us a pep talk.

"We have to rise to the occasion," Simpson concludes. "I'm innocent. I'm going to win."

"I've got to say something," Shapiro says the moment the speaker clicks off. "I need to clear something up."

Everyone turns to the humiliated lawyer, who is fidgeting slightly in his seat. Shapiro speaks very deliberately.

"I've learned for the first time what it is to be wrongfully accused," he begins. "I've learned that all of you thought I had leaked O.J.'s police interview to the *Star*. I understand why you thought I did this. I was seen in a restaurant receiving a bottle of champagne from an editor of the *Star*."

Shawn Chapman watches closely. He looks sheepish, she thinks. Not at all his usual expression.

"It was innocent, and it took on a sinister meaning," Shapiro continues. "I can see how all of you distrusted me, how you thought I was doing something that I was not in fact doing. It hurts me so much to realize this. I don't blame any of you, but you were wrong."

Members of the team are trying to glance at each other without being too obvious. Is anyone buying this? Kardashian wonders. The faces around the table are closed. No signs of sympathy. There had been, after all, nothing damaging to O.J. in that transcript—the leak merely discredited its source. Those who believe Shapiro engineered the whole thing, Bob decides, aren't changing their opinions one iota.

"I can see that you were very angry with me," Shapiro continues, "and I just-apologize for the way I acted. I was very upset that everybody seemed to be turning against me. So I spoke to O.J. before Christmas. I tried to establish my relationship with him. I was very upset."

Carl Douglas interrupts: "I need to say something about that." Douglas speaks in precise, hammering tones. "In the years I've been a lawyer, there has been a cardinal rule in big cases. You never dog another lawyer to the client without that lawyer being there to defend himself."

The hostility in the room is now thick enough to touch. People look nervously from Shapiro to Douglas.

"I do not appreciate it when my colleagues and I are working sixteen hours a day on this case while you are out socializing and at sporting events, and you tell our client that we are not doing our jobs. After that, I cannot trust you."

Nobody moves. A major and public reprimand from an attorney Shapiro has obviously considered his inferior. Shapiro takes only a moment to choose his reaction.

"You are absolutely right," he says. "Carl, I apologize to you for having done that. I apologize to each and every one of you. I did all of this because I felt insecure. I felt everyone was turning against me. Now I understand why you were. You thought I'd leaked the transcript to the *Star*."

For all his humility, real or assumed, Shapiro can't conclude without a counterattack, a veiled one, against Lee Bailey:

"Someone I've considered a friend my entire life has betrayed me," he adds. "I can never forgive him for that. I don't know that I can ever talk to that person again."

At the lunch break, Bailey asked Shapiro into an empty office near the conference room.

"Bob, we've got to get this thing straightened out," he started. "It looks terrible. I have suggested to Johnnie that you handle the demeanor witnesses."

Shapiro seemed depressed and wary, but said, "I appreciate that."

So much for never talking to "that person" again, Bailey noted.

"Frankly," Shapiro continued, "I shouldn't be worrying so much. I've got plenty of money; I can retire. I'm sick of this whole business. I'll finish off this case. I don't need to practice after that."

After the break the atmosphere was different. The lawyers were carefully civil to each other. It seemed for the moment that they had crossed a treacherous wilderness and finally emerged, weary, but on their feet.

Shapiro, Bailey, and Barry Scheck distributed their strategy briefs. Shapiro addressed his relatively short sixteen-page memo to Simpson.

> In spite of the pre-game jitters, I am convinced that we
> have a well-balanced team of experts and trial lawyers who
> will be able to present this case to the jury in a manner that
> will create more than reasonable doubt for your acquittal.

Bailey's "Trial Overview," footnoted to tell the reader it was "written on British Airways 215 from LHR [London's Heathrow Airport] to BOS [Boston], strictly from recollection," concluded that Simpson "has one strong force going for him in his quest for liberty. It is the quantity and quality of intellect and experience which has been assembled to serve him, to RLS's everlasting credit."

Scheck's was the memo of the day. He had turned his late-night anxiety into a forty-page strategic examination of every piece of DNA evidence. Carl Douglas choked for a moment at his first sight of the single-spaced mass of detail, looked again, and realized that Scheck had broken through, laid out *everything* in clear, logical order. We can deal with this evidence, Douglas thought. At first glance, he didn't understand every detail, but the gist of Scheck's thinking was obvious.

It could be demonstrated, he wrote, that something odd, suspicious, or just plain wrong had occurred during the collection or LAPD lab testing and handling of just about every drop or smear of blood evidence. "The DNA and forensic evidence simply cannot be trusted," Scheck concluded.

For the first time, the whole team joined the DNA discussion. Scheck had pulled them past a critical point on the learning curve. They were all following now.

"PCR testing is very new and very sensitive," he explained. "The LAPD people at the crime scene and laboratory personnel who collected, processed, and tested the evidence were outrageously untrained and extremely sloppy. They had no idea how to provide appropriate safeguards."

Ed Blake cut in to suggest recruiting expert defense witnesses to study LAPD lab methods, and then testify about the LAPD's ineptitude. Others wondered aloud if the troubling blood in the Bronco arrived via careless cops who had carried it over from Bundy.

"It's very easy to contaminate blood samples under the best of conditions in a medical laboratory," Scheck said. "Then, in PCR testing, you amplify the wrong DNA. Some of the nation's best crime laboratories are testing in ways that are still controversial among scientists."

But the theoretical problems were merely a backdrop for the key strategic issue. "We will show," Scheck said grandly, "that the LAPD laboratory is a cesspool of PCR contamination. We'll demonstrate they had no special procedures for collection and handling of biological evidence. And we will show they broke the few rules they had for whatever kind of test was going to be used."

Johnnie sat back and smiled. Carl Douglas was feeling better.

"Furthermore, we can show that the police who investigated this case and someone at the very top of the LAPD lab didn't play it straight." Scheck was wound up now. "This wasn't a neutral, let-the-chips-fall-where-they-may investigation. Someone leaked false information to that reporter, Tracie Savage. Someone in the lab seemed to know the DNA test results before the samples were even sent to the outside laboratory!"

* * *

Scheck's job was to demonstrate that there was a reasonable doubt about the integrity of the evidence and to establish the possibility that someone did indeed tamper with it. The cross-examination of Fung and Mazzola, the criminalists who collected the blood samples, and of Yamauchi and Matheson, the LAPD lab technicians, would be crucial. More than crucial, Scheck said. The defense might have won or lost by the time they left the stand.

But Scheck wasn't saying everything on his mind. He remembered his depression one night shortly before Christmas in Shapiro's deserted office. He had looked out the eighteenth-floor window at the blinking lights of the city below. O.J. is very persuasive when he talks about his innocence, he said to himself. The time line works in his favor. But the blood evidence, Scheck knew then and now, was something else. Barry knew that either somebody tampered with a whole lot of that blood evidence, or Simpson committed the murders.

Of course, simple logic indicated that both possibilities could be true.

As a defense attorney, Scheck knew that his only job was to present his case truthfully and persuasively to the jury: the facts as he could determine them, his theories, his reasoning, and the evidence to back up those theories. The jurors would draw their own conclusions. Their opinions, reactions, and gut feelings mattered. Professionally speaking, Barry Scheck's opinions about his client's guilt or innocence were irrelevant. Whatever he might conclude in the privacy of his mind, everything he did as an attorney was based on his presumption of Simpson's innocence.

Barry Scheck dominated the afternoon's proceedings. But the team was surprised to hear an authoritative new voice.

For the first time, Bob Shapiro was discussing the evidence in detail. He spoke knowledgeably of times, dates, hair and fiber evidence, specific blood swatches, and other crime-scene issues. Scheck theorized that the unusually large amount of DNA on the Bundy back gate and on the bedroom socks was evidence that someone had tampered with the swatches. Shapiro contributed in detail, down to specific nanogram counts.

Johnnie Cochran was surprised that Shapiro was finally up to speed. He must have done his homework in Hawaii, Cochran thought.

That evening Shapiro again visited Simpson, this time with Alan Dershowitz. They reviewed Bob's offer to resign if that was what O.J. wanted. By the end of the meeting, Shapiro was still on the defense team.

9

GETTING OFF THE PLANE ON JANUARY 3, PAT MCKENNA and Howard Harris decide to scope things out at Shapiro's office before going to Cochran's.

Nobody's around. They open the conference room door and find Bonnie Barron and Bill Pavelic. McKenna gives Bonnie a big hug. She doesn't hug back. Hey, Happy New Year. He gets a thin smile.

"Where are the files?" Pavelic asks.

"What do you mean, where are the files? The files are in Florida," McKenna replies.

"They weren't supposed to go to Florida."

"Who says?"

"And the pictures, where are the crime-scene pictures?"

"They're in Florida. Packed up. We're shipping everything back."

"Well, I'm very glad. Where are they being shipped to?"

"To Johnnie's office. That's what we were told to do."
Pavelic turns to Bonnie.

"Bonnie, take a memo. I am against this. They should be sent here. They are the property of Bob Shapiro."

"Hey, Bill, what's going on? What are you talking about?"

"Have you read the New York *Daily News?*" Pavelic asks. As if the connection should be obvious.

"I never read it in my life, much less today," McKenna tells him.

That same morning, January 3, Simpson makes his usual call to Johnnie's office during the defense meeting.

"You know, there's been all these leaks," Simpson says on the speakerphone. "I keep reading about my attorneys fighting."

Everybody at the table stared at the phone rather than at Shapiro and Bailey.

"We can't have this," O.J. continued. "We can't leak stuff to the press. We can't *talk* to the press."

By now, everyone had looked at Bailey and Shapiro at least once.

"Everyone on the team should be aware of all statements before they are issued," O.J. concluded. "No one should make a statement without prior consultation with the team. People are saying conflicting things."

Everybody agreed, as usual. They had to work together.

Sitting to one side of Johnnie, Carl Douglas worried. So far, the most important secrets were safe: the second set of shoe prints; the wet blood swatches; O.J.'s missing reference blood; other crucial details of the blood evidence. The heart of their case was still a secret.

The meeting's final hours were productive. Jo-Ellan Dimitrius suggested a shadow jury. Two options: a full-time group sitting through the entire trial. Forget it; too expensive. The second: a group working only on specific witnesses. That might be possible.

Johnnie then told the group that Dr. Lenore Walker, the

psychologist who specialized in spousal abuse and had coined the term "battered woman syndrome," was flying in from Denver to interview Simpson. Months earlier, Alan Dershowitz had predicted that Walker's theories would make it impossible to link Simpson's off-again, on-again abuse of Nicole to murder. Cochran had worked with Dr. Walker before and was enthusiastic about bringing her into the case.

But Bailey warned that the D.A. would see Walker's clinical notes in the discovery if the defense called her as a witness. This would, he observed, "no doubt lead to extensive studies by a prosecutorial psychiatrist." Dr. Bernard Yudowitz posed the same problem for the defense, Bailey reminded them. Presenting an expert witness who says the client doesn't *think* like a murderer will inevitably bring to the witness stand a legion of prosecution psychiatrists saying the opposite, and it is questionable which set of experts the jury will believe. Beware of using psychologists as experts, Bailey concluded.

The team then considered the likely prosecution argument that Mark Fuhrman had made most of his racist remarks ten or more years ago and that they were therefore not relevant.

"Racism persists over time," Gerry Uelmen told them. "It is therefore unlike some other characteristics which can be excluded due to remoteness." Everybody agreed.

That night CNN reporter Art Harris called Carl Douglas at home. Just to chat, he said. As the lawyer dodged serious questions, the reporter said he heard that Carl had eaten a big plate of Chinese food at today's lunch break. Douglas felt a chill. There's a leak from the inside, he thought. This reporter knows what I have for lunch. Does he know about the shoe prints, the swatch transfers, and who knows what else?

Carl called Johnnie at once. They decided on a code phrase to use when a sensitive matter came up in a meeting: "Let's not talk about that now." The topic would then be discussed only in Johnnie's office, between Cochran and those he chose to include.

He has spent a year fooling the nation, this lawyer. He has made them all believers that he is a heroic, hard-working lawyer in the hunt for a grand, fantastic verdict.

Unfortunately, Robert Shapiro is your typical Hollywood invention—a character only tan-deep in makeup and significance.

The nation knows his face. After his client, Shapiro had the most prominent expression in the country last year. He was a gentle pat on an accused posterior. And Shapiro couldn't have been happier.

"Just keep those newspaper clips coming," he told his staff.

His secretaries attached articles about stilettos and mailed out autographed photographs of the lawyer.

While the lawyers huddled around O.J. at Christmas, Robert Shapiro boarded a plane with his wife and kids. He flew to Maui. The kids sat in cabin, their dad in first class. Shapiro kept walking back to see his kids. At each sight of the celebrated counselor the plane rocked with approval. Shapiro waved, and shook hands. . . .

When the plane landed, Shapiro did a radio interview and then checked into the Grand Wailea Hotel. He registered under an alias, Tony De Milo. Unlike Venus, this De Milo was headless. You could've called and checked it out. We did.

The other members of the defense team were incredulous. They were equally astounded by a Christmas fax. Shapiro said he could be reached through his alias. Then he infuriated everyone by sending out DNA for Christmas—the $38 cologne. When O.J. inquired, Johnnie Cochran reportedly explained, "I think Shapiro has gone off the deep end."

An entertainment lawyer, Shapiro has been in over his head all along. He has never tried a murder case in front of a jury. That kind of thing takes preparation. And Shapiro isn't interested in that sort of thing.

Shapiro couldn't be bothered. He has amazed members of the defense team with his unfamiliarity with the facts.

. . . Here is what Robert Shapiro wanted to know:

"How many minutes did it take Ronald Goldman to walk over to Nicole's from the restaurant?" He demanded of the investigators at [one] point.

"Gee, Coach Shapiro," they explained. "Ronald Goldman didn't walk to the murder scene from the restaurant. He went home, changed and drove a borrowed car to the murder scene."

Shapiro could disappear quietly now. But the lawyers working with him are appropriate, decent men. Cochran will not crush Shapiro. But they will hold all future meetings in his office, not Shapiro's. F. Lee Bailey has been reluctant to hurt Shapiro, too. That is loyalty at work, incidentally. He was charged with DUI in California. Shapiro handled his defense and won. Bailey won't forget. But now he is on the case. Even Cochran defers to his judgment now.

Simpson is a little afraid of firing Shapiro completely. In yesterday's three hour meeting at which Shapiro was benched, Shapiro, at one point, said he was quitting. But the others talked him out of it in part for public relations reasons. Simpson is afraid that Shapiro will sell him out to one of those absurd tabloid shows. The *National Enquirer* and the *Star* eat regularly off Shapiro's plate. So O.J. lets Shapiro stay on as quarterback on a non-passing team. Better to keep your enemies close.

—Mike McAlary, New York <u>Daily News,</u>
January 4, 1995

Wednesday, January 4, was their first day back in court. McAlary's column had hit the streets on the East Coast before the sun rose in California. When Bailey got wind of it, he phoned John McNally in New York and asked him to fax it directly into the courtroom. But Lee had left by the time it arrived. During a break, Shapiro read it and exploded.

"Lee must *go*," he told Kardashian. "He is responsible for the leaks. He is orchestrating my removal from the case."

"Every week, there's a different leak," Kardashian told him. "It's either coming from you, or Lee, or Johnnie. I know it isn't coming from me."

"Bailey and McNally did it," Shapiro insisted. "I know it. Check their phone bills. They are the only ones with New York connections. McKenna is involved, too. These people deal with the media constantly. Look in McKenna's phone directory. He's got every one of the tabloid phone numbers."

Shapiro announced he would take Bailey's name off his letterhead. He would change his office locks. "I will not be in the same room with him. I will not ride in the same car with him. I will not speak to Lee Bailey again."

That evening Johnnie and Carl asked Shapiro into Johnnie's office. They wanted him to meet with Bailey. Bob started screaming: "He raped me, he fucked me, I won't go to him." Then he turned to Douglas. "He raped me. What if he raped your son? That's what it feels like to me. I'll never sit in the same room with him."

Carl could see that Shapiro was crazed. Time to back off. There was no reasoning with him now. Douglas got the impression that Shapiro cared more about his image than the fate of O.J. Simpson. Carl wouldn't forgive that.

The next day Kardashian gave it a try. He asked Shapiro to meet with Bailey and Cochran to clear the air. Shapiro refused again.

"Come on, Bob!" Kardashian exclaimed. This was getting exasperating. "Let's work together for O.J.'s sake. Meet with us. Talk to Lee."

"If I go into that room," Robert Shapiro said solemnly, "there will be blood all over the walls."

Pat McKenna knew John McNally had all the gossip from Bailey. Then McNally talked to McAlary, back in November, off the record. Didn't figure he was giving the guy a story.

396

McAlary had written about the case before, but never like this. The wires and TV picked it up. For a day or so, the feud got national coverage.

McKenna was now locked out of Shapiro's offices. He had to beg Bonnie Barron for the suits he kept there. She wasn't inclined to do him any favors. "Even when my wife kicked me out," he joked desperately, "she let me take my clothes." At least he got a laugh from Bonnie. And his suits.

Even Cochran was now upset. He knew *somebody* close to Bailey was responsible for this. But nobody seemed angry at Lee's team. By this time, the team was directing all its anger toward Shapiro. Any blunders by the Bailey crew seemed minor. Johnnie's big concern was future leaks.

SIMPSON LAWYERS DROP PLANS FOR
DNA HEARING; MOVE IS A STRATEGY SHIFT
FOR THE DEFENSE, WHICH CAN STILL
CHALLENGE HANDLING OF BLOOD DROPS.
JUDGE TO SEQUESTER JURY.

—Los Angeles Times, January 5, 1995

Thinking about it on the evening of January 5, Carl Douglas suspected that the arguments about dropping the damned Kelly-Frye hearing had merged into a wonderful, if accidental, strategy.

Marcia Clark and her DNA experts, including a new arrival from northern California, Rockne Harmon, made it clear they were unhappy with the waiver. They'd wasted a lot of time preparing for the hearing. They were sufficiently annoyed to insist on having O.J. himself tell them he knew what he was giving up.

"While this development is not surprising," Rock Harmon insisted to Judge Ito, "we would like the court to assure itself and everyone in perpetuity that Mr. Simpson appreciates what he is waiving."

If you say it's not surprising, Douglas thought, I'll assume it is. I'll assume you're pissed off.

Bob Shapiro told Ito that Simpson had read a list of the

397

rights he was giving up "and fully understands the document."

Ito asked, "Mr. Simpson, is that correct?"

"Your Honor, that's correct. I have read it and I have full confidence in my lawyers, and we withdraw the previous motion. I understand the waiver."

"Gee, I wish you'd told me this before Christmas," Ito said wistfully to Johnnie Cochran. "I spent two weeks reading up on this stuff." Now the court's own DNA experts were also out in the cold. Just what Barry Scheck and his colleagues wanted.

The publication of Simpson's book, *I Want to Tell You,* would be announced in just a couple of days, on January 8. It would be in the stores by the end of the month. Most of the team had never heard of the project until this moment.

"My God, this is a nightmare!" Barry Scheck exploded. "What if the interview tapes get subpoenaed? They may be inconsistent with Simpson's police interview. What if O.J. testifies? He'll be limited by what he said to Schiller."

"I've read the manuscript." Lee Bailey's voice was heavy with authority. "Nothing in it will harm us."

Johnnie and Carl concurred with Bailey. Bob Shapiro disagreed vehemently. This is a disaster, he insisted.

In the end, the client's book was simply one more odd reality to absorb in This Fucking Case. No one could recall another murder case, ever, in which the defendant published a memoir *before* he went to trial. TFC, Carl Douglas thought. But the good news was, the publisher's advance was paying a substantial part of their fees.

None of the defense lawyers wanted the job of breaking the news to Ito. Barry Scheck objected to telling him at all. Ito's hostility to the New York lawyers was well known. We have no obligation to tell him anything, Scheck said.

The others argued that Ito should be given the chance to sequester the jury before the book was available. But who would be the messenger?

Kardashian, of course. He was a *business* lawyer.

* * *

Ito looked at the book as Kardashian stood before his desk the next morning. "What's the publication date? Or more to the point, when will copies be available to the media?" the judge asked.

"At the end of the month," Kardashian replied. Ito didn't have a problem with that, he told Kardashian. The jury would be sequestered by then.

10

ON THE EVE OF TRIAL JOHNNIE COCHRAN HAD A MANAGE-ment problem: Two of his top lawyers weren't speaking. Never mind embarrassing stories in the media. How do you run a tight, focused defense when two of your major players are pissing on each other?

The obvious solution was to jettison either Bailey or Shapiro. No doubt that Cochran wanted to boot Shapiro. The last five months had rubbed Johnnie very raw, starting with Shapiro's snobbery. Johnnie never felt that Shapiro was pulling his weight. He hadn't even put together useful files on witnesses. Then *this* week. Cochran was deeply offended that Shapiro had pretended Simpson wanted him in charge. On a personal level, it was an easy call.

In public and professional terms, Shapiro's exit was quite another matter. Shapiro had put the team together; no escaping that. From the beginning, he'd been the visible leader. The jurors had seen him on television for months. They'd spoken to him during the voir dire. You couldn't have the jury wondering why he'd suddenly disappeared from court. They'd assume the worst.

And Robert Shapiro would fight. Cochran remembered an ugly phone call from Bob after the McAlary column appeared. Even Shapiro's wife, Linel, had barked at Cochran on the phone: Why did Bailey have a full-time seat at the defense table? First time in his life Johnnie'd ever had to explain himself to a colleague's wife. Open conflict made Cochran deeply uncomfortable. But he had to weigh his options. He'd even consulted with Wilmer Harris, one of his partners.

TO: Johnnie L. Cochran, Jr.
FROM: Wilmer J. Harris
DATE: January 7, 1995

California Rule of Professional Conduct 3–700(B)(3) requires an attorney to withdraw from representation when, inter alia, "the member's mental or physical condition renders it unreasonably difficult to carry out the employment effectively."

California Rule of Professional Conduct 3–700(C)(3) states that an attorney may withdraw from representation if his "inability to work with co-counsel indicates that the best interests of the client likely will be served by withdrawal."

Given the facts that you related to me today, it seems that, at a minimum, an attorney who is unwilling even to speak to his co-counsel should consider terminating his employment pursuant to rule 3–700(C)(3). Furthermore, it seems that there is a strong argument that withdrawal is mandatory under rule 3–700(B)(3) if the relationship is so strained as to make it impossible for either attorney to represent the client effectively.

Nevertheless, Cochran concluded that Shapiro must stay. Kardashian knew that he didn't want it to look like he had pushed Shapiro out after becoming lead attorney. To Johnnie, his own image was everything. That left Bailey. Cochran and Douglas met privately to discuss it. The mess with the *Daily News* was reason enough to get rid of him. Plus there were other concerns. That driving-under-the-influence arrest years back. Everyone saw Bailey's hands tremble occasionally. At lunch, he often had a couple of drinks. At dinner, he always had something. But he was working for free. Possibly not an easy man to fire.

Bailey's obvious replacement, Cochran decided, was Barry Scheck. Bailey wanted to do the DNA work. Lee was brilliant in meetings, but those were friendly territory. Cochran worried that Lee might stumble in court. And he knew Scheck could do the science better. Barry had obvious fire, though he hadn't practiced in California. The other lawyers were stunned one day when Barry walked unthinkingly through the "well," a space between the attorneys' tables and the bench. You don't do that in Los Angeles, Scheck was told, without an invitation from the judge.

Johnnie approached Scheck. "Will you substitute for Lee?" Barry said no thanks. He wasn't interested in that third seat at the counsel table. I'd rather watch on TV and work on the case, he explained. Someone has to review the new discovery that's still coming in; there are DNA tests still in the works. Johnnie had seen for months that Scheck knew his stuff. Now he discovered that Barry was also a remarkable man. He had just turned down a starring role in the trial of the century.

Johnnie then came up with Plan B. In a few days the hearing on excluding Simpson's past domestic troubles would start. These past incidents, the defense would argue, formed no reasonable link to homicide. The defense brief argued that the 911 tapes, reports of the 1989 New Year's Eve beating, the smashed-windshield incident, the stories that O.J. had pushed Nicole from a moving car, his alleged stalking of her, and Nicole's diary entries should all be declared inadmissible. Dr. Donald Dutton, a prominent domestic violence expert, was a key prosecution witness.

"Let's see how Bailey does with Dutton on cross," Cochran suggested to Douglas. "The jury won't see it. And let's see if we get more leaks."

Bailey thought it odd to be assigned Dr. Dutton's cross-examination on such short notice. The fainthearted might hesitate. But he was happy. He considered himself bulletproof.

Before Dutton took the stand, Bailey approached the doctor. Bailey had written books. So had Dutton. Perhaps they might exchange copies. A cool start, Carl thought. Never let them see you sweat. Then Bailey listened to the direct examination. He saw at once that Dr. Dutton was poorly prepped.

Bailey had a good corner man, maybe the best on the subject: Dr. Bernie Yudowitz, who had visited O.J. before the holidays and was now, at Bailey's request, watching Dutton on TV. At a break, Bailey called Dr. Yudowitz in Massachusetts and took his suggestions.

In beginning his cross, Bailey aimed at Dutton's premise that abusers were generous only when strings were attached. Well, Doctor, what if a man *didn't* attach strings? What if, like Mr. Simpson, the man paid for everything, gave unequivocally with no payback, and lost his temper occasionally? Wouldn't that fly in the face of your theories?

Dutton admitted that it would. Bailey, seeing his opening, went on. He asked Dutton how he distinguished between a spousal batterer and a good-hearted, generous husband who occasionally lost his temper. How, more to the point, do you link such behavior with murder?

Piece of cake, Bailey felt.

Carl Douglas watched Bailey in wonderment. Lawyers like F. Lee Bailey, the giants, were his heroes. They did it all. The first rule for young lawyers is: Impress the witness with your memory. Bailey did that perfectly. He worked completely off the top of his head, razor-sharp, firing questions at the poor guy at top speed. Bailey carried no notes. Never did. He appeared to know Dr. Dutton's theories by heart. Bailey was killing him.

Douglas smiled when the older lawyer sat down. "Welcome aboard, brother," he said. He'd always liked this man. He knew now that Cochran wouldn't fire Bailey. They'd solve the management problem some other way.

When the hearing concluded, Ito took Simpson's past abuse of Nicole under consideration. The judge would issue a written ruling soon.

*   *   *

402

That evening, January 12, Cochran and Pavelic sat in Skip Taft's office with a small, stoop-shouldered Salvadoran woman. They liked her. Her English was poor and they had to work to follow her story. But they found it worth the effort.

Rosa Lopez, the housekeeper for O.J.'s neighbors, might be able to turn the case around. Johnnie listened carefully. Pavelic had interviewed her twice before. He knew the basics of her story. Mrs. Lopez told them she had been walking her employer's dog near Simpson's property line and noticed the Bronco parked in front of Simpson's house after ten P.M. on June 12: exactly when the prosecution said O.J. was committing murder.

The news got better. Mrs. Lopez's room was barely twenty-five feet from the spot where the bloody glove had been found. She was awakened by noises around 4:40 A.M., she said. She was scared of prowlers. But suppose, Pavelic suggested to Cochran, she had been confused on being awakened? What if she really heard the noises later? Say at 6:30 A.M., around the time Fuhrman found the glove? Pavelic was excited.

Best of all, Mrs. Lopez said that Mark Fuhrman had interviewed her the morning of June 13. Pavelic knew that Fuhrman's notes from the Bundy crime scene were detailed and meticulous. He did his paperwork well. But there was nothing about Rosa Lopez in any of the LAPD's reports. How would Fuhrman explain that? Pavelic was convinced the woman was a treasure.

That same week Barry Scheck is deeply impressed by Mary Anne Gerchas. "She saw four men running away!" Scheck exclaims to Pat McKenna. "It's electrifying!"

But McKenna is edgy. He needs to investigate. So he visits this lady at home and starts his routine. Ask about small things, try to trip her up. The night of the murders she went to the supermarket, bought some food, and went to mass, right? Then she went house hunting and saw those four guys. He asks what groceries she bought. Try to remember. She mentions something unlikely, maybe ice cream or milk, something you wouldn't buy if you weren't going straight home. McKenna feels that she isn't straight. In fact, he *knows* she isn't, but he can't pin it down. He has a bad reaction, but nothing he can tell the lawyers.

Two days later McKenna and Howard are shopping at night and end up in the mall where Gerchas owns a jewelry store. Let's drop in, McKenna said. Introductions all around, small talk. Then McKenna asks if he can use her bathroom. The floor is stacked high with *National Enquirers* and other tabloid rags, full of O.J. stories. We're out of here, McKenna tells Harris.

Meanwhile, other members of the team decide Gerchas could be important. Owns a respectable business. Went to church that day. She looks good. Scheck's excitement is contagious. Pavelic is keeping her on call; she's willing to be interviewed.

Johnnie asks McKenna for a final opinion. "Go with her, Johnnie," McKenna says. Cochran tells everyone she'll be a great witness. McKenna knows in his bones that he should see her again, check into her past before vouching for her. But he doesn't. So much to do and so little time.

11

EVERYONE WAS BACK IN COURT ON FRIDAY, JANUARY 13. Shapiro and Bailey were now riding in separate cars and pointedly avoiding eye contact. After Bailey's performance with Dutton, Cochran put that problem aside. Important business today. Almost all the defense attorneys attended: Shapiro, Cochran, Uelmen, Dershowitz, Bailey, Scheck, Blasier, Douglas, and Kardashian. Today the issue was Fuhrman's background and the evidence that he used the word "nigger." The prosecution had filed a motion arguing that Ito should exclude "remote, inflammatory and irrelevant character evidence" from the trial.

That meant ignoring Mark Fuhrman's past, including the psychiatric evaluations in which he used racial slurs. If the prosecution won, they surely would exclude witnesses like Kathleen Bell, who wrote the defense saying she would testify that Fuhrman boasted to her that he'd invent excuses to stop cars with racially mixed couples. He'd like to see "all niggers gathered together and killed," Bell would tell the jury. Unless the prosecution won.

The defense strategy was obvious: Portray Fuhrman as a violent racist who hated to see any black man—including O.J. Simpson—sexually involved with a white woman. That dramatically enhanced the credibility of the defense argument that the glove Fuhrman found at Simpson's home was the linchpin of a police conspiracy.

For prosecutors, the stakes were equally high. Put a racial slur in the mouth of a key witness, and their complex construction of physical evidence will be undermined by rage and distaste. A celebrity is on trial. The evidence is largely circumstantial. For the prosecution to prevail, the jury must accept the story the evidence tells. It's a serious problem indeed if the jury believes the detective handling critical evidence is a raving bigot.

Deputy D.A. Cheri Lewis attacked the defense position:

"Early on in this case the defense planted the idea, the wish, frankly, that a detective with the Los Angeles Police Department planted evidence—the glove—at Rockingham.

"Now, the trouble with this wish, and I'm not calling it a theory because it doesn't even rise to the level of a theory," she said contemptuously, "the trouble with this wish, this dream of the defense team, is that there is absolutely no evidence to support that theory." She reviewed Fuhrman's involvement in the police investigation step by step.

Finally, Lewis addressed Fuhrman's use of the "N-word."

"It is self-evident, to a certain extent, of course, when someone issues the 'N-word' or any other racial epithet in front of anybody, and especially in front of a member of that minority group, it has an inflammatory effect that is incomparable, and to that specific issue Mr. Darden wishes to address the court."

Darden, who had participated very little so far, rose.

"Your Honor, I think the best indication of just how inflammatory the use of this word is is the fact that it appears that Mr. Cochran and I, the only two black lead lawyers on each side of the counsel table, are somehow dragged into this issue to argue it before the court.

"It is a dirty, filthy word. It is not a word that I allow people to use in my household. I'm sure Mr. Cochran doesn't. . . . It is so prejudicial and so extremely inflammatory that to use that word in any situation will evoke some type of emotional response from any African-American within earshot of that word."

Johnnie Cochran was dumbfounded. "This is offensive," he whispered to Douglas. "This is how he feels? Or is he just trying to win a motion?"

Cochran's astonishment quickly turned to anger. Darden was insulting the black community. Cochran had heard the word "nigger" in plenty of civil cases against abusive cops. Black jurors don't faint when they hear it; Darden's suggestion was infantile. Simpson was equally stunned. O.J. stared at Darden, shaking his head in disbelief.

"It is the filthiest, dirtiest, nastiest word in the English language," Darden continued with growing intensity. "It has no place in this case or in this courtroom. . . . It will do one thing. It will upset the black jurors."

Many reporters were astonished. The D.A.'s office had been accused of bringing Darden into the case solely because he was black. Now he was offering an argument a white prosecutor could never make. By taking this approach, Darden seemed to acknowledge he had been brought into the case because of his race—after insisting, of course, that race had no bearing on it. It was disingenuous, to say the least.

Darden was far from finished.

"It will give them a test, and the test will be, Whose side are you on?" he continued with mounting passion. "The side of the white prosecutors and the white policemen, or the side of the black defendant and his very prominent and black lawyer? That is what it is going to do. Either you are with the Man, or you are with the Brothers.''

Darden was now extremely emotional.

"Can you believe this guy?'' Douglas whispered to Johnnie.

"When you mention that word to this jury or to any African-American, it blinds people. It will blind the jury. It will blind them to the truth. They won't be able to discern what is true and what is not. It will affect their judgment. It will impair their ability to be fair and impartial. It will cause extreme prejudice to the prosecution's case.''

Cochran was furious. Douglas could almost feel the heat of his anger as they huddled. "What the fuck is he talking about?'' Douglas snapped.

"It is a race case, then,'' the prosecutor went on. "It is white versus black, African-American versus Caucasian, us versus them, us versus the system.''

Darden finally sat down. It was Cochran's turn. "Go kick his ass,'' Douglas whispered to his boss.

"Okay, son.'' Cochran walked to the podium, a study in calm fury.

"I would be remiss were I not to take this opportunity to respond to my good friend, Mr. Chris Darden,'' he began. "His remarks this morning are perhaps the most incredible remarks I've heard in a court of law in the thirty-two years I have been practicing law. His remarks are demeaning to African-Americans as a group.''

Douglas liked this. This was Johnnie talking from the heart. Impromptu. Without plan or strategy. He was pissed.

"And so I want . . . to apologize to African-Americans across this country. Not every African-American feels that way. It is demeaning to our jurors to say that African-Americans who have lived under oppression for two hundred plus years in this country cannot work within the mainstream, cannot hear those offensive words.''

Carl glanced at the prosecution table. Darden looked dumbfounded.

"What we are talking about this afternoon, Your Honor, is words out of the mouth of Mark Fuhrman . . . and I am ashamed that Mr. Darden would allow himself to be an apologist for this man."

Now Darden clutched the arms of his chair. He started to rise and object, then thought better of it.

"All across America today, believe me, black people are offended at this moment." Cochran was winding down. "So I say this was uncalled for. It is unwarranted and most unfortunate for somebody that I have a lot of respect for. Perhaps he has become too emotional about this."

Darden wasn't taking this well. No surprise, Douglas thought. Cochran had called him an apologist for Mark Fuhrman. That translated as "traitor," with overtones of "Uncle Tom." Of course, both lawyers were performing for TV. But Cochran had been called Darden's mentor. Now they were adversaries.

Shapiro was pleased with Cochran's fiery reply. Douglas wanted to applaud. He'd never been so proud of Johnnie. "This is the greatest day," Shawn Chapman thought. "I love this." This trash-talker, Darden, had been cut down to size. A message had been sent: Don't play games with us. This is serious.

In the car afterward, Cochran, Douglas, and Chapman couldn't stop debating whether Darden had meant what he said. Chapman was convinced the prosecutor believed every word. Her boss was more forgiving.

"That can't be how he really feels," Cochran insisted. "He must have been saying that to win the argument."

But on one thing they all agreed: They could push Chris Darden's hot button any time they wanted.

BLACKS DEBATE ISSUE OF RACE IN SIMPSON CASE

"I am angry and all black people should be angry," Cynthia Vernon of View Park said Saturday outside the Baldwin Hills/Crenshaw Plaza shopping center. "These issues are some of the exact same things that Dr. Martin Luther King was talking about."

In barbershops and bookstores, over fax machines and phone lines, the talk in Los Angeles' black community . . . centered on the heated and high-profile courtroom exchange. . . .

Eddie McNeil of View Park bitterly denounced Darden's argument, saying: "They got the black boy to throw the brick while the white man hides his hand."

Cecil Fergerson . . . said most people he has talked to "are appalled by Darden's position . . . [It] had nothing to do with O.J. . . . It had to do with a black man who is a prosecuting attorney who one day might have my son up there."

Gloria Alibaruho . . . who was one of Darden's professors at San Jose State . . . [said,] "When Chris made his statement, I knew where he was coming from. He's a person with a conscience. He has honor. He has courage. He has dignity. . . . There are instances when the N-word can be softened but it is only intraracial, not interracial."

—Lisa Resper, Henry Weinstein, and Edward J. Boyer,
Los Angeles Times, January 15, 1995

On Sunday, January 15, Dr. Lenore Walker, the expert in spousal abuse, and her colleague Geraldine Dailey were in the visiting room interviewing Simpson when Kardashian arrived with a picture of O.J. that Johnnie planned to use in his opening statement. He stayed just long enough to get Simpson's okay while Walker and Dailey waited. Kardashian, like the others, hoped Walker would find the abuse issue exaggerated and show that spousal battering couldn't be linked to homicide in O.J.'s case.

12

2 SIMPSON JURORS LIKELY TO BE REPLACED BY ITO

Ito made his tentative decision known in a closed-door session Friday afternoon, according to sources, after investigators from the Sheriff's Department delivered reports about the jurors—a 48-year-old Inglewood man who works for the Hertz Corp. and a 38-year-old Norwalk woman employed as a letter carrier.

The woman's ability to serve was challenged by the defense, which alleged that she had not fully disclosed her experiences with domestic abuse. Ito found that the woman had been candid, a source said, but tentatively has decided to excuse her after a "recent incident."

The male juror facing dismissal is black; the woman is Latina.

—Andrea Ford, Los Angeles Times, January 15, 1995

THE DEFENSE HOPED THAT JUROR 320 WAS ON HER WAY home. They'd gotten an anonymous phone call that she had discussed the case at her job. That was clearly against Ito's rules. Jo-Ellan Dimitrius was convinced that this juror leaned toward the prosecution. Then number 320 came to court one day in December with a swollen lip. When Ito spoke to her in chambers she said, "He beat the shit out of me the day before I came here." The judge's investigators found the assailant, her boyfriend, who admitted beating

410

her. On her questionnaire, she hadn't mentioned problems with domestic abuse. Exit Juror 320. Good riddance.

The team liked Juror 228, the Hertz employee. Carl Douglas felt that shaking hands with Juice in a reception line wasn't prejudicial. Ito's investigators had found people who'd seen the incident. It was just a handshake, they said. The juror said he had no memory of the meeting. But his questionnaire had said nothing about meeting Simpson. Ito was immovable: Don't surprise me after you've filled out the form.

SHAPIRO, BAILEY RIFT ERUPTS, SPLITS SIMPSON TEAM

On the last weekend before O.J. Simpson goes on trial for murder, two of his celebrated lawyers are on the outs, with veteran litigator F. Lee Bailey being ejected from Robert L. Shapiro's suite of offices and his name removed from the letterhead of the Century City firm, Shapiro confirmed.

"We can't have snakes in the bed trying to sleep with us," Shapiro said.

Last week, when Bailey cross-examined a witness for the first time, at a hearing on whether allegations of domestic abuse should reach the jury, Bailey and Shapiro sat as far from each other as possible at the defense table.

—Andrea Ford, <u>Los Angeles Times</u>, January 16, 1995

The first reporter to call Bailey was David Margolick of *The New York Times*.

"We have a comment from Bob Shapiro. Do you want to answer it?"

"No."

Then Dominick Dunne, who was covering the trial for *Vanity Fair*, called.

"Shapiro's really sticking it up your ass," said Dunne.

"Oh my God!"

Bailey regained his composure quickly. Made a dignified

and firm statement: This case is not about Bob Shapiro. It is about O.J. Simpson. He faxed a copy to Johnnie.

That evening Simpson called Bailey. "I hope you didn't respond."

"O.J., I can't let something like this snake-in-the-bed business go unanswered. But I kept my response very tight."

"Okay, but please don't say anything more."

"I don't intend to."

After reading the morning papers, Carl Douglas was convinced Shapiro had to go. Johnnie didn't need persuading. Six days earlier, Cochran had circulated a long memo about the infighting. He'd asked everyone "to pledge that there will be no backbiting and speaking ill of any other person on the team." Now this.

But Simpson still didn't want to fire Shapiro. He told Cochran that afternoon that it would play wrong. The public would think the team was falling apart. Worse, Shapiro might run to the tabloids and sabotage the case. Better to keep him sitting on the bench.

Rosey Grier, who had read the newspapers, called Cochran. "Do you mind if I call Bailey and Shapiro?" Johnnie was all for it. So was O.J. Grier reached Bailey first. "Will you agree to forgive Bob Shapiro?" he asked.

"Absolutely," Bailey answered. "But he won't talk to me."

Rosey called Shapiro next. He reminded the lawyer of the time they met during Grier's first visit to the jail. "Remember why you came here," Shapiro had advised Grier as he was about to be overrun by the press. Don't be distracted by the barrage of questions. Be clear on *your* purpose.

So why was Shapiro working on this case now? Rosey asked. To help O.J., Shapiro replied. Rosey suggested he and Bailey get together again for O.J.'s sake. Shapiro agreed.

"I want to ride down with you," Kardashian said to Bob Shapiro on the phone at 6:30 the next morning.

Kardashian reached Shapiro's house at 7:30. The two

men talked in the backseat of Shapiro's Mercedes while Keno, Shapiro's driver, took them to Cochran's parking lot, where the team met.

"You've got to cut this out," Kardashian began.

"You don't understand. He was godfather to my son. I am *so angry.*"

"You have to do it for O.J. After all, you're getting paid by him."

This basic point didn't seem to register. "Bailey's such a putz," Shapiro continued. "He's trying to take over. Trying to resurrect his career at my expense."

"Bob, cut it out. Worry about O.J., not yourself."

Pulling up in front of Cochran's building, they saw Bailey. Kardashian seized the moment. "Bob, get out of the car and shake his hand. Hug him. Do something, Let him know everything is *okay.*"

Kardashian had no idea what Shapiro would do. Shapiro exited the car, walked toward Bailey, and stuck out his hand. "I believe we can work together to help O.J."

"I'm delighted you have that attitude." Bailey returned the handshake. They hugged each other. Then Kardashian walked up to Bailey with as much authority as he could muster. "You guys don't have to be best friends, but you have to work together for O.J.'s interests." Then Cochran arrived.

"They've kissed and made up," Kardashian announced.

Johnnie congratulated them both and said little else. Riding downtown, Shapiro and Bailey decided to put on a show for the press. Past reporters and cameras, they entered the courthouse arm in arm.

At lunchtime, Cochran assembled the team in the jury room and sent out for deli food. "We are now on the eve of trial," Cochran began. "We must start fresh from here."

Both Bailey and Shapiro were asked to speak. Then Cochran, who had invited Rosey Grier, asked him to read from the Scriptures. Grier gave an impromptu homily on forgiveness and brotherhood. Everyone joined hands and bowed their heads.

"Let us take pride in ourselves," he prayed. "Let us work

413

together as a team and permit no evil spirit to invade our domain. God is with us.''

This was a first for Carl Douglas. He had never prayed with his colleagues in a murder trial before. Or in any kind of trial. He didn't want to be racist, but what was happening now was very black.

13

ITO SAYS JURY CAN HEAR STALKING,
ABUSE CLAIMS; RULING IS MAJOR VICTORY
FOR PROSECUTION

Handing prosecutors in the trial of O.J. Simpson their most important victory to date, Superior Court Judge Lance A. Ito ruled Wednesday that they may tell the jury about more than a dozen incidents in which the former football star allegedly beat, frightened and stalked Nicole Brown Simpson during their tempestuous relationship.

Ito also ruled that jurors may hear a slightly edited tape of a 1993 emergency call in which Nicole Simpson pleads for help as a man she identifies as O.J. Simpson tries to break down her door.

—Jim Newton and Andrea Ford,
Los Angeles Times, January 19, 1995

That evening, Shawn Chapman, Bill Pavelic, and Pat McKenna visited O.J. to discuss each episode of domestic violence that Ito ruled could be admitted. On the surface, some of them looked pretty bad.

Incident by incident, they listened again to O.J.'s versions. But by now, the investigators had checked out Simpson's stories, witness by witness. And one by one, their client's recollections were corroborated.

By the end of the evening it was apparent that Simpson was their best witness on each domestic violence incident. No problem in getting his story on the record, Shawn mused. O.J. was eager to be the star witness.

The next day, January 20, Lee Bailey ignored the fact that the defense had waived the Kelly-Frye hearing. He stood in Cochran's conference room, running through the DNA material to show the team how he planned to present it during the trial. As he talked, the lawyers looked at one another unhappily. Bailey wasn't making sense.

"Lee, what in the hell did you just say?" Johnnie asked. "If we can't understand it, how will the jury?"

"Complicated, it is," Bailey admitted, apparently unruffled. "Pray allow me sufficient time to make a further explanation."

Bob Blasier winced. It'll be a nightmare if Lee tries to handle this evidence, he thought. He and Scheck had anticipated this: Lee was trying to cover up his lack of knowledge with oratory. That had been his approach to DNA all along.

Blasier remembered one December day when Bailey facetiously explained how he'd present the DNA evidence. The dots on the PCR testing strips would flummox the jury, he said. He would attack them as "voodoo dots." You can't accept *dots* as representative of anything, he'd argue. They're just dots on a piece of paper.

"He doesn't know *anything*," Scheck said afterward.

Last month, when he was still hoping to give part of the opening statement, Shapiro had asked Bob Blasier to explain DQ-alpha typing.* Blasier spent nearly an hour coaching him. Shapiro learned fairly quickly to parrot what Bob said.

---

*This PCR-based test measures the genetic marker identified as DQ-alpha on the DNA strand.

He practiced his explanation on Michael Baden and several other team members. But then the details began to slip away. Shapiro was smart enough to abandon the effort within days. None of the lead lawyers understood the intricacies of DNA testing, Blasier realized. High time they faced that.

It was now evident that Barry should take over. Separately, various team members suggested as much to Johnnie.

"Bailey can't do the DNA," Kardashian said. "Nothing personal against Lee. He just doesn't know it."

"I agree," said Cochran. "Barry's got to do it."

Johnnie asked Bailey into his office.

"Lee, we have to talk about the DNA role in this case. We've just decided we have to go with Scheck."

Bailey protested. But there was little real emotion in his statement.

"These guys are getting paid to know this stuff," Johnnie said. "They're the experts. We should let them do it."

Bailey had no fight in him. Not for this battle.

"Don't worry, we'll give you other witnesses," Cochran said. "You've got Fuhrman."

ITO ALLOWS USE OF "N-WORD"

"If the challenged racial epithet was used in a relevant incident, it will be heard in court," Ito wrote Friday in a five page ruling.

—Associated Press, January 21, 1995

On Saturday, January 21, Jo-Ellan Dimitrius addressed Johnnie directly as the team listened. "They're not a stupid jury," she said. "Don't talk down to them."

Opening statements were less than a week away. Cochran was back from the Napa Valley resort where he'd gone to pull his thoughts together. Carl Douglas had outlined the team members' ideas for him. Shawn Chapman was assigned to collect the raw materials Johnnie needed; she asked Pavelic for Rosa Lopez's and McKenna for Mary Anne Gerchas's statements, plus the witness reports relevant to the time line. Kardashian had enlarged a photo of Simpson smiling with his daughter Sydney at the June 12 dance recital.

As the deadline loomed, a sense of family grew. Nobody imagined that the grudges and rivalries had vanished, but for three days the drafting of the opening statement eclipsed personalities; they brainstormed, wrote memos, argued, one-upped each other.

Johnnie was supremely confident. He had so much to talk about. So many tactical and strategic issues to shape into a rich narrative. Moreover, the client was a celebrity who hoped to resume his public life. That compelled Johnnie to address the TV camera as well as the jury.

But the abundance of material bothered Carl Douglas. Opening statements should be lean, he felt. Avoid anything you could trip over later.

Barry Scheck, whose influence seemed to grow daily, opened an intensive discussion of juror theory, joined by Dimitrius and Blasier. Scheck cited a common professional notion that jurors decide innocence or guilt based on "likelihood ratios." The idea was that jurors ranked evidence depending on their view of the defendant's probable guilt or likely innocence. At trial's end, they added up the numbers.

That wasn't how it worked, Scheck insisted: "What people really do, is listen to testimony and turn it into a story that makes sense to them. Psychologists believe this is how people usually absorb information. So it's critical in an opening statement that everything you say is consistent with your overall narrative. Both sides will put forward competing narratives. The key is to get the jurors to integrate all the information into *your* story line."

Even Johnnie, confident of his courtroom prowess, listened intently. Scheck was a fine lecturer.

"That's why the media reality of a trial is so different from the jury's reality," Scheck continued. "The public narrative consists of sound bites from a multitude of sources. Inside the courtroom, the juror gets information from only two competing sources. So knowing *all* the details of a case becomes crucial. That way you can keep everything consistent with your narrative."

Start with the time line, Scheck suggested. If you can show that Simpson didn't have the *opportunity* to commit the crimes, the juror will build his scenario from there.

"In New York, I might do a musical comedy on that," Barry joked. "Use a little sarcasm. First he goes there. Then he goes there. Next he goes *there?* And where else? The jury begins saying, Hey, is any of this possible? Then you work on demeanor. Would a guy like this do it? The jury starts questioning the basic logic of the whole thing. Then the forensic evidence comes in. If all these other things are impossible, how did this stuff get here?"

Cochran loved it. Musical comedy wasn't his style, but he *was* a storyteller. He would construct a convincing narrative for the jury.

A day earlier, Carl Douglas had bumped into an old friend, a public defender. "You know," she said, "I've never had a case where the time of death is based on the wailing of a dog." Today Douglas passed the remark on to Johnnie for his opener.

"How about saying the LAPD lab uses wagon train technology in a twentieth-century world?" Blasier said.

Cochran smiled. "That's nice," he said to Blasier. "I like that."

Bob Blasier had said little since arriving in L.A. He wanted to pick up the nuances of team politics before jumping in. Then, during this brainstorm session, the wagon train metaphor hit him. He'd been a prosecutor for fifteen years and he knew the old-fashioned image would hurt the D.A.s.

Scheck and Blasier got along well personally, but they disagreed over whether to present the full complexity of DNA to the jury. Blasier argued for keeping it simple, especially in the opening statement. Let the prosecutors wallow in arcane science.

Scheck, however, was convinced the jury would understand the technology. "We have to give them specific details so they can absorb the case we're making," he insisted.

"Barry, it's foolish to assume they'll understand the nuances," Blasier protested. "They won't. Shapiro, Bailey, and Cochran don't. Keep it simple. Let the other side make it complicated."

Cochran agreed with Blasier's minimalist approach. Vivid phrases like "wagon train technology" made sense to him. DQ-alpha typing strips didn't.

On an even more important issue, Blasier and Scheck were in agreement: The so-called Dream Team didn't know its case. True, each lead lawyer did well in his own area: Lee Bailey fully understood the time line. Johnnie was an obvious expert on the race issue, whatever they chose to call it. Carl Douglas was well organized, generally. Bob Shapiro's twenty-five-page memo showed a surface understanding of the case work, although some of his "facts" weren't nailed down.

But Barry couldn't shake a sense of impending doom. Blasier soon shared it. Along with Peter Neufeld in New York, they decided they would have to learn the whole case on top of their DNA work. Someone had to. Scheck had already begun by the time Blasier arrived. Now Blasier plunged into the discovery with him.

Semantics were hotly debated. A strategy called Blunders in Blue highlighted every LAPD investigative and evidence-collecting mistake. Coroners' errors would be called Blunders in White. Scheck objected strenuously.

"Blunders in Blue creates a Keystone Kops image," he insisted. "Pratfalls. Circus stunts. It's funny. We need *malevolent* images." We're saying these cops tampered with the evidence. Do you want the jurors thinking of innocent, fun-loving clowns? We're talking about something far worse than incompetence. You must keep the opening statement consistent with our overall narrative in tone as well as content. Scheck could see that Cochran got it. He gave Johnnie a rough drawing of his concept, which he called Integrity of the Evidence. A shaded box labeled "LAPD Black Hole" was surrounded by outside entities: the FBI, Cellmark Laboratory, the California Department of Justice lab. Arrows showed that everything tested by Cellmark, California DOJ, or the FBI had first passed through the

"Black Hole." At the bottom of the drawing, he wrote: "Contaminated, compromised and corrupted."

Cochran loved it. In his office, he would explain the chart to an imaginary jury. "Contaminated," he said gravely. Then "Compromised . . ."—even more seriously. Then he would break character to flash what Barry called his "Johnnie smile" before continuing.

"And there is something *more* sinister," the lawyer intoned. Significant pause. Eye contact. *"Corrupted."*

The previous day, Marcia Clark had thrown the defense a curve. It was customary for the prosecutors to pass along the names of their first few witnesses so the defense could prepare for cross-examination. The D.A.s, Clark told Cochran, would start with domestic violence. Their first witness would be a 911 operator. Next, the police officer who responded to the 911 call. Ron Shipp, a former police officer, would be their third witness.

The D.A.'s decision to open with domestic discord was somewhat unexpected. The defense team had forgotten Dershowitz's prediction months earlier.

"Portraying O.J. as a caring father must remain our central theme," Uelmen argued when he heard how Clark would begin her case. Show the photo of Simpson with his daughter at the recital: "It presents the question we want haunting the jury throughout. Could this man have brutally murdered the mother of his children as this same little girl lay sleeping in an upstairs bedroom—only three hours after this photo was taken?"

Mary Anne Gerchas, flaky or not, becomes part of an unrelated debate. Johnnie wants to name her in his opener. Bob Blasier and a few others oppose that. Johnnie likes specifics; he says juries like them. He also plans to mention Rosa Lopez and Dr. Kary Mullis, the primary developer of PCR testing. Mullis is willing to say the tests are too delicate to be reliable. Johnnie also says he'll mention Dr. Lenore Walker, whose preliminary conclusion is that Simpson doesn't fit the profile of a typical abuser.

Cochran intends to *call* these witnesses, he says. Why not name them? Blasier is flatly against it. It's a trap, he insists. If something changes, if they don't testify, the jury remembers. More important, the prosecution will also remember. Don't do this, Douglas argues. It will be a horrific mistake.

As the evening goes on, Carl reports again on the prosecution's display boards for their opening statements. As case coordinator, Carl had visited the district attorney's office to examine the prosecution displays. He had briefed the team earlier in the week. Now the D.A. expected to see the defense displays. Reciprocal discovery rules required it. Carl was shocked when Barry Scheck argued otherwise.

Stall them; they've been stalling us, Scheck had been saying all week. The boards give away too much of our case. Scheck even considered leaving out the defense's contention that there was blood missing from Simpson's reference sample. This part of their case should remain secret, he argued.

"We're sandbagging them. I'll catch hell for this!" Douglas protested.

"It's about the client," Johnnie said.

"I'll get slammed for this tomorrow," Carl complained.

"Carl, it's not about you," Johnnie said evenly. "It's for the client. You'll have to fall on your sword. Go and do it." They agreed to hold the material until the last moment.

A defining moment. Douglas understood. He'd expected to play hardball in this case. That was okay. But this moved beyond hardball; it was bending a rule to gain advantage. Of course, they were obeying a larger rule: Act in the client's best interest.

Late that night, after almost everyone left, Carl Douglas began assigning witnesses to various attorneys. It was a headache. Who should Bailey have? It was obvious whom Scheck should cross-examine, but no final assignment was made. Carl took Ron Shipp because Cochran couldn't: Shipp was his distant cousin. Johnnie would take the rest of the cops, since that was his territory. Before Johnnie went home he dropped in on Carl.

"Shapiro wants Denise Brown," Carl said to Johnnie. "Should we do that? He keeps saying O.J. wants a white male to cross Denise."

"I don't believe him," Cochran answered.

"Look, he did a solid job at the prelim. I feel bad giving him so few witnesses."

Douglas, though still angry at Shapiro, was impressed by his unfailing dignity. Since the power shift, Shapiro rarely complained. He often worked alone at his office. He was hardly one of the gang, but he was remarkably diplomatic now. Other lawyers complained constantly about their witness assignments. Shapiro never did.

Carl suggested adding Kato Kaelin to Shapiro's list. Let's get Shapiro reinterested in the case, he said.

"All right," Johnnie replied.

On Sunday, January 22, as the rehearsals ground on, Bailey, for all his towering self-confidence, admitted he was bothered by Ron Goldman's blood in the Bronco. "By no means damning evidence," he insisted. "But an obvious problem. Goldman should never have been in that Bronco." But there was a way to deal with it, Bailey said. The glove was the exculpatory key. "If Fuhrman walked over to the Bronco, wiped the glove around inside it, then deposited it behind the house intending to find it, we are comfortable, gentlemen," he explained.

As the team filed into the final pretrial session on Sunday afternoon, they found a memo suggesting that Johnnie wasn't the only lawyer in the room with preacher's credentials.

FROM: F. Lee Bailey
TO: My Advocate Colleagues
SUBJ: The trial, the public, and our profession

Ladies and Gentlemen:

Suffice it to say that the jury trial we are about to commence will be scrutinized and reviewed throughout its progress more thoroughly and by more viewers than any other trial in prior history. . . . Simply put, we are about to make important history. . . .

All of you—each and every one—are trial lawyers of skill. Some are stars already, and the rest will be before this trial ends if each "stays the course" of living within the canons, the parameters of professionalism, and the boundaries of human decency. . . . it seems to me after more than forty years of living in courtrooms that the "high road" is as likely to produce victory as any combination of less desirable measures. In the heat of battle, and while honestly pursuing their objectives, lawyers in court often appear to be too acerbic, self-righteous, pompous and snarling. I think we owe a duty to everyone—the parties we represent, the public, our country, and the profession we revere—to try more deliberately than have any lawyers in history to stand tall.

Hopefully, when a conclusion is reached and a verdict has been returned, what millions have seen will leave them convinced that we did our jobs well. . . .

Never let it be said that F. Lee Bailey lacked a sense of occasion.

14

THE BIG DAY, MONDAY, JANUARY 23. NO MORE PRELIMI-naries. Opening statements would begin. Kardashian picked up Bob Shapiro at 7:30 A.M. and drove to Johnnie's office. Lee Bailey was waiting as they pulled in. A light rain was falling. Johnnie was late, as usual.

News helicopters rattled over the courthouse. Satellite trucks stood everywhere. Vendors were hawking T-shirts, buttons, watches. Evangelists carried signs asking Jesus to save us all. The earlier media circus was a small-town carnival compared to today's madness.

The L.A. County sheriffs had roped the press off on each side of the descending stairs. The defense team entered unmolested. Kardashian put on his "game face," stoic, solemn. Stepping into the VIP elevators, he found himself staring straight into the hostile eyes of Marcia Clark. He nodded and smiled. A simple reflex. She stared at him coldly.

The courtroom was jammed. Kardashian walked through the small door into the holding cell and told the bailiff he wanted to say a prayer with Simpson. They hugged, then joined hands.

"Lord, Thy will be done," Kardashian said. It seemed the only thing to say.

In the courtroom the defense team were pumped like athletes ready for a big game. No sign that they had all been up until 2 A.M. listening to Johnnie's speech. Simpson emerged from the holding cell and sat between Shapiro and Cochran.

Judge Ito took the bench. The TV camera panned down from the seal of the State of California and the trial began.

Then, to everyone's amazement, more pretrial wrangling consumed the day. The D.A. filed yet another motion about whether Kathleen Bell could testify about what she'd heard Fuhrman say. The prosecution wanted Judge Ito to listen to Bell's testimony first, outside the presence of the jury, and rule whether it was admissible. In legal jargon, this was a 402 hearing. Lee Bailey presented the defense's reply. In thunderous oratory, he declared that Fuhrman's failure to report his interview with Rosa Lopez, whose information might be advantageous to their client, proved that his racism required the most thorough scrutiny.

"If Detective Fuhrman decided to 'get' Mr. Simpson for his boldness in keeping company with a Caucasian woman,"

Bailey charged, "certainly an attempt to smother this evidence would further his purpose."

This anti-police heresy enraged the prosecutors. But Ito ruled for the defense. "I will allow cross-examination on that point," he stated. Kathleen Bell was in. A touchdown for the defense, and Bailey had carried the ball.

Cochran asked the court to let O.J. speak to the jury for one minute as part of the opening statement.

The defense request startled many seasoned trial reporters. The formal motion cited incredible precedents: Clarence Darrow handling his own case. The Angela Davis trial. Many were surprised that Ito was even considering Cochran's motion: Most judges would have denied it on the spot. That afternoon he denied Simpson's request but ruled that he could walk up to the jury box, lift his trousers, and show them his injured and arthritic knees. A radical break with custom. An amazing moment. The team had added an extra point to their touchdown.

Now the defense showed the prosecution the display boards, which Scheck had held back until the last moment. Marcia Clark exploded when she saw the chart documenting Simpson's missing blood. A major defense argument was being revealed for the first time and would soon be presented to the jury. "That's a lie, that's not true, this information is all wrong!" Clark shouted in the courtroom.

As he stood beside the board, Scheck was nervous. He had documented his presentation meticulously. Two weeks earlier he, Bob Blasier, and defense criminalist Mark Taylor had remeasured all the various reference tubes used by the LAPD lab in the presence of police serologist Greg Matheson. But he was still afraid Clark would come up with some plausible explanation for the missing blood. She didn't.

Minutes later, bare-knuckle fighting began in earnest when prosecutors protested Carl Douglas's list of thirty-four new witnesses. The discovery rules require that witness lists be exchanged well before trial so each side can prepare. The previous Friday, the defense had protested that prosecutors sideswiped them with a new list including salespeople from

425

Bloomingdale's department store in New York City and previously unmentioned witnesses on spousal abuse.

It wasn't the prosecution's fault, Cheri Lewis had argued. "Before we took the holiday recess, it was anticipated that opening statements in the case would take place approximately two months hence. . . . On January fourth, suddenly the defense comes up with this surprise announcement that it is withdrawing its Kelly-Frye motion. . . . This was a surprise to the prosecution, so suddenly what we had to do was to come up with an additional list . . . which we have voluntarily provided to the defense. . . . We are in fact put in a surprise position, which was undoubtedly a tactical decision of the defense." Scheck's Kelly-Frye plan had worked. So it seemed to the defense: That day Ito had ruled that Clark and Darden could not mention the new witnesses in their opening statements.

Now, on Monday, Douglas was giving prosecutors a list of new defense witnesses. Not one or two last-minute additions, but—count 'em—thirty-four. That took brass, was the reaction in the pressroom.

Carl knew the discovery problem was going to be unpleasant. He sat quietly and absorbed Hodgman's protest. Ito had ordered discovery and witness lists to be exchanged as early as August. Not Carl's responsibility back then. He'd assumed Shapiro's people were handling the discovery.

When the paper mountain had fallen on his desk three weeks earlier, he was briefly overwhelmed. He had no idea what had been sent to Hodgman's office already. Pat McKenna told Douglas horror stories about times when he, McNally, Howard Harris, and Sara Caplan boxed up discovery willy-nilly for the district attorney's office, furious that Bob Shapiro wasn't supervising them. Buried under a landslide of other work, Douglas made an executive decision: Hope for the best. Assume that whatever had been shoved into those boxes was enough. To be candid, with so much else to do he didn't care.

Bad decision. Bad assumption. It wasn't enough. The

prosecution had something to say. So did the judge. He evened the score: Cochran couldn't use twenty-four of the new witnesses. But Ito allowed ten, including Dr. Lenore Walker.

15

ON TUESDAY, JANUARY 24, THE COURTROOM WAS PACKED again. Simpson's mother and his daughter Arnelle were in front-row seats. The Goldman and Brown families were in the first and second rows. There was so little room that Barry Scheck had to take a spectator seat.

Chris Darden rose to make the first statement. "We're here today to . . . settle a question that has been on the minds of people throughout this country these last seven months," he began. Darden was wearing a dark blue suit. He moved his hands as he talked, spreading his fingers. "Did O.J. Simpson really kill Nicole Brown and Ronald Goldman?

"The evidence will show that the answer to the question is yes," he said in a surprisingly flat monotone. "O.J. Simpson murdered Nicole Brown Simpson and Ronald Goldman."

The defense team watched. Simpson sat up straighter than the others, eyes alert, immaculate in a gray wide-shouldered suit. He shook his head silently and often. Shapiro hovered behind him. Carl Douglas and Lee Bailey filled the other counsel chairs. Johnnie Cochran and Bob Blasier were in seats slightly away from the table, while Kardashian, Shawn Chapman, Sara Caplan, and Jo-Ellan Dimitrius had seats by the railing.

"What we've been seeing, ladies and gentlemen, is a public face, a public persona, a face of the athlete, a face of the actor," Darden continued. "We also have a private side, a private face. . . . The evidence will show that the face you see, and the man you will see, is the face of a batterer, a wife-beater, an abuser, a controller."

Carl Douglas felt that Darden lacked polish. He sways, Douglas thought. Uses too much slang. He'd expected more poise from Darden.

Cochran leaned over. "Weak," he whispered. Johnnie was convinced that spousal abuse wouldn't impress this jury. It doesn't equal murder.

Behind him, Bob Shapiro appeared equally unimpressed. He whispered to Simpson—something about "no evidence."

"He killed her for a reason as old as mankind itself," Darden was saying. "He killed her out of jealousy. He killed her because he couldn't have her. And if he couldn't have her, he didn't want anybody else to have her. He killed her to control her."

"That's a lie," Simpson whispered to Cochran.

". . . The more control he gained, the more abusive he became. . . . You're going to be hearing evidence regarding domestic abuse, violence, intimidation, physical abuse, wife-beating, public humiliation."

Unlike the defense team, the press was generally giving Darden high marks. Many felt he was digging himself out of the grave that Johnnie dug for him during the "N-word" exchange. He had the emotional part of the opening, and he was letting you know he felt strongly. Darden gave the impression of forcing a professional calm over his disgust and anger at Simpson. The narrative was dramatic; he was doing it justice. Pretty obvious it was written well in advance. Nothing impromptu here.

Jo-Ellan took the measure of the jurors. They just sat there. Little obvious reaction. At the break, she told Johnnie the jury wasn't very impressed.

Darden delivered a tight conclusion: "He was obsessed with her. He could not stand to lose her. And so he murdered her. And as you hear the evidence in this case, it will become clear that, in his mind, she belonged to him. If he couldn't have her, nobody could." Darden paused. "Thank you."

Marcia Clark followed Darden.

"The evidence will show that on the night of June 12, 1994, the defendant had an hour and ten minutes of time in which his whereabouts are unaccounted for," she began.

Clark had the harder job of presenting the physical evidence. "And we will show that it was during that hour and ten minutes that the murders were committed . . . at ten-fifteen, a dog [was] heard barking . . . the evidence will show [it] was Nicole's dog, [and that barking] fixes the time at which the murder occurred."

Shawn Chapman wondered why the prosecution insisted on so precise a time of death. They're locked into one theory, she mused. Johnnie made a note. The prosecution had made a major mistake, Douglas felt. Bailey was delighted. Now it would be his time line against theirs.

Clark worked her way methodically through the evidence, by showing slides of bloodstains on the Bronco's center console and side panels. "The blood on the panel here matches the defendant," she said.

Another slide. "The blood on the console matches the defendant."

Another slide. "The item number thirty-one on the console is consistent with a mixture of the defendant and Ron Goldman."

Another one. "This bloodstain on the console was recovered later in time, after the fourteenth. That is consistent with a mixture of the defendant, Ron Goldman, and Nicole Brown."

The litany become ominous, a kind of grim verse.

"On the Rockingham blood trail . . . blood spot number six matches the defendant.

"The blood drops found just inside the front entry of the defendant's home . . . matches the defendant."

She showed the socks: one spot matching Simpson, another Nicole. The Rockingham glove had blood consistent with a mixture of Simpson, Nicole, and Ron.

Shawn Chapman glanced at Johnnie. The effect of the word "matches" was starting to register.

Clark offered a slide of the third blood drop leading away from the bodies. "Matches the defendant."

The fourth drop. "Matches the defendant."

The fifth and last drop. "Matches the defendant."

This is impressive, Carl Douglas thought. The visual, the sound of that one word. Pretty good.

Blood where there should be no blood: in Simpson's car, in his house, on his driveway, and even on the socks at the foot of his bed.

Then the conclusions. The strongest images. The slides of the two bodies drenched in blood. Simpson stared at the ceiling, drawing deep breaths, while the Goldman and Brown families sobbed openly. Arnelle Simpson leaned her head on her mother's shoulder and burst into tears. Spectators gasped as the slides showed a river of blood pocked by the dog's paw prints.

Carl Douglas had to admit that Clark had done well. Better than well. Well enough, he thought, that he wasn't about to ask Juice for a reaction. Not a good moment to bother the defendant.

The pressroom's collective verdict was positive. Very well done. Very businesslike. Very low key. Chris had the more dramatic story, the heart of the case. But Marcia had the evidence, the proof.

Without much discussion, the defense lawyers decided against visiting O.J. that evening. No doubt he'd be glad for company, but the situation was too delicate. Simpson would certainly want their appraisal of the prosecution's opening. Darden and Clark had had impact, no question. And O.J. had been distraught over the photos of Nicole. Tonight, it would be too easy to say the wrong thing. One ill-chosen word could send their client into further despair. Much better, they all felt, to look at the whole picture after Cochran's opener.

16

NEXT MORNING JOHNNIE COCHRAN WALKED UP TO THE jury box. He stood close to the jury, a commanding figure in his dark blue suit, burgundy tie, and striped shirt. He started preaching at once. Early on, he used his favorite Martin Luther King, Jr., line: "Injustice anywhere is a threat to justice everywhere."

Then Cochran went on the attack.

"Darden said yesterday that in Richmond, California, and someplace in Georgia, people were asking questions. Well, I'd like to think in my hometown of Shreveport, Louisiana, my mother-in-law in New Orleans, and other places throughout this country today, they're asking: Why did Mr. Darden spend all that time on domestic violence? This is a murder case. Why'd he do that?"

Johnnie started naming future witnesses. "Let me just talk briefly about the witnesses they didn't talk about yesterday," Cochran said. "There's a lady who works next door to Mr. Simpson on Rockingham. She will indicate that when she came out to walk her dog at about eight P.M., that Bronco was parked at the curb there."

For the most part, the trial reporters liked Cochran's style but felt he was wandering too much. After telling jurors that Rosa Lopez walked her dog at eight, he lost the order of his episode. First O.J. and Kato Kaelin go to McDonald's, fine. Then prowlers. But when? Was that later? He moved back to Lopez hearing Simpson leave for the airport. Then forward to overhearing men's voices on the Rockingham property after midnight. Everyone was waiting for the 10:15 P.M.

sighting of the Bronco parked at the curb. That was the point, wasn't it?

"I hope I told you that when she came out to walk her dog at ten-fifteen that same night," Cochran finally said, "the Bronco was parked exactly the same way at that curb."

Cochran had found his rhythm again. "And one of the most unique things about this lady is the fact that the morning of June thirteenth, that Monday morning, a police officer came over to her residence, asked her what she'd heard. . . . And she can identify that officer as Detective Mark Fuhrman. Detective Mark Fuhrman will play an integral part in this case for a number of reasons."

Everybody at the defense table agreed that Mark Fuhrman should be dumped at the jury's feet as often as possible.

"It's very interesting that the prosecution never once mentioned his name yesterday. It's like they want to hide him. But they can't hide him. He's very much a part of this case. And we ask ourselves, Why didn't they mention him?"

Cochran had just challenged the prosecution to put Fuhrman on the stand. Dershowitz had predicted Clark would hide him. Any smart prosecutor would. Now Johnnie was making sure the jury knew all about Fuhrman's role in the case. If the prosecution didn't call Fuhrman, the defense would remind the jury that the cop who climbed the wall to Simpson's estate and who found the bloody glove was nowhere to been seen. Present or absent, Fuhrman would be a major defense target.

"There's another witness, Mary Anne Gerchas," Cochran continued. Kardashian noticed Marcia Clark turn to Chris Darden with a gleeful expression at exactly the moment he mentioned Mary Anne Gerchas. Marcia was laughing! She was having trouble keeping her composure. What on earth was going on?

". . . Sometime after ten-thirty in the evening, she's walking down Bundy Street," Cochran went on. ". . . She sees four men who come within ten feet of her, two of which appear to be Hispanic and the others are Caucasian, several of which have knit caps on their heads."

Kardashian got it. Something was wrong with the witness.

"And that's what this lady was trying to tell the police, trying to tell the district attorney, trying to tell anybody who will listen," Johnnie continued. "They didn't want to listen because they made that decision and this rush to judgment."

No question in anyone's mind that Cochran was a story-teller. Many marveled that poorly organized material didn't undercut his ability to mesmerize. He had the jury listening, taking notes, leaning forward. Now Johnnie had the display board showing the photo of O.J. with Sydney at her recital practically on top of the jury.

Cochran explained that Simpson wasn't in an ugly mood hours before Nicole died. Look at how warm he is in that picture. Never mind what Darden's witnesses say.

Then Johnnie went to the experts: "Dr. Lenore Walker . . . will talk about the fact that life-threatening violence usually precedes a homicide incident, and she does not find that in this case. Stalkers don't go all across the United States working, doing commercials, shooting movies, having a new girlfriend, going on with their lives."

Many of the veteran reporters compared Cochran's opener to what they'd heard at other big trials, from other lawyers. Those opening remarks were dry, even boring, but they took you down a straighter road. Cochran's presentation was disjointed. His material revealed no pattern. He has O.J. chipping golf balls, men running to a car, Rosa Lopez walking the dog again and again, Kato doing this or that. Seemed like he was throwing out every piece of information he had, just to see what stuck.

Cochran couldn't resist using Blasier's analogy as he attacked the blood evidence. "That this is, by all accounts, twenty-first-century cyberspace technology that is used by these police departments with covered-wagon technology."

As the lunch break neared, Cochran kicked the wailing dog one last time. Deadline time for East Coast newspapers and nightly TV news. He had pointed out earlier that you don't rely on a dog to tell you when someone died. Now he repeated the point. The prosecution was depending on a dog for vital information "when a man's life is at stake." The jury could ponder that over lunch.

When court reconvened that afternoon, Cochran carefully set up the day's biggest moment. Simpson would speak to the jury without saying a word.

"The problems with his hands were so severe he could not shuffle the cards when he played gin rummy," Johnnie said. Then he directed Simpson to the jury box.

O.J. rose and walked the length of the courtroom, head high. He made eye contact with as many jurors as he could. He held up his left pant leg and looked away uncomfortably as Cochran described his damaged knee. The jurors in the front row were close enough to touch him, although none did. The sports-induced arthritis made it impossible for Simpson to have killed anyone in a struggle with a knife, Cochran insisted.

"Thank you very much," Johnnie concluded. "I would ask you to keep an open mind until tomorrow, until we have a chance to finish."

After Johnnie finished, Judge Ito excused the jury for the day. The court went back to a discovery violations hearing over the witness lists. Hodgman was mad over the thirteen witnesses the defense never shared with the prosecution.

He began his list of complaints by citing Cochran's statements about unknown witnesses, missing reports, and late discovery. The D.A. was demanding a full discovery report, and Shapiro was refusing to provide it. Hodgman had just started a strong protest when Ito called a break. When the hearing resumed, Bill Hodgman was shaking with anger.

Part of Cochran's opening statement, the prosecutor said with barely controlled rage, was very, very prejudicial to the people. Hodgman was turning colors. He's almost blue, Kardashian thought.

Hodgman was stridently asking Ito to "admonish the jury to disregard that." Then he paused. ". . . And, Your Honor, we will . . ." He took a longer pause. ". . . talk about discovery. . . ."

Then Hodgman stopped suddenly. The last pause was out of synch with his words.

"Excuse me. I need to slow down myself a little bit, Your

Honor. Give me just a moment." Another longish pause. Now the whole courtroom was staring. "Yesterday or the other day, the court had to take a deep breath. Allow me to take one, too."

Hodgman quickly got himself back to normal.

Ito swung a steely gaze toward Carl Douglas. "Mr. Douglas, are you going to address these discovery issues regarding witnesses?"

Douglas took a deep breath. He was pretty sure how this was going to play, and the prospect wasn't pleasant.

"The court is well aware that we have been working diligently in this matter," he began cautiously. "We have not coordinated all of our defense efforts as well as I would have liked."

Douglas felt the prosecutors staring at him.

". . . I will represent to the court as an officer of this court that Miss Gerchas's statement I saw for the first time only five minutes ago. It is a copy of a statement that was taken in July of 1994."

Carl had assumed Shapiro's firm had given the D.A. what the law required. Now he was in bad trouble. The prosecutors were enraged. The judge was glaring. Reporters were scribbling in their notebooks. Millions were watching on TV. There was nothing to do but plod on.

Douglas said desperately, his voice rising despite his efforts to sound calm, "I tell this court, looking the court straight in the eye with all seriousness, that it had been an oversight. I am embarrassed by it and I take full responsibility. It is my obligation as the coordinator of the evidence to be better on top of the witness flow. . . . It is my blame and my blame alone. I take full responsibility."

Carl Douglas read out and spelled witness names, thirteen in all. It seemed to take an eternity.

Ito gave him a brittle smile. "I have to say, Mr. Douglas, I've had long experience with Mr. Hodgman. I've known him as a colleague, as a trial lawyer, and I've never seen the expressions on his face that I've seen today."

The day got no better. Hodgman pulled out another list: Simpson's dyslexia. Arthritis reports. Medical records on the cuts. Dr. Lenore Walker's reports. Paperwork from Baden and Henry Lee.

"This is supposed to be a fair proceeding," Hodgman said angrily. "Where are the reports? I don't think in the history of jurisprudence have we ever had anything occur like what happened today in this courtroom."

Now Carl was starting to lose it. He imagined the TV commentators that night. The newspaper articles.

"Your Honor, I will fall on my sword." Douglas was nearly out of control. Furious. ". . . I acknowledge when I am wrong, but there has not been any malice. This is not the most preposterous thing in jurisprudence. This is a mistake. This is a function of dealing with hundreds of witnesses . . . of there being twelve lawyers, five investigators, twenty-two thousand pages of evidence."

Douglas couldn't remember feeling so low. He had done what Johnnie wanted. He had covered for Shapiro's office. It was all for the client. Cold comfort in that thought right now. He was enraged. As the hearing ended for the day, Hodgman—a decent man, no question—walked over to Douglas and offered his hand. Hodgman's eyes seemed to say, "A fight's a fight, after all."

Douglas couldn't even look at him. He waved the prosecutor off and walked out, still incensed.

Late that night, Douglas heard on the news that Hodgman had been taken to the hospital. The media were saying "chest pains," carefully not calling it a heart attack. Carl immediately felt terrible about snubbing him. Bob Shapiro was shocked. Johnnie sent flowers.

Kardashian turned off the news and wondered about Johnnie's opening statement. One thing for sure, he thought, feeling a little guilty at his pleasure, we've already got the prosecutors on the defensive.

KEY PROSECUTOR'S ILLNESS MAY DELAY
TRIAL; WILLIAM HODGMAN IS HOSPITALIZED
WITH CHEST PAINS. GARCETTI SAYS HE MAY
SEEK TO POSTPONE PROCEEDINGS.

Deputy District Attorney William Hodgman, 41, complained of chest pains during a trial strategy meeting at the Downtown Criminal Courts Building and was taken by paramedics to California Medical Center, Garcetti said at a news conference.

Garcetti said Hodgman was seated next to him at the strategy meeting when he asked to be excused. "He told me he was not feeling well," the district attorney said. "He said he was disoriented and felt chest pains."

"There was no definite evidence of a heart attack," said emergency room physician Dr. Jim Gregg.

—Los Angeles Times, January 26, 1995.

On the eve of the publication of Simpson's book, O.J.'s coauthor, Larry Schiller, appeared on *Larry King Live*. Simpson and his attorneys were worried about how Schiller might answer the obvious question: Was O.J. guilty?

KING: Did you surmise guilt or innocence?
SCHILLER: You know, in a way, that's an unfair question . . . [because the evidence has not been presented in court]. But I've been asked that question many, many times, and let me put it to you this way. If O.J. Simpson is involved in the death of his ex-wife, I don't think it exists in his mind. But there are very, very few people that can take an event like that and put it out of their mind.

—Larry King Live, January 27, 1995

Schiller knew that question was inevitable and had thought hard about how to answer it. He had spent many hours with Simpson and had seen how he could win over an audience. Now that the media were saying O.J. wasn't the charming man the public thought he was, what was left for Simpson? Schiller had come to feel that Simpson had retreated deep within his public persona, to a place where he could exclude anything that challenged his chosen image. That was how Schiller had come to his answer. "If he did it, it doesn't exist in his mind."

* * *

On Friday, January 27, Ito called a recess until Monday to let Bill Hodgman recover.

The following day, Skip Taft called a meeting with Kardashian and Cochran. He seemed oblivious of the awkward timing: Johnnie was preoccupied with the second half of his opener and wanted to rehearse. But Skip couldn't wait. They had to cut expenses.

Taft wanted Shapiro to absorb the monthly retainer for his co-counsel, Sara Caplan. Johnnie paid Shawn and Carl from his fees. Why shouldn't Bob pay Sara?

At first, Cochran was fascinated, then infuriated. He asked for the first time who was getting what. As lead attorney, he now had a right to know. When Skip said Shapiro took home $100,000 a month, Johnnie could hardly contain his anger. Six months earlier, when Cochran met him at the Beverly Hills Tennis Club, Shapiro had implied he was making half that. Only a million dollars was available for fees, he'd said. On that understanding, Cochran signed on for $50,000 a month—which covered Shawn, Carl, and his support staff.

Anyway, the real issue was not Caplan but Shapiro. He was no longer in charge. Within days, Taft proposed a 50 percent cut to Larry Feldman, the attorney who had negotiated for Shapiro. Bob has a contract, Feldman told Taft. Nothing will change.

Taft then told Feldman that he would no longer pay Sara Caplan's salary. That was up to Shapiro now. Caplan left the case shortly after. About Shapiro's fee, they said nothing. They all knew what O.J. would say: Just don't pay him. Let him wait. Cochran left the meeting still seething about Shapiro's lack of candor with him.

Bailey's situation was troubling. They had thought Shapiro would take care of him. Just like me, Kardashian joked to Taft and Cochran. Bailey contributed a lot, and he wasn't getting a dime. They decided to pay his expenses and offer him participation in any lawsuits Simpson might file after the trial.

Days after its release . . . "I Want to Tell You" tops the nonfiction and general interest lists released . . . by the Wall Street Journal and heads USA Today's hardcover best-seller list. The New York Times reported the book will top its nonfiction list for February 12, based on sales for the week ending January 28.

. . . Publishing industry sources have said the book drew an advance of more than $1 million.

—Associated Press, January 29, 1995

On Sunday, January 29, the team assembled at Cochran's office at 10:30 A.M. for one last rehearsal of Johnnie's opening statements. Spirits were high. Kardashian was surprised when Bob Shapiro walked in. A few days earlier, Shapiro had thrown his arm around him in court. Said he had Super Bowl tickets. Did Kardashian want to fly to Miami with him? No, thanks, he said, and added that Los Angeles was a more exciting town this weekend. Apparently, Shapiro concurred.

That same morning, Mary Anne Gerchas's questionable background got heavy play in the media. The D.A.'s office had leaked the story. After Johnnie's enthusiastic introduction, she was now an embarrassment. Pat McKenna had supposedly checked her out.

"You know, Pat, I relied on you," Cochran told the detective in front of everybody. Johnnie was angry, but, as always, polite.

"I'm sorry, Johnnie. I thought she was okay." That wasn't good enough, but it was all McKenna could say.

SIMPSON DEFENSE CALLS COLLECTING OF EVIDENCE "SLIPSHOD"; COURT JUDGE ITO CONCLUDES THAT DEFENDANT'S ATTORNEYS DELIBERATELY HID INFORMATION ABOUT WITNESSES. HE ALLOWS THE PROSECUTION TO RESUME ITS OPENING STATEMENT.

O.J. Simpson's lead trial lawyer, his opening statement interrupted largely by defense conduct ruled deliberate and illegal, belatedly resumed his address to the jury Monday with a ringing attack on what he called the "careless, slipshod, negligent collection" of evidence against his famous client.

Prosecutors said that Mary Anne Gerchas, a jewelry store owner Cochran said would testify that she saw suspects other than Simpson fleeing the crime scene, used at least three different names and Social Security numbers and that she is an avid fan of O.J. Simpson. They also promised that they could produce witnesses who would say that Gerchas told them she was not in fact walking along Bundy Drive looking for a condominium on the night of the murders as Cochran claimed last week.

Although he [Ito] did not grant the prosecution request for a delay in the trial, he did tell the jury about the violation—reading an admonition that legal experts said could damage the defense.

In his admonition, Ito told the jury that Cochran—whom the judge referred to only as "defense counsel"—had "mentioned witnesses who had not been previously disclosed to the prosecution or whose written statements were not given to the prosecution before trial as required by law. This was a violation of the law. . . ."

"It's devastating for a defense lawyer to start a trial with the judge telling the jury that you violated the law," said Gerald L. Chaleff, a prominent Los Angeles defense attorney. "It sends a message that you are not to be trusted."

—Los Angeles Times, January 31, 1995

By Tuesday morning, January 31, Johnnie was prancing all over his offices. The grand marshal again. Just like the day he got the case. Newspaper stories didn't bother him.

Jo-Ellan Dimitrius said he'd impressed the jury very positively. The phones at Cochran's firm were ringing off the hook. Nothing but applause. Shawn told her boss that the evening before, total strangers had approached her at her gym. "Oh my God, he's innocent," they said. "I had no idea." So much enthusiasm.

The press, the establishment, even the court, could say whatever it pleased. Johnnie Cochran knew his audience. He knew his jury. And they were the only audience that counted.

LAWYERS WEIGH O.J. WITNESS

Prosecutors in the O.J. Simpson murder trial said they want to call as a witness a retired policeman and domestic violence expert to question him about private conversations with Simpson.

Ronald Shipp is featured prominently in the book "Raging Heart," which says Simpson dreamed about killing his ex-wife.

In the book, author Sheila Weller uses the pseudonym "Leo" for a person who talked with Simpson in his bedroom June 13, the day after Nicole Brown Simpson and Ronald Goldman were killed.

—Associated Press, January 31, 1995

PART FIVE

Adversaries Alike

1

ON TUESDAY, JANUARY 31, CARL DOUGLAS DRIVES
Johnnie, Shawn Chapman, and Bob Kardashian to court in
his Lexus. Shapiro and Bailey will arrive in their own cars.
The trial that Shapiro put on a fast track eight months ago
will finally start today, when the prosecution calls its first
witness to the stand.

The defense's seating plan separates the feuding attorneys, Shapiro at the far end of the table, on O.J.'s left;
Johnnie and Carl on O.J.'s other side; Bailey next to the
podium, almost in the center of the courtroom.

Cochran has taken six of the first nine witnesses so the
jury will know straightaway who the lead attorney is.
Shapiro has two, Douglas one. The other witness assignments aren't settled. Bailey isn't sure whom he'll get besides Fuhrman. Barry Scheck prefers to work at the office for
now.

For days the team has debated general tactics. How
aggressive should the lawyers be? Bob Shapiro argued that
less is more. Ask a few key questions; get out. Johnnie and
Carl are convinced that black juries like a show, a lawyer
fighting hard for his client. No question where Bailey comes
down in that debate. Scheck and Neufeld are fighters, too.
Blasier is calmer. Most of the team, Douglas knows, will
fight bare-knuckle when necessary.

Only Simpson might object. He hates confrontation.
Johnnie expects to be in witnesses' faces. He will push every
button he can find on Darden and Clark. Johnnie knows that
sooner or later, Juice will understand this is a brawl, not a
ballet.

The media have announced that the prosecution will open with domestic violence. The defense plan is to show on cross-examination that the incidents are exaggerated or even nonexistent. Jo-Ellan Dimitrius has told Johnnie that this jury won't be shocked by domestic violence. Douglas isn't so sure. Others share his concern. If the prosecution makes a strong battering case, Simpson will have to testify, risky as that may be. He's their best witness to convince the jury that the abuse never happened.

Kardashian walks into the holding cell just before nine A.M. O.J. is pacing and talking to himself.

"How'd you get here, Juice?" Simpson says to the wall. "Let's go," he mutters. Kardashian can feel Simpson's edge. Starting today, the D.A. will parade the worst parts of O.J.'s life before the TV camera and jury. He isn't scared, Kardashian knows. *Apprehensive,* maybe?

Bob interrupts O.J.'s monologue. "Take it easy. We know a lot of bad stuff will come out. Don't worry about it." Simpson keeps pacing. Kardashian knows that O.J. hates the thought of being portrayed as a wife-beater.

"We'll deal with it," Bob continues. "We'll deal with whatever comes out. This is what we've been waiting for."

Simpson has his own personal strategy, he's told Kardashian. He'll wear suits every day. Stay inside his public face. Be someone they like. Take the stand, Johnnie had said to him. You're the best possible person to explain yourself. You know the truth.

Judge Ito called the packed courtroom to order. The defense team took their places. Bob Blasier, Shawn Chapman, Sara Caplan, Howard Harris, and Kardashian sat by the rail.

Marcia Clark and Chris Darden were at the prosecution table. Bill Hodgman, still in the hospital, was noticeably absent. Scott Gordon, a domestic violence specialist; Jonathan Fairtlough, the D.A.'s technical assistant; and Cheri Lewis took the remaining prosecution seats.

* * *

Douglas knew that new discovery would land on their desks daily. Sooner or later, a prosecution witness would astonish or embarrass the defense. Neither he nor Johnnie knew what the case would look like in three months.

Sharon Gilbert, the 911 operator who took Nicole's call in 1989, is the prosecution's first witness. Her testimony gives the D.A. a chance to play one of the 911 tapes again. For the first time, the jury will hear Nicole's fear and Simpson's rage.

The prosecution must convince the jury that Simpson hit his wife in 1989. They claim you can hear a slap on the tape. Johnnie is not so sure. If the defense can create doubt by cross-examination, that will weaken the first battering incident presented to the jury.

Cochran's job begins after Darden finishes direct examination. Johnnie needs to make Sharon Gilbert switch sides, at least a little. He addresses the witness with exquisite courtesy. Simpson watches, impassive. O.J.'s account of this incident is straightforward. He pleaded no contest to the charges, did community service, made his apologies. Nothing to hide.

"I heard a female screaming, and then I heard what I thought was a slap," Gilbert testified during Darden's direct examination.

On cross, Cochran questions whether she could hear a slap through the static and other background noise of that phone call. He starts by questioning her accuracy.

"And where we see 'apartment' up there," Johnnie says, referring to Gilbert's log, "to the right of your statement—that was a mistake because your previous call had been from an apartment, is that right?"

"Right."

"And as we listened to that tape, could we hear you typing?"

"Yes, you could," Gilbert says.

"And so there's no mistaking about it, your typing was not anybody being struck, was it?"

447

"No."

"And since you didn't talk to anybody, you don't know whether or not there [were] blows being passed between two people, or what the situation was, do you?"

Gilbert insists she heard screaming and blows.

"But . . . you hadn't talked to anybody, so you don't know what was taking place at that location, do you?"

"No, I do not," Gilbert says.

"We heard typing and we heard static," Johnnie continues. ". . . I believe at some point that you became excited as you heard this, is that correct?"

"Yes."

All this to dilute the impact of that possible slap. Douglas looks at the jury, hoping to see perplexity. A terrified woman is screaming on the tape, yes. But there's no clear picture here of a man beating a woman. Carl calls the first witness a draw.

Next on the stand is Detective John Edwards, the uniformed cop who responded to the 911 call in 1989. The detective tells a brutal story. Edwards is effectively conveying the horror Nicole experienced. For years Simpson has told his friends this incident was a "mutual-type wrestling match." Detective Edwards describes something different:

". . . A woman came running out of the bushes to my left, across the driveway. She was wearing a bra only as an upper garment. . . . She ran across and collapsed on the [gate] speaker . . . and started yelling, 'He's going to kill me. He's going to kill me!' "

"Liar!" Simpson writes on a notepad. He passes it to Cochran.

". . . I said, 'Well, who's going to kill you?' She said, 'O.J.' . . .'I said, O.J. who? Do you mean the football player, O.J. the football player?' "

"It's not true!" Simpson whispers to Johnnie.

But nothing Edwards says is as damaging as the three Polaroid snapshots of Nicole he took that night at the West L.A. station. Darden displays them on a huge video screen. He passes the originals to the jury. Nicole's face is red with scratches. Her expression is blank, numb. She seems almost ghostly. Simpson shakes his head, and complains again as the Polaroids work their way around the jury.

"You know, do you not, sir," Johnnie asks on cross, "that if somebody gets into a fight, on occasion there may be bruises on both sides?"

"Oh, yes."

"So you talked to Nicole Simpson, you talked to O.J. Simpson, but you had made your decision [to arrest Simpson] . . . before you talked to O.J. Simpson, isn't that right?"

"Yes."

Minor victories, Douglas decides.

It was late in the day when Mike Farrell, the detective who investigated the same incident, was sworn in. On direct examination, he offered Simpson's explanation. "He told me that it turned into a mutual-type wrestling match and that was basically it." Farrell recalled another occasion when Simpson apologized and promised to get counseling.

Then Farrell gave the defense what it wanted. Johnnie asked if other West L.A. cops had gone to Rockingham on domestic dispute calls. Farrell said that in 1989 he polled the station house.

"And you got a report from *one* officer, did you not?" Cochran asked.

"That's correct."

"And that officer's name is Mark Fuhrman?"

"That is correct."

Double-edged sword here, Carl mused. The prosecution wanted to establish that the cops were cozy with Simpson and didn't take Nicole seriously. They'd done that—but they'd also given the defense the opportunity to introduce Mark Fuhrman, the only cop in the division who involved himself with O.J.'s and Nicole's problems. Win some, lose some.

2

The next day, February 1, Douglas will cross Ron Shipp, the African-American ex-cop and Rockingham hanger-on who claims that O.J. confided to him that he had dreamed about killing Nicole. In his pretrial interview with Shipp, Carl heard nothing like that. "What's the worst you can tell me about O.J.?" Carl had asked. Shipp didn't volunteer a thing.

The defense expected Shipp to testify that Nicole had asked him to counsel O.J. about domestic violence. He'd taken an LAPD course on the subject. That could be bad.

Weeks after first interviewing Shipp, Douglas heard about Sheila Weller's book *Raging Heart*, another "inside story" of the case. In the first chapter, Simpson's close friend "Leo" says Simpson invited him to his bedroom the night after the murders. According to "Leo," O.J. didn't want to take a lie detector test; he'd dreamt of killing Nicole. The prosecutors gave Carl a tape of their interview with Shipp. But no transcript. By the time the tape was transcribed, Marcia Clark had told Johnnie Cochran that "Leo" was Ron Shipp.

Simpson insisted that Shipp wasn't in his bedroom that night. His sister Shirley and her husband, who were, could vouch for that. And Shipp wasn't a close friend, just an errand boy. By the way, O.J. added, he has a drinking problem.

On the morning of February 1, Bill Pavelic turned on his office TV at nine. His job was to monitor the direct testimony. He knew the team was nervous about Shipp, who

450

claimed to be an insider. No one doubted he was at Rockingham on the night of June 13, and of course he had helped with security the day of the funeral. Over the years Shipp had brought West L.A. cops to Rockingham and used Simpson's tennis court and Jacuzzi.

O.J. told Pavelic that Shipp admired Nicole and that his friends told him that Shipp was in love with her. To Pavelic, that made Ron Shipp suspect as a prosecution witness. Simpson admitted he discussed his dreams freely with his jail visitors, and Pavelic learned that O.J. had mentioned his dreams to Joe Kolkowitz, one of his old friends, and that Kolkowitz had told Shipp.

Today Ron Shipp seemed deeply distressed. He avoided eye contact with O.J. as he walked to the witness box.

"Do you and the defendant remain friends today?" Chris Darden asked.

"I still love the guy," Shipp replied. "But I don't know. I mean, this is a weird situation I'm sitting here in."

The ex-cop testified that in early January 1989, Nicole asked to see lesson plans from a police academy class he taught on domestic violence. She was especially interested in the profiles of batterers and their victims. She asked Ron to show them to O.J.

Kardashian wondered again why he'd never known any of this. Why his friend didn't confide in him. Why O.J. didn't get help.

". . . I told him [Simpson] Nicole had advised me that he had hit her," Shipp said to Darden, "and that after looking at the profile she felt that they [the characteristics of batterers] all fit him to a T."

"What was the defendant's reaction?" Darden asked,

". . . He denied that any of those were him except for maybe one."

"And which one was that?"

"The jealous. He said, 'Maybe I might be a little jealous.' And that was it."

Shipp had established a possible psychological background consistent with a motive for murder. Shipp testified that O.J. told him about his dreams at about eleven P.M. That's impossible, Kardashian tells himself. I was there, too. O.J. went to bed at 9:30. I made sure Shirley and Benny were in his room because we worried that O.J. might kill himself. They never left him alone. Why is Ron Shipp doing this?

When Darden finished, court recessed. In the holding cell, Simpson reviewed the testimony with Shapiro, Carl, Kardashian, and Johnnie. "We never played tennis," he said. "We never went to dinner. We never played golf. *We weren't close friends*. It's all lies!"

"Kick his ass," Johnnie told Carl.

Carl Douglas started quietly. Why hadn't the witness mentioned Simpson's dreams last July, when Marcia Clark and Phil Vannatter interviewed him? What about the interview with Douglas himself?

"So did you lie when you didn't tell me about that dream?"

"I sure did," Shipp replied.

"You've lied a few times, haven't you, sir?"

"Never in court."

"You've lied a few times concerning what you know about Mr. Simpson, true?"

"Yeah, I'd say."

That set the tone. Carl's voice got more strident.

"Have you in the past shared intimate secrets about a friend with somebody writing a book?" he asked.

"Never," Shipp answered.

"Never before?"

"Never," Shipp repeated.

". . . You say that the conversation with Mr. Simpson was eating you up. Is that your statement?"

"That's correct."

"And did you hope to exorcise this pain from your body by talking to [*Raging Heart*'s author] Sheila Weller?"

"Yes, I did."

"You didn't think that you could exorcise this pain from your body by talking to the police department?"

Cochran was signaling, but Douglas didn't notice.

"Stop that shit, Carl!" Cochran hissed. Douglas was giving Shipp a perfect setup for a dramatic attack of conscience.

"Johnnie, make him stop!" Simpson whispered furiously. Douglas didn't hear. He was too caught up in taking Shipp down.

Carl established that Shipp was a fledgling actor and then accused him of testifying "to enhance your profile around the world."

"I'm doing this for my conscience and my peace of mind," the witness fired back. "I will not have the blood of Nicole on Ron Shipp."

Bailey was sitting closest to Carl. He tugged on Douglas's coat. "Shut him up, shut this guy up," Bailey almost shouted.

"I can sleep at night, unlike a lot of others," Shipp concluded.

Carl finally realized that his questioning had backfired.

Moments later, Shipp turned toward Simpson. "This is sad, O.J. But no, this is really sad."

Douglas took one last shot.

"You drink a lot, don't you?"

"I used to."

"You've had a drinking problem, haven't you?"

"In the past I have."

Douglas turned to Judge Ito. "We can stop now, Your Honor."

That night, Carl Douglas sat with his wife and watched the TV news. He went into shock as one white commentator after another denounced him. He was sarcastic, they said, mean-spirited, overharsh. On NBC, defense attorney Gerry Spence, once asked to join the team, was particularly critical. But then reporter Andrea Ford and attorney Leo Terrell, both black, insisted Douglas was on target.

Embarrassment and depression settled over him. Now I *feel* it, Douglas thought. Race *does* define this trial. Black folks loved what I did. White folks are dogging me. TFC.

453

Johnnie phoned, disturbed by the TV analysts. Tone it down tomorrow, he said.

A trial lawyer whom Douglas considered a friend rang up: "Don't watch TV after you've had a witness. You'll start questioning what you are doing."

The next morning, Johnnie drove his Rolls-Royce, with Carl in the passenger seat, Kardashian and Shawn in the back.

"I guess you see what it's like now," Johnnie said. "The press second-guesses us, criticizes everything. I don't read the papers or watch the news." The ride turned into a discussion of cross-examination techniques. Douglas remained silent.

In the holding cell, Simpson gave Carl a list of questions. Ask these, he said.

Everyone was astonished. No one had ever seen Simpson give his lawyers direct orders before.

"He never ran license plates for me," Simpson insisted. "He did it for Nicole. Ask about that."

Shapiro put in: "I don't think you should do that, Carl. You're the attorney, not him. You should ask the questions you want."

Johnnie interrupted, so aggressively that Kardashian was startled: "If the client wants them asked, we'll ask the questions. He's the client. He knows what went on. Ask the questions, Carl."

Douglas felt his hackles rising.

Simpson's next item: Carl's tone. Too loud, Simpson said, perhaps too aggressive—and, he added, Douglas had objected too often during Darden's direct examination. "We sound like the prosecution during the opening statements."

Then O.J. instructed Douglas on diction, inflection, accents. "I taught all the guys on the teams how to talk," he explained. "I taught Marcus. I taught Lynn Swann. There's something in your voice. You get loud, screechy. The inflection is wrong. You need a different tone."

Douglas said nothing aloud.

We are now required to consult with O.J. and kiss his ring before finishing up with a witness, he thought.

Lee Bailey wandered in. "When this is over," he said mildly, "I think we can open an office in West Palm Beach. Bailey & Simpson."

Fifteen minutes into the proceeding and already there's trouble. Bob Shapiro rises to address the court.

While others were at sidebar, he tells Ito, Ron Shipp was "staring at us, mouthing some type of words." Shipp also made "unusual facial expressions that would go from a grimace to a smirk, and it was in front of the jury."

After Ito's staff checks with Court TV, the judge agrees that Shipp has made a gesture or an attempt to communicate with Simpson.

Darden announces he'll ask Shipp to tell the court what he said when the jury returns. Douglas objects: The statement is not evidence. Ito agrees. But Lee Bailey jumps up before Douglas can catch him.

"Can we hear what he said?"

Ito orders Darden to tell everyone.

"He said, 'Tell the truth,'" Darden announces. The prosecutor can't conceal his pleasure.

"Can you believe he said that?" Simpson says to Kardashian. "Of all the people to tell the truth! Why doesn't he tell the truth?"

Shapiro muttered that he'd do better. He'd be nice. Cochran and Douglas are in the prosecutors' and the witnesses' faces, too pushy, too tough. Shapiro says it's not good for Simpson. O.J. is now upset with everyone.

Marcia Clark gets up while the jury is out and asks Ito to let Darden ask a certain question again. Mr. Darden stated it improperly, she says. You have to live with it, Ito replies.

Johnnie sees an opening to push Darden's buttons. "She's given you up, pal," he jokes to Chris. "She's given you up."

Darden smiles. But it's not a joke. Cochran is saying that the white prosecutors will throw you out with the trash when this is over.

* * *

A.C. turned on his TV to watch the trial. He knew Ron Shipp had eyes for Nicole. He'd always considered Shipp a possible suspect. It upset him to watch the proceedings. Cowlings began to feel feverish. He started to cry and shake like a leaf. After all these months, it was real. He was out of control, trembling, weeping. He called his mother and told her he thought he was going crazy.

Get your Bible, his mother said. She made him read to her. She talked him through it. It took him a long time to calm down.

"O.J. really gave me shit," Cochran tells Carl that evening. "He wants only me and Shapiro to do the witnesses."

That sounded about right. Douglas knew Simpson couldn't say it to his face. But he'd had the feeling Shipp would be his last witness for a long while.

"Okay, that's fine," Carl said. It was all about the client, he reminded himself.

3

ON THURSDAY, FEBRUARY 2, DARDEN SHOWED THE pictures of Nicole's injuries and bruises that had been found in Nicole's safe-deposit box. The defense had seen the contents in discovery. They knew the most damaging items were O.J.'s letters to Nicole. One apologized for the 1989 beating. "Let me start by expressing to you how wrong I was for hurting you," Simpson wrote. "There is no acceptable excuse for what I did."

But the defense also had Nicole's letter to O.J., which

Arnelle had retrieved from New York. Nicole had written, in effect, that she shared the blame for the couple's problems. The defense had no way to introduce that letter now: It was the prosecution's turn to present its case. They would have to wait.

The next witness, Terri Moore, was the 911 dispatcher during the 1993 Gretna Green incident. She gave the D.A.s another chance to show Simpson at his worst: They played the tape of him yelling after kicking the door. Simpson listened. Douglas glanced at the jury. Would they buy the prosecution line that these incidents of domestic discord led to murder?

The next day, Nicole's Gretna Green neighbors, Catherine Boe and her husband, Carl Colby, took the stand. The prosecution wanted to establish Simpson as a stalker. The couple had dialed 911 around 10:30 P.M. in late April 1992, to report a man lurking around Nicole's property. Colby looked out his window and saw a black man pacing on the sidewalk. He didn't recognize the man as Simpson, and his story sounded vaguely racist: "I said to myself, What is a man of this description doing outside at this time?"

After calling the police, he recognized O.J. "I was embarrassed that I'd called 911 because I didn't feel Mr. Simpson was a threat to me or anyone else in the neighborhood."

Douglas felt that the D.A. had proved the defense's point. Without a clear picture of Simpson as a menacing figure, it would be hard for the prosecution to prove that domestic violence led to murder.

Douglas assumed Keith Zlomsowitch would be the next witness. His testimony could establish O.J. as a Peeping Tom, a stalker spying as Nicole and Keith made love. That would hurt. Zlomsowitch was in the courthouse, ready to take the stand, but Chris Darden called Denise Brown, Nicole's older sister, instead. The defense was surprised but assumed the D.A. passed on Zlomsowitch because Nicole's neighbors had failed to set up their stalking theory.

Nicole's sister, the tenth domestic abuse witness, took the stand on the afternoon of Friday, February 3. Denise Brown was practically the murdered woman's dark-haired double. Carl Douglas wondered if the jury would see Nicole in that witness box.

"We were all drinking and goofing around and being loud and dancing and having a great time," Denise testified about a night at the Red Onion restaurant. "And then at one point, O.J. grabbed Nicole's crotch and said, 'This is where babies come from, and this belongs to me!'

"And Nicole just sort of wrote it off as if it was nothing, like she was used to that kind of treatment. I thought it was really humiliating, if you ask me."

Shapiro jumped up. "Move to strike that last part as being nonresponsive, calling for speculation, narrative."

Ito overruled.

"That's a lie!" Simpson hissed. Shawn Chapman could hear him from her seat inside the rail. "I'd never say that," Simpson continued. "She had C-sections! If I grabbed her there, it would have been playing, friendly."

Darden pushed on. "Did the defendant appear mad or angry or upset when he grabbed your sister's crotch and made these statements in front of these strangers?"

"No, he wasn't angry. . . . It was like, 'This belongs to me. This is mine.'" Denise looked as if she might cry.

Cochran asked for a sidebar. "Your Honor," he said, leaning on the railing, "we're going to ask the court to move to strike this last part. . . . This lady is hostile. It's not fair to this defendant. We're trying to, you know, keep him under control."

"Can I make a suggestion?" Darden asked, "Are we adjourning at three o'clock?"

"Boy, I sure hope so," Ito said.

Darden looked at Denise Brown. "If you look over at the witness, I don't think she's going to make it."

"She's all right. She'll make it," Ito replied.

"I don't think she's going to make it," Darden insisted.

"Then she will have the weekend," Ito concluded, "to stiffen her upper lip."

"I would rather not enter the weekend with her breaking down crying," Johnnie answers.

Nicole's sister was already on the verge of tears. "Are you

all right?'' Darden asked her. She nodded. He led her through the story of Simpson losing his temper at Rockingham after a long evening of nightclubbing: O.J. was throwing pictures and clothes, and finally he picked up Nicole and threw her against the wall and then out of the house, Denise said. ''She ended up falling . . . on her elbows and on her butt. . . .''

That image of Nicole pushed Denise over the edge. She was choking out the words. She took a moment to compose herself, then went on. ''We were all sitting there screaming and crying, and then he grabbed me and threw me out of the house.''

Simpson was enraged. ''Hey, she lived on welfare for six years!'' he spat out. ''I paid her money. I gave her things. She's a slut!'' His bass whisper carried. Douglas wondered if the jury could hear him.

''Are you okay, Miss Brown?'' Darden asked. Denise was still crying.

''Yeah, it's just so hard. I'll be fine.''

The prosecutor suggested ending for the weekend. Ito agreed. A perfect Friday finish for the D.A., Kardashian thought. The jurors would see her tears all weekend.

4

AT JOHNNIE'S OFFICE THAT FRIDAY EVENING, THE PHONES and faxes were hot. Many African-Americans were outraged. She was lying, callers said angrily. A lying bitch. Fake tears. She kept fingering a crucifix. Religious bullshit! Some even threatened to kill her.

Johnnie smiled as he entered the conference room. It was

the first gathering of the full team since the prosecution case began. The big question was whether Denise's eerie resemblance to Nicole was getting to the jury.

Douglas had been watching the black jurors and sensed that they weren't comfortable with Denise Brown.

Kardashian had checked faces, watched body language. They just don't believe her, he thought. Maybe the white jurors are buying this. Not the blacks.

Despite the community reaction, everyone knew Denise could hurt the defense. Bob Shapiro would cross-examine her on Monday. Should he be tough or friendly? She'd cry if he pushed her the wrong way. Count on it. Would the jury see him as a bad guy? Imagine he was abusing *Nicole?*

Shapiro was worried about the jury's perception, and Douglas thought he'd go light on her. That was his style.

As the defense met that Friday night, a treasure sat next to the VCR in Cochran's conference room, a tape that had surfaced only days before. The team watched it now with mounting excitement. A vacationing stockbroker had noticed Simpson standing outside Paul Revere Junior High School after the dance recital the day Nicole and Goldman were murdered. The stockbroker turned on his video camera and taped Denise Brown kissing Simpson enthusiastically. Then he shot O.J. kissing Judy Brown, smiling and greeting the Brown family, lifting up Justin.

Denise had testified that Simpson was menacing and gloomy at Sydney's recital. If that was true, why did she say good-bye so warmly?

The stockbroker had sent the tape to the prosecution, but it never showed up in discovery. As the first witnesses took the stand that week, the broker called Cochran's office.

"What about my tape?" he asked Carl Douglas. "Aren't you going to use it?"

The defense called the D.A.—and lo and behold, the tape was found and turned over. Denise Brown's testimony gave them the opportunity to use it.

* * *

On Monday morning, Chris Darden continued his direct examination of Denise Brown.

"Did you see the defendant's face immediately after you told him that he took your sister for granted?" Darden asks.

". . . His whole facial structure changed. I mean, everything changed about him. . . .

"Then all of a sudden the eyes got real angry. His whole jaw . . . his whole face just changed completely when he got upset. It wasn't as if it was O.J. anymore. He looked like a different person. . . ."

Douglas sees that the prosecution is trying to establish Simpson as a Jekyll-and-Hyde killer.

Simpson is agitated. He scribbles notes and shoves them toward Shapiro and Cochran. Most are questions he wants asked. He instructs Shapiro in an aggressive stage whisper.

"Go easy on her, Bob. I don't want a confrontation with her."

Johnnie listens to O.J. attentively. Shapiro looks straight ahead. He doesn't want interruptions while he's listening to a witness he's about to cross-examine.

Shapiro finally turns to Simpson and says, *"I'm* the lawyer. This is what you're paying me for. If you want to run things, you don't need me."

Shapiro began his cross-examination gently. "Miss Brown, as you know, I have to ask you some questions."

Knowing the answer is yes, he asks Nicole's sister if she and Darden have rehearsed her testimony. He politely questions her memory. Does she recall dates? Does she know if the incident at Rockingham occurred before or after O.J. and Nicole were married? Denise acknowledges that she had a few drinks that night.

". . . And you had margaritas then at the house, did you not?"

"We had more drinks at the house," Denise replies.

Shapiro brings up Simpson's no-smoking house rule, suggesting it might account for his anger. Denise's date, Ed McCabe, smoked. Wasn't Nicole a "part-time closet smoker"? Wasn't she getting cigarettes from McCabe? Then he moves on to the crotch-grabbing incident at the Red Onion.

"It's too soft," Simpson now whispers to Cochran.

"At that time were you still drinking?" Shapiro asks.

"Oh, I was drinking at that time, yes."

". . . I don't mean to embarrass you, but this particular evening, could you tell us how much you had to drink, if you recall?"

"Oh, I don't recall how many drinks, no."

After lunch, Shapiro shows the stockbroker's video. "Do you recognize what is depicted in that brief video?" he asks Denise.

"I saw us saying good-bye to O.J."

Shapiro stops the tape. Freeze frame of Denise embracing Simpson with obvious enthusiasm.

". . . And what were you doing at that time?"

"I gave him a kiss good-bye."

Shapiro cues the video further. Simpson kisses Judy Brown and shakes hands with Louis Brown. O.J. is animated, smiling. Now he's lifting Justin, kissing the boy. Finally he shows the enlarged picture of a smiling Simpson posing with Sydney.

"Is that the way O.J. looked after the recital?" Shapiro asks Denise.

"I wasn't there when the picture was taken."

"I said, Is that the way O.J. looked after the recital?"

"I guess," Denise admits.

Shapiro sits down. Now Darden will present his redirect.

O.J. glares at Shapiro. "I want you to do this!"

"I think you're foolish," Shapiro snaps.

The two of them are carrying on as if they're alone in the courtroom: "I want you to play the video again where I'm picking up Justin!" Simpson says angrily. "I'm showing pain because he's too heavy. I'm saying ouch. I almost drop him. Ask Denise about that."

"It doesn't mean anything. You *could* pick him up. The tape doesn't show you grimacing so badly that you almost drop him. That's absurd."

"I *want* you to play it," Simpson insists. "I was in pain."

462

Shapiro refuses again. "O.J., I'm the lawyer. I'm getting a hundred thousand dollars a month from you. Do what I tell you."

"I want to show it!"

"I don't think it should be shown again!"

The defense lawyers, in shock, barely notice that Darden has finished.

"Mr. Shapiro?" Ito calls.

Shapiro looks up. "May we have a moment to confer, please?"

The team huddles.

"You've hired me to do a job," Shapiro argues. "I'm the heart surgeon. I'm operating. Do you want to be awake giving instructions?"

"I'm the client. I want you to do as I say."

"Bob, do it," Cochran cuts in. "O.J. is the client. Do it."

"Okay." Shapiro scowls. "I think it's very foolish."

Robert Shapiro rises stiffly. Doesn't even glance at the defense table.

"Your Honor, may we cue up to the one portion of the video where O.J. is picking up his son? I would like the witness to see if she can refresh her memory whether O.J. is screaming with a little pain when he lifts up his son."

He's sticking it to Johnnie, Kardashian thinks.

"Stop there," Shapiro tells the technician.

"Were you able to discern from his mouth movements and his voice," he asks Denise, "that he appeared to be in pain when he was lifting his son?"

"No," she replies.

"Thank you; nothing further."

Shapiro says nothing to Johnnie or O.J. as he sits down. One question and he sits down? Kardashian wonders. That's the loudest fuck-you I've heard in years.

5

IN THE TWELFTH-FLOOR PRESSROOM, REPORTERS DEBATE the impact of Denise's testimony. She was the prosecution's best eyewitness to several key domestic incidents. The grabbing-the-crotch story was something you couldn't make up.

The mostly white press corps has made no secret of its feelings all along. Simpson did it. Reporters had expected Denise Brown's testimony to be almost as harrowing for the spectators as for the witness. Instead, she came across as strangely detached, even lifeless.

Several days before, Denise had appeared on the Barbara Walters show, telling Walters much of what she said on the stand. Same words, same inflections. Something didn't ring true. You'd expect her to seem wounded, vulnerable; she didn't.

As the reporters watch the trial on TV in the pressroom, the air is thick with disparaging comments. AP's Linda Deutsch shares the general view. But she worries that her negative assessment may be off. "What did you think of Denise's performance?" she asks another reporter afterward.

"That's the word. It was a performance," her colleague replies.

Johnnie Cochran has two goals in all his criminal trials. Winning an acquittal for Simpson was his top priority, of course. But restoring O.J.'s freedom would be only a partial victory. The second goal was to restore the defendant's

464

reputation. An important thing for any client, but especially for O.J., whose livelihood depended entirely on his good-guy image. When Denise Brown finished testifying, Johnnie told Carl their second goal was a lost cause. Johnnie felt privately that O.J. had been so convincingly established as a wife-beater over the last two months that his days as a corporate spokesman were over. Of course, Cochran said nothing to Simpson, who was not ready to accept that fact. The first order of business remained, as always, to get Simpson home.

The next day, Tuesday, February 7, there are problems with the jury: An elderly white woman on the panel shares an arthritis specialist with Simpson. The doctor may be one of the defense witnesses. A conflict? More important, the woman's been arguing with her fellow jurors. No one will force her to vote for acquittal, she's said, no matter what the majority thinks.

Ito dismisses her because of her doctor and ignores the rest. He says he's been told the jurors aren't getting along, but he gives no details.

While the attorneys meet with Ito in chambers, Kardashian sits with Simpson in the holding cell. Again O.J. rehashes the years leading up to his 1993 divorce. He is furious with Nicole. How could she preserve those terrible pictures and his letters in a safe-deposit box?

"What if we got back together, then were both killed in a plane crash?" he explains. "They'd find those pictures from '89. What would our kids think of me? It's not right for the kids!"

Bob and O.J. talk about the jury trip to Rockingham scheduled for this Sunday.

"Everything's got to be just right," Simpson said. "The place has to look good. Like why would I give up such a terrific place?"

Court reconvenes just before eleven A.M. The prosecution has finished with domestic violence. The subject may come up again, but for now the battering-as-precursor-to-murder strategy seems to have fizzled. The D.A. didn't succeed in making a stalker of Simpson. Denise's tears were probably wasted on black jurors. So far, the prosecution case hasn't worked well.

Next, Marcia Clark will present ten witnesses to establish the time of death. First to the stand is Tia Gavin, who waited on Nicole at Mezzaluna that night. Gavin says that Nicole and the Browns left the restaurant at about 8:45 P.M. In cross-examining her, Shapiro tries to place Ron Goldman's arrival at Bundy as late as possible. This would move the time the murders occurred closer to eleven, giving Simpson no time to kill two people, dispose of his weapon and bloody clothing, and be at Rockingham by 10:55.

Shapiro had finally given up on 10:02 as the time of death and on multiple-time-line stuff. In recent meetings, as the team reviewed Bailey's time line, Shapiro had been virtually silent. It was hard to tell whether he was conceding, indifferent, or sulking, but Douglas had no great interest in Shapiro's inner feelings. He was handling his assignment according to plan. That was all that counted.

Bartender Stewart Tanner testifies that he last saw Goldman at about 9:50 P.M., before he left Mezzaluna. They planned to go to a Marina del Rey bar that night. Tanner said Mezzaluna was a five-minute walk to Nicole's condo. Goldman's apartment was also five minutes from the restaurant. The D.A.'s message to the jury is clear: Ron could easily have gotten to Bundy in time to be murdered at 10:15 P.M.

Karen Crawford, Mezzaluna's manager, got a call from Juditha Brown at 9:37 P.M. asking about a pair of lost eyeglasses. Crawford found them outside the restaurant and put them in a white envelope. Five minutes later, Nicole called, asking for Ron Goldman, who then asked Crawford for the glasses.

"He told me he was going to drop the glasses off at Nicole's," she testified. "He left at about ten minutes to ten."

* * *

The day's last witness, writer Pablo Fenjves, may be the most important prosecution witness so far. The D.A. expects him to nail down the time of the murders, which will eventually dovetail with the period during which Simpson's whereabouts are unaccounted for.

The writer and his wife live seventy yards north of Nicole's, sharing a back alley with her. Fenjves was watching the ten P.M. Sunday news in his bedroom when he heard the Akita's "plaintive wail."

"And for how long did you watch the news?" Clark asks.

"Well, about fifteen or twenty minutes into it," Fenjves answers, "I became aware of a barking sound. . . ."

"So it was approximately fifteen minutes after the news," Clark asks, "that you started to hear a dog barking?"

Cochran objects. "Your Honor, that misstates what he just said."

Fenjves makes the correction. "Fifteen, twenty minutes *into* it, I heard a very distinctive barking. . . . As you may recall, I described it at the time as a plaintive wail. Sounded like, you know, a very unhappy animal."

Then Johnnie shows off his distinctive cross-examination technique: Diffuse the original account, confuse the witness, and suggest a parallel reality. Cochran likes to set up a diffuse-and-confuse moment with a question about truthtelling.

"And of course, in addressing and talking to the police officers, you told them the truth about everything as best you knew, right?"

"Yes, sir."

Did Fenjves sense the setup? Hard to tell.

Cochran approaches, LAPD report in hand, and quotes from it.

" 'At approximately 10:15 to 10:30 P.M., witnesses [Fenjves and his wife] heard a dog barking uncontrollably to the rear of their residence.' Do you recall so indicating to the police?"

Fenjves answers only about the location of the sound. Cochran repeats the time-line question.

"As I told you," Fenjves says, "I told them that I heard the dog barking between 10:15 and 10:20."

"So if they have that wrong," Cochran persists, "*they're* wrong. Is that right?"

"That is possible," Fenjves says doggedly, "because I did not say that."

Cochran takes the witness through all his movements, upstairs and downstairs, in bed, watching television. Then questions his sense of direction, of color, of sound.

But Fenjves doesn't waver. He heard the dog between 10:15 and 10:20.

Carl smiles to himself. The defense has its own witness to a possible time of death. Robert Heidstra was walking his own dogs and heard the Akita begin to bark around 10:45. His turn on the stand will come during the defense case.

The next day, Eva Stein, another neighbor, tells how she woke up to "very loud, very persistent" barking at 10:15 P.M. Couldn't get back to sleep. Her roommate, Louis Karpf, returned from a trip about 10:45 and went to the mailbox. The Akita approached him, "barking very profusely." He ran behind his gate.

Stephen Schwab left his Montana Street apartment to walk his dog after a *Dick Van Dyke Show* rerun ended at 10:30 P.M. He saw the Akita at 10:55 P.M.; he was certain of the time. Carl Douglas knows the defense will point out that the murders could have occurred minutes before Schwab encountered the dog.

By Wednesday evening the prosecution has the jury on the edge of their seats. The barking-dog testimony is dramatic. The press sees pure melodrama.

The reporters recall Johnnie's opening statement: How absurd it is, he said, to build a murder case around a barking dog. For now, the dog has become the prosecution's star witness.

TO: Johnnie Cochran
FROM: Michael Schneider [Alan Dershowitz's associate]
DATE: February 9, 1995

We had an interesting tip . . . says that the prosecution's theory is based on two Perry Mason stories by Erle Stanley

Gardner: 1) The Case of the Howling Dog!!! and 2) The Case of the Buried Clock. This might be useful as a reference in a closing argument: although the prosecution would have you believe that this is the Case of the Howling Dog, real life is not like a Perry Mason novel, etc.

6

FEBRUARY 12 WAS MARKED WITH A HUGE RED CIRCLE ON every attorney's mental calendar. The jury would visit both the crime scene and O.J. Simpson's home. Impossible to overestimate that Sunday's importance.

The defense needed the jury to see the cramped space where Nicole and Ron died. It should be clear to anyone visiting the courtyard that the thin blood smears and tiny bits of trace evidence connected to Simpson could not be the logical aftermath of *this* crime: Goldman's defensive wounds suggested a fierce struggle. The assailant would have been bruised, or worse. And a single killer stabbing and slashing two people in that space would be covered in blood.

Jurors also needed to see the position of Nicole's body. She had fallen barely fifteen feet from the public sidewalk, her body clearly visible through the open gate. Cochran would call witnesses who had walked by shortly after the time prosecutors insisted the murders were committed. Those witnesses had seen nothing.

The interior of Nicole's condo told its own story. Sydney and Justin's bedrooms were close enough to the crime scene for the children to have been wakened by the struggle. Would

Simpson kill his children's mother in a place where those same children might catch him in the act? The defense wanted the jury to *feel* the proximity, to walk the short distance from the kids' rooms to the courtyard.

The condo's interior offered another advantage for the defense. Jurors would see empty rooms—no furniture, bare walls. The home Nicole had made for herself and her children, her pictures, her candles, the music she liked—these were all gone. The empty apartment would reduce the dead woman to an impersonal abstraction. Not good for the prosecution.

At Rockingham, the defense wanted to show the jury that no man would give up all this over a woman. Johnnie said it to Carl so often it was practically a mantra. This was a man with everything to lose. Whatever his anger or jealousy, he would never throw it all away.

The defense also wanted the jury to see where the bloody glove was found, far away from Simpson's alleged blood trail at the house. The area *around* the blood-soaked glove had been pristine—no blood trail led either to it or away from it.

Cochran also wanted jurors to see the heavy shrubbery and bushes overgrowing the fence where the glove was found. To climb that fence would be extremely difficult. Anyone standing in that walkway would see that a climber would have been scratched, the shrubs would have been disturbed and branches broken. But in the crime-scene photos, the foliage was intact. How did the glove get there?

The jury would see the other discreet entrances into Simpson's home. Two side doors. A gate by the pool patio. A low fence near the back of the house was fairly easy to climb. The prosecution didn't even know about the secret pathway that Kardashian and Simpson had used two days after the murder to get O.J. past the press. The defense had no obligation to tell anyone. If Simpson had been sneaking into the house like the shadowy black man the limo driver saw on the night of the murders, why would he use the front door?

The prosecutors, meanwhile, still hoped the jurors

470

wouldn't enter Simpson's home or Nicole's condo. They'd argued hard in Ito's chambers the previous week. Comparing Nicole's empty condo to Rockingham is prejudicial, they told the judge. The mansion is vivid and colorful. Simpson comes alive for the jurors. At Bundy, we see bare walls, empty rooms. Nicole becomes more distant, less sympathetic. The comparison was unfair, they insisted. And all the evidence was outside.

"The jurors are intelligent people," Ito finally said. "They can appreciate that these people are dead and the house had to be cleaned out." Carl Douglas restrained a smile. The jurors knew that *intellectually*. But that didn't change the emotional impact. Ito had to know that too. His decision was a win for the defense.

All day Saturday, members of the defense team are hard at work establishing O.J.'s African-American identity at Rockingham.

Cathy Randa and Arnelle have worked hard on the project. Rockingham is now sparkling, the furniture arranged for maximum effect. O.J. wants a fire in each fireplace. A thousand dollars' worth of flowers have been ordered. The American flag must fly on the flagpole out front.

A nude portrait of Paula Barbieri vanishes from its spot near the fireplace in Simpson's bedroom. There will be no pictures of white women in O.J.'s bedroom. A silver-framed picture of O.J. and his mother goes on his bedside table.

Justin's homemade Father's Day card tracing his tiny handprint and footprint still hangs on the bathroom door in Simpson's bedroom. "Keep this and remember it, Daddy," the card reads, "because when I grow up, you'll see how small I was."

The white women on the walls have to go, and the black people have to come in. All along the wall on the curving stairway, pictures are taken down. Ditto for the photos of white women downstairs. A few pictures of white female movie stars are left near the bar. Simpson always surrounded himself with photographs of his friends. Rockingham's walls, end tables, and shelves overflowed with them. The faces were overwhelmingly white. That's not the way to please a jury dominated by African-American women.

"We've got to have pictures of his family, his *black* family, up there," Cochran says.

Kardashian has photos enlarged at Kinko's, then framed nicely. One is even carefully placed in the kitchen. The jurors won't notice that they are color photocopies.

We're getting manipulative here, Bob thinks. He is embarrassed. Then he resolutely shoves the feeling aside. If the prosecution is too dumb to check the photos they took of those walls the day after the murders, it's not our fault, he decides. If they can't figure out that we'll show the jury O.J.'s proud to be a black man, too bad.

Cochran wants something depicting African-American history. "What about that framed poster from my office of the little girl trying to get to school?" he asks.

Johnnie means Norman Rockwell's famous 1963 painting, *The Problem We All Live With,* in which a black grade school girl walks to school surrounded by federal marshals.

As the picture is brought into the house, Kardashian finds himself saying to no one in particular, "I think O.J. also had that painting. Some years ago. It's probably in storage." Now he feels better.

They hang the framed poster at the top of the stairs, where the jury can't miss it as they go up to Simpson's bedroom. Everyone is pleased. This has little to do with a search for the truth. This is stagecraft.

7

ON SUNDAY MORNING, FEBRUARY 12, THE FREEWAY IS A moonscape without cars. Motorcycle cops with flashing lights clear the sixteen-mile route to Brentwood. Two police cars lead. Simpson follows in a van with deputies, followed by another van full of cops. Judge Ito rides alone in the next car. The jurors' bus, with barred, tinted windows, follows. Then the defense team, followed by a van carrying the prosecutors. Then a press bus with photographers. More police cars bring up the rear. Helicopters flap overhead. The media are waiting.

The lawyers are thunderstruck at the empty freeway. Drivers passing in the other direction are waving at them. Crowds have gathered on freeway overpasses. Some hold up three fingers of one hand and two of the other to show Simpson's football number, 32. So this is what a presidential motorcade feels like, Shawn Chapman thinks.

Once off the freeway, the convoy ignores stop signs and red lights and pulls up in front of Ron Goldman's apartment building. A brief pause. People gather on balconies with their Sunday morning coffee and wait on street corners. The convoy drives to Mezzaluna and stops at a nearby intersection. Hundreds of spectators are massed in front of the restaurant. Most take pictures of the bus. The media are everywhere.

Bundy Avenue is empty as the caravan moves south to the crime scene and stops at the condominium. One prosecutor and one defense lawyer are assigned to each group of five jurors. The ground rules impose total silence once the lawyers and jurors are in proximity. The attorneys cannot speak to the jurors. The jurors cannot ask questions.

The Brown family had requested that Simpson be kept outside Nicole's condo. O.J. agrees: He doesn't want to go in. He's driven around the corner.

"May I sit with O.J.?" Kardashian asks Judge Ito.

Kardashian is frisked and told to leave his cellular phone on the grass. He slides into the car's front seat next to a deputy. Simpson is in back, handcuffed. Another officer is beside him. O.J. carries his *Living Letters* Bible. He reads Kardashian passages from Isaiah 54.

"The Lord's hand is on your life," Bob says when Simpson is finished. "The Lord is in control."

They talk about a favorite topic, their ex-wives.

"We took these two average middle-class girls and gave them bracelets and Mercedes and diamonds," Simpson laments. "We gave them all this stuff, and look what happened. And Nicole became a different creature."

Kardashian spends an hour with O.J. Then he takes a tour. Again, he is surprised by the tiny killing area. To fight here would be like fighting in the shower. Goldman's fist was so bruised that it's hard to see how O.J. could have killed him and walked away with no marks.

The prosecution, Bob knows, sees it differently. They want the jurors to see that this lethal cage allowed no exit, no room to fight. One man, they'll argue, could surprise two people here, kill them easily.

Douglas and Marcia Clark are making a last inspection of Rockingham while the jurors wait outside. "Goddamn you, Carl!" Clark exclaims. "You know there have never been as many black people on these walls in his life as there are today."

"Marcia, how dare you think that," Douglas answers mildly enough.

Clark is angry. She complains about the fires. Ito orders them extinguished. She objects to the bedside picture with his mother. No luck on that. To Carl's surprise, Clark doesn't notice the Rockwell reproduction at the top of the stairs.

Outside, deputies uncuff Simpson and take him to Sydney and Justin's play area in the front of the house. O.J. is at ease with his captors. Deputies stand with their prisoner like guys hanging out on a street corner. They've gathered around Sydney's dollhouse as Simpson's maid, Gigi, brings out sandwiches, potato chips, and Cokes. Simpson talks proudly about his property, special trees he's had planted, his rose garden, the blooming dates of various flowers.

Everybody's best friends, Chapman marvels.

A pretty alternate juror walks by, dressed casually in Levi's. Because of her long hair, reporters call her Jeannie after the heroine of the late-sixties TV sitcom *I Dream of Jeannie*. Deputies and lawyers prefer "Fufu."

"Check out Fufu in jeans," one deputy cracks.

"Oh, man, look at her in those pants." Simpson is leering. "I want to get *at* her."

"Yeah, she's hot," another deputy agrees, "but she's so stupid."

"I don't care how stupid she is," Simpson says. "Look at her in those jeans!"

The usual nonsense, Chapman thinks. Just like guys everywhere. But one is a prisoner, and the others are his guards.

For Johnnie Cochran the day offers a rare chance to view key locations with his client. When the jurors are finished, he and Simpson take their own tour.

"Let me see where you were chipping golf balls," he says.

Simpson takes him to a spot in the front yard.

"Where are the divots?" Cochran asks.

"They've grown back by now," O.J. answers.

Cochran, Carl Douglas, Kardashian, Simpson, and several deputies enter the house. There are fresh flowers on a table in the entry, next to a picture of Simpson and Justin. They climb the staircase past twenty-seven pictures of Simpson, his black family, and his black friends. Staring at them from the head of the staircase is the Rockwell painting from Johnnie's office. O.J. leads the way into his bedroom. The deputies allow him to enter the walk-in closet and bathroom. He looks at Justin's Father's Day card on the door.

"Someone took down the green towels and put up white ones," O.J. observes. "That's the only thing different." He's been gone eight months. With everything that's happened, Douglas thinks, he remembers *towels?*

Down to the kitchen, out to the garage. They all enter the side walkway. Simpson asks where the glove was found. Prosecutors are hoping jurors will agree that the fence and the narrow alley make it easy for someone scrambling over the fence to crash into Kato Kaelin's back wall or run into the air conditioner, thus explaining those mysterious thumps Kaelin reported.

"Johnnie, there's no way I or anybody could climb over this fence," Simpson says. "Look at it. And look at this air conditioner. There's no way I would hit that."

They walk back to the front yard. Simpson looks up.

"You forgot to put up the flag," he complains. "The American flag should have been there."

8

On Monday, February 13, the day after the jury's trip to the crime scene and Rockingham, the entire defense team assembled for a strategy meeting. The prosecution was entering the next stage of its case: the discovery and collection of the physical evidence against Simpson. First on today's agenda was Marcia Clark's direct examination of Robert Riske, the first LAPD officer at the crime scene. Last

Thursday, minutes after putting him on the stand, she posed a routine question.

"In the course of your training, sir, at the academy," Clark had asked, "were you trained in crime-scene preservation?"

"They kind of gloss over it," Officer Riske answered. "They don't really train you."

The defense team chortled over this answer: The first cop at Bundy tells the jury that LAPD training isn't geared for the high-level scientific demands of DNA testing. Robert Riske had jump-started the "compromised-contaminated-corrupted" strategy. On cross-examination, the defense could now start to attack the validity of the blood evidence before the prosecution even introduced it.

Johnnie wanted some African-Americans on the defense's expert-witness list. Shawn Chapman reported she'd found Dr. H. Range Hudson, an emergency-room physician at L.A. County Hospital who was an expert on cuts and wounds.

"He was very skeptical of O.J.'s innocence," Shawn explained. "He wasn't sure he wanted to be involved." But after Hudson reviewed photos of the cuts on Simpson's hands, he agreed that Simpson's injuries were more likely inflicted by broken glass than by a knife blade. On that point, he backed O.J.'s story. But Hudson hadn't made up his mind about testifying, Chapman warned. He might not work out.

As usual, O.J. phoned during the meeting. "Before you take on a witness, come and talk to me," he insisted. "You guys are taking on witnesses without getting my input." Simpson's voice on the speakerphone was pushy, hard. "We can't be having so many sidebars," he went on. "We've got to speed up this trial."

No one was ever quite sure what to say when Simpson took command. Now and again his tactical suggestions were sharp. But this went far outside a normal attorney-client relationship. More like orders from the high command. General Simpson spelling it out.

In court Simpson talked endlessly whether anyone listened

or not. He expected his lawyers to accompany him to the holding cell at lunchtime and breaks. "Who's going back to lockup with O.J.?" Johnnie would ask. Kardashian was everybody's hero. His ability to endure, even sympathize with Simpson's monologues was bottomless. He became the audience for O.J.'s nonstop lectures on domestic violence.

The one lawyer who could get Simpson off that subject was Barry Scheck, whose own trial work had involved many cases of spousal abuse. But Barry never let on that he was deeply troubled by Simpson's attacks on Nicole. We have to discuss blood evidence, Barry would say, managing to distract Simpson.

Shawn was upset that O.J. couldn't drop the topic of domestic violence. The prosecutors had fumbled the issue during the first week of the case, then moved beyond it. But Simpson wouldn't let go. The crotch-grabbing testimony made him furious. That *wasn't* where his babies came from. He insisted that his lawyers bring up Nicole's cesarean deliveries. He pestered Shawn constantly. She counted the times he brought up the subject. At least in the hundreds.

Douglas knew that sometimes you just had to cut Simpson off. "I don't care, O.J.," he said more than once. "We're not going to do it." But Johnnie always backed Simpson. You have to listen to the client, Cochran kept saying. "You'd better go talk to O.J. before he gets mad at you" became a running joke.

"Another thing," Simpson was saying on the speakerphone, "don't ever ask for another lawyer's consent to do something. I didn't like it that day when Bob asked Judge Ito to wait until he consulted with Alan Dershowitz and Gerry Uelmen. We seemed stupid. We have ten lawyers in the room. We have to consult with two more?"

The lawyers listened silently.

OFFICE OF ALAN DERSHOWITZ

TO: Michael Schneider
FROM: Lisa Green
DATE: February 13, 1995
RE: Tips received

A caller pointed out that Fuhrman repeatedly stated that he lifted the bloody glove with his pen and that the droplet on the door of the Bronco was around the size of an eraser or the top of a pen.

9

LEE BAILEY HAD BEEN IN COURT ALMOST EVERY DAY SINCE the prosecution called its first witness, and he still hadn't cross-examined anyone. Sometimes Cochran thought of taking Fuhrman away from Bailey, of cross-examining the detective himself. What bothered him was that Bailey's hands shook at times. One day early in the trial, he openly poured something into a cup out of a small silver thermos that sat on the defense table in plain sight.

Of course, Judge Ito had quietly relaxed courtroom protocol. Lawyers at trial usually observe a level of decorum suitable to a church service. Now, however, the judge ignored the thermoses that attorneys on both sides stashed under their respective tables. Court sessions were long. Everyone needed the occasional jolt of caffeine. And all the lawyers—with one flamboyant exception—were discreet.

But a silver thermos sitting on the defense table looked terrible. One day when Bailey left the courtroom, Kardashian leaned over and sniffed. He smelled coffee. Nothing *but* coffee.

Whatever Lee Bailey's thermos held, one of the world's most famous lawyers had very little to do. One day, reporters spotted him designing a letterhead on his laptop. One of his computer programs calculated the distance between points on a map. He worked out the number of feet between Mezzaluna and Ron Goldman's apartment. He calculated the distance between the West L.A. police station and the crime scene. He had nothing better to do. Most of the defense team took copious trial notes. Bailey didn't.

Carl Douglas liked Bailey. He remembered the early days of the case. Bailey had *authority*. He made cameo appearances, a knight on a white horse. He dazzled them. The defense team reminded Douglas of the L.A. Lakers when Magic Johnson returned. At first they were in awe of him; soon enough, he became a mere mortal again. Bailey endured a similar fate. The other lawyers suspected he was hard of hearing. His drinking, real or supposed, bothered some.

Still, a few weeks ago, Bailey had brilliantly cross-examined Dr. Dutton, the D.A.'s expert on battering. Douglas assumed that after such a strong performance Johnnie would assign Bailey more witnesses. But Cochran held back. Then, with virtually no notice, Sergeant David Rossi, the watch commander on the night of the murders, was scheduled to testify. The prosecution was clearly worried about Mark Fuhrman. They knew the defense would suggest that he had carried the Bundy glove's mate to Rockingham, and they wanted Rossi to bolster other testimony that Fuhrman had never been alone in the courtyard with the Bundy glove.

Who better to take this last-minute witness than a lawyer who never took notes? Let Bailey have him, Cochran told Carl.

The defense plan for the next day—Tuesday, February 14—was to use Rossi to attack the LAPD's entire evidence-gathering process. Scheck wanted to suggest that the crime scene had not been preserved properly. As watch commander, Rossi had been present only to safeguard the security of the crime scene. Bailey, however, wanted to create the impression that the silver-haired cop was somehow responsible for the entire investigation.

"Do you know the difference, Sergeant, between a footprint and a foot impression?"

"No, I don't."

"Assuming, if you will, that a footprint is a two-dimensional residue of someone having walked somewhere with a wet outer shoe, and a foot impression is a three-dimensional residue, would you think those worth preserving for the benefit of the detectives who might be called upon to solve the case?"

"Yes, I would."

Douglas watched in amazement.

Carl leaned over to Shawn Chapman. "He's really good, isn't he?"

"Are you kidding? My panties are wet." Chapman laughed.

Douglas smiled back. "Mine, too."

Bailey moved on.

". . . Did you know that some footprints can't be seen except when shown with an oblique light?"

". . . I suppose that's possible."

"If you're careful where you walk, what does that mean? That you avoid stepping on things of significance?"

"That's correct."

"And if something significant can't be seen, can you avoid stepping on it?"

"If I can't see it, no."

Shapiro turned angrily to Simpson. "This is ridiculous overkill," he said. "Lee's making a fool of himself."

Driving back to the office after court, even Johnnie had to admit that Bailey put on a good show. That evening, Johnnie told Douglas that he had decided to leave Fuhrman with Bailey. Was race the reason Johnnie was bailing out? A black attorney going after a racist cop, in this case, wouldn't look good.

Carl confirmed that his sister and her friends loved Lee Bailey. "She's my focus group," Douglas explained. "Black people like big."

Besides, Bailey had plenty of criminal experience, knew cops as well as Johnnie did. Now F. Lee Bailey would have something to do.

10

A.C. HAD SEEN SYDNEY AND JUSTIN A FEW TIMES SINCE the murders. They adored him. A few weeks ago, in January, he had driven down to Dana Point to visit them.

Sydney had remarked to the cops at West L.A. station that Nicole had argued with "her friend" the night she died. Everyone assumed that friend was Faye Resnick, who said in her book she'd phoned Nicole that evening. And O.J. had insisted from the beginning that the real killer or killers would be found among Resnick's addict and dealer connections. Her call to Nicole from a residential drug treatment center would tie into that theory. So the defense wanted A.C. to ask Sydney who her mother was talking to on the phone the night of the murders. Any detail the child could offer might be helpful.

But Judy Brown forbade A.C. to mention Nicole's death to Sydney. O.J.'s kids still spent a wonderful day with A.C. Then Arnelle tried to persuade the Browns. No luck. Time was running out.

Johnnie approached Marcia Clark. Maybe the Browns would listen to her. Clark said she would help, but there was no way to tell what she would actually say to Nicole's parents. A few days later, Marcia told Shawn Chapman: "The Browns won't allow it."

Johnnie had to approach O.J. for permission to call Sydney as a possible witness. Not in open court, of course; not in front of any cameras, Cochran reassured him. She could testify on the record in chambers. O.J. refused. Absolutely not. Johnnie wasn't about to push on this one.

* * *

Throughout February, Simpson continued to pester his lawyers about the abuse issues, becoming more aggressive every day. When things got really bad, Kardashian would talk him through a fantasy golf tour in the holding cell. "You remember that Wednesday morning we played the Riveria Country Club?" Bob laughed. "You swung so hard and whiffed it? You almost fell down!

"Put your clubs in the car," he would begin. "Drive to Riviera. Change your shoes in the locker room. Go to the driving range for a few practice swings. Get up on the first tee. You remember how it's elevated. You look north, getting ready for your first drive. Take four hours to play it," he'd say. "Play thirty-six holes if you can." Some days Kardashian talked O.J. through the entire course.

"Bobby, that really took me away from the case," Simpson said, pulling out of his reverie. "First time I've been able to do that in a while."

"You think they'll let you back in a country club after this?" Kardashian asks. "You're accused of doing this, *and* you're black."

"Probably not," Simpson says. "I'll have to buy a condo in a gated community with club membership included."

Inevitably, they come around to the trial again.

"Why is there so much interest in this case?" O.J. wonders.

"Because everyone who's been divorced has probably thought about killing his ex-wife." Bob laughs.

While the prosecution proceeded with its case, Scheck and Blasier were working in their hotel until well after midnight every night. They sat before VCRs watching tapes of the Bundy crime scene and Simpson's Rockingham place. Cochran's office gave Bob Blasier an old VCR without a remote. The hotel TV was no better, with more snow than a Canadian winter. Night after night Bob paced between his chair and the VCR to stop and start the tapes. Before long he developed eyestrain. Barry Scheck also suffered, studying different tapes in another room on equally poor equipment. Between them, they watched hundreds of hours of unedited news footage the defense had obtained.

Little by little, they found gold. One tape seemed to show an *ungloved* hand at the crime scene picking up what looked like the bloody envelope holding Judy Brown's glasses. Another showed people crowding together near Nicole's body who had no business there. A third video showed the LAPD photographer rummaging through Nicole's mailbox. Another clip, from Rockingham, gave them criminalist Andrea Mazzola carrying a plastic garbage bag to the evidence truck. What was in the bag? Someone had to know. Little by little, Scheck and Blasier started to piece together important information about what happened at the crime scenes.

On one tape, Blasier noticed a video cameraman shooting on the grounds of the Rockingham estate. Who was he? There was nothing about him in the discovery material—no tape, no name, no description of a video being made. When the defense asked, the prosecution replied that *it* had no work product from that cameraman. However, the discovery rules required the prosecutors to give the defense everything they collected whether they planned to use it or not. So Ito forced the prosecutors to find the tape. Then the D.A.s argued that the tape was taken for insurance purposes, in case Simpson ever claimed the police had damaged or stolen something. It was never intended as evidence. Ito dismissed that argument. When Scheck received the tape, he saw that it included Simpson's bedroom. There were no bloody socks on the floor.

Some videos didn't give up their secrets easily. Scheck and Blasier watched one clip thirty times before they noticed two coroner's assistants in a crowded background *dragging* Ron Goldman's body out of the crime scene by the feet. They had missed it time after time. Suddenly it popped out at them.

When they finished, they sent all one hundred hours of unlabeled tape to the prosecution as discovery. They added a note that they would present portions of each as evidence. That was all the law required. Let the prosecutors have fun deciding what to look for.

* * *

484

Now that the prosecution was presenting crime-scene evidence, Scheck, Blasier, and Neufeld became the experts. Their strategy had to shape the cross-examination of almost every witness. The testimony of criminalists Dennis Fung and Andrea Mazzola, they knew, would largely determine whether the blood evidence against Simpson could be discredited. If Fung came off as an incompetent field technician making serious mistakes, it would be easy for the defense to convince the jury that the LAPD's evidence had been contaminated and corrupted. Then the future testimony of the prosecution's science witnesses would automatically be suspect. But if Fung escaped unscathed, the aura of legal authority around the LAPD lab and the DNA experts would be harder to damage. The cross-examinations of Detectives Lange and Vannatter had to lay the foundation for the defense attack on Dennis Fung.

Scheck and Blasier spent whole evenings coaching Cochran and Shapiro for these critical cross-exams. Very precise questions had to be asked of each witness. Their answers would be crucial to Fung's cross-examination. The videotapes, too, would play an important role when the detectives were crossed.

11

ON WEDNESDAY, FEBRUARY 15, JUDGE ITO SAID THAT HE expected a letter from Bill Hodgman on discovery claims and counterclaims. Hodgman was no longer a trial regular. His chest pains the night after his rage at Carl Douglas proved not to be a heart attack, but his wife, Janet, wanted him to stay out of court. Hodgman was now the case manager, working in his office upstairs.

At the moment of Ito's announcement, Hodgman walked into the courtroom. "Speak of the devil," Ito joked.

Bill Hodgman smiled.

Ito smiled.

". . . I feel some responsibility for your absence for the last several days," the judge said.

"Don't take any responsibility on yourself, Your Honor. I think the responsibility was mine. I appreciate the thought."

Sitting by the railing, Shawn Chapman remembered the morning after Hodgman had been hospitalized. "One down, two to go," Carl and Johnnie had joked. The competition between the two teams was now brutal. Whenever Chris Darden trash-talked the defense, the blood lust returned. Darden and Cochran often traded insults—ostensibly good-natured ones. Except they weren't. Push his buttons, Cochran and Douglas said.

That same day, prosecutor Rockne Harmon, the aggressive DNA specialist imported from the Alameda County D.A.'s office, was ready to call Cochran's bluff.

Johnnie had charged in open court that O.J.'s blood from the Bundy back gate and Nicole's blood on the socks in Simpson's bedroom had been spiked with blood from the reference samples taken after the murders. Both stains contained far more DNA than most of the other blood evidence. The assertion was, of course, a logical follow-up to Johnnie's remark in his opening statement that there was blood missing from O.J.'s reference sample. The missing blood, he implied, might have been used to plant those two stains. But Cochran's comment had made Scheck and Blasier nervous. It was premature; that blood was missing was highly likely, but not yet proven to their satisfaction.

"There is a preservative named EDTA in those [blood] tubes," Johnnie had argued before Ito a week earlier. "The [tubes] are premanufactured [with] a specified amount of that preservative" in them. So if EDTA turned up in the blood evidence, it would strongly suggest that the "evidence" was really Simpson's reference blood. These charges of LAPD tampering infuriated the prosecution.

"Mr. Harmon," Ito now said, "I have just received your letter . . . indicating that the Federal Bureau of Investigation will conduct the EDTA tests that they propose on Monday, February 20." That was five days from now.

The prosecution was doing what the defense had been afraid to do: testing for EDTA. The D.A. was ready to gamble that the FBI would not find EDTA in the blood-stains. "We intend to pursue that with all of our vigor to refute the allegations, which have cast a cloud over many of the people who worked on this case," Harmon declared.

Bob Blasier thought it would take several months for the tests to be completed. Both sides could only guess at the results. There could be no middle ground, just a clear win for one side or the other. EDTA in the blood from the Bundy back gate and the bedroom sock would strongly support the defense argument that those stains came from O.J.'s reference blood. If there was no EDTA, that part of the defense case collapsed.

Meanwhile, both sides were still waiting for the RFLP-DNA results from the rear gate at Bundy, the Bronco console, and the Bronco carpet. FBI agents were searching the world for shoe styles matching the bloody patterns at Bundy. The criminal investigation was still in progress, even as the trial proceeded. Such a thing was almost unheard of. Shapiro's insistence on starting trial within sixty days of Simpson's arraignment, which had benefited the defense, might also let the prosecution introduce new evidence at the eleventh hour.

At the end of the day, while examining Detective Ron Phillips, Marcia Clark again made the point that Mark Fuhrman had never been alone with the evidence. Score one for them, Douglas thought. Then Clark had Phillips, Fuhrman's supervisor, tell how he notified Simpson in Chicago. The detective said Simpson exclaimed, "Oh, my God, Nicole is killed!" But O.J. never asked about the circumstances. The prosecutor suggested that Simpson already knew how Nicole died.

In cross-examination, Johnnie quoted from Phillips's report, according to which Simpson asked, "What do you mean, she's been killed?" Phillips replied lamely that he'd had no chance to answer the question: Simpson was hysterical.

A very effective cross, Douglas thought.

JURY IN O.J. CASE IS SHOWN
THE GLOVE AND SKI CAP

Ending the day's testimony in powerfully dramatic fashion, the prosecutor . . . gave the jury its first look at the physical evidence Friday, gingerly lifting a blue knit cap and a bloody leather glove out of two wrinkled shopping bags. . . .

—Linda Deutsch, AP, February 17, 1995

On Friday, February 17, thirty crates of evidence and their police escort arrived in Albany, New York—on several planes, because a single commercial flight couldn't accommodate that much baggage. Drs. Baden, Wolf, and Lee were there to receive the crates. Months earlier at the LAPD lab, they'd had a brief look at pictures and paperwork but weren't allowed to touch the evidence. Couldn't even turn over the socks. Now Judge Ito had finally responded to defense pleas and allowed the defense scientists to make their own study of the physical evidence.

Today, the weather was brutally cold. One LAPD officer, born in Hawaii, had never seen snow before and insisted that Baden take his picture in it.

On Saturday the eighteenth, the crates were unpacked at Dr. Wolf's lab in the pathology department at Albany Medical Center.

The team had been granted three days to work through all thirty crates. Baden was reminded of Dr. Watson asking Sherlock Holmes what he was looking for. I'll tell you when I find it, Holmes replied.

The moment the three started opening the crates, they

488

were shocked by how badly the evidence had been processed and maintained. One lens from Judy Brown's eyeglasses was missing. When informed of this, the LAPD accused the doctors of losing it. The remaining lens was smeared with blood, dirt, some unidentified pink material, and a possible fingerprint. The envelope containing the glasses clearly showed an imprint resembling what Lee had identified from photos as a possible second shoe print. Lee also confirmed the wet transfers on the bindles that Blake and Gary Sims, of the California Department of Justice, had found.

The autopsy described Ron Goldman's stomach contents as fluid. Now the doctors found pieces of tomato peel, raisins, and other food particles. On Ron and Nicole's clothing, they found undocumented foreign hairs and threads.

Some of the packages wrapping the blood samples were bloodstained from improper drying. The wrapping on one thigh scraping was sealed with blood-encrusted Scotch tape, which presented the possibility of cross-contamination. Paperwork showed that blood swatches returned from testing were given new identification numbers.

But the scientists found no obvious treasure—no one clue, no single trace of this or that to exonerate Simpson or identify another killer. There was one possible exception: On Goldman's jeans Henry Lee found a striped pattern that looked to him like further evidence of a second shoe print which he hadn't been able to see in the coroner's photographs.

The real value of the three-day labor lay in the abundant data Baden, Wolf, and Lee found to support the defense argument that the LAPD's handling of the evidence was sloppy. It was obvious that the physical evidence had been extremely vulnerable to contamination.

The following Monday, the defense complained in chambers that the blood evidence had been renumbered in an attempt to slow the defense down. Rockne Harmon eventually indicated that this was so: The prosecution had meant to cause confusion.

12

On the same day the evidence arrived in Albany, KMEX-TV broadcast live from a working-class neighborhood in East Los Angeles. Rosa Lopez, the Salvadoran maid Johnnie had mentioned so prominently in his opening statement, had been discovered at her daughter's home.

"We found a worried Rosa who didn't know what to do," correspondent Maria Villalpando told her TV viewers. "It was very sad to find her feeling so alone. Rosa Lopez resigned her job after being identified by the press as a key witness for the defense of O.J. Simpson."

Lopez felt besieged when satellite trucks gathered outside her employer's home next door to Rockingham. Eluding a Pinkerton man hired to keep track of her, she vanished. For several days the defense had had no idea where she was.

Johnnie Cochran liked this tiny woman with downcast eyes and a leathery peasant face. She'd worked at the bottom of society since childhood, borne children of her own, fled the war in El Salvador when her son was killed. He knew a jury of black working-class women would listen to Rosa Lopez.

Walking her employers' dog the night of the murders, she saw the Bronco parked at Rockingham at 10:15 P.M. Her testimony would make it hard to imagine that Simpson killed two people more than two miles away at the same time.

Mark Fuhrman had interviewed Lopez but never filed a report. This was another indication of his deviousness, an important element in the defense strategy.

McKenna drove over to Rosa's daughter's house to find out why she'd fled and what her plans were. Lopez insisted

490

she wanted to go back to El Salvador. When they were alone, she said "Mr. Johnnie" was wrong when he told the jury 10:15. It was closer to ten P.M., maybe a few minutes later.

Her daughter had seen Johnnie on TV and remembered that her mother had told her ten P.M. Was her mother supposed to get up on the stand and lie? Did Mr. Johnnie expect that? Rosa's daughter got angry. Rosa wasn't sure she wanted any part of this.

McKenna thought Pavelic might have played a part in stretching the time to 10:15 when he first interviewed Lopez a few weeks after the murders. Cops often pushed witness testimony in useful directions. If Rosa saw the Bronco at ten she wouldn't be much help. Maybe Pavelic had pushed a little.

Rosa now told Pat McKenna she looked at her watch just before she took the dog out. It was ten. She made a cup of tea, put a collar on the dog. After several retellings, she added that she heated the water in the microwave and took the tea outside with her. Suddenly it was clear to McKenna. A microwave boils water in forty-five seconds, about the time it takes to put on a collar. That made it a minute or two after ten when she took the dog and her tea outside. Pavelic must have assumed Lopez had heated water on the stove, which would have taken longer, *then* put the dog's collar on—more time—and *then* drunk the tea. Pavelic's assumptions put Lopez outside around 10:15 P.M. Unfortunately, his assumptions were wrong.

"I am so mad at Mr. Bill," Rosa said in her heavy accent. "I never say this. I never *say* ten-fifteen."

McKenna calls Pavelic. "Bill, where'd you get ten-fifteen? I've been talking to this woman for two or three days now. She says it's ten o'clock."

"I have a taped statement saying ten-fifteen P.M.," Pavelic answered.

McKenna went to see Johnnie and Carl. He assumed they had the tape, so he didn't mention it. The only issue was the time. "Look, you guys," he told them, "we have a problem with ten-fifteen. We can say 'after ten.' But that's all."

By the end of the week everything was a mess. The media were chasing Rosa Lopez stories. Another neighborhood maid said Rosa expected to make money from her testimony. The *National Enquirer* said, amazingly, they didn't believe her story. Wouldn't buy it.

At an all-day hearing, Cochran asked Judge Ito to let Lopez testify immediately. A defense witness five weeks into the prosecution's case. It's unusual, Johnnie said, but my witness is like a bird about to fly back to El Salvador. Not surprisingly, the court wanted to hear about this from Ms. Lopez herself.

JUDGE ORDERS TESTIMONY FROM DEFENSE WITNESS WHO THREATENED TO FLEE

A housekeeper who could give O.J. Simpson an alibi for the night of the slayings promised to return to court and testify on Monday—right in the middle of the prosecution's case—rather than flee the country.

"I will do it for you, Your Honor," Rosa Lopez, speaking through a Spanish-language interpreter, said as she sobbed at the lectern.

—Linda Deutsch, AP, February 24, 1995

Chris Darden questioned Lopez during this extraordinary hearing outside the presence of the jury. He asked for proof that she really intended to depart for El Salvador. She said she'd made a plane reservation on the country's national airline, Taca. While Darden continued his questions, Cheri Lewis checked.

"Ms. Lopez, we just called the airline," Darden said. "They don't show a reservation for you."

"Because I am going to reserve it, sir. As soon as I leave here I will buy a ticket. . . ."

"You lied to us, didn't you?"

Darden had damaged Lopez's credibility before she could utter a word of actual testimony.

Ito ruled that Lopez could testify Monday, on videotape, without the jury present. If later on the defense wished to use Lopez in presenting its case but she was unavailable, it could show the tape to the jury.

13

ON MONDAY MORNING, AS JOHNNIE AND CARL PREPPED Rosa Lopez in Ito's jury room for her testimony, the prosecutors suddenly demanded more discovery on her. Carl Douglas noticed that the D.A.'s copy of the Lopez interview didn't bear the same date as the report he had in his hand. So the defense must have two different reports from her interviews. Lopez had spoken with Pavelic, then with McKenna and Pavelic together, and a third time with Cochran and Pavelic. Those were the interviews Douglas knew about. He had thought one report covered them all. But now he understood that the report turned over in discovery was not the same as the one he had. I am going to catch hell, Douglas thought. Again. How many times do I have to go through this?

"We know that she has been interviewed extensively by counsel," Marcia Clark declared. "I cannot believe for one minute that there was no note taken, any statement taken [of those additional interviews]. . . . And if defense counsel want to get up and deny it again, we're going to revisit it again."

The TV cameras panned toward Carl as he stood up. "It was only this morning, Your Honor," he said, "that I saw for the first time that the two-page interview that we had given to the prosecution was not the same two-page interview that I had been using in my notes.''

Clark and Darden had already accused Douglas of hiding the second report. A sidebar was called. Darden asked: ''Any other reports? Any tapes?'' Douglas felt a chill. What *did* the defense actually have? He knew of nothing and said so. Johnnie backed him. ''We never taped, Your Honor,'' he insisted.

Back to open court. ''There are no notes that have not been turned over,'' Douglas stated. ''There are no tape-recorded statements of Miss Lopez. . . . There is no tape recording of Miss Lopez by any of our investigators.''

At home Bill Pavelic was working on his computer with one eye on the TV when he heard Judge Ito say to Douglas, ''Are you sure?'' Then: ''. . . tapes.'' Ito asked whether the team had taped an early interview with Rosa Lopez, and if so, why wasn't it in discovery?

Suddenly, Pavelic felt ill. He had the tape. He'd forgotten all about it during the chaotic move from Shapiro's office to Johnnie's. He faxed a message to Shapiro in court: Call immediately. Twenty minutes later, he was on the phone.

''Bob, I fucked up,'' Pavelic said. ''I have a tape of Rosa Lopez from my first meeting with her. I never mentioned it. It's not in the discovery report. But goddammit—I have it. I just wanted to bring it to you guys' attention.''

''Come to court,'' Shapiro said.

''Now or tomorrow?''

''Right now.''

Pavelic jumped into his wife's car and sped downtown. Clark and Darden hate my guts, he thought. I've never lost a case before them. They'll love this. They'll wait for the day I'm late with a library book so they can lay a felony on my ass.

Shapiro walked into the jury room, where Johnnie and Carl sat with Rosa.

''I just talked with Pavelic,'' Shapiro said. ''He has a tape. He's coming down to court.''

Douglas felt flushed. I'm a defense lawyer for fifteen

years, he thought. I've read hundreds of witness interviews. I can't remember ever seeing a report that didn't flag you in the first or last paragraph that it was also recorded. Or that notes were available. I will look like an idiot, he told himself bitterly. Ito will announce there is a tape. The camera will pan toward me. It will look like my fault.

Shapiro and Cochran were discussing the matter with Ito when Pavelic entered the courtroom. Ito looked up.

"Go back," the judge said. "We'll call you."

Ito called Pavelic a few minutes later. At the prosecution table, Marcia Clark was fuming. She had been accusing the defense of deliberate misconduct, and now she had evidence. The judge looked down at Bill Pavelic.

"Any rough notes, anything you wrote down, anything handwritten?" Ito was clearly impatient.

It was an awkward moment. "I may possibly have some notes in regards to the statement I took," Pavelic said carefully.

"Do you have any tape recordings of any statements?" Ito asked.

"I tape-recorded the first statement, which was the July statement," Pavelic answered.

Pavelic heard gasps around the courtroom. Carl Douglas sat grimly.

Ito ordered Pavelic to bring the tape and his notes to court.

"I shall do my best to get those items," Pavelic answered, looking up at Ito's high bench.

"No, don't do your best," the judge shot back. "*Have* them here tomorrow!"

"How the hell could this have happened?" Cochran demanded of Carl that evening. Johnnie was through with Pavelic: I don't want him doing any further investigations. He's a liability.

Bill Pavelic wasn't the only investigator making mistakes: McKenna hadn't checked Mary Ann Gerchas's background. Both that and the Lopez tape were major screwups. But McKenna was the kind of guy Cochran could forgive. Pavelic was considered Shapiro's man.

495

Nevertheless, Carl knew, Pavelic was an excellent resource. No one knew LAPD procedures as well. Douglas tried a balancing act.

"I'll back off completely," Pavelic offered when Carl phoned him.

"Bill, continue what you are doing," Douglas said quietly. "We'll still need a lot of analysis. Just be very low key. Stay out of active investigations. Stay out of court. Perhaps you should stay out of our office. But be available by phone and fax."

When Kardashian got to the courthouse the next day, he saw Bill Pavelic in the first-floor cafeteria, looking somewhat the worse for wear. Bob sat down with him.

"The real problem is this defense isn't being run properly," Kardashian told Pavelic. "If we were a business, and Rosa was a product we wanted to market, somebody would have been with her every moment, protecting our asset."

Pavelic didn't seem particularly cheered by this.

Kardashian went upstairs to visit Simpson. O.J. was reading a Lawrence Sanders detective story. He'd just finished a Robin Cook mystery. Neither one took his mind off Rosa Lopez.

"You know we really step on our dicks every time," Simpson grumbled. "It isn't the evidence that's getting us. It's ourselves."

Meanwhile, in Ito's chambers, Johnnie was playing Pavelic's tape of Rosa. On the tape, Pavelic walked Lopez through the statement she'd just given him. At one point on the tape, she said she'd seen the Bronco at "approximately" 10:15.

The judge gave prosecutors an hour to listen and make copies.

During that time Carl came into the holding cell. For once he was openly angry. "I don't want to fall on my sword again!" he told O.J.

"You shouldn't have to," Simpson agreed. He made an executive decision: It was Shapiro's turn to apologize to the court.

* * *

For days the Rosa Lopez examination inched forward in open court. The jury was absent. The spectators, the press, and people who watch Court TV heard it all.

Lopez's videotaped testimony was a struggle. Chris Darden noticed her new clothes, asked if Johnnie Cochran was paying her. How about the tabloids? Wasn't there a $5,000 payment? Lopez denied it.

"Isn't it true that you told Sylvia Guerra [a friend of Lopez's] that if she would say that she saw the Bronco, she would also get paid five thousand dollars?" Darden asked.

"No mí recuerdo," Rosa Lopez replied. She didn't remember.

Lopez gave the same answer to dozens of questions. Reporters chided the defense. For the rest of the trial, *"No mí recuerdo"* was guaranteed a laugh.

14

ON THE PREVIOUS SUNDAY, FEBRUARY 26, DR. LENORE Walker, the defense's expert on domestic violence, arrived at Cochran's office to present her report on Simpson to the team. Following her was a TV newsmagazine crew. Right into Johnnie's conference room. For months we try to stop the leaks, Pat McKenna thought, and now a TV crew comes into Johnnie's offices? Cochran seemed indifferent, but to everyone's surprise Shapiro said he wanted them out or he'd walk. Johnnie told the crew to leave.

The defense had been waiting for weeks to hear Walker's opinion on spousal abuse.

Practically the first thing she said was that Simpson did not fit the profile of a batterer who murders: "He has good control over his impulses. He appears to control his emotions well.''

Dr. Walker explained that there are three general categories of batterers. One common type is mentally ill. Another group is violence-prone, in and out of the home. The third, less pathological, group seeks power and control. Simpson's problems fell into the third category.

Dr. Walker told the team that O.J. and Nicole's history should be viewed in three distinct periods. Before 1985, Simpson felt secure and in control. Nicole was his girlfriend. Rockingham was his house. He and Nicole enjoyed passionate sex, travel, and fun.

Phase two, Walker said, brought radical changes: marriage and children. Nicole was a devoted mother. O.J. was no longer the center of her life. Simpson missed her attentiveness and wanted to continue the spontaneous sex, the impulsive traveling. She preferred staying home with Sydney and Justin. He was no longer the master of his domain. Rockingham was now his *family's* house. Simpson stepped up his extramarital sex. He felt out of control, abandoned.

The New Year's Eve beating in 1989 frightened Simpson, the doctor explained. He was shocked by his capacity for violence. And he knew that as a black man, he faced double condemnation, first as a batterer, second because he had beaten a white woman. This might destroy his career as a pitchman. His offer to tear up the prenuptial agreement if he beat her again wasn't aimed at reassuring her. He was setting up a penalty system for himself. Now a failure to check his violent impulses could cost him millions in a divorce. O.J. wrote that letter as much for himself as for Nicole.

The third phase began post-divorce. Simpson suffered deeply from his loss of control over Nicole, over his life. Yet he wasn't a classic stalker. Walker had studied Simpson's calendar. Stalkers don't travel to golf tournaments, she explained. They don't see other women. They don't redecorate the bedroom and bath for a new girlfriend, as Simpson was doing for Paula Barbieri. Stalkers are single-minded, monogamous.

498

O.J.'s pattern was closer to that of a heartsick lover, Walker felt. The incident with Keith Zlomsowitch was more a matter of jealousy than of stalking. Simpson could control his anger. He had a bad temper, but he yelled and and left, or just left. Walker had administered a battery of tests: the Minnesota Multiphasic Personality Inventory, the Rorschach test, the Wechsler Scale of Intelligence test. Simpson's cognitive functioning was normal. His intelligence was in the superior range. His social skills were remarkable.

McKenna is thinking the bottom line here is, O.J. has problems dealing with women, but he's not a wife-beater. That should take care of it. But no, all these people sit around so respectfully while we hear hours of this stuff. They don't know what she's talking about, but they're afraid to say so.

Simpson has made remarkable progress, Dr. Walker continued. At first he had no self-awareness of his violent behavior. He insisted that the 1989 incident was as much Nicole's fault as his. By the time we finished working together, he was able to admit he had battered Nicole that night. He saw that he was responsible for the violence. Even one incident, he understood, characterized him as a batterer.

But Mr. Simpson is not an *end-stage* batterer, as the prosecution charges, Walker added. At worst, he might fit the beginning stage. Battering spouses tend to murder when a separation begins, but Nicole died after the couple had been apart for years.

It is possible, she continued, that he murdered in a disassociative or "fugue" state, a disturbed state that the sufferer cannot afterward recall. Indeed, Walker believed that this was the *only* possible way O.J. could be guilty. Someone who kills in a fugue state has no sense of being at the murder scene, no memory of the crime. But Walker considered this scenario unlikely: Simpson had no history of fugue states.

* * *

After Dr. Walker left, Shawn Chapman said she thought Walker would be a great witness. Walker was usually on the side of abused women. Speaking for O.J., she'd have wonderful credibility.

Johnnie knew better. The defense was ahead now. The prosecution had run out of gas on domestic violence when Denise Brown played so poorly. If Walker took the stand, it would be open season on O.J.'s mental state. The abuse incidents Ito ruled inadmissible might be brought in. Lee Bailey agreed: Put Walker on, and the other side will bring in their own experts. Our expert says he's not a killer; theirs will say he is.

The team agreed to put her on hold. If the prosecution brought in its own domestic violence expert, the defense would use Walker to testify to a hypothetical case that fit the defendant's scenario. The jury would still get the message, but Walker would never mention Simpson. And so the D.A. couldn't, on cross-examination, ask about her tests or interviews of him.

Simpson calls the team on schedule. Today he is thoughtful, subdued. "I really want to work with a therapist now," he says. "Dr. Walker did show me that a lot of the behavior I had was, you know, like a batterer. I really was a batterer," he goes on, haltingly. "I am responsible for that."

Simpson's lawyers know they are finally hearing something revealing from O.J. on domestic abuse. Shawn Chapman remembers her long days listening to Simpson on that "mutual-type wrestling match." Nothing was his fault, then. Now he sees the truth.

"I really need to deal with it," Simpson continues. "I need to come to terms with it."

Chapman is assigned to find Simpson a therapist.

Kardashian wonders if this breakthrough will last.

Dr. Bernard Yudowitz, the forensic psychologist who had evaluated O.J. at Bailey's request, eventually heard about Simpson's remarkable phone call. He knew it wasn't the whole story. Dr. Walker had told him Simpson became

500

increasingly despondent during their interviews. A natural result, Yudowitz thought, of realizing he was a batterer. That he wanted a therapist, Walker and Yudowitz knew, meant only that he wanted relief from his depression. The two doctors knew that owning up to his misdeeds probably wasn't Simpson's primary goal.

15

PROSECUTORS REMOVE JUROR WHO SAYS THEY'VE MADE "PRETTY STRONG CASE"

Prosecutors succeeded in ousting a black juror from the O.J. Simpson trial Wednesday, apparently because they thought he was biased toward the former football star. But the man quickly told reporters he thought the prosecution has made "a pretty strong case."

Michael Knox, a 46-year-old courier, was the subject of numerous complaints over several weeks that led to a dispute during the jury's visit to Simpson's estate.

. . . it was reported that before Knox was chosen as a juror, he'd bet a week's salary that Simpson would be acquitted.

Then he showed up at the jury's trip to the murder scene and Simpson's mansion in a sweatshirt with the logo of the Los Angeles Raiders and a cap with the logo of one of Simpson's former teams, the San Francisco 49ers. . . .

—Linda Deutsch, AP, March 1, 1995

The defense team hated losing Knox. His wardrobe sent them obvious signals. One day he wore a red suit with red shoes. Shawn Chapman smiled to herself: A man from the 'hood; count on him. Everybody agreed.

When Knox told a press conference he thought the prosecution had made a strong case, they assumed he was playing with the D.A. He's mad at them for booting him, Johnnie and Carl agreed. Sending them a message: You made a mistake, fools. I'd have voted guilty.

Because of the Rosa Lopez examination, the jury had not heard testimony for almost a week. Now that she was gone, Detective Tom Lange returned to the stand on March 6. The defense liked him. Sometimes he stopped at their table to chat.

Barry Scheck had coached Johnnie Cochran carefully. Every word in your cross-examination matters, he insisted. You must ask questions that will help me attack the evidence collection. You're laying the foundation. It will pay off with Dennis Fung.

"You would always prefer to have the evidence collected as soon as you see it, or as soon as possible," Johnnie had asked Lange ten days earlier. "Isn't that correct?"

"We would prefer that," Lange answered in his slow, methodical way, "but it doesn't always happen that way."

What about blood collected belatedly on the Bundy back gate? The detective said he had asked Dennis Fung to collect it.

"In fact, it was not done until July third, three weeks later," Cochran said. "Isn't that correct?"

"Yes."

"Are you aware that this crime scene at Bundy had been washed down at some point on June thirteenth or June fourteenth?" Cochran then asked.

"I am aware that the front walkway was washed down," Lange responded.

The jury now knew that someone had initially missed a significant bit of blood evidence. Had that evidence ever really been there at all? Had the washing down of the crime scene included the back gate? Cochran left the possibility dangling. Later he asked Lange if the blood on the back gate was collected the day after the murders.

Lange replied evenly, "My information is that it was not done."

Cochran was putting the foundation in place: sloppy work by the LAPD's criminalists. Perhaps bad crime-scene supervision by Lange.

During lunch, Kardashian sat with Simpson in the lockup. For twenty years, their delight in practical jokes had been one of their bonds. Now Deputy Roland Jex was handcuffing Simpson to the chair in the small room next to the holding cell. Kardashian stood off to one side. Suddenly O.J. turned to Kardashian and barked, "Get him!"

In an eyeblink, the tall black deputy stuck his foot in front of Simpson's chair, then exploded into a combat stance. Kardashian was impressed. Very fast reflexes.

Simpson and Kardashian cracked up. A glorious goof. But Jex glared at them. It wasn't the joke O.J. and Bob thought it would be. Jex could have hurt them.

Once again Tom Lange stood by the defense table during a break. Everybody was relaxed.

"Maybe I'll tell them you live in Simi Valley, Tom." Cochran laughed. "I'll ask you: Did you bring those shoes back from your house in Simi Valley?"

Everyone laughed. Chapman thought Johnnie was having fun. After a mostly white jury in Simi Valley acquitted four policemen in the 1991 beating of Rodney King, the city's name had become local shorthand for pro-cop white racism. Lange had indeed taken Simpson's Reeboks home to Simi Valley from Rockingham on the night of June 13. That could matter to this jury.

Once court resumed, Cochran didn't waste time.

"And then you drove from your home in Simi Valley down to the location," Cochran asked. "And how long did it take you to get from Simi Valley to the location in Brentwood?" Johnnie continued.

"Perhaps fifty minutes, an hour."

Any point worth making was worth making again.

During Sergeant Rossi's earlier testimony, Lee Bailey had run a tape of news footage that Scheck and Blasier had found. It showed a policeman walking right on the bloody pathway and thus suggested unimaginable sloppiness. Now on Tuesday, March 7, the prosecutors ran an earlier sequence from the same video showing cops taking down the yellow security tape. Bundy was no longer a "crime scene." The police on that walkway were doing nothing wrong.

Johnnie then brought up another video that showed a white sheet or blanket that had been placed over Nicole's body. Blasier's wife, Charlotte, had pointed out how outrageous it was to use and then abandon a blanket that could easily carry trace evidence.

"When . . . the crime scene was broken down," Cochran said, "that sheet was just left on the ground."

"That is my understanding," Lange answered.

"As an experienced investigator . . . [you] do attempt to preserve any possible trace evidence; isn't that correct?" Cochran asked.

"Trace evidence, certainly," the detective said carefully.

Cochran went on, "And [the blanket] was never preserved or kept or booked by anyone, as far as you know . . . is that correct?"

"That's correct," Lange replied.

Later in the day, Lange testified that he himself had covered Nicole's body with the household blanket. Who could possibly know what had been on that blanket before Lange laid it over Nicole's body? Simpson could have slept on it during an overnight visit. Trace evidence from O.J. on the body—hair, for example—could have come *from the blanket*. The point had been made to the jury. Weeks later the defense learned that the blanket had been laundered the day before the murders. But for some reason, the prosecutor never mentioned that fact to the jury.

* * *

On Wednesday, March 8, Alan Dershowitz was in Boston, watching Cochran's cross-examination of Lange on TV. He faxed Johnnie in the courtroom. Autopsy photos had shown that Nicole's throat was slashed so deeply that her head nearly came off. Colombian drug killers do something like that, Alan said. It's called a Colombian necktie. Here, finally, was support for O.J.'s theory that Nicole's murder was somehow caused by Faye Resnick's contacts in the drug world. Cochran read the fax once and went on the attack immediately.

"Let me ask you some questions about your theory about this not being a drug-related homicide," Cochran said to Lange. "Have you ever heard of something called a Colombian necklace?"

"I believe so."

Cochran asked if it meant "a situation where drug dealers will slice the neck of a victim, including the carotid artery, in order to kill the victims and to instill fear and send a message to others who have not either paid for the drugs or have been informing to the police?"

"I heard that," Lange replied.

Then the court recessed for lunch. During the break, the detective learned that Cochran had it wrong. He meant Colombian *necktie*. A "necklace" was a form of mob execution in South Africa. Lange decided to play with Cochran a bit.

"What is a Colombian necktie?" Johnnie began that afternoon. Now he had the name right.

"My information is that it is a tire that would be put over someone's neck and set afire," Lange answered. He was explaining a "necklace."

Johnnie stopped short. That wasn't what Alan Dershowitz had said in his fax. Try again.

"Have you ever heard of a Colombian necktie being a situation," he asked, "where in a drug killing a person's throat is slashed and their tongue is pulled down through the neck area?"

"No," Lange answered.

It didn't much matter who'd won the round. Johnnie was

controlling the courtroom. And the media had something new to talk about.

By the time Johnnie was finished, Lange had admitted that Mark Fuhrman had mentioned Simpson's past history of wife-beating to him. So at the time Fuhrman climbed the Rockingham wall, O.J. must already have been a suspect.

As usual Shapiro wasn't happy. Johnnie's cross-examination was too long, he told Simpson. Too many useless questions, too much posturing.

That same day, Shapiro's wealthy friend Michael Klein turned Kardashian and Taft down for a loan. Simpson was now out of cash. Klein didn't mind lending his guest rooms to the defense attorneys, but forget about a loan. Not even with O.J.'s home as collateral.

Then Hawthorne Savings and Loan came to the rescue. O.J. owed $675,000 to Bank of America on his Rockingham home, nothing on his New York condo. The savings and loan gave O.J. a $3 million line of credit, secured by both properties. The loan fee was almost $90,000. Nobody else was willing to do business with O.J. Now Simpson had to turn out a steady stream of autographed photos and footballs to make his interest payment every month.

On Thursday, March 9, Detective Mark Fuhrman was ready to take the stand. The defense had branded him a racist cop, accused him of planting the bloody glove at Rockingham. Alan Dershowitz had been wrong: The prosecution was going to use him, despite his questionable background.

For weeks the defense had been hearing that Chris Darden would examine Fuhrman. "There is no way that Chris should take Fuhrman," Johnnie had told Carl two weeks earlier. "It would be awful."

"Fuck him," Douglas argued. "If he wants to do it, let him."

"Carl, he's still black," Johnnie insisted. "He's still a young lawyer. He has to be black when he leaves here. I'm going to tell him he shouldn't do it."

Cochran had humiliated Darden once, but he wanted no

more trouble for African-Americans in Ito's courtroom. Don't do the white man's work here, he wanted to tell Chris Darden. You're already being called a traitor. If you examine Fuhrman, you'll be forced to protect a racist.

As the day of Fuhrman's appearance approached, Cochran took every opportunity to talk to Darden. No verbal jousting now, but straightforward advice, black man to black man. Once he put his hands on Darden's shoulders and whispered into his ear during a break. Another time he wrapped an arm around Darden as they stood together. Each time the message was the same: You know Fuhrman's a bad guy. Don't let them sucker you into this. Let the white folks deal with Fuhrman. Darden was unyielding. I'm a prosecutor, he told Cochran. I won't make decisions because of race.

The preceding Monday, *Newsweek* had reported that prosecutors had staged a mock cross-examination of Fuhrman in a grand jury room. In Ito's chambers, on the morning Fuhrman was to be sworn in, the defense demanded whatever transcript existed from that rehearsal. The transcript should be turned over as discovery, the defense argued. Clark insisted the rehearsal was not an interview but witness prep, therefore ''work product'' and not discoverable. Ito agreed.

Meanwhile the defense heard rumors that the prosecutors didn't want Fuhrman to pretend he'd never said ''nigger.'' They heard from inside the D.A.'s office that a former girlfriend saw a stainless-steel swastika decorating Fuhrman's Christmas tree. There were also Fuhrman's clashes with Peggy York during her command of the West L.A. station. And Fuhrman's psychiatric records from the early eighties were in hand. Ito had excluded them, but they provided valuable background. The defense had plenty of ammunition in reserve.

Waiting for court to begin, Linda Deutsch of the Associated Press recalled a moment during the July 1994 preliminary hearing when Fuhrman had described his feelings on first seeing the glove at Rockingham.

''When I found the glove back here on this pathway,'' he

testified, pointing out the back walkway on a map, "I have to admit to you that the adrenaline started pumping. . . . My heart started pounding, and I realized what I had probably found."

Fuhrman's statement set off warning lights in Deutsch's mind: This is a seasoned detective, not a rookie on his first case. He's cool and professional until he talks about finding the glove. Something is very odd here.

When Fuhrman arrived in court, O.J. stared hard at him. Chris Darden rose to start the direct examination. Johnnie shrugged. Suddenly the prosecutor turned to Johnnie and let the older lawyer see his middle finger. Then he sat down. Johnnie figured Darden had taken his advice. But he had to get the needle in, Carl Douglas thought.

Marcia Clark rose to address the witness.

Douglas looked at the tall cop sitting rigidly in the witness chair and thought: He *is* capable of framing an innocent man. Simpson sat quietly.

"Detective Fuhrman, can you tell us how you feel about testifying today?" Clark began.

"Nervous," Fuhrman answered. He also admitted he was "reluctant" to take the stand.

"Can you tell us why?" Clark asked.

"Throughout, since June thirteenth, it seems that I have seen a lot of the evidence ignored and a lot of personal issues come to the forefront. I think that is too bad."

Lee Bailey felt Clark was coddling him. Detective Fuhrman, are you upset at these personal attacks? She's treating him like a little boy, he thought.

Bailey knew Fuhrman the ex-marine would be a tough witness. The detective's responses were direct, precise. He hardly blinked. He knew everything cold. No hemming and hawing. He seemed like a perfect cop, a perfect prosecution witness. But, for the first time in the trial, Marcia Clark appeared nervous.

Clark tried a preemptive strike, introducing the letter Kathleen Bell wrote to the defense. Now Bailey could probe

Fuhrman's alleged racist remarks on cross-examination. Bailey would take full advantage of the invitation.

Fuhrman then testified to going over the wall at Rockingham, to interviewing Kato Kaelin, to finding the blood on the Bronco, to discovering the glove at Rockingham, to finding the other glove and ski cap back at Bundy. Piece by piece, he explained how the evidence pointing to Simpson was found, much of it by him.

After two days of direct examination, Clark ended on Friday afternoon with testimony suggesting that Simpson had planned to bury Nicole in a big plastic bag. She asked Fuhrman to show the jury three items found in the back of Simpson's Bronco: a long-handled shovel, a dirty towel, and a plastic bag large enough to hold a body. She didn't ask Fuhrman to explain their possible use. The implication was obvious. The media had a new headline.

At home that evening Kardashian's phone rang. "I'm an LAPD officer," the caller began. The male voice was bass and aggressive. Kardashian assumed the man was black.

"The plastic bag is standard equipment in the back of a Ford Bronco," the cop said. "The spare tire is stored in it."

Kardashian laughed.

On Monday morning, March 13, Lee Bailey arrived early. Today he would cross-examine Fuhrman. He went directly to the holding cell for O.J.'s input. He saw Simpson alone.

Bailey emerged ready for the "Fuhrman funeral," as he called it. He carried six fat ring binders bursting with transcripts from Fuhrman's preliminary hearing. One for the prosecution, another for Judge Ito, *three* for the defense, and one for himself. The pages Bailey planned to use were printed on orange paper. We know your previous statements better than you do, those binders declared. They were intimidating.

Nobody on the defense team knew Bailey's plan.

Bailey was a master at finding a witness's fatal flaw. Years before, in the Coppolino murder case, he convinced the jury that an eyewitness was actually a woman scorned, with a motive to lie. Coppolino was acquitted.

In the courtroom this morning, Bailey and Fuhrman were two marines under fire. Would Fuhrman make the mistake of refusing to give an inch? Would he be too cold, too dispassionate, when a touch of humanity might make him more convincing?

Carl Douglas could only guess how Bailey planned to attack the detective. Ironically, Carl thought, Bailey might have more in common with his witness than he'd readily admit: Bailey could also be immovable when flexibility would serve him better.

Marcia Clark had discovered the plastic bag mistake. She corrected it before the defense started its cross. Then Bailey began by underlining the error.

"Good morning, Detective Fuhrman," he opened. "Could you tell us when it was that you were enlightened as to the fact that the plastic bag you saw in Mr. Simpson's Bronco comes with the car?"

"I believe it was Saturday," Fuhrman replied.

"So that after nine months of investigation, you discovered on Saturday that this important piece of evidence was perfectly innocuous, is that right?"

Bailey was on first base.

Bailey took the witness through the Bundy crime scene, probing for inconsistencies, trying to lay traps.

"Now, is that the sum total of the observations you made on that little excursion?" Bailey asked. "You saw a knife wound, and that is it?"

"Yes, sir."

"Nothing else?" Lee asked.

"I don't believe so, no."

"How about a couple of gloves, Detective?"

"Excuse me?"

"Did you see a couple of gloves up there?" Bailey hammered quickly. Maybe he could get Fuhrman to admit to seeing two gloves—one of which, the defense would argue, he later planted at Rockingham.

"No, I saw one glove."

Bailey knew Fuhrman would *insist* that he never found two gloves at Bundy. Well, let him swear to the jury that he

510

didn't take a glove to Rockingham: It would only count against him when Bailey destroyed his credibility.

The courtroom seemed to hold its breath. Everyone present expected Bailey to prove that Fuhrman planted the glove. He'd told the media he was going to tear Fuhrman up. Even his colleagues at the defense table were waiting for a breakthrough. Instead Bailey moved on to Kathleen Bell, the young woman who had heard Fuhrman express racist views at a marine recruiting station.

Bailey ran a video of Bell on the Larry King show, then a picture of Bell. The woman was ready to testify that Fuhrman had used the word "nigger." Fuhrman insisted he had never met her.

"You say you're sure you never met a woman named Kathleen Bell?" Bailey asked.

"Yes, sir." Fuhrman stayed cool. "I do not recall ever meeting this woman in the recruiting station or anywhere else."

"Well, I'm trying to get the distinction," Bailey continued, "between a lack of recollection, a faded memory, and an absolute certainty that you have never seen this woman until you saw her on television. Which is it?"

"I do not recognize this woman as anybody I have ever met," Fuhrman said.

"Did you say at any time . . . in the presence of any female, including Kathleen Bell, that you'd like nothing more than to see all 'niggers' gathered together and killed?"

"No."

By day's end, Bailey had still not set Fuhrman up for the "N-word."

On the second day, Bailey made Fuhrman justify everything he'd done at both crime scenes. He took Fuhrman through his movements that night again and again. Why not take other cops along to explore Rockingham's dark back walkway? He was worried about finding a suspect, wasn't he?

The old lawyer flipped open his notebooks to the orange pages, searching out the smallest inconsistencies between Fuhrman's pretrial testimony and his current testimony. He questioned Fuhrman's confusing preliminary-hearing statement about seeing the Bundy glove, or gloves, through a fence. Bailey read from the transcript:

" '. . . through that iron fence you can get very close to the male victim, and looking down there I could see *them* down at his feet.' " Bailey leaned hard on "them."

The detective never missed a beat. "I was referring to the knit cap and glove," he said.

"Show me anywhere on that page where the knit cap is mentioned. Can you?" Bailey asked.

"That page, no."

Bailey was into microsurgery: no detail too small. To others, it looked like two marines arm-wrestling to a draw. Lots of grunting. No movement. No blood.

LOW KEY BUT STRONG START FOR BAILEY SEEN

. . . The question of the moment is: Does F. Lee Bailey still have his fastball?

Right ballpark. Wrong metaphor.

Cross-examination rarely depends on speed. Usually it calls for junk-curves, sliders, change-ups and, if you're clever enough, the occasional spitter. They're the sort of pitches that flirt, dance and deceive before they hit the catcher's mitt with the thud of awful finality. . . .

As Detective Mark Fuhrman may yet discover, when it comes to throwing junk, 61-year-old defense attorney Bailey still has a lot of stuff. . . .

—Henry Weinstein and Tim Rutten,
Los Angeles Times, March 14, 1995

On the third day, March 15, Bailey can see several ways to lead Mark Fuhrman to the "nigger" question. He isn't sure which would be best. By now, he knows the detective is tough.

For days the jury has been stone-faced. Even O.J. has controlled himself. He makes a point now of not consulting with Bailey in front of the jury.

The defense wants the jury to see Fuhrman as a man desperate to stay in the case, desperate to be a star, desperate to punish a black man who flaunted his sexual involvement with a white woman. Today Bailey wants to show the jury that Fuhrman was a bad cop promoted to bad detective. And this bad detective was the first detective at Bundy. First at the Bronco. First over the wall. He decided to go out back, alone, to investigate a suspicious noise. And he found the glove.

Lee Bailey wants to demonstrate that Mark Fuhrman had motive and opportunity to take a bloody glove from Bundy to Rockingham. He had motive and opportunity to rub that glove around the interior of O.J. Simpson's Bronco and plant it on the walkway behind the house.

Didn't you go out to the Bronco, wipe the glove on it, and dump the glove behind the house? Bailey asks. Fuhrman insists he didn't, says he didn't even try to open the car door. Fine: the more details on the record, the more chances for impeachment down the road.

That a police detective might plant evidence is hard for most people to imagine, especially if they think O.J. Simpson is guilty. But now the idea is before the jury. Let them think about it.

Next, let Fuhrman deny being a racist. For three days the detective has admitted nothing. Now Bailey comes to *the* question. How best to phrase it? Perhaps like this: Have you used the word "nigger" in the last ten years? Ten, a good round number. Ito has ruled against introducing Fuhrman's psychiatric records from 1983. Bailey can't ask about events twelve years ago. But Ito has admitted the 1987 incident Kathleen Bell described in her letter to the defense. We can go back eight years, so why not ten? Then let Fuhrman deny it. If we show he lied about this, then the jury may question all of his other responses.

Even if Fuhrman admits saying the word, Bailey can still do a hard follow-up: You don't like black people, do you? Is it fair to say you disliked O.J. Simpson intensely when you saw him holding a baseball bat while his attractive white wife cried over her broken windshield? Fuhrman's answer won't be all that important. The best question in a cross-examination is one where you don't care what the witness answers. The jury gets the message: Mark Fuhrman uses racial slurs and hates black men who are involved with white women. Perhaps he hated O.J. Simpson enough to frame him.

Bailey goes back to Fuhrman's dress rehearsal.

"Did you tell the lawyers in that room that you never used the word 'nigger'?" he asks.

"It was never asked," Fuhrman replies.

"Do you use the word 'nigger' in describing people?" Clark objects. Ito allows the question.

"No, sir," Fuhrman says. He refuses to give an inch.

"Have you used that word in the last ten years?"

Bailey waits for Marcia Clark to object, to insist he can go back only to 1987. She doesn't.

"Not that I recall, no," Fuhrman says.

Bailey exults silently. The defense has just gained the right to examine two extra years of Fuhrman's history. And Fuhrman finally has said: I don't remember.

Then Bailey asks if Fuhrman might have forgotten. The detective pretends not to understand the question. Bailey tries again.

"I want you to assume that perhaps at some time, since 1985 or 1986, you addressed a member of the African-American race as a 'nigger.' Is it possible that you have forgotten that act on your part?"

"No. It is not possible."

Bailey is certain that no juror will believe for a moment that *this* cop hasn't used that word in a decade. Certainly the black jurors won't believe it. How many white men, cop or civilian, could make that claim? If Fuhrman lies about this, would he lie about the glove? Simpson looks pleased. He is content to leave Bailey alone. No coaching from the owner's box today.

"Are you therefore saying that you have not used the word in the past ten years, Detective Fuhrman?" Bailey thunders now.

"That's what I'm saying, sir."

Fuhrman is cool. He's calm. He's mine, Bailey thinks. I have him now.

"So that anyone who comes to this court and quotes you as using that word with African-Americans would be a liar." Bailey is setting the stage for the team's future witnesses.

"Yes, they would," Fuhrman says.

"All of them, correct?"

"All of them."

That afternoon, the prosecution argued that before Fuhrman could be questioned again on that point, the defense must present witnesses to impeach his testimony that he hadn't used the word "nigger" in the last decade. How could Fuhrman be cross-examined on material the judge had not even ruled admissible yet? To everyone's surprise, Ito agreed with the D.A. and decided to conclude Fuhrman's cross-examination, subject to recall. Fuhrman would have to take the stand again after the defense presented its impeachment witnesses. The right to recall the detective was open-ended. Fuhrman was planning to retire to Idaho, but was still under subpoena; he could be escorted back to court, if necessary.

Johnnie and Carl were amazed to hear Bailey say "nigger" so often. The team had discussed this. We don't want a white guy throwing this word around on television, Johnnie had said. They'd assumed Bailey would use it sparingly, if at all.

Douglas and Cochran agreed it was a good cross, but not a great one. Lee didn't shake Fuhrman, much less break him. Everyone had expected a Perry Mason moment. All we've been hearing for weeks is Fuhrman, Fuhrman, Fuhrman, Chapman thought. I'll demolish this racist cop. Just you watch. It will be clear he planted the glove. Nothing in Bailey's cross came close. Shawn felt let down.

We'll impeach him on the "N-word," Johnnie said that night. But it doesn't take us the distance. We need to show this guy as a monster.

The press, too, had expected more from Bailey. Where were the fireworks? Where was the third-act drama, when the witness crumbles and admits everything? What happened to the Fuhrman funeral? Was Fuhrman just one tough witness? Or did Bailey blow it? In the twelfth-floor pressroom, the consensus was that F. Lee Bailey had, in fact, lost his fastball. The reporters had no way of appreciating the groundwork he had laid for the defense attack on the LAPD.

16

On Friday, March 17, St. Patrick's Day, Bob Shapiro arrives in his Mercedes. As the press surrounds the lawyer, his driver, Keno, notices a strange piece of metal pipe in a newspaper rack on the street. He points it out to the cops before driving away. The courthouse is sealed off.

Everyone is out on the street, including Shapiro and Kardashian. Forty-five minutes later, the bomb squad blows up the metal pipe. An anticlimactic end to all this hurry-up-and-wait. As Kardashian enters the hallway outside the courtroom, he sees talk-show host Geraldo Rivera. "Bob, how are you?" Rivera calls out cheerily. As if they were old friends.

"Hi," Kardashian answers without breaking stride. He gets into the courtroom and lockup quickly, and finds O.J. in high spirits. Juice has pulled another practical joke.

Simpson explains that he was kept in the holding cell during the bomb scare. He hid in the one corner of the large dark cell that couldn't be seen from the doorway. After the all-clear, Deputy Guy Magnera came in and called to O.J., "Time to go."

Simpson didn't answer. Magnera stopped, confused. He couldn't see O.J. in the corner. Had his prisoner slipped away somehow during the bomb scare? Then Simpson emerged, smiling. Magnera thought it was funny. Thank God it wasn't Deputy Jex, Bob thinks. And he laughs, but he's preoccupied.

"We've got to talk about Shapiro," he says. "He sits at the end of the table bitching about the other lawyers. He distracts people. He wrecks morale."

"Let's wait," Simpson says.

"Everybody on the team is mad at him," Kardashian argues.

"He put the team together, Bobby," O.J. insists. "The jury's seen him. They'll wonder what happened. They'll think we've got another fight on our hands. We don't need that."

Simpson is immovable. Shapiro will stay. Anything else would look bad.

Still determined to do something about Shapiro, Kardashian approached Cochran in the courthouse cafeteria at lunchtime.

"I'm with you, Bob," Cochran said. "He's really hindering me. But you've got to talk to O.J."

Kardashian went back to the holding cell. No lunch for him today.

"O.J., it's in everyone's best interests that he be terminated. Johnnie feels very strongly about this. He asked me to talk to you."

"We've got to wait," Simpson repeated. "I can't do it that easily. He got the trial going quickly, he got me Michael Baden. He got me Henry Lee. Scheck and Neufeld. If it wasn't for him in the beginning, I wouldn't be as far down the road as I am today."

Kardashian knew Shapiro hadn't assembled the team all by himself. But he *had* moved in the right direction during those first weeks. It was pointless to argue specifics. The facts didn't matter. O.J. never fired anyone.

DISMISSED JUROR: BAILEY A "MASTER,"
FUHRMAN TELLING TRUTH

> The fifth juror dismissed from the O.J. Simpson trial
> said Friday he was impressed by defense lawyer F. Lee
> Bailey, but ultimately believed Detective Mark Fuhrman
> was telling the truth. . . .
>
> [Tracy] Kennedy said he had not made up his mind
> about Simpson's guilt or innocence, and feels that others
> on the panel are also keeping open minds until they
> hear from both sides. . . .
>
> —Linda Deutsch, AP, March 17, 1995

Tracy Kennedy had unnerved the defense. He sometimes
stared at Simpson. The team assumed he was antagonistic to
their arguments; they suspected he was writing a book on the
trial. His fellow jurors complained he was eavesdropping on
their dinner table conversations while pretending to listen to
music on a Walkman that contained no tape. Two deputies
said Kennedy had asked *them* to keep notes. Exit Mr.
Kennedy.

The defense was glad to see him go. But they didn't like
his replacement, a tough-looking white woman. They
learned in voir dire that she had once turned an entire jury
around, from 11–1 against her to 12–0 in favor. She must be
something in deliberations. Then again, on another occasion
she'd sided with African-Americans in a racial conflict. The
defense wasn't reassured. She just didn't look likable sitting
in seat number 3. Before long, Johnnie was calling her the
Demon.

On Saturday, March 18, Cochran, Bailey, Dershowitz,
Scheck, Bailey's partner Ken Fischman, Dimitrius,
Douglas, Blasier, McKenna, Chapman, Harris, and Kardashian gather in Johnnie's conference room. Fuhrman's
televised appearance on the stand has produced new witnesses willing to testify against him. McKenna is assigned to
do background checks—*complete* background checks, this
time. And no tape recorders. Robert Shapiro's cross-
examination of Detective Phil Vannatter, the lead investigat-

ing officer, is scheduled for the next court day. But Shapiro isn't at the team meeting.

The defense wants to find a key to Vannatter. Johnnie knows cops; that's his business. Most cops, he says, are single-minded. They start on a path and stay with it. They won't go back. If a cop gets caught, he forges ahead and covers it up. Example: Vannatter says O.J. was not a suspect at first. He says he sent Fuhrman over Simpson's Rockingham wall because he thought someone might be bleeding. To get a formal search warrant, he states O.J. left town on an unexpected trip. He says the next day he took O.J.'s blood from police headquarters to Rockingham to give it to criminalist Dennis Fung. But how did he know that Fung was there? Maybe the criminalist was at Bundy.

Bailey says Vannatter is an old-fashioned cop: He thinks justice is what he decides it is. Cops like him do whatever they want to do and hide behind the code of silence. If Fuhrman lied, Vannatter will cover for Fuhrman. If we show he lies routinely about small stuff, Bailey says, we can make the jury wonder if he lies about big things.

The team reviews Thursday's and Friday's direct examination of Vannatter. The burly detective had been relaxed and comfortable while Chris Darden questioned him. But he let you know where he stood.

Darden began with preemptive damage control on areas he knew the defense would attack. He established that a jail nurse had taken blood from Simpson to be used for comparison with any evidence collected. Vannatter had then taken Simpson's blood vial to Rockingham. That would certainly be a defense target.

"Why did you take the sample to Rockingham?" Darden asked.

"I knew that the criminalist was at Rockingham," Vannatter answered. ". . . I hand-carried it to him for the chain of custody and to protect that piece of evidence."

". . . Could you have booked the evidence at Parker Center?"

"I could have booked it," the detective replied. "But I

didn't have a DR [Division of Records] number. I didn't have an item number. If I would have done that, it would have been sitting there with no control over it.''

Darden was on the defensive, trying to cover as many bases as he could. He wanted to show that the detective was safeguarding the reference blood, not using it to plant or enhance evidence.

On Monday, March 20, Shapiro arrived at the courthouse wearing a small blue pin on his lapel. City councilwoman Laura Chick, LAPD commissioner Art Maddox, and the Police Protective League, the LAPD's rank-and-file union, had launched a campaign urging people to support the LAPD. They were giving out these little pins. A month before, Dennis Zine of the PPL had given Shapiro one. That same day he wore it and nobody noticed. But today huge billboards around town featured the blue ribbon. Now Shapiro was wearing one, and he would cross Vannatter. The media noticed it and were all over him.

At the defense table, Johnnie Cochran stared at Shapiro. ''Bob, what are you wearing that pin for?'' he asked incredulously. Shapiro said something about a friend giving it to him.

Cochran dropped it. But he knew the jury would see the pin. Would they know what it meant?

O.J. didn't like the pin either. But he said nothing.

As Shapiro rose to address Vannatter, he might have been the old cop's neighbor. His plan was to keep the cross friendly and light. To make his points while the jury enjoyed a painless ride. He started with the LAPD's lack of technical sophistication.

''Since the time that you have become a police officer twenty-six years ago,'' Shapiro began with a smile, ''I would imagine that there have been drastic changes in scientific evidence in criminal cases.''

''Yeah,'' Vannatter said. ''There have been changes. Yes.''

''Would you describe them as drastic?''

''Probably, yes.''

This was foundation for the attack on criminalist Dennis

Fung, who collected the physical evidence. Fair enough, Carl Douglas thought, but could we display a bit more vigor? Simpson began writing notes. He wanted a stronger tone.

"Are you familiar with the proper techniques of the collection of DNA evidence?" Shapiro asked.

"I am not a criminalist," Vannatter said, huffing a little, "and I am not an expert in that, no."

Shapiro was setting things up for Barry Scheck. "Are you aware that a trainee was sent out to the crime scene?"

"Yes."

". . . Is that the type of person you would like collecting your evidence under your direction?"

Vannatter reddened a bit. "That's the person who was sent."

Shapiro repeated the question. Did Vannatter understand what he'd been asked? Over Darden's objection, Ito allowed this.

"I really have no control over that," Vannatter finally answered. "Of course I would like to have the most qualified person do everything for me, but that is not the practical world." The cop was annoyed.

During the lunch break the team was amazed to see Shapiro chatting with Vannatter. He was still wearing the pin supporting the LAPD. They talked like old friends.

After lunch Shapiro continued to pick away at the LAPD's competence in high-tech evidence collection.

"What are the dangers of entering a crime scene if you're not trained properly?" he asked.

"Destruction and contamination of the evidence," Vannatter said warily. They'd been over this before.

"DNA evidence is minute, sometimes even microscopic, isn't it? Shapiro asked.

"I don't know," Vannatter admitted. "That's way out of my field of expertise. I really don't know that."

O.J. started sending notes to Shapiro at the podium. Shapiro ignored them. O.J. conferred with Johnnie. Ask O.J.'s questions, Cochran whispered to Shapiro. Shapiro said nothing.

"Isn't it true, sir, that one of the reasons that you wanted to leave the crime scene and go to the Simpson residence," Shapiro asked, "was because you had information that there had been previous instances of domestic violence and you immediately suspected the ex-husband as being the person responsible in these cases?" Finally there was real force in Shapiro's voice.

"No, that is not true," Vannatter answered. But his broad face was tight and red.

Johnnie knew there was no way this jury would identify with Vannatter. This business of going over the wall supposedly to check for additional victims was an affront to their common sense, a transparent excuse to intrude without a search warrant. Carrying the blood vial to the crime scene was also strange. Blood should be stored in a lab refrigerator, not in a cop's pocket. That was rudimentary. Vannatter had done some very unusual things.

Carl Douglas knew the prosecutors hadn't yet grasped what this defense team could do to their witnesses. The D.A.'s office thought they had an open-and-shut case. Marcia Clark had talked about the blood results as if they settled everything. Now the defense was dismantling the prosecution's case piece by piece. Prosecutors aren't trained to search out the kind of loopholes a good defense team can find. And by this time the Simpson defense had brought together fourteen attorneys whose combined experience was awesome.

On Tuesday, March 21, Bob Shapiro worked his way through a second day of cross-examination. Simpson wrote another question on a Post-it note. This time Shapiro agreed it was worth asking.

"Did you ask Arnelle Simpson, 'Where's O.J.?' " Shapiro began. He was referring to the predawn meeting with Simpson's daughter after the detectives entered the estate.

"She gestured toward the house and said, 'Isn't he here?' " Vannatter testified. "And I asked her, 'Is he? Do you have a key? Can we go check?' And she took us into the home."

Shapiro made his move. "Did you ask her where O.J.'s bedroom was?"

"No, I did not."

"If you were concerned about O.J., wouldn't you want to go up to his bedroom and see if he was still sleeping?"

Vannatter insisted that Simpson was already "accounted for." But now he was contradicting himself. When Arnelle let them into the house, she had not yet told the cops to contact Cathy Randa for her father's schedule. For all she knew, her father might have been in the house sleeping.

"But he wasn't accounted for immediately, was he?"

"No, sir, he wasn't."

Shapiro had hit paydirt. The cops had justified their going over the wall without a warrant as a search for someone injured and bleeding. So why didn't they check the house thoroughly? Particularly Simpson's bedroom? Shapiro had demonstrated the possibility of a "rush to judgement."

Now Shapiro was ready for a serious gamble. The team had discussed this. Vannatter was an old-style, by-the-book cop. A man of habit, he'd investigated crime scenes and handled evidence the same way for decades. During his career, had he taken reference blood from many persons? Of course. Had he carried such blood with him to a crime scene before? The defense didn't know.

Shapiro was about to break the rule that you never ask a question unless you already know the answer. The case demanded it.

"How many times have you taken blood from Parker Center out to a crime scene?" Shapiro asked almost casually.

If Vannatter had never carried blood to a crime scene before, then his taking it to Rockingham delivered a powerful message: He might have taken some blood out of the tube in the intervening time.

"I don't know," the detective replied. "This may have been the first time. I don't know. I can't recall right now any other time that I have done that."

Vannatter's waffling and discomfort were plain to the jury.

The question was now firmly established: What happened to O.J.'s blood sample in Vannatter's custody?

One last question. No gamble here. "Did you walk into any blood evidence while the crime scene [at Bundy] was still secure?" Shapiro asked.

"No, sir."

Shapiro turned to Howard Harris at the VCR. "May we show the video, please?" It was another clip from Scheck's and Blasier's marathon viewing.

"Can you identify the person," Shapiro asked, "that appears to be standing on a sheet covered with blood?"

Vannatter reddened. "Yes. That is myself."

Johnnie smiled. Even Simpson was pleased.

17

THE D.A. HOPED TO PROVE BEYOND ALL DOUBT THAT THE Bronco contained Goldman's blood mixed with Simpson's. There wasn't enough of anyone's DNA in any one stain for the most accurate but lengthy RFLP typing. By March 20 the prosecution received permission from Judge Ito to combine blood from several stains in the Bronco for future RFLP testing. The prosecution now wanted the most definitive DNA test available. Results that might be unassailable. But these tests would take months to do. More discovery-during-trial for the defense to deal with eventually.

Drs. Lee and Baden continued to insist they were *not* advocates. Presenting the facts to advantage was Johnnie Cochran's and Marcia Clark's proper work. The scientists were above the fray. They dealt with objective, quantifiable data; their first loyalty was to scientific truth. Lee discussed his observations freely with LAPD lab people. Gary Sims from the DOJ lab spoke openly with Ed Blake, who was observing DOJ's testing for the defense, long before the results became official.

It was a different story with the DNA lawyers—Barry Scheck, Bob Blasier, and Peter Neufeld on one side; Rockne Harmon, Woody Clarke, Lisa Kahn, and Cheri Lewis on the other. All of them wanted to win as badly as Clark and Cochran.

During Neufeld's absence in New York to complete another trial, Scheck immersed himself in the facts of the case. In December the defense brought in William Thompson, a professor at the University of California-Irvine who was both a lawyer and a forensics specialist. Thompson huddled with Scheck and Blasier to study the prosecution's presentation of scientific material.

In January, Marcia Clark had incorrectly characterized each blood identification as a "unique" match—this is *her* blood; that is *his* blood—which implied that the DNA typings were positive identifications like fingerprints. Scheck and Thompson knew that was scientifically inaccurate.

On Monday, March 20, the defense had filed a motion objecting to the prosecution's language of "unique" identifications. No more "match," the defense brief requested. Use "consistent with." The defense wanted to prevent the prosecution from linking DNA test results to specific individuals. As William Thompson argued, that can't reasonably be done. DNA testing is an elimination process. It is not a positive identification of any one individual. It is not a fingerprint. If blood test results were properly explained, it would be clear that Nicole's and Ron's and O.J.'s blood shared characteristics with blood from other persons.

The defense knew the D.A. would call Robin Cotton, the lab director of Cellmark Diagnostics, to explain the DNA science to the jury and announce test results from her lab. Scheck and Thompson knew what was coming. Cotton would list probabilities: Simpson was the only one in millions who could have left the blood on the walkway.

The defense needed a target, but Robin Cotton and

Cellmark wouldn't do. Her lab and its work, like Sims and DOJ, were unassailable. But the meaning of the numbers was fair game.

Thompson and Scheck hoped to force the prosecution to put a statistician on the stand to explain the astronomical numbers. On cross-examination, Barry Scheck knew, the defense could score crucial points.

Ito issued no formal ruling, but as a practical matter the defense won. They had demonstrated Clark's error in using the word "match" so convincingly that thereafter, the judge was much more likely to sustain the defense's objections. No question now that the prosecution would have to present an expert witness to explain what the DNA numbers meant.

On Tuesday, March 21, Carl Douglas wondered why the prosecutors were presenting Kato Kaelin. Fuhrman, Phillips, Lange, and Vannatter had told the jurors when the evidence was found. Next, the D.A. should have used the testimony of the two criminalists, Fung and Mazzola, to explain how it was collected. Instead, here was Kato Kaelin, a time-line witness. The prosecution expected him to establish the last time O.J. had been seen the night of the murders.

Douglas wondered if the prosecution had foreseen the shape and scope of the defense attack aimed at Fung and Mazzola. Did the D.A.s need extra time to prepare their criminalists?

Marcia Clark showed Kato the same gentle solicitude she had demonstrated with Fuhrman. "You feel a little bit nervous today?" she asked.

"Feel great," mumbled Kato. "Little nervous."

Douglas knew that Kaelin would testify that he'd last seen Simpson at 9:37 P.M., when O.J. stood at the driver's door of his Bentley at Rockingham. Kato didn't see him reenter the house. No other witness saw Simpson again until limousine driver Allan Park loaded his luggage seventy-eight minutes later. In cross, Bob Shapiro could only hope to show that Kaelin had no idea what Simpson did next.

The defense also wanted to remind jurors of their Rockingham tour. Kato Kaelin heard thumps that the prosecutors—having implied that Simpson climbed the fence to sneak back onto his property—insisted was the defendant slamming into the guest bedroom wall. The jury had toured that walkway. They saw that the chest-high cyclone fence was overgrown by thick trees and shrubs and couldn't be scaled without breaking branches and leaving a trail. The police found no sign of entry or of a trail immediately after the murders. Nor, eight months later, could the jurors. Further, Allan Park had seen a shadowy figure—O.J., the prosecution would say—enter the front door of Rockingham. The jurors would remember from their tour that going from the walkway where the glove was found to the front door was a roundabout way of entering the house, one that ignored two closer, less visible doorways.

On Wednesday, March 22, Marcia asked Kato about the thumps he heard during the night of June 12. Early on, the defense had theorized that the three knocks on Kato's wall at 10:40 P.M. might have been a signal or had come from whoever dropped the glove to implicate O.J. Those thumps would get Kaelin's attention and set him up as a witness. But Detective Fuhrman, who according to the defense had planted the glove, knew nothing of the case until he was called at approximately two A.M. He was on the other side of town when Kaelin heard those thumps. The defense wanted to forget those noises. They hoped the jury would, too.

Simpson was still protective toward Kato. Months earlier, he'd quashed speculation by his attorneys that Kaelin could have been the murderer. His houseguest would be no problem on the stand, he said. "Kato's gonna tell the truth," he told Kardashian. "Kato's not going to hurt us at all. He'll do the best he can."

"And so," Clark asked, "approximately what time was it when you heard the thumps on the wall?"

"At about ten-forty," Kaelin answered.

* * *

Later that day Kato testified about helping Simpson load luggage into the limousine that evening.

"I'd put the golf bag in already," said Kaelin, "and I was going to go get the knapsack to put it in."

Did he mean the "dark knapsack" lying near the Bentley? Clark asked. Yes, Kaelin said, but Simpson stopped him.

"What did he say?" Clark asked.

"I'll get it."

Clark was trying to plant the idea that O.J. wouldn't let Kato touch the "dark knapsack" for sinister reasons. "That small dark bag," Marcia Clark had told the jury in her opening statement, "was never seen again." Kardashian knew otherwise.

As court ended that afternoon, Kardashian told Johnnie the knapsack was in his daughter's closet. And he'd told Shapiro months ago that Simpson's golf bag was in his garage.

Cochran asked Kardashian to ask Simpson what had happened to the knapsack between the night of June 12 and now.

The "dark knapsack," O.J. explained, was actually a dark blue golf-shoe bag. Simpson said that while Allan Park loaded the limousine, he had dropped it by the Bentley to load it with new golf balls from the car's trunk.

Simpson told Kardashian that he repacked his bags for Chicago in the trunk of the limousine. He dumped the golf balls from the "dark knapsack"—that is, from the blue leather shoe bag—into his golf bag, then stuffed the empty shoe bag into the golf bag as well. During his hours in Chicago he never touched the golf bag. When he returned from Chicago he carried the Louis Vuitton bag and the black duffel bag. The golf bag with the shoe bag inside followed on the next flight.

At Rockingham on June 13, Kardashian took the Vuitton bag from Cathy Randa. When police wouldn't let him take the bag inside, Bob threw it in the trunk of his car and took it home. Then he brought it back to Rockingham the next morning, June 14.

The same day, Simpson left Rockingham with Kardashian and picked up the golf bag at the airport. At some point during the next three days, Simpson took the "dark knapsack" out and put it in the closet of the room he was using at Kardashian's house. Bob could vouch for that. He'd found the bag there after Simpson's arrest.

One day in July, Bob Kardashian and Al Cowlings had secretly inspected the golf bag. Then, as now, it was leaning against the back wall in Kardashian's garage. The tabloids were saying the murder weapon was inside. The two men closed the garage door, opened the travel cover, and carefully pulled all the clubs out. They turned the bag upside down. No knife fell out. They shook it. Still nothing. They shined a flashlight inside, looking for blood. Then they opened each of the side pockets. They pulled out a windbreaker, golf balls, golf gloves, tees. Kardashian ran his hands around the interior of each compartment, feeling for sharp objects.

Both men stood for a minute in silent relief. The bag was clean.

Now Kardashian reported this to the defense team. Cochran agreed it was time to get the luggage. Kardashian still had the golf bag and the "dark knapsack." Cochran asked Ito to appoint Judge Wong again to observe.

The question that stymied the defense was why, since the prosecution had accused Kardashian of disposing of bloody clothes, they hadn't asked for the bags during the last nine months. They could have run tests for blood traces, pulled the luggage apart looking for hair and fiber evidence that might link O.J. to the murders.

Of course, the tests might also come up negative. Maybe the D.A. had decided it was better to let speculation about the "missing bag" linger.

On Thursday, March 23, Kato seemed lost. His answers became vague, and in response Marcia pushed him. He resorted to some lame silliness. That didn't sit well with Clark. She pushed harder. On cross, Shapiro came to his rescue.

". . . And you have done the best you can to try to recollect what took place," Shapiro said, "but you can't be absolutely certain of everything you testified to, can you?"

Kato seemed about to cry.

"I have been honest in everything I remember," he said woefully, "and I answered that way."

By Monday, March 27, Marcia Clark, now on redirect examination, was out of patience with Simpson's house-guest. She was angry when Kato soft-pedaled Simpson's behavior after the June 12 recital. Simpson was "upset" about the tight dress Nicole wore, Kato had admitted.

How upset? Clark asked.

"More upset with the Sydney statement," Kaelin answered. Kato was referring to something Simpson said at the recital about wanting to spend more time with his daughter. "But maybe just a bit with that."

"Just a *bit?*" Clark asked incredulously.

She then read Kaelin his earlier testimony about Simpson's comment on Nicole's attire.

"Are you changing your testimony now, Mr. Kaelin?" she asked. Her anger was obvious.

"No," Kaelin answered.

"Was he upset, or wasn't he, when he talked about Nicole and her tight dresses?" Clark asked.

"No, not real upset . . ."

Clark cut Kaelin off and asked the court to make Kato a hostile witness.

Douglas knew the defense had to be gentle with Kato: If Marcia isn't happy with him, let the jury think we are.

For a change, Bob Shapiro's buddy-buddy style was exactly what was needed.

18

LEE BAILEY HAD BEEN LOBBYING TO CROSS ALLAN PARK, the limousine driver who picked up Simpson and took him to the airport. He'd learned that Park's mother worked as a lawyer on Catalina Island. Since he planned to study Simpson's Rockingham home from the air, he invited her to join him in the helicopter. The old warrior and Mrs. Park enjoyed a pleasant talk.

"I've talked to his mother," Bailey said to Carl Douglas more than once. "We've gotten along quite well." Douglas, who oversaw witness assignments, understood the message. He also knew that Johnnie planned to cross-examine Park himself. The helicopter ride didn't help.

On Tuesday, March 28, Allan Park took the stand. Cochran and Douglas knew this witness could create trouble: He was sincere. He hadn't taken a dime from the tabloids. He had no ax to grind.

Simpson told Cochran he thought Park was honest, but mistaken. As Park told his story, O.J. scribbled a constant stream of notes: I *never* told Park I was sleeping. Ask him! Johnnie resisted: If this young man thinks you said you were sleeping, let it go. It sounds fine. We don't need to get into a spat with young Abe Lincoln.

"I never forget these things!" Simpson hissed. "I don't care if I lose. I'm not lying. I wasn't sleeping!"

For once, Cochran ignored him. Simpson said it again. But Johnnie waited him out. Simpson eventually moved on. The witness said he saw two cars—one a Bentley—inside the gate at eleven P.M.

"There weren't two cars there," Simpson's Post-it note read. "There was only one. Ask him."

The second car, Arnelle's, wasn't at Rockingham until she got home—two hours after Park left with Simpson. Park had to be remembering what he saw on TV the next day. Now Park didn't remember seeing the Bronco outside the gate, but he did remember seeing a car that wasn't there. We can do something with this, Simpson insisted.

This time Johnnie agreed. "You have previously testified that you did see two cars in that driveway?" he asked Allan Park.

"Yes," Park said.

Cochran repeated the question twice more for emphasis. Then he asked Park to describe the two cars. The driver said one was a Rolls-Royce, the other "dark."

". . . If I were to tell you that that second car did not arrive in that driveway until about one o'clock A.M.," Cochran said, "would that in any way refresh your recollection that there was only one car when you looked in there?"

"No," Park answered.

So much hinged on the Bronco. Did Park see the car while he was at Simpson's home? Simpson had told Cochran the Bronco was there. Now Cochran had to shake Park's confidence.

"[When you arrived] you were focusing on the address and on the house," Cochran said. ". . . You were not focusing on any cars, particular cars parked there. Isn't that correct?"

"Yes," Park admitted.

"And you cannot tell this jury *positively* that a vehicle was parked there outside the Rockingham gate or not," Cochran hammered. "Can you?"

"No," Park said.

A breakthrough. Cochran had read Park's testimony at the preliminary hearing and before the grand jury, plus his original LAPD interviews. In each case, Park remembered *no* Bronco when he pulled out of Rockingham to take Simpson to the airport. Prosecutors had told the jury Simpson had driven the Bronco to Rockingham from Bundy minutes before, parked it, and entered the estate at Rockingham. The defense, of course, maintained that the Bronco had been there all the time.

In either case, the Bronco *must* have been parked at the curb when Allan Park pulled out and left with Simpson for the airport: Police found it there in the morning.

"When you left the Rockingham gate, sir, and you were going to pull out to head to the airport . . ." Cochran asked carefully, "at that point you don't recall whether or not you saw any parked cars [on the street], isn't that correct?"

"That's correct," Park admitted.

". . . And at all times throughout your testimony," Cochran said, "you have always tried to be as accurate as you could, isn't that correct?"

"Yes," said Allan Park.

The defense scientists' favorite villain was Rockne Harmon. "Rock" was one of their small tribe, a science-expert lawyer. He was also a former navy officer who always seemed ready to ram his ship into yours. The team had a running joke: Give Rock enough time, and he'll step on his dick.

On Thursday, March 30, Bill Thompson and Rock Harmon argued before Judge Ito over the scope of the cross-examination of Kary Mullis, a potential defense witness on PCR-DNA typing. Thompson maintained that the prosecution was trying to restrict the defense's inquiries into DNA generally. Also, Mullis would tell the jury that PCR testing was unreliable when blood was collected from locations like the Bundy crime scene and the Bronco and tested by a lab like the LAPD's. A Nobel laureate, he was first among the developers of the PCR technique; he should know. Naturally, the defense considered him a valuable witness.

But they knew Harmon planned to attack Mullis's credibility. And unfortunately the scientist was an easy target. He talked publicly about his LSD trips. He seemed to devote his life to surfing and chasing women. He was so aggressive toward a female writer for *Esquire* magazine that she devoted portions of her article to his relentless, if fruitless, efforts at seduction.

During the hearing, Thompson asked Ito to exclude questions about Mullis's personal life and nonscientific pursuits. He also objected to the D.A.'s leaks concerning Mullis's lifestyle.

Ito turned to Harmon, who was clearly annoyed.

"I am happy that Dr. Mullis might be cross-examined on whether he's consumed LSD on the day of his testimony," Harmon responded. ". . . Or perhaps they get him in a detox center for a period of time, so that when he testifies I won't be able to ask him that."

Rock had gone too far. Everyone in the courtroom felt it. The defense attorneys sat stone-faced. Inwardly they rejoiced: Harmon had stepped on it. Judge Ito's voice was angry. "Mr. Harmon, I really don't need to hear that sort of thing."

Afterward Thompson and Neufeld walked into the ninth-floor men's room, where they saw Harmon finishing up at the urinal. Neufeld was known for a cutting wit. That was the means. Now he had motive and opportunity.

"Rock, that must be painful after what you just did to yourself," Neufeld said.

Furious, Harmon zipped up and, in a hurry to leave, slammed into the closed door.

Mr. Kardashian,

Why are you helping O.J. Simpson get away with MURDER? You have helped him with evidence and probably would have helped him escape from your home.

You are being watched by us. When you get up on the witness stand, you better tell the truth, or we'll let all the world know where you live, and where your children live. You need to become *afraid* or else you and your attorney friends can think that you're all above the law. We also know where Mr. Shapiro lives. Your [sic] destroying our City and we're not going to let you get away with it. STOP THIS TRAVESTY—NOW!!!

[letter unsigned]

FROM: William G. Pavelic
TO: Robert G. Kardashian

Please be informed that the aforementioned letter does constitute a crime and you have the option of making a crime report or file it away . . . like so many other dubious communications . . . .

As you probably know, the author of this letter provided the wrong name and address [on the envelope only]. In fact, the [false] return address is a block away from O.J. Simpson's Rockingham residence.

On Wednesday, April 5, Johnnie and Carl sat in Judge Ito's chambers. "They're using the powers of the Sheriff's Department and the LAPD to kick our good jurors off," Johnnie complained angrily.

It did no good. Ito said the matter was settled. Juror 462 was dismissed. In 1988 she had obtained a restraining order against a boyfriend or husband, but hadn't mentioned it in her juror questionnaire.

Back in October, Jo-Ellan Dimitrius had told the defense that number 462 was among the five most pro-O.J. jurors in the entire pool of three hundred. As the trial progressed, it was obvious she liked the defense. Juror 462 relaxed and smiled whenever Johnnie talked. She stiffened and stared at the ceiling when Marcia Clark questioned witnesses. Her dismissal was a loss for the defense.

The pool of alternate jurors was down to six from the original twelve, and there was no telling how long the trial would last.

That evening Jeanette Harris, Juror 462, appeared on KCAL's news broadcast with Pat Harvey, who asked Harris's opinion of the prosecution. "They're not necessarily saying anything," Harris replied.

The team realized losing Harris wasn't all bad. Now she was giving them accurate reports on the jury. Other dismissed jurors, like Michael Knox and Tracy Kennedy, had been cautious with the press—but Harris, bless her, was outspoken. She didn't think domestic violence was an issue. "That doesn't mean he's guilty of murder," she said on TV.

Better yet, she didn't believe Fuhrman. Do you think someone who makes racial slurs could plant evidence? the interviewer asked. "Yes, I do," she answered. Fantastic, Shawn Chapman thought. But did the other black jurors agree with Harris?

Jeanette Harris was "quite impressed" with O.J. "He's gone through a lot," she told the interviewer. ". . . He's got two minor children at home that he's not allowed to comfort. . . . It totally amazes me that he's able to handle it."

When Simpson heard about the interview he said, "You tell her if she isn't married, I'll marry her."

Harris's remarks—especially her vague comments about racial tensions within the jury—sent shock waves around the courthouse. A week later Ito asked her to explain her televised statements on this point. Harris took the stand in a closed session.

The situation was far more serious than the defense had realized. Harris told the court that the jurors had split into antagonistic black and white groups which ate and exercised separately. They watched videos in different rooms. She told stories of shoving, even hitting. One day a Hispanic juror asked to open a window, saying she couldn't breathe the same air as African-Americans. Some deputies were prejudiced, too, Harris added. They gave whites more telephone time, better shopping opportunities.

A week later, KCAL reporter David Goldstein would testify that Harris also said she "was with a group of five or six other jurors, that they had discussed the case, and that at that time, they believed that he [Simpson] was not guilty." Of course Harris had not identified the others.

If Harris was telling the truth, the jurors had violated Ito's order not to discuss the case in any way before formal deliberations.

Ito said he would investigate. He wanted to be as thorough as possible: "We should err on the side of caution."

Cochran and Douglas were startled by the vehemence of

Harris's views. They'd lost her, but she brought good news. The defense felt fairly confident they had a hung jury. Those pro-defense black jurors could never be swayed by the stern, pro-prosecution white woman in seat number 3 who had turned another jury her way. They could only hope that pro-Simpson jurors would withstand Ito's investigation.

19

MEMORANDUM

FROM: FLB
TO: Skip Taft
SUBJ: Out of State Witness Interview
DATE: 4-5-95
COPY: Johnnie Cochran

TOP SECRET—EYES ONLY

Pat McKenna and I are about to embark on a road trip to conduct "pretestimony" interviews of a number of critical listed and prospective defense witnesses. . . .

Andrea Terry, Provo, Utah: She was with Kathleen Bell . . . when Bell encountered Fuhrman for the second time. Terry heard Fuhrman declare that whenever he saw a "nigger" with a white woman he would arrest him, and that all "niggers" should be put in a pile and burned.

Natalie Singer, Nashville, Tennessee: On Tuesday morning of this week Pat and I interviewed Carol Hannak of Sherman Oaks. In 1987 these two women were roommates in Los Angeles. Singer was taken to the hospital with a kidney stone, and Hannak accompanied her. While waiting in the emergency room, Hannak met Mark Fuhrman and his partner, Tom Vittraino. She subsequently dated Vittraino (but did not have an intimate relationship with him), as a result of which Fuhrman came with Vittraino to her apartment on several occasions. Fuhrman continually berated "niggers" and extolled the virtues of the work of Adolf Hitler. He confided that he kept a bowling ball in the trunk of his car to whack suspects in the head, and liked to put his pistol against "niggers' " heads until they were so frightened they would urinate involuntarily. Ultimately, Singer threw Fuhrman out of the house. . . .

Roderic Hodge . . . Hodge was arrested and prosecuted by Fuhrman together with two other blacks; he was subsequently tried for a drug conspiracy, and acquitted. When he was arrested, he was ordered to strip (with his colleague) and bend over, whereafter Fuhrman said, "All you 'nigger' assholes look alike to me."

When Mark Fuhrman finished testifying, the phone calls started. McKenna took most of them. People now remembered Fuhrman. Natalie Singer, for instance, whose roommate had dated Fuhrman's partner, had a fantastic story, if it checked out. Roderic Hodge was black. If Singer and Hodge looked good, the defense had Mark Fuhrman by the balls.

Then Bailey's office got a call from a judge in Texas. She'd been driving in L.A. one night and asked directions of a police officer walking on the street. He was very polite to her. During their conversation, a Corvette pulled up with a black guy and a white girl inside. They also needed directions. The police officer gave them the information, but rudely. After they left he said to the jurist, "I hate these goddamn niggers." When she saw Fuhrman on TV she recognized him as that officer.

538

20

ON APRIL 5, THE DAY THAT JEANETTE HARRIS WAS dismissed and made headlines, Barry Scheck began the second day of Dennis Fung's cross-examination.

Fung was the witness O.J. Simpson's acquittal depended on, the key to discrediting the blood evidence. Behind Fung, already examined, were Vannatter, Lange, and Fuhrman. Ahead were Andrea Mazzola and Colin Yamauchi. But Fung was the key.

Under Scheck's tough exterior he was beset by doubts. For months, respected colleagues and close friends had badgered him with their misgivings: Ask a few questions and sit down, they said. *Don't* suggest a frame-up. It's ridiculous to think that someone tampered with the evidence. Cochran and Shapiro have set you up as the fall guy. They won't attack the LAPD, you will. And you'll be humiliated.

The night before Scheck began his cross he had a full-blown anxiety attack. His heart raced. He hyperventilated and sweated. He knew that when he and Neufeld finished with Fung, Mazzola, and Yamauchi, the case would be won or lost.

He'd plotted two alternate lines of questioning for Fung. If the witness was willing to criticize Vannatter, Lange, and Fuhrman, even to admit his own errors, the cross would follow Plan A. If Fung protected those who came before and after him, Scheck would attack.

"You'll attack him?" Gerry Uelmen asked incredulously. When Uelmen had crossed Fung in the preliminary hearing, the criminalist had been calm and professional.

"He's covering up for a lot of people," Scheck replied. "I have it on videotape, and I have it in the records."

On the first day of his cross, Scheck charged that Fung had recklessly risked contaminating evidence to please Detective Lange, and had abandoned proper procedure rather than annoy the detective.

"Mr. Fung," Scheck said harshly, "when Detective Lange requested that you bring the glove into the middle of the Bundy crime scene to show it to him, you had concerns that there was a terrible danger of cross-contamination?"

"I knew there was a danger for cross-contamination, yes," Fung said.

"And at that Bundy crime scene," Scheck demanded, "did you at any point have reluctance to question Detective Lange's judgment about what should be done in terms of gathering evidence?"

"Did I have—yes. Yes, I did," Fung stuttered. ". . . I did question his judgment." Fung was lost.

In establishing this point, Scheck had constantly fought prosecutor Hank Goldberg's objections. Time and again Scheck rephrased and sharpened his questions. Sometimes he even shouted. He asked about the possibility of "terrible cross-contamination" six different ways before Fung's answer satisfied him. Then he followed with variations of the question seven *more* times to drive the point home.

As the second day came to a close, Scheck scored another major point. Earlier, Fung had insisted that he collected all the evidence himself or supervised his trainee, Andrea Mazzola. Using video clips that showed Mazzola working alone, Scheck forced Fung to admit that the trainee collected many of the Bundy bloodstains without Fung's supervision. And this was only her second murder case.

Fung's vital testimony was interrupted by a curious diversion. A well-dressed Chinese man sat in one of the defense's guest seats. Around eleven in the morning, this gentleman's aide passed leather-bound menus to the defense. What's this? the lawyers asked. Shapiro explained that the Chinese millionaire had paid $5,000 at a charity auction to have lunch with the defense team. He had two chauffeured limousines waiting downstairs. They'd have lunch in a private room at the Tower restaurant. Order now, please. Everyone did.

It is now Tuesday, April 11. Almost a week has passed without testimony while court recessed to let several jurors recover from the flu. Meanwhile, Ito questioned those who were well about Jeanette Harris's charges of racial tension and her statement that jurors had discussed the case in violation of the judge's order. Dennis Fung has enjoyed a five-day rest from his ordeal. Now he is back on the stand.

Barry Scheck cues up a video clip.

"Mr. Fung, that is you getting the prescription glasses envelope from Andrea Mazzola and grasping it with your *bare hand*," Scheck asks, "isn't it?"

Fung replies that it could be "any number of things."

"If that is not you grasping the envelope with the prescription glasses in your bare hand," Scheck says impatiently, "what, pray tell, is it?"

Fung fights back. Fingerprint the envelope, he challenges Scheck. "I know that my fingerprints are not on that envelope."

Scheck itemizes the Bundy evidence. If Fung is holding neither the hat, nor the glove, nor the pager, nor the keys, nor Nicole's ring, nor blood evidence, he asks, what *is* in his hand?

"Notepad, maybe," Fung answers lamely.

Scheck runs the video again, this time in ultra-slow motion.

"There. There! How about that, Mr. Fung?" Barry is shouting now.

"Is that a question, Mr. Scheck?" Ito interrupts, trying to calm things down.

Scheck isn't fazed. "How about that picture, Mr. Fung? Does that refresh your recollection that you took the envelope from Andrea Mazzola with your bare hand?"

Fung *still* fights. It can't be the glasses envelope, he insists, "because we did not start picking up evidence until well after the coroners were gone."

A bad mistake: Scheck then shows a video of Mazzola

541

picking up the bloody glove and reminds Fung of the time by pointing out a coroner's assistant still at the crime scene.

"So you did begin evidence collection before the coroners left? . . . So what you said before wasn't true?"

"It was, to the best of my recollection at the time."

First Fung's bare hands on evidence, now his faulty testimony about when they started collecting that evidence. And Barry Scheck's day isn't over.

"You did not count the number of swatches you collected for each bloodstain, did you?" Scheck asks.

"That's correct," Fung answers. The numbers "varied."

Scheck is reaching past Fung to the time when the defense will present its case. Failure to count the blood inventory is sloppy, of course, but the real importance of these questions is the foundation they establish for later examinations, especially for Edward Blake and DNA expert Gary Sims, who discovered the mysterious "wet transfer" from swatches in one bindle that alerted the team to the possibilities of tampering. And the foundation is also being laid for Henry Lee's testimony, much later.

"And you have absolutely no record of how many swatches you put into the plastic bag for any bloodstain collected in this case?" Scheck continues.

"The stain is the evidence, not the swatch," Fung insists. "I didn't record the number of swatches."

Fung also says he didn't record totals either in the field or in the lab where test tubes were used to dry the swatches and bindles used to segregate them.

Simpson sent only a few Post-it notes in Scheck's direction. Like the other lawyers, Scheck saw his client each day before court while he was handling a witness; but with Scheck, O.J. stuck to stage direction. Simpson wanted dramatic moments before each break, at the mid-morning and mid-afternoon recesses, and something bigger before lunch. Then something hot at day's end. Something *monstrous* for the weekend. Simpson wanted maximum press coverage.

* * *

Later that day, Barry Scheck moved to Simpson's blood on the back gate—the blood that appeared out of nowhere several weeks after the murders. The defense has been waiting for this.

As Scheck approached the witness, he remembered that day in December 1994 when they made the discovery. Scheck, Bob Blasier, and Bill Thompson had been in Laguna Beach, at the office of molecular biologist Simon Ford. Surf crashed outside the window as Ford and the others examined several pictures of a blood spot on the Bundy back gate. Fung had collected a sample from it almost three weeks after the murders.

"Hey, wait a minute," said Ford. "Where is it?" They all looked at a photo of the gate. There was no blood spot.

"It must have been taken later," Scheck said.

But the picture was dated June 13, 1994, the day after the murders. The four men exchanged puzzled glances.

Out came a magnifying glass. "This has got to be a mistake," someone said. The original blood spot would appear under magnification. But it didn't.

At first the men couldn't accept what they'd found. Bill Thompson thought of the movie *Blow-Up*. In that film, important evidence, missed by eyewitnesses, appears only in an enlarged photo. Now here they were with a magnifying lens, and the reverse was happening. Nothing was there.

Now it was time to nail Fung on this issue. "You say on direct examination that you don't recall Detective Lange directing you [on June 13] to look at that rear gate for blood drops?" Scheck asked.

"I don't recall him specifically telling me to do so, no."

Twice more, Scheck asked the criminalist whether Lange mentioned blood drops on the back gate that day. Fung didn't positively recall that he did, but said he "might have."

Fung said he did not see blood on the back gate on June 13. Suddenly Scheck pulled out a photograph of the gate area taken on July 3, the day Fung collected the blood.

"You see what is marked . . . as a blood drop on the rear gate?"

"Yes."

"That's what you saw on July third?"

"Yes."

"Let's look back at the picture of the gate on June thirteenth." The photograph was projected so the entire court could see it. Scheck looked directly at Fung and raised his voice to make his point:

"Where is it, Mr. Fung?"

"I can't see it in the pic—photograph," Fung admitted.

It was 4:30. Scheck had given Simpson his big bang to finish the day. The words "Where is it, Mr. Fung?" appeared in every media broadcast and story that day. Perry Mason had arrived.

21

THE NEXT DAY, APRIL 12, SCHECK ASKED FUNG: "DO you recall that we discussed Barry Fisher's *Techniques of Crime Scene Investigation?*"

Fung remembered it. Scheck began reading.

" 'It is a certainty that wet or damp bloodstains packaged in airtight containers such as plastic bags will be *useless* as evidence in a matter of days.' " Scheck leaned hard on "useless." Did Fung recall this passage? The criminalist said no.

Rapidly, Scheck read other passages. Storing damp blood in "warm environments" accelerates deterioration. Air-drying the sample, then storing it at room temperature—or, best of all, under refrigeration—preserves it far longer. The value of blood for testing, Scheck read, "begins to diminish almost immediately." For maximum benefit, Scheck read, "one should air-dry the samples at the scene."

Then Scheck walked Fung through the Bundy collection process. He and Mazzola started at 11:30 A.M. They put blood swatches into plastic bags, which were stuffed into coin envelopes. The envelopes went into brown paper bags, which were deposited on the floor of their truck.

Scheck asked if the sun was shining. Fung said it was.

"And it was hot inside that truck?" he asked.

"There were periods when I went out to see the truck to make sure it wasn't getting too hot."

"Well, by what means?" Scheck demanded. "By opening the doors and waving your hands there?"

The swatches stayed in the truck in plastic bags in the gathering heat of a June day for seven hours. Fung took them downtown at 6:30 P.M.

Fung insisted, ". . . I feel that was the proper way to collect and preserve that evidence."

Why didn't he use the truck's refrigerator? "It stops working after several hours," Fung admitted.

That week Bill Pavelic had been watching Scheck on TV. Now he saw Scheck turn to the four mysterious red stains on the lower exterior of the Bronco door. The stains continued on the door's interior.

These thin, linear "stains" had bothered Pavelic from the beginning. Fuhrman had testified about "three or four little lines" that looked like a "brush mark." Today Fung was saying that he did not recall that Fuhrman mentioned them when calling him over to the Bronco on June 13. If the tiny red lines were blood evidence, Pavelic knew, Fuhrman would have told Fung to collect it.

For months Pavelic had searched for the missing part of this story. Did Fuhrman *open* the Bronco door and find the red-stained lines so far down on the door panel that they weren't visible from the outside? If so, he couldn't admit it: He had no search warrant to enter the Bronco at that time. More important, if he had opened the door, he would have had the opportunity to wipe a bloody glove from Bundy around the car's interior, leaving behind Nicole's and Ron's blood. Fuhrman couldn't leave himself open to *that* charge.

Pavelic had looked for a more conventional explanation than evidence planting for the presence of Nicole's and Ron's blood in the Bronco. If there was such an explanation, so much the better. Any jury prefers the commonsensical to the exotic. Almost accidentally, Pavelic discovered the answer in the Bronco impound report: The officer who wrote the report had noted that the alternator and battery were in working order before the car was towed. That meant he either started the engine or opened the hood, which required someone inside the car to pull the hood-release handle or turn the key. So someone *had* to have entered the car while it was still at Rockingham even though the cops said it was locked.

Working backward through police radio logs, Pavelic discovered that a pair of uniformed cops named Gonzales and Aston had been at Bundy just after the bodies were found; before the sun rose, they'd been assigned to Rockingham. Pavelic found that Westec Security had seen the two officers pull up at Rockingham at 5:25 A.M. The Westec man saw the two LAPD officers beside the Bronco, without a flashlight. But Pavelic hadn't seen any reports from Gonzales or Aston in the official discovery.

Months earlier, clandestine LAPD sources had given Pavelic two reports from Gonzales. The first covered the cop's Rockingham duties. The LAPD had buried it, Pavelic speculated, because the officers were originally sent to Simpson's neighborhood to knock on doors for witnesses. From this it followed that the police considered Simpson a suspect immediately, something they weren't about to admit; Vannatter's story was that he didn't, at that point, consider O.J. a suspect. The report stated that Fuhrman asked Gonzales and Aston to secure the Bronco as evidence. That meant filling out an impound report. And the report revealed that someone had to have entered the car, or Gonzales could not have stated that the battery and alternator were in working order.

When the trial started, Pavelic got Gonzales's second report. The cop wrote that earlier that night at Bundy, he stepped into the garden area to look at Nicole. The Akita was still there. Gonzales played briefly with the dog and noted its bloody paws. Pavelic reasoned that Gonzales might have gotten blood on his shoes and perhaps even on his hand. In the Rockingham report, Gonzales detailed the blood he saw in the Bronco: He noticed a smear inside the driver's-side door panel, blood on the driver's seat, a smear on the steering wheel, a light smear on the passenger-side door panel, and two drops on the center console. This list was a second indication he had been inside the Bronco. So Gonzales could have tracked Ron and Nicole's blood into the Bronco on his shoes or—less likely—transferred it from his hands.

Walking through the Bundy condo with the defense team in July of 1994, Pavelic had found Gonzales's LAPD business card in Nicole's desk drawer. He'd never found an explanation for that.

Gonzales remained a mystery to Pavelic. Assuming that Gonzales had transferred the victims' blood to the Bronco, Pavelic still had no idea how Simpson's blood got there— unless it, too, had been transferred by Gonzales from the crime scene.

Vannatter had testified that he took Simpson's blood vial to Rockingham on June 13. It was logged in at the LAPD lab on June 14. When did Vannatter give it to Fung? Scheck asked. Fung said the exchange took place at Simpson's home. But there was no written record. Suddenly, in the middle of Barry's cross, the prosecution came up with ABC-TV news footage showing Vannatter, inside Simpson's hallway, giving Fung the reference sample. For a moment this unsettled Scheck. He'd thought he had demonstrated that Vannatter might have kept the vial of reference blood long enough to take blood to frame Simpson. Now the question had become: What happened to the blood once Vannatter gave it to Fung?

On Thursday, April 13, as his grinding cross-examination of Dennis Fung continued, Scheck zeroed in on a video of Andrea Mazzola carrying a plastic garbage bag out of

Rockingham. Fung had said he took the vial of Simpson's blood from Vannatter at Rockingham, but didn't place it in his lab kit. Fine. But where *did* he put it? Fung could not remember when he'd taken it out to the van. When Scheck showed him the video, Fung hesitated. "I think it's the blood vial" inside the plastic garbage bag, he finally admitted. Until then, the defense had not known Simpson's reference blood was in that bag. Why didn't the criminalists use a standard LAPD evidence bag?

Scheck's implication was clear: Simpson's blood sample left Rockingham concealed in a garbage bag, as strangely as it had arrived. Were the criminalists deliberately hiding it? Was the blood vial actually in the bag? Or had someone else taken Simpson's blood to plant as evidence?

TV, LEGAL WRANGLING
BOG DOWN SIMPSON TRIAL

"Why is it taking so long?"

In slightly less than three months of trial, according to The Times' calculations based on court transcripts, Ito has allowed 436 sidebars through Tuesday—an extraordinary number, most legal experts agree. Meanwhile, about 41% of all the available court time has been consumed by proceedings for which the jury was not present. . . .

". . . Why is it taking so long? The answer is contained in one word: television," said defense attorney Gerald L. Chaleff. . . . "Everybody involved in this trial knows that everything they do or say is being seen or heard by millions and millions of people."

—Henry Weinstein and Tim Rutten,
Los Angeles Times, April 16, 1995

On April 17 Judge Ito observed during a sidebar that he'd never before seen a witness so thoroughly destroyed as Dennis Fung. He asked Scheck to stop. The lawyer respectfully refused. He wasn't finished. He still had foundation to lay for future cross-examinations.

Even Simpson was bored. "We ought to take a video of Fung's testimony and market it to insomniacs," he joked to Kardashian. He began focusing on Hank Goldberg's questions; the attorney's professorial monotone was also sleep-inducing. "The Jewish cadaver," Simpson called him. Kardashian didn't like the ethnic slur.

That day Bob Shapiro brought a bag of fortune cookies to court. "These are from the Hang Fung restaurant," he joked as he gave them to reporters. Shapiro offered one to Chris Darden. The D.A. refused. The bag had barely been emptied when the media struck. Shapiro's bigoted joke was covered in depth on the dinnertime TV news. Johnnie's milder wisecrack, "We're having Fung now," was largely ignored. The Asian community expressed its outrage.

Shapiro swallowed hard and apologized publicly.

Carl Douglas shook his head. Who makes anti-Asian jokes while trying a case before a Japanese-American judge? Some guys have a talent for sticking their foot in it.

As Linda Deutsch watched Dennis Fung dissolve under Scheck's attack, she was struck by the irony that the blood evidence the prosecution was sure would convict Simpson was actually becoming a defense tool to win an acquittal.

In fact, Scheck *was* hanging Fung. On April 18, he zeroed in on Hank Goldberg's redirect from the previous day.

"Now, is one of the habits you have when you testify, umm, selective memory?" Scheck demanded archly. ". . . Do you have a habit of being vague when you think it is going to help the prosecution's case?"

Fung denied it.

Then Scheck attacked him for not closely examining the socks collected in Simpson's bedroom. Goldberg had explored that topic with Fung to explain why the LAPD hadn't found blood on the socks until seven weeks after they were collected.

Why *not* examine the sock closely? Scheck wanted to

know. "Now, when you looked at the ankle areas of those socks on June 13, did you not see a smear of blood?" he asked.

"I did not look that closely, so I didn't see any smear of blood," Fung responded. He had sidestepped a "no."

Wasn't Fung looking for evidence such as bloody clothing? Weren't the socks in a suspicious place?

"And you were concerned, were you not," Scheck continued in a rising voice, "that they might have been socks worn by the assailant?"

Dennis Fung admitted that was a "possibility."

Then Scheck turned to the LAPD video that the D.A. had recently been ordered to turn over to the defense.

Did Fung know the camera had panned over the bedroom? Did he know the tape had a time stamp? The witness knew. Did he know the video did not show the socks on the bedroom floor?

"I remember looking for the socks in the videotape," Fung answered gamely, "and they weren't there." He went on to argue that the socks wouldn't have been visible from that camera angle.

Because the tape hadn't been shown during Fung's direct testimony, the defense couldn't introduce it on cross. They would have to delay screening it for the jury until their own case.

Nothing prepared the team for Dennis Fung's last act.

They'd expected the criminalist to bolt from the courtroom the moment Scheck finished. But Hank Goldberg managed to get in a last gentle word.

"Mr. Fung, have you ever testified before in a case where you were on the witness stand for eight days?"

"Never."

"Are you glad to be off?" Goldberg asked.

"Very."

Then Dennis Fung climbed out of the witness chair and walked straight to the defense table.

"You guys did a great job," he said. He shook hands all around, including with Simpson. "Good luck to you."

The lawyers stared at him in awestruck silence. Kardashian wondered if this was a case of a victim bonding with his oppressor. Or was it simply a naturally courteous man's manifestation of extreme relief?

Barry Scheck left the courthouse on a wave of congratulations. "I have to get prepared for the next witnesses," he mumbled. He would be closeted in his hotel room tonight, working late.

Carl Douglas decided it had been, by far, the trial's best cross-examination. Shapiro was telling everyone how proud he was of Barry. Even Johnnie Cochran, always uncomfortable when others enjoyed the spotlight, was pleased. He looked at Scheck and the other DNA lawyers with new respect.

As for Scheck, he felt some regret. Fung handled himself with dignity under difficult circumstances, he thought. And Scheck himself had been the "difficult circumstances." But this was a murder trial. The LAPD had to be accountable, and attacking Fung was the way to attack their incompetence. Scheck decided the TV commentators and the jury were seeing different dramas. The press had been using words like "vicious" and "mean-spirited" all week, and predicted a backlash against the defense. Barry Scheck felt otherwise; he hoped the jury did. His first obligation was to defend his client. Exposing the errors in evidence handling was critical. That meant attacking Dennis Fung. There was no avoiding it. It was nothing personal. Maybe, he thought, recalling the final handshake, Dennis Fung understood that too.

Some may think Scheck has gone on too long. But this is a jury that has been sequestered to suffocation, bored, shut up and shuttled around and Scheck is the best show they've seen so far. He's focused, dramatic and getting results. His examination is directed to the jury and to one specific point: The path to a reasonable doubt concerning the scientific evidence. Scheck's strategy with Fung has been brilliant and daring.

—Gigi Gordon, Los Angeles Times

22

WHILE DENNIS FUNG WAS ON THE WITNESS STAND, A newspaper reporter gave Johnnie Cochran something useful in hopes of eventually getting something in return. The reporter told Cochran that Lucienne Coleman, a lawyer in the D.A.'s office, had information on what the prosecution knew about Mark Fuhrman just after the murders. Johnnie asked Shawn if she knew Coleman. "She's wonderful, she's honest, she's great," Chapman replied. "Will you call her?" Johnnie asked. Shawn did.

On Tuesday, April 18, Shawn Chapman picked up Coleman outside the Hall of Administration in downtown L.A. Coleman had been a colleague of Shawn's, but today she didn't want to be seen with the defense attorney. For years she had also been Marcia Clark's friend. Coleman and her husband were married at the same time Marcia was. The two couples had double-dated.

Sitting at the Cobalt Cantina on Sunset Boulevard, they talked about the case. Coleman confirmed what the defense had long suspected.

When Clark first got the case, she was confident that O.J. was guilty. Lucienne had asked Marcia what evidence she had.

"There is a glove behind here [Simpson's house]," Clark had said, "and there are a couple of blood drops at the house and whatever."

"That's not really enough for you to be this adamant," Coleman had said to Clark. Then Marcia exploded.

"You don't know what you're talking about," Marcia

told Lucienne. It was strange, Coleman said, for Marcia to be so certain, so early. It wasn't like her.

Three weeks later the *New Yorker* article appeared naming Fuhrman as the cop suspected of planting the glove. To a few cops she worked with, Coleman remarked on how far-fetched the article's accusations seemed. One of them, Andy Purdy, didn't think they were far-fetched at all.

"I worked with him and he is bad news," Purdy told Coleman. "I was married to a Jewish woman and he drew a swastika on my locker. . . . He's a racist and I wouldn't put it past him." Purdy also said that Fuhrman may have lied under oath at a preliminary hearing in another case.

Coleman told Chapman she was stunned. The next day, an officer named Maxwell told Coleman that Fuhrman was at a picnic or barbecue bragging about seeing Nicole's "boob job" and how great it was. Maxwell couldn't nail down the date; it was some years back. Naturally, Coleman said, she wondered how Fuhrman knew the victim and what kind of relationship they had.

So what did you do? Shawn asked.

I told Marcia, Coleman answered. She was with Hodgman. She listened to it all and said, "I don't want to hear any of this bullshit. It's all bullshit put out by the defense. I'm sick of other D.A.s getting involved in my case for their own self-aggrandizement. Just get out of my office."

Lucienne was shocked. First of all, Marcia was supposedly her friend. Second, she hadn't said anything inconsistent with Simpson's being guilty. But Marcia hadn't spoken to her since.

Chapman thought the whole episode was a breach of ethics and a violation of the law. Coleman knew it too. The D.A. has a legal obligation to investigate potentially exculpatory information, information that may show that someone other than the defendant is responsible for the crime. A key witness's possible relationship with the murder victim certainly fit that category. Whatever the D.A. knows must be turned over to the defense. Nothing concerning this matter ever was. Coleman told Shawn that seven months later, in February of 1995, just before Fuhrman took the stand, she was interviewed by LAPD Internal Affairs—but that body had no obligation to reveal to anyone what it was investigating or its findings.

That evening Shawn told Johnnie the entire story. She said Lucienne Coleman was prepared to testify for the defense and name the officers. Coleman felt this was clear misconduct on the part of the prosecution. It shouldn't be ignored even if O.J. was guilty.

What the defense now wanted to know was whether the D.A.'s office had deliberately refused to investigate the incident themselves so there would be nothing to give the defense. Or was Marcia just burying her head in the sand? Whatever the motive, if Coleman's story was accurate, the facts of the prosecution's misconduct were clear.

Of course, Cochran would have to wait for the defense's case to present Coleman's information. Or perhaps her charges against the D.A. warranted a special hearing. Either way, there was no doubt the defense would use Coleman's disclosure when the time was right.

When Dennis Fung finished his testimony, Judge Ito started interviewing the jurors individually in chambers about the allegations of ex-juror Jeanette Harris. Now other jurors were naming the same three sheriff's deputies whom Harris had accused of exacerbating racial tensions. Ito was concerned and told both sides he would interview the deputies as well.

The judge had barely begun questioning Juror 453, a black flight attendant, when she asked to be released immediately.

"I can't take it anymore," she told him as defense and prosecution attorneys listened. Then she started to cry. ". . . The way I've been treated by some of the deputies these last three months . . . I really wish you would change them. That would make me feel more comfortable maybe." Ito asked her to step outside while he spoke to the attorneys alone.

Darden remarked that this was "an easier problem" to resolve. Perhaps he meant it was easier to reassign deputies than create harmony among the jurors. Ito voiced some concern about fairness to the deputies.

"You've always said the most important thing is the comfort of these jurors," Cochran told Ito. "[Now] you want to salvage these deputies' feelings at the cost of losing another juror?"

Johnnie was fighting hard to keep Juror 453. He pointed out that the last four black jurors interviewed also felt they were being treated differently from the nonblacks. Darden agreed with Cochran. Ito told the sheriff's department that he wanted the three deputies transferred within the hour.

The judge sat quietly as Juror 453 returned. "I have asked the sheriff's department to change three deputies," he said. "They are going to change them immediately." The young black juror was visibly relieved. "Oh, thank you very much," she told Ito. He asked her to start from square one, "take a deep breath, step off the van and say, Hey, nice hotel . . . like getting off the flight attendants' bus at a new hotel, new airport. You know how that is."

She said she knew and would continue as a jury member.

On Friday, April 21, the jurors went on strike. They refused to come to court and waited for Judge Ito to come to their hotel for a meeting. Ito finally agreed to meet with them as a group, but only in the courtroom.

When they left their hotel, thirteen of the eighteen were wearing black. By the time they arrived at the courthouse the media were buzzing about the "jury revolt."

Ito canceled the court session to meet with the assembled jury. A number of the jurors said it was unfair that the deputies had been removed and asked Ito to reconsider. Ito heard them out, but there was no turning back.

The "jury revolt" sent different signals to various members of the defense. Carl Douglas was dumbfounded. Three black jurors were crying over the loss of the deputies. He wondered if the defense team was reading the black jurors all wrong. In a phenomenon known as the Stockholm syndrome, a hostage may eventually bond with his captors. If these jurors had become virtual hostages of the legal system and were defending the deputies, were they also bonding with the police? It wasn't much of a stretch from bonding with law enforcement officers to identifying with the prosecution. Could that really be happening to their "dream jury"?

Douglas was especially concerned that some black jurors obviously resented the fact that other black jurors defended the deputies. Were the black jurors splitting into factions? That scared Shawn Chapman.

Chapman heard another reason why thirteen jurors had shown up in court in black that day. She was told the pro-deputy jurors suggested they all wear their "California Pizza Kitchen" T-shirts. The jury had been guests of the restaurant for dinner, and they'd all been given free T-shirts. If Ito was being unfair to the deputies, some jurors felt, the trial could wait while they lodged their protest and gave their favorite restaurant some free publicity by wearing their T-shirts to court. Other jurors refused and wore black instead. So the black clothing was an "anti-revolt" gesture.

Any way you looked at it, Johnnie said, this was worrisome. The message was clear: Get these eighteen people sufficiently upset and they'll stop the trial cold. But Shapiro, Scheck, and Bailey figured they were looking at a hung jury, and for now this was good news. Any major conflict in the jury, no matter what, was good for the defense.

TFC, everyone said. But maybe this deserved its own category: mega-TFC.

23

Now that Barry Scheck was through with Fung, Peter Neufeld, who had returned from New York, went to work on Andrea Mazzola. The prosecution had no choice but to present her. She had collected most of the blood swatches and was crucial to establishing the chain of custody of the evidence. The defense planned to question her competence—by bringing up her lack of experience and her status as a trainee—and to establish that Fung's sloppiness wasn't unique. The plan was to show the jury that work on all the evidence had been slipshod. That meant, the defense would later argue, that the DNA test results were far less reliable.

Andrea Mazzola would be Peter Neufeld's first witness before the jury. Carl's private "focus group"—his sister and her friends—said Scheck had done fine. Everyone liked him. Neufeld, like Scheck, would be relentless with witnesses. Ito had said during voir dire that he didn't like Neufeld and hoped he wouldn't return from New York. Barry made sure he did. It was time for Ito to appreciate New Yorkers.

On the previous Thursday the prosecution had completed Mazzola's testimony in just three hours. No doubt the D.A.s anticipated another brutal cross. But Neufeld had barely started when the jury "revolt" shut down the court. Now, on Tuesday, he resumed.

Since the beginning of the trial and through Fung's endless testimony, Ito had been patient to a fault. It was clear he had a highly volatile jury to consider. He became markedly tougher on the attorneys. "I don't want to hear about that . . . Move on . . . Ask your next question" came from the bench. No more sidebars. He wanted Cochran to limit complaints to sixty seconds. Judge Ito took charge aggressively for the first time.

Not that things went appreciably smoother. Carl Douglas was upset because Neufeld read his questions. "Horrendous, hate it," he grumbled, but there was nothing he could do. Ito also complained: Neufeld spoke too fast for the court reporters. "Both your pace and your Brooklyn accent—they have difficulty." Neufeld found himself apologizing for mispronouncing Mazzola's name as "Massoler," but then noted that he didn't like Clark's giggling during testimony. "Mr. Neufeld is on some other planet," Clark snapped. Tension was high.

On Wednesday, Neufeld forced Mazzola to admit that in many instances the prosecution's display boards were "incorrect" as to who collected which samples at Bundy. The D.A.s had credited Fung and Mazzola with the collection and implied that Fung had supervised all the trainee's work. Now Mazzola set the record straight: She had done her work alone, without any supervision. Under Neufeld's questioning, she explained that she and Fung had met after the defense's Griffin hearing on August 23 to review all the blood evidence and to clarify who had actually collected what.

"And after that discussion you made certain entries in your field notes next to each one of the items, correct?"

"Yes."

Neufeld noted that the D.A.'s display boards reflected none of these corrections from the criminalists.

Then he tackled Mazzola about carrying the garbage bag to the criminalists' van. Mazzola acknowledged that she didn't know until the next day that the bag contained a blood vial; indeed, she never had detailed knowledge of the contents. She simply placed the garbage bag in the front seat of the evidence truck. Without supervision.

Mazzola admitted that she had never seen the blood vial at Simpson's home on April 13. Neufeld attacked her for napping briefly on Simpson's couch during a break, while Vannatter supposedly handed Simpson's blood vial to Fung.

"Well, Miss Mazzola, at any time did you ever carry or handle O.J. Simpson's blood vial?" Neufeld asked.

"Not to my knowledge."

"And that is still your position as you sit here today?"

"It was . . . not to my knowledge at the time. I was not told that I was carrying the blood vial," she responded.

Neufeld then used Mazzola to lay the foundation for the planned defense attack on the bindles that contained the "wet transfers." The defense had discovered that Mazzola's initials were missing from the bindles, although she had previously testified that she marked them. On cross, she admitted that her initials were missing.

"Would you agree that without proper documentation, it's easy for someone to tamper with them?" Neufeld asked.

"Yes," Mazzola said.

"So did the absence of your initials raise in your mind [the possibility] that the original evidence may have been tampered with?" Neufeld's question needed no answer.

Scheck and Neufeld understood you can't insult the jury's common sense. You can't expect the jury to believe that all these oddities in handling Simpson's reference blood were pure chance.

At the end of the day, Neufeld and Scheck went home happy.

While the prosecution suffered through Mazzola's cross, Bob Kardashian had his own troubles. He often played gin in the holding cell with Simpson or talked with O.J. while he played solitaire. During the morning break they went back to their card game. Bob took his coat off. Time passed quickly. Before they knew it, Deputy Guy Magnera appeared; "Time to go," he said.

O.J. got up as Bob put on his jacket. By the time Kardashian turned to leave, Simpson and Magnera were gone and the door was locked.

At first he thought it was a joke, payback for their own practical jokes on the deputies. He knocked on the door; no answer. He pounded on the wall, but lightly. Court was now in session, after all. Nobody answered.

Kardashian decided to play solitaire and wait for someone to show up. As the minutes crawled by, he understood what O.J. must feel.

An hour passed. He knocked on the door again. Still no response. Then a sheriff opened a door from an adjoining courtroom. Deliverance! Bob walked through the other courtroom and into Ito's, and went straight to Magnera.

"You locked me in. What was that for?"

Magnera was startled. He hadn't seen Kardashian. It was pure accident. He hadn't heard the knocking on the door. He was honestly sorry.

At lunchtime Bob smuggled in a sandwich for O.J.—his daily assignment. Pastrami today. By now he was a pro at this. He was always afraid O.J. would play a joke on him, tell the deputies or something. Might be worth forfeiting the contraband to see the look on Bob's face. Today the deputy stopped him. "Smells like Chinese food," Magnera said with an all-knowing smile.

"Yeah, we just ate Chinese food," Kardashian said as he walked past. They were onto him. Time for the torch to be passed.

Next day Douglas smuggled the sandwich—and got caught. This time, Carl fell on his fork for the client.

During the week Fung and Mazzola were on the stand, the defense filed a motion accusing the prosecutors of improperly using police to investigate pro-defense jurors and force enough "selective" disqualifications to cause an eventual mistrial. If the total number of jurors fell below twelve, either side could insist on a mistrial unless both agreed to proceed with fewer jurors. With the integrity of the blood evidence under attack, the prosecution stood to gain from a mistrial. A mistrial was not what the defense wanted. The defense also requested that social workers, rather than officers of any law enforcement agency, replace the Sheriff's Department as jury custodians.

Judge Ito denied the motion and said he would continue to

interview the jurors. But he also asked the defense to investigate the possibility of social workers replacing the deputies. Somewhat later, Douglas had to report to the judge that no organization was willing to take on the job.

24

By now, Scheck and Neufeld knew that the prosecutors considered Dr. Henry Lee their most formidable opponent. The latest discovery revealed that the D.A. had tapes showing Lee at a crime scene in street clothes with no white lab coat. Improper procedure, they would charge. Barry and Peter had attacked Fung and Mazzola's competence at the crime scene; now Lee would receive similar scrutiny. The prosecution was also saying Lee removed blood evidence from the back gate when he visited Bundy in June 1994. That had never happened, and Lee signed a sworn statement to that effect. Foreseeing the likely cross-examination, Scheck began to worry. Lee was a formidable witness for the defense. Baden was another.

Shapiro and Cochran both sense they are ahead. They're sure of a hung jury; it's the real chance of acquittal that makes them edgy. Disagreements between them flare again.

It was already obvious from Shapiro's cross-examination style that he was cautious by nature, avoiding anything even slightly risky. Now he's even more cautios. Although the defense case is three months away, he's already saying he doesn't want any witnesses whose credibility isn't 110 percent. Play it safe, he urges.

Cochran mentions Rosa Lopez. Shapiro responds with a flat no.

Then Shapiro says he wants to exclude Robert Heidstra, their best time-line witness. He is afraid the D.A. will call the manager of Heidstra's apartment, who'll say Heidstra never walks his dogs at a set time so his time estimates could be off by thirty minutes. Why take a chance?

Johnnie's tolerance for risk is much higher. The black jurors are used to people like these, he tells Bob again. Heidstra lives in a converted garage? So what? That doesn't make him unreliable. To this jury, Heidstra and Lopez are real people, people they can relate to. Shapiro can't see it. Johnnie asks himself whether Bob Shapiro has ever had a client or a witness remotely like these two people.

On Monday, May 1, Ito called all the attorneys into his chambers before court for a ninety-minute meeting. More problems with Juror 453, the young flight attendant. Once again she had insisted to the judge, "I can't take it anymore." She explained that after the deputies were removed at her request, things only got worse. The other jurors blamed her for the transfers. She was ostracized.

Now Ito let her go. Neither side fought to keep her: During deliberations, someone so fragile might cave in immediately. Within an hour the world knew her name—Tracy Hampton.

Shawn was disappointed with Hampton. "That's not the way a black woman should comport herself," she told Johnnie and Carl. "Who would want her?" Johnnie also believed black women were strong; this one wasn't.

When it came time to pick the next juror, Ito's clerk, Deirdre Robertson, reached into the large manila envelope and withdrew the paper for Juror 1427, a twenty-eight-year-old Latino real estate appraiser for Los Angeles County. They were now down to five alternates and the prosecution had not even presented two thirds of its case. Johnnie had lost a black juror. Now there were seven blacks, three whites, and two Hispanics.

* * *

That day, Scheck, Neufeld, Blasier, and Bill Thompson filed a motion demanding the prosecution call Thano Peratis, the nurse who drew Simpson's reference blood. The D.A. was legally required to demonstrate the "chain of custody" of all the blood evidence before presenting the results of DNA testing done on that evidence.

The defense had to show that Peratis had drawn 8 milliliters of blood from Simpson on the day he returned from Chicago. It was necessary to establish the original amount if the defense was to prove that blood later was missing. If Peratis now said he had drawn a smaller amount, the defense would impeach him with his own testimony from the preliminary hearing and before the grand jury.

Later that day, LAPD serologist Greg Matheson was testifying about O.J.'s reference blood. Under Bob Blasier's cross, he acknowledged the LAPD didn't keep accurate records of the amounts of blood drawn from living persons for testing. There was no need to, they reasoned: More blood could be taken if the technicians exhausted the first sample. This was further evidence of chronically sloppy work in the LAPD lab.

Blasier's cross-examination of Matheson was highly technical. Such minute dissection of lab procedure might be edge-of-the-seat stuff for a scientist, but the defense found it sleep-inducing.

Some days Simpson could hardly handle the boredom and considered waiting in the holding cell till the end of the day. "It wouldn't look good," Carl told him. Why should the jury listen if the *defendant* can't be bothered?

The numbers at the defense table dwindled. Bailey, Kardashian, and Chapman stayed away from the courtroom occasionally, but Shapiro and Cochran were there every day.

25

KARDASHIAN, COCHRAN, BAILEY, AND SHAPIRO VISITED O.J. in jail when court adjourned during Greg Matheson's testimony.

Dr. Robin Cotton of Cellmark would testify next for the prosecution. She was about to deliver the official DNA test results. What better way to take your mind off the blood evidence than to talk to Simpson again about taking the stand? O.J. wanted to do it. Johnnie and Shapiro were still on opposite sides of the issue.

Minutes into the conversation, Johnnie suddenly turned to O.J. "Mr. Simpson, did you commit this horrible crime?" Looked at him hard. Steel in Cochran's voice.

"I would never hurt Nicole," Simpson blurted. Within seconds, his eyes were glistening with tears. "She's the mother of my children. I could never do anything as horrible as they said I did. I'm just not capable of doing something like that. I would *never* do it."

The attorneys were silent as O.J. slowly calmed himself. The discussion continued: How could he be prepared? Was his testimony needed? Would the prosecution end its case with more incidents of domestic abuse? The answer to that question would determine whether Simpson testified. He was the defense's best witness on this subject.

O.J. agreed with the lawyers that they were ahead, the jury hung for sure. But Johnnie was still concerned with O.J.'s post-trial life. If he walks out a free man, Cochran insisted, he also needs to walk out an innocent man, a decent man. He can't be stigmatized as a wife-beater forever.

Privately, Johnnie wasn't optimistic about clearing Simpson's name. But he had to try.

As the attorneys left the jail, Cochran turned to Shapiro. "See how good he is?" he said enthusiastically. "See how convincing he is?"

"There's no way I'd let him take the stand," Shapiro replied. No more was said.

In court the next day, May 10, Dr. Robin Cotton pointed to films of DNA patterns. "That pattern is consistent," she said, "and looks to be the same as the pattern from Mr. Simpson. . . ."

After two days, the director of Cellmark Diagnostics in Germantown, Maryland, had testified that Simpson's blood seemed to be in all the wrong places. Results showing Nicole Brown's and Ron Goldman's blood were equally incriminating. The defense team listened and awaited its turn.

Prosecutor George "Woody" Clarke led Cotton through a primer in DNA. The team knew that only three jurors were college graduates. Clarke hoped to convince them the science was not only valid, but irrefutable. Of course, the jurors had to be awake to be convinced of anything. Listening to Dr. Cotton describe the four bases—adenine, guanine, thymine, and cytosine—that made up DNA, Carl Douglas was restless.

The day before, Clarke had tried to preempt the defense strategy. In his cross of Dennis Fung, Barry Scheck had raised a dark vision of mishandled and ruined blood evidence. Now the jurors had to be convinced otherwise. Clarke asked Dr. Cotton: Could degraded blood mimic someone else's DNA? Could sunlight, humidity, or rain change DNA from one type to another? Impossible, she said. "You may degrade the DNA so much that you can't type it," she explained. "But you won't just change types from one to another. Doesn't happen."

Then Cotton identified other DNA matches between Simpson's blood and the drops at Bundy and Rockingham. Every drop had DNA patterns "similar" to Simpson's blood.

How often does Simpson's DNA pattern show up in the

population? Cotton was asked. She cited a Bundy blood drop, item 52, which contained enough DNA to be tested by the slower, but more definitive than PCR, RFLP process. Simpson's DNA characteristics would occur only once among every 170 million whites or African-Americans, Cotton explained. If you added "western Hispanics" to the group, she said, the pattern would occur only once in 1.2 billion people.

Carl Douglas watched in dismay as jurors busily took notes. There were involuntary reactions all through the panel. These numbers were astronomical!

The statistics on the remaining drops were less startling because those drops contained only enough DNA for the less precise PCR tests. One in 5,200 blacks, or 1 in 56,000 whites, would have the same characteristics. This was less damaging, Douglas knew, but hardly good news.

When Clarke got to the blood on the socks in Simpson's bedroom, the figures seemed unreal. The same DNA would be found in 1 in 6.8 billion western Hispanics, Cotton said. For whites the figure was 1 in 9.7 billion. African-Americans? "That number is one in five hundred thirty billion." Carl Douglas had to shake his head. Did that many people even exist?

By May 15 the defense was so busy with new discovery that it was almost impossible to plan strategy for anything except the science. Scheck, Neufeld, Blasier, and Thompson had the DNA material in hand and were planning their own tactics. Cochran and Douglas knew that at least this area was in good order.

Every day brought a new mini-crisis. One day bloody clothing was found at the hotel Simpson had stayed in in Chicago and Chapman immediately asked O.J. about it. He told her, "Nothing to worry about." Somebody said O.J. was driving on Sunset the night of the murders. Simpson said, "No way." Then the D.A. tested O.J.'s blood for methamphetamine. It came up negative. But Shawn still worried about O.J.'s coke use back in the Buffalo Bills days.

Now she had to concentrate only on admissible evidence.

All that mattered was the jury. If something wouldn't affect the jurors, forget it.

As she listened to the evidence in court, Chapman did her best to evaluate it as if she had no idea of the upcoming defense. The D.A.'s case against Simpson centered on blood. All that blood. Blood everywhere. Here's a man who never had blood in his car until the day after his ex-wife was murdered. It was hard to ignore that thought. Goldman's blood in the Bronco was almost irrelevant. The simple fact of blood in Simpson's car the day after the murder made Chapman question O.J.'s innocence.

Shawn was depressed. Sometimes she couldn't shake the thought that he was guilty.

Then she would see O.J.—and as soon as they started talking, her doubts vanished. All of them. Completely. His intensity, the depth and consistency of his sincerity, dissolved Shawn's doubts. "What was I thinking? O.J., I'm so sorry." She had to apologize, if only in her own mind.

26

JOHNNIE HAD HAD MORE THAN HIS FILL OF SHAPIRO by now. When they drove to court together, Bob sat in back dictating into a small recorder: notes for his book on the case.

You're talking too much, Shapiro told Johnnie. Stay away from the press. You could make five million dollars. Johnnie scoffed at the idea that a book would bring five million. But Shapiro continued: You're undercutting your commercial possibilities. Cochran let him go on. Remain Mr. Nice Guy.

All along Johnnie assumed he'd eventually write a book, but he wasn't about to count the dollars yet. And he had no idea how much speaking engagements might bring. But the operative word was "eventually." Winning his case was the immediate task.

Whenever they arrived at court, Shapiro went into press mode, buttering up the media. Johnnie's frustration was intensifying: He felt Bob was undermining the team. He'd worn that support-the-police blue ribbon, while telling the press that racism wasn't involved in the case. Johnnie thought the man was a hypocrite. He'd do anything for a headline.

Peter Neufeld started his cross-examination of Dr. Robin Cotton on Thursday, May 11, with a question about a tiny database of black-donated blood from a Red Cross office in Detroit, Michigan, that Cellmark used for population statistics. The lab had made its billion-to-one RFLP estimates by comparing the DNA patterns from Nicole's and Simpson's reference blood and the DNA from the blood on the sock with the DNA patterns of African-American blood from only 240 donors.

Carl Douglas struggled to follow this. He was sure of one thing. When the jury heard that these astonishing statistics came from fewer than 300 black people in Detroit, it would be suspicious.

"Would you agree, Dr. Cotton," Neufeld said, "that there has been substantial controversy in the scientific community about that assumption that you've just described?"

The question was too argumentative, Ito ruled. Never mind. Douglas knew the jurors got the idea.

Barry Scheck felt that the defense's contamination theory had not yet been demonstrated convincingly enough. In defense meetings he insisted it was not enough to theorize for the jury; you had to show them exactly how the events in your theory could have occurred, show them that your scenario was not just possible but *probable*.

Scheck, Thompson, and Neufeld approached the problem methodically. They worked long hours exploring different theories. After days of friendly debate they decided the contamination must have occurred inside the LAPD crime lab. Then they focused tightly on LAPD criminalist Collin Yamauchi, who had handled the blood samples on June 14 before the first testing began.

Some months earlier, the defense had hired Dr. John Gerdes to evaluate LAPD crime lab procedures in the year before this case. He concluded the lab was a "cesspool of contamination," and he would testify to that. Gerdes had also discovered that the vials containing the reference samples from Nicole and Goldman were contaminated with Simpson's DNA. That fact and its implications were crucial.

The swatches collected from the Bundy walkway placed O.J. at the crime scene more convincingly than any eyewitness. The defense had to show that somewhere, somehow, by accident, by design, or both, Simpson's reference blood was transferred to the Bundy swatches.

During the first two weeks in May, Barry went through all of Yamauchi's notes in the discovery material with a fine-toothed comb. Months earlier, Bill Pavelic had shown the team a photograph in which the outside of Simpson's reference vial was stained, even caked, with blood. Beyond a doubt, that vial had been carelessly handled. That was Scheck's starting point.

Scheck wanted to determine the sequence of events in the lab on June 14. The LAPD would not allow the defense to interview Yamauchi, but after days of shuffling and reshuffling, Barry assigned what seemed to be the correct order to Yamauchi's notes, some of which bore no dates.

Yamauchi had worked with O.J.'s reference sample immediately before he handled the Rockingham glove. If Yamauchi got blood on himself, or if he got some on the table when he opened O.J.'s vial—a real possibility, considering the bloodstains *on* the vial—he could have transferred O.J.'s blood to the glove.

Then Scheck worked out from the lab notes the order in

which Yamauchi handled the Bundy blood swatches. Scheck compared that order to the amount of Simpson's DNA found on each sample.

Paydirt. For the first time Scheck and his team could see that the Bundy swatch with the largest quantity of O.J.'s DNA, swatch number 51, was the first one that Yamauchi touched after he handled the Rockingham glove. The swatch containing the second-highest quantity was the second one he touched. And so forth.

Common sense indicated that Yamauchi *had* to have gotten some of Simpson's blood on his own glove, or on the table, or both. It was like stepping into a mud puddle, then continuing onto dry ground. Your first footprint leaves a lot of mud; the next one leaves a bit less; the third leaves still less. Scheck could see Yamauchi's "footprint" on the glove and Bundy blood swatches.

The sequence was clear: Yamauchi gets O.J.'s reference blood on his gloved hands. Maybe on his worktable. Then he transfers O.J.'s blood to the Rockingham glove. Next he handles the Bundy swatches and contaminates them with Simpson's blood.

Scheck knew this was a bombshell. Top Secret—Eyes Only.

But there was also blood from *someone* on the swatches before Yamauchi ever touched them. What about the original DNA in the blood on the Bundy swatches? The jury already had that answer, but it hadn't been explained to them yet. When Fung left those swatches in the hot van all day, Scheck would argue, the original DNA, possibly the killer's, had degraded so much that it no longer showed up in testing.

The tide was now shifting in favor of the defense. Barry's theory that O.J.'s DNA was unwittingly transferred to the swatches by Yamauchi stood up to scrutiny. It was scientifically valid. It also reinforced the defense's assertion that the first PCR test results that incriminated Simpson were unreliable, like everything else that came from the LAPD's "Black Hole."

Johnnie and Carl didn't have to stretch their imaginations to believe that those first tests might have given some cops the impetus to plant, fabricate, or doctor other evidence. This guy's guilty. Don't let him get away with it. Make it stick.

The only question left was: What exactly happened to O.J.'s reference blood on June 14, the day Yamauchi worked on the glove and the Bundy swatches? Scheck would have to get his answer in his cross-examination of Collin Yamauchi.

Back on February 15, the D.A. had told the court that the FBI would be testing the Bundy back-gate swatches and O.J.'s sock for the preservative EDTA, which could be found only in Simpson's reference blood. The defense knew the D.A. wasn't rushing the FBI; the prosecution wasn't eager for bad news.

Now in mid-May, Judge Ito asked the prosecution for an update on the FBI's tests. Apparently he had been doing his homework, because he also asked if these test results would include printouts from gas chromatography, a method of analyzing the chemicals present in various substances. Gas chromatography was not widely used to determine whether EDTA was present. Ito was asking, in effect, if after this long wait, the results would finally settle the issue.

In reply, Rock Harmon rambled, answering more than Ito had asked. "It sure—it did—No. There's no question that there's a flicker of hope that there's something in there that they [the defense] could get somebody to say something that they'd like. But it is not going to be Special Agent Roger Martz [of the FBI], the only witness we intend to call [about these tests]."

The defense read between the lines: So there was EDTA in the swatches from the Bundy gate and the socks. Scheck and Neufeld would go after Martz on cross-examination. And if the prosecution did not put him on the stand, the defense would call him as a hostile witness.

Harmon's statement was the first real hint that Simpson's reference blood, containing EDTA, may have been used to spike or accidentally transfer O.J.'s blood to existing blood swatches—or to create new evidence. Had the prosecution known this? Or had the LAPD done its best to conceal it from the D.A.? Did one or more rogue cops tamper with evidence? Who had access to the reference blood?

Barry Scheck hoped that he could eventually answer these questions for the jury. Once again, it was important to demonstrate not only that evidence tampering *could have* occurred, but that it *probably did*.

27

ON FRIDAY, MAY 19, BARRY SCHECK WAS ON THE attack again, but no one knew it. His target was the well-liked, much-respected DNA scientist Gary Sims, a senior criminalist from the State of California's crime lab. The epitome of the conscientious scientist, Sims gave straight answers. He was sincere. Scheck knew that he would shade nothing.

Barry began aggressively. "Mr. Sims, are you part of any conspiracy to tamper with evidence in this case? Are you?"

"No. No, I'm not." Sims almost smiled.

Gary Sims belonged to the world of Scheck, Bill Thompson, Bob Blasier, Henry Lee, Ed Blake, Rock Harmon, and Woody Clarke. He knew that Scheck understood the science and carried a big stick.

"To your knowledge," Scheck went on, "Dr. Cotton from Cellmark is not part of any conspiracy to tamper with evidence in this case?"

Now Sims really smiled. "No, I don't believe she is."

Scheck went on to establish for the jury Sims's thorough and careful DNA lab procedures. Later, he would use this standard to contrast to the LAPD lab's poor technology and slipshod practices.

Sims had already done well for the prosecution. On his first day, May 16, he told prosecutor Rock Harmon that three stains lifted from the Bronco's center console matched mixtures of Nicole Brown's, Ron Goldman's, and O.J. Simpson's blood. For the first time, the jury heard that Ron Goldman's blood was found inside the Bronco, something almost impossible to explain innocently.

Another stain on the console, Sims stated, matched a mixture of Goldman's and Simpson's blood. On the driver's-side carpet, Sims identified Nicole's blood. He said the Rockingham glove's lining showed blood with a strong possibility of being Goldman's. After Sims looked at genetic markers from Nicole Brown's DNA and the blood on the socks, Harmon asked, "What opinion did you reach?" Sims answered that there was a match.

But today Scheck posed the really important question:

"Do you know from your own personal knowledge how and when that blood got on the sock?"

"No," Sims replied.

Scheck's job today was to lay part of the foundation for the defense's "garbage-in, garbage-out" theories on the blood testing. If the blood evidence was contaminated "garbage" when it was sent from the LAPD lab to DOJ, all of Sims's clean, careful tests were irrelevant.

For hours Scheck asked Sims pointed questions about safeguards against contamination. Soon Collin Yamauchi, a young LAPD technician with limited DNA experience, would testify. Scheck wanted Yamauchi's presentation to suffer by comparison.

Scheck also raised the specter of cross-contamination between the Bundy and Rockingham blood samples. He was setting up Henry Lee's future testimony about the "wet transfers" on the paper bindles.

For Kardashian the discussion was impossibly technical. He'd made it through law school and passed the bar, yet he simply couldn't understand this. Could the jury follow it?

During the break Scheck headed straight for Carl Douglas. "Did you get it?" he asked.

"Barry, I don't know what the fuck you've been saying for the last forty minutes," Douglas replied. "It's like you and Sims are having a private conversation." Douglas was Barry's litmus test. If he got it, the jury got it. If he didn't, there was no hope the jury would.

On Monday, May 22, Scheck was so enmeshed in technical abstractions that he lost even Gary Sims.

"Let us assume that this is cross-contamination with Sample 52 from a reference sample or from another swatch containing Mr. Simpson's blood that had a high DNA content," he began.

"Okay," Sims said.

"And let us further assume that the starting material on swatch number 52 had DNA that was degraded."

"Okay," Sims repeated.

"Would not a result, assuming that 1.3 dot is a real dot, not an artifact . . ." Scheck paused. "Are you with me?"

Sims smiled, said yes.

"Would not the reading on *this* strip be consistent with that set of assumptions?"

Rock Harmon jumped up to object. The question was an "improper hypothetical."

"Do you understand the factors involved in this question?" Judge Ito asked Sims.

"I think I understand the first half of it"—Sims grinned—"and then I kind of lost it on the second half."

Carl Douglas knew he'd lost the first, second, third, and fourth halves.

Eight days had passed. Sims was back on the stand after attending a funeral. Rock Harmon wanted the jury to view the actual bedroom socks under a microscope so they could follow Sims's testimony.

As courtroom theater, this made sense. "There's a large number of small stains on there," Sims had testified two weeks earlier, when Harmon questioned him, "and it's only when you get under the stereomicroscope that you can really appreciate how much there is.''

Barry Scheck objected, complaining that jurors would now see evidence that Sims hadn't mentioned on direct. The test cuttings from the fabric were indicated only by a rectangular hole in the socks; on cross-examination, Sims had said nothing about the number and size of the stains. ''I don't see how that's within the scope of the redirect examination at this point,'' Barry insisted. Redirect was supposed to confine itself to issues that had come up in the cross-examination.

Bill Thompson smiled as Ito overruled Scheck's objection. He could easily imagine Barry discovering how to use this turn of events to the defense's advantage.

Thompson knew Scheck hadn't been planning to show the sock to the jury, but now an important opportunity presented itself. For months, the LAPD lab had insisted that on three separate occasions it failed, purely by accident, to see the bloodstains on the socks. Dennis Fung saw no blood when he collected them on June 13. LAPD lab supervisor Michele Kestler saw nothing on June 22 when Michael Baden and Barbara Wolf had been standing by as observers. Baden and Wolf saw no blood. Finally, on June 29, Ito requested an inventory of blood samples so he could rule on whether to give the defense team ''splits'' for their own tests. That day's LAPD notes said of the socks: ''blood search, none obvious.''

Three times, the prosecution said, criminalists and lab technicians missed the blood Gary Sims was now describing because the socks were dark and the lighting was poor. Nobody noticed the DNA-loaded sock stains until August 4: Lab notes for that day mentioned the stains. The delayed discovery was an oversight, the LAPD insisted.

Scheck and the other defense scientists didn't believe it. Someone had spiked the socks with reference blood between June 29 and August 4. Nothing else made sense. How could the LAPD science experts have missed the blood three times? Scheck first became suspicious when he learned the blood from the sock had contained a large amount of DNA, enough DNA for an RFLP test, just like the DNA-loaded blood swatch from the Bundy back gate—the blood that had also eluded police until July 3, when Dennis Fung returned to collect it.

When the prosecution produced the socks, Scheck picked up the one with the bloodstain and brought it straight to the jury. Laid it out right there for them to see. Nobody needed a microscope.

The jury looked very carefully. The bloodstains were clearly visible even in the courtroom's imperfect light. Scheck knew the jurors' common sense would tell them the LAPD was lying.

28

WHILE SIMS WAS ON THE STAND, KARDASHIAN MET Howard Weitzman for lunch at The Grill. It was the first time the two had really talked since O.J.'s arrest.

They had been friends for most of their adult lives. Since O.J.'s arrest, they had been drifting apart. All the awkwardness back when Shapiro was hired seemed to be the reason. Now Bob wanted to clear the air.

I think O.J. is guilty, Howard said right off. Most people think he's guilty. Bob wasn't surprised. He knew that at a national conference of criminal defense lawyers two weeks earlier, Howard had joked about how smart a move he'd made by leaving the case. Weitzman repeated the remark now. "You're right," Bob said. There were certainly easier clients to defend.

But Kardashian spoke up in O.J.'s defense. "I don't feel

he is guilty. You're acting like everybody else, believing the press. I wasn't at the crime scene either, so I don't know what happened.''

''What about all the DNA?'' Howard asked.

''You know, John DeLorean was caught with cocaine in his briefcase, on film, and you got him off,'' Bob pointed out. ''You of all people shouldn't believe the press.''

''Remember the early morning on Tuesday in O.J.'s closet,'' Howard said firmly. ''Remember what Juice said to me.''

Bob remembered a conversation on Monday evening, the day after the murders, not on Tuesday morning. Either way, he had been there during the whole conversation in O.J.'s closet. What on earth was Howard talking about? He asked but got no response: Weitzman changed the subject.

Bob wouldn't let it pass. ''I don't remember O.J. saying anything about his doing it or being guilty,'' he said. ''O.J. was talking about the missing money and the missing glove, that's all.'' Weitzman didn't answer.

''What are you talking about?'' Bob repeated. Again, Howard refused to answer.

The conversation went in circles. Nothing was settled. But they remained friendly. As far as Kardashian was concerned, when you've known someone for thirty, thirty-five years, you discuss all sorts of things without anger. Their friendship would survive Simpson.

MEMORANDUM

TO: Simpson Defense Team Members
FROM: Johnnie L. Cochran, Jr.
DATE: May 23, 1995

As we begin serious preparation for the Defense's presentation of evidence, we must develop and finalize a consistent theme to be presented to the Jury for the Defense. . . . I would ask that each attorney provide me, in writing, any and all items of evidence which you feel should be reviewed and addressed.

، . . . Let me have your memo by Tuesday, May 30, 1995, at 5:00 P.M. before our meeting with experts on Saturday, June 3, 1995.

Although Cochran wanted a unified strategy, the defense still had to track any number of scattered details. It took time, but ignoring seemingly small leads could be dangerous.

The same day Cochran sent his memo, tips that the killings were actually drug-related were still arriving. Dershowitz's office had heard that Goldman had been dealing drugs and selling to Faye Resnick and Nicole. Something for McKenna to check.

Shawn Chapman noticed in the discovery that Jean Leighton, the American Airlines employee who directed O.J. to a baggage carousel for his golf bag the day after his return to L.A., was prepared to say that she found it strange that O.J. personally retrieved the bag. Celebrities usually send someone or have delayed luggage delivered. Chapman thought the prosecution might call Leighton.

The next day the defense was warned that another juror might be on the way out. Carl had written a memo on anonymous calls their office was receiving about various jurors. One caller said that a female juror's boyfriend expressed his firm belief in O.J.'s guilt whenever he visited her. The same juror allegedly suffered domestic abuse in previous relationships, abuse never disclosed on the jury form. On April 7, a caller said a juror's sister was giving coworkers information about the case, which she got while visiting the juror. A third call, on April 20, said yet another juror had formed an opinion about O.J.'s guilt before sequestration. Carl took all the information to Judge Ito. Why not get rid of the jurors who'd already decided O.J. was guilty?

29

ON WEDNESDAY, MAY 24, JUDGE ITO RECEIVED AN anonymous letter dated May 12. The following day, he read it to prosecutors and defense lawyers in his chambers.

> Dear Judge Ito:
>
> I have been debating over and over what to do with this information. . . . I work for a literary agent. I'm only a receptionist . . . but I know for a fact that my boss has entered an agreement with a juror and her husband.

The anonymous writer couldn't name the juror: "I can only identify the juror as female, once an alternate, husband became ill, about 40 years old, a white woman. . . ."

The likely suspect was Francine Florio-Bunten, Juror 353. The defense team had nicknamed her Touchy-Feely after she described herself that way when Ito asked the panel about conjugal visits.

"The working title for the book proposal is *Standing Alone, a Verdict for Nicole*," the letter continued. "It is obvious to me that the woman and her husband came to the conclusion of Mr. Simpson's guilt and sold the book with that agreement."

The defense hated Florio-Bunten. Not only had she replaced one of their favorites, Michael Knox, but she seemed to be at odds with jurors they liked. Ex-juror Jeanette Harris claimed that a white female juror kicked her one day. The same juror, entering the box, also purposely

579

stepped on the foot of one of Harris's allies, African-American juror Willie Cravin, Harris said. On another occasion, the same woman hit Cravin on the head. Harris didn't name anyone, but the target of her allegations was probably Florio-Bunten.

If Florio-Bunten went home, eight jurors would have been dismissed in four months. Only four alternates would be left.

On the other hand, the defense had assumed Touchy-Feely would vote against Simpson. One anonymous call, which Douglas had noted, said that before sequestration she allegedly told friends that the blood evidence convinced her. Her voir dire profile wasn't promising. This could be a very good day, Carl Douglas thought.

Parts of the letter rang true. Ito had already talked to Florio-Bunten about her husband's medical problems. The writer mentioned the Inter-Continental Hotel, where the jury was staying. This was hardly public knowledge. Yet everyone felt the letter was odd. Maybe it was all too perfect. This mysterious receptionist said that Florio-Bunten believed in Simpson's guilt. Someone fabricating a story meant to get rid of an anti-O.J. juror *would* say that.

Ito called Juror 353 into chambers.

"It has been brought to my attention from a credible source," he told her, referring to the anonymous correspondent, "that one of our jurors has been in contact with a literary agent or publisher."

This person planned to write a book whose title suggested he or she believed in Simpson's guilt, Ito continued. He repeated the title, adding that the juror's "spouse, boyfriend, or husband" was making the arrangements.

"Are you that person?"

"No."

"All right. Do you know anything about this?"

Florio-Bunten said that her husband had talked to a male juror's girlfriend on conjugal-visit night. *That* juror was writing a book, her husband told her. The defense speculated it was a single juror who sat in the front row.

Ito then asked about reports of conflict at the Inter-Continental.

580

"There's always conflict." Florio-Bunten shrugged. "There's always little things. You know, 'She gave me the hairy eyeball today,' or 'He stands too close to me.' . . . I probably have offended quite a few people here on a number of occasions, and quite a few people have offended me. . . ."

Ito asked, "Do you think you can put aside any of those petty things and work together?"

"I sure hope so," she replied.

"How's your husband?" the judge asked almost casually. "There was some illness problem."

Florio-Bunten said he was doing better. Was he contemplating writing a book? Ito asked.

The juror laughed, startling everyone.

"Why do you laugh?" Ito asked.

"Because you don't know my husband." She smiled. "He's just an ordinary guy."

Ito asked her to wait outside.

It was a long day. Reporters were milling around the ninth floor, waiting to learn why Ito and the lawyers had been closeted in chambers for hours. A deputy had brought Ito a note scribbled on a newspaper. Now its alleged writer, the young Latina juror, number 1427, was being grilled.

"Did you write any notes to anybody?" Ito asked her.

"No. I didn't say anything."

Ito asked if she'd written a note on a newspaper and shared it with another juror. "I asked 353 for something, and then I wrote something down."

Ito showed her the newspaper page. "Is that the note?"

"Yes, I scribbled that."

Florio-Bunten was asked to return to Ito's chambers.

"Did another juror before you came in here write you a note about our discussions?" She denied it.

Ito showed her the note. "Was that note shown to you?"

"No."

"You're sure?"

"I'm positive."

Ito had trapped her. Number 353 had lied. Johnnie was

silently elated. Florio-Bunten would have been a problem. So what if the anonymous letter was weird? It was no longer the reason for her dismissal.

Carl Douglas thought Florio-Bunten's lie about the note was only a convenient excuse for Ito to get rid of her. The Latina juror had also lied point-blank to Ito, but she wasn't dismissed. Of course, none of the jurors had a bad word to say about that young lady. Florio-Bunten, however, seemed to be the target of two jurors' animosity.

Douglas was convinced that Ito was actively trying to stabilize the jury as a harmonious, effective working group, not just a bunch of stoics who would stay the course. Ito needed a jury able to hold on through final arguments, maybe four months from now. He didn't want long-held grudges and simmering resentments to create a crisis at the last moment. And he wanted the jury to do more than survive deliberations without bloodshed or breakdown: He wanted it to reach a verdict. From now on, Douglas suspected, the judge would be looking very closely at personality conflicts.

Johnnie had begun worrying that at this rate, there might not be twelve jurors left. The trial could proceed with a smaller number, but only if both sides agreed. Such agreement might be hard to come by, and Ito could call a mistrial. Carl thought: TFC.

OUSTED JUROR DENIES SHE WAS
PLANNING TO WRITE A BOOK

... Friday afternoon, Florio-Bunten told her side of the story on a radio talk show hosted by attorney Gloria Allred. ...

She thought the prosecution's case "was going pretty good. They would need a lot more evidence to convince me. I would definitely need something to tie Mr. Simpson in with the blood drops. ... For me the compelling evidence is finding Ms. Simpson's blood on Mr. Simpson's sock. And of course the glove with Mr. Simpson's blood on it. That's pretty compelling."

582

Florio-Bunten said she thought the controversial DNA evidence "was the most interesting part. I was enthralled. It was like a puzzle. I thought they explained it fairly simply. I was able to understand it."

The former juror reported a strong reaction to a defense allegation against Los Angeles Police detective Mark Fuhrman. "Even though he was a racist, would he plant evidence? That was the thought that went through my mind . . . I didn't know what to think of that evidence. I was kind of shocked that I would be listening to it."

—Tim Rutten, Henry Weinstein, and Andrea Ford
Los Angeles Times, May 27, 1995

30

BARRY SCHECK BEGAN TO SUSPECT THAT COLLIN YAMauchi might help the defense. The young lab technician was unpolished. More important, he was honest. He was certainly no politician. Rock Harmon discovered this to his dismay on Yamauchi's first day of testimony, May 24.

"Based on what you've heard in the media before you did the tests in this case," Harmon began, "did you have an expectation what the outcome of these tests would be?"

"I heard on the news that he's [O.J.] got an airtight alibi," Collin Yamauchi replied. "He's in Chicago, and it's his ex-wife, and I go, Oh, well, he's probably not related to the scene."

There was a moment of stunned silence before Ito called

an urgent sidebar. Agitated prosecutors and defenders rushed to the bench. The defense argued that the mention of Simpson's alibi opened the door to bringing in the tape of the statement Simpson made to Vannatter and Lange when he returned from Chicago on June 13, 1994. Ito ruled against it, saying the door had not yet been unlocked.

Scheck heard something else in the lab technician's reply. To convince jurors that Simpson's DNA got into the Bundy blood drops via contamination in the LAPD lab, he needed an honest witness, someone willing to admit that serious procedural errors occurred. The contamination scenario he and Bill Thompson had worked out was complex and fragile; it was an explanation, not a proof. In presenting it, Barry would have to ask questions to which he didn't already know the answers—always a serious risk. He would have to ask Collin Yamauchi how he handled the blood; he couldn't predict the answer.

Yamauchi's unpolished manner might help. Or it might not. Many an otherwise honest person would lie to protect his professional reputation. Or possibly Scheck's scenario was wrong. Yamauchi might insist—truthfully—that the vial of Simpson's blood, his table, his gloves, were spotless. Much of Scheck's theory depended on how well he had unscrambled Yamauchi's notes. Maybe Scheck would discover in questioning Yamauchi that he had missed something vital. These possibilities did nothing to reduce his anxiety.

On Tuesday, May 30, Barry Scheck began questioning Yamauchi, using the chronology that he and Thompson had worked out from the lab technician's jumbled notes.

"Now, on direct examination," he said, "you specifically remembered that you received Mr. Simpson's reference tube after a conversation with Dennis Fung, right?"

"That's right," Yamauchi replied. "I've had chances to look over my notes more carefully and try to piece together that issue."

Scheck talked him through the work area at the end of his lab table. Had he taken Simpson's reference tube to that spot? Did he write up a card to denote the blood swatches that would be made using blood from the tube?

"Yes, I recall making the blood-swatch card in that area," Yamauchi answered.

Did he write a card before examining the Bundy glove?

"Judging by the continuity of my notes . . ." Yamauchi answered thoughtfully, "I would say, yeah, that's the most likely scenario."

Yamauchi had made a card to reference O.J.'s tube, Scheck repeated carefully, "*before* you did cuttings of the Bundy blood swatches?"

"Yes," Yamauchi said. "That goes in line with the continuity."

Carefully, Scheck established that Yamauchi removed a milliliter of Simpson's blood with his left hand, leaving the tube in a lab stand rather than placing it where it was less likely to spill. Had he changed gloves afterward? Yamauchi insisted he had. Scheck asked if Yamauchi's memory of handling Simpson's blood vial had "improved" since reviewing his notes.

The witness paused.

"The way you're making me think about it right now . . ." he said, "I now recall I had those gloves in my hand. They had blood on them. I would have to get rid of them . . . and, somehow or other, that reminds me of taking off my gloves at that point."

"This just occurred to you as we're talking right now?" Scheck asked. *Blood on his gloves!* Barry hid the elation he felt.

"You're bringing me back to that time and place where I was doing that," Yamauchi said, "and yes, it helped my recollection."

"Did it come to your attention that mishandling Mr. Simpson's reference sample in relation to the crime-scene specimens could be a significant error?"

"Argumentative," Rock Harmon objected. Ito agreed. Scheck returned to his contamination scenario.

"Did you get blood on your gloves when you opened Mr. Simpson's reference tube?"

"Yes," Yamauchi said, "soaked through the paper."

"You remember that now?" Barry was being gentle. He felt that the young man really was remembering this for the first time in months.

"Yes, I do."

"Didn't you testify before that as you opened the tube, you did it with a Chem-wipe?" Scheck asked.

"Yes, and blood soaks through the Chem-wipe."

Scheck continued, still carefully, "So now you are saying that you have an independent recollection that the blood soaked through the Chem-wipe?"

"Along the tip edges, yes."

"And when you gave that [earlier] description," Scheck went on, "did you include the fact that the blood went right through the Chem-wipe, got your gloves dirty?"

"No, I don't believe so."

Scheck was flying now. "In our discussion here on cross-examination, this came to you for the first time?"

Yamauchi agreed it did. Talking "in that much detail" helped, he said.

Scheck's nights of studying the disorganized lab notes had paid off. By walking the witness step by tiny step through his handling of the blood vial, Scheck had reopened Collin Yamauchi's memory bank. Yes, he'd spilled Simpson's reference blood, he remembered. It had leaked through a Chem-wipe onto his lab gloves.

The criminalist insisted that he then threw the gloves away, but the jurors now had grounds for reasonable doubt: He had shown that his memory for detail was imperfect.

After the spill, Yamauchi next examined the Bundy glove, then each Bundy blood-drop swatch. The swatches decreased in Simpson DNA content in the same order in which Yamauchi examined them. Was Yamauchi tracking the DNA from the reference blood through the Bundy swatches the way a kid with muddy shoes would leave disappearing footprints on a clean floor?

Scheck turned back to Yamauchi.

"In reviewing your notes, you agreed that you could have cut samples from the glove before you cut swatches from the Bundy samples?"

586

"Yes," Yamauchi answered.

Done, Scheck thought. He had established the possibility of a blood-contamination trail. First Yamauchi had admitted he spilled O.J.'s reference sample on his gloved hands. He said he then changed his gloves, but Barry could point to his other memory lapses as leaving room for doubt. Scheck could then argue that, while wearing the bloodstained gloves, Yamauchi handled the Bundy glove and transferred O.J.'s blood to it. *Then* the criminalist touched the swatches from the drops leading away from the bodies.

Now all Scheck had to worry about was whether the prosecutors could explain these facts some other way. Scheck knew he hadn't exonerated Simpson. However, he could now plausibly demonstrate that O.J.'s DNA might have found its way onto the swatches through contamination. But what about the blood *originally* on the swatches, the blood that had degraded in Dennis Fung's hot van? In crossing Fung, Scheck had established that the long delay before the blood was refrigerated had compromised the accuracy of future tests. The blood Fung collected at Bundy was very possibly the killer's blood. And there was no way on earth, Barry knew, to prove that that degraded blood—the blood on the swatch before Yamauchi contaminated it—wasn't *also* Simpson's.

Barry Scheck now felt that Henry Lee's testimony on the possible second shoe prints at the crime scene was enormously important. The blood-contamination scenarios that Scheck had just demonstrated supported the often-ridiculed hypothesis that more than one killer was at work that night. The *original* blood on those contaminated Bundy swatches could have come from more than one person. Henry Lee's discovery of a second shoe print in several locations at Bundy supported that possibility. Beyond presenting the contamination expert, microbiologist John Gerdes, Barry Scheck would take on no additional chores. He would concentrate all his efforts on preparing Henry Lee for the stand.

31

ON SATURDAY, JUNE 3, THE DEFENSE HELD ITS LARGEST meeting so far. The team had been planning it for over a month. The prosecutors had told Johnnie they'd be finished by the end of June, and the defense lawyers had been given what they thought was a complete list of remaining prosecution witnesses.

Time now to plan the defense case in detail. Today every defense expert, some important expert witnesses, and all the attorneys were present. Kardashian counted over twenty people in the tiny conference room. Enough talent to start a forensics think tank.

Carl said that security and confidentiality were now critical. After every defense meeting so far, the prosecution had seemed to know immediately what was going on and had been able to harass defense witnesses. Johnnie agreed that some members of the team were talking too freely. It had to stop. Some things could be discussed only in Johnnie's private office, among a select group—especially now that the defense case would begin in a month.

Barry Scheck presented an overview of the case. He went through the integrity of the evidence, the degradation of the blood drops, the cross-contamination of the glove, the missing 1.8 milliliters of Simpson's reference blood, and the big blood spot found high up on the sock recovered from O.J.'s bedroom. The location of that stain suggested it had been planted.

"If O.J. was Michael Jackson," Dr. Lee joked, "maybe he could get blood way up on that sock." He was referring to Jackson's trademark short pants. "All my clients have only one glove,'' Johnnie put in. Kardashian suggested that everybody come to court one day in short trousers and white socks to illustrate the Michael Jackson Defense. The team had two days of serious business to handle, but a little humor was welcome after six months of TFC.

Scheck gave the defense some good news: The tests done by the FBI showed EDTA in the blood swatch from the Bundy back gate and in the swatch from Nicole's blood on Simpson's sock. The presence of EDTA in the Bundy back-gate drop was an overwhelming indication to the defense that the blood had been spiked with O.J.'s reference sample. This may be the single strongest thing we have, Scheck said. Shapiro agreed: This was *real* evidence. But he nevertheless suggested that the defense spend minimal time on DNA during its case. Just get in and out. We'll never be able to prove innocence. The jury is already bored stiff. Let's present our case in a month or less.

The issue of the jury's stamina had to be considered. Only four alternates were left, with at least two months to go. This jury was fed up and exhausted; Ito wanted to speed up the trial. Shapiro had suggested cutting down the team's witness list, and today he presented the idea again. Maybe less would be more. Johnnie seemed to agree.

Next, Dr. Robert Huizenga, who had examined O.J. two days after his return from Chicago and had photographed his body, presented O.J.'s medical history, at length, in jargon nobody understood. Then he summarized all the medicalese: "O.J. looks like Tarzan, but acts more like Tarzan's mother."

"You've got to use that," Johnnie said.

"We've got to acknowledge that O.J.'s *capable* of doing it," Peter Neufeld pointed out. "Otherwise, you lose credibility."

Almost everyone agreed Huizenga should not try to create the impression that O.J. was physically incapable of committing the murders. It was enough if he dispelled the notion that O.J. was physically fit. Shawn could see that Johnnie wasn't listening to these nuances. He was taken with the handsome Huizenga; he thought women jurors would love him. To Cochran, that was all that mattered. Put him on. Carl assigned the doctor to Shapiro.

Then Dr. Bertram Maltz, a rheumatologist, spoke about O.J.'s damaged joints, his osteoporosis, his arthritic flare-ups in 1991, 1992, and 1993. Use this, he said, to create reasonable doubt about his ability to commit the crimes. Then Maltz discussed the family history of osteoarthritis, which had put O.J.'s mother in a wheelchair. Johnnie's face lit up. Maybe we should call Eunice Simpson. I can see her being wheeled up to the witness stand, he said to Shawn. All that was needed was O.J.'s okay.

After that, Dr. Lee gave his crime-scene analysis, reviewing everything that had been presented in court so far.

"Lot of blood everywhere, should be a lot of blood on murderer," Lee said. "Should be a lot more in Bronco." What Lee said next was the heart of the matter: "If they collected evidence properly, real killer would be identified. They didn't do their job from day one. They fucked up." Scheck could hear that line in Lee's testimony, expletive deleted.

Lee pointed out that Goldman's murder could have taken several minutes. "Twenty-five wounds in matter of seconds? Random wounds? With movement, murder takes time." Lee pointed out that Goldman's pager was over *here*, his keys over *there*. Look at the photographs: The scattered objects showed movement. The more bloody the scene, the better for the defense. One glove was dropped. One of the killer's hands was bare. But there were no bloody fingerprints. How come only a few drops of blood on the glove, with a murder like this? Scheck could see that Lee's testimony would raise reasonable doubt. For sure.

Lee pointed out that two other sets of gloves from Simpson's home showed no wear. But the gloves from the crime scene were very worn. Not in character for a rich man to keep worn gloves. A small point, but good.

Johnnie cut off Dr. Lee abruptly when he started to talk about the second set of shoe prints. There were too many people present. Cochran had to protect Henry's testimony against leaks.

Shawn thought Dr. Lee seemed more guarded today. He

emphasized that he wouldn't present conclusions. Had the prosecution's case affected Dr. Lee as it had Shawn? All those 1-in-170-million blood matches had shaken Chapman. Now the discovery showed that fibers from O.J.'s Bronco were found at the Bundy crime scene. They could rest assured the D.A. would make the most of that. Shawn had had her moment of doubt; she felt that Lee was entitled to his. Lee had been arguing right up to his professional limit but wouldn't go beyond it.

Barry Scheck then suggested that another criminalist, Dr. Larry Ragle, could testify on some points. Take some of the burden off Dr. Lee.

Dr. Herb MacDonell, an expert in blood-spatter analysis, discussed the blood on the sock, particularly the blood he had found on the sock's interior. The large photograph he showed made it clear that the socks had to be lying on a flat surface, possibly a table or lab counter, when the blood soaked through to the third surface.

The team next considered the question of discovery. Did they have to turn over all the notes of defense experts who were going to testify? Gerry Uelmen had written an opinion that it might be best for the experts to prepare only a final report, submit that to the team shortly before they testified, and give it to the prosecution immediately. That way, he said, the defense lawyers could state truthfully that they had requested and received only one final report from their experts. Scheck knew that sooner or later MacDonell's notes, like Dr. Lee's, would have to be turned over, and then the prosecution would know just about everything the defense was going to present. Barry wanted to hold back as long as possible.

Dr. Baden's report went on and on. The prevailing view was that Dr. Wolf would testify instead. But nobody had yet told Baden that. Shapiro couldn't get him to shorten his remarks. Kardashian, as usual, wished for a stun gun. Dr. Wolf finally had to tell Baden to stop. Her manner, as always, was concise and impressive. Johnnie told Carl he wanted Dr. Wolf to testify. We need some women, Cochran said. Maybe they could use Baden and Wolf for different topics.

Bailey made his presentation on the time line. He and McKenna had done their job well. Heidstra and his dogs checked out: He had heard a "Hey, hey, hey" at 10:40 P.M. Bailey also brought up a new potential witness, Francesca Harman. She had driven by the Bundy address at about 10:30 P.M. and had not heard a dog barking. Finally, Ellen Aaronson and Danny Mandel were perhaps the most important time-line witnesses for the defense. They had been on a blind date the night of the murders, and had never seen each other again, but they told the same story. They walked right by Nicole's condo at 10:25 P.M. and saw nobody. Heard nothing.

Next, Bailey turned to hair and trace evidence. "It can't convict him, and it won't prove innocence," he said. Twenty percent of the hairs on the knit cap were consistent with O.J.'s. The rest belonged to third parties. As for the Bruno Magli shoe prints at Bundy, the D.A. couldn't connect O.J. with a purchase of such shoes at Bloomingdale's or any other place. The prints wouldn't convict him, wouldn't prove innocence.

Johnnie liked what Bailey had done and assigned him three new witnesses to cross, including Douglas Deedrick, the FBI's hair and fiber expert.

Since Ito had made it possible to recall Fuhrman during the defense case, Bailey planned to impeach him at that point. Bailey went through the pros and cons of each witness he planned to call. Not only could the prosecution attack aspects of Kathleen's Bell's background, but also there was another problem with her: If she hated Fuhrman, why did she supposedly introduce him to her closest friend, Andrea Terry? Then there was Max Cordova, a former marine sergeant, who admitted he remembered Fuhrman only in *his* dreams. Forget him, Lee said. Natalie Singer's roommate was dating Fuhrman's partner and heard Fuhrman use the word "nigger." Nothing for the D.A. to attack in Singer's background. And then there was Roderic Hodge, whom Fuhrman had called "nigger." He had spent time in jail; surely the D.A. would try to discredit him. But the jury had to hear his story. Johnnie said he wanted every one of these witnesses checked. *Thoroughly* checked. No more of this "She's great" stuff after one interview, he said, looking straight at McKenna.

By the end of the second day the only question left was O.J.'s possible testimony. One strategy was to get as much of O.J. as possible in front of the jury without actually putting him on. Use the exercise video. His family. His friends. Anything and anyone else that created the right image. Then O.J. got on the speakerphone and said he wanted only the most reliable people on the stand—his entire family, if possible; maybe A.C. But Cochran said he wanted to wait on Cowlings. His testimony would undoubtedly lead to the events surrounding the Bronco chase.

Uelmen had written a memo on O.J.'s possible testimony. There were risks, he wrote, "that his demeanor will incriminate him and there was a risk it will open the door to damaging evidence that was previously kept out." The dangers in O.J.'s behavior on the stand, Uelmen now said, could be minimized by careful preparation.

Shapiro repeated that he didn't want O.J. to testify. He recounted once again how badly the client had handled himself when Shapiro had tested him. He looked to Kardashian for support; he'd been there. But Kardashian said nothing. Johnnie had also begun to think that Simpson shouldn't be called—the case was going so well; Scheck was doing a great job—but on the other hand, Simpson might be needed. The prosecution was threatening to end its case with domestic violence. Johnnie was always thinking of O.J.'s future as much as the trial.

Bailey would not listen to any waffling. "Start preparing him and give him a real chance," he said. "He's innocent. Let my partner, Fischman, prepare him."

Scheck's position was that in a criminal case you don't put the defendant on unless you absolutely have to. "And we *don't* have to. In the context of this case, it doesn't make any sense," Barry said. But he agreed with Bailey that O.J. should be prepared anyway. "You prepare him even if you're not going to use him. You always prepare the defendant, just in case." Then he added, "O.J. interacts differently with women than with men.'' Shawn Chapman knew what he meant. O.J. was automatically boastful and flirtatious with women. That wouldn't necessarily impress a female prosecutor.

To prep Simpson, the team needed its own Marcia Clark—sharp, tenacious, and on their side. O.J. had to learn to relate to a female attorney as a professional. Scheck suggested Cristina Arguedas from Emeryville, near San Francisco. One of the best criminal lawyers in the country, he said. Barry had worked for her when he was in law school. Shawn said she would make the call.

Cochran and Shapiro viewed Barry Scheck, Peter Neufeld, and the other science attorneys with new respect. Their initial discomfort with PCR and RFLP and the other exotica was insignificant now. Scheck had turned the seemingly incomprehensible into a devastating weapon that had neutralized the D.A.'s most incriminating evidence. Scheck and his colleagues were winning the case before the defense even called a witness.

Johnnie Cochran, Bob Shapiro, and Lee Bailey had to accomplish as much. Thanks to Scheck and Neufeld, the D.A. could no longer use O.J.'s blood to put him at the crime scene. The other defense attorneys had to use the time line for the same purpose.

Shawn checks with O.J. before calling Arguedas. "Fine" is his answer; he's ready to take the stand. Shawn calls Emeryville. Arguedas likes the idea and agrees to a modest fee plus travel and hotel expenses.

As they talk, Shawn wonders if Arguedas thinks O.J. is guilty. The attorney never says so, but Shawn can feel she's not a fan.

"Send me all the statements he's made, the police statement, the suicide letter. Any material about admissible incidents of stalking or abuse," Arguedas says. She needs the tough stuff to do her job properly. Shawn decides Arguedas will be an effective D.A.-surrogate. O.J. won't know what hit him.

32

On Monday, June 5, Kardashian and Simpson were playing gin rummy in the holding cell when Cochran and Shapiro hurried in. Lawyers on both sides had been in chambers arguing with Ito about two jurors.

"We got fucked," Cochran barked.

Juror 1427, Farron Chavarria, and Juror 1489, Willie Cravin, were out. Johnnie, a relentless optimist, had imagined Cravin would survive Ito's latest investigation of quarreling among the jurors. Now he was furious. "Ito had no grounds to get Willie," Johnnie went on. "He based his decision on the testimony of two white jurors who were dismissed for lying!"

Four days earlier Ito had discussed Chavarria, the Latina real estate appraiser, with both sides. The defense was pleased that Ito wanted her dismissed: Chavarria appeared to be pro-prosecution.

During Judge Ito's earlier investigation that ended in Francine Florio-Bunten's ouster, Chavarria was the juror who, in defiance of Ito's order, warned Florio-Bunten about the judge's inquiries. When Ito asked Chavarria about this, she answered evasively.

"She lied, and she has to go," Johnnie had argued during Ito's earlier investigation. "The time is now."

It was hard for Marcia Clark to defend a juror who had lied to the judge, but she felt obliged to try. "She's been targeted by the defense, as was 353 [Florio-Bunten]," she argued. "They've been very successful in getting rid of those they don't like." The prosecutors had lost Florio-

Bunten; they were about to lose Chavarria. So it was no great surprise that they now attacked a pro-defense juror.

Clark said she wanted Cravin, a postal manager, dismissed. The defense wanted to keep him.

"Here is a man who has systematically harassed and intimidated other jurors," Clark stated. ". . . Is this the kind of person that can actually deliberate with other jurors in a meaningful and adult fashion?"

She was deliberately leaning on the exposed nerve Ito had revealed in his recent jury investigations. It was obvious to both sides that the judge was trying to create a group that could bring in a verdict.

Clark now worked on Ito's anxieties. "He is a very severe and grave danger to the integrity of this jury and to their ability to evaluate the evidence."

Johnnie understood Ito's anxieties as well as Clark, but feared the judge would dismiss Craven as a trade-off for Chavarria.

Johnnie had been right. Both jurors were out.

Cochran tried to save the day by arguing that Ito should delay the trial while the defense asked the Court of Appeal to overturn his ruling. In addition, Johnnie wanted Cravin held in the jury room of the courthouse.

Darden and Clark insisted that the defense couldn't hold Cravin. If Ito ruled wrongly, they said, the only remedy is a mistrial. But the last thing the defense wanted at this point was a mistrial.

"Somebody knows a lot more about this than probably all of us," Cochran said to Ito.

"Who?" Darden asked.

"Alan Dershowitz."

"What has he ever won?" Clark shot back.

Cochran requested a forty-eight-hour delay for Dershowitz to write his brief. Ito gave the defense until the end of the court day. Detaining Cravin longer, he said, would be "tantamount to arresting him."

By five o'clock the Court of Appeal had ruled against the defense. Cravin was out. Two African-American women replaced the dismissed jurors. Both were young and seriously overweight. By the next day a member of the defense team had nicknamed them Two Tons of Joy.

Now there were only two alternates left. The prosecution still had a month to go on its case and the defense anticipated two months after that before the jury got the case. Now both sides had to consider proceeding with a jury smaller than twelve, or declare a truce in their battle of attrition over the jurors.

Of the remaining alternates, one was an elderly gentleman who always wore a suit and tie. The defense had nicknamed him Calhoun. They were disappointed that he hadn't been seated by now. He was a solid African-American. A rock. His face said everything. They knew he'd taken serious abuse from whites as a child in the Deep South. "Damn bastards," he'd said during one of Ito's juror investigations. "They've been treating me like that all my life."

The last alternate was Fufu, whose jeans had captured O.J.'s attention during the jury visit to Rockingham. She reminded everyone of Nicole.

33

On Tuesday, June 6, Simpson sat with Kardashian in the tiny attorneys' room next to the holding cell. The autopsy pictures were being shown today. Simpson was distraught. "Nic would have been calling my name," he choked. "She would have been calling for my help."

Kardashian listened as his friend tried to pull himself together.

"Why didn't anybody help her?" Simpson sobbed. "Didn't anyone hear her?" He could barely get the words out. "I can't believe I couldn't help her. I wasn't there to help her."

Kardashian watched Simpson, handcuffed to the chair and crying, and pondered his own questions on O.J.'s innocence. Moments like this restored his faith. He felt O.J.'s tears were real.

The Los Angeles County coroner, Dr. Lakshmanan Sathyavagiswaran, a polished, friendly man, had begun testifying the previous Friday. Brian Kelberg, the prosecutor assigned to present him, started by tidying up loose ends. Since no L.A. County pathologist had gone to the crime scene, Kelberg prompted Sathyavagiswaran to agree that to go was "good practice" but that tight budgets often required sending a lower-ranking coroner's investigator instead. As department head, Sathyavagiswaran repeatedly took responsibility for coroner Irwin Golden's flawed autopsy. "He made some mistakes, yes," the witness said, pointing out error after error.

The first day had been a tedious recital of technicalities, and so was the beginning of the second; Sathyavagiswaran explained arcane details of mortuary science. "If I did commit this crime," a bored Simpson joked to Kardashian, "I'd be confessing right now."

Kardashian was surprised when Sathyavagiswaran approached him during a break.

"I think you are a great friend," the coroner said. "I want to tell you, I wish I had a friend like you."

"Thank you," Kardashian said after a pause. "That's very kind of you." He was so surprised he could hardly manage an appropriate response.

"I am only doing my job," Sathyavagiswaran said and walked away.

In contrast to the coroner's remark, Kardashian remembered that a few days before, while driving on the freeway, he'd put the top of his Mercedes down. "Hey!" someone shouted. He turned to see a woman in a car in the next lane moving her finger across her throat. "Murderer!" she yelled.

Today, Tuesday, Sathyavagiswaran's job was to explain exactly how Nicole and Ron died. Ito had warned the jury that the pictures "are not pleasant to look at." He added, "If at any time . . . you feel unusually uncomfortable or if you need to take a break, feel free to let me know."

Brian Kelberg was known as a master of heavy-handed interrogations. No grisly detail escaped him. He followed a classic prosecutorial technique: Make the murders overwhelmingly real. Make the jury want to punish someone.

"I need you to sit at the table and block me from the camera," Simpson said to Bob. "It's zooming in on me. This is very difficult, and I don't want them to see my reaction. Will you?"

"Sure," Kardashian said.

In the late afternoon of June 6, the photos arrived on huge display boards; silence settled over the courtroom. Kardashian watched as jurors struggled visibly for composure. One woman covered her mouth. Another juror breathed slowly and deeply. Others refused to look and stared fixedly at their notebooks.

Both the defense team and the victims' families had asked that the display boards be exhibited only to the jury. Simpson wished to be spared the view, his lawyers said. The Goldmans and Browns asked Judge Ito to respect the privacy of their loved ones. The television camera and court spectators, including the press, saw nothing.

But there was no escaping the images evoked by Dr. Sathyavagiswaran's testimony. When Kelberg asked about the gaping wound in Nicole's neck, the coroner explained that her carotid artery and jugular vein were "transected."

How does the body react when that happens? Kelberg asked.

"Bleeding," answered Sathyavagiswaran, "and you could have a sudden loss of [blood] supply on one side of the front of the brain. You could have seizures, and then ultimately you could die because of the rapid bleeding from this large vessel.''

As he listened to the chilling details of how his ex-wife died, Simpson furrowed his eyebrows, rocked in his chair, and worked his jaw slowly, wincing, staring stiff-necked into space.

How did the fatal wound occur? the prosecutor asked.

"My opinion is that Miss Brown was on the ground facedown when this wound was inflicted," Sathyavagiswaran answered. "My opinion," he said, "is that the head was extended backwards and the knife was used to cause this incised stab wound from left to right." He suggested that Nicole did not resist.

"Doctor," Kelberg said, ". . . if you could use me and my head and hair, would you demonstrate what is your opinion as to the manner in which that last major incised stab wound was inflicted?''

The coroner pulled Kelberg's head back by the hair to expose his neck. He drew a ruler across it like a knife. Instinctively, Kardashian put his hand on Simpson's shoulder. The athlete's muscles were rigid.

The defense was starting to despise Kelberg for his theatrics.

Sathyavagiswaran answered Brian Kelberg's questions for five more days with the jury surrounded by tall display boards of autopsy pictures. The defense team was rigid with tension. This is like living in a dark cloud, Kardashian thought. The only relief was boredom during the long discussions of autopsy and morgue procedure.

In midweek, the prosecutor asked Sathyavagiswaran to approach him and clench his fist as if holding a knife. Could he plunge the imaginary blade into Kelberg fifteen times in fifteen seconds? Yes was his answer. Kelberg hoped to underscore a prosecution theory that the killings happened quickly.

On Thursday, June 8, Ito called a court break when one juror, clutching a handkerchief, asked to be excused. Other jurors sat rigid, with their eyes closed. The elderly black alternate, Calhoun, gagged and appeared to be choking as he reached for a handkerchief to wipe his face. Chris Darden asked about moving one of the boards farther back. "We can't move the board back," Kelberg said.

"All right, let's call it a day," Ito said.

Though the display boards were turned away from the cameras, crime-scene pictures occasionally turned up on the defense table's closed-circuit monitor.

"Don't look!" Kardashian hissed, seeing a shot of Nicole lying in blood.

It was often too late. More than once O.J. caught glimpses of Nicole's body. He grimaced, fought back tears, and rocked hard in his seat, breathing rapidly and deeply to maintain control.

On Wednesday, June 14, Bob Shapiro began his cross-examination. He told Simpson it would be short. Less will be more, he repeated.

"Isn't it true, Doctor, after eight days on the stand," Bob Shapiro began, "there's only four facts you can testify to within a reasonable degree of medical certainty based on your education, background, experience, as to how these two people died?"

Shapiro's tread-lightly style was perfect here. He had read the mood in the courtroom. Everyone was drained and exhausted after eight days of horror and tedium. The jurors were numb, the victims' families beyond tears. Resentment simmered beneath the unnatural calm. The jurors seemed on the verge of another revolt.

Shapiro quickly asked summary questions. Sathyavagis-waran knew that Nicole and Ron were homicide victims, right? They bled to death from stab wounds. They died between nine P.M. and 12:30 A.M. the night of June 12–13, 1994. Is that correct? The coroner agreed. But he couldn't "for a certainty" determine the number of killers. He testified that one person using a single-edged knife "could be" the murderer, but he couldn't exclude a second person with a double-edged knife.

That was the answer Shapiro wanted. He had reduced the

coroner's eight grueling days into a sound bite. A win for Shapiro and the defense.

On Thursday morning, Shapiro finished almost before he had started. He challenged Sathyavagiswaran's testimony that the angle and direction of slash wounds indicated how they were inflicted.

He held up a knife. Slashing the air, Shapiro described different stabbing motions. He demonstrated other ways to grip the knife. The coroner admitted that under such conditions it was difficult to establish with certainty how a stabbing took place, or even whether a killer was right- or left-handed.

In redirect, Kelberg hit back at Shapiro. Is the evidence at Bundy, Kelberg asked, "consistent with one killer, six foot two, two hundred and ten pounds, athletically built, with the element of surprise, with a six-inch-long single-edged knife, killing Nicole Brown Simpson and Ronald Goldman? Would you . . . stake your reputation on that?"

The coroner said he would.

For nine days, Linda Deutsch and other reporters watched the stricken faces of the jurors and the backs of the display boards. What did the jury see? Reporters wondered how the grisly pictures affected the jury's view of the evidence. What did the pictures show? The press felt they had to know in order to write intelligently.

At first, Judge Ito refused to let reporters view the autopsy photos. Their interest, he grumbled, was little more than prurient. First Amendment lawyers came to court and argued that, whether the judge liked them or not, reporters were the public's representatives. Trials in America are supposed to be public events for good reason. The press had a right to see this evidence, however gruesome.

Ito ruled that one reporter from each publication or TV or radio station covering the trial could see the photos. The viewing, split into two shifts, took place in an empty courtroom after Dr. Sathyavagiswaran left the stand.

Linda Deutsch was stunned. She and other reporters

stared speechlessly at a vast mural of horror. The bright blue display boards bore large pictures of Nicole and Ron. The blue of the boards framed the bloody, lifeless bodies and made them appear larger and more vivid. In many shots Nicole's eyes were open. Those pictures were almost unbearable. Her head had been propped back to show the cut in her neck, so deep that the knife had actually nicked her spine. In the picture the wound was a ghastly canyon. No one spoke. Very likely no one could. Ito, Brian Kelberg, and several junior prosecutors sat off to one side.

Writer Dominick Dunne, whose daughter had been stabbed to death years earlier, became red-faced and sat down. Shoreen Maghame of the City News Service sat beside him. Some reporters were momentarily unsteady on their feet. The normally noisy press was as silent as if in church.

In all her years of covering trials, Deutsch had seen nothing this bad. She felt the prosecutors might have overdone it: How easily this jury could resent this. We're not stupid, they might think. Show us the pictures for five minutes, an hour, but not a week! Why are you subjecting us to this horror?

34

WILLIAM G. PAVELIC

FACSIMILE

TO: Carl Douglas
DATE: June 13, 1995

Since July of 1994, on numerous occasions, Richard Aaron called Bill Pavelic, Pat McKenna and John McNally regarding his telephone conversation with Nicole Simpson on June 12, 1994, shortly before 11:00 o'clock in the evening. Mr. Aaron indicated he was talking with Nicole when someone rang the door. Nicole excused herself and opened the door. Nicole came back on the line and informed Mr. Aaron that she had to leave. Prior to terminating their telephone conversation, Mr. Aaron heard voices in the background involving more than two individuals. . . . Their accents [were] Hispanic.

Mr. Aaron has been very elusive. . . . When I spoke to Aaron he was reluctant to turn over his telephone records.

I am bothered by the fact that Mr. Aaron alluded to Nicole's drug usage and that his phone number is registered to a Hispanic family.

On Thursday morning, June 15, Dr. Sathyavagiswaran ended his epic testimony. Minutes later, Brenda Vemich, a buyer from Bloomingdale's department store in New York, was sworn in. The D.A. wanted to link the bloody gloves to O.J. Simpson. This witness was the first link in the chain of evidence concerning those gloves. She identified Nicole's credit card receipt for two pairs of Aris Isotoner gloves. The prosecution said one pair was of the same type found at Bundy and Rockingham. Presumably, Nicole had bought them for O.J.

Most of the defense team was in court that day: Shapiro, Cochran, Bailey, Dershowitz, Chapman, and Kardashian. Lee Bailey, who had been interviewing potential witnesses, was present to cross-examine the prosecution's shoe-print expert, scheduled to follow their "glove witnesses." Clark had not indicated on her witness list how much time each would require, so Bailey took the precaution of showing up early.

For months Bailey had studied Simpson's hands and, whenever possible, the actual gloves in evidence. He had concluded that those gloves wouldn't fit Simpson. He was waiting for the right opportunity to satisfy himself about that.

Today the prosecution called Richard Rubin, a former Aris Isotoner executive in charge of the glove-manufacturing division. The FBI had searched for the store where the Bundy-Rockingham gloves had been purchased. So far, no luck. Now they called the man most knowledgeable on the manufacture of these particular gloves. He would point out all the gloves' unique features, so that ultimately the D.A. could place them on Simpson's hands. The defense expected that the prosecution would next introduce photographs of Simpson wearing gloves like those Rubin would describe. The defense knew from the discovery that Rubin was not in Simpson's corner. Watching the glove executive describe the evidence, Bailey decided this witness was enjoying his moment of fame.

Meanwhile, Bob Shapiro had a plan. Rubin himself was immaterial, but Shapiro was banking on the fact that the witness would make his points while referring to the actual gloves. Sure enough, as Rubin talked, the gloves sat out in plain sight. During a break, Shapiro walked over and picked them up. Kardashian watched in amazement as Shapiro pulled them on. They were a snug fit. He removed them and walked quickly into the holding cell, where he compared his hand to Simpson's. O.J.'s hands were far bigger.

''They'll never fit you,'' Shapiro said.

Shapiro told Cochran what he had just done, and later in the same break Johnnie duplicated the experiment. Cochran's hands were slightly bigger than Shapiro's, but smaller than Simpson's. The gloves fit so tightly that he had to pull them off finger by finger. At some time in the future, Shapiro and Cochran would have O.J. put on the gloves in front of the jury.

As the break was ending and Darden entered the courtroom, Bailey saw his moment.

He walked over to the prosecutor and whispered, ''You've got the balls of a stud field mouse.''

Lee Bailey was enjoying himself thoroughly.

He had cultivated a chatting relationship with Darden, sometimes serious, sometimes anything but. Earlier in the trial, when the young prosecutor risked a contempt citation by refusing to apologize to Ito for an ill-tempered remark at sidebar, Bailey had tried to help. "Hey, simmer down, my friend," he had whispered. "I've been there."

"You're not going to have our client try these gloves on, are you?" Bailey said in a friendly tone. "They probably won't fit, and you may not wish to know. But if, as I suspect, you lack the balls to find out, we might find out for you."

Darden smiled and said nothing.

When Rubin resumed his testimony, Darden asked a series of questions about a pair of extra-large Aris Isotoner gloves Rubin had brought along. Cochran asked for a sidebar.

"Your Honor, I wasn't clear what counsel was trying to do," Johnnie said.

"I would like to lay the foundation to show they are the exact same size, similar make and model, so that perhaps we can have Mr. Simpson try them on at some point," Darden answered.

Cochran objected that the defense wasn't prepared for such a surprise demonstration. Johnnie was setting his trap carefully. "At some point, if Mr. Simpson testifies, and we want to have him try on the gloves in evidence," he began, "that is one thing."

Ito unwittingly played into Cochran's strategy when he ruled that Darden could go ahead. "I think it would be more appropriate," the judge continued, "for him to try the other gloves on." He was referring to the gloves found at Bundy and Rockingham.

"That was exactly my point," Cochran added quickly.

Ito helped again. "I mean the real gloves that were found," he said.

"The only problem is," Marcia Clark said warily, "he has to wear latex gloves underneath because they're a biohazard, and [the latex gloves are] going to alter the fit."

Minutes later, Darden committed himself.

"We would like to have Mr. Simpson try on the original evidence items," he told Ito.

Johnnie requested another sidebar. The timing was "inappropriate," he insisted. Of course, he added quickly, his client had no objection and would do it. Just one thing: Could Simpson wear latex gloves underneath and make the demonstration away from TV camera? "He doesn't want this to seem like he's giving some kind of performance," Cochran explained.

Darden interrupted, rising to the bait. "I would just say that he was more than willing to walk over to the jury and show them his hand, and show them his knees and everything else that suits his purposes."

"This is far different from somebody exhibiting injuries," Cochran charged. "They just got caught trying to bring some ringer gloves in here," he said, referring to the new gloves.

Darden protested that he'd shown the new gloves to F. Lee Bailey. The transcript would read like a typical sidebar skirmish. The defense knew otherwise.

The courtroom day was nearly over.

"Your Honor, at this time," Darden announced, "the People would ask that Mr. Simpson step forward and try on the glove recovered at Bundy as well as the glove recovered at Rockingham."

Johnnie Cochran smiled. "No objection, Your Honor."

Simpson rose and walked to the jury box. Marcia Clark remained seated. Two deputies walked close behind Simpson as if he might escape.

First Darden gave Simpson the Rockingham glove and requested that he step forward so the jury could see clearly. Then Darden handed him the Bundy glove.

Simpson couldn't fully get the glove on his hand. The outer surface of a latex glove is unusually smooth, and the Rockingham-Bundy gloves had cashmere liners. Even so, he couldn't get the first glove on completely. The deputies were peering over Simpson's shoulders to see what was happening. Judge Ito asked them to step back.

Simpson tried the other glove, struggling for several minutes before the jury and the TV camera. Marcia Clark turned white but did not move from her seat.

Simpson tugged persistently, raised his eyebrows, pursed his lips. His body language made his difficulty plain. The gloves appeared not to fit.

Darden had taken a staggering blow.

"May he [Simpson] show his hands in front of the jury so that they can see—" Darden asked. Ito said yes.

The jurors not directly in front of Simpson craned their necks. Clearly, they were spellbound. Marcia Clark was still pale. Her expression suggested that she grasped the full extent of this disaster.

Simpson then said out loud, "The gloves are too small; they don't fit. Too tight." O.J. continued to try to work the gloves over his hands. At Darden's request, he straightened his fingers, but that seemed to move the gloves only a little further toward his wrist.

Ito asked Simpson to show the gloves to the jury once again. He did.

Darden made one last attempt.

"Could we ask him to make a fist . . . with his right hand while the gloves are on. . . ."

O.J. did.

"Could we ask him to grasp an object in his hand, a marker perhaps. . . ."

Simpson held a blue marker and lifted it slightly upward. Now Darden wanted him to raise his hand high in the air while holding the marker.

Cochran objected. The image Darden wanted to show the jury was obvious. Ito agreed. Simpson smiled a little.

The certainty of a hung jury now became the possibility of an acquittal. Bailey had been saying all along that nothing mattered if the gloves didn't fit: If they don't fit, they're not his gloves.

Shapiro had been telling Kardashian for months that whoever didn't step on his dick would win this case. Now Shapiro was gloating. This was the prosecution's second fatal mistake. Backing Fuhrman had been the first. That's what makes it all so exciting, Shawn thought. You never know what will happen in court. No matter how well you prepare, you just never know.

At the end of the day, the team sat in the empty courtroom savoring their victory. The prosecutors had left. The reporters were gone, the TV camera dark. They were still flying and no one was ready to come down to earth yet.

The bailiff let Simpson stay a few minutes. Ito was working at the bench. Could Simpson try on the gloves? Shapiro asked the judge. No latex undergloves this time. Ito consented.

The gloves were carried to Simpson at the defense table. Cochran, Douglas, Shapiro, Bailey, Kardashian, and Chapman stood in a circle.

Simpson tried to pull them on again. They still didn't fit.

"I knew they wouldn't fit," O.J. said, looking up at his lawyers. "These gloves aren't my size. I've got really big hands. I told you that."

35

THE DEFENSE WAS SURPRISED THAT THE PROSECUTION DID not present photographic evidence showing Simpson wearing the gloves. It was sure to come later.

On Monday, June 19, 1995, Kardashian saw O.J. in the holding cell. Simpson was reading Nicole's diary, which had been recovered from her safe-deposit box. She had written it during their divorce. O.J. was pensive.

"Well, I couldn't pick them up today because I just flew

in late at night," he was saying to his dead wife when Kardashian entered. Simpson was going through each entry justifying to Nicole why he had or hadn't done this or that. Bob thought that to some extent this was just another of O.J.'s conversations with Nicole. But it was also severely practical. Simpson knew that if he took the stand, he'd have to answer questions based on the diary.

One minute he was talking to Nicole, the next to Kardashian. He told Bob how much he missed Nicole. "She's thirty-six today. [Simpson had apparently forgotten that her birthday had passed a month earlier.] What would she be doing today if she was here?" Simpson had asked A.C. and Arnelle to put a rose on Nicole's grave. Then he lashed out at the Browns. They would be on Geraldo Rivera's show today. Promoting themselves, he said. He was sure the tabloids would photograph them at the grave. Kardashian knew O.J. had that detail right. He could easily imagine the photographs.

That same day, June 19, the FBI shoe expert, Bill Bodziak, took the stand. Bodziak had supervised a worldwide search for the shoes that created the bloody prints at the crime scene; he had tracked the waffle-patterned design to a small factory in Italy that manufactured soles for Bruno Magli shoes, an expensive and uncommon make. He'd decided that the bloody tracks had been made by a limited-edition style of Bruno Magli loafers which sold for $160 a pair.

Bodziak compared the shoe prints to Simpson's size 12 Reeboks and concluded that the Magli prints at Bundy were the same size. He said that 299 pairs of those loafers had been distributed to forty stores in the United States. There the trail ended. Bodziak and other agents could find no salesperson who remembered Simpson or Nicole purchasing a pair. He could say, however, that only 9 percent of American men wear size 12 shoes, and the wearers tend to be six feet tall or more. O.J. was six-one. Another implication was obvious: Bruno Magli customers were wealthy, like Simpson.

The defense felt little concern. They were all still high

from the glove demonstration yesterday. Richard Rubin had returned to the stand earlier to say that the gloves had shrunk because of the blood and that the latex undergloves made the fit impossible. But Rubin's statements didn't weaken the impact of yesterday's demonstration.

In the afternoon, Lee Bailey started his cross-examination of Bodziak. Bailey had made the usual predictions to his colleagues: He'd flatten Special Agent Bodziak. Step on him with a pair of his own shoes. Bob Blasier had helped Bailey prepare and said he was ready. Carl Douglas was looking forward to the fireworks.

Johnnie was less confident. During Goldberg's direct examination of Bodziak, Bailey had objected very little. He was letting things stand unchallenged that Johnnie would have stopped. When Johnnie mentioned it, Bailey, of course, insisted this was part of his strategy. As usual, he didn't explain. He took no notes while Goldberg worked. Cochran decided this was bravado: Bailey was possibly hard of hearing. Add to that his drinking and trembling hands—very old news by now—and Johnnie Cochran was worried.

During his plodding direct examination, Goldberg gave Cochran something else to worry about. The young prosecutor brushed up against the defense's tightly held secret, Henry Lee's second set of shoe prints. How much did the other side know?

Bodziak said there was no indication that more than one pair of shoes was involved. He confirmed that he considered Simpson someone who could have worn the Bruno Magli loafers that made the bloody shoeprint impressions.

Bailey's cross fell apart as he and Bodziak followed a diagram of the shoe prints that led from the bodies to the back gate. Bailey asked about the prints labeled "M" and "O," which appeared to be at a 45-degree angle to each other.

"Would you say that 'O' and 'M' could have been made by the same person?" Bailey asked.

Bodziak agreed.

"Standing with one foot askew?"

"Yes."

No problem yet. But Bailey had started badly. He tried too hard to confuse and embarrass Bodziak. The witness didn't budge, but Bailey persisted when he should have moved on. Then Bailey got the shoe size slightly wrong. He even once called Bill Bodziak by the wrong name, Deedrick, that of the FBI fiber expert scheduled as his next witness. Cochran and Douglas watched in growing alarm. During the midafternoon break, they took him aside and demanded a tighter focus. They might as well have asked water to run uphill.

Bailey now pushed Bodziak to admit that shoe prints pointing in a different direction from others pointing toward the back gate meant their owner might have turned around and headed back. Bodziak admitted the "possibility" but added he doubted that was what the difference indicated.

"Well, without any evidence of turnaround," Bailey said suddenly, "supposing you had two people with the same brand and size of shoe?"

Unlikely, answered Bodziak, who appeared amused. Bailey asked for his reasoning.

"Because in all the cases I've worked," Bodziak explained, "I can count on one hand the number where a common shoe . . . both in size and design, was shared by two persons simultaneously at the crime scene."

Bailey wouldn't let go. "You're making an assumption I didn't ask you to make," he thundered, "and that is that the pairs were *coincidentally* similar. . . . It could have been *deliberate,* couldn't it?"

"I don't believe that, either."

At the defense table, Simpson was scribbling notes frantically and rocking in his chair. Cochran leaned over to him, glancing at Bailey. Bailey didn't see their consternation. He asked Bodziak if, knowing that shoe prints can be traced, two career criminals "might arrange to arrive at a crime scene in the same footwear, make and model?"

The witness was incredulous. "You're suggesting that they intentionally did it?" he asked.

"Absolutely," replied Bailey.

Even sophisticated killers wouldn't buy two pairs of *rare* shoes, Bodziak said, after a startled pause. "They would do that with a common shoe,'' he continued. ''They would not be searching for hundred-and-sixty-dollar to hundred-and-eighty-dollar Bruno Magli shoes where they had to go to different states at the same time to buy them in the same size. . . .''

''But it's possible?'' Bailey insisted again.

The FBI agent refused to play along. ''In my opinion, it's not even possible because it's so ridiculous.''*

Watching the trial at home, Kardashian was furious. This is *asinine,* he thought. We look stupid! It's embarrassing.

Simpson called him that night.

''I don't want Bailey doing witnesses anymore,'' he began. Bob didn't argue.

''He's lost it!'' Simpson growled.

O.J. told Kardashian he'd met Bailey alone after court in the holding cell and raged at his stupidity. What is wrong with you? he demanded. How could you do something so damaging? Why don't you take notes like the other lawyers, get your facts straight?

''I want him out of there,'' Simpson said now to Kardashian. ''He's done with witnesses. I don't want him screwing up again.''

Simpson told Bob that Bailey insisted he had done more than O.J. realized. He wasn't really pushing a theory that there were two killers in Bruno Magli shoes. Simpson hadn't recognized the *deeper* strategy. Cross-examination, Bailey lectured his client, is about what happens up the line, not just today. Bailey was laying the foundation for Dr. Lee's second-shoe-print testimony. He was also planting doubts about Bodziak. The jurors needed to see Bodziak's ignorance about professional killings. Assassins disguise their work, lay false trails. They make plans to fool the cops. The cross was a big win for the defense, Lee Bailey insisted.

*Seven months after the end of the trial, a photograph of O.J. Simpson taken at a September 26, 1993, Buffalo Bills game was published in the *National Enquirer*. In this picture, Simpson is wearing Bruno Magli loafers of the same design that could have left the shoe prints found at the murder scene. Thirty additional photographs of Simpson wearing the identical shoes, taken at the same football game, were introduced into evidence during the civil trial in which Simpson was held responsible for the deaths of Nicole Brown Simpson and Ronald Goldman.

Kardashian stayed home the next morning and faxed Cochran and Shapiro in court. When the day ends, he said, call me. It's urgent. Skip and I want a meeting. Court ended that day around lunchtime. When Cochran called back, he suggested they meet at three at Marino's restaurant, near his office. Douglas and Chapman came along. Marino's, already closed, gave the team a private lunch.

"We must do something about Lee Bailey," Kardashian started bluntly. "He is an embarrassment to the team."

Nobody was about to dispute that.

"Skip and I have talked to O.J.," Kardashian continued. "We want his witnesses cut. We want him pretty much removed from the case. The jury doesn't need to hear any more disasters from Lee Bailey."

Cochran agreed. "O.J. told me how upset he is with Lee. They had a shouting match in the holding cell. Bailey knows he screwed up."

Kardashian noted Bob Shapiro's broad smile. On this issue, he was in total harmony with Johnnie.

One problem, Cochran added. Lee has Deedrick, the FBI hair and fiber expert, later this week. We just don't have time to prepare someone else.

36

MEMORANDUM

TO: Dr. Henry Lee
FROM: Pat McKenna
DATE: June 19, 1995

Pursuant to instructions . . . from Mr. Bailey after consultation with yourself, a forensic experiment was conducted in order to test the likelihood that a blood smeared glove—similar to those allegedly recovered at Bundy (left) and Rockingham (right)—could sit in the night air for more than seven hours and still have a "moist" appearance (as testified by Detective Fuhrman when he found the glove at about 5:30 A.M.).

A black leather glove . . . was ultimately purchased by me . . . on June 12th, 1995.

At about 10:30 P.M., on the evening of June 12, 1995 . . . two gloves were placed upon the counter [of Simpson's Rockingham home kitchen]. Dr. Heizenga [*sic*] drew 3 cc's of blood from my arm . . . smeared the blood on one glove and then the other. The entire sequence was videotaped.

The left glove was placed in a plastic "Ziploc" bag. Then both the bagged glove and the glove not bagged were carried to the spot identified by Detective Fuhrman. . . . The right glove was placed on the ground. [The left glove, still in the bag, was also placed on the ground.]

. . . No one was allowed to touch the gloves, or to enter the area where they were positioned until . . . morning.

At 5:30 A.M. on June 13, 1995 . . . Mr. Bailey and I returned to the Simpson home. . . . We opened the gate . . . and photographed the gloves once more, after opening the bagged left glove and observing that the blood on it was still wet. The right glove [left in the open air overnight] was completely dry. The photographs described above are submitted with this report.

On Wednesday, June 21, Shawn Chapman was working in her office while watching the trial on TV. The defense had a secure fax machine in the courtroom plus a phone they could use. Now Carl called Shawn: Send me page 3476 from the files. Chapman found the page and faxed it back to Carl. On her TV she watched Carl receive the fax and hand the document to Johnnie. Moments later, Cochran used it. Interactive law. The electronic trial. The future was here.

Sometimes Peter Neufeld would drop in. Like Scheck, he didn't like being in court unless he was working a witness. Since Barry's virtuoso performance with Fung, Neufeld had existed in his partner's shadow. He was no egomaniac, but he was eager for his own "Fung moment."

Pat McKenna was also working in Cochran's office. He thought this DNA stuff was lost on the jurors but he enjoyed Peter Neufeld's company. Neufeld was always digging, always learning something new. Pat loved the way Neufeld would lay it all out in plain language. You'd never guess he was some scientific egghead. He was more like a good, ballsy blue-collar guy from Brooklyn.

Today Peter was going through all the charts and hieroglyphics trying to figure out how he'd cross-examine this expert, a certain Dr. Weir, a statistician from New Zealand. McKenna could see Neufeld would rather be with his kids, but Peter was one of the best trial lawyers he'd ever seen.

Then Peter showed the printouts to Shawn. She couldn't believe all these strange symbols in a row. Peter said he was learning for the first time how those huge DNA numbers involving samples containing blood from two or more persons were calculated. He had to master a lot of new material.

The defense had filed a motion in March to challenge the method of calculating these so-called mixture statistics. Now the hearing was scheduled for tomorrow.

On Thursday, June 22, the prosecution brought Dr. Bruce Weir to the stand for a hearing outside the presence of the jury. Dr. Weir was the prosecution's population geneticist, a New Zealand-born professor of statistics and genetics at North Carolina State University. The court would rule on whether his statistical computations were admissible. The issue was determining how frequently within a population a particular DNA pattern would occur.

Ito required the prosecution to present its statistics on mixtures separately from the single-person DNA results. Dr. Weir had come up with a fairly novel method for calculating results in mixed samples and had given the defense a series of reports on his work. This was uncharted territory to most forensic scientists. The problem was, Weir kept changing his calculation procedure from report to report. He had, in effect, calculated the frequency of each sample by a slightly different method. Thompson and Neufeld found it hard to keep up with his changes.

So the defense decided to challenge the admissibility of *all* of Weir's calculations on mixed samples. Bill Thompson handled the defense argument. He was nervous: This was the first time he had cross-examined a witness on national TV.

After hearing arguments and Weir's testimony, Ito ruled that test results based on the "frequencies" approach were admissible. Dr. Weir would testify.

Thompson was dejected that he had not done a better job in the hearing. Walking into the Bel Age Hotel, he was still clutching one of Weir's reports. It contained one particular formula he hadn't checked before cross-examining Weir earlier that day.

As Thompson watched the late news on TV, he was still brooding about Weir's numbers. Then it hit him: Weir hadn't taken into account an alternative form of a gene which in DNA testing is called a masked allele. Each allele has a marker. But in the DNA-DQ-alpha system of testing that Weir was working with, not all alleles have *separate* markers. Some alleles must be inferred from the presence of other data. Thompson knew that in a stain containing blood from two people, an allele from one person can mask or cover one from the other person. Weir had ignored this possibility and had assumed that Simpson's allele was present when it might *not* have been. As a result, Weir underestimated the frequency with which the combination would occur. For example, Weir might conclude that a certain mixed stain could occur only once in 10,000 samples. But an accurate finding might have been closer to once in 5,000 or 1,000. Ignoring the possibility of masked alleles rendered most of Weir's calculations for a whole group of samples incorrect. More important, the mistake showed a strong bias against Simpson. Thompson let out a shout.

Neufeld was in his room preparing for his own cross-examination of Weir before the jury, which was scheduled for tomorrow. Bill raced down the hotel hallway, shouting "Peter! Peter!" and waking up Japanese tourists in adjoining rooms. Heads came popping out of doors.

Bill soon calmed down and showed Peter the problem in Weir's calculations. Then Peter got excited, too. Big grins on their faces. The colleagues spent hours pondering the mistake and wrote a series of new questions for Neufeld's cross, less than twelve hours before he would face Dr. Weir in court.

As Neufeld began his cross the next day, he dropped a number of hints to the jury that something big was coming.

"During your career, sir, have you ever made any mistakes as a professional?"

"Oh, I'm sure I have."

"Have you ever made errors in either calculations or computations?"

"I'm sure I have." Now Dr. Weir seemed a bit edgy.

"And would you also agree, Doctor, that perhaps you have even propounded theories that at some time in the future ultimately were refuted?"

Weir moves away from his "I'm sure"'s.

"I don't believe so. I don't—I can't think of any published refutations of any of my papers."

Neufeld noted the careful phrasing and moved to the next step. He reminded Weir that he had taken into account the DNA results supplied by Cellmark, the FBI, and the California DOJ. Had he also considered the DNA profiling done by the LAPD? "That is omitted from your statement, is it not?" Weir agreed. Now Weir knew that Neufeld understood that he had written his report without all the information he needed.

"And are you aware, sir, that the Los Angeles Police Department conducted DNA profiling in this case?" Neufeld asked.

"I became aware about eight P.M. last night."

Now Peter moved to the error that Thompson discovered last night.

"But this time, sir, unlike the other items on the glove, you chose not to include the frequencies of those pairs of markers, assuming the 1.2 allele wasn't there—isn't that correct?" The 1.2 allele was the masked allele Thompson had pointed out last night.

"I think you found my mistake, Mr. Neufeld." Dr. Weir tried to maintain his unflappability. No matter.

Everyone looked at the witness. Had this highly credentialed expert, who was supposed to confirm the enormous odds against a match for the mixtures of Goldman's and Simpson's blood, made a major error?

Neufeld asked a series of questions: Weir admitted he did not consider all the data. Peter then summed up: "The numbers that are arrived at by you and put on that board are biased against Mr. Simpson, isn't that correct?"

"As it turns out, it looks that way, yes."

Neufeld repeated his point for good measure and moved on.

Carl Douglas could see that the jury understood that Neufeld had just impugned the integrity of the huge numbers the D.A. had been throwing at them. Johnnie was smiling. Disbelievers in DNA now had a basis for their disbelief.

Thompson knew the real problem was that though Weir was a great statistician, he didn't understand the genetic system he was working with.

Weir spent the weekend recalculating his numbers. His original result was that the DNA in the mixed stain would occur once in 3,900 times; the corrected figure was 1 in 1,600 times. His corrected results were still impressive. But now the jury had reason to wonder if the result meant anything at all.

37

WILLIAM G. PAVELIC

TO: Johnnie L. Cochran
          Robert L. Shapiro
          Carl E. Douglas
          F. Lee Bailey
DATE: June 23, 1995

Please be advised that on June 23, 1995, at approximately 1200 hours, I received a phone call from Mr. Tom McCullum [*sic*] who advised me of the following.

In December of 1990 or 1991, Nicole Brown Simpson gave him a pair [two pairs were actually given] of Aris Isotoner gloves as a Christmas present.

Mr. McCullum is in possession of a brown leather Aris Isotoner glove with a cashmere liner and a black Aris Isotoner glove with a fur liner.

Mr. McCullum is a good friend of the Brown family as well as O.J. Simpson and wants to maintain his neutrality.

TELEVISION COVERAGE OF THE TRIAL HAD PROMPTED SEVERAL people to approach the defense with evidence of Fuhrman's racism. Now the coverage brought them Mr. Thomas C. McCollum III. Three days after his phone call to Pavelic, McCollum wrote to the D.A.'s office and sent it one glove from each pair. "I saw the news regarding O.J. wearing gloves similar to the fur lined gloves and the dark-brown snug fitting cashmere lined glove [which] seems to resemble

620

the gloves found at Bundy and Rockingham. . . . The dark-brown ones I received in either 1990 or 1991.''

Nicole had purchased two pairs of the gloves, which matched McCollum's in every detail, at Bloomingdale's on December 18, 1991. The defense couldn't prove that those same gloves became McCollum's Christmas gift, but the circumstances were, as lawyers say, ''highly suggestive.''

The defense team, convinced it was far ahead now, had no immediate use for this information. Cochran and his colleagues felt the prosecution wouldn't introduce the ''McCollum gloves'' in any case.

On Wednesday, June 28, FBI Special Agent Douglas Deedrick, an expert on hair and fiber, testified as the prosecution's final witness. He discussed various hairs and fibers found at the crime scene, on the knit cap, and in the Bronco.

The prosecution hoped to end with compelling testimony, stronger than even the DNA evidence, that would place Simpson at the crime scene. Scheck and company had scored heavily against the blood evidence, and the other side could not rebut until after the defense presented its own DNA witness. Deedrick's trace evidence was easier to explain to the jury, far less exotic and technical. It was also highly visual.

The defense had been worried that Clark would end her case with more domestic violence witnesses. Such an ending would, after all, be dramatic. Had Clark finished by recapping O.J.'s troubled history with Nicole, she would have forced Simpson to testify. So when Carl Douglas got the final list of the D.A.'s witnesses, he sighed in relief. Maybe the D.A. had finally realized this was a murder case, he thought.

''This dog won't hunt,'' Carl said to his colleagues: Domestic violence doesn't prove homicide. There would be no Keith Zlomsowitch to portray O.J. as a stalker and voyeur. No limo driver to describe Simpson hitting Nicole. No witnesses from an incident at Victoria Beach, where he also supposedly hit her. Not even testimony from the victim's mother, Juditha Brown. Maybe Clark had also been listening to the dismissed jurors. Now the only reason for O.J. to take the stand would be to rehabilitate his image.

For the last month, Bailey had been preparing to cross the hair and fiber expert. But after Lee's performance with the FBI shoe expert, O.J. was still furious. Simpson threatened to reassign the Deedrick cross. In the end, Johnnie stayed with Lee. There was no time for someone else to prepare. He assured O.J. that Bailey could handle Deedrick. That settled it.

Bailey knew that Deedrick couldn't be demolished as Fung had been. His best approach was to cast doubt on the value of the evidence itself. Black hairs on the knit cap? They might have been O.J.'s, granted. But they might also have come from any number of other persons.

The defense saw Clark's display boards for the first time just before Deedrick took the stand. The presentation would be illustrated with enlarged photographs of hair and fiber. The defense also hadn't seen Deedrick's notebook. Bailey insisted these were major discovery violations.

Ito agreed but couldn't come up with an appropriate sanction this late in the prosecution case. With that, Ito recessed for the day.

At nine the next morning, Thursday, June 29, Johnnie Cochran was at the podium. The day before, he said, ''we had to ask Your Honor to order Mr. Deedrick, the FBI agent, to turn over his notebook, and we now know why. . . . Contained in that notebook is a five-page single-spaced report which makes the [previous] discovery violations . . . seem like child's play.''

Cochran asked that Ito grant the defense time to review the discovery report and find an appropriate way to address the issues raised. Clark did not object.

After the break Cochran asserted that what had been recorded in Deedrick's papers and withheld from the defense was perhaps the most damaging evidence so far against Simpson. Had the prosecution planned to spring it on the defense in the final hours of its case?

The report in question explained that the beige fibers from

the carpet in Simpson's Bronco were extremely rare. That same rare beige fiber was found at Bundy: a strong indication that someone with access to Simpson's car had been at the murder scene. The beige fiber had also been found on the knit cap at Bundy and with other hairs from Nicole and Ron Goldman on the Rockingham glove. However, the defense also knew that an LAPD criminalist, Susan Brockbank, had admitted that a piece of carpet taken from the Bronco was stored in the same evidence box as the cap and gloves. Bob Blasier now pointed out to Ito that this looked like more cross-contamination.

The withholding of Deedrick's Bronco-fiber report was a deliberate manipulation and an attempt to avoid discovery, Cochran argued. Privately Johnnie was willing to give the prosecutors the benefit of the doubt; the D.A.'s office was dealing with so much material that this report could have been overlooked. Shapiro and Bailey thought the report's absence from discovery material was deliberate. Carl Douglas said the FBI was trying something slick and got caught at it.

Johnnie argued that the judge should exclude Deedrick's testimony or at least forbid the prosecution from using the report or referring to it. The defense knew that Deedrick's information on the rare beige fibers was crucial if Clark was going to show the jury that there was more than blood from Simpson at the crime scene. The fibers from the Bronco carpet had the potential to neutralize Barry Scheck's attack on the blood evidence.

Clark insisted that she only became aware of the report at the same time the defense did. She had never requested that it be prepared. She insisted that the discovery violation was not willful, despite the defense's allegations. If anyone was to be penalized, she said, she herself should be, personally. "Don't penalize the proof of the case," she pleaded.

After reading Deedrick's report, Ito said it was compelling. "It really narrows it down to where the carpet fiber came from."

He then delivered his ruling.

"The prosecution will be precluded from presenting any evidence that is contained in the report." The judge was clearly angry that he had to exclude what was possibly the most damaging evidence against Simpson in the entire trial, but he had little choice. The rules of discovery were clear.

Without question, the prosecution had taken a major blow. The defense saw Ito's decision as the first major ruling in their favor. Chapman knew the carpet-fiber evidence would have been worse than the "1-in-170-million" blood results. She didn't know how the defense could have explained it away. Even Johnnie's optimism would have failed him at that point.

For the next three days Special Agent Deedrick testified without being able to mention the rare fiber. However, he did explain that hair resembling O.J.'s was found inside the knit cap and that hair similar to Nicole's was on the outside. Another hair similar to O.J.'s was discovered on Goldman's shirt. The Rockingham glove carried hairs comparable to Nicole's and Goldman's, in addition to hairs from unidentified third parties.

The defense watched with some misgivings as Bailey approached Deedrick. During Clark's direct, it had seemed once more that he wasn't hearing well—or, worse, wasn't paying attention. On several obvious occasions he again failed to object. When Bailey started his cross he questioned the agent's truthfulness and elicited testimony that, unlike fingerprints, hairs were not unique. This was rudimentary. It was clear to the defense that Bailey lacked a command of the subject. Johnnie was severely disappointed, and Douglas saw that his friend was not as assured as he had been earlier in the trial.

Bailey had now lost both men's support. They agreed it looked as if he hadn't done his homework. Dershowitz, too, thought Bailey was contributing very little to the case these days. And word got back to Carl that Bailey had gone home to Miami the weekend before simply to relax. Hardly the way to prepare for cross-examining the final prosecution witness.

There would be no more witnesses for Lee Bailey. Carl gave him the bad news over lunch. He told Bailey how displeased everyone was about his performance with Deedrick.

38

WHILE DOUGLAS DEEDRICK WAS ON THE STAND, SHAWN Chapman drove to the airport at the beginning of the July 4 weekend to pick up Cris Arguedas, the attorney Scheck recommended to test O.J.'s ability to testify, and Arguedas's partner, Penny Cooper. The visit had been approved by Ito, *ex parte*, under seal. Nobody would know of it, not even the prosecution.

The attorneys' room was opened for the visit. Bob Blasier met the lawyers at the Biltmore Hotel and took them to the jail where O.J. was waiting for them, charming as usual.

Their greetings were cold. They made no small talk, no attempt to ingratiate themselves. Simpson got the message: Say hello and get right to what we're here for. Shawn and Bob Blasier sat and watched.

Cris Arguedas started with questions about Simpson's relationship with Nicole. O.J. replied as usual, relying on his thousand-watt charm. "Mr. Simpson, is there some reason you find this funny?" Arguedas asked. Simpson just smiled again.

"Isn't it true you were married when you met this young girl, isn't that true?" she asked.

"Yeah, but you know, Marquerite and I were kinda, you know, we were kind of . . ." Simpson answered lightly. He smiled, a worldly "Must I really explain this?" smile.

Again the attorney asked, "Do you find it amusing that you were married to someone at that time?"

Simpson couldn't be O.J. with Arguedas and Cooper. His charm was useless. Every time he tried his usual routines they cut him off immediately. When the lawyers got tough,

Simpson got uncomfortable. When they got tougher, Simpson got more entrenched in his usual ploys. Shawn found it horrible.

Simpson's answers weren't inconsistent. He wasn't scrambling his stories or getting caught in lies. It was just that he couldn't put his usual spin on everything. Every light, smiling answer earned him a sharp "Do you find that amusing?" or "Why do you find that funny?" Now he had to explain difficult and awkward matters precisely and in detail, and he couldn't.

Arguedas and Cooper moved to his arguments with Nicole.

"You know, we were just scuffling." His standard opening. By now Shawn could recite his lines herself.

Arguedas asked, "Well, how is it that she had bruises on her?"

"Well, you know, I think that we were in the mud and she fell, oh, she fell down."

"How did she fall down?"

Shawn sat there grimly while O.J. tried to joke his way through every serious subject. She started to hate him. Just plain hate him. She knew anyone else would hate him too. Including, of course, the jury.

Finally Chapman couldn't take any more. She left the room to call Johnnie.

"Baby, you're kidding," he said.

"No, I'm not. It's horrible. Just distasteful," Shawn said.

Later that day, Carl came into Johnnie's office as Shawn was repeating the story. "Oh, shit" were the first words out of Carl's mouth. Let's think about it, Johnnie said, calm as always.

That night, O.J. called Shawn at home. "Who *were* those women that you sent down here today?" He started laughing, and Shawn eventually laughed too.

"So they kicked your ass, didn't they?" Shawn finally said. O.J. agreed. "You know, Marcia would never be like that," he said. O.J. wasn't about to concede that he had failed.

O.J. called Kardashian that night, too, "Come down tomorrow and see how I do," Simpson said. By the end of the conversation, Bob knew O.J. wasn't looking forward to his second day on "the stand."

The next morning, Johnnie was there to see for himself. Kardashian watched as Arguedas and Cooper went after O.J. again. Shawn saw that his "testimony" was no better, no worse, than the day before. Cochran agreed with Shawn's conclusion: horrible. Kardashian had to give his friend an "F." O.J. had failed the Shapiro test, the Cochran test, and now the Scheck test. Douglas knew the defense didn't have time to coach Simpson. Kardashian felt they were ahead and the last thing to do now was to take risks. On that point, Shapiro was right.

Bailey was the only one who still felt Simpson should testify. Ultimately, O.J. would make the decision.

However, Scheck got word from Arguedas that Simpson could be prepared. He could be a good witness if the defense had to put him on—provided he was trained. Cris didn't seem to think the experiment was as big a disaster as Simpson's attorneys did.

Bailey, who was almost out of the case himself, repeated that Simpson had to testify for his future. It had been improper not to prepare O.J. for his test with Arguedas and Cooper. Bring on the coaches. Who better than a professional athlete to understand directed, supervised practice? Bailey kept lobbying for his partners Ken Fischman and Dan Leonard to come out to California and work with O.J. Even if he, Bailey, paid for it. He begged Johnnie.

Johnnie said, Let's wait.

PROSECUTION RESTS CASE IN SIMPSON TRIAL

After five months, 58 witnesses and 10 dismissed jurors, O.J. Simpson's prosecutors today completed their part of a trial that has transfixed the nation with its legal theatrics. . . .

The prosecution built its case on blood and fibers and the mournful wailings of a barking dog but in the end still had no eyewitness, no murder weapon and no definite motive. . . .

Johnnie Cochran Jr. said he planned to call his first witness Monday morning. . . .

—<u>Los Angeles Times,</u> July 7, 1995

Had the prosecution proven its case beyond a reasonable doubt? Was it airtight? Actually, they'd left holes big enough for the defense to walk through. Scheck and his colleagues had gone directly to the heart of the D.A.'s case: the blood evidence. And nobody, Johnnie hoped, could forget Simpson trying to put the glove on.

PART SIX

Don't Spike
the Ball

1

ON SATURDAY MORNING, JULY 8, CARL DOUGLAS WAS reviewing the case alone in his office. He knew Johnnie always saw the glass half full. He preferred to see it half empty. The prosecution had presented more circumstantial evidence against Simpson than Carl had ever seen amassed against a client in his fourteen years as a criminal attorney. As Carl saw it, the prosecutors were so afraid of losing that they overwhelmed the jury with mind-numbing detail and weakened the impact of their case. If you ask them what time it is, Johnnie said, they'll tell you how to make a watch.

That afternoon the defense started a weekend-long meeting to prepare for Monday. All the attorneys were there, plus some of the experts. Dr. Lee was on the speakerphone.

Rosey Grier opened the meeting with a prayer. Johnnie then said that they were in a better position today than he'd ever expected. They should all be elated—but not complacent. Now, could they present their case in four to five weeks? That was Cochran's goal.

Shapiro pointed out that reasonable doubt and lack of motive should be their message from now on. Let's not take risks, he said. Kardashian, however, wanted to go for an acquittal. Take some risk. Attack.

"We can't get an acquittal, because of the Demon," Shapiro replied, referring to the older white woman still glaring at them from Seat 3. Kardashian became more adamant: "If you want a hung jury, Bob, play it safe, but that isn't what we're here for." The conversation slowly turned toward going for a win.

On the speakerphone Simpson repeated that he wanted the jury to know that he wasn't a batterer; he'd never stalked his ex-wife. He was still determined to repair his public image. O.J. wanted to call Marcus Allen, who was alleged to have had an affair with Nicole. Allen would confirm that O.J. was not a jealous husband: After all, he allowed Marcus to be married at Rockingham. But Marcus had recently told O.J. in a phone call he definitely didn't want to testify. Simpson felt abandoned.

The attorneys wanted to forget Allen: a lot of hassle for very little payoff. Do anything to drive him crazy, O.J. said. Just drive Marcus crazy.

Then there was Keith Zlomsowitch. The D.A. had promised to call him, then didn't. Maybe the defense should. He had told the cops that in confronting him and Nicole about making love on the couch, Simpson wasn't really angry; he was more upset about their proximity to his kids.

The vote was unanimous: Close the door forever on domestic violence. Stay with O.J.'s demeanor before and after the murders. Deal with the time line. Let Scheck and his colleagues continue to undermine the blood evidence.

Blasier reported on the disastrous mock cross-examination by Cristina Arguedas and Penny Cooper. O.J. didn't care, he still wanted to testify. When he got off the phone, they all agreed that he would have to be convinced otherwise.

Then the team reviewed the demeanor witnesses: O.J.'s golfing buddies, plus Dr. Christian Reichardt, Faye Resnick's former boyfriend, whom Johnnie especially liked. Reichardt had spoken to Simpson on the phone about an hour before the murders. The people from Los Angeles International Airport and O'Hare and on the planes to and from Chicago were ready to go. The prosecution had avoided all of them. Bailey had all the time-line and "Fuhrman funeral" witnesses in place and checked out.

The next day, Sunday morning, Shapiro, Cochran, Blasier, McKenna, and Kardashian drove over to Rockingham to meet with Simpson's family. His daughter Arnelle, his sisters Carmelita and Shirley, and his mother would be the defense's lead witnesses.

Arnelle would cover events during the week before the murders, until she was awakened by the police early on June 13. Carmelita would follow, and then Johnnie would call Eunice to the witness stand. Wheelchair and all. Eunice Simpson's presence would be powerful. The jury would have to respect her.

The real issue that Sunday morning was how to place Nicole's letter to O.J. on the record. This letter, the one in which she took partial responsibility for their marital problems, had been the defense's ace in the hole ever since Arnelle retrieved it from O.J.'s New York apartment. They wanted to present it without opening the door to Nicole's state of mind. If they opened that can of worms, the D.A. could present evidence on Nicole's fear that O.J. might kill her. The defense wanted to use the letter only to rebut the prosecution's assertions that O.J. had a "motive," "intent," or "plan" to kill Nicole.

The only way the defense could accomplish that would be through a witness to whom O.J. had shown the letter. Simpson couldn't recall if there was such a person. Now Johnnie asked each family member, but nobody remembered it. The defense's last resort was to bring it out if O.J. took the stand.

After lunch the attorneys rejoined the rest of the team at Johnnie's office. They knew the prosecution had photos of O.J. wearing gloves resembling the Aris Isotoners. Tom McCollum, who had received two pairs of Isotoners as a gift from Nicole, was now someone to consider calling. Nicole's purchase of the gloves at Bloomingdale's was only a week before McCollum received them. The lawyers agreed, however, that O.J.'s demonstration with the gloves had said it all. But they still had to be prepared on these peripheral issues. This was no time for complacency.

The next topic was O.J.'s missing blood. The prosecution hadn't called Thano Peratis, the nurse who had drawn the reference sample from O.J. He was too ill to testify, the D.A. said. Pavelic, whom Johnnie had barred from defense meetings after his blunders with Rosa Lopez, had recently learned that Vannatter received Nicole's and Goldman's reference blood from the coroner's criminalist, Gary L. Siglar, around noon on the fourteenth of June, but hadn't booked the blood into the LAPD lab until the next day. It was clear that Vannatter had been carrying not only O.J.'s blood but also both victims' blood samples containing EDTA. Suddenly there was a lot to hang Vannatter with. EDTA had become a critical issue, as Blasier had said it might. The prosecution's own tests had now found EDTA on the swatches from the Bundy back gate and Simpson's sock. The defense allegations that someone had spiked the swatches with reference blood had real substance.

The prosecution, however, hadn't called Roger Martz, the FBI agent who had done the EDTA tests. Obviously they didn't want to advertise they'd found EDTA in the blood swatches. So the defense put Special Agent Martz on their witness list. They also decided to call their own expert, Fredric Rieders, to confirm the FBI's findings.

By Sunday night, witness assignments were given out. Johnnie approved them all; Carl broke the news. The new rule was that nobody could present a witness unless he had personally interviewed him. Nothing could be left to chance.

2

O.J. SIMPSON'S DEFENSE BEGAN ON MONDAY, JULY 10. Shapiro, Cochran, Douglas, Uelmen, Chapman, Blasier, and Kardashian were in court.

Some of the defense team wanted to begin with the time line. Bailey argued to establish immediately that Simpson didn't have time to commit the murders. But Cochran had been adamant that the Simpson family should be their lead witnesses. He was immovable: Female African-American jurors are the heart of our strategy. We'll lead with black women who love O.J. Simpson.

The first defense witness was Arnelle. Cochran thought jurors might sense Simpson speaking through this proud, beautiful young woman. She projected vulnerability, sincerity, and concern for her father. The black women on the jury would connect with that. So the defense hoped.

Cochran's questions were honeyed. Are you the oldest of the Simpson siblings? Arnelle was. Was there anything special about her birth date, December 4, 1968?

"I was born the same day my dad won the Heisman trophy," Arnelle replied with a smile.

Like the rest of the Simpson women, his ex-wife, Marquerite, wore yellow that day. Denice Shakarian Halicki, Kardashian's fiancée, had suggested the color as a show of solidarity that the women in the jury might like.

Then Cochran wanted to show that *all* the black women in Simpson's life supported him. Even Arnelle's mother, Simpson's ex-wife.

"Is she [Marquerite] present in court today?" Cochran asked.

"Yes, she is."

"Is she the lady with the flower on with the yellow?" Cochran asked.

"Yes, she is," Arnelle answered dutifully.

She seemed to be doing very well.

At the defense table, Arnelle's father wasn't pleased. The team had to take the offensive now, he insisted. No more scuttling through holes in the prosecution's line. His team had to march down the field and score.

Simpson wrote nitpicking notes to Johnnie about everything Arnelle said. Why didn't Arnelle say he'd never beaten Nicole? *Why didn't she say that?* Why didn't Arnelle say that Gigi, the housekeeper, sometimes drove the Bronco? Johnnie whispered it wasn't important, but Simpson was upset, shaking his head, making faces.

Kardashian felt that Arnelle was doing exactly what they hoped for. She was sympathetic to her father. Was Dad usually late when limo drivers arrived? It was "an ongoing joke within the family," she said. ". . . He will get dressed in the last fifteen minutes before we would have to leave. He has done this for years."

Her father was extremely busy in 1994 with broadcasting chores, she testified, implying that Simpson had no time for stalking Nicole. He was considerate to Nicole even though they were estranged. He'd gone to Bundy to take her chicken soup when she was sick.

Simpson had been distraught the night after Nicole's death, Arnelle said. "He kept talking to the TV, saying, 'I can't believe this.'" She'd never seen him so upset. Cochran moved on to evidence issues—the police had found fibers at the crime scene which might be from a dark blue jogging suit. But, said Arnelle, her dad didn't own a dark blue or black sweat suit.

Then Cochran came to Ron Shipp, with whom the prosecution had begun its case some five months ago. He had testified that he was alone with O.J. in his bedroom the night after the murders, and that Simpson had told him about dreams of killing Nicole. The defense had to destroy Ron Shipp's credibility without putting Simpson on the stand. The testimony of family members present that night might be even more effective than Simpson's.

Under Carl Douglas's cross, Shipp had admitted to having a drinking problem. Now Arnelle said that she saw Shipp drinking beer at the Rockingham bar the night of June 13.

"Did you ever see Mr. Shipp that evening when he didn't have a beer with him?" Cochran asked.

"I can't say."

When it came time for cross-examination, Marcia Clark took the same approach Shapiro had used with Denise Brown: Get in and out fast; don't get rough with a sympathetic witness. Clark knew that Arnelle wasn't home the night of the murders and couldn't attest to her father's whereabouts. Clark stuck to issues that could not be challenged in redirect.

"And you did not see Mr. Simpson between ten and eleven o'clock at night on June the twelfth; is that correct?"

"Yes," Arnelle answered.

Point made. Simpson had time to commit the murders.

Next on the stand was Carmelita Simpson Durio, Simpson's youngest sister. Bob Shapiro's job in examining her was to discredit Ron Shipp's testimony. Shipp drank beer at Rockingham, she told Shapiro, "from the time I was there until the time I left."

More important, Shipp was in Simpson's bedroom for only "a couple of minutes," Carmelita said. He was never alone with O.J. Shirley Baker, Simpson's other sister, and her husband, Benny, had also been in the bedroom all the time.

On cross, Chris Darden evened things up a little. After Carmelita said Shipp had "glassy" eyes and was "muttering to himself," Darden asked if she had any idea what his face looked like when he cried. She didn't. Did she know if he was crying out of grief for Nicole that evening? She didn't know. Sitting in the family room most of the evening, could she see everyone who went upstairs to Simpson's bedroom? She admitted she couldn't.

Johnnie then called Eunice Simpson. She was sitting in her wheelchair in the front row. The entire courtroom turned toward her.

Bob Blasier had planned to escort her to the stand, but Carl Douglas felt that would look wrong. He got up and offered his arm to Mrs. Simpson. She rose from the wheelchair, leaning heavily on Douglas, and walked slowly past the prosecution table, past the jury, and onto the stand. Douglas had to help her into the witness chair. Every step of her painful progress was caught by the TV camera.

Eunice Simpson projected extraordinary dignity. Johnnie had known ever since their June strategy meeting that she would be perfect. The thin, elderly woman suffered from rheumatoid arthritis, a crippling condition affecting her entire body. Rheumatoid arthritis is a far more drastic illness than osteoarthritis, which usually stiffens only a few joints. Mrs. Simpson had been in court often, her wheelchair always parked in the aisle by the family's seats.

Johnnie was theatrically gentle. He let Eunice explain to the court that she'd raised her four children mostly alone, working nights for twenty-eight years as an attendant in San Francisco General Hospital's psychiatric ward. She'd asked for the night shift so she could be with her children during the day.

"We were gripping each other," she said when Cochran asked how she'd spent the time with her son that night at Rockingham after the murders. Mrs. Simpson said O.J. had held her hand all evening until he went to bed.

Cochran worked his way slowly to Ron Shipp.

He asked for her impressions of the ex-cop. "He appeared to be spaced," Eunice Simpson explained.

"What was that word again?" Johnnie asked. " 'Spaced,' did you say?"

"I would say spaced."

"What do you mean?"

"He didn't appear natural," she replied.

Not only was he "spaced" that night, the elderly woman said, but she'd seen the same demeanor during earlier visits. "He always appeared to be kind of starry," she said.

Carl Douglas was smiling. He and Johnnie wanted the female jurors to see conflict between Ron Shipp and Eunice Simpson. If this impeccably respectable matriarch doubted Shipp, they would, too. He knew the prosecutors wouldn't dare attack her on this point.

Johnnie closed by having Eunice mention that O.J. had rheumatoid arthritis "most of all" in her family.

Chris Darden rose. "Your Honor," he said, "we have no questions for Mrs. Simpson."

The defense had moved fast, finishing its first three witnesses by mid-afternoon. Shirley Baker was scheduled for the next day. She'd say that she and Benny spent the entire night in O.J.'s bedroom and heard no conversation between Shipp and Simpson about dreams.

Speed was a major element in the defense strategy. Get

the witnesses in fast, fully prepped. Don't allow anything on the record for the prosecution to attack. If we don't open the door, the D.A. can't walk in. Then get the witnesses out fast. Let the jury feel that things are finally moving. Maybe Shapiro had been right after all.

Johnnie wanted to complete the entire defense case in four to five weeks. Scheck said six to seven. More important, Cochran was once again at the helm, reestablishing contact with the jurors. The first day he presented the jury four black witnesses. Through the five months of the prosecution case, they had seen only five African-Americans on the stand.

Just before lunch, Lee Bailey cornered Carl Douglas. "I don't feel a part of things," he complained. "I've got no witnesses."

Every attorney wanted more witnesses. Shapiro was always extremely polite, rarely nagged. Douglas respected him for that. The daily exchanges with Bailey were becoming more difficult; he wasn't unpleasant about it, but accepting defeat was not his nature. Now he pushed hard and often. Douglas tolerated it out of respect for the man's legend. But since the fiasco with Bodziak, the FBI shoe expert, Simpson had been adamant: Cut Bailey off! "I understand how you feel, but it's not me," Douglas answered now. "Johnnie makes policy on this."

"Carl, I know better than that," Bailey countered. "Perhaps I should return to Florida. My place may be at home."

Carl found it hard to be tough with Bailey. After all, he liked him. He told Bailey he'd ask Johnnie to give Lee one more witness.

The next witness for the defense was songwriter Carol Conner, wearing a vest that looked like a piano keyboard. After her, interior decorator Mary Collins would testify. Johnnie Cochran hoped these two women would establish Simpson and Paula Barbieri as passionate lovers. O.J. had moved on; he had no reason to harbor jealous rage at his ex-wife.

Conner had watched Simpson tenderly stroke Barbieri's

face at a $25,000-a-plate black-tie charity dinner the night before Nicole was murdered.

Mary Collins, in turn, told of coming to Rockingham to give Simpson and Barbieri an estimate on redecorating his bedroom. Paula was moving in. O.J. gave Collins a deposit. The prosecution treated both witnesses gently. Their one-note testimony offered little for cross-examination.

By this time, the defense knew that Paula had called Simpson's cellular phone to break up with him the day Nicole died. She'd left a strong message on his voice mail, but the cops, not knowing this, never questioned Simpson or Barbieri about the call.

Simpson's phone bill showed that he'd called former Raider cheerleader Gretchen Stockdale that same afternoon. He'd left a message that he was "totally, unattached with everybody. Ha haaaa!" The D.A. knew about the call to Stockdale, but seemed less interested in Barbieri's call. In actuality, O.J. Simpson had no romantic life on the night Nicole was murdered. As far as their friends knew, Barbieri and Simpson hadn't split. Now Barbieri seemed to be protecting O.J., visiting him often. Whatever their current relationship, she was unlikely to testify.

On Tuesday morning at 7:30, Bailey phoned Kardashian.

Carl had assigned him the American Airlines pilot, Wayne Stanfield, a demeanor witness—*if* O.J. agreed. Stanfield, who had asked for Simpson's autograph en route to Chicago, was scheduled to testify the next day, July 12. But Simpson still had to give Carl or Johnnie the word.

The previous evening, Bailey had practically begged Bob to speak to Simpson, but O.J. hadn't called Kardashian that night. Now Bailey was upset. Bob was wary. He said he'd talk to Simpson before noon. An hour later, while riding to court with Shapiro and Cochran, he brought up Bailey's request. No more witnesses for Bailey, they all agreed.

When Kardashian reached the door of the holding cell he asked the deputy, "Anybody back there?"

"Lee Bailey."

Bailey was making his case that he should examine the

airline pilot. He also wanted his Boston partner, Ken Fischman, to fly in and start prepping Simpson to testify. Bailey insisted that *he'd* pay Fischman's expenses. When Bailey left, Simpson just shook his head.

"Make sure Fischman doesn't come out," O.J. said. "I've got enough attorneys." But he agreed that Bailey could have the pilot.

3

THE DEFENSE ATTORNEYS WOULD NOW PRESENT *their* time line. McKenna and Bailey had done a good job of finding witnesses to bolster the defense theory that the murders took place after 10:30 P.M.

If Nicole and Ron had been killed around 10:15, as prosecutors insisted, the defense's first two time-line witnesses, Danny Mandel and Ellen Aaronson, should have seen Nicole's body through the open gate, just as Sukru Boztepe and his wife did two hours later.

Danny Mandel had taken Ellen Aaronson to Mezzaluna for dinner on a blind date. They never socialized again, but both of them related to Pat McKenna the same story. They walked right past Nicole's gate at about 10:25 P.M. the night of June 12. Photos of the crime scene showed Nicole's body only fifteen feet from the sidewalk. A decorative outdoor light shined on her corpse. If the crimes had been committed by 10:15 P.M., Mandel and Aaronson should have seen the body or been confronted by the howling Akita. More important, there should have been bloody paw prints on the sidewalk by then.

The defense knew the prosecutors would argue that

Mandel and Aaronson hadn't been there. Early police reports indicated that the two first thought they'd taken a different route home, then changed their minds. Douglas expected Marcia Clark to attack these witnesses, whose testimony raised solid reasonable doubt.

"Is there any question that you walked by that area?" Bob Shapiro asked Mandel.

"No."

"When you walked by that area, did you notice anything unusual?"

Mandel said no. Did he hear anything unusual? He didn't. Did he hear a barking dog? No.

Shapiro put up a picture of the bloody crime scene. Did Mandel see any blood?

"No, I did not."

"Did you see the shape or silhouette of the body of a person when you walked by?" Shapiro asked.

"No, I did not."

"How can you relate what time it was?" Shapiro asked.

Mandel said he glanced at his watch as they approached Aaronson's apartment a few minutes later. It was close to 10:30 P.M.

Marcia Clark seemed furious as she listened to Mandel. She began her cross with an attack.

"Now, Mr. Mandel, your first statement, actually your first belief, was that you were at the location of 875 South Bundy at about eleven o'clock, correct?"

Mandel denied it. Clark asked if Aaronson had made this statement. He didn't know.

"And initially when you spoke to the police," Clark continued, "you believed that you had walked back from the Mezzaluna by a different route than you have explained to us today, correct?"

Mandel denied it.

Clark held him to his first impression. He'd changed his mind, hadn't he, to get fifteen minutes of fame? Mandel denied it.

* * *

"Bob, you have to stop this," Johnnie whispered to Shapiro. "Object more! She's badgering the witness."

Shapiro refused. *Marcia* looks silly, he argued. The jurors see it. I'm letting it go on.

"You have to protect the witness," Cochran insisted.

Actually, Danny Mandel appeared unruffled by Clark's badgering. But Cochran didn't like it. However the witness reacts, you don't let the other side get away with badgering him. Shapiro ignored Cochran.

Then court recessed. In the holding cell, Shapiro and Cochran came close to shouting. The start of the defense case had raised the tension level markedly. Simpson, too, was enraged by Shapiro's passivity: "Wait until it's Johnnie's turn!" he bellowed at the lawyer. "Marcia can't be hassling our witnesses. Johnnie will show you how it should be done."

The tension continued through the end of Mandel's testimony and spilled into the lunch hour. Kardashian had never before seen the team members so on edge. Simpson was screaming at Shapiro over trivia, irate that he hadn't thanked Mandel for his testimony.

In the afternoon, Clark attacked Ellen Aaronson, implying that she, too, had changed her story to gain notoriety. But Aaronson held firm and confirmed Mandel's account.

Francesca Harman and Denise Pilnak, the next two witnesses, didn't fare as well under cross-examination. Harman told Shapiro in direct that after leaving a dinner party on nearby Dorothy Street she drove past the Bundy gate at 10:20 P.M. She saw and heard nothing: no bodies, no blood, no barking dog. On cross-examination Chris Darden made Harman admit that her window was open a crack and she had been listening to the radio, which would have prevented her from hearing the dog. She said she was watching the road, not the sidewalk.

Then Denise Pilnak opened a floodgate of trouble for the defense. Living on Bundy, Pilnak testified that long before she heard barking she looked at a household clock and saw it was 10:18 P.M.

"And are you sure it was that time?" Johnnie Cochran asked.

"I am a stickler for time," Pilnak answered proudly. "I don't go anywhere without two watches when it's important."

She pulled up her left sleeve and displayed a gold dress watch and a plastic digital model.

But under Clark's blistering cross, Denise Pilnak crumbled. Clark suggested she was working from a "script." She confronted the witness with interviews she'd given to police and reporters saying she heard the barking nearer to midnight. She asked what time Pilnak arrived at court today. Pilnak smiled sheepishly at the jury when she couldn't remember. Clark bore down and repeatedly suggested she was another wannabe.

With only an hour left before adjournment, Robert Heidstra, perhaps the most important time-line witness for the defense, was sworn in. His face showed years of a hard life.

Kardashian thought of Rosa Lopez, who had faltered so badly in her videotaped courtroom interrogation. Like Lopez, Heidstra was poorly dressed and appeared uncomfortable in court. He waxed and cleaned luxury cars for a living. Called detailing, this process was a necessity for L.A.'s status-car set.

Johnnie Cochran liked Heidstra. Working-class jurors, Johnnie said endlessly, understood witnesses like Heidstra, his life, his problems. They'd listen to him.

Mandel and Aaronson had set up one end of the defense time line. Now Heidstra would establish the other. He had to be believable.

At 10:35 P.M., as he walked his two dogs in an alley across the street from Bundy, Heidstra heard the Akita bark. Then, at 10:40, he heard voices from Nicole's yard yelling, "Hey, hey, hey!" Mandel and Aaronson had seen and heard nothing unusual when they walked by the Bundy gate at 10:25. If Heidstra was right, the murders commenced ten minutes later. The limousine driver, Allan Park, spotted Simpson at Rockingham at 10:55. Heidstra's testimony would establish that it was almost impossible for Simpson to commit the double murders.

The defense knew that prosecutors had told Heidstra he'd be a key witness. They'd even sent him a letter saying how valuable he was. Then they dropped him without explanation. He felt abandoned, angry at the prosecution. Johnnie could exploit that.

But Heidstra's testimony also raised serious problems for the defense. He said he'd seen a "white wagon car" leave the murder scene. Sometimes he called it "Jeep-like." A white Bronco? It might be a Chevy Blazer, he'd said.

"Whatever you do," McKenna and Bailey kept telling Heidstra, "don't call it a Bronco." But they decided to take the risk of using him.

Heidstra's testimony today was brief. He had two old, slow-moving dogs, a collie and a Hungarian sheepdog. Most evenings he walked them at 10. On the night of the murders, he'd started late, around 10:15. Walking on Gorham toward Bundy, he heard the Akita barking wildly at 10:35. From his nightly walks, he knew the dog and the condo where it lived.

Instead of continuing south down Bundy, Heidstra said, he turned around, worried that the Akita would attack, and went into an alley parallel to Bundy. The Akita continued barking. A neighbor's dog began to bark as well.

"And at that point you are in the alley," Cochran said, "and it is ten-forty on June 12, 1994. What happens next?"

"I was listening to the dogs and all of a sudden I heard two voices," Heidstra answered. "The first one I heard was a clear male young adult voice that said, 'Hey, hey, hey!'"

What then? Cochran asked.

"I heard another voice . . . talking back to him, to the person who said, 'Hey, hey, hey!'"

But Heidstra couldn't hear what the other man said over the barking dogs. The argument lasted about fifteen seconds, he guessed.

"Then I heard a gate slamming . . . around ten-forty, I would say," he continued. He "recognized the gate immediately . . . where the Akita is behind all the time."

Then he walked down the alley toward Dorothy and turned northeast toward his apartment. Arriving home, he stayed outside a moment; he still heard barking. He learned about the murders the next morning on the radio.

Darden just stared at Heidstra as court ended for day. Tomorrow he would cross-examine.

That night, when Denise Pilnak returned to her apartment, her telephone answering machine held twenty-eight death threats. Over the next few days she called McKenna and Carl Douglas eight times to complain that her life had been turned upside down.

When McKenna called Kardashian about Pilnak's problems, Bob thought of his own. He'd endured hate mail and death threats since the beginning. Hardly a day passed without a public confrontation of some kind. "Guilty!" people muttered at him in supermarkets and restaurants. "You have blood on your hands!" strangers shouted on the street.

The letters and phone calls that reached him at home were the worst.

"If that nigger walks," one letter said, "you die!"

"We know where your children live," a late-night caller growled. "We know where your children go to school."

"Watch your rearview mirror," Kardashian told his oldest daughter, Kourtney. "Be careful how you drive. Don't come home late at night."

On Wednesday morning, July 12, Johnnie did preemptive damage control concerning the "wagon car" Heidstra was about to describe. First, he wanted to establish that on Memorial Day Heidstra had been visited by Darden and two other men from the D.A.'s office.

"How were you treated by Mr. Darden and these men who came out to see you?"

"Pretty cruel."

Darden began objecting angrily.

"Did the subject of where you came from ever come up?"

Darden objected again. Tension was rising between the

two lawyers. Cochran asked for a sidebar. Darden had asked Heidstra what he was doing in America, Cochran told the judge, and Darden suggested he should return to France. Chris Darden angrily denied this. He insisted that he'd asked Heidstra when was "the last time he'd been home."

"I'm extremely disappointed, Your Honor, in Mr. Cochran, that he would resort to this type of character assassination of myself," Darden added in muted fury. ". . . This is low. . . . Mr. Cochran is desperate. None of this happened."

Ito agreed and told Cochran to try other questions. But a fight between Cochran and Darden was brewing.

Before jurors Johnnie asked whether Heidstra saw a "vehicle" that night. Yes, Heidstra had seen something.

"I saw from the west side of Dorothy, the side of Nicole's condo, a white car came out of the darkness into the light. . . ."

The car stopped at Dorothy and Bundy and turned south, Heidstra said. Simpson's Rockingham estate was north.

Carl Douglas had misgivings about this "wagon car." Douglas felt that a smart guy with an urgent need to get rid of a knife and bloody clothing might very well drive south a few blocks to find a dumpster. Cops might not search in that direction, and O.J. would still have time to get back to Rockingham by 10:55 P.M.

Could Heidstra describe the car?

"It appeared to be a wagon car, Jeep-like car."

". . . To you it appeared to be light in color?"

"Could be Blazer or Jeep Cherokee," Heidstra answered.

Johnnie ended his direct examination minutes later. Darden was ready. You could see it in his eyes.

"When you talked to the police initially," Darden began, "you told them that you thought the vehicle might be a Blazer, is that correct?"

Heidstra agreed.

"You also said that it resembled a Ford," Darden said. "Is that correct?"

"I don't recall that."

"Well, did you tell the police that the vehicle resembled a Ford Bronco?" Darden said, raising his voice.

"Never." Heidstra was adamant.

Darden reminded Heidstra of an interview he gave the local CBS station. "Did you tell the reporter that the vehicle looked like a Ford Bronco?"

Heidstra said he didn't recall the interview. Darden pressed hard. "I don't recall," Heidstra said in exasperation. "I don't recall. *I don't recall!*" Darden asked if he knew a woman named Patricia Baret, who worked in his veterinarian's office. "Did you tell Patricia that the vehicle looked like a Ford Bronco?"

Heidstra paused, shaken. ". . . Might have said maybe a Bronco. I don't recall that."

Carl Douglas squirmed. Whatever you do, they'd told him, *don't say it was a Bronco.* So what's happening? The first time this guy is asked, he says it's *like* a Bronco.

Darden then asked about the voices Heidstra heard. "Hey, hey, hey!" was spoken by what sounded like a young voice? Heidstra agreed.

"When you heard that voice, you thought that was the voice of a young white male, didn't you?" Darden asked.

Johnnie objected. He knew where this was going. "How can he tell if it was a white male?" Cochran demanded.

Ito told Cochran to sit down.

Hadn't Heidstra said that to a D.A.'s investigator? Darden asked. Heidstra denied it.

"And that second voice sounded deeper than the first voice, didn't it?" Darden said. Heidstra agreed.

Darden asked Heidstra if the second voice was "older." Cochran objected again.

"The second voice that you heard sounded like the voice of a black man, is that correct?" the prosecutor asked.

Johnnie leaped to his feet. "Objected to, Your Honor, I object!"

"Sustained, sustained," Ito barked.

"Of course not!" Heidstra cut in, ignoring Ito.

Ito stopped the proceedings. He ordered the jury out of the courtroom, then Heidstra.

Ito asked Darden to explain himself. Darden said that the veterinarian's assistant told the D.A.'s investigators that Heidstra bragged he'd heard "the very angry screaming of an older man who sounded black."

"I resent that statement," Cochran snapped. "You can't tell by somebody's voice whether they sounded black. . . . That is a racist statement."

The entire courtroom could see the fury in Darden's eyes. Johnnie had pushed the prosecutor's deepest button again.

". . . And I think it is totally improper in America at this time in 1995 we have to hear this and endure this," Cochran concluded.

Barely suppressing his fury, Darden tried to explain that identifying a murderer was the issue. If the statement was racist, it was Heidstra's statement. Darden himself had never said such a thing. "But that is what *you* are suggesting." Darden was on the verge of losing his temper completely.

"I didn't say that," Cochran insisted.

"That is what has created a lot of problems for myself and my family," Darden continued. Now he was out of control. "Statements that you make about me and race, Mr. Cochran!"

"Wait, wait, *wait*," Ito interrupted. "I'm going to take a recess right now because I am so mad at both of you guys I'm about to hold both of you in contempt." He called a fifteen-minute break so everyone could cool off.

Carl Douglas was deeply uncomfortable. He pulled Cochran aside. "If you said that to rattle Darden, it was brilliant," Douglas told his boss. "If you said it because you believe it, I disagree."

Cochran brushed him off. Douglas refused to drop the matter.

"It was both," the older lawyer insisted. "Of course I wanted to rattle him. But I also think it was racist to say that about how a voice sounds."

"Johnnie, that's bullshit," Douglas retorted.

Who better qualified than Carl to pass that judgment? He'd enjoyed watching Johnnie needle the opposition many times. It was a normal courtroom game. The prosecution certainly indulged: Marcia was always trying to steamroller them. Darden trash-talked heavily.

But Darden's complaint that the taunting was hurting his family had stopped Carl cold. With the TV camera watching and the stakes impossibly high, his boss had forgotten there was life outside this trial. Chris Darden was part of *their* community. They'd crossed a line. Darden's protest came from a deeper level than they'd ever expected.

During the break, Cochran, Shapiro, and Kardashian went to the holding cell with Simpson to read Patricia Baret's statement. " 'I know it was O.J.,' " she said Heidstra told her. " 'It had to be him.' " Bad news for the defense lawyers. They assumed the prosecution would call Baret during their rebuttal phase. As it turned out, the D.A. never did call her, but the prospect now drove the tension level higher.

Suddenly Shapiro started screaming at Simpson. The two men stood toe to toe.

"Why are you allowing Lee Bailey to do the pilot?" Shapiro demanded. "He stole all my files and took them to Florida while I was in Hawaii." Shapiro's voice rose even higher. "He got his employees into it. He's a snake. He's responsible for all the press leaks. I don't want him involved in the case anymore."

Kardashian worried that they could be heard in the courtroom.

"If you listen to Lee," Shapiro shouted, "he's the one who can turn this into a guilty verdict! Why are you letting him do the pilot when Johnnie and I are getting along so well now?"

Johnnie just listened, didn't say a word.

This thing is killing all of us, Kardashian decided.

4

ON THE AFTERNOON OF WEDNESDAY, JULY 12, F. LEE
Bailey sat at the defense table, waiting for the next witness to
be sworn in. As for tomorrow's headlines, Darden and
Cochran had locked them up. Bailey's job today was simple.

American Airlines captain Wayne Stanfield had stepped
out of his cockpit during the Los Angeles–Chicago run in
the predawn hours of June 13, 1994, carrying his personal
flight log. He wanted O.J. Simpson's autograph.

Bailey had to get on the record that Stanfield saw no cuts
on Simpson's hands. He'd already told the defense that
Simpson was friendly and certainly didn't act like a killer.
Cover those points, thank the witness, and sit down: That
was all Bailey had to do.

Bailey got through the demeanor material with no problem. Simpson had signed the log and added, ''Peace to
you.''

But then Bailey went off track. He himself flew planes,
had even written a book on the subject. He couldn't resist
showing off. He asked Stanfield to look at a screen projection of the page in the captain's log Simpson signed and
started asking about the technical information also visible.

The aircraft was an MD-80, number 215, departure Zulu
time 0645, actual takeoff 0656, Stanfield explained.

''When you say 'Zulu time,''' Bailey asked, ''would you
translate that for the members of the jury?''

It meant Greenwich Mean Time, the international standard, Stanfield answered. Bailey asked for a translation from
Greenwich time to Los Angeles time, then to Chicago time
for the landing.

Johnnie waved Bailey over.

"Zulu time! What the fuck are you doing?" he hissed.

Bailey started to explain. He had a reason. Count on it, he *always* had a reason.

Johnnie interrupted. "The jury doesn't understand anything you're saying," he whispered angrily.

Simpson watched, even more upset than Cochran.

Clearly finishing up, Bailey started to ask whether Stanfield mentioned the meeting to his copilot after returning to the cockpit.

This time, Cochran ran over to him.

"The whole reason we called this witness," Johnnie whispered, "was so he could say he saw no cuts on O.J.'s hands."

Bailey started to explain.

"You didn't ask him the most important question in this case!" Cochran said. "Ask it now!"

Bailey turned to Stanfield. Had the pilot noticed bandages or injuries on Simpson's hands? Anything unusual at all?

"My only observation is that he has a much larger hand than I would have expected," Stanfield answered, "but nothing as far as cuts or anything."

Bailey ended the interrogation.

After Darden finished a short cross, Bailey left the courtroom quietly. Everyone at the table was stunned. A simple, straightforward chore—and he had almost blown it. Bailey didn't know it, but Carl knew Cochran's original decision was back in force: This was his last witness.

That same day, Pat McKenna checks a stack of phone messages that Johnnie's receptionist, Jan Thomas, has taken over the last three days. Some are bizarre. McKenna handles the anonymous ones first. Most of them are from crooks out to hustle the defense for one thing or another, he assumes. He finds one from San Francisco, not anonymous; he gives the guy a code name, "Brian," and calls him back.

"Brian" says he's a film producer. Won't give his real name. He has something about a woman named Laura, who's written a screenplay. He's rejecting it—but, more important, it's based on some tapes with a cop called Fuhrman. The producer tells McKenna he's seen partial transcripts. "You should listen to them. They'd be very relevant to your case." Laura lives in one of the Carolinas, maybe North Carolina, he says, and gives Pat her number. McKenna thinks, Could Fuhrman have been taped using the "N-word?" Is it possible? Come on! He doubts it, but calls Laura anyway.

"I'm begging you, please don't hang up on me," McKenna begins. He's said this maybe two hundred times so far in this case. "I believe in my heart of hearts that O.J.'s innocent. We really need to hear those tapes."

The woman won't give her last name. She directs McKenna to her lawyer, right here in Century City.

When McKenna hears the lawyer's name, he decides to play his "Jewish card." Minutes later he's on the phone with Matthew Schwartz, Esq., and telling him about Fuhrman— the swastika story, the racial epithets. Schwartz is a bit shaken.

"If you get those tapes to me, I'll make sure you're protected," McKenna promises. "I served with the Ninth Marines in Vietnam. I'm not afraid of anything." The attorney says he's going out of town but will be back on Tuesday, July 18.

What Pat McKenna doesn't know is that Bill Pavelic has heard rumors from his cop friends that Fuhrman has done interviews for a book. Quite some time back, years ago. Bill couldn't get anything more; the lead was dead. Then, around the first of July, Bob Shapiro's assistant, Bonnie Barron, got a call for Shapiro from Stephen Heiser in San Francisco. Heiser was a disbarred attorney who'd given Pavelic information on Faye Resnick's former fiancé fleeing the country, plus material on killings and drugs during the time Resnick lived in the Bay area. When Pavelic called back, Heiser told him about tapes of Mark Fuhrman on which he used the word "nigger" repeatedly, talked about beating blacks, talked about *framing* blacks. Pavelic thought it was too good to be true.

"How do you know they're authentic?" he asked.

"I know they're authentic because one of the tabloid TV shows is already negotiating with a lawyer who represents the writer."

Pavelic set up a sting operation on the spot: "Tell them I'm willing to pay three hundred thousand for the tapes. I want to flush out the attorney. Put it out through the grapevine," he told Heiser. "Don't say who your source is."

Three days later, just around the time "Brian" and McKenna talk, Matthew Schwartz takes Pavelic's bait. Pavelic gets his phone number and address. Pavelic then calls Carl Douglas's secretary, tells her he wants to subpoena some tapes, and gives her the bare-bones information. Cathy Randa's son, Gary, gets the job of serving the subpoena on Schwartz. The young man who answers the door tells Randa, "Mr. Schwartz is on vacation." The young man is actually Schwartz.

At the same time, Pat McKenna goes to Carl Douglas. "I can't tell anyone about this. I can't even tell Bailey, and if he knows I'm not telling him he'll kick my ass." McKenna explains his conversations with "Brian," Laura, and Schwartz. "Bullshit. Not true," Douglas says immediately. But the next day he and McKenna tell Johnnie. Cochran sends a letter to Schwartz and tells Shapiro.

McKenna can't hold out any longer; he calls Bailey. Bailey wants in, of course, but when he calls Schwartz, Schwartz says he's already received a letter from Cochran and will meet with Shapiro and Cochran on July 18.

On Wednesday, July 12, the defense continued presenting demeanor witnesses. Arriving at the L.A. airport on the night of the murders, Simpson's limousine pulled up next to a van belonging to couriers Michael Norris and Mike Gladden, blocking them in. They were annoyed until Simpson stepped out.

Norris called out, "Hey, what's up, O.J.?"

"Hey, what's happening?" Simpson answered.

In prep sessions, Norris told the team he'd seen the athlete stuff something into his golf bag. That had to be the "dark knapsack" prosecutors thought suspicious. Norris was fuzzy about details concerning the small bag. Cochran settled for letting the jury see that his client didn't act like someone who had just committed two gruesome murders.

Next, Mike Gladden took the stand. He confirmed Norris's story, adding small details. The next day Darden would cross-examine him.

On Thursday, July 13, Ito started the morning by denying several defense motions. They couldn't call the D.A.s who prepped Mark Fuhrman for his appearance on the stand. They couldn't present the travel agent who heard Simpson, in Chicago, complain about cutting his finger. That testimony would be hearsay and thus inadmissible. They couldn't ask Faye Resnick's ex-boyfriend Christian Reichardt about her cocaine addiction to introduce the "drug-killing" theories.

Though Chris Darden rose slowly to cross Gladden after the rulings, he was clearly impatient. "This was the first time you had ever been face to face with the defendant?" The courier agreed. "So you really can't tell us, then, how he normally behaves?"

Douglas thought Darden would try to bludgeon Gladden. Plainly, the prosecutors knew they were about to lose the biggest case of their careers. They are pissed, Douglas said to himself; we're kicking their asses. As a federal public defender, he'd never once met a prosecutor who lost gracefully. Now, the atmosphere in court had changed. There was none of the semi-sincere camaraderie everyone had been at pains to display back in February. The opposing attorneys hardly spoke to one another now. Even the trash talk had slowed down. No more of this search-for-truth bullshit. Clark and Darden were down to the basics: Attack, attack, and then attack again.

Simpson knew the game his team was playing. But as team owner he reminded them, "Don't anyone get cocky." He had said it all the way back when Barry Scheck destroyed Dennis Fung in April. "I played football for twelve years, and I never spiked the ball after a touchdown," he told them. "I just handed it to the ref, or I dropped it. Don't you guys get cocky." It was an almost constant refrain.

655

Wise words, Douglas thought. A wounded dog is the most dangerous dog, completely unpredictable. Letting down your guard could be fatal.

The defense wound up its demeanor phase. Howard Bingham, a noted photographer, and Steve Valerie, a business-school student, had both been on the plane to Chicago with Simpson. He was calm and relaxed, they said. Hertz rep Jim Merrill, who met Simpson at the Chicago airport, testified that he seemed relaxed on arrival. Dave Kilduff, the Hertz VP who drove Simpson back to the airport a few hours later, told jurors how distraught O.J. was. Mark Partridge, a lawyer who sat next to Simpson on the flight back to Los Angeles, said the athlete was grief-stricken during the flight, but somehow able to sign autographs.

On Friday morning, July 14, orthopedic surgeon Robert Huizenga was sworn in. A Harvard Medical School graduate, he had served as the Los Angeles Raiders' team doctor. Now he practiced medicine at UCLA. Shapiro had hired him to examine Simpson two days after the murders.

Cochran and Shapiro agreed on Huizenga's testimony: The doctor would tell the jury that Simpson's arthritis kept him from moving well. Further, he had found no cuts and bruises during that examination, except small cuts on Simpson's fingers. In a few weeks, Henry Lee would testify that in his expert opinion, a murderous fight with Ron Goldman in the tiny Bundy yard should have left the killer badly bruised and cut. The jurors, particularly the ladies, would like Huizenga, Johnnie decided.

Huizenga began well. Shapiro first raised issues he assumed the prosecutors would highlight. Was Simpson strong? Yes, but not unusually so. Could he hold a knife? Yes. Shapiro then put the exam photos up on the screen. Simpson was in his underwear.

"This appears to me as a layperson to be a man in pretty good shape," Shapiro said. "Would that be your evaluation?"

The doctor, smiling and at ease, explained that some people present a fit appearance without being so.

"Although he looked like Tarzan," the doctor continued, "he was walking more like Tarzan's grandfather."

The courtroom enjoyed this. Douglas noticed that several normally deadpan jurors smiled, even the Demon.

With less than an hour before the weekend recess, Brian Kelberg started cross-examining Dr. Huizenga. Everyone at the defense table relaxed. Kelberg was known to put the jury to sleep.

But suddenly Kelberg was scoring points. The doctor admitted he'd seen no evidence of any serious disability that would limit movement. No "acute" flare-ups of rheumatoid arthritis or osteoarthritis. No orthopedic symptoms. The litany of negative findings went on.

"Doctor, was there *any* finding," Kelberg finally asked, ". . . which in your opinion would have prevented him from murdering two human beings using a single-edged knife on June twelfth of 1994?"

"No, there was not," Huizenga answered.

Kelberg had a nice closer for the weekend. Everybody knew it.

5

On Saturday, July 15, the defense gathers again in Johnnie's conference room. Cochran begins by announcing that he's told the prosecution the defense will be done by August 11. He tells the team he really wants to be finished on the fourth.

Carl Douglas informs the group that Thano Peratis, the nurse who took O.J.'s blood sample, cannot be called as a witness. He's had a heart attack and is still in the hospital. That's not really bad. Now they can introduce his testimony from the preliminary hearing and before the grand jury to establish the amount of blood drawn from Simpson. Johnnie says he's been told privately that the D.A. might do a videotaped interview with Peratis. Let them do their end run around us, Cochran says; then we can tell the court we weren't invited to ask our questions. Everyone likes that.

The next topic is the continuing testimony of Dr. Robert Huizenga. Shapiro wants to make sure the doctor dispels the notion that O.J. is still a consummate athlete. "The truth is that he'd come in last in a hundred-yard dash," Shapiro says.

Then they discuss the cuts on O.J.'s hands, a subject Johnnie can't get out of his mind. Huizenga has told the jury that he saw and photographed cuts on Simpson's fingers. "O.J.'s never been really clear about these cuts," Johnnie says. Shapiro digresses to questions about the Rockingham blood-drop pattern. Where did the trail of drops really start? In the foyer? Or in the kitchen? Kardashian reminds everyone that O.J. said he went out to the car and cut himself there. That would explain the drops in the car.

Douglas asks if there's anything in O.J.'s police statement inconsistent with that. They check the transcript. There isn't.

Someone suggests that the defense doesn't have to say O.J. was bleeding before he left. But that doesn't explain the blood in O.J.'s foyer, Kardashian says. Maybe it's not this cut but some old cut. He's got more than one cut. Out come the photographs of O.J.'s cuts. The subject is sure to be raised again on Monday. Can the doctor be helpful? A decision has to be made.

"It's not a *decision*, it's what O.J. remembers," Bob Kardashian says firmly.

His memory is that he may have cut himself in the kitchen, he's not sure, and he may have cut himself in the Bronco getting the phone out, Bob Blasier says, paraphrasing the interrogation transcript. "Somewhere after the recital, somewhere when I was rushing to leave the house," O.J.

said. The team likes that version, right from O.J.'s own mouth. Forget about Huizenga.

Johnnie then lets the entire defense team in on the Fuhrman interviews. They view a tape of last night's *Inside Edition*, which broke the story about the Laura McKinny screenplay. *Inside Edition* managed only a sketchy report, with none of the audiotapes. There's no mention of the story today in the morning papers or on any news program. Maybe the media just didn't believe it.

Johnnie points out that the good guys, the police, are really the bad guys here. "It may never be the same in this country, if this information is true." Johnnie says Schwartz has agreed to a Tuesday meeting, but Carl knows McKinny will have to be handled carefully so she doesn't panic when the media find her. McKenna adds that she has to be protected: Now there's a cop out there who would love to kill her.

Douglas starts to say something, but Shapiro interrupts: "Name that race!" It's been the team's running joke since Cochran and Darden had their face-off in court over Heidstra's "Hey, hey, hey!" Carl chuckled. This was gallows humor at its best.

Blasier reports he's been working on the EDTA test results. The FBI charts are confusing and complicated. The paperwork is terrible. Of course: No way would the prosecution supply road maps to the FBI findings Rockne Harmon had alluded to in court. Blasier tells the group that in some of the charts he found "spikes" that represent EDTA. The fact that EDTA was present in the reference blood was buried in the reports. Blasier then said he was "ready to take on Harmon" and the EDTA issue.

Johnnie then tells everyone he wants to recall Pablo Fenjves, the prosecution time-line witness. Fenjves said he heard the dog "wailing" about 10:15 P.M. on June 12. The defense now has information that this witness is a former reporter for the *National Enquirer*. That's good. He once wrote a screenplay using the phrase "plaintive wail of police

659

sirens.'' That's better. Well, maybe it's a stretch from sirens to a dog. Carl Douglas has to smile. He can picture Johnnie going after the now-pitiful wailing dog again. The consensus is that Ito won't let in the new information. They decide not to recall Fenjves. Why show that the defense is worried about his statement?

The big question still open is how to end the defense case. Dr. Henry Lee should be the last witness, Scheck says. Kardashian thinks Lee is a better showman than even Simpson in his prime: ''He'd be better than O.J.,'' Bob says, ''even if Simpson hadn't been arrested for the murders.'' Nobody disagreed.

6

O.J. TEAM SEEKS TAPES OF COP

O.J. Simpson's lawyers are investigating the possible existence of audio tapes that could put Detective Mark Fuhrman back on the hot seat.

Fuhrman's lawyer, Robert Tourtelot, told the Daily News . . . the detective worked on a fictional script . . . but had no knowledge of any conversations that were taped.

—Michelle Caruso, New York Daily News, July 17, 1995

ON MONDAY MORNING, JULY 17, KARDASHIAN FOUND Bailey in the holding cell arguing that he should be more involved with the Fuhrman tapes: He was the only attorney on the team who understood the ex-marine. Minutes later,

Simpson was talking to Paula Barbieri on Bailey's cell phone. Bring the prisoner toys, Kardashian thought. Lend him your phone. Maybe he'll be grateful.

When Bailey left, Kardashian and Simpson settled into a gin rummy game. By now, Simpson owes Kardashian over a thousand dollars. "Lee is always trying to position himself." O.J. said. He smiled, looked down at his cards. "He wants to do more witnesses. I don't think so."

When court convened, Kelberg started by asking Huizenga what he'd learned of Simpson's mental state.

His insomnia, the doctor replied, was probably caused by "this incredible, incredible stress that maybe no other human being short of Job has endured."

The defense team winced. Simpson as a biblical hero? Kelberg would exploit that. The prosecutor let a few minutes pass before he struck.

"Is it your characterization," Kelberg asked harshly, "that Mr. Simpson is in a situation which to your knowledge only Job has suffered more?"

Huizenga, flustered now, said that Simpson had endured a "change in his life status that very few, if any, people have experienced."

"And if he had murdered two human beings, Nicole Brown Simpson and her friend Ronald Goldman," Kelberg shot back, "would that be the kind of thing that would cause a great weight to be on a man's shoulders?"

"If someone hypothetically killed someone," Huizenga replied carefully, "they certainly would have a great weight on their shoulders."

Hadn't Huizenga said Simpson had the strength to hold a knife? Kelberg asked a few minutes later. The doctor agreed.

"Would he also be able, in your opinion," Kelberg said loudly, "to grab the hair of Nicole Brown Simpson and yank her head back to hyperextend her neck area prior to taking a knife and slashing at her throat area?"

The doctor agreed Simpson could do it "in a stationary situation."

* * *

Shapiro had known that Huizenga would say that O.J. could hold a knife. Douglas wondered if Bob should have asked the question first to undermine Kelberg's impact. Carl knew the defense team was feeling cocky. Their overconfidence had weakened their long-term strategy of setting things up for Henry Lee by showing Simpson, two days after the crimes, looking as if he'd never been near a bloody fight.

Kelberg had won this round. The jury hadn't been put to sleep. And Huizenga had said Simpson was strong enough to kill two people.

At the lunch break Kardashian smuggled a turkey sandwich into the holding cell for Simpson. "I don't know how much more of this I can take," Simpson said. He looked at the contraband, but he obviously wasn't in the mood to eat. "I should have just shot myself," he growled. "We wouldn't have gone through all this aggravation for a year."

As Kardashian listened, O.J. began a dialogue with himself.

"No, it's better *this* way," he said. "If I'd shot myself, the Goldmans and Browns would have sued my estate and taken all my money. This way they can't get it. This way at least *I'm* spending it."

Bob was feeling a little moody himself.

"If I knew how tough this was going to be on me and my family," Kardashian said, "I'd have stayed home that Monday morning."

Both men looked at each other hard.

Testifying for the prosecution, FBI expert Doug Deedrick had said the hairs found at the crime scene showed traces of dye but no dandruff. On Tuesday afternoon, July 18, Johnnie called Simpson's hairdresser, Juanita Moore, who testified that she never dyed O.J.'s hair and that, furthermore, he sometimes had dandruff.

Next, Officer Donald Thompson took the stand. He was the senior uniformed cop at Rockingham, the one who had handcuffed Simpson. Johnnie called him to establish the LAPD's rush to judgment. The direct examination worked well.

Then Chris Darden started his cross.

"Do you understand the meaning of the term 'probable cause,' Officer Thompson?"

Johnnie Cochran objected. "That's not an issue, Your Honor. I object. Improper."

Ito called another sidebar, then sent the jury out.

Darden explained that since Cochran had suggested that Thompson and the LAPD had no cause to arrest Simpson that day, he would show that the cop had been at Bundy, where he saw the bodies. He knew that Nicole had been married to Simpson; he had seen blood at Rockingham. Darden was going to replay all that for the jury.

Ito said Darden could do it in "three questions." Fifteen would be more dramatic, Darden joked. "But we're not here for drama," Ito said impatiently.

"I'm not," Darden said quietly. "Not anymore."

"Yeah, after the gloves!" Cochran sniped.

Ito turned on Cochran. "That was a cheap shot!" he barked.

"Did Mr. Cochran apologize?" Darden asked.

"Not yet, but he will," Ito said firmly.

Johnnie didn't. Instead he gave a long list of reasons why his objection should be sustained. Along the way he baited Ito. His tone was pleasant, but the content was brazen: "The fact that the court can ask those questions in two or three questions, that's very nice, Your Honor," he said. "But then, Your Honor is no longer in the district attorney's office. That's their job."

Carl Douglas held his breath. Everyone waited for Ito to sanction Johnnie. Nothing happened. Johnnie wound down. Then everyone waited for the apology.

"I don't think it was a cheap shot," Johnnie insisted.

It was, Ito repeated. Cochran disagreed. Ito insisted, again.

"Well, it's your court," Cochran said defiantly. "So if you think it was, then I apologize. But I don't think it was a cheap shot."

"Mr. Darden and I were discussing a matter," Ito said, visibly irritated, "and you piped in with that. Which I took to be a cheap shot."

"Well, I didn't think it was a cheap shot."

Ito called a recess and stormed off the bench. "Mr. Cochran, you think about that!"

The defense team stifled a collective gasp, then smothered a smile. Johnnie had driven Judge Ito from his own courtroom! He had the upper hand.

Johnnie was loving it.

The day ended with John Meraz. The towing company used by the LAPD to store the Bronco had fired him for entering the car and stealing "souvenirs" from the glove box. Cochran knew Meraz was iffy, but his souvenir hunting made an important point: Many people had access to the Bronco. Anyone with Simpson's reference sample could have smeared his blood in the car.

Cochran couldn't resist asking the witness what he *hadn't* seen in the Bronco. Meraz was looking for blood, he said. He'd read about it in the newspapers. He didn't see any.

Marcia Clark came out snarling. She got Meraz to admit he'd lied to his boss about taking items from the Bronco and had changed his story several times before being fired. Clark hurt his credibility badly. Still, the defense had established that the Bronco was readily available to anyone bent on planting evidence.

The next day LAPD detective Kelly Mulldorfer helped the defense again: She'd investigated the storage yard and discovered they hadn't kept a log of who entered the vehicle, legitimately or otherwise, for months.

7

ON TUESDAY, AFTER COURT, COCHRAN, SHAPIRO, AND Douglas walk into an office in Santa Monica. There will be no record of the meeting. No bill. No paper trail. The use of this office is a favor to Cochran, who wants someplace confidential and leakproof. Two young lawyers are already waiting; they might be fresh out of law school. Eager. Big smiles. They're obviously enjoying being involved in the trial of the century and are impressed by meeting Cochran and Shapiro.

Matthew Schwartz and Ron Regwan said they'd listened to the tapes. They confirmed that the voice was Fuhrman's. "One incident he describes could start a riot if it got out," they say. Shapiro asks many questions. No, Fuhrman doesn't talk specifically about planting evidence. Yes, the "N-word" is used throughout. They won't confirm the full name of their client. Cochran and Shapiro already know she is Laura Hart McKinny; McKenna has all the information they need.

Schwartz explains that their client only wants to sell her screenplay, based partly on Fuhrman's interviews. They've had big money offers for the tapes, but she's not selling. Never. And she's not eager to help the defense: She thinks Simpson is guilty.

Schwartz and Regwan suggest that Cochran file a motion asking the court to compel their client to provide the tapes. She won't volunteer them, but she won't fight a court order.

As Shapiro and Cochran leave, they know the road ahead may be rough. Johnnie isn't ready to click his heels and celebrate. Shapiro says he'd like to travel to North Carolina with Johnnie; Carl understands that Bob, no less than Johnnie, is willing to play the race card. But Douglas knows Cochran won't share that issue.

On Wednesday, July 19, at the end of the day, the defense called another LAPD officer, Willie Ford, a black man who made the Rockingham video for the LAPD's Scientific Investigation Division.

The defense now wanted to prove to the jury that the socks in Simpson's bedroom, stained with Nicole's blood, could have been planted by the police.

Barry Scheck had noticed this official-looking guy carrying a video camera months ago on a news-video clip taken at Rockingham. They'd found no tape from him in the discovery pile. Prosecutors had explained to the court that Ford's tape wasn't included because he'd made a visual record of Simpson's property so no one could claim the LAPD stole or damaged anything during the search. The tape was "administrative," not "evidence."

If you believe that, Barry Scheck from Brooklyn has a bridge to sell you, someone joked. Ito must have shared this skepticism, for he ordered the tape given to the defense.

"And when you got to his bedroom, did you see any socks on the floor at the foot of his bed?" Johnnie asked Ford.

"No," said the cameraman.

"If you *had* seen the socks there," Johnnie continued, "you would have shot them with the camera, wouldn't you?"

Ford said he would have.

The time stamp on the tape showed that Ford shot the bedroom scenes at 4:13 P.M. on June 13, 1994. Dennis Fung and Andrea Mazzola's records said they'd collected the socks around 4:30.

To Scheck the socks had always been suspect. Starting with Fung, LAPD criminalists examined them three times and found no blood. It was only on August 4, almost two months after the killings, that someone finally noticed blood. Scheck had enjoyed one of his best courtroom moments displaying the socks to the jury. *Anybody* could see the blood. How could a trained criminalist and the LAPD's crime lab personnel miss seeing blood *three* times unless it simply hadn't been there?

Bill Pavelic was told these were thin dress socks, which he assumed Simpson had worn to the fund-raiser with Paula Barbieri that Saturday night, June 11. He knew O.J. was compulsively neat: He wore only freshly laundered clothes and changed them constantly. The rest of his clothes from Saturday evening were in the nearby laundry hamper. He wouldn't have left the socks on the floor.

Weeks earlier, Carl Douglas and Pat McKenna had examined the video carefully. They saw the camera pan across parts of the rug at the foot of Simpson's bed. Did it take in the entire rug? They froze several frames. As if assembling a jigsaw puzzle, they matched sections of the woven pattern to see if Ford had really photographed the whole rug.

He hadn't. The camera angle missed the section of the rug where the socks were found and later photographed by the police.

As Johnnie ran the video in court, Carl Douglas wondered if Clark and Darden knew it didn't show the most important part of the rug. Johnnie didn't care: Ford hadn't seen any socks, period. He'd said so in an evidence hearing. He'd said so to Johnnie personally. Now he had testified to it. So it didn't matter if the video gave a partial picture of the rug—except that Marcia might make something big and nasty of it to soften the impact of Ford's testimony.

"Stop it there. . . ." Johnnie positioned the frame on the rug. "Any socks on that rug that day, Mr. Ford?"

Ford said no.

"You didn't videotape any, and there were none there," Cochran added for emphasis. "Is that correct?"

A dramatic end to the day. If Ford saw no socks, why were they lying there twenty minutes later when Dennis Fung came in? Had someone taken them from the hamper and thrown them on the rug? Two months later, did someone spike them with Simpson's reference blood? Ford's video included a bonus: It showed some type of suspenders on the bed. In the discovery material, the defense had found LAPD pictures showing the suspenders in a different position. That meant that evidence had been moved or the photo was taken at a different time, or both.

When Ford returned to the stand the next morning, Thursday, July 20, Cochran showed him the LAPD's official evidence photos with the socks lying on the rug.

"You never saw what is depicted in that photograph, right?" Johnnie asked.

Ford said no. Johnnie knew the jury liked this man; he was one of them. A workingman. A black man. Obviously an honest man, who was saying something his superiors wouldn't like.

On cross-examination, Chris Darden repeatedly reminded Ford he was assigned to Rockingham "to show the way it looked after the *search*," implying that Ford made his video after Fung and Mazzola collected the socks. But Darden never asked whether Ford had videotaped the section of the rug where the socks would have been. Now that the position of the socks was known, Ford's answer would have been no.

When Willie Ford stepped down, the defense was caught without a witness to present. Obtaining the Fuhrman tapes had distracted everyone on the defense team, adding one more burden to their workload. It was only Thursday, but Scheck and his colleagues needed the entire weekend to complete their preparation of the scientific evidence. However, Ito wanted someone on the stand now. The jury was dead tired, and days off did not move the trial forward. The judge demanded they produce a witness. They called the detective who searched Simpson's laundry hamper.

Detective Bert Luper had pulled a glove like the one at the crime scene out of one of Simpson's drawers and left it on a table under a Tiffany lamp. The defense had seen it in Ford's video. Maybe the jury would assume the detective also dropped the socks on the rug. It was a stretch, but Johnnie needed to kill time.

What Cochran forgot was that Darden could turn this into something else: Luper had also *found* the socks.

"Did you see those socks before Mr. Ford arrived?" Chris Darden asked.

"Yes, sir," said LAPD Detective Adalberto Luper.

Darden continued, "Do you recall what time of the day it was that you first saw those socks?"

"It was between twelve-thirty and twelve-forty that afternoon."

If Luper was to be believed, the socks were on the rug nearly four hours before Willie Ford made his video. Now it was Luper's word against Ford's. The defense hadn't thought this witness through, and they were paying for it. Darden scored.

8

ON FRIDAY, JULY 21, ITO RULES AGAINST THE DEFENSE: While Dr. Herb MacDonell may testify, he may not discuss the drying time of blood on sock material since the experiment was conducted at his home. The defense then tells the court it has run out of witnesses for the day. A small retaliation.

Also a good time for a defense meeting. At eleven A.M. the core attorneys get down to business.

Alan Dershowitz points out that "a role reversal was now obvious in the trial." Marcia Clark and Chris Darden have "learned a hell of a lot in the last six months." They are becoming more effective in attacking the defense witnesses. The defense lawyers have given the prosecutors a master class in cross-examination techniques.

Shapiro says they shouldn't overreach themselves, shouldn't attempt too much. They must keep their witnesses to a minimum. "It's critical now to anticipate the downside of every person we put on," Kardashian adds. Deal with any downside on direct before the prosecution cross-examines. Everybody agrees.

Case in point: Should they call Dale St. John, the limo driver who usually took O.J. to the airport? In the plus column, he can testify that O.J. traveled a lot and was always late. On the downside, St. John might say he never saw O.J. playing golf in his front yard, never waited more than two or three minutes for an answer when he rang the house on the gate phone, never saw O.J. pick up his own luggage. The vote is unanimous: Dale St. John doesn't testify.

Scheck mentions the discovery quandary over their experts' notes again. With Dr. Henry Lee's testimony perhaps only two or three weeks away, Barry is worried they may have to turn over Lee's notes any day now. Then the prosecution will know all about the "second shoe print" and "wet transfers." The more time the D.A. has to plan a counterattack, the worse for the defense. "But if we don't comply with discovery rules," Johnnie says, "we'll be punished." Scheck insists Lee's notes reveal too much. Shapiro sides with Cochran here: Play it safe. Turn the notes over. "It would be terrible if Ito excluded Henry Lee's entire testimony," Johnnie says. Kardashian remembers Marcia Clark's stricken face when Ito excluded all the evidence on the rare fibers from the Bronco carpet. The judge isn't lenient on discovery violations.

Finally they decide: Get Lee on the stand, but hold back his notes as long as possible without risking damaging penalties. A misstep to either side of this tightrope could be costly.

On Monday, Bob Blasier will present Dr. Fredric Rieders, their EDTA expert; he will be followed by the FBI agent who performed the tests showing the preservative in the blood swatches. Then Dr. Herb MacDonell will explain to the jury that Nicole's blood was found on the *interior* surface of

Simpson's sock and lay out the implications of his findings. Blasier expects those three witnesses to take the entire week.

Barry Scheck then delivers bad news: Gary Sims of the California DOJ lab, who already testified for the prosecution, now has some preliminary results from the more sophisticated RFLP-DNA tests. They show both Goldman's and O.J.'s blood in the Bronco.* "Just when we thought there couldn't possibly be any worse DNA findings, there are," Scheck says. The final results may be a month or two away.** What to do? Should the defense reemphasize the lax security in the tow garage? They've just presented John Meraz, the garage employee fired for stealing from the Bronco, and Detective Kelly Mulldorfer, who had investigated the matter. They decide these two are enough to make the point. Concentrate on Fuhrman as the person who planted the blood in the Bronco. Don't complicate the issue needlessly. The trial may end before the new RFLP test results are final.

While they're on the subject of Fuhrman, Johnnie reports that Laura Hart McKinny is being served a subpoena as they speak. At a hearing in North Carolina on July 28, the defense will argue that the tapes are material evidence and ask the court to order McKinny to produce them in Los Angeles. Johnnie will travel to North Carolina with Shapiro and Gerry Uelmen. Cochran is excited, as if he sees the headlines already.

---

*Earlier, PCR-based tests on the three blood smears from the console revealed that there was a mixture of Simpson and Goldman blood. Performing the RFLP test on the combination of the stains provided more powerful results.

**RFLP tests typically deal with four or five different genetic markers on a strand of DNA. In general terms, the chance is about 1 in 10 that two people carry the same genetic marker. When you combine that with the results for a second marker, also with approximately a 1-in-10 chance of being shared, the likelihood that two people share both markers drops to 1 in 100. Because the likelihood that two people share the same array of genetic markers drops so far so quickly, no more than four or five different markers are usually tested.

"Eleven hours of tapes, from March 1985 to February 1995," he tells the team. "It's explosive. He uses the 'N-word' very frequently. There is more stuff about what he did in West Los Angeles. He's like a KKK." But Douglas knows that nobody on the team has heard the tapes. Cochran's glowing reports are based on hearsay from McKinny's own attorneys.

Barry Scheck is skeptical. "They never, *ever* say anything you think they're going to say, Johnnie," Scheck tells him. Let's get to work on the case we have. We need you here, not in North Carolina.

During a break, Bailey grabs Cochran. "The worst guy in the world to go with you is Bob Shapiro," he says. Bailey points out that he's won every Fuhrman motion he's argued before Ito. Uelmen has always lost. I tried cases in North Carolina in the fifties, Bailey says. And then his standard trump card: I'll pay my own way.

"Don't worry about it," Johnnie says, *"I'm* going."

Carl knows Shapiro and Uelmen aren't actually making the trip; Johnnie just doesn't want Bailey. Douglas takes Lee aside. "It's no big thing: Johnnie will handle it." He can see Bailey isn't convinced. The old man can be absurdly persistent once he fixes on an idea.

Scheck and Cochran now find themselves at odds on the last defense witness. Scheck has always wanted Dr. Henry Lee to end their case. But Johnnie is already saying he wants McKinny or Fuhrman for their big finish—assuming the tapes are all they're cracked up to be. "I'm not a believer in the tapes," Barry repeats. This defense should not rest on someone's taped voice.

"We get Fuhrman on tape being a racist and you can't believe that?" Johnnie is incredulous.

"That I can believe," Barry replies. "I can't believe that it's our case."

"Well, you know, right does have a way of working out somehow." Johnnie is beaming. Nothing more is said: How do you argue with faith in cosmic justice?

9

THE DEFENSE TEAM WANTED THE PROSECUTORS TO BELIEVE they were putting Simpson on the stand. Get them busy preparing for something that wouldn't happen. Now they launched a quiet but diligent effort to plant disinformation with the media: Simpson's prep session with the attorneys from San Francisco over the July Fourth weekend was leaked. Not the results, just that it happened. At least, that was how it was supposed to go. Carl Douglas wasn't smiling as he watched the ABC-TV evening news, which reported that Simpson had been taken aback by the intensity of the questioning by Cristina Arguedas and Penelope Cooper. They had lit a small wildfire. But today Carl didn't enjoy being the arsonist.

On Monday, July 24, the defense began presenting its scientific case. Scheck said it wasn't enough to demonstrate that something could have happened. These jurors had to believe that blood tampering *probably* occurred.

Microbiologist Fredric Rieders was sworn in. He was the man Scheck had selected to undermine the two most damaging pieces of blood evidence the prosecution had against Simpson—namely, the Bundy backgate blood drop and Nicole's blood on the sock.

Rieders's testimony would strengthen the defense assertion that there was reasonable doubt. Dennis Fung had not seen the blood spot on the back gate in June, nor had an LAPD photographer. But Detective Lange had. Fung didn't collect the mysterious drop until July 3. So was it really there on June 13? The bedroom socks were also collected on June 13, but no one found blood on them until August. Both blood samples contained incriminating amounts of DNA.

The defense goal was to establish that these two pieces of evidence contained EDTA, the chemical used to preserve the reference blood drawn from Simpson, Nicole, and Goldman. And the blood-spiking theory was supported by the FBI's finding that EDTA was present in these two pieces of blood evidence.

The EDTA test results were a gift from the prosecution. During the pretrial hearings, when Scheck and his colleagues theorized about planted blood, they knew they couldn't risk testing for EDTA. If the results were negative, the media would surely find out, weakening the defense claim of police corruption. Instead, the defense pushed the prosecution into ordering the tests. Rockne Harmon was indignant at the allegation of evidence tampering. Test it, Rock, the defense lawyers taunted. If the FBI test found EDTA, the gamble would pay off. If the test results were negative, Scheck had a fallback position: He'd charge bias and claim that the FBI test methods had precluded conclusive results.

As it turned out, the FBI found just enough EDTA to provide what Harmon called a "flicker of hope" for the defense. From the disorganized discovery material on the test results, Bob Blasier dug out what he needed and sent the test results to Fred Rieders. Now Blasier needed one simple statement from the scientist: that the tests showed EDTA, period.

Definitive results would have required a determination that the EDTA levels in the back-gate blood and the sock blood matched the EDTA levels in the LAPD reference samples taken from Simpson and Nicole. However, EDTA bonded chemically with the metal, reducing the amount that could be found in the back-gate blood sample. Exactly what percentage had remained on the metal gate when the blood was collected, no one knew. Testing for EDTA was a relatively new lab procedure. *Real* results, results that would have settled the corruption question to someone's disadvantage, weren't technically possible.

EDTA is also an anticoagulant. Everyone agreed that the blood from the reference tubes contained a high-enough proportion of EDTA to have made anyone walking around with similar levels bleed to death from a paper cut. All this had to be summarized for the jury. When the prosecution was looking for its own EDTA expert, the first name on most lists was Dr. Rieders. And like Dr. Ed Blake, he'd already been retained by the defense.

Now Bob Blasier asked Rieders if, on the basis of his review of the FBI tests, he concluded that EDTA was "present in the stain from the back gate."

"In my opinion, yes," Reider replied. EDTA was in the blood swatch from the socks, too, he said.

Blasier's next witness would be FBI lab analyst Roger Martz, who ran the tests. He would provide "foundation" that the tests had occurred. Blasier also expected Martz to argue that the quantity of EDTA he'd found wasn't surprising. There was a little EDTA in most people's blood, from food preservatives or chemicals in the environment. Blasier knew from his visit to the lab at FBI headquarters that Martz had also tested his *own* blood and found the same levels of EDTA as were present in the blood evidence. Since Blasier knew the levels of EDTA in the sock and back-gate blood samples would never match the levels in the LAPD reference blood, he wanted Rieders to establish that such a match was nonetheless plausible.

Could the quantity of EDTA found by the FBI in the evidence have "come from a purple-top tube?" he asked Rieders, referring to the tube containing Simpson's reference blood.

"Yes, of course it could," Rieders answered firmly.

Carl Douglas was surprised to see Marcia Clark, who had no science background, rising to cross-examine Rieders. He had expected one of the DNA experts, Rockne Harmon or Woody Clarke, to do it. Carl speculated that Marcia Clark wanted the jury to see her again, since Darden had handled the previous seven witnesses.

Clark attacked Rieders like an avenging angel. Agent

Martz had tested his *own* blood, she told him, and it contained the same amount of EDTA as the evidence. She showed him the paperwork.

"Isn't it true, Doctor, that [Martz's] own unpreserved blood came up very similarly in results to the bloodstains on the gate and the sock?" Marcia Clark asked. "Isn't that true?"

"Surprisingly, yes," he admitted.

Clark repeated *that* point again and again throughout her cross.

Driving home that night, Kardashian and Shapiro wondered aloud about loose ends. Tonight the topic was Kato Kaelin.

Why had Simpson called Kato from the airport limousine and told him to reset the house alarm? O.J. had never done that before. Kato said he had set the alarm, but Arnelle said it wasn't on when she let Detective Vannatter into the house in the early hours of June 13. Were both of them telling the truth? Or had Kato never set the alarm?

Of course, it also made no sense that Simpson let Kato live rent-free at Rockingham. Not exactly a guest, not exactly an employee—was Kato a connection between O.J. and someone else? Questions, always questions.

10

ON TUESDAY MORNING, JULY 25, FBI SPECIAL AGENT Roger Martz took the stand. "Everyone is saying that I found EDTA," he began. "I have never said that, and I don't believe Dr. Rieders ever said that." His manner was relaxed but definite.

Martz had made it clear to Bob Blasier during his visit to FBI headquarters that the peaks or "spikes" on the graphs of the test results "could be" EDTA. Not "were," but "could be." He also told Blasier he assumed that the tiny amounts of EDTA in the blood from O.J. and Nicole came from routine eating and drinking. The blood from the reference samples would have levels of 2,000 parts per million, he'd said. The back-gate and bedroom-sock blood swatches had only 2 parts per million.

"Martz is a mixed bag," Blasier had written in a memo to the team immediately after his visit to the FBI lab. "There may be EDTA in the evidence, but he will strongly state that it could not come from purple-top [reference vial] blood. Do we still call him? Is it enough for us to present arguments that their system is not sensitive enough . . . ? The fact that his own non-EDTA blood shows spikes similar to our evidence is troubling. How do we deal with this?"

The defense decided to ride it out. Were the test results from the back gate and sock, Blasier asked, "consistent with the presence of EDTA?"

"Yes," Martz answered.

But after a morning recess, Martz suddenly turned very tough. He insisted he had not found EDTA. Then he went further. "I am not convinced that EDTA *is* present on that sock," he said, "and I want to make that very clear."

Blasier had to wonder if Martz had gotten a call from Washington. He had been neutral and easygoing before the break. Now the change in his attitude was dramatic. He said his data had been "misinterpreted by somebody else."

Blasier began a series of questions to challenge Martz's test data. "The raw data," he said, meaning the information from which the graphs were drawn, "what happens to that?"

It was stored in a computer, Martz answered.

For later analysis?

It was erased after the FBI finished its testing on the case, Martz admitted, "because we only have so much [computer] space." *Erased.* A piece of luck. Blasier turned on him.

"Where is the raw data that you did that formed the basis for all these charts right now?"

"It no longer exists." Now the FBI agent was flustered.

"It was erased off the computer when the case was dictated [completed in written form]."

"It has been destroyed?"

"Well, yes."

Blasier was excited. More suspicious behavior by law enforcement.

On cross-examination Marcia Clark returned to the raw data. "Now if someone wants the digital data that backs up the graphs you have generated," she began, "could you go back and test the evidence again and retrieve that data?"

Clark apparently shared Blasier's view: Missing data looked bad. But Martz said he could retrieve the data.

"When Mr. Blasier visited you in Washington, D.C., did he ask you to do that?"

"No, he did not."

Clark detoured to sideswipe Rieders. "Dr. Rieders has done nothing more than take your test results and give his own interpretation to them. Is that your understanding?"

"That's my understanding," the FBI agent agreed.

By Wednesday afternoon, July 26, Agent Martz was even more unfriendly, and Ito allowed Blasier to classify him a "hostile" witness. Blasier asked why Martz had changed his demeanor so drastically. "Did you decide at the break that you needed to be much more of an advocate?"

Martz said no.

More aggressive, then?

"I think I decided that I had to be more truthful," he replied. "I was not telling the whole truth with yes and no answers."

As Blasier had predicted in his July memo, the agent was a "mixed bag." His testimony gave the defense a difficult two days. They'd gotten the EDTA theory in front of the jury, but Martz had hurt them.

Bill Thompson knew that after Rieders and Martz, the jury had to weigh conflicting opinions. Martz said the EDTA in the blood evidence could have gotten there normally. Rieders said it could have come from a reference tube. How could twelve nonscientists resolve that kind of question? The prosecution couldn't lose this point if it wanted to win the case. Thompson was certain that the other side would present a rebuttal witness, but none was ever called.

As it turned out, Agent Martz's testimony involved more ambiguities than Bob Blasier had ever anticipated. During the last week of the trial, Blasier learned that the U.S. Department of Justice had reprimanded Martz for stating, before the Simpson jury, that he alone had developed the specific technique he used to determine the presence of EDTA in blood. The jury would never know that certain FBI personnel felt that Martz might have misrepresented the facts. A mixed bag, indeed!

11

ON THURSDAY, JULY 27, DR. HERB MACDONELL, THE expert who would establish that Nicole's blood was found on the "third surface" of Simpson's sock, was to testify.

Claiming to have scandalous personal information about MacDonell, Marcia Clark had told Johnnie several days earlier that the prosecution would "destroy" him on cross-examination. Carl knew she was daring the defense to call him. It's terrible, what she's saying, Douglas thought. Here a man adopts a bunch of kids, is a good Samaritan, and Marcia is going to trash his character, all for a win. Pretty sick. Douglas knew, whatever the allegations, that they weren't admissible. But he felt that Clark had gone beyond trash talk. He checked with Peter Neufeld: "Nothing to worry about," Peter said.

MacDonell testified. And Marcia Clark never attacked him personally.

Peter Neufeld took Dr. Herbert MacDonell step by step through his testimony. The doctor held one of the team's most tightly guarded secrets, and it was critical that the jury understand its implications.

Examining the socks the LAPD had found in Simpson's bedroom months earlier, MacDonell, aided by Henry Lee's photos, concluded that the quarter-sized stain containing Nicole's blood did not result from crime-scene activity. If Simpson had gotten Nicole's blood on his socks during the murders, the doctor explained, the microscopic pattern he and Dr. Lee examined would probably have suggested splashing, or "spatter." "I did not find any distribution of blood that I consider a spatter," he testified.

Instead, he saw a blood pattern which suggested that someone pressed something bloody against the socks. What about an accidental swipe? Neufeld asked. MacDonell saw no "feathering out on either side" to suggest a lateral motion.

Slowly, carefully, Neufeld worked toward the surprising conclusions MacDonell had drawn. The doctor decided that the sock must have been lying on a table when the stain was created. The implication—MacDonell wouldn't say it outright—was that someone in the Los Angeles Police Department had dabbed or pressed a bloody cotton swatch against the socks.

How do you know it was a compression transfer? Neufeld asked.

Spatter projects itself "between the fibers," MacDonell explained. A compression transfer stains "only the top part of the weave." In any given wet transfer, some blood may soak between the fibers at the stain's center. But the edges of the stain will have blood only on the surface. The stain on Simpson's socks looked like that, MacDonell said. "It is classic."

The witness was halfway there. Neufeld nudged him toward the strategic objective step by step, asking about blood on "the inner surface of the opposite side of this sock."

The defense knew that MacDonell had found Nicole's blood on that inner surface. Yet there was no blood on the outer surface of that side of the sock.

If Simpson had worn these dress socks at Bundy and Nicole's blood splashed on them, as prosecutors contended, a transfer to the opposite inner surface—and only the inner surface—was impossible. Simpson's ankle would have blocked it. Blood could gather on that second inner surface only by soaking through from the opposite outer surface.

The sock's opposite side had no blood on the outside. MacDonell's conclusion: Someone laid the sock on a lab table and pressed something soaked with Nicole's blood against it. The "compression transfer" released enough of her blood to soak through to the inner surface of the opposite side in amounts visible under the microscope. MacDonell and Henry Lee had spotted it. Now their findings were displayed in enlarged color photographs to the jury.

Neufeld had arrived at the critical moment. "What conclusion did you make about whether the ankle was in or outside that sock at the time the transfer occurred?" he asked.

Marcia Clark jumped up to object. Speculation without foundation. Ito agreed. Neufeld rephrased it. Ito again sustained Clark's objection and called a sidebar, which ran into lunch hour and would, in fact, continue through the following Monday.

Peter Neufeld, the tall New Yorker, had grown in stature on the team. Cochran's secretaries hated him at first. He wanted everything *now*. He interrupted conversations. Always abrasive; smart, but arrogant.

In Shawn Chapman's mind, Neufeld had evolved into the unofficial chairman of most strategy sessions. "Johnnie, we've got to stop this," Neufeld was always saying. "We're veering off." Like Scheck, he had joined the defense as a DNA specialist. Soon enough, he had an opinion on just about everything. Most of those opinions, the team knew, were on target.

12

It's lunchtime, and O.J. is fretting and fussing about the Fuhrman tapes, which nobody has heard. Nobody will get a look at the transcripts or the tapes except by court order, Matthew Schwartz says. Johnnie tells O.J. he will be in North Carolina the next day to argue the defense motion before the local court.

The defense is using the midday break to hold a meeting in the jury room. During lunch, Juror 247, the black male alternate, becomes dizzy and is taken to the hospital. Court is canceled for the day. Now they don't have to race back.

The defense has learned the prosecution wants the audiotape from Gretchen Stockdale's answering service, which recorded the message Simpson left the day of the murders. The D.A. wants to show the jury that O.J. was finished with Nicole, had a relationship with Paula but was unfaithful to her, and was wandering.

In September 1994 the tape was in Shapiro's office. Now it's missing. "We searched the office, we can't find it," Shapiro says. "We'll look like assholes." They trace out the tape's complex itinerary. The bottom line, according to Shapiro: McKenna took it from his office, probably sent it to Miami during the "famous" Christmas holidays.

"Within six hours we'll see a motion for sanctions," Shapiro says. Johnnie agrees. "It's obstruction of justice, secreting evidence," Shapiro continues. Kardashian adds that the D.A. will probably want a jury instruction reprimanding the defense. Finally the team reads the transcript of the tape they found in Shapiro's files.

Uh, hey, Gretchen, sweetheart, it's Orenthal James who is finally at a place in his life where he is like totally, totally, unattached with everybody. Ha haaaa! Azz, in any event, um, I gotta Sunday evening, uh I'd love. . . . I guess I'm catchin' a redeye at midnight or somethin' to Chicago but I'll be back Monday night. Uh, if you leave me a message leave it on 310–613–3232. That's 613–3232.

"This is much ado about nothing," Johnnie concludes. "We're not calling her; we're not impeaching her; we can produce the transcript." That's it.

Shapiro then turns to another sticky subject: whether Baden or Wolf should testify. He doesn't want to call either of them. "You know it's a potential problem," he says. Michael's wife is dying, and he's working in another city. Will Marcia try to make something nasty of that? After her threats about Herb MacDonell, it's hard to believe she has any scruples about intimidating defense witnesses.

Kardashian, sounding like Shapiro today, says, "Less is more: Get in and get out." Then Shapiro surprises everyone: "Baden is too excitable and goes on too long." Nobody disagrees with that. They all remember him in meetings. Johnnie says, "Even if you do two hours of direct, this asshole Kelberg will do three days of cross." Then we'll lose him; Baden will go crazy. "But his notes have already been turned over to the prosecution," Johnnie reminds everyone. They wind up not voting, deciding to wait.

Johnnie says this may all be academic by the time he gets done with Fuhrman and Judge Ito's wife, Captain York of the LAPD. Then he reads an unsigned statement from a veteran cop, Donald Evans, who worked with Fuhrman.

Captain York was also directly involved in internal affairs investigations which centered on Detective Fuhrman that [concern] alleged gender and racial bias. Captain York also personally counseled Detective Fuhrman regarding these issues while I was stationed with the two of them at West Los Angeles station, but I have read her declaration and she is factually inaccurate.

Now they know Captain York may have lied in her sworn declaration: She did know Fuhrman. "What are we trying to accomplish here?" Cochran asks. "The point is, what will happen if we file a signed declaration about York?"

The team decides to investigate the cop, Donald Evans, before doing anything else.

On the issue of the Fuhrman tapes, Cochran says he has spoken to Laura McKinny and is off to North Carolina this afternoon. "I can tell you it's totally legitimate. He's talking about breaking some guy's legs, used 'nigger' like eight hundred times." Johnnie is really excited. Then Shapiro learns that Lee Bailey, now in New York, will join Cochran back east and gets angry. "I was going to go, and now I hear Lee's going," Bob says. If Lee is there, everything will get out to the press, Shapiro adds.

"I agree, that's what scares me," Johnnie replies. "I'll tell Lee again if anything leaks he'll be held liable."

13

THE NEXT DAY, FRIDAY, JULY 28, JOHNNIE COCHRAN SAT in Superior Court Judge William Wood's chambers in Winston-Salem, North Carolina, listening to Mark Fuhrman's voice on tape for the first time. Cochran, Bailey, local counsel Robert Craig, and Laura Hart McKinny sat in a row. On the other side of the room, behind a tape recorder, were McKinny's L.A. attorneys, Matthew Schwartz and Ron Regwan, along with Judge Wood. Johnnie had warned Bailey he would be held responsible if anything leaked to the media.

This was the first step in obtaining the tapes from

McKinny. Judge Ito had ruled that the tapes were material to the Simpson case. If a North Carolina judge agreed with Ito, the tapes were on their way to Los Angeles.

Johnnie had asked himself many times why the Lord wanted him on this case. Listening to Fuhrman use the Ku Klux Klan title "Grand Dragon," allude to "Hitler's celebration," and talk of "beating niggers" and of "dumb niggers," Johnnie had his answer. The Lord wanted him to show America the evils among our police, he decided.

It was obvious that Fuhrman hadn't been tricked or coerced into making these tapes. He was answering McKinny's questions based on his own experience. He was clearly a racist cop. That was how Johnnie saw it. Robert Craig could see that Judge Wood was outraged at what he heard.

In chambers, everyone agreed the tapes should go back to Los Angeles. Johnnie stood over the judge's shoulder pointing out sections in the transcript. "I've seen enough," Wood said before long. "We need to give up the tapes," Matthew Schwartz said. He was ready to stipulate that his client would appear in Los Angeles with the tapes. A done deal. Johnnie had won before the hearing was over.

Then Judge Wood said to Johnnie, "We're still going to put on the evidence here. I just want to make a record." The judge didn't want stipulations. No secret deals behind closed doors.

Then McKinny took the stand in open court to explain on the record how the tapes were made. Bailey could see she didn't want to be embroiled in legal proceedings and ordered to release her tapes to the world. She hated losing her writer's privilege of protecting a source. She was now teaching screenwriting at a local college. How would she look to her students? Moreover, she believed O.J. was guilty. Now her own research might slip out of her control and help him go free.

Laura McKinny answered Johnnie's questions; she told how, why, and when the tapes were made, but she didn't give him much help. She said the views Fuhrman expressed were not necessarily his own. "I don't know that it reflects his feelings about African-Americans."

Then Matthew Schwartz presented his objections. The tapes were work product and in addition were protected under the First Amendment. Fuhrman had provided creative consulting services. The tapes had commercial value to his client, which would be lost once they became part of the public record. He did the job his client wanted; he was not rolling over for the defense.

Then Cochran presented his arguments, concluding: "It would be a travesty not to find material whether this man [Fuhrman] committed perjury. Who could argue that it doesn't bear on Mr. Simpson's guilt or innocence?"

The tapes themselves were not played in open court. No transcripts were read into the record.

Judge Wood ruled that Fuhrman had been a technical adviser on a work of fiction. He agreed with Schwartz that the tapes were not material to Simpson's case. He would not compel McKinny to testify in Los Angeles or to turn over the tapes. Schwartz and Regwan misunderstood Wood's statement. They walked over to Bailey and Craig to congratulate them. "What are you congratulating us for? You won the motion," Craig told them. Schwartz was stunned. So was Regwan. For a moment they couldn't grasp the judge's ruling.

Craig told Bailey that Judge Wood was known in North Carolina for inconsistent rulings and was unlikely to rule in favor of Simpson's attorneys. The judge had asked some days earlier why a local attorney couldn't argue the motion: "Mr. Craig, you're quite capable of handling this. . . . I don't know why we need these out-of-state attorneys." Nonetheless, Cochran and Bailey turned up in his courtroom. And Wood was apparently offended by Johnnie, who wore a dark suit with a tie of African kente cloth. Judge Wood didn't like the showmanship. He wanted his own fifteen minutes of fame.

Cochran was shocked. He could not understand how the judge could rule on materiality when the case wasn't even his.

14

Monday morning, July 31, Kardashian drove to the courthouse with Bailey and Shapiro. "I'm sorry I couldn't go to your party, Lee," he said. "I just didn't feel I should with O.J. still in jail."

"Rest easy, my friend," Bailey replied oratorically. "O.J. called me Sunday and asked how it went. I told him wonderfully. He thanked me for seeing to it that Shirley and Carmelita had a fine time."

Now Kardashian was *really* upset. Like everyone else, he had been invited to Lee Bailey's thank-you dinner party at Michael's, a trendy restaurant, the previous Saturday night. But a week earlier Simpson had said the defense team shouldn't be celebrating while he sat in jail: The press might think it was a victory party.

"I have decided not to go," Skip Taft told the team. "I think it's a bad idea." Everyone agreed. Johnnie told Carl and Shawn to back out.

But within a few days Bailey had convinced Johnnie that Simpson's sisters would be disappointed. Then Cochran told Shawn and Carl to go. Kardashian was torn. Finally, out of respect for O.J., he stayed home.

Bob was furious as he walked into the holding cell. "Skip and I missed this party for you!" Kardashian told O.J. "Then you call Bailey and thank him for doing it? What's the matter with you?"

Simpson seemed bewildered. "I thought the party was nice. What's the big deal?"

"Oh, fuck you, O.J.!" Bob yelled.

"Bobby, take it easy," Simpson answered, as if humoring a child. "It's no big deal."

Kardashian was hot with anger. His voice started to rise. He felt used. "You know what? I'm just going to do what I want from now on! I'm not going to concern myself with what's going on around here."

"Go ahead, do whatever you want," Simpson answered sullenly.

Bob decided this was not the time to tell O.J. that he and his fiancée were breaking up. The strain of the trial, the loss of time together, were too much for both of them. The decision had been made. Now he and Denice were just working out the logistics; she was house-hunting.

That same morning, July 31, Ito ruled that Peter Neufeld could continue with the question he'd put to Herbert MacDonell.

Was finding blood on the sock's opposite inner surface "consistent with a bloodstain passing through one side of the sock to the other?" Neufeld asked, adding, "When the sock is not on the foot and is instead lying flat on a surface?"

"Yes, it would be consistent with that," MacDonell agreed.

"And why, sir, is that?"

Normally, MacDonell explained, "there is something like a foot inside the sock." Unless there is "a tremendous hole right through the ankle, there is no way that anything can go from one side of the sock to the other."

Carl Douglas noted with satisfaction that ten jurors were taking notes.

In an angry cross-examination, Marcia Clark managed to suggest a damaging alternative.

"If someone wearing the socks that you saw were to step near to the body of the victim Nicole Brown Simpson—near enough for the ankle bone to come in contact with her bloody hand," Clark asked in biting tones, "could that cause a compression transfer?"

"Certainly," answered MacDonell.

"If she were to reach a bloody hand out and touch her

thumb or finger or hand to the ankle of Mr. Simpson wearing those socks,'' Clark asked again, ''could that cause a compression or a swipe?''

It could, MacDonell admitted. The image of Nicole's bloody hand was devastating. But Carl Douglas still felt that the defense had won the day.

The next day, August 1, Bob Shapiro ''called'' Thano Peratis, who was still too ill to appear.

The defense needed Peratis's testimony on the record to show that he had said he withdrew about 8 cubic centimeters of blood from Simpson. That fact was basic to Scheck's theories about blood missing from O.J.'s sample. The prosecutors had never called the nurse, though he had been healthy while they were presenting their case.

Today the defense wanted to plant that quantity, 8 cubic centimeters, firmly in the jurors' minds. First the transcript from the grand jury hearing in June of 1994 was read into the record, and then videotape from the preliminary hearing in July of 1994 was played in open court. Peratis wasn't fuzzy at all.

''How much blood did you withdraw from Mr. Simpson?'' Shapiro asked on the tape.

''Approximately 8 cc's,'' Peratis answered.

''When you say, 'approximately,' you did not measure the amount?''

''Well, it could have been 7.9 or it could have been 8.1. I just looked at the syringe and it looked at about 8 cc's. I withdrew the needle from his arm,'' Peratis said. ''It's just routinely about the amount I usually draw,'' he explained.

They had ''8 cc's'' on the record.

The defense knew the prosecutors planned a taped-at-home interview with Peratis for the trial's rebuttal phase, when last-minute witnesses could be introduced to counter Scheck's arguments. They assumed Peratis would say he had only ''eyeballed'' the amount of blood in the purple-topped tube and had probably taken less than 8 cubic centimeters.

The defense planned to complain that the taping was done secretly. Cochran could make that sound conspiratorial.

* * *

When the defense finished with Peratis, they called microbiologist John Gerdes. He would confirm and amplify Barry Scheck's "cesspool of contamination" characterization of the LAPD lab, which Johnnie had announced in his opening remarks. The defense had been laying the groundwork for this witness ever since Dennis Fung's testimony.

But Ed Blake, one of the team's DNA experts, had argued against calling Dr. Gerdes. He opposed using PCR tests in forensic work: He thought they lacked adequate controls. Blake warned the team that Gerdes had a reputation for stating his professional convictions vehemently and might launch an attack on DNA technology. He could be off-putting. So Scheck didn't know what to expect of him.

He asked Gerdes to evaluate the operations of the LAPD lab. Did it have serious and effective contamination controls?

"I found that the LAPD laboratory has a contamination problem that is persistent and substantial," Gerdes replied. The contamination was "chronic." He found it "month after month": Test tubes leaned against each other in lab racks; that offered potential for contamination. On blood-typing strips, he had seen more serious contamination: He had found faded dots where no dots belonged. That suggested that one sample's DNA had seeped into another sample's test. "That represents human DNA that shouldn't be there," Gerdes said. "That is what our definition of contamination is."

Both the defense and the prosecution knew that Gerdes hadn't specifically evaluated the LAPD's test work on the Simpson case. He'd looked at the lab operations generally. Prosecutors had earlier argued that general lab contamination did not prove that any given evidence—say, that in the Simpson case—was contaminated. Still, Scheck had to emphasize the defense's "cesspool" image while downplaying Gerdes's inability to link it directly to this case. Fortunately, the Denver microbiologist's style was dramatic.

A responsible oversight agency, Gerdes charged, "would shut the lab down with this level of contamination."

Was it the worst lab Gerdes had inspected?

"Definitely, by far," the doctor replied.

Scheck had an indirect way to link the LAPD's sloppy lab

work and the Simpson evidence. He put a set of typing strips from Cellmark on the screen. They showed several faded dots among the darker dots indicating DNA. How did Gerdes interpret that image?

The strip suggested evidence of a "second gene system," he told Scheck. The faded dots were "consistent" with Simpson's DNA "finding its way into Nicole Brown Simpson's sample and then not being detected until it gets to Cellmark. . . ."

"Speculation," prosecutor Woody Clarke objected.

Ito agreed, but still allowed Gerdes to explain the "significance of this pattern of typings." Gerdes saw two possibilities. Either Simpson's blood was mixed with Nicole's and Ron's at the LAPD lab, or the Cellmark environment had somehow introduced "contaminants and artifacts" similar to those at the LAPD lab. Now Scheck had linked the LAPD errors with the Simpson evidence.

On Thursday, August 3, Woody Clarke began his cross of Gerdes. Bill Thompson eyeballed the jury and liked what he saw.

Thompson had chosen his bellwether jurors a while back, a few who he thought leaned toward acquittal, some others who might convict. The Demon was everybody's choice for the most serious pro-prosecution threat. She sat happily through Robin Cotton's lengthy testimony on the Cellmark test results, while the faces of jurors who supported Simpson visibly tightened as Cotton reeled off numbers.

Yesterday and today the jury reactions shifted. As Gerdes outlined the mess at the LAPD lab, the Demon shook her head several times and rapidly took notes. She seemed perplexed. Thompson saw the supportive group relaxing. Now we have an explanation, he imagined them thinking. They looked relieved.

We're scoring big points here, he decided.

Thompson knew how big when he saw that during cross-examination Woody Clarke offered no alternative explanation for the faded dots on the test-result strips.

Here was a scientist with a doctorate in microbiology

saying the LAPD's lab is a disaster and the prosecution's test results at high-class labs like Cellmark probably show cross-contamination. Gerdes was destroying the prosecution's blood evidence case, yet Woody Clarke went after him almost diffidently. Clarke began by challenging Gerdes's credentials. Routine. Then he had Gerdes admit he hadn't studied forensics or worked directly with criminal evidence. He's trying to make him a hired gun, Thompson thought, a paper-pusher who reads other people's test results.

"Isn't it correct, Dr. Gerdes," Clarke challenged, "that every time you've been retained to review another laboratory's work, it has been with the intent, if possible, of attacking that evidence?"

Thompson glanced over at two jurors who seemed to like Simpson. They were almost nodding off.

An entire day passed before Woody Clarke scored seriously. On Friday morning he forced Gerdes to acknowledge that Collin Yamauchi had not extracted DNA from the blood samples that went to Cellmark and emerged with faded dots: Those samples went directly to the outside lab. Didn't this mean, Clarke asked, that no LAPD "contamination" occurred?

Gerdes worked hard to hold his ground. "[There might not have been contamination] at the [DNA] extraction stage, but there are earlier stages," the microbiologist insisted.

This was unresponsive, Clarke complained. Ito had already barked, "Answer the question, Doctor."

"If you restrict it to the extraction stage, that is true," Gerdes finally said.

On Monday, Clarke scored one final point. If PCR tests match the more reliable RFLP testing, he asked, "isn't that a significant example of validation?" Gerdes admitted he had agreed to that in principle in the past.

It was too late, Thompson decided. Clarke's point didn't seem to have much impact. Gerdes had done the job. The Demon was obviously upset. The jurors who supported Simpson appeared ready for a good weekend. Thompson assumed this would settle the Kary Mullis question: Was the maverick PCR inventor really needed now?

Carl Douglas was more than satisfied. Gerdes had been one of the most effective witnesses of the trial. He and Cochran were very pleased.

NEW DNA TEST ON BLOOD FROM BRONCO REVEALED

In a revelation that rocked an otherwise slow court session, Deputy Dist. Atty. Rockne Harmon disclosed Friday that a new DNA test suggests that O.J. Simpson's car was smeared with a mixture of his blood and that of murder victim Ronald Lyle Goldman. . . . Harmon said [this] during a brief hearing outside the jury's presence. . . .

If confirmed by the further analysis and allowed into evidence, the RFLP test . . . would have an extra advantage for prosecutors.

—Jim Newton, Los Angeles Times, August 5, 1995

15

ON SATURDAY, AUGUST 5, MOST OF THE DEFENSE EXPERTS are in town for a meeting. Some are staying at the Hotel Bel Age, just off the Sunset Strip in Hollywood. Dr. Henry Lee, Kary Mullis, Larry Ragle, and John Gerdes have all flown in; Scheck, Neufeld, Blasier, and Thompson are the hotel regulars. The work is draining; everyone is under the gun. But the hotel is a fun place to stay.

Thompson walks in on Neufeld, who's getting ready for the meeting. "You won't believe what just happened to

Gerdes and me in the elevator,'' Thompson says. Neufeld answers, ''A woman wearing a skimpy bikini and a cobra tattooed on her belly invited you to a party. And she was gorgeous.'' They both laugh. Then Neufeld adds: ''And she invited me to a party yesterday.'' No time, alas, to consider her offer.

By the time everyone gets to the meeting at Cochran's offices, the cobra lady is just a distant memory. Johnnie, back from North Carolina, is optimistic. The defense will appeal Judge Wood's ruling, of course.

It has been a month since Johnnie told Judge Ito he planned to end the defense case by August 11. He'd really intended to be finished by August 4. Yesterday. And here they are with a month's worth of witnesses still ahead. Shapiro says the defense has to finish fast. But how?

Today they'll review the case ahead, week by week.

First up, this coming week: Should they call Kary Mullis?

Mullis has been sitting in the courtroom for days waiting to testify. Johnnie mentioned him in his opening statement; Rockne Harmon is waiting to cross-examine him. Harmon has even grown a beard and says he won't shave until Mullis takes the stand.

The defense knows Mullis is the right man to make the point that PCR testing was never intended for police forensic work: It is too vulnerable to contamination. In Mullis's opinion, PCR is not reliable under conditions present in the LAPD lab. Whose opinion could possibly carry more weight? Dr. Mullis had won the Nobel Prize for his work on the PCR process.

The defense is well aware there's a downside to using Mullis. He has strong political beliefs, and he claims that HIV doesn't cause AIDS. Rumor has it that he has photos of naked women on the refrigerator where he keeps LSD. He's a maverick, eccentric and outspoken. Can he be controlled? Shapiro adds that Mullis doesn't look like a kook. He really looks like a Nobel Prize winner; that's all that matters.

''I spent the last two weeks with Kary,'' Scheck tells them. ''I love this guy, one of the smartest people walking the planet. He's wired.'' So far, so good. But there's more:

"We went to a jazz club and talked about Yamauchi spilling the blood, item fifty-two from the walkway, and he says, 'What's RFLP?' He starts banging on the table. 'Now, *what* is RFLP?'" The smiles of the defense team vanish as Scheck continues, "He forgot what RFLP was, and everything we discussed. I couldn't tell if he was kidding me."

Shawn is laughing to herself. The other day, Barry Scheck had phoned her with a tale of woe. While Bob Shapiro observed, Scheck and Neufeld had been prepping Mullis for the stand—a cross-examination rehearsal on the roof of the Bel Age hotel. "I don't know what I'm fucking going to do," Scheck had lamented to Shawn. "Shapiro just gave Mullis a beer, he's drinking, he's not concentrating. I don't know what to do."

Scheck was freaking out. Barry's high-intensity worrying was the team joke, but this was a whole new order of magnitude. "He forgot *again* what RFLP means." Shawn had to chuckle. It was funny—except it wasn't.

Peter Neufeld points out that they don't need Mullis to discuss the evidence in *this* case. "He can just talk about the PCR technology."

The bigger question is what Rockne Harmon will do to Mullis. It doesn't matter, Peter Neufeld says. The jury is turned off by Harmon. "Just let him cross Mullis and we win."

But Scheck's misgivings can't be ignored. The vote is to use Mullis only as a last resort.

In the week of August 14, Scheck plans to attack the handling of evidence at the crime scene. He'll use Larry Ragle, a retired criminalist who worked in southern California.

Barry Scheck begins listing his problems. There are serious contradictions in the defense attack on the LAPD. "If the LAPD was the Keystone Koroners, the Keystone Kriminalists, and the Keystone Kops, how can we argue that this is an elaborate conspiracy? The LAPD can't be stupid and corrupt at the same time—that's bullshit." The only answer, Scheck says, is a witness "who says when you screw up the chain of custody records, it gives people an opportunity to tamper with the evidence." Let's find one.

Then Scheck says he's worried about the white blanket the police used to cover Nicole's body at the crime scene. He'd questioned Dennis Fung at length about the blanket. The LAPD then started an investigation of where the blanket came from. Now discovery shows that Detective Lange asked Officer Thompson to find something to cover the body. Thompson took the blanket from a cupboard near the children's room. Later Nicole's maid confirmed that it had just been washed. The defense has been expecting the prosecution to use that fact to counter the defense argument that a household blanket thrown over the body could have transferred trace evidence to the crime scene. The recent washing is a good argument for the prosecution. What's going on here?

Larry Ragle, the expert on crime scenes, tells the team that the LAPD's real mistake was not saving the blanket. In that case, he says, "they could have explained it away. What I see are lots of blunders on top of blunders."

Dr. Lee, who's been sitting quietly, now adds, "Doesn't matter if a blanket laundered or not laundered. Laundering doesn't remove trace evidence that may have been on it already. It adds other trace evidence from dryer." So maybe the D.A. is as smart as Dr. Lee? Everyone laughs.

The third week will be Mark Fuhrman's funeral—with or without the tapes.

Johnnie is all smiles when anyone mentions the Fuhrman tapes. Today Cochran discovers he has a new friend in "his" camp, the pessimist Barry Scheck. Barry is concerned that the Demon will be the holdout "Guilty" vote. The Fuhrman tapes, Scheck believes, could guarantee her vote for acquittal.

"If we can't get these tapes into evidence, we can lose this case. And you know, all bullshit aside, that's the truth," Scheck tells them. Alan Dershowitz, who's on the phone from Boston, adds that the defense can lose only if it "maintains" the Demon on the jury. Should the defense look for a way to get her removed?

For the first time the team openly discusses investigating a juror themselves. No question they want to get rid of the Demon. Scheck agrees with Dershowitz's idea of investigating her. Alan notes, "A dismissed juror wrote a letter back to the Demon and said, 'Stick to your guns, don't let them push you around.'" Jurors' mail is read by the deputies to censor outside material about the case. Sometimes interesting tidbits get back to the defense. Does this note to the Demon disqualify her? Is an investigation worth it with only two alternates left? Carl Douglas says no and reminds everyone that Ito has ordered both sides to keep away from the jurors. Cochran says "No way" should they investigate the Demon.

Why Barry's sudden change of heart about the Fuhrman tapes? "We must put those tapes on the record," he says. He's visibly upset. There is nothing else in the defense case, he believes, that will *guarantee* a win on appeal. "I mean, we can't screw around," he says.

Johnnie agrees that "the tapes are the most important thing we've got." Bailey reports that Fuhrman was taped saying things like "'You tear up his driver's license, then you get him for not having identification.' Now, that's not for any play, that's what he's doing out there."

Johnnie recaps the situation. Ken Spalding, a respected black lawyer in Raleigh-Durham, worked with Joe Cheshire, another attorney, to put together the motion to overturn Judge Wood's ruling. It was filed last Tuesday. Word is that on Monday, August 7, the appellate court will rule.

Shapiro points out that Michael Baden has added another asset to his credentials: He and Dr. Wolf have just finished testifying in another case for the same D.A.'s office that is prosecuting Simpson. Not bad, when the D.A. asks if Baden or Wolf is an independent expert.

But the question of who should testify, Baden or Wolf, remains open.

* * *

Now that the case is nearing its end, conjugal and family visits to the jurors—and the inevitable "pillow talk"—are becoming important. Pillow talk must be considered both a potential tool and a possible hazard. Most important, it can't be ignored. Shapiro and Cochran are checking the TV reports daily, something Scheck, Neufeld, and their colleagues have not been doing.

Today Johnnie is incensed because Geraldo Rivera and CNN are both calling him a liar. Cochran had said O.J. was bleeding at Rockingham and had cut himself there. O.J. had told Vannatter he cut himself in Chicago. Rivera claims these are mutually contradictory statements.

"All these pundits don't understand that there are different cuts," Johnnie fumes. Scheck questions whether the two stories about the cuts are inconsistent. But it doesn't matter, Cochran says: We shouldn't commit ourselves to one explanation to the exclusion of the other.

Alan Dershowitz points out that the prosecution has never yet "set out their theory of the case. They've implied it, but haven't set it out." What about the D.A.'s inconsistent treatment of the three bangs on Kato's wall? Is O.J. coming in the front door, coming in the back, or climbing over the fence? Cochran says, "Vannatter's theory starts in the car, goes to the back where the glove is left, and then into the house. That's inconsistent with the D.A.'s other theory that O.J. climbs over the wall."

Scheck points out that the prosecution has to deal with the inconsistencies. "We have to be prepared to hit them in a way that they cannot effectively answer in rebuttal."

Johnnie still has Fuhrman on his mind. "Assume Fuhrman is a lying racist. Assume Vannatter goes out there and they think O.J. is guilty. I really believe that *they* believe he's guilty. The case against him is strong. They decide, 'We're going to lean on O.J., we're going to make a case with this guy.' Now it's Fuhrman who's taken off the case and he despises Nicole.* I mean, people who hate, don't just hate

---

*At approximately 2:40 A.M. on June 13, Detective Mark Fuhrman was informed by his supervisor, Detective Ron Phillips, that the LAPD's Robbery-Homicide Division would take over the case. This was about half an hour after Fuhrman arrived at the crime scene.

O.J., they hate her just as much for hanging around with a black guy. So he does all these things. And I think Vannatter and Lange are forced to cover up for him. This guy is a lying racist. And nobody had the courage to come forward and say this guy is lying."

They have heard all this before. Nobody minds hearing it again.

16

WHILE JOHN GERDES WAS FINISHING ON THE STAND, F. Lee Bailey sent a two-word fax to the courtroom: "WE WON." Johnnie wanted to jump up and down right in front of the jury. Carl brought the fax to Simpson. Kardashian said to him, "What a lucky guy you are."

RULING COULD OPEN WAY TO CHALLENGE
FUHRMAN; NORTH CAROLINA COURT SAYS
PROFESSOR CAN BE MADE TO TESTIFY ON
TAPES OF DETECTIVE USING RACIAL EPITHETS

A North Carolina appellate court delivered a major boost to O.J. Simpson's legal efforts Monday, issuing a ruling that could clear the way for his lawyers to put on evidence that Detective Mark Fuhrman may have lied on the witness stand. . . .

Barry Scheck said of the decision: "Huge, huge. It could be the case."

—Jim Newton, Henry Weinstein, and Tim Rutten,
Los Angeles Times, August 8, 1995

Even with the McKinny tapes on the way to Los Angeles, the defense knew there was a long road ahead before they could be heard by the jury. Would Ito allow all the tapes to be heard? If not all, which portions? In what context? Would a transcript be read into the record, or could Fuhrman's voice be played in open court?

Then the chicken-and-egg issue: Which would come first, Fuhrman himself or the tapes? Douglas knew Ito would make that call.

Johnnie knew the Fuhrman tapes would trigger investigations of every case in which Fuhrman had testified. Once the snowball started downhill there would be no stopping it.

Johnnie asked Douglas to handle security when the tapes arrived. "I don't want anybody to see them," Johnnie told Carl. "Lock them in the safe, tapes and transcripts." Bailey pointed out the problem of turning over the D.A.'s copy of the tapes under discovery. "We can only do that," Bailey says, "under an order signed by Ito, naming the specific people who will have access to them. Then they won't be leaked."

At this point the defense was sitting pretty. When Fuhrman testified, Ito had not allowed him to answer any questions about Bell or Terry because the defense had not yet presented those witnesses. In effect, he suspended Fuhrman's cross.

"Thank God we didn't finish," Bailey now said. "If we had, Fuhrman could refuse to come back, and the jury would never know. Now he's still in cross-examination. If he refuses, the jury will know all about it." Johnnie wanted to present the tapes to the jury first, then call witnesses to other incidents of racial abuse or bias. They'd confirm that the way Fuhrman talked during his extended conversation with McKinny was not an isolated event.

Johnnie knew the Fuhrman tapes weren't O.J.'s sole salvation, but he felt they put Simpson on the threshold of an acquittal.

Now O.J. Simpson would never have to take the stand.

Scheck knew that if Simpson testified, the burden of proof would inevitably shift. Forget whether the D.A. had proved its case beyond a reasonable doubt. For the jury it would come down to whether or not you believe O.J. Besides, if O.J. testified for two weeks, the rebuttal would take at least two months. There'd be no jury left to vote. Scheck would go down fighting before he'd let this client take the stand.

Despite his months of dogged determination to speak his piece to the jury, Simpson now agreed with Scheck and his colleagues. He saw it for himself: His testimony would kill their case.

17

IT WAS TUESDAY, AUGUST 8, AND THE DEFENSE HAD TO call a pathologist in less than thirty-six hours. They still hadn't decided which pathologist.

The prosecution had formally requested Baden and Wolf's notes under discovery. Ito ordered the defense to produce them by nine A.M. on August 10 if either witness was going to testify. Baden was worrying loudly because he wasn't being prepared.

So who would it be? A little late to be making up our minds, Kardashian thought. He listened as Cochran called Peter Neufeld and Barry Scheck at their hotel. Lee and Carl joined Johnnie and Bob in the conference room.

"Peter, we're using Michael, right?" Johnnie begins. Neufeld is noncommittal. Either Michael or Barbara, he answers.

"Carl says he talked to a defense lawyer in Wolf's last

case. She comes across like a schoolteacher. Shapiro says he talked to Al McKenzie, another prosecutor in the same building as the D.A. He thought Michael was good. A veteran." Johnnie says O.J. will follow their lead on this.

Maybe the real problem here isn't the choice of pathologist; maybe it's Bob Shapiro, who'll present the witness, Cochran thinks. Now Shapiro doesn't want to call either of them. He feels the defense has accomplished enough in crossing Lakshmanan, the medical examiner. Nothing our own pathologist could say would advance the case.

"Tell Bobby this is one of the times he's got to use his personality," Cochran says. "He's got to be more compelling than that asshole Kelberg. He can't let Kelberg have a field day with Michael—if it's Michael. He's got to deal with the duration of the killings. The number of perpetrators. The different kinds of weapons that could have been used. The wounds on Goldman's hands, consistent with striking his assailant. This man stood up for a period of time and bled and the perpetrators had to have a lot of blood on them."

"Which of the two would you want?" Cochran asks Scheck.

"Tough call," Barry says. Neufeld won't commit, either.

Johnnie tries again. "Make your call from the standpoint of the jury."

"Henry Lee felt very strongly it should be Michael instead of Barbara," Neufeld answers. "Michael's had to stand up to people like Kelberg before."

"No question he's the foremost pathologist now in America," Barry adds. "He discovered all of Golden's errors that Lakshmanan testified to." Scheck seems to be leaning toward Baden.

"Tell Michael to be strong," Johnnie says. "Tell Bob this one time he has to be real strong, because Kelberg needs to be beaten." Cochran seems to be sidling into a decision.

"You know, Bob Shapiro was lobbying against Baden testifying," Neufeld says.

"I know. And if he still has any questions about it, we'll have someone else do it," Johnnie concludes.

"Okeydoke," Scheck says.

It's settled: Baden will take the stand for the defense on Thursday.

Now the real work began. Scheck knew Baden was overflowing with information about the case. The problem was getting him to focus. Scheck, Neufeld, and Blasier rehearsed his testimony with him, topic by topic, until dawn. They took special care on the subject of Ron Goldman's wounds.

The defense agreed with Lakshmanan that Goldman's first wounds were probably to the neck and that his final injuries were in the lung area. But Dr. Baden pointed out that there was no blood in Goldman's lungs. If the last stab wounds had been inflicted soon after the first, most of his blood would still have been in his body, and so his heart would have pumped blood into his injured lungs. However, if the struggle had been protracted, almost all the blood would have left his body before death and little or none would have entered his lungs. Baden concluded that Goldman died only after a lengthy struggle. This was exactly what the defense wanted. Heidstra had testified that he first heard the barking Akita around 10:40. Now Baden's expert opinion meant Ron Goldman might still have been locked in combat with his killer at 10:55, when limo driver Allan Park spotted O.J. at Rockingham. Baden's testimony on this point virtually exonerated Simpson. It had to be presented with maximum impact.

Bob Shapiro's style was a potential problem. Until now, the team practically had to drag him into prep sessions. He didn't like working from notes. He said he knew the case. All of it. But Scheck and his colleagues were firm: This testimony had to be different. Scheck prepared a lengthy outline for Shapiro to follow precisely. Shapiro still balked. Johnnie backed Scheck: Using Barry's script was nonnegotiable. Shapiro agreed. Reluctantly.

18

NEWS LEAK IRRELEVANT TO DEFENSE CONSPIRACY THEORY

The O.J. Simpson trial judge removed a rung from the ladder of evidence supporting the defense's conspiracy theory Wednesday, ruling that a news leak [Tracie Savage's report on NBC that tests on the sock from O.J.'s bedroom would show Nicole's blood, a report aired before the sock was sent for testing] wasn't material to the murder case.

While acknowledging the defense has presented extensive material to show blood could have been planted on a sock at Simpson's home . . . Ito said the defense failed to show that whoever prematurely revealed test results to journalists also likely tampered with evidence.

—Linda Deutsch, AP, August 9, 1995

ON THURSDAY MORNING, AUGUST 10, DR. MICHAEL Baden was sworn in. Johnnie was still wondering if they had made the right call on this witness. Barry Scheck could still hear Shapiro arguing against putting on *any* pathologist.

Carl Douglas knew the defense underestimated Baden. He was a veteran—not just an expert witness, but an expert at being a witness.

Shapiro took nearly an hour to run through Baden's credentials. Today he was unabashedly playing the race card. Hadn't Baden done autopsies in cases involving important

African-American figures such as Martin Luther King, Jr., and Medgar Evers? Yes. Hadn't he helped locally in the case of the African-American football player Ron Settles,* one of Johnnie's early triumphs? Yes. The autopsy on President Kennedy was mentioned, of course, as was the fact that Baden and Wolf had been down the hall a few weeks earlier, testifying for the prosecution in another case.

At lunch, Shapiro admitted to embarrassment. Was he too obvious on the racial issue? No. Well, then, he joked, had he forgotten anybody? No, Scheck said, deadpan.

In the afternoon, Shapiro used Barry's outline. Any lawyer armed with the script, Douglas thought, could have presented Baden. Courtroom expertise was needed only if Baden went off on tangents, as he had done so often in defense meetings. But today he was on target. Baden dismissed Dr. Lakshmanan's opinions as "possibilities," nothing more. He said the autopsy evidence didn't show how many killers were involved, whether one or two knives had been used, or whether the knife or knives were double-edged or single-edged. Baden kept his answers tight, sharply focused.

Shapiro asked Baden if he saw blood while examining the Rockingham socks at the LAPD lab twelve days after the murder.

"No," he answered firmly.

Scheck's outline emphasized that Ron Goldman had fought his killer at length. Baden felt the prosecution's contention that Goldman died quickly was simply a convenient way to explain why Simpson had so few cuts and no suspicious bruises. Baden's theory of a prolonged struggle required establishing that Goldman's jugular vein was severed before he received the stab wounds to the chest.

"The cut wound to the neck came first," Baden explained. That was demonstrated by the fact that Goldman's lungs contained very little blood, he said.

*Ron Settles was a college football player who was arrested on a traffic violation and jailed. The authorities claimed he hanged himself in his cell. A private autopsy later revealed he had suffered a beating and then died.

"How much blood is contained in an average adult male?" Shapiro asked.

"About five quarts."

Coroners had reported that only 100 to 200 cubic centimeters of blood, about a cup, had leaked through the lung wounds into Goldman's chest cavity, "a very small amount of blood to bleed from stab wounds of the lung," Baden now said.

Why so little blood? Because so much had gushed from Goldman's jugular vein that he had no blood pressure left to fill his lungs. He had lost more than 1,000 cubic centimeters of blood. It would have taken about ten minutes, Baden said.

Since the jugular wound drained downward, drenching Goldman's shirt and shoes, Baden concluded that he was upright when the vein was severed. He was probably still standing when the killer stabbed him in the chest. Most likely, they were struggling.

"It would take at least five, ten minutes for the heart to stop pumping effectively once he started bleeding from the jugular vein," Baden explained.

As long as fifteen minutes? Shapiro asked.

"It could be," Dr. Baden answered.

In one vivid image, Baden made a key defense argument come alive. If Baden was right—and his credentials argued that he was—Goldman lived long enough to fight his killer. He had knuckle bruises and a swollen right hand. Prosecutors argued that the bruises came from banging into the metal fence or a nearby tree as Goldman quickly expired. Baden's scenario was more compelling. Ron Goldman stayed on his feet and kept fighting. He hit his attacker hard enough to leave his own right hand swollen. He almost certainly left marks on his killer.

After lunch Brian Kelberg carried five boxes of transcripts into court. He started his cross at maximum volume. Douglas watched happily. Kelberg looked foolish. Ito shushed him: "The jury is only six feet away."

But Baden didn't get through cross-examination entirely unscathed. Kelberg doggedly forced him to admit that a single knife could have caused all the wounds. Baden also admitted that the widely publicized mistake of throwing away Nicole's stomach contents didn't really matter; they wouldn't have revealed a precise time of death. Then Kelberg asked if Baden had ever informed deputy coroner Irwin Golden about the mistakes found in the autopsy.

Baden saw his chance to take care of a personal matter. Months before, he had unwittingly engineered Golden's humiliation by coaching Shapiro on technical questions, something he regretted to this day. Now he paid a debt of conscience to Irwin Golden.

"Look, I don't want to trash Dr. Golden," Baden said. "He did a fine job. . . . His autopsy is better than most autopsies and better than the autopsy of President Kennedy."

Nonresponsive, Kelberg objected. Ito struck the remark from the record.

Nonetheless, Michael Baden had said what he wanted to say. On national television.

19

THAT SAME MORNING, THURSDAY, AUGUST 10, 1995, while Dr. Baden was waiting to testify, Matthew Schwartz and Ron Regwan appeared before Judge Ito to deliver the original and copies of seven audiocassette tapes and four microcassettes along with Laura Hart McKinny's original transcripts.

Ito turned the copies over to the defense and ordered them not to duplicate, disseminate, or publish the tapes or transcripts. He named Johnnie and Carl as the only members of the defense team allowed access besides those persons making transcriptions under their direction. The tension in Johnnie's office was at its highest since the day of the murders, when the staff wondered if Johnnie would get the case. Now, as they waited for the Fuhrman tapes, they were no less excited.

Just before noon Carl walked into the office, smiling. He carried the set of duplicate tapes that McKinny's attorneys had given the court for the defense.

Cochran's office had never handled anything like this before—transcribing eleven hours of tapes in, say, two or three days. Carl gave the tapes to his assistant, Carmen Qualls. He soon saw this was no one-person job, so he added a second typist, but she could only work nights. A third worked half days and half nights: Even at five in the morning, someone was transcribing. To hire outside typists was impossible, of course.

That Thursday night, Bailey stood around waiting for something to read. Cochran had a driver deliver a copy of McKinny's transcripts to Gerry Uelmen at his hotel.

"How come you're not sharing a copy with me?" he asked Carl, reminding him that he and Uelmen were working together on the presentation to the court, asking the judge to allow excerpts from the tapes to be played before the jury.

"I've got my marching orders on this one," Carl replied.

Bailey stood before Carl. Mad. Getting madder every second.

"It's demeaning," Bailey said, "insulting to me as O.J.'s attorney."

Then he turned and left. Douglas had never seen his friend this upset.

By the next afternoon, Friday, August 11, only two tapes had been finished. Their audio quality was poor; much of the dialogue couldn't be heard because of background noise, and in some cases, different transcribers heard the same section differently. This would never do.

Kardashian suggested that Carl consult Larry Schiller, the

writer who had helped Simpson with *I Want to Tell You*. Larry was also a TV motion-picture director. He should know something about sound.

Schiller represented a risk. Carl considered him a journalist. How could you trust any writer not to take the tapes for his own purposes? But Kardashian vouched for him, and Kardashian was the closest person on the team to Simpson.

That same evening, two security guards took the first five tapes to a sound studio in Burbank, where Schiller was waiting amid the most modern computer programs and sound-reduction equipment to filter out background noise. State-of-the-art *Star Wars* stuff. Through the weekend, from ten at night till four in the morning, Schiller worked on the tapes until he had completed all eleven hours of tape. Before sunrise each morning he gave the defense improved copies for transcribing.

On Monday, August 14, Simpson sits in the holding cell, waiting for his attorneys. Over the weekend the prosecution and the defense have independently transcribed the Fuhrman tapes. Kardashian can feel the tension when he arrives at the courthouse with Johnnie. One reporter shouts, "What do the Fuhrman tapes mean? Is it enough to get your client off?" Cochran is quick: "No, it's all the evidence that's going to get him off." He and Carl know the snowball is now an avalanche.

Douglas and Kardashian walk into the holding cell and give Simpson some of the transcripts. Outside, in the courtroom, Shapiro, Scheck, Blasier, Neufeld, and Uelmen are sharing two other copies.

O.J. starts reading aloud to Kardashian, paging through quickly. "Can you believe this?" he keeps saying. "Listen to this." Simpson is totally absorbed.

Outside the holding cell, Marcia Clark calls for a meeting in Ito's chambers.

Cochran, Shapiro, Scheck, and Neufeld sit down with Clark and Darden. Marcia begins by telling the judge that she's read the D.A.'s transcripts over the weekend. From the expression on her face it is clear that she is the bearer of bad tidings.

"Mark Fuhrman discusses Lieutenant York," she tells Ito. "He makes derogatory comments." Ito says he has no problem discussing this potential conflict in open court. But Ito doesn't know what the tapes actually say about his wife. Cochran does: Fuhrman says York "sucked her way to the top" and was "an asshole." Another example: Fuhrman brags of how he defied her—"You're a joke, I'm not going to listen to you." Cochran hinted about "inconsistencies" between Fuhrman's remarks and York's signed declaration. The tapes confirm that they knew each other.

But there's worse on the tapes than mindless name-calling. Cochran gives Ito examples of Fuhrman's character-izations of blacks and Mexicans.

Scheck then quotes Fuhrman: "The job of the police officer is to lie and create probable cause." Clark calls Scheck a liar, insists that the remark isn't on the tape. Barry stands his ground. "No question. This man is talking about his view of the job of the police officer and how that all ties into racial attitude."

Ito wants to return to the legal issues, "because we may be talking mistrial." The judge explains: "It's a double prob-lem because if he is disparaging (a) of my wife, and (b) of Internal Affairs, where my wife is now the commanding officer . . . that makes it a double whammy here. This is obviously a problem that we will have to broach first. Fuhrman may have to testify."

Cochran makes it clear he doesn't want a mistrial.

Marcia then surprises everyone. She tells Ito that the D.A. may want to call York to testify in Fuhrman's behalf.

Conflicts multiply every time someone opens his mouth.

"You know how to get around this, Marcia," Ito tells Clark. Her face is one big question mark. She doesn't get Ito's point. Cochran interrupts angrily. "Your Honor, you've already been telling them how to run their case." It's obvious to the defense that Ito is suggesting that the prosecution withdraw all of Fuhrman's testimony: Then he can't be recalled.

The D.A. can't really do that, Douglas thinks. The jurors have already seen Fuhrman. *Maybe* they think he lied. Now the D.A. withdraws his testimony? The prosecution would be going out of its way to damage its case. Carl thinks the D.A. should quietly file perjury charges against Fuhrman, that's all.

Ito is at a loss here. He hasn't heard a moment of the tapes or seen a page of transcript. Nothing is officially before the court yet. He can only outline hypothetical options. He can have someone else deal with the tapes, he says, but "I don't see how another judge can step in and make an admissibility call in this context." That brings them back to a possible mistrial.

"If the prosecution declares a mistrial, we don't agree to it," Johnnie declares.

"I don't want a mistrial," Clark says. "I just want a clean record."

Cochran can't restrain himself. "If you want a clean record," he snaps at Marcia, "you should have kept Fuhrman shut up."

With nothing resolved, Ito concludes the meeting and convenes court. Fredric Rieders will testify first, and Michele Kestler, a supervisor at the LAPD lab, is scheduled to follow. How can anyone concentrate?

As Rieders takes the witness stand, Simpson is buried in the transcripts, oblivious to anything happening in court. He reads steadily and slowly. Fuhrman admits on the tapes that the cops have manufactured evidence in other cases. For the first time, Simpson sees evidence that Fuhrman could have planted the glove at Rockingham. This is no longer hearsay. He holds one bad cop's own words in his two hands.

Simpson, like Scheck, had at first been skeptical. This was too good to be true. Don't put too much hope in the tapes, O.J. kept saying. But now the transcripts are overpowering.

As O.J. read, Kardashian said to himself: Only O.J. and Fuhrman know whether Fuhrman planted it or he didn't. Then Bob revised his thought: God knows, and whoever left the glove knows.

Simpson was mouthing the words he read. Some reporters started trying to read his lips.

All the while, Blasier dealt with Rieders on the stand. The

forgotten men. It was a safe bet only the court reporter was listening.

O.J. wasn't alone in his preoccupation. Despite Ito's orders, almost everyone on the defense team was reading the transcripts in court. Kardashian kept leaning over to look at Johnnie's copy. Carl walked over to Kardashian several times: "Read this, read this."

I used to go to work and practice movements. Niggers. They're easy. I used to practice my kicks.

—McKinny tape no. 4

Go to Wilshire division. Wilshire division is all niggers. All Niggers. Nigger training officers, niggers . . . with three years on the job.

—McKinny tape no. 5

How do you intellectualize when you punch the hell out of a nigger? He either deserves it or he doesn't.

—McKinny tape no. 9

Leave the old station. Man, it has the smell of Niggers that have been beaten and killed in there for years.

—McKinny tape no. 10

[Referring to U.S. aid to drought victims:] You know these people here, we got all this money going to Ethiopia for what. To feed a bunch of dumb niggers that their own government won't even feed.

—McKinny transcript no. 1
[McKinny no longer had the tape]

Kardashian can't find the word "black" or "blacks"—much less "African-American"—anywhere in the transcripts. The detective seems to know one word only: "nigger."

At the lunch break, the defense again meets in the jury room. That York is Ito's wife and may have lied about knowing Fuhrman in a sworn declaration gives the defense

712

grounds for a mistrial. But where is the advantage? Douglas says the reason Marcia is threatening to call York is that the D.A. seems to be losing and wants a mistrial. But can Clark justify scuttling a $6 million case and committing the People to a retrial? Wouldn't that be political suicide?

Neufeld and Scheck are worrying that Ito will fuck them over and rule the tapes inadmissible. Blasier agrees. But Johnnie wants to turn the publicity groundswell to advantage. He talks about playing five or six hours of tape in open court. In your dreams, Kardashian thinks.

Johnnie tells them he's meeting with McKinny and her attorneys at 6:30 in his office. He asks Scheck, Shapiro, Uelmen, Bailey, and Douglas to attend. Johnnie says that McKinny's interview with Fuhrman in July 1994 will guarantee that O.J. walks—*if* Ito admits it as evidence. In this interview, recorded after the murders, Fuhrman calls Shapiro "the Jew" and talks about how he's going to take the lawyer's swimming pool away when he wins his lawsuit over the allegations in the *New Yorker* article. More important, he talks about the glove: "I am the key witness in the biggest case of the century. And, if I go down, they lose the case. The glove is everything. Without the glove—bye-bye."

Everyone knows that by now, the entire prosecution team has also read those words.

FUHRMAN'S LAWYERS DEMAND ACCESS TO INTERVIEW TAPES

Detective Mark Fuhrman sent his lawyers into battle at the O.J. Simpson trial, asserting the detective's right to tape recordings the defense lawyers say will prove he is a liar.

"There could be further injury and defamation to Detective Fuhrman, and he has no ability whatsoever to rebut any of this because he's been denied any access to his own voice," [Laurie] Butler [Fuhrman's attorney] argued.

One of McKinny's attorneys, Ron Regwan, said . . . his

client likely would allow Fuhrman to review the tapes and transcripts at the attorneys' office.

—Linda Deutsch, AP, August 14, 1995

20

ON TUESDAY, AUGUST 15, THE AVALANCHE ARRIVED ON Judge Ito's doorstep. Ito called all the attorneys present into his chambers.

Carl Douglas was convinced Ito had discussed the tapes with his wife. LAPD Internal Affairs, which she now heads, learned of the tapes over the weekend. Carl couldn't fathom anything of such importance not being discussed between husband and wife.

Now the judge started by reading the lawyers the relevant portions of the civil procedure code. "If my wife is a material witness," Ito told them, "then under this code section, I'm required to disqualify myself and perhaps declare a mistrial at this point." Clark repeated her desire to call York.

The defense knew Clark was pushing them all toward a mistrial. Could another judge take over for Ito? What would the inevitable delay do to the jury? By now the room was full: Cochran, Shapiro, Neufeld, Douglas, Blasier, and Scheck for the defense, and Clark, Darden, and Hodgman for the prosecution.

The York issue could not be dealt with, Marcia said, without a ruling on whether and how much of the Fuhrman tapes were admissible. Clark felt another judge should rule on all the tapes, not just the York sections.

Johnnie spoke up: "We would like to argue this in open court." He wanted the publicity. Then he assured Ito the defense would never call Captain York as a witness, "because we don't want a mistrial."

For nine months the knowledge that York might have lied in her declaration had been the defense's hidden weapon. They could have used it themselves to cause a mistrial if they had seen a conviction coming. Now Johnnie relinquished it once and for all. A necessary trade-off to get the Fuhrman tapes before the jury and prevent a mistrial.

"We propose that the tapes be given to you with the parts [about York] redacted," Cochran continued. "These tapes prove it [Fuhrman's perjury] in his own voice, and Peggy York has nothing to do with it." Johnnie is working hard to save a winning case. "We want to go forward. Captain York will never be called as a witness by us. I want to make sure everybody knows where we stand on this. We want to do this in open court."

Cochran wants his message made public. Enough wasted time. There are twelve jurors waiting to hear evidence. He makes his key point: "On July 28, 1994, Mark Fuhrman says, 'I am the key witness in the trial of the century. They know it. If I go down, their case goes down, bye-bye.'" He wants this statement to leak to the media.

Scheck speaks for the first time. "We think this is a deliberate effort to create a mistrial," he says, referring to Clark's earlier statements.

"I don't think Mr. Scheck should be allowed to be heard," Clark replies immediately. She probably means that Scheck is violating the court's "one lawyer to an issue" procedural rule. But they are in chambers. All parties know the rule doesn't apply here.

Scheck is furious.

As the private conference ends, Marcia says that she will oppose the admissibility of the tapes, no matter what their content. Barry repeats that the D.A. is acting in bad faith.

"Shut up, Scheck!" Clark snaps as they leave chambers. Bill Hodgman looks on in dismay.

* * *

Judge Ito sent the jury home while he held the open hearing Cochran had requested. No question, the matter before the court now was more important than the scheduled testimony.

Johnnie was sure Marcia wanted another bite at the apple. A new trial. One in which Fuhrman never set foot in the courtroom, one in which all the LAPD errors were neutralized. The trial could be held in West Los Angeles, where the jury pool would provide few blacks. Most important, Douglas figured, the defense would lose the element of surprise. "Just put all our secrets in your briefcase," Carl said. "Take a year and figure out how to deal with them." The second time around, the prosecution won't make the same mistakes. Ito's wife was the prosecutors' exit from a disaster, and they could blame it all on Fuhrman.

In mid-morning, what had been said in chambers about York for the past two days was repeated in open court.

At 1:50 P.M. Ito heard final arguments from both sides.

"I've heard enough, I've heard enough," he finally said. "When a concern is raised regarding a court's ability to be fair and impartial, it is not the actual existence of impartiality or partiality that is the issue, it is the appearance. I love my wife dearly and I am wounded by criticism of her, as any spouse would be." Ito's voice was choked with emotion. "I think it is reasonable to assume that that could have some impact.

"I therefore recuse myself from the issue of the tapes themselves and specifically whether or not Captain York is a material and relevant witness. This matter is therefore . . . transferred . . . for reassignment.

"I suspect I won't get a Christmas card from the judge who gets this case," Ito concluded. He hardly looked happy, but he managed the wry comment with aplomb.

SIMPSON TRIAL THROWN INTO CHAOS

"This is a blockbuster! This is a bombshell!" defense attorney Johnnie Cochran Jr. said [of the Fuhrman tapes]. "This is perhaps the biggest thing that's happened in any case in this country in this decade."

Marcia Clark said the judge might have to surrender the bench [to another jurist] for the rest of the trial. . . .

"There is no ability to sever this issue," Clark said. "All rulings involving Fuhrman witnesses become suspect."

—Linda Deutsch, AP, August 16, 1995

That evening at six the defense gathered in Cochran's conference room. Dershowitz, on the phone from Boston, opened the meeting by stating that if Clark had been the lawyer in the Rodney King case, she would have said that *that* tape was immaterial. They were all still on edge from the day's events, and Alan's wisecrack was a welcome, if brief, respite.

Johnnie told Dershowitz, "Ito was almost in tears when Marcia told him face to face in chambers, 'We think we want to recuse you.'"

"She sandbagged him too," Alan replied.

What to do now? Judge John Reid in Department 100 had the transcripts. Clark wanted Ito removed from the case.

Johnnie's first concern was the jurors. "They are going to get really pissed. They don't know totally what is happening yet, but they will by tomorrow. It's visitation day."

"What if the jury rebels like they did when the bailiffs were thrown off?" Shapiro wonders.

"Then it's not our fault," Neufeld says.

"We have to keep on saying this is bad faith on the D.A.'s part," Scheck added.

"I suspect," Dershowitz says, "if this case were to go to an appellate court for an advisory opinion they would rule that Ito should come back after this is over."

Barry still wants to find a way to litigate the recusal issue, since it was bogus in the first place. "All Clark wanted to do was derail this trial. Yesterday she was willing to stipulate that a witness lied under oath. Today she wants Ito out." The defense should challenge the issue of recusal, Scheck insists.

"We've got to find a way," Alan says, "and maybe the

717

forum is the judicial council. Let's just assume the prosecution comes in tomorrow and says, 'We don't back off. We need Peggy York.' Therefore, Ito's recused. Then we have the right to take it to the judicial council, not about who the new judge should be, but about the fact that there is no basis for a full recusal.''

"You may be right, Alan," Johnnie says.

Bailey wants to know if there is such thing as a partial recusal. "Just tell the jury Fuhrman lied," he says. "He can't give valid testimony.''

"Ito's already made a finding that there's an appearance of impropriety in his deciding certain issues," Neufeld says. "Finally the issue is simply whether or not there's such a thing as a partial recusal.''

Neufeld reminds the team of a Chris Darden comment: "I said to Darden, 'You don't have to worry. You guys own the courthouse.' Darden said, 'Well, we own the courthouse, but there was one part we didn't own. Now we do, and that's 103.' He's saying they own Ito now.''

21

On Wednesday, August 16, Kardashian drove to the courthouse with Cochran. Even though Ito's recusal was the first order of business, the subject didn't come up. Right now they had to decide whether to call to the stand Howard Weitzman, O.J.'s attorney for the first thirty-six hours after the murders. They wanted Weitzman to testify that Vannatter wouldn't allow Simpson to have an attorney present at his taped interview with the police and that O.J. insisted he didn't mind being questioned without his attorney present.

But Howard wasn't giving them much help. Johnnie was angry. At first, the defense team had thought Weitzman was wary because he was in line for a high-level corporate job. But that excuse had evaporated. "You've got the job at MCA now, motherfucker," Johnnie said as if Weitzman were in the room. "You're going to testify." Kardashian pointed out that Weitzman's boss, Ron Meyer, was a good guy, wouldn't hold it against Howard if he testified. So how hard to press the matter? O.J. would have to make the call on that.

Before Johnnie visited O.J., both sides convened in Ito's chambers. Shapiro, Cochran, Uelmen, Darden, and Clark were present. The session was off the record, with no court reporter. It would later be made public. Ito seemed to be in a better mood; he would soon have a few days off.

"I haven't vented in a long time and I would like to," Darden said immediately. "We think you have been unfair with us," he told the judge. "It started with Kelberg; you cut him off. You allowed Mr. Cochran six days of cross-examination and you would not allow Mr. Kelberg his cross-examination. You embarrassed him. You ridiculed him in front of the jury, and we don't like that. You continued to do that the next day with Miss Clark. You vilified her in front of the jury. We don't like that."

Later, Carl Douglas had to shake his head when he heard about this outburst. Darden was acting as if his buttons had been pushed when no one had said a word. True, Johnnie had crossed Detective Lange for six days—but Marcia's redirect had taken place during those same days. And when had Ito "vilified" Marcia? It was hard to follow the specifics of Darden's accusations.

At the off-the-record chambers meeting, Cochran became indignant. So did Shapiro and Uelmen. They found Darden's attack on the judge reprehensible.

"I'm not going to sit here and listen," Cochran said to Ito. "You can if you want." He ordered Shapiro and Uelmen to leave with him.

As they walked out of chambers, Shapiro said, "They want to play with their ball, on their field, with their referee, and as soon as anyone disagrees with their position, he's out." Had Chris Darden revealed the real reason the D.A. had sought Ito's recusal? Did the prosecution actually believe Ito favored the defense?

Minutes later Scheck, Neufeld, Kardashian, Douglas, and Blasier gathered around Johnnie at the defense table. Johnnie had fire in his eyes. Shapiro suggested presenting the facts in open court, since Cochran was so upset.

Ito convened court at 9:40 A.M. to continue the hearing on the recusal issue.

Marcia Clark opened by saying the prosecution had examined all the relevant cases and the issues of conflict raised by the Fuhrman tapes. The issue before the court was not race. The evidence must decide the case, not the use of the "N-word," she stated.

"We have to be concerned with the public perception that these proceedings are conducted fairly," Clark went on. "We are entitled under the law to seek the course of recusal, but we have determined that it is not the only course. We have determined that our faith in this court's wisdom and integrity has not been and will not be misplaced." Carl Douglas had to shake his head again at Darden's attack on Ito half an hour ago. Had Chris been trying to get his complaints aired while the judge felt vulnerable?

The prosecution, no doubt with Gil Garcetti's approval, had made a 180-degree turn overnight. Clark now agreed that Ito could determine the admissibility of the tapes with the exception of the portions mentioning York. And she proposed that Ito get a redacted version of the tapes for his ruling—just what Johnnie had suggested in chambers the day before.

Judge Reid would decide on whether York was a material witness. But he would confine his ruling to that one point, Ito added.

"We may not even desire to call Captain York after we know what the ruling is, so we need to get that resolved first," Marcia added.

Ito ordered the defense to provide its motion arguing for the admission of the tapes the next day, so that the trial could move ahead.

Then Shapiro asked that the conversation that had just taken place in chambers be put on the record. Ito allowed him five minutes. Shapiro went step by step, quoting Darden's statement and the defense's interpretation.

Darden was allowed his turn, and he hit hard. "For a year now, these defense attorneys have been holding over your head the issue of Captain York. It is extortion," he said. "It has been a year-long extortion to get you to allow as much racist and irrelevant and inflammatory incidents into trial as possible." Darden couldn't have known it for sure, but he was half right. The defense had never used its knowledge of the York-Fuhrman connection in any way at all, but having the option might have lent it a psychological edge. Darden's intuition outweighed his ability to make his point calmly.

Douglas knew the most intriguing question would never be answered. Had Ito known for almost a year that his wife lied about knowing Fuhrman? Or had he just found out now, through the Fuhrman tapes?

After three long days the trial seemed to be back on track. The D.A. had backed down. The defense had relinquished the York issue for good.

That evening Cochran, Douglas, and Kardashian sat in Johnnie's office listening to the news.

> It's not clear exactly why prosecutors would move in that direction [to recuse Ito], except for their stated concerns about a possible conflict of interest. Judge Ito's wife, a police captain, is a target of disparaging remarks by Detective Mark Fuhrman, on tapes that may be introduced as defense evidence.

"*May* be introduced?" Kardashian said with a big smile.

Cochran was more interested in the fact that the ACLU was now on Fuhrman's case. The city council was calling for an investigation. The police commissioner wanted the tapes. The *Los Angeles Times* planned to print transcript excerpts. After that, the Justice Department would want all the tapes. The Fuhrman tapes had taken on a life of their own.

BACK FROM THE BRINK;
PROSECUTION WON'T SEEK ITO'S OUSTER

. . . Prosecutors retreated from their threat to seek his ouster and essentially embraced the defense position that Ito should rule on the tapes after hearing edited versions of them.

[The move to recuse Ito] "amounted to prosecutional extortion of the judiciary," Shapiro said. "This is unethical conduct at its highest."

"This case is a circus! And they've made it a circus," said Darden. . . . "If Mr. Shapiro and Mr. Cochran want to refer me to the state Bar, fine, because . . . I'm going to be referring defense attorneys to the United States Attorney's Office!"

—Michael Fleeman, AP, August 16, 1995

The next morning—Thursday, August 17—Kardashian and Douglas are sitting with O.J. in the holding cell discussing the jury's impending second visit to the crime scene, planned for the same time of night the murders took place. How can they arrange the lights to the defense's advantage?

"There's a light that's supposed to light up the address in the mailbox area," Kardashian notes. "Facing toward the bodies." But there won't be any bodies.

Then Simpson hits on the real problem with the night jury view: "If there's nothing to see it doesn't matter what lights are on. Assume the bodies are already there, and you've also got to assume the dog is barking. The prosecution's witnesses said the dog started barking and never stopped. It's not what they *saw*," he says, "it's what they *heard*."

"That's a great argument to be made to the jury," Bob says.

That afternoon the defense called LAPD fingerprint comparison expert Gil Aguilar. If Simpson was the murderer, and if one hand was bare at least some of the time, as the single glove suggested, why were his fingerprints absent? The LAPD had dusted Bundy and lifted numerous latent prints, none of which was Simpson's.

722

Better yet, out of seventeen prints lifted, the LAPD found nine sets of prints they couldn't identify at all. They had printed every cop, county employee, and friend of Nicole's who had been at Bundy—fifty-eight people in all. Nine sets of unidentified prints are something for the jury to think about.

"Did you have occasion to look at the seventeen prints lifted from Bundy and compare those prints yourself with those of Mr. O.J. Simpson?" Johnnie asked.

Aguilar did.

Cochran asked what he found.

"That none of the latent prints recovered from the scene were identified to Mr. Simpson."

On cross Chris Darden asked, "Mr. Aguilar, you wouldn't expect a person wearing a pair of gloves to leave fingerprints at a location, would you?"

"No," Aguilar replied.

Watching on TV, Pavelic thought about Kato Kaelin and Marcus Allen. Had their prints been matched to those found at Bundy? He checked with Dennis Payne at the LAPD, who would know. The answer was no.

That evening at Cochran's office, Johnnie says he's sure the D.A. will concede that Fuhrman's a racist, but insist that he didn't plant the glove. That won't work, Johnnie tells the team. They can't have it both ways.

Henry Lee's been calling from Connecticut. He wants to get on the stand soon. That would mean Laura McKinny or Fuhrman might be the last witness for the defense. Johnnie doesn't like that. Douglas agrees: "McKinny's not an expert witness, Lee is," he says. And McKinny is talking to the D.A. as much as she's talking to the defense. Johnnie doesn't want to end with something iffy.

Carl Douglas is getting pissed off at Henry Lee. One day Lee's in Indonesia or Micronesia; who knows where he'll be next week? Thank God Barry Scheck has the job of baby-sitting the criminalist. They like each other.

"Strategically, he'll be a much better witness early next week than a week later," Scheck points out now. Lee's testimony will introduce the defense's last two critical attacks on the physical evidence: the "wet blood transfers" in the bindles, and the second set of shoe prints. The doctor's notes have been turned over to the prosecution; it's not smart to give the D.A. time to find alternative explanations.

"Get him saddled up, get him out here," Bailey says. They all agree that Dr. Lee shouldn't be delayed.

This leads to Bailey's plan for the "Fuhrman funeral." Who should come first: Laura Hart McKinny, Mark Fuhrman, or Kathleen Bell?

"We need to decide tonight," Johnnie says. We know, he went on, that we're going to call all three of them. "To question Fuhrman, we've got to get Bell on first," he suggests. Bailey agrees that Bell and Andrea Terry must come before Fuhrman. That leaves McKinny either first, third, or last. We can decide that on Sunday, Bailey says.

"When Fuhrman takes the stand, can he invoke the Fifth Amendment in front of the jury under California law?" Barry asks. "Or is that something that takes place outside the presence of the jury?"

Uelmen says, "He cannot be called and simply take the Fifth in front of the jury."

Actually, Fuhrman is in the middle of his cross-examination. He's being recalled. This prompts more questions from Barry. "In cross-examination, when it might show he was involved in criminal conduct, and he takes the Fifth, then is that before the jury, or outside the jury? Does he have a lawyer?"

Dershowitz says he thinks the defense is better off if Fuhrman doesn't take the Fifth. Let the entire country watch him try to explain away his own taped voice. "Remember what a terrific liar he was, how everybody in America was conned? That was because he's a trained liar."

So far, the prosecution has been saying publicly that Fuhrman's statements on the tapes don't refer to actual incidents. Rather, he made up stories, solely for dramatic purposes. The defense maintains that what Fuhrman said is true; he has done the things he described to McKinny. To support their position the defense has suggested to the *Los Angeles Times* that the paper independently investigate one of the excerpts that they hoped to use but that has not yet been made public.

ON TAPE, FUHRMAN DESCRIBES INCIDENT SIMILAR TO '78 EVENT

. . . Sources say the Los Angeles Police Department has now uncovered records of a Nov. 18, 1978, incident in Boyle Heights that matches many details [of a bloody beating spree after two policemen were shot] described by Fuhrman in that audiotape. . . .

"They knew damn well I did it," he said. . . . "But there was nothing they could do about it. Most of the guys worked 77th [Street Division] together. We were tight. I mean, we could have murdered people. We all knew what to say. . . .

"Two of my buddies were shot and ambushed, policemen. . . . Both down when I arrived . . . and we kicked the door down, grabbed the girl . . . stuck a gun to her head, and used her as a barricade." . . .

Fuhrman said the beating continued until "we had them begging that they would never be gang members again" and included throwing some of them down two flights of stairs.

"We basically tortured them. . . . We broke 'em. Their faces were just mush. They had pictures of the walls with blood all the way to the ceiling and finger marks of trying to crawl out of the room."

Afterward, . . . "We had blood all over our legs."

—Jim Newton and Henry Weinstein,
Los Angeles Times, August 18, 1995

THE RELEVANCE OF THE DETECTIVE'S TAPES

. . . From what is now known about the detective's taped comments, they seem clearly germane to the trial and ought to be admitted into evidence, notwithstanding their highly inflammatory content. . . .

Whether the tapes will further the pursuit of justice is not clear. If Mr. Simpson is innocent, then discrediting this detective and raising reasonable doubts with the jury may help him prevail. But if Mr. Simpson in fact murdered his former wife, Nicole Brown Simpson, and her friend Ronald Goldman, the tapes help a guilty man go free. Mr. Goldman's family has already complained bitterly that defense lawyers are diverting attention from a mound of evidence against Mr. Simpson by putting Detective Fuhrman on trial rather than the celebrated athlete.

—*New York Times* editorial, August 18, 1995

Alan Dershowitz remembered his early prediction that Marcia Clark would play it smart and never call Mark Fuhrman as a witness. He'd been wrong. She had put Fuhrman on the stand, his testimony was televised, and the tapes had surfaced.

"It's unimportant how many segments Ito will ultimately let in," Alan told Johnnie. "What's more important is that the prosecution knows we have the tapes. They can no longer attack Kathleen Bell." The Fuhrman tapes would corroborate Bell's testimony and prove Fuhrman's perjury. That was excellent. But Johnnie also knew it was just a small slice of the pie.

JUDGE ITO'S WIFE IRRELEVANT TO SIMPSON CASE

[Judge] Ito's wife can offer no relevant testimony in the O.J. Simpson murder trial, . . . cementing Ito's role as trial judge.

The decision by . . . Judge John H. Reid also settles the conflict-of-interest dispute prompted by the taped interviews of former Detective Mark Fuhrman.

As the tapes continue to rock the trial . . . no testimony was given Friday and jurors were sent to the beach.

—Michael Fleeman, AP, August 18, 1995

22

ON SUNDAY, AUGUST 20, THE DEFENSE GATHERED IN Cochran's conference room. The defense case would be over in two weeks at most.

"I know it's our job to get Simpson off," Johnnie began, "but I think our legacy should be to show this country that the cops will do just about anything. They will lie because they believe that the end justifies the means." Johnnie was chronically distressed that the average white person always thinks he knows what's going on—while being, in fact, deeply naive about police corruption. The Fuhrman tapes gave Johnnie another weapon for his lifelong battle.

Cochran and Neufeld then clashed over the use of the media. Johnnie was ready to let the team members appear on TV. Peter disagreed sharply. "It's not that I'm opposed to the press," he said. "But I want to speak only when we can control the forum. It's a mistake to go on shows like *Larry King* or *Nightline,* where someone else can define the parameters." Johnnie listened carefully. He respected Neufeld's acumen. "What you say in the courtroom and at a press conference is what matters. It's a strategic mistake to make yourself available to the shows."

Cochran didn't see it that way. "If Goldman gets up there and says, 'Simpson butchered my son,' fuck him. He's not

727

on the fucking jury and I won't take that shit. My heart goes out to him, but he's simply wrong. The client is presumed innocent. That's the bulwark of our system. I am not going to take a backseat to anyone anymore. If I get on the *Nightline* show, I'll answer anything he asks. I'm not going to let the other side take the day." But there was, of course, a case to finish. In the end, Johnnie agreed with Peter that the work had to come first and everyone should stay off TV.

On Sunday evening Larry Schiller spoke to Douglas about how to present the Fuhrman tapes in court. Don't play them alone, Schiller said. Don't let the jury just read transcripts. Carl thought this guy was becoming a pain in the ass.

Schiller continued: Let the jury relate to the material as they relate to TV news, to a sound bite.

When Douglas heard "sound bite," he decided to listen more closely. Douglas still didn't trust Schiller: The guy was a writer. Let me see what you have in mind, Carl said. Of course, security went along.

Meanwhile, on Monday, August 21, the question of whether Howard Weitzman would testify is before O.J., and Simpson can't understand why Weitzman won't take the stand.

"I've known Howard for forty years," Kardashian tells him. "He will not, under any circumstances, embarrass himself publicly." Howard's potential testimony—that he gave in lamely to a naive client and a bullying cop—may occasion some laughter at his expense. He's now a full-time member of the establishment in a high-level corporate job.

"He's got the media support and he's now got the backing of MCA," Bob explains. "He's concerned only with his image."

But Simpson needs Weitzman's testimony on that one point. Vannatter will lie. Count on it. If the defense can get Howard on the stand, Weitzman won't lie. So fuck him. Subpoena Weitzman.

When Johnnie and Peter leave for the courtroom, Kardashian and Simpson quickly get back to their gin rummy.

"When you walk out of here, Juice, with a pay-per-view deal," Kardashian says while looking at his cards, "your take will be thirty-five million. With my twenty percent commission, you'll still have twenty-eight million left.''

"I'd be the happiest fucking man in the world," O.J. replies. *"If* that happens.''

"You'd better have security everywhere you go," Bob tells him. "You're going to need some protection.''

"I'll go to New York, because they don't give a shit about anything back there," Simpson says. "It's hard to be a redneck in New York City." They both chuckle.

Then Kardashian falls silent. It's not going to happen, he says to himself. Nobody in his right mind will pay to hear O.J. tell his story.

When Ito called the court to order that same day, the public learned that over the weekend the prosecution had withdrawn its request for a night viewing of the crime scene. The lighting showed either too much or not enough. The defense was delighted.

Then McKinny's attorneys, Schwartz and Regwan, requested that the court investigate the *Los Angeles Times* publication of verbatim quotations from the Fuhrman tapes. Ito denied the request on the grounds that the leak had more than likely come from the defense's motion supporting the tapes' admissibility as evidence. The motion had been filed under seal on August 17, the day before the *Times* publication. There was no need to investigate.

At lunch, Bailey told Cochran he was taking Laura McKinny flying. "Now, Lee, I don't mind your flying," Johnnie told him. "But don't take Laura. I don't want her killed in a plane crash now." Bailey, of course, was trying to ingratiate himself with McKinny. He was still pitching to do her direct examination. "If there has to be a crash, you make sure she's not in it." Cochran's tone was light, but his resolve was iron. No more witnesses for Bailey. Not even if he chartered the Concorde.

That morning and after lunch, Larry Ragle, the former head of the Orange County crime lab, testified that the LAPD forensic work in the Simpson case was substandard. On cross, Hank Goldberg was able to bring out nothing worse than the fact that Ragle had retired in 1989 and had not been involved with major crime investigations since 1976.

As Ragle left the stand he walked over to Vannatter, whom he'd known for years, to say hello. He put out his hand.

"You're a traitor, a disgrace as a former police officer," Vannatter growled. "You're a *traitor*." Ragle was startled.

Cochran was blunt: Vannatter was a "motherfucker."

On the way home, Johnnie, Carl, and Kardashian are still preoccupied with the Vannatter incident.

"He called him a traitor," Johnnie says.

"They stick together, don't they?" Kardashian adds. "Maybe we'll call Ragle back and say Vannatter was intimidating a witness," Johnnie suggests, seeming tickled by the possibility.

Carl, playing devil's advocate, says Vannatter might have thought Ragle was provoking him. Johnnie laughs.

"Someone said, 'You're going to get hurt, boy,' when I walked past the crowd today," Johnnie says more somberly. "We have to increase our protection. From now on, we all go down to court en masse and with an armed guard. We're getting toward the end of this case. I'm going to lock up my house." The three lawyers fall silent. "I think it's the best insurance."

Johnnie deliberately lightens the mood. "When O.J. gets out, the best insurance for him is to get a black date."

Right, says Kardashian, somebody with a big Afro. Carl starts laughing.

"I want somebody dark," Johnnie says.

"Can't be cream color or bronze," Bob adds.

Then Kardashian notices a girl just outside the car: "*There's* a girl for O.J."

"Not dark enough," Johnnie says. "I want a black woman with black, black hair. Got to be *real* black." Johnnie can't stop laughing. "Yeah, with a wide ass. And he has to say, 'I love this woman for who she is inside.'"

O.J.'s got to love her for her personality, her heart, Bob adds. "That's part of his punishment."

"O.J. been *saying* he wants a change," Johnnie replies.

"When his neighbors hear he's moving back to Brentwood, they'll buy his house." Kardashian can't contain himself. "They'll all chip in. He'll move to New York or Hawaii with his kids."

"He's got a major battle coming with the Browns to get his kids home," Johnnie reminds them. The levity is over. It never lasts long.

"When he gets out, he'll get his kids," Bob says. "They can't keep them."

"Terrible, this case from hell," Johnnie sighs.

"To get out of jail and not be able to have your kids," Kardashian says sadly.

"We've seen everything," Johnnie says. "Boy, I tell you, we could write a book just about how crazy this case is."

Carl adds his TFC. By now it's the defense team's "Amen."

On Tuesday, August 22, the defense filed its final brief for the Fuhrman tapes to be admitted as evidence. The first set, filed on the seventeenth, had been rejected because the transcript references did not coincide precisely with the actual tapes. Now Ito said he would need a week to review the material and make a finding on the tapes' relevance.

On the ninth floor, outside Ito's courtroom, everyone was still reading *Time* magazine and the *Los Angeles Times*. Both featured major stories on the Fuhrman tapes and quoted them at length. Fuhrman's statements were based on verifiable incidents, the articles stated. No fictional episodes invented for a screenplay here.

Douglas knew the publication of the Fuhrman excerpts benefited Simpson and left Ito little maneuvering room. If the judge now excluded the tapes, it would look like a cover-up.

But what about the jury? By now, the defense had a catchphrase, "pregnant Fridays": Be sure to make headlines on Friday, like the story of the Fuhrman tapes in the *Los Angeles Times*. The jury would be certain to find out on Saturday during conjugal visits.

* * *

O.J. was smiling when Howard Weitzman appeared in court to answer his subpoena. By now Simpson just wanted to make life difficult for Weitzman. As he had planned, after Howard showed up, O.J. told his attorneys to withdraw their request to have Weitzman testify. A conference took place in chambers, and then the court canceled the subpoena.

Then Christian Reichardt, Faye Resnick's ex-boyfriend, testified, while Dr. Henry Lee stood in the hallway waiting his turn. Reichardt told the jury he spoke to O.J. several hours before the murders and everything seemed okay.

23

DR. LEE WAITED TO TAKE THE STAND AS HE HAD DONE IN hundreds of other cases. But this one had taken a toll on him. He had swung back and forth like a pendulum. One week he wanted to testify, the next he didn't. Now, finally, he was going ahead, because he believed in what he would say. It had nothing to do with O.J.'s guilt or innocence and everything to do with the facts as he saw them.

Lee always felt the heart of the case was the evidence. Don't try to challenge someone's credentials. Don't try to impeach a person on something he goofed up six years ago. That wasn't his style.

He hated waiting. He remembered when Carl Douglas had phoned him in Seattle at a scientific conference. Come to L.A. right away. Come look at the socks. Lee had said, No way, I'm in an international meeting. But still, the next day he left his hotel at four in the morning to catch an early flight to L.A. He was taken to the LAPD laboratory, where he waited in the hallway for hours. They couldn't find the socks. The police lab couldn't find important evidence in an important case? That was when Lee first said to himself, "Something is fucked up on this case."

He wondered if the prosecution was trying to wear him down, frustrate him. These were his colleagues. Good people. Then the prosecution had him followed, sent people to listen to his speeches. He thought they were trying to get him to leave the case. He approached his observers directly. Told them he couldn't be frightened off. They apologized to him.

Dr. Lee took the stand late on Tuesday afternoon, August 22. Barry Scheck planned, after establishing Lee's credentials, to take up the second set of shoe prints.

The issue was tricky. For Scheck, it brought several strategic problems into worrisome focus. A year ago, Lee had examined poor-quality copy prints of the crime-scene photos received from the prosecution and noticed bloody parallel imprint lines on the walkway. Later he also saw similar lines on Goldman's right trouser leg and on the bloody envelope. They were consistent with a shoe other than a Bruno Magli, he said. Lee's observation stayed a well-kept defense secret until Scheck had to provide the information to prosecutors. Despite threats of judicial sanction, he had waited until the last minute.

When Scheck finally turned over Lee's notes, the D.A. figured out his probable testimony and had new photographs taken of the Bundy walkway tiles.

When the prosecution's new pictures reached the defense team's discovery pile, Scheck and Lee couldn't tell if the prosecution photographer had shot exactly the same tiles or others. The new and old pictures didn't match well. The new photos suggested that some of the lines Lee was about to identify as potential shoe imprints might have been trowel marks made by cement workers when the condo was built. Did the defense now have a mix of blood lines and old trowel marks? Or possibly just trowel marks? Nobody had ever checked Lee's discovery by comparing the original LAPD photos to the original tiles.

Whatever the case, Dr. Lee's secret was suddenly less

dramatic. But since he'd also seen similar lines on the torn envelope, and on Ron Goldman's pants leg, the theory of a second set of shoe imprints remained viable.

Lee was a showman. His English was awkward, but his reasoning was clear. Juries loved this avuncular, affable man.

Dr. Lee prided himself on scientific neutrality. He'd tell you what he saw, but pull back if asked to speculate about what it meant. Scheck knew not to ask Lee to draw conclusions. However, they both agreed he would use a G-rated version of his pungent summary, "Something's fucked up here."

When Scheck finished with Lee's professional and honorary titles he set up the Bundy walkway pictures and asked Lee about his first visit to the crime scene thirteen days after the murders.

First, Lee noted seeing the Bruno Magli imprints. Then he saw something else, he told jurors. "I notice a different design, a parallel-line design type of pattern," Lee said.

Scheck moved carefully, noting that these were either trowel marks or evidence suggesting another set of shoes. Lee described the Bruno Magli patterns and "a series [of] linear designs that is consistent with an imprint." On the tenth tile, counting from the staircase, he identified another "parallel-line design."

"This one is more complete," said Lee, "It's a pattern resembling [that] on a shoe."

Scheck had to protect Lee's statements against the eventual testimony of FBI experts in the rebuttal case who might contradict him. He asked if Lee had done chemical tests to enhance and clarify the imprints he identified.

"No, I did not."

Why not?

"The [court] order is very strict. I only can photograph, measure, and do simple tests, cannot add too many chemical or remove the whole walkway."

Scheck moved on to imprints that couldn't be trowel marks, those on the bloodstained envelope containing Judy Brown's glasses and on an uncollected scrap of paper Lee had noticed in the crime-scene pictures.

"In a close inspection of this envelope and this piece of paper," Lee said, "I discover this imprint-like pattern on the paper."

Could the new "pattern" have come from a Bruno Magli shoe? Lee said no. How about from Ron Goldman's boot? Lee said the victim's footgear had a "completely different" sole pattern.

So far, so good. Then Scheck asked if the bloody lines on the paper were consistent with the lines on the cement. Lee backed off. He could give only "a very limited conclusion" because he could not examine the uncollected scrap of paper.

The next morning Scheck showed the jury a picture of Ron Goldman's bloody jeans laid out on a lab table and showing the last of the "second-shoe" imprints. Lee described three linear patterns.

Again, Scheck risked asking for a conclusion. "Is the parallel-line pattern that you've circled there consistent with a partial shoe print?"

"I cannot definitively say that is a shoe print," Lee answered. "It could be."

To bolster Michael Baden's testimony suggesting that Ron Goldman fought his killer for five to ten minutes, Scheck then had Lee describe the tiny Bundy yard. Lee's line of reasoning also involved blood. But Lee had reached his conclusion by reconstructing the crime scene, not by medical analysis.

"Now, Dr. Lee, looking at the bloodstain patterns and the impression evidence in this closed-in area," Scheck began, "is it consistent with a prolonged struggle between Mr. Goldman and assailant or assailants?"

"I cannot tell you exactly how long," Lee replied. "It is not a short struggle."

Scheck asked why.

"The bloodstain pattern, the deposit of the key, beeper, in different locations," Lee explained, reminding jurors of pictures he'd shown them. "The bloodstain smears, contact pattern under the boots, and vertical droplet in different locations which shows a movement."

Anything else? Scheck asked.

"No," Lee answered firmly.

Scheck asked Lee about the time he flew to Los Angeles to examine the Rockingham socks before they went to the FBI for testing.

"Who were you with?" Scheck asked him.

"Uh, you and attorney Neufeld."

The doctor had it wrong. Scheck and Bob Blasier had accompanied the criminalist that day. Do you mean Mr. Blasier? Scheck asked.

"Oh, maybe him," Lee answered, smiling. "You all look alike. I don't know."

Laughter rolled through the courtroom. This was not the first case at which Lee had made such a gibe. Scheck guided the witness back to his visit to the LAPD lab. After waiting nearly three hours, Lee had been met by five prosecutors and a surly technical staff who provided a microscope in "terrible shape . . . I can't even focus."

Then Lee had asked for guidance on lab procedures. "Laboratory scientist say, 'You're the expert. You should know it,' in a very mean manner and unprofessional."

Lee's face, kindly all morning, now darkened. His scientific opinions were almost anticlimactic. He immediately saw that both socks were stored in a single bag.

"You pick up the socks, put in one envelope, you already contaminate both socks," Lee said. "You have a cross-contamination."

The prosecutors had made an issue of pictures showing Lee, the famous criminalist, examining the socks in street clothes at the LAPD lab. No lab coat or hair net. "I wasn't provided with a lab coat nor hair net," Lee explained with annoyance. "Both socks already put in one envelope. Doesn't matter what I wear, space suit, body armor. Still contaminated."

Kardashian smiled. The next time this guy comes to call, he thought, they'll give him a decent microscope.

* * *

Scheck moved on to Herb MacDonell's testimony.

Through microphotography, MacDonell found that blood from a quarter-sized ankle stain had drained to the opposite inside surface of the sock found in Simpson's bedroom. He'd found no blood on the outside of the opposite side. The blood couldn't have reached that "third surface" with a leg inside the sock.

Lee analyzed MacDonell's pictures and supported this conclusion. The particles of blood on the sock's inner opposite surface looked like tiny red balls. Some pictures were so enlarged they showed only one microscopic ball. Had Lee accounted for all the blood? Scheck asked.

"Eating spaghetti, I find one cockroach," Lee explained. "I look at it. I find another cockroach. It's no sense for me to go through the whole plate of spaghetti, say there are 13,325 cockroaches. If you find one, it's there."

Scheck finally got to the point. Professor MacDonell testified that the sock stains were "consistent with a transfer stain starting when the socks were lying on a flat surface and no leg was in the sock. Are you aware of that?"

"That's his testimony," Lee answered. "I have nothing to dispute with him."

Spoken like a scientist. But Scheck knew the jury needed a straight-ahead statement. Did Lee agree with MacDonnell?

"I agree," the doctor answered.

One sour note was struck that day. Judge Ito read aloud his formal response to prosecution protests that the defense hid Henry Lee's material from them for almost a year.

"Once a trial has begun," Ito wrote, "the statutory discovery obligations must be complied with immediately."

He promised "significant and substantial monetary sanctions" and gave Hank Goldberg extra time to prepare for cross-examination. He advised both sides he'd tell the jury what happened. Carl Douglas wasn't worried. How seriously would this jury take a reprimand from the establishment?

On Friday morning, August 25, Scheck addressed his last major topic: the wet transfer marks discovered by Ed Blake and Gary Sims and confirmed by Dr. Lee. The intricate wet-transfer story was a major part of the defense allegations of police tampering.

Blood from the Bundy crime scene, earlier prosecution witnesses had explained, was collected on cotton swabs, or "swatches," that had been moistened with distilled water. Criminalists Fung and Mazzola stored the bloody swatches in plastic bags in their truck, then took them to the LAPD lab. Following standard laboratory practice, they placed the swatches in test tubes overnight to dry. In the morning, Andrea Mazzola said she packed the swatches in paper wrappers—bindles—and initialed each of the bindles.

Lee explained that he saw no initials on the bindles when he reviewed the LAPD lab's work. He also noticed that four of the seven swatches had made a "wet transfer" of blood onto the paper bindle. Blood swatches take about three hours to dry. These had been left fourteen hours before being wrapped. Lee also noticed that some wet transfers were not "mirror images" of the swatch originally bearing the blood.

Had someone removed four of the original swatches after Mazzola packaged them and substituted new swatches with "spiked" blood? Were the spiked swatches rewrapped in new paper bindles? If so, it would explain why the swatches smudged the bindles. Either way, the new ones weren't dry when wrapped. This would also explain why Mazzola's initials were absent: She wasn't there when the swatches were rewrapped.

Scheck knew Lee wouldn't speculate for the record about tampering. As a scientist he'd say only that something wasn't right about the swatches. They'd worked on the exact wording for weeks.

"What is your opinion about the existence of these transfer stains?" Scheck asked.

"Only opinion I can giving under the circumstance," Lee said in his imperfect English. "Something wrong."

Scheck saw Johnnie Cochran signaling to him frantically. He knew what Johnnie wanted. During the planning sessions, Simpson had insisted that saying "something's wrong" at the end wasn't strong enough. Have Dr. Lee say it again and again, O.J. said. Scheck resisted. Now it was Friday noon. The weekend was starting. Simpson wanted a big finish. Scheck went to the table for a huddle. Ask him *what's* wrong, Simpson hissed. Cochran and Douglas agreed.

"You don't understand," Scheck argued. "It's better to say something's wrong, period. Don't get complicated. It's better to end it this way."

They wouldn't accept that. The argument soon became so heated that Scheck asked Ito for a short break. The jury left. When they returned, Scheck had capitulated.

"Dr. Lee, the last answer that you gave this jury . . . is 'Something is wrong,'" he said to Lee carefully, turning his eyes to the defense table. "Could you please explain what you mean?"

Lee was ready. "What I mean, there are seven swatches . . . four imprints."

Seven dry swatches should leave no blood on the paper wrapping, Lee said. Perhaps all seven weren't dry. If so, he should see *seven* transfers.

"I only see four," Lee concluded. "The number did not add up. Maybe there be reason to explain. I don't know."

Now Scheck was finished. Ito sent the jury to their hotel for the weekend. Goldberg would start his cross-examination the following Monday.

24

THAT SAME FRIDAY EVENING, AUGUST 25, LARRY SCHILler arrived at a sound studio in Burbank with all the Fuhrman tapes, a complete set of transcripts, and the offer of proof listing the order in which the excerpts should be presented. By now Carl had decided that Schiller didn't need a security guard at his elbow. So many excerpts had been published that their commercial value was almost zero.

For Schiller the trick was to give the text a rhythm. Use subtitles for everyone to read as the words were heard. Make sure the written words were easy to follow and kept up with the spoken word. Put some low-frequency sound between the excerpts. How long an interval should there be between excerpts? How to arrange the words on the screen? Lots of variables to work out. Schiller had all sorts of state-of-the-art equipment, but only the right creative decisions would produce an effective presentation.

It took three days to complete. The bill came to a bit more than $28,000 for studio time alone. Schiller didn't charge the defense for his services. He was laying the groundwork for a book he planned to write.

On Saturday, August 26, the defense had another meeting. By now they were almost daily occurrences. Dr. Lee seemed unstoppable, and now the Fuhrman tapes gave the defense their first real opportunity to get the media on their side.

Gerry Uelmen had persuaded one of his former students to write an op-ed piece for *The New York Times*. "I spent four hours on the phone with him," he said.

"I'm going to talk to the *L.A. Times* today," Johnnie added. "And I'm going to suggest they write something for this Sunday"—namely, an analysis of all the black ministers' statements and the Urban League press conference scheduled for tomorrow.

Then Cochran tells the group he's talked with Daryl Mounger, a well-regarded criminal attorney who's now representing Mark Fuhrman.

"Fuhrman will take the Fifth," Johnnie says.

By now nobody on the defense really believes that Fuhrman will continue answering questions. The one unresolved issue is whether he will be required to take the Fifth in front of the jury. Despite Dershowitz's and Uelmen's arguments, some defense members say that the jury will never see Mark Fuhrman again.

"We'll give the D.A. notice we want him back. Now,"

Johnnie says. Let him stand up there in front of the country and squirm.

Johnnie went on to suggest that Uelmen present the defense arguments concerning the Fuhrman tapes—the hearing is scheduled for Tuesday, August 29—since Laura McKinny's testimony might be limited to the circumstances surrounding the tapes. Who would handle Bailey's "Fuhrman funeral" was still up in the air.

"Now that Fuhrman's dead," Bailey said to Douglas, "I really don't care who does the embalming." If Lee had been a young lawyer looking to make his name, being shut out of the Fuhrman presentation would have hurt. But Bailey didn't need the Simpson case to become famous. Maybe this case had finally become a pain in the ass for Bailey. TFC, Carl thought.

On Monday, August 28, the defense was amazed when Goldberg let Henry Lee repeat his strongest statement twice.

"Now is it your view, Dr. Lee, that often science cannot provide explanations for every phenomenon?" the prosecutor asked.

Lee agreed. Goldberg pushed on: If you can't explain something as a forensic scientist, he asked, does it mean something's wrong?

"Yes. There is something wrong," Lee answered firmly.

Whoops. Goldberg marched doggedly on. "Isn't it often that you look at something and you can't explain it?" he asked.

"If everything right, it should be explainable," Lee insisted. "If something I cannot explain . . . doesn't matter what. You see a wet transfer which means something wrong."

Nonetheless, the quiet prosecutor managed several solid successes. Goldberg asked Lee for endorsements of DNA testing and got them, particularly on the controversial PCR testing. No one at the defense table was surprised. By now, they knew Lee's views well. Strategically, his statements served the defense anyway. This scientist, whom the jury

741

clearly liked, supported the DNA tests. Lee really *was* objective. That strengthened his testimony in support of defense theories.

Goldberg then asked Lee about his most famous case. An airline pilot was convicted of killing his wife and using a wood chipper to scatter her body across a snow-covered riverbank. Lee had used DNA tests to identify the victim's remains and help convict the husband. Cross-contamination hadn't been a problem, even though tiny bits of the corpse were mixed in collecting buckets with deer bones and other riverbank refuse.

"And despite that, sir, it was proper . . . to attempt DNA technology on this evidence, is that correct?" Goldberg asked.

"That's correct," Lee said.

Carl Douglas decided that Goldberg scored some points.

"Sir, if a person were to wrap their hand around someone's throat [from behind] and slit that person's throat," Goldberg asked, "and the blood spurted forward, would you expect the assailant to be covered in blood?"

"Probably not," Lee admitted.

Firing from several directions, the prosecutor also took solid shots at the second-shoe theory. First, he showed Lee a sharp new photograph of the Bundy walkway.

"And now that you see that photograph," Goldberg said, "does it appear that the parallel lines are in fact trowel marks or scratches in the surface of the pavement?"

"Could be," Lee said.

"Does that appear to be the most reasonable explanation?" Goldberg pushed.

"Yes, right," Lee agreed.

The prosecutor played videotapes of detectives walking in the crime-scene area, suggesting they might have left the patterns. If a police officer or citizen left the imprints, would that be relevant to the case? Goldberg asked.

Now Lee was annoyed. His answer veered close to sarcasm. "If in blood," he said tightly, *"that's* significant."

Goldberg ended with a second mention of the FBI

footwear and imprint expert, Bill Bodziak. Scheck assumed that during their rebuttal, prosecutors would recall Bodziak to attack the second-shoe theory directly. Had Lee read Bodziak's report concerning blood patterns on Ron Goldman's blue jeans? Goldberg asked. The scientist said he didn't recall the details.

"Didn't you take that into consideration before you got on the witness stand and testified?"

"Well, different expert have different opinion," Lee countered. ". . . Have imprint, imprint in blood. If he don't call that a footprint, I have nothing to argue with that. He entitled to his own opinion."

Goldberg was doing well, Douglas thought.

"Are you saying, sir, that that is a footwear impression now," Goldberg asked Lee again, "or are you saying it could be any kind of impression?"

"No, I'm still saying that's an imprint. An imprint . . . consistent with a footprint. It could be footprint. It could be other imprint."

No question, Henry Lee was one of our best witnesses, Carl Douglas decided when it finally ended.

25

On Tuesday, August 29, the Fuhrman tapes were front-page news. Every television station headlined the story. Now the defense waited to find out how much Judge Ito would allow the jury to hear. And what Mark Fuhrman would do when he was recalled to the stand.

For the last year, two trials had proceeded simultaneously:

one inside the courtroom, for the jury, and another for the rest of the world. The "outside" trial of public opinion was always just below the surface in the mind of every defense attorney. All along, the defense had to be careful not to let this "outside" trial influence courtroom strategy. But today the two trials would merge.

Ito had been reviewing the Fuhrman material for almost a week. At one point he'd asked Gerry Uelmen to withdraw Fuhrman's remarks on Ethiopia as not really relevant. Johnnie didn't like it, but Uelmen agreed with the judge.

Now Ito wanted oral arguments from both sides on the tapes' relevance and their presentation to the jury. Were they too old? Too tangential? Were there witnesses who could testify to the same things? Did the court and jury need to hear Fuhrman's voice?

Ito sent the jury back to their hotel until Thursday. This morning an army of attorneys packed the courtroom: Clark, Darden, and Cheri Lewis, for the prosecution; Cochran, Shapiro, Douglas, Blasier, Scheck, Bailey, Uelmen, Neufeld, and Kardashian, for the defense; city attorneys James Hahn and Mary House, representing the Los Angeles Police Department; Kelli Sager, appearing on behalf of various media organizations; Douglas Mirell, for the ACLU; Schwartz and Regwan, for McKinny.

Simpson's family were in their assigned seats. So were the Brown and Goldman families. Vannatter sat just inside the rail, next to the prosecution table.

Gerry Uelmen was ready to present Laura McKinny. Lee Bailey sat quietly. Johnnie didn't want a marine-to-marine battle today.

"Let's launch into the McKinny matter," Ito said just after nine A.M. Laura Hart McKinny was sworn in.

The slender, longhaired woman, now a filmmaker-in-residence and professor of screenwriting at the North Carolina School of the Arts School of Filmmaking, walked slowly to the stand. Her manner was low-key, her expression pained. Throughout her testimony she spoke in a quiet, sometimes hesitant voice. Some spectators had to lean forward to hear her.

Uelmen began with the basics: When were the tapes made? Over a period of ten years, McKinny replied, 1985 through 1994. The purpose of her interviews? To research a screenplay about women in the police force. Point by point McKinny validated the tapes.

"Now . . . in the interviews that were taped, was the word 'nigger' ever used?"

"Yes," McKinny replied.

". . . Is it because that word was spoken by Officer Fuhrman?" Uelmen asked.

"Yes."

Uelmen moved on to the material the defense wanted admitted. Was it offensive to McKinny? Yes. Why not tell Fuhrman his language was offensive? Not appropriate; she was in "journalistic mode," she replied.

Then Uelmen introduced the videotape the defense had prepared to present each excerpt. Ito could read the text on the screen while hearing Fuhrman's own words. Gerry Uelmen was ready to play forty-one excerpts.

"Do you think I really need to contemplate all forty-one of these?" Ito asked. Gerry suggested seventeen at first, then asked for all forty-one.

At ten A.M. the first ten excerpts were read into the record. These passages existed only in transcript form. McKinny herself had inadvertently erased the tape years ago.

We got females and dumb niggers and all your Mexicans that can't even write the name of the car they drive.

Uelmen took McKinny through each excerpt. Then, at 10:20, he started playing the actual audiotapes.

Fuhrman's words filled the courtroom and were broadcast by Court TV. He boasted of police brutality and of manufacturing evidence. Fuhrman used the word "nigger" so much that it almost lost its impact.

Simpson was hearing the tapes for the first time. Fuhrman's voice had a matter-of-fact quality—bland, careless, even casual—which made his offhand recital of heinous acts even more chilling. Carl Douglas could see that O.J. was angry. So was Shapiro. Vannatter turned red. Kim Goldman, Ron's sister, wept softly. Marcia Clark sat quietly as Chris Darden objected periodically for the record. Her expression was icy.

> I used to go to work and practice movements. Niggers. They're easy. I used to practice my kicks.
>
> —McKinny tape no. 4

> We stopped the choke [choke hold] because a bunch of niggers have a bunch of these organizations in the south end, and because all niggers are choked out and killed— twelve in ten years. Really is extraordinary, isn't it?
>
> —McKinny tape no. 4

> These niggers, they run like rabbits. . . . Some police- men just sit there and they look, you have to tell them what to do.
>
> —McKinny tape no. 7a

"I don't need to hear any more," the judge said. "I have read the offer of proof. I've heard the tapes. I've read the transcripts." He called a sidebar conference.

"I know what you're talking about," he told Uelmen. "What's the need to take up court time?"

Uelmen pushed. He had to lay the foundation for every excerpt since Ito hadn't decided which ones would be admitted. Ito relented.

Uelmen moved on to show "probable cause" that Fuhr- man manufactured evidence. On that point, Fuhrman had said of his job as a cop in the field: "You're God."

Simpson's face darkened. He held himself rigid. He looked directly at McKinny.

Ito called a fifteen-minute recess.

The judge returned to the bench a changed man: calm, deliberate, with some tough decisions made. First he un- sealed the defense's offer of proof. He said he would make it available to the media at the lunch break.

"Secondly, Mr. Uelmen, over the recess I had the

opportunity to sit and contemplate for a few moments . . . I think that there is an overriding public interest in the nature of the offer. I don't want this court ever to be in a position where there is any indication that the court would participate in suppressing information that is of vital public interest."

The defense had won. Like fire, like the wheel, like the principle behind the airplane, the Fuhrman tapes belonged to no one individual. The judge was saying, in effect, that society's interest came first.

"I suggest . . . you play your video presentation to the court in its entirety without further interruption. That will be for the purpose of public dissemination of this information."

Douglas couldn't stop staring at Ito. The judge looked as if he had just come down from Mount Sinai with the tablets.

Then Uelmen played the excerpt that had appeared in the *Los Angeles Times:* ". . . We basically tortured them."

For over an hour Mark Fuhrman's voice filled the courtroom as the detective boasted about police brutality and repeated the word he swore he hadn't used in ten years.

When Ito recessed for lunch, nobody moved or spoke for several minutes. Vannatter was enraged. As he left, his first words were to Larry Schiller: "You just gave Simpson his freedom."

No, *you* did, when you had Fuhrman go over the wall, Schiller thought as the detective walked away.

During the break, the Goldman family held a press conference to attack Ito's ruling. The first floor of the courthouse was packed, as was the entire balcony.

"This is now the Fuhrman trial," Fred Goldman said. "It's disgusting. My son, Nicole, our families, have a right to a fair trial. And this is not fair."

"This case is over," Shapiro told Cochran. "This is the case."

"Bob, just settle down," Johnnie said. "We've got a long way to go."

Barry Scheck was worrying over ways Ito could still screw the defense. After a moment, Simpson repeated his first rule for the team: "Don't spike the ball. Remember that."

Douglas had been assigned to handle the press during lunch. His press conference would be in the ninth-floor men's bathroom, the scene of countless unofficial media briefings throughout the trial.

Johnnie loved using the breaks this way. He could talk and talk, while the reporters were unable to take notes. Of course, the female reporters were annoyed that they didn't have equal access. One day a woman TV producer asked a male *Los Angeles Times* writer to check out something from Douglas about a potential defense witness. The two stood side by side at the urinals, exchanged a few words. The reporter didn't mind helping out his television colleague: he was also learning something he hadn't known. He and the producer joked about teaming up in the future. The problem was, Marcia Clark never used the ladies' room on the ninth floor.

Today, writers Joe Bosco and Joe McGinnis and reporters Furnell Chatman and David Goldstein followed Carl into the men's room. Carl was gloating. He was ready. In the past he had talked about the power of the tapes without quoting them. "Chilling" and "terrible" were the two words he'd used. Nothing more. As Douglas stood by the urinal, none of the journalists said a word to him. The tapes themselves had said everything.

In the afternoon the rest of the tapes were played. Marcia Clark argued against their admissibility. McKinny had testified that in her opinion the tapes did not exonerate Simpson. Nothing Fuhrman said on the tapes made her feel he had planted evidence in Simpson's case.

"This may well be the most difficult thing I've ever had to do as a prosecutor," Clark began. "I don't think that there is anyone in this courtroom, in this country, that could possibly envy me. I cannot afford the luxury of being Marcia Clark the citizen. I am Marcia Clark the prosecutor and I stand before you today . . . not in defense of Mark Fuhrman, but in defense of a case, a case of such overwhelming magnitude in terms of the strength of the proof of the defendant's guilt.''

The arguments went on for hours. Clark was eloquent.

''This is not something I can rule on from the seat of my pants,'' Ito finally said. He had admitted the tapes to the ''outside'' trial, the public forum. It still remained to be seen what he would admit to the ''inside'' trial.

26

ON THURSDAY, AUGUST 31, THE DEFENSE IS STILL WAITing for Judge Ito's ruling on the Fuhrman tapes. Word is it will come sometime today. At Cochran's office, the day starts slowly.

Daryl Mounger has informed the defense that Mark Fuhrman has returned from Sand Point, Idaho, where he now lives. Mounger is also waiting to see what Judge Ito will let in.

While the team waits, they review the blood evidence, the heart of the prosecution's case.

Blasier points out that the June 14 LAPD lab blood results do not clearly put Goldman in the Bronco. Look at the dates, he continues. The blood from the back gate was collected on July 3; the blood on the sock from O.J.'s bedroom was found on August 4; and Goldman's blood in the Bronco was collected on August 26. The prosecutors are always saying, Look at everything. Well, let's take their overview ourselves. Why does the evidence keep getting stronger against O.J. as time passes?

''In the end, we will have to argue that Fuhrman was in

the Bronco," Johnnie says. The team agrees that Fuhrman's presence in the car could account for the blood from Nicole and Goldman on the Bronco's console.

Carl Douglas reports that Lori Menzione, an airline reservation operator in Chicago, is now willing to testify for the defense. "O.J. is telling Menzione that his wife has just died," Carl says, "and asks how soon he can return to L.A.—'Just give me a new ticket'—then he says, 'Wait a minute,' and she hears a sound over the phone like someone clearing off a table." According to Menzione, Carl reports, O.J. came back on the line and said, " 'I'm sorry, I just broke a glass and I'm bleeding.' In a sort of calm way."

Scheck wants to know if Menzione heard the breaking glass.

Yes, Carl says, a cracking sound.

"Is there a telephone in the bathroom?" Barry asks.

"No," Douglas replies.

"So where is he talking to her from when the crashing sound is heard?" Scheck wants to know.

"He says he put the phone down," Johnnie answers.

"The phone is supposedly in the bedroom by the bed and he goes into a separate room, and she can hear that sound?" Barry says. "Did he go into the other room to break the glass?"

"Well, we don't know that one," Johnnie concedes. Where and when the cuts appeared on O.J.'s hand is a quagmire. Every time the defense thinks it's finally found solid ground, the earth shifts.

What interests Dershowitz, who's on the phone from Boston, is what Simpson has already told the cops about this. Did he break the glass in Chicago when he heard the news about Nicole's death from the cops, or was it when he was speaking to the operator?

Scheck points to a conflict here. O.J. has said he cut himself in L.A. Did he also cut himself while he was cleaning up in Chicago?

"That's not what he said to the reservation operator," Johnnie says.

Kardashian says they'd better ask O.J. again.

"I'm starting not to believe him," Cochran says. " 'I broke the glass, I cut myself and I'm bleeding.' " Now Johnnie sounds upset. How could O.J. break a glass in the hotel bathroom while talking on the phone in the bedroom?

"We have pictures from the hotel room of broken glass in a sink with no blood," says Scheck. "Not only did he cut himself, but he cleaned it up and washed all the blood down the sink?"

"Well, we knew we had a problem here," Johnnie agrees. "Barry, we can still argue that the glass was broken in the sink, and he washed his blood down into the sink. That's our argument."

Nobody is satisfied with this, but it's the best they can come up with for the moment.

Kardashian sees that O.J.'s contradictory accounts are getting to Cochran. Bob knows Johnnie has been troubled about the cuts for some time, and his doubts are only getting worse. Kardashian remembers what Wayne Hughes told the police about O.J. almost a year ago: "O.J., believe me, is a guy that can deal with people better than any person that I've ever known. . . . He turns the right phrase. . . . I've never known a person of his equal in my life." Kardashian agreed: Juice made a living by his persuasive charm. "He makes Shapiro and these guys look like klutzes," Wayne also told the cops. Kardashian smiled when he read it.

There is nothing to smile about now. What bothers Bob most is that O.J. has had months to sort out his recollections about his cuts, yet every time he discusses them, his story grows more confusing—so much so that even Cochran is now visibly upset. What the hell is going on? Kardashian knows as well as Hughes that O.J. can put a charming spin on anything. Why have Simpson's skills deserted him on this critical issue? The implications frighten Kardashian.

At four P.M. Judge Ito's clerk, Deirdre Robertson, calls Johnnie's office. She is ready to fax them the judge's ruling on the Fuhrman tapes.

"You're not going to be happy," Deirdre tells Carl. Okay, Douglas thought, it's two of Fuhrman saying he planted evidence, and only five or six of the other.

Word has spread throughout the office and everyone moves to the conference room. Carl Douglas stands by the fax as the ruling comes through. Johnnie emerges from his office and Carl hands him the first copy. The single-spaced type is so small that Johnnie goes back to his office to read it. Everyone is on edge, excited. Carl comes into the conference room with copies for everyone.

Little by little the excitement turns to amazement. Then anger.

"He's fucking us!" Gerry Uelmen says. The normally calm scholar is almost shouting. "He's allowing only two things in! *Four lines.*" From eleven hours of tape that yielded hundreds of pages of transcript.

Ito has not admitted any of the excerpts about the manufacture of evidence—the most important issue for the defense. Much more important than any one "nigger," Carl knows. Even one incident would support the defense argument that the glove was planted.

Ito is willing to deal only with the issue of Fuhrman's sworn testimony that he has not used the word "nigger" in the last ten years. The two incidents the judge has admitted would corroborate other testimony the defense plans to introduce. Ito has ruled that the other excerpts submitted by the defense would outrage the jurors more than the evidence merits: This case doesn't involve name-calling, police beatings, and revenge. Some of the material he considers fiction. He ruled that the prosecution's recent stipulation that Fuhrman said the word "nigger" forty-one times is sufficient.

Bailey, sickened, says the excerpts Ito picked mean absolutely nothing.

The ruling reads, in part:

The defense may play and display the following excerpts as impeachment:

8: "We have no niggers where I grew up."

752

13: Q: "Why do they live in that area?"
A: "That's where niggers live."

The court finds the probative value of the remaining examples to be substantially and overwhelmingly outweighed by the danger of undue prejudice.

Before long Cochran returns to the conference room. "It doesn't matter," he tells the group. "We'll get over this, too. They can't stop us. Fuck them."

Shawn Chapman starts to cry and runs into her office. Peter Neufeld follows her, with Scheck close behind. "It's like the Rodney King decision," she says, weeping.

"Get everyone down here," Johnnie snaps in the hallway. "We're having a press conference." Peter Neufeld doesn't want Johnnie to take questions. Say what's on your mind and walk away, is always his policy. Today Cochran agrees. Carl faxes Shapiro the ruling. Shapiro wants Cochran to delay the press conference until he can arrive from the west side.

Fuck, no, we're not waiting, Carl thinks. He says as much to Shapiro, but politely.

The elevator is small. The whole defense team wedges itself in. There is deep sadness under the fury. TV cameras are massed outside the glass doors of the building. Johnnie lifts his head and walks briskly toward the media.

Cochran, in black shirt and lavender jacket, stands before a battery of TV cameras with the defense team behind him. He says Lance Ito's ruling is one of the cruelest, most unfair decisions ever rendered in a criminal court in this country. Ito, he says, is "misleading this jury. That is dishonest. All of the world knows who this person [Fuhrman] is, but now our jury won't. O.J. Simpson is a man who has been wrongfully accused and, we believe, framed. The cover-up continues."

When Cochran has finished his statement he turns immediately, reenters the building, and goes up to his offices.

In the conference room, Dershowitz is now on the speakerphone. "Ito's saying these jurors don't have the intelligence, do not have the judgment, do not have the sense of fairness to analyze this evidence.'' Uelmen is pacing as he looks for a way to get more excerpts admitted.

Johnnie is on one phone, talking to a *Los Angeles Times* reporter. Carl is on another. They can't call Simpson. Surely he will get the news on TV and call them. "Here's a court that has let dreams in, has let the worst autopsy pictures in, has let domestic discord for eighteen years in. . . ." Cochran is on a roll.

In a quiet moment, he turns to Bob Blasier. "When I read the ruling I had this feeling, like the sick feeling when you lose a loved one. I don't want to go into Ito's chambers anymore. I don't trust the guy."

"Look, Johnnie, we've never trusted him," Blasier says. "We have to focus on the jury now, and getting an acquittal."

The team had to get back on track. Let's get witnesses Singer and Hodge ready to go on Tuesday, Johnnie thinks aloud. Or maybe Kathleen Bell should be the first witness. And let's ask Laura McKinny to come in for another conversation.

"By the way, Carl," Johnnie says to Douglas, "are we really ready?"

Carl doesn't say a word. He knows Johnnie has forgotten to assign anyone to present Bell, Terry, and Singer.

Cochran answers Carl's unspoken question. "If Bailey is up to it, I say we come back here tonight to prepare. If he's up to it, it's his."

Douglas smiles.

"I want Fuhrman down at the courthouse," Johnnie adds. "I just want to fuck with him."

Uelmen points out to the team that for the last nine months Pavelic has been asking for contact sheets of the color pictures taken at Bundy by LAPD photographer Rolf Rokahr. The prosecution wouldn't turn them over.

"The lighting on the pictures where Fuhrman is pointing to the glove always raised the possibility that the photo might have been taken earlier than the time Fuhrman testified to,"

Gerry explains. If the photograph was shot before Fuhrman went to Simpson's home at 4:40 A.M., the photo would prove he had access to the glove or gloves at Bundy and lied about that fact.

Dershowitz says the defense should argue that if the jury believes there has been one instance of tampering with the evidence, they should distrust the rest of the prosecution's case.

Neufeld says he's finally seen Rokahr's contact prints but doesn't know if the set is complete. Tomorrow he and McKenna will visit the LAPD photo lab.

"The first contact sheet, of the first roll of film shot, shows the order in which the pictures were taken, and also shows Fuhrman pointing at the glove," Scheck says. "The pictures on the contact sheet taken before and after the glove photos show they were taken at night." Fuhrman testified that the picture in which he is pointing at the glove was taken at seven A.M. or later. "Fuhrman testified that he was never near the glove before he went to Rockingham at four-forty," Barry adds.

Dershowitz is excited by the new discovery. Scheck starts pounding on the table. "His finger in the photograph is *three inches* away from the glove. God only knows how close it was when the camera wasn't shooting."

Scheck explains that the sun rose about 5:30 that day. Fuhrman was seen walking out of Rockingham by a Westec Security guard at 5:30 A.M. The defense can now argue that Fuhrman climbed over Simpson's wall earlier than he said on the stand. Or "we can argue that Fuhrman went back and forth," Scheck says. "It's all new information."

The important thing now is to interview the photographer, Rolf Rokahr, and then call him to the stand.

Johnnie says, Subpoena him. Now.

O.J. finally calls, loud and agitated. "I've been five hours in the attorney room, listening to Nicole Pulvers. Not one visitor. I don't know what the hell the ruling is, except he fucked us."

"He fucked us totally," Kardashian says.

"I want to call Fuhrman tomorrow," Simpson tells them. "You ask him if he lied in this case."

Douglas cuts O.J. off. "Right now we're all running on emotion and anger. We're not thinking rationally," he says. "I don't think that calling Fuhrman is in your best interests, at least not tomorrow. We have not adequately thought through our plans."

Uelmen tells O.J. they'll attack Ito's ruling tomorrow in open court. "We're going to tell Ito his ruling indicates he thinks you are guilty," Gerry explains.

"I don't want Ito attacked," Simpson answers. "It's a three-day weekend, a holiday. It's going to get back to the jury. Their families will tell them what you said." O.J.'s voice is intense. "Some of these women like Ito. The jury respects him. I don't want anybody hearing us say, 'Ito thinks O.J. is guilty,' even though we know he does."

"The Juice is right," Uelmen says, backing down.

"Keep talking, Juice," Carl says. "We'll stop you when you're wrong."

Bailey tells Simpson, "Ito told me months ago that we may not cross Fuhrman about what a witness said until that witness has testified. That means we have Hodge, Terry, Singer, and Bell to testify tomorrow if need be."

Then we'll think about Fuhrman, Uelmen adds. "Nobody will attack these witnesses now that the tapes have been heard publicly."

"I got him, I got Fuhrman!" Scheck shouts to O.J., referring to Rokahr's photos.

Bailey doesn't understand. "I've been living with this fuck for a year," he says. "Tell me how you got him."

"I have Rokahr's photo log here. I have Fuhrman's testimony here. Peter has seen the D.A.'s set of Rokahr's contact sheets, and it shows that the picture of Fuhrman pointing to the glove was taken at night."

Barry is over the top now, yelling, pounding the table. *"Now we got proof, now we got proof!"*

"Bill Hodgman said he remembers me making a formal request for the contact prints seven months ago," Neufeld adds. "They held back evidence. If we hadn't gotten a ruling from the judge we might never have gotten them."

Scheck is still pounding on the table.

Simpson says he remembers that Rokahr once said he took the pictures about four in the morning. Something in his original statement to the police.

"That's right. His initial statement is consistent with the photographs," Scheck says. "Then he tells a different story and the D.A. suppresses the contact sheets."

"Juice," Bailey says, "we got lots of work. We're not putting Fuhrman on the stand tomorrow. Next week we'll call Rokahr. And Rokahr should be on the stand before Fuhrman ever gets there."

Scheck agrees. So does Simpson.

"You bet your ass we can now talk about the suppression of evidence," Scheck says. "Ito had better investigate and reconsider his ruling on the tapes because we now have indisputable proof that Fuhrman perjured himself about his movements that night. We can prove it." Barry can't control his excitement. *"We can prove it!"*

"I'm so frustrated sitting here," Simpson says. "I mean, a game show came on TV. There was no news."

27

ON FRIDAY MORNING, SEPTEMBER 1, TEN ATTORNEYS FOR the defense were in court. The prosecution was represented by four. The jurors were upset. Ito said their trip to Catalina Island hadn't gone well: They came back barking at the seals, they got seasick. "I've got a jury going nuts," the judge said glumly. Within an hour he sent the jurors back to their hotel for the long Labor Day weekend.

Cochran immediately asked the court for clarification of its ruling of the previous day. "There are some parts that are incoherent," Johnnie stated. Ito said his ruling was very clear. Johnnie replied it wasn't clear to the defense.

Cochran told Ito that he intended to file a motion for reconsideration of Ito's ruling on Tuesday, the next court day.

Then Johnnie gave the court the order of their next witnesses: Natalie Singer, Roderic Hodge, Kathleen Bell, and Andrea Terry. Ito warned Cochran that he didn't want any repetitious witnesses after Bell and Terry. Nothing redundant. This trial had to end.

Call Bell, Terry, and McKinny, the judge told them. Argue that Fuhrman's a liar and a racist. But Ito considered Hodge and Singer overkill.

The defense wanted Hodge first. Hodge's testimony gave the defense "the only incident where Fuhrman talks directly to a black man," Uelmen said. "And O.J. is black." He knew Ito would have to buy that.

But Ito's big concern was to end the trial quickly. He didn't care who the defense called first, he said. "But at some point in time, enough is enough."

Darden, who had been watching these exchanges with obvious anger, finally rose. The D.A. was also unprepared for witnesses today, he said. The prosecution had prepared for all forty-one excerpts from the tapes, in case Ito admitted all of them.

This made no difference to the judge. "You're being jammed because I've got a jury that's going nuts," he told Darden.

Darden said he had no discovery on Hodge and Singer. No notes or statements from investigators. He wanted them now.

"Are you ready to proceed with them?" Ito asked Darden.

"Am I ready? No, I'm not ready," Darden responded angrily. "Frankly, I don't feel I'm competent to represent the People of the State of California this morning, as it relates to Mr. Hodge.''

Ito still wanted to proceed with Hodge. Nobody else did. He called a break.

The defense gathered in the holding cell and decided to call Darden's bluff. He'd said he was unprepared only for Hodge, not for Kathleen Bell or the others. Once court reconvened, Bailey announced that he was calling Singer.

Ito was angry: He'd expected Hodge. ''Call Mr. Hodge,'' he ordered. Not Bell, Singer, Terry, or anyone else.

Everyone was unprepared and backed off.

''They can put the defendant on the witness stand. We can handle *him* today,'' Darden said. ''We're ready for that.''

''*He's* here,'' Marcia Clark added.

This broke the tension slightly. At least Ito was amused. ''Nice try,'' he said.

Outside the courtroom, Bailey told the press that Fuhrman said to Hodge, ''I told you I'd get you, nigger.'' He also announced that Lucienne Coleman would testify that she was told Fuhrman discussed Nicole Simpson's breast enlargements with another officer and that she was informed that he scrawled swastikas on the locker of a fellow officer after the man married a Jewish woman. More news for the jurors' conjugal visits.

28

WHILE JOHNNIE WAS IN COURT THAT MORNING ARGUING about tapes and witnesses, Pat McKenna and Peter Neufeld drove to an LAPD-approved photo lab on Jefferson Boulevard. Today they would receive a complete set of contact sheets from Rolf Rokahr's shoot at the Bundy crime scene.

Pavelic had been the first to realize the contact sheets' importance. Michael Baden had also wanted them from the first day he arrived in Los Angeles. Back then, the defense just wanted to be sure they had a print of every image taken.

Ito finally ruled that the defense was entitled to the contact sheets if they existed. Sure enough, the D.A. found them. The photo of Fuhrman pointing to the glove was taken with a flash, but the background lacked any distant objects to show whether it was shot in daylight or at night. The only way to be sure was to place this one image in the sequence in which it was taken.

An investigator from the D.A.'s office was waiting for McKenna and Neufeld at the lab. He brought out the contact sheets immediately—plus all the rolls of film Rokahr had exposed on June 13, 1994. Neufeld and McKenna wanted their set to be in the order the photos were taken. In fact, they wanted several sets. And they wanted to be present while the sets were printed.

The process took all morning and into the afternoon. Neufeld and McKenna asked about the type of film used, the lighting, and similar information, which they would need when they interviewed Rokahr.

Just after lunch the D.A.'s investigator handed them the

finished work. Outside the building they finally opened the envelope.

The first roll had been shot at night. The first exposures showed streetlights still on in the background, in front of black skies. The second roll also began with night shots, the streetlights lit up against a black sky.

On the first roll was the shot of Fuhrman pointing to the glove. It had been taken well before sunrise. There was now no question that Mark Fuhrman had lied about when the picture was shot. Only the photographer could give the exact time, and they would interview him on September 4, Labor Day.

Neufeld was amused by how excited McKenna had been as they looked at the contact sheets. "This happens all the time," Peter told him as they drove away. McKenna knew that. But he also wondered what else the D.A. might be holding.

The team was in the conference room at Cochran's office when Neufeld arrived with his big news. He passed a set of contact sheets around the conference table.

"We now have a sequence of photographs, row by row," he explains. "The last two shots on the first roll are taken at night. In the middle of June, the sun rises about five-thirty. Fuhrman left at twenty to five to go to Rockingham. Then, Fuhrman says, he goes back to Bundy at about seven to take pictures of the glove. By seven A.M. the sun is bright outside. You wouldn't have streetlights on. But when you look at roll two, at all the photos that followed the two of Fuhrman with the gloves, it's still night."

"What advantage do we get from this?" Shapiro asks.

"He lied," Neufeld answered. "He was inches away from the glove before he ever went to Rockingham at twenty to five. That means one of two things: Either Fuhrman made two trips to Rockingham; or he made one trip and had an opportunity to grab a glove somewhere in that area before going there. He said he was never near the glove before his trip to Rockingham. He lied on the stand."

"All right, let's move on," Johnnie says. "Mounger now

says *maybe* Fuhrman *won't* take the Fifth. I think he's lying and I think Fuhrman will.''

"If Fuhrman takes the stand," Shapiro says, "and after we ask him if he works for the LAPD, then we ask, 'Have you ever lied under oath?'—of course he's going to take the Fifth.''

Johnnie says: "If Fuhrman comes back on a cross-examination, Lee will have to take him. If he comes back on an evidentiary hearing, Gerry will take him. We need two different sets of questions." Uelmen and Bailey say they'll get to work.

"Lee, I'm not going to be embarrassed," Johnnie adds in front of everyone. "I want to know what you're doing in advance. Nobody is going off on any tangents. Everybody understand that.'' It was Friday evening. Johnnie said he wanted all the preparations done by Tuesday morning.

Time for Cochran to watch the evening news. He turns on the conference room TV.

> In court Shapiro wasn't even making ardent huddles at the defense table this morning. Yesterday, Shapiro was conspicuously absent at Johnnie Cochran's press conference.

Everyone laughs, including Shapiro. "Like, you know, I missed one fuckin' press conference," Shapiro says.

> Shapiro has long opposed the race issue as an issue in terms of defense.

"Get out of here," Kardashian says to Shapiro as the laughter continues.

"See, I told you not to hold the press conference until I arrived," Shapiro jokes. But the undertone is serious.

"I couldn't wait any longer," Cochran says. "Tuesday morning I'll be late to court. You can hold the press conference.''

* * *

When Cochran turns off the TV, Carl asks Uelmen, "Did you see Darden today?" Uelmen had.

"He's insane, he's insane," says Johnnie. "I saw him pushing people out of the way in the hall."

"He was cursing on the way out," Douglas adds. "Calling all kinds of people 'motherfuckers.' I don't know what his problem is, but he needs some serious therapy. Maybe we should make a motion on the therapy issue." The lawyers start laughing all over again.

"Maybe Shawn should videotape Darden," Johnnie says.

"Just remember what his family is going through," Douglas reminds Johnnie. Suddenly the laughter stops.

The next morning, Saturday, September 2, Johnnie visited Simpson to update him on all the Fuhrman issues.

Johnnie began by explaining Ito's ruling and what they would do about it, if anything. He filled O.J. in on his conversation with Daryl Mounger on whether Fuhrman would take the Fifth. Johnnie was now sure he would.

O.J. had something else on his mind. He wanted to testify. If Fuhrman would never be heard by the jury, O.J. felt he should be. "If the fucking liar isn't seen by the jury," he said, "I want them to see me."

As it happened, the formalities were in place. Johnnie had put Simpson's name on the witness list for the last week of their case, just to confuse the prosecutors. O.J. liked that. The defense wanted to occupy the other side with useless tasks. It was working. Take a look at Chris Darden, Johnnie said.

Cochran again listed reasons why O.J. shouldn't take the stand: The case was strong without him. The glove demonstration—think of the impression it must have made on the jury. Dr. Lee had been impressive. So had the EDTA argument. If you ignore all those so-called experts on TV, he told O.J., you'll see you don't have to testify.

O.J. said he was still prepared to gamble. Where was the absolute assurance he would walk out of jail when this was over?

Douglas and Kardashian had discussed O.J.'s possible testimony. If—the worst-case scenario—they had a hung jury, O.J. would almost certainly take the stand in a second trial. Why give the D.A. a preview of his testimony now? Dershowitz had also told Kardashian that if O.J. testified every one of his lawyers should be disbarred. At this point in the case, no thoughtful lawyer would let him get within a mile of the witness stand. To put Simpson on would distract the jury from Fuhrman's perjury and from Vannatter walking around with a vial of O.J.'s blood.

"Putting you on the stand," Alan had told O.J., "tells the jury that this case is no longer about what the LAPD did. Now it's all about what you did. They'll forget about Fuhrman. They'll focus on your spousal abuse."

O.J. was getting the message.

Johnnie needed his client's decision today. Simpson was the owner of the team. What were Cochran's marching orders? Only one week left in This Fucking Case.

O.J. suggested recalling Arnelle. The jury loved her. He wanted the jury to know that he never hit Nicole. His daughter was the best person to tell them.

"I'm not going near that subject," Johnnie said.

But Cochran could see Simpson was edging away from testifying. Don't push him, Carl Douglas had told Johnnie. Don't push him, and he'll back away on his own.

Then Bailey visited O.J. Right up to this day, he'd wanted O.J. to testify. Never budged from his position.

But today Bailey said, "O.J., we are in a position now where you should not testify. If you do, it will be a whole new case." He explained to Simpson that the D.A. wanted a mistrial in the worst way and couldn't get one. The prosecution's last hope was juror attrition. If we lose more than two jurors, Bailey said, there will be fewer than twelve. Darden has stated he won't go on with fewer than twelve. We're willing, the law permits it, but Darden is saying no. And unless both sides agree to finish with a smaller jury, it's a mistrial. Bailey went on: Scheck has already told you that putting you on the stand will lengthen the trial by at least a month. How can you gamble that this jury can hold on that long?

"I'm the saddest guy in the world today," Bailey told

him. "I always wanted you on the stand, but I had to vote that you should not testify." That Lee Bailey had finally capitulated said a lot to Simpson.

"Close the case and get out" was Bailey's final advice to his client.

2 LAPD OFFICERS SUSPENDED
FOR FALSIFYING EVIDENCE

Two 18-year veterans of the embattled LAPD were suspended Friday for falsifying evidence in a murder case, forcing prosecutors to drop charges against two men and jeopardizing as many as 100 other cases the officers investigated, officials said. . . .

The suspensions come just days after release of the taped comments of former LAPD Detective Mark Fuhrman, who boasted of fabricating evidence, beating suspects, and singling out minorities for mistreatment. The usual public announcement was part of a department effort to restore public confidence and show its commitment to rooting out bad officers. . . .

—Alan Abrahamson and Jodi Wilgoren,
Los Angeles Times. September 2, 1995

DEFENSE'S NEW FUHRMAN WITNESS
ADDS TWIST TO CASE

. . . Lucienne Coleman, a 17-year veteran of the [D.A.'s] office and former head of its sex crimes division, has told fellow prosecutors, Internal Affairs investigators, and now members of O.J. Simpson's legal defense team that police officers had told her and several other deputy district attorneys about allegations that Fuhrman had committed an act of anti-Semitic vandalism and boasted of an intimate relationship with Nicole Brown Simpson. . . .

Early in August, 1994, Coleman met with the prosecutors in Clark's office. . . . "[I] told them what I had heard. . . . When I told Clark and Hodgman what I knew, Clark stated, 'This is b—!'"

29

ON MONDAY MORNING, SEPTEMBER 4, LABOR DAY, PETER Neufeld and Pat McKenna are surprised: Prosecutor Alan Yochelson is delivering LAPD photographer Rolf Rokahr, exactly as he said he would. Until now, the D.A. had refused to let the defense interview Rokahr. Today Yochelson has some doughnuts and coffee waiting at Parker Center. The atmosphere is casual: Peter and Pat wear blue jeans.

McKenna and Rokahr sit side by side, the contact sheets laid out on the table. Neufeld and Yochelson sit across from them. The interview is taped.

Neufeld takes the photographer through the entire evening at the crime scene, step by step: When did you arrive? Who directed you to take the pictures? When and why? Then Rokahr tells Neufeld and McKenna that at one point he was standing at the back gate talking to Detective Ron Phillips, who had been directing him, when Detective Mark Fuhrman came up to both of them. Fuhrman was alone. He wanted to have evidence pictures taken at the front gate. Rokahr and Fuhrman walked around the block to the front gate. Fuhrman was alone? That sticks in McKenna's mind.

McKenna knows that other cops have testified that Fuhrman was never alone at Bundy before he went to Rockingham at 4:40 A.M. Now Rokahr says that before Fuhrman went to Rockingham, he approached Phillips and Rokahr by himself to have pictures taken at the front gate. It was Fuhrman's idea, Rokahr says, to show him the evidence, which included the glove.

Bingo! That's it, McKenna says to himself. Yochelson isn't even paying attention. Rokahr doesn't grasp the significance of what he has just said.

Then Neufeld points to the last two frames on roll one. These are dark, Peter says. Maybe the lighting is wrong, maybe the film is wrong, maybe it's really six in the morning? No, Rokahr says, those two pictures were taken at around four in the morning. One shows Fuhrman pointing to the glove.

Bingo again. Fuhrman has lied for sure. He said he'd pointed to the glove at seven A.M. Now the LAPD photographer can impeach him.

Then, Rokahr says, he left Fuhrman alone next to the glove and moved on to take other pictures. He just lost sight of the detective. The other pictures are on roll two.

Neufeld and McKenna are poker-faced. They take their time finishing up. No rushing out of the building. Rokahr will be on the stand tomorrow, September 5.

When they finally get to the front door, it's hard not to sprint to their car. As the doors swing closed behind them, Neufeld turns to McKenna. They give each other a high five, right there in front of Parker Center. They have nailed Mark Fuhrman.

Late on Labor Day afternoon the defense has a short meeting. Their defense of O.J. Simpson is nearly over. The jury is barely hanging on. No matter what, they will finish this week. Bailey is a restored man. He has at least two or three witnesses to present and is anxious to take on Ito.

The atmosphere this afternoon is a mix of elation, anxiety, and fatigue. The end is in sight, but the outcome is still uncertain. Time to let off a little steam.

"I'll guarantee you, Fuhrman will take the Fifth," someone says, and proposes a gentleman's bet. Neufeld is the first in: Fuhrman will not. Scheck agrees. Shapiro says, Of course he will. The odds are now 10 to 1 against Fuhrman taking the Fifth.

Bob Blasier says he wants the detective to try on the gloves.

Suddenly the power in the building goes out. Cochran is stuck in the elevator. First time he's been late for a meeting since he joined the team. Douglas says, Let him walk all ten flights. By the time he gets here we'll be done with the meeting.

"Looks like you lost five pounds," Kardashian says when Johnnie finally comes in. The unflappable Mr. Cochran is out of breath. *"Shit,"* he says. Everyone is now laughing.

Bailey brings up last week's suggestion of working with a focus group for closing arguments. Shawn Chapman says that this time the defense should ask about the important elements of the case. For example, " 'What has made the defense's case most believable to you?' That's what I mean," she says. "Then the same questions from the prosecution point of view: 'Was there anything about Simpson's defense you did not believe?' " The others agree.

"What's important is how did their opinions change, if at all," Shawn adds. She reminds them of their focus group on Rosa Lopez. Johnnie wanted to use the videotape or bring her back from El Salvador. "Everyone in the focus group said they hated her, overwhelmingly," Shawn reminded them. "That's the only thing that convinced Johnnie not to play the tape." Douglas agrees. Let's get going right away, the team decides.

To establish that Fuhrman lied about access to the glove, Barry Scheck wants to make sure Rokahr testifies before him.

"We've been kicking back for six days," Bailey says. "We have to come out now with a bang, let the jury see what they've been waiting six days for." Scheck and Cochran agree. Bailey wants to start with Rokahr. Uelmen wants Bell. The problem with Bell is that Ito might just say: I've given you Bell, I've given you Terry, I've given you the right to say Fuhrman's used the "N-word" forty-one times. Now Rokahr? Enough is enough.

Barry points out that Rokahr isn't redundant. Bell and the others all address Fuhrman's racism. The photographer is a totally different story.

Barry goes on: They must find a way to keep Fuhrman from taking the Fifth. "We have to create an escalating series of questions," he suggests, "first dealing with his attitudes about lying, about manufacturing probable cause. If we start with those, he can't take the Fifth. If he denies those, then we impeach him with the tapes." Blasier says Ito will rule that those questions are not relevant.

Scheck, spacing his words very slowly, emphatically, but not loudly, says, "Let—him—rule—those—aren't—relevant."

"Let's just waltz into court and call a witness." Blasier says. "Call the jury, and call a witness at 9:05."

30

On Tuesday morning, September 5, Carl Douglas, Johnnie Cochran, and Robert Kardashian drove to the courthouse together. As Johnnie put it, "This is the morning for white women." Kardashian listed them: Bell, Singer, Terry, and McKinny.

As they pulled up to the courthouse a sign caught Johnnie's eye. " 'LAPD plus Ito equals corrupt!' " Cochran shouts. "I just love it!"

After the usual meeting in the holding cell, Lee Bailey looked confident as he called Kathleen Bell to the stand. Fuhrman, who had recently retired and moved to Idaho, was in the building today waiting to be called.

Anything negative the prosecution might have on Kathleen Bell had been eclipsed by the Fuhrman tapes. Bailey has only to ask Bell some key questions and get her off the stand. He starts by taking her back to her first meeting with Fuhrman at the Marine Corps recruiting station. Trouble started, she said, when she told Fuhrman she had a white girlfriend named Andrea Terry who admired Marcus Allen.

"What happened when you mentioned the name Marcus Allen to Mark Fuhrman?" Bailey asked her.

"His demeanor changed, and his attitude toward me changed," she answered, settling comfortably into the witness chair.

"And what, if anything, did he say?" Bailey asked.

"He said that when he sees a black man with a white woman driving in a car, he pulls them over." Bell testified that she asked Fuhrman, "What if they didn't do anything wrong?" How did Fuhrman answer? "He said he would find something," she said. And if the couple was in love? she asked the detective. "That is disgusting," Fuhrman had replied.

Cochran and the others worried that something might still go wrong. What if prosecutors decided to attack Bell, regardless of the tapes?

"After the word 'disgusting' was uttered, what was said next by either of you?"

"I just kind of paused," Bell replied, "and then he said, 'If I had my way, all the niggers would be gathered together and burned.'"

Kardashian saw that nearly every juror was taking notes. In the back row, a woman scowled. Another stared at Bell as if in a trance. Two in front jerked their heads nervously back and forth between Bell and Bailey. It reminded Kardashian of watching a tennis match.

Bailey repeated the original phrase, asking how Bell reacted when Fuhrman said he'd "gather all the niggers together and burn them." Then he rephrased it.

"Did you respond in any other way . . . when Mr. Fuhrman told you what he would like to do with reference to burning an entire race?" he asked.

"I kind of got teary-eyed and left," the witness said.

Chris Darden opened his cross-examination by asking Bell if she, too, was horrified by the "N-word." She said yes. He jostled her a little, asking why she introduced her friend Andrea Terry to Fuhrman later on if she was so horrified.

Bell denied introducing them. She'd never do that, she said.

Then Darden asked about her letter to Judge Ito. Months earlier, Bell had written to the judge saying she'd rather not testify. She believed Simpson was guilty and didn't want to help him.

"You didn't want to help the defendant in this case?" Darden asked.

"No, I did not," she said.

"Okay," Darden said slowly. "And that is because you think he—"

Cochran and Bailey objected. Ito instructed Darden to move on.

Andrea Terry was waiting in the hallway to be sworn in as the next witness. Johnnie asked for a short recess. The team huddled in the holding cell with Simpson. Could she be trouble? With an acquittal in sight, each potential witness required intense scrutiny. Could Terry hurt them? On the stand, Bell had vehemently denied that she'd introduced Terry and Fuhrman in a bar a few weeks after hearing Fuhrman's racist rants. Andrea Terry would say Kathleen Bell had introduced them. The prosecutors had interviewed her, Terry said. They knew.

Johnnie and Carl sent Andrea Terry home.

"The older lady in the back *looked* at me," Shawn told Douglas during the break. "On her way out, right in the eye, with this warm smile." Chapman couldn't contain herself. A juror had *smiled*. It had to mean something good.

"Just calm down," Carl said. "We've still got closing arguments."

* * *

The defense next called Natalie Singer. In 1987, Mark Fuhrman had visited her West Los Angeles apartment.

Watching television in Nashville, where she now lived, Singer had been astonished to hear Fuhrman testify he'd never used the word "nigger." She called Shapiro, Cochran, then Lee Bailey's office in Boston. Pat McKenna finally called back.

When Singer lived in L.A., she had been hospitalized for a kidney stone. Her roommate met Fuhrman and his partner, Tom Vittraino, while visiting her. A few weeks later, when Singer was back home, the two cops came calling. Singer was so shocked by Fuhrman's statements that she eventually banned him from the apartment.

"Did he use an epithet well known to the world that denotes black people and begins with 'n'?" Lee Bailey asked.

Singer said yes.

How did she react? Bailey asked. She was "shocked, stunned. I'd never met anyone who talks that way."

Kathleen Bell had already testified that Fuhrman used the "N-word" and hated African-Americans deeply enough to wish for their immolation. She had told jurors that he boasted he'd "find something" to justify stopping a black man in a car with a white woman. In other words, he might falsify evidence. Now Singer would establish that Fuhrman's racist boasting wasn't an isolated incident.

"What did he say?" Bailey asked.

"Is it okay to say that?" Singer asked in surprise.

"Yes."

"He said, 'The only good nigger is a dead nigger.' "

Marcia Clark spent less than ten minutes cross-examining Natalie Singer. The prosecutor faltered during one question. She excused herself: "I'm sorry, this is not a great day for me, speaking-wise." Clark was clearly upset.

Bailey scored again on redirect. *How* did Fuhrman use the words?

"When he says the things," Natalie Singer said of Mark Fuhrman, "it is bolstered and held up and pushed out of his mouth with hatred and arrogance and despicability. And that is what hurts. That is what hurts.''

Forget the tapes, Bailey thought triumphantly. This Jewish gal from Brooklyn has done the job. Fuhrman's burial is at hand. If Mark Fuhrman takes the Fifth now, we don't really care.

The team decided to hold back on Roderic Hodge for now. Don't force Ito into ''Enough is enough.''

The prosecution, of course, had been expecting Hodge. Instead, the defense called Rokahr. Peter Neufeld began by asking Rokahr when he had arrived at the Bundy crime scene. What type of film had he used? What shots did he take first? Rokahr confirmed what he'd told Neufeld the day before at Parker Center: He finished the first series of crime-scene shots at about 3:50 or 3:55 P.M.

''What was the next thing that happened after you completed shooting these location shots?'' Neufeld asked.

''I believe at that point I met up with Mark Fuhrman.''

Rokahr then testified that, as he had told McKenna and Neufeld, he met Fuhrman at about 4:10 A.M. (Later in his testimony, he confirmed that Fuhrman was alone at the time.) Neufeld pinned Rokahr down on the exact time he and Fuhrman arrived at the front gate. Between 4:25 and 4:40, he replied. The photographer then stated that he, not Fuhrman, suggested the picture in which Fuhrman pointed at the glove.

''[Did] you ask Detective Fuhrman to point to the item . . . because it was nighttime [and] the glove was difficult to see?'' Neufeld asked.

''That is correct.''

The defense was almost home free. They had established that the picture was taken before 4:40 A.M. and that Fuhrman was alone when the two men met.

The Fuhrman pictures were numbered 34 and 35 on the first roll of film. ''And those were the last two pictures you took on that first roll of film . . . in the early morning hours of June 13, 1994?'' Neufeld asked.

''That is correct,'' Rokahr answered.

Neufeld gave the jury the contact sheet to pass around. He had not mentioned Fuhrman's testimony that he was never alone at Bundy. Douglas wondered if the jury understood the implications. Scheck didn't care. He was in seventh heaven.

On cross, Darden managed to establish only that Rokahr sometimes had a bad memory, was in poor health, and took thirteen medications daily.

Neufeld had forgotten one point, which he picked up on redirect.

"In terms of how light it is, is there an obvious difference between a photograph taken an hour to an hour and a half before the sun rises, and a photograph taken an hour to an hour and a half after the sun rises?"

"Yes, there's a difference," Rokahr answered.

"If the sun rose that morning at five forty-one A.M., you would be able to tell the difference, without being precise, whether the photograph was a nighttime shot, shot perhaps an hour, hour and a half before sunrise, and one shot an hour and a half after sunrise, wouldn't you?" Neufeld asked.

"I would like to think so."

Neufeld had delivered.

Then, outside the presence of the jury, Gerry Uelmen asked the court to reconsider the ruling on the tapes. Uelmen pointed out that one of the two excerpts admitted was almost inaudible: Background noise made it hard to recognize the word "nigger," robbing the snippet of its dramatic impact. And this was the only live audio excerpt Ito had approved.

"I will agree that that particular excerpt . . . is not audible in a real sense," Ito ruled. He substituted one of Uelmen's suggestions.

31

Laura McKinny sat with her husband in the nineteenth-floor conference room the defense used for its witnesses. She was nervous as she waited to testify. Her upcoming court appearance had reduced her to tears.

The defense team briefed her gently. Gerry Uelmen and Johnnie both warned that Darden would accuse her of moneygrubbing, trying to sell tapes a good citizen would have turned over to the prosecutors long ago.

Mark Fuhrman was also on her mind. McKinny told Cochran and Douglas she was afraid he might kill her. She felt she was risking her life. Still, she managed to pull herself together, and she never mentioned backing out.

When Laura McKinny took the stand, she still looked worried.

Bob Shapiro had watched the jurors carefully when McKinny's name was called. They sat up slightly, edging forward. News of the tapes had gotten to them; they knew something important was coming.

McKinny told Cochran she'd met Fuhrman in a West Los Angeles café in 1985. She had been sitting at an outdoor table, transcribing notes on a laptop.

"A man dressed in street clothes came up and asked me about my computer," she said.

Fuhrman and the dark-haired woman were both single at the time. He let her know he was a cop, and the connection was instant. She told him she was researching a screenplay about the tensions between men and women in uniform. Fuhrman offered to consult. McKinny asked him to describe the job's "frustrations" and the resulting "cover-ups." The young cop was eager. She convinced him the interviews should be taped.

Carl Douglas saw that the jurors were alert and taking notes.

How many times did Fuhrman use the word "nigger" during the years of taping? Cochran asked.

"Approximately forty-two," she said.

Forty-two times? Cochran asked for emphasis. McKinny confirmed it.

"During the forty-one or forty-two times that Mr. Fuhrman used the word 'nigger,' " Cochran asked a few minutes later, "could you tell us how he appeared?"

"When Officer Fuhrman used the word 'nigger,' it was in a very casual, ordinary pattern of speech," McKinny said. She said it was "in a serious manner. It was not light-hearted."

"Was it insulting?" Cochran asked.

Fuhrman used it "in a demeaning, derogatory fashion." Disparaging? Cochran asked, pounding his theme. Yes, McKinny said, he used it "in a disparaging fashion."

Now Cochran was ready to present Excerpt number 8, in which Fuhrman talked about his youth in Washington State. He passed out transcripts to the jury, and Howard Harris turned on the overhead projection screen. McKinny had accidentally erased this tape years ago, Cochran explained. Only a transcript remained.

"And the quote by Fuhrman is, 'We have no niggers where I grew up,' " Cochran read solemnly. "Do you recall him saying that?"

It was during their first interview, on April 2, 1985, McKinny said.

Douglas saw the jurors writing rapidly in their notebooks.

Cochran couldn't resist a jab at Ito over the sanitized presentation of the tapes. "Can you compare that with the other forty-two times or so that he used this [word] in the course of your interviews?"

"There is a significant difference here," McKinny said. "This particular example is the least offensive and inflammatory, in comparison to the others."

Ito ordered the jurors to disregard McKinny's statement. It didn't matter. They had heard it.

"Let's move down to the second incident we have been allowed to use of Fuhrman speaking," he said. He read the transcript first.

" 'They don't do anything, they don't go out there and initiate a contact with some six-foot, five-inch nigger that has been in prison for seven years pumping weights.' "

If you heard it on tape, could you identify Fuhrman's voice? McKinny said yes. The tape was played.

Do you recognize the voice? Cochran asked.

"Officer Mark Fuhrman."

". . . And that was his voice, is that right?"

McKinny confirmed it. No doubt? Cochran asked.

"No doubt about it," she answered.

The next day, Wednesday, September 6, Cochran, Douglas, and Kardashian drive to court again in Carl's car.

As they turn off Broadway onto Temple Street, they notice new signs in front of the courthouse: "Get the KKK out of the D.A. and L.A. Police."

Near the curb, the crowd notices Cochran, and the chant begins: "Johnnie, Johnnie, Johnnie."

"Grab your seat," Kardashian says to Johnnie. "We'll go around back to the parking lot."

"I'm not the President, I'm just Johnnie," Cochran replies. He begins to open the door, and the crowd outside cheers. The sound is deafening. "Johnnie, Johnnie, Johnnie."

Now the crowd is so thick around the car that Cochran can't open the door. Douglas wants to head for the parking lot. So does Kardashian. Carl thinks it's getting too crazy.

Finally Johnnie gets the door open.

"Good morning, good morning," Cochran says. He disappears into the sea of reporters and spectators.

Laura McKinny returned to the stand for Chris Darden's cross-examination.

"Isn't it true that Mr. Regwan and Mr. Schwartz have

been attempting to sell those transcripts and those tapes?''
Darden began.

McKinny denied it. "Have you ever discussed with
anyone selling the audiotapes for one-half million dollars?''
he asked.

She hadn't, she said. Had she told her attorneys to
negotiate a tape sale? Darden asked. Now he was becoming
hostile.

"I have authorized my attorneys to determine the value of
the tapes, yes.''

Darden moved suddenly to the racial epithet. How did she
feel the first time she heard Fuhrman use the word
"nigger"?

McKinny said she didn't recall.

"You don't remember . . . not being offended by it?''
Darden demanded.

Cochran objected to Darden's "tone of voice." Ito
sustained him.

"You understand that that is the most vile word in the
English language?'' Darden pushed.

"I think it is *one* of the most vile words in the English
language, yes,'' McKinny replied.

"You think there are worse?'' Darden asked sarcastically.
McKinny stared at him.

"Why are we having this adversarial relationship?'' she
asked him. Her tone was both tearful and enraged. "I don't
understand that. It is a vile word. Why do I have to define it
more so than it is?''

Darden pressed on. Did she use the word in her screenplay?

Yes, she answered.

"You are using that word in your screenplay to help make
money, right?''

Ito sustained Cochran's frantic objection. Darden rephrased. "Are you trying to make money off the use of that
word?'' Ito allowed that. But Darden didn't follow up. He
asked McKinny if any of her screenplays had been filmed
and moved quickly to a short film she and her husband, a
director, had made for Playboy Productions.

"And this piece was what, sort of a soft-porn kind of

piece?'' Darden asked. The contempt in his voice was hard to miss.

Ito sustained Johnnie's objection. Darden tried another direction. When Fuhrman used the word "nigger," he asked like an angry parent, "why didn't you just tell him to stop?"

Cochran objected and was quickly overruled.

"For the same reason I didn't tell him to stop when he told me of police procedures," she snapped, "cover-ups, other information that I felt was important for me to have. . . ." She didn't try to hide her anger.

She stuck it to him, Douglas exulted. Maybe the door is open to the rest of the tapes! At the least, it was now possible for the defense to ask about manufacturing evidence and covering up.

Douglas glanced at the jurors. They were absorbed. Darden had so enraged Laura McKinny, who was initially reluctant to help the defense, that she deliberately said "cover-ups" in the same breath as "police procedures." This was a witness who chose her words carefully. Douglas was convinced she understood the implications of her answer.

Darden was still attacking. Was McKinny's relationship with Fuhrman "only professional"? He was only a "technical adviser for the screenplay," she insisted.

"And *that* is it?" he asked sarcastically.

"Yes."

Clark and Darden huddled for a moment. Then Darden attempted some damage control. Did McKinny recall how she'd defined "cover-ups" during her meeting with the D.A. last month? Did she say she meant Fuhrman had said the LAPD was covering up "the fact that female officers did not perform well in violent situations"?

McKinny agreed. Darden finished soon after.

Cochran began his redirect. "Who was expressing these views of cover-up?"

McKinny replied, "Officer Fuhrman." Darden objected, and Ito overruled him.

"With regard to cover-up, he talked to you, did he not?" Cochran asked.

Darden objected again. This time Ito supported the prosecutor. Startled, Cochran demanded a sidebar. Ito asked, "What is your intended question?"

"He opened the door, Your Honor," Cochran said quickly. ". . . There are many other cover-ups that took place, and we have a right to bring that up. I didn't bring that up. You limited us, and I didn't do it. I sat down."

Ito asked Darden why he'd brought it up.

"She unloaded that on me," Darden complained. "That wasn't in direct response to a question. She unloaded that on me in front of the jury. She is their witness. It is obvious she is biased for the defense."

"So what are you going to ask in response to this, Mr. Cochran?" Ito said.

Cochran, still agitated, said, "I have the *right,* it seems to me, to ask the question."

"That is *not* what I asked," Ito snapped. "I asked you what you are going to ask."

"Your Honor, I resent that tone!" Cochran snapped back. For the first time in the trial, he had lost his composure. "I'm a man just like you are, Your Honor. I resent that tone, Your Honor. I resent that tone, Your Honor."

Ito ordered Cochran and Shapiro into chambers and brought the court reporter along for an on-the-record rebuke. The judge was furious. So was Cochran. The real issue, everyone knew, was Ito's ruling to allow so little of the Fuhrman tapes into evidence and Cochran's harsh statements about Ito at his press conference.

"Mr. Cochran, let me just express to you some concern that I have regarding our personal relationship at this point in time," Ito announced from behind his desk. "I have chosen up to this point to ignore your press conference last Thursday and what I consider direct contempt of this court."

For once, Cochran kept quiet.

Perhaps Cochran took "umbrage" at the interruption minutes earlier, Ito said. "Well, let me tell you something: I take umbrage at your response and your reaction." Did he mean the courtroom argument or the press conference? No one was sure. "I'm going to suggest that you and I both take a deep breath, take a recess, and come back and talk about this again." Judge Ito relaxed a little. "You are involved in the heat of battle. I understand that."

Cochran couldn't let go. "I was just saying I didn't want to be talked to like a schoolkid. I said I felt that we do have a long relationship, and I felt we were the ones who were being put upon on this whole issue, and I was trying to explain it. So I will take a deep breath," Cochran wound down. He paused. "I am prepared now to try to tell you what I am trying to do."

"No, I need to take a deep breath, too, Mr. Cochran," Ito insisted. The judge ordered the mid-morning recess.

Simpson's holding cell is crowded. All nine of the defense attorneys in court are present, half crazed, trying to work out a plan.

"Ito said last week that Fuhrman wasn't discussing a fictional character," Neufeld begins. "He was talking about himself. Now Darden is trying to undermine the obvious inference that any person would draw from listening to the tape!"

Scheck is on fire. "Darden is saying McKinny wanted to get into show business, she was exploiting racism! She wasn't just maintaining her journalistic role!" Barry looks at his colleagues. "I say to Darden, Fuck you!"

"You're too loud," Simpson interrupts, glancing at the door.

Bob Shapiro, always cool, adds, "Isn't that the whole point of his cross?"

"Johnnie, you have to tell Ito, 'I'm too emotional to argue this now: I don't want to create a problem with you,'" Scheck continues. "Let Dean Uelmen argue that Darden opened the door."

Barry pauses. "Then Uelmen will get up and say, 'Your Honor, Fuck you!'" The tension dissolves in laughter.

"I'm glad Johnnie got mad," Simpson says as the laughter fades. "Fuck this *shit*."

"Johnnie, you let Ito give you a whipping," Bailey warns. "Don't let it happen again."

Cochran smiles. "I've been beaten up by a white man today." Referring, not quite accurately, to Judge Ito.

Gerry Uelmen warns him to calm down, stay serious.

"I'm really *mad,*" Cochran insists. "I got sidetracked. I got fucked around. I apologize for this. Bob and I approached the bench. I said the door was opened. He unloaded on me, and I told him off. Well, all right," Cochran says quietly, his fatigue showing. "I think we're ready."

"Mr. Cochran, did you wish to make any further comment?" Ito asked after the recess.

"I would ask, Your Honor, would the court allow Dean Uelmen to make that for me at this point?"

Ito wasn't having any. "We are in mid-sentence in your argument, counsel," he observed. ". . . I would prefer that you conclude it."

Johnnie finished the sidebar without incident. The judge opened the door a crack but limited Cochran's questions to "that statement made in the district attorney's office" which Darden had brought up on cross.

When the jury returned, Cochran let some time pass, inquiring first about McKinny's experiences when the tapes were subpoenaed. Then he returned to the cover-up issue.

"What did you mean when you talked about cover-up as it relates to men against women in this screenplay that you ultimately wrote?"

McKinny began to answer, but Darden objected. Another question, another answer began, another objection. On Cochran's third try, McKinny said, "Some women on the police department were not willing to adhere to some of the cover-ups that men were—" Darden objected again. In all, he made thirteen objections before Cochran gave up. The jury had heard enough partial replies to get the general idea. Johnnie moved on to the "horrible" "N-word" and asked for yet another sidebar.

"There are certain portions of the tape which I think are now open that deal with men against women," he said. Cochran offered to search the tapes for the right moment during lunch and bring McKinny back.

"If she returns after lunch," Darden threatened, "I will impeach her with her love letters to Mark Fuhrman."

"This is how we got into this problem, by attacking her," Johnnie retorted. He was tempted to challenge Darden's trash talk. Cochran had asked McKinny what her relationship was with Fuhrman. She said it was purely professional. He believed her. Now he let the issue pass. This wasn't the moment to push his luck with Ito.

"We got into this problem because we are chasing down issues that have nothing to do with this trial," Darden threw back at him. He looked at Ito. "If Mr. Simpson is acquitted because Mark Fuhrman uttered an epithet, then there is no justice, Judge."

32

AFTER LAURA MCKINNY LEFT THE WITNESS BOX ON September 6, the defense called Roderic Hodge. On the previous day, the prosecution had argued that Hodge's testimony was redundant. Ito ruled against them.

For the last four days the defense had debated putting Hodge on the stand. Bailey, Cochran, and Gerry Uelmen wanted him. Kardashian had doubts. Carl Douglas and Shawn Chapman, former public defenders, thought Hodge's past might hurt them. Police records labeled him a onetime crack dealer involved with a notorious local gang, the Playboy Gangster Crips. Cochran was vehement: They had to use Hodge. Johnnie had searched in vain for a black witness outside Simpson's family. Uelmen wanted Hodge. He was, after all, a black man, and Fuhrman had called him "nigger." The cop hadn't been bragging or posturing to third parties. The team voted 6 to 2 for Hodge. Simpson didn't like him, except for the fact that he was black. Johnnie said the client's vote counted as much as all six. But this time Simpson waived his veto power. When the team voted again, Hodge won.

Fuhrman and his partner had arrested Hodge on January 11, 1987, more than eight years ago. He now lived in Dalton, Illinois, south of Chicago, where he worked as a phone-repair technician.

"Will you tell the ladies and gentlemen of the jury what Officer Fuhrman said to you on [that] date in January of 1987?" Cochran began.

"Yes, sir," Hodge replied. "At that time Officer Fuhrman turned around, looked at me, and told me, 'I told you we would get you, nigger!'"

Fuhrman's tone of voice?

"Anger, hatred, just something from deep inside, if you would, just very ugly."

And how did Hodge feel? Cochran wanted the jury to feel it.

"Belittled, scared, very, very angry."

Chris Darden wasn't calm. He wanted Hodge's head. He asked Hodge whether Fuhrman and his partner had arrested him only once. Cochran objected.

Ito called a sidebar and lectured the prosecutor.

"Why wouldn't you at this point say, 'Mr. Hodge, you were offended, that was a horrible thing. Thank you very much, good-bye'?"

Darden insisted that Hodge had a record of police trouble, that he'd filed excessive numbers of police abuse complaints.

That would open a door, Cochran said. The defense could show next that Hodge was acquitted of the charges brought the day Fuhrman arrested him.

Darden countered that Hodge's abuse complaint from that day hadn't mentioned racial epithets. He had the document. Ito allowed Darden to go ahead.

"Nowhere in this Internal Affairs complaint is it mentioned that you complained of Fuhrman's use of any epithets," Darden said. "Is that correct?"

The young black repairman asked to read the eight-year-old interview. Ito gave him the lunch hour.

"Did you see the epithet indicated here in these documents?" Darden asked when court reconvened.

"No, sir."

But Cochran had noticed something else during the lunch break. Ten of the report's pages were missing: more suspicious behavior from the LAPD. On redirect, Johnnie first asked Hodge if he had "any doubt" that Fuhrman called him a nigger.

"Sir, there's no doubt in my mind whatsoever," Hodge replied.

Then the LAPD Internal Affairs report. "Do you know what happened to pages 7, 8, 9, 10, 11, 12, 13, 14, 15, and 16?" Cochran asked.

"No, sir," Hodge said solemnly, "I would have no idea."

The Fuhrman funeral was proceeding well.

33

NATALIE SINGER HAD BEEN F. LEE BAILEY'S LAST WITness. At lunchtime he quietly left the courthouse.

Uelmen would now present Mark Fuhrman.

After the break, Fuhrman's attorney, Daryl Mounger, asked to be heard by the court. Ito was hearing arguments outside the presence of the jury on other issues, but turned his attention to the lawyer.

A key issue, Ito told Mounger, was whether Fuhrman should be recalled "for additional testimony." He asked for Mounger's "observations."

If his client knew what defense lawyers planned to ask,

Mounger replied carefully, it would help, "because of the position that Detective Fuhrman was in."

Mounger had defended one of the cops accused of beating Rodney King. He was an experienced police lawyer with a straightforward duty today: to protect Mark Fuhrman from himself.

Gerry Uelmen spoke for the defense. "We don't believe a witness is entitled to a preview of the questions . . . to be asked on cross-examination," he responded tartly.

At Ito's direction, Uelmen grudgingly gave Mounger a copy of the defense's offer of proof. "It's not exactly a mystery as to what we're talking about here," Ito said to Mounger. The brief didn't list questions, but Fuhrman could see in general what the defense had in mind. Mounger took it upstairs to the eighteenth floor to consult with his client.

Mounger soon returned. In his conversations with Cochran a week earlier, he had vacillated. His client might take the Fifth, or might not. "I have advised Mr. Fuhrman that he should not answer any questions before this court," Mounger now said. ". . . He will assert his Fifth Amendment privilege if asked any questions."

Mounger said he hoped that both sides would agree for the record that Fuhrman would not testify, and would let him stay on the eighteenth floor.

"No, Your Honor," Uelmen responded. "We believe it's necessary for him to assert the privilege from the witness stand in response to a question."

If we can't get Fuhrman physically in front of the jury, Carl Douglas thought, a hearing in open court still puts him there through pillow talk.

Ito agreed that the defense was entitled to a hearing and ordered Fuhrman to appear. "He will be here shortly, Your Honor," Mounger said.

The first of Fuhrman's three bodyguards entered the courtroom alone. He walked briskly to the railing and checked the entire room.

Then Mark Fuhrman came in. In the press section, Linda Deutsch of the Associated Press wondered if he'd lost weight. He looked terrible. He seemed thin; there were dark circles under his eyes. But he maintained a military bearing: shoulders back, head high. Even in disgrace, he had star quality. The courtroom was silent, raw with tension. Deutsch half expected to hear a solemn drumroll in the background.

The reporter looked over at Simpson. He had turned in his chair to glare as Fuhrman marched past. The detective sat down at a table on the prosecution's side of the room. Time seemed to stop. Ito directed Mounger to stand next to his client. Then the judge looked down at the tall cop.

"Detective Fuhrman," Ito said, "would you resume the witness stand, please?"

In all her years of court watching, Deutsch had never seen a human being so isolated. Chris Darden had turned his back. Marcia Clark pointedly looked away. She'd made it clear in the day's arguments that she and Darden wished Mark Fuhrman didn't exist. He was damaged goods. If she lost the case, Fuhrman would be the reason.

Deutsch assumed Fuhrman would answer some routine questions before taking the Fifth. She remembered 1976, the Patty Hearst trial, when Hearst took the Fifth forty-two times in front of the jury. Now she waited for Fuhrman's first answer.

"Detective Fuhrman, was the testimony that you gave at the preliminary hearing in this case completely truthful?" Gerry Uelmen asked.

Fuhrman conferred with his attorney before answering. "I wish to assert my Fifth Amendment privilege," Fuhrman said.

Deutsch was disappointed. Uelmen hadn't left Fuhrman room for any other answer.

"Have you ever falsified a police report?" Uelmen asked.

Again Fuhrman leaned over to Mounger; then he sat up stiffly.

"I wish to assert my Fifth Amendment privilege," he repeated.

Simpson was rigid with tension. His shoulders shook slightly, but otherwise he did not stir.

"Is it your intention to assert your Fifth Amendment

privilege with respect to all questions that I ask you?'' Uelmen asked.

Deutsch noticed movement at the defense table. Cochran was signaling Uelmen urgently. Fuhrman leaned down to Mounger one more time.

''Yes,'' he said.

Panic reigned at the defense table. Uelmen was ending it too soon! He seemed to have forgotten a prepared question. Carl Douglas was nearly out of his seat, trying to catch Uelmen's eye. He mouthed, '' 'Did you plant evidence?' '' Then he whispered as loud as he dared, '' 'Did you plant evidence?' That's the question you want to ask him!'' Even Simpson was gesturing toward Uelman.

''Come here, Gerry,'' Johnnie hissed. ''Come *here!*''

Uelmen finally noticed Cochran's frantic signal. He asked Ito's permission to break off for a short conference.

''Gerry, ask him if he planted the *glove!*'' Johnnie hissed furiously as they huddled. ''Ask the fucking question! What the fuck is wrong with you?''

Daryl Mounger moved into the vacuum. Further questions ''[wouldn't] serve any purpose,'' he told the judge. His client had already said he wouldn't answer them. ''Anything further can only be a show,'' he said.

Had Uelmen blown it?

''I have only one other question, Your Honor,'' Uelmen said.

Ito allowed it.

''Detective Fuhrman, did you plant or manufacture any evidence in this case?'' he asked.

Cochran and Douglas groaned. He didn't mention the glove!

''I assert my Fifth Amendment privilege,'' Fuhrman said for the last time.

A few objections and a sidebar later, the detective was gone, escorted by three bodyguards and Mounger. Fuhrman walked out with his head high, eyes straight ahead.

The long-awaited drama had played out so fast that Deutsch felt cheated; the last act of the decline and fall of Mark Fuhrman had been disappointing. As Deutsch wrote her story, she realized the prosecution had kept Fuhrman away from the jury. That had been the D.A.'s triumph.

Downstairs, a police van carrying Fuhrman pulled out of the underground parking garage. Its windows were blacked out.

Afterward, in the holding cell, Simpson's stoic mask crumbled. As soon as he was alone with Kardashian, he wept.

"This fucking bastard plants a glove and commits perjury," he said, his voice breaking. "He gets to go home, and I have to stay here!"

All day, Kardashian had watched O.J. restrain himself. No one could carry that kind of tension indefinitely, Bob knew. In recent weeks, Simpson had rarely revealed this much vulnerability. Among friends, he joked, showed a little temper. That was all. Today he cracked.

Simpson cried. Kardashian sat with him silently.

34

BEFORE FUHRMAN'S APPEARANCE, WHEN MOUNGER WENT to consult with his client, Robert Shapiro approached Larry Schiller, who was sitting in his usual place in the first row behind the rail. Could Schiller drive him home at the end of the day? The writer was surprised.

Over the last several weeks Schiller had repeatedly invited Shapiro for lunch, breakfast, dinner. The answer never varied: No, I'm busy. Always polite, always negative.

When court ended, the two men walked down the locked hallway to the VIP elevator. Marcia Clark was waiting there alone, her arms piled with stacks of folders. Shapiro said hello. She didn't lift her eyes. There was no reason to introduce Schiller; she knew who he was. Clark was obviously going upstairs to the eighteenth-floor offices; they were going down to the parking lot. When the doors opened, Schiller entered after Clark. Shapiro followed. The elevator went up first, then back down. Schiller thought Clark looked as if all the life had been drained from her.

As they drove, Schiller asked Bob Shapiro a few questions about Fuhrman, the topic of the day. Eventually they got to the subject of books. Bob said he was writing one; so would Schiller. They talked for almost thirty-five minutes as they drove to Shapiro's home in Benedict Canyon. This was the first informal conversation Schiller had had with the attorney. He hoped there would be more.

Shapiro was the first in a long list of defense participants whom Schiller would interview over the next eight months. That night, he called Robert Kardashian and set their first interview.

On Friday morning, September 8, Simpson and Kardashian are in the holding cell. O.J. is emotional. "What's left of my privacy?" he asks. "I'm planning to be back with Sydney and Justin. I want to be home by my daughter's birthday."

The tension is growing. Today may be the last day of the defense case. At that moment Johnnie comes in from Ito's chambers.

"Ito says he wants you to give a clear waiver on the record that you're not taking the stand," Cochran tells him. "This is a good time for you to make a statement."

Ito will not shut O.J. down as long as he is succinct and to the point, Cochran says. "It will be the story of the day."

"And it's the last time you're going to talk without being paid," Kardashian says. "Same goes for you, Johnnie."

O.J. isn't listening to Kardashian: He's drafting his statement. "I maintain I'm innocent," he says aloud.

"No, you're one hundred percent innocent," Kardashian reminds him.

"I'm *totally* innocent; I did not do this; I am concerned about what is left of my privacy and Nicole's," O.J. says aloud.

"And what's left of my future," Bob adds.

"And I know if I took the stand," Simpson continues, "this trial would go on. I miss my two younger children. I'd like to be home for my daughter's birthday."

"'When are you coming home, Daddy?'—remember that," Kardashian adds.

"'How much longer are you there, Daddy?'" O.J. says, quoting Justin.

In the courtroom, O.J. is still working on his speech. Uelmen, Neufeld, Shapiro, and Cochran gather around the defense table as Simpson runs through his statement for them.

"I've got a family, I have kids, two young kids I haven't seen in sixteen months."

"Yeah, it's powerful," Johnnie says,

"I have stated from day one: I'm one hundred percent innocent," Simpson continues.

Johnnie then shows Simpson Ito's draft of an instruction to be read to the jury about Fuhrman's absence. "Okay, my brother, here it is," he says. Both sides now have a chance to comment on the text before Ito reads it to the jury.

It reads: "Detective Mark Fuhrman is not available as a witness for further testimony in this case. His unavailability for further testimony is a factor which you may consider in evaluating his credibility as a witness."

O.J. reads the statement quietly. "Ito's played it both ways," he finally says. "We can't argue; he really didn't help the other side."

Then Simpson returns to his rehearsal, oblivious to the fact that he's sitting in a public courtroom. The fine-tuning continues for almost ten minutes.

Gerry Uelmen tells Ito that the defense accepts the jury instruction as submitted. Marcia Clark announces that the prosecution does not. She will take Ito's decision to read the instruction to the Second Appellate District Court of Appeal within hours. Naturally, she doesn't want the jury told they can consider Fuhrman's "unavailability" in determining whether to believe him. The jury is bound to figure out that Fuhrman perjured himself. Ito agrees to wait; the prosecutors have the right to object to a higher court.

By the end of the day, the state appellate court has ruled that Judge Ito must abandon his jury instruction entirely or explain to the appellate court why he thinks he can give it. Ito kills the instruction rather than respond. The prosecution has won the day.

Then Cochran tells Ito that the defense will go to a higher court to get this ruling overturned. He maintains that Fuhrman is still a witness under cross-examination and that the defense has not concluded its case.

O.J.'s speech will have to wait until after the jury instruction issue is settled.

In the evening, the defense team meets in Johnnie's conference room. Johnnie says there's no way the defense is resting its case until Fuhrman is before the jurors. He has fifteen more witnesses to call if he needs to stall.

"The defense will never rest," Cochran declares.

"The D.A. knows they've lost the case," Bob Shapiro says. "What we have to protect against is a mistrial."

"All they want is a mistrial," Johnnie adds. But he still wants Fuhrman to appear.

"First of all," Shapiro continues, "all these remedies are nice: Grant Fuhrman immunity, strike his testimony, play more tapes. You can ask for anything, but they're all going to be denied, denied, denied, and denied."

Everyone is caught up in the Shapiro-Cochran exchange.

"This judge will say, 'Call your next witness,' and you know we have no other witness that will *advance* this case," Shapiro insists. "We're going to say we can't rest without a witness, but we must rest."

"I'm not resting. Ito wants O.J. to waive his rights." Johnnie is getting angry.

"And if he asks for a witness on Monday," Shapiro

snaps, "are you going to call O.J.? We must rest!" Shapiro's cool is evaporating.

"I'm not sure," says Johnnie. "I'm not sure Ito can force me to rest."

"Of *course* he'll do that." Shapiro is almost shouting now. "Let's be realistic. Forget the anger. Let's deal with the new DNA results coming in." Shapiro has everyone's attention.

"They're going to bring back the good, the bad, and the ugly in rebuttal," Shapiro continues. "We need to focus on the bad and the ugly and use them to our advantage."

Then Shapiro pulls an idea out of thin air. "Maybe we should talk about June seventeenth and O.J. trying to commit suicide."

"No way in the world!" Johnnie explodes. "Why are you bringing this stuff up?"

"Johnnie, I am throwing things out off the top of my head," Shapiro says calmly. "I want us to *think* about it."

Now Johnnie is really angry.

"You have the wrong attitude, Johnnie," Shapiro says.

"No, I don't."

"We do have a rebuttal in the heart of our case, which is the scientific evidence," Shapiro says. "We have to start to reevaluate our position. Then reevaluate our strategy, and look at it intelligently."

"*Thank you*, Bobby," Johnnie says, still angry. "Let's move on. I want to talk about our appeal on the jury instruction and how we're going to assign the prosecution's rebuttal witnesses. Bob, you're going to be mad, but that's the way it is."

"No, I'm saying rethink our plans before we rest," Shapiro points out.

"I'm not going to rest. Fuck it, I'm not going to rest!"

"All our appeals will be denied," Shapiro insists. "Deal with it now."

"We have to say, 'Next witness, Mark Fuhrman,'" Scheck throws in.

"Do we have the right to call Fuhrman again in front of the jury," Carl asks, "and have the jury hear the request denied?"

"Why not say, 'Judge, we're going to call the jury,'" Shapiro says. "The jury comes in, then, 'Excuse me, Judge—we call Mark Fuhrman!'"

That gets some strained laughter. The room is filled with tension and exhaustion, along with a residue of good humor.

Alan Dershowitz has been listening from Boston. "I've got a great idea!" he says now. "This is very serious. Put O.J. on the stand for direct examination. Then after he finishes direct, call a break, and out of the presence of the jury . . ."

"Have him take the Fifth Amendment," Shapiro finishes.

"It's brilliant, think about it," Alan adds.

Johnnie is now laughing. "Nice going," Cochran says. "Just keep in mind, Alan, Ito will never do right by us."

35

ON MONDAY, SEPTEMBER 11, THE TEAM AND O.J. ARE IN the holding cell, still debating the Fuhrman issue.

"I think we want to call Fuhrman," Neufeld says, "for a limited purpose: having him identify his voice on McKinny's tapes."

"We have to get him in front of the jury," Johnnie says. "I spoke to his attorney; Fuhrman's still in L.A."

"This is nonevidentiary testimony," Neufeld explains to O.J. "McKinny's credibility was attacked by Darden and she is the one who identified Fuhrman's voice. What we're doing is providing additional evidence that it's Fuhrman's voice."

"Let Fuhrman hear his own voice saying 'this nigger,'"

Cochran adds. ''But''—and Johnnie is obviously frustrated—''Ito is not going to let us call him. We bring the jury in for the rebuttal today, and I say my next witness is Mark Fuhrman. Ito will just say, 'Mark Fuhrman is not here today,' and it's over.''

''Good try,'' Simpson tells him.

In court Ito wanted to know what the defense's plans were. ''All right, Mr. Cochran, what is your position on the defense, since you haven't rested at this time?'' Ito asked impatiently.

Johnnie was in fine form. ''As the court is aware, the defense really never rests,'' he began. ''But, more specifically, in this case, we *cannot* rest . . .''

Cochran said he was taking a writ to the appeals court on the issue of the jury instruction.

And one last request: McKinny's credibility had been impugned during the cross-examination, Cochran said. ''We would like to call Mark Fuhrman to the stand and specifically have him utter those words that were played on that tape. So that once and for all we can determine that it is his voice,'' Cochran explained, ''and the jury knows that it is his voice.''

Ito denied Cochran's request to call Fuhrman but allowed the defense to delay resting. He ordered the prosecutors to begin their rebuttal case, their opportunity to refute points the other side had raised. Marcia Clark protested: She and Darden couldn't rebut a case they hadn't seen in its entirety.

''I want to get witnesses in front of this jury,'' Ito said angrily. He paused theatrically. *''Now.''*

As Ito started to ask for the jury to be brought in, Cochran interrupted. Would the court care to rule on bringing Fuhrman back to read the transcripts?

''All right,'' Ito barked. ''The request is denied.''

Now the prosecution again attempted to put the gloves on O.J. Simpson. The first try had become the D.A.'s biggest mistake of the trial. Today they would call several photographers who had shot Simpson wearing the same kind of

795

gloves at various sports events. Then Richard Rubin, the glove expert, would be recalled to identify the gloves in the photographs.

The defense had avoided mentioning either the Aris Isotoner gloves or the Bronco bloodstains, so prosecutors couldn't raise the issues in their rebuttal. But the glove photos hadn't arrived when Clark and Darden finished their case on July 6. Because the pictures were new evidence, Clark asked to reopen the prosecution case briefly, to call the photographers and Gary Sims. Ito granted the request.

To enhance the glove photographs, Clark and Darden had planned to use high-tech computer techniques normally reserved for satellite surveillance. Barry Scheck threatened to challenge the technology with a time-consuming Kelly-Frye hearing. Clark and Darden backed down and decided to present their "glove witnesses" minus the computer-assisted visuals.

Mark Krueger, an amateur photographer, led six quick witnesses for the prosecution. Each had taken pictures showing Simpson bundled up and wearing gloves while covering winter football games. All the gloves looked like Aris Isotoner Lights. Krueger's photo was taken at a 1990 Chicago Bears game.

Shawn Chapman and the others waited for Richard Rubin, whom the defense called the Glove Man. He had already looked at the six sets of pictures and said the gloves were Aris Isotoners, identical to the murder gloves.

Rubin was scheduled to testify the next day, and the prosecution's discovery on him had just arrived, although the defense had been asking for his notes for weeks. Finally a letter from Rubin to Clark and Darden was supplied. Johnnie opened it while Blasier read over his shoulder.

Blasier pointed to one sentence. Both men smiled.

On Tuesday, September 12, Rubin took the stand, clearly pleased to be back. Darden ran a video of Simpson smiling and jostling Cincinnati Bengals quarterback Boomer Esiason at a Bengals-Oilers game. Could Rubin identify Simpson's gloves?

"Based on what I've seen, I would say that is Style 70263, size extra large, brown," he replied.

"How certain are you of that?" Darden asked.

"I'm one hundred percent certain."

The jurors watched closely as Rubin looked at pictures and fingered the bloodstained gloves Darden brought to him. This particular style is "quite rare," he said, and the size was manufactured in "very limited" quantities.

"Are the gloves worn by the defendant in these . . . photographs the same style as the gloves found at Bundy and Rockingham?" Darden asked.

"Yes, they are," Rubin said.

"Mr. Rubin, have you tried to be completely impartial in this case?" Bob Blasier asked.

"Absolutely."

"Now, you haven't been currying favor with one side or the other?" Blasier said.

"Absolutely not."

In the angry maneuvering that had become commonplace in this trial, this slap at Richard Rubin was really aimed at Chris Darden. Johnnie and Carl hadn't forgotten his harsh cross-examination of Laura McKinny. Now they would discredit *his* witness.

The amazing thing, Douglas thought, was that Darden must have seen this coming. But while he had Rubin on the stand, he did nothing to neutralize it.

"You don't have any agenda here for one side or the other?" Blasier continued.

"I do not," Rubin answered smoothly.

The prosecution had sent Rubin the pictures in July, asking for his evaluation. He'd replied that Simpson was wearing Aris Isotoner Lights.

Blasier asked the question a fourth and last time. "You haven't tried to shade your opinion in any way to favor one side or the other?"

"Absolutely not," Rubin said.

Blasier let the witness relax, asked an innocuous question about Rubin's letter to the prosecution. Then he asked: Had

797

Rubin closed the letter by saying, "Maybe I can make it to the victory party!!"?

For a moment Rubin was startled. "Correct," he finally answered.

"Now, was this party planned before the defense started?" Blasier continued.

"This statement was made in jest," Rubin replied, regaining his smooth delivery, "no differently than on the first day that I testified here. As I walked out, I wished Mr. Simpson and the crowd the best of luck. It meant nothing."

Blasier ignored him. He asked the question again. "Had the victory party been planned before the defense started?"

"Absolutely not."

"Were you expecting an invitation to it?" Blasier asked deadpan.

"No, I was never expecting an invitation to it," Rubin answered helplessly.

Blasier had him rattled now. Did he consider himself a member of the prosecution?

"No, I do not," he said.

Kardashian saw several jurors who had paid close attention to the damaging pictures enjoying Rubin's embarrassment.

36

DESPITE ALL THE DAMAGE IT SHOULD HAVE DONE, THE September 12 testimony by DNA analyst Gary Sims seemed to have little impact on the jury. The jurors listened, Kardashian saw, but they took few notes. He assumed they were tired. Sims's testimony was heavily technical. Bob could barely follow it himself.

The defense had known for a week that bad news was coming from Sims. He'd combined three PCR-tested bloodstains from the Bronco console and obtained enough DNA for a more reliable RFLP test. The results showed both Simpson's and Goldman's DNA present in the blood swatch.

Now Rockne Harmon presented Sims.

"Mr. Sims, have you conducted additional testing that you are here to provide the results on in this case?" he began.

Gary Sims said yes.

For "context," Harmon walked Sims through his previous testimony involving PCR tests on the same stains.

The jury seemed indifferent.

"Mr. Sims, what is the impact of your RFLP results on the combination of 303, 304, and 305 on Dr. Gerdes's criticism about the 1.3 allele in item number 31 from the center console?" Harmon asked.

Sims began his answer: "Well, I think the RFLP results do tend to undermine that because they do show consistency with what I originally called item number 31."

Did anyone understand this? Finally, Harmon asked Sims for his results and conclusions.

"The finding of that pattern in the console is consistent with a mixture of the banding pattern of the defendant, Mr. Simpson, and also the contribution from Mr. Goldman," Sims said.

The defense wondered how much of this message got through the fog of verbiage.

ITO RAISES DISPUTED SOLUTION
TO JUROR PROBLEM

. . . Although Richard Rubin dominated the day's testimony, legal wrangling and new jury problems continued to dog the trial and keep it on its precarious course toward conclusion. In the morning, one juror threat-

ened to leave the panel because she needed to attend to a
rental property that has been vacant and is losing
money, . . . but was persuaded to stay when . . . Judge
Lance A. Ito said he would consider having the county
pay her losses.

The defense, which favors the recusal of that juror—a
retired white woman who sits in the front row of the
jury box—immediately objected. Simpson's lawyers later asked for that juror to be dismissed and filed a motion
urging Ito to reconsider his offer to financially help her.

—Henry Weinstein and Jim Newton,
Los Angeles Times, September 13, 1995

The juror was the Demon. The defense would have been
happy to see her go. Clark and Darden wanted to keep her at
any cost. Though public opinion was strongly opposed to
giving money to any juror other than the statutory daily fee,
it was not unprecedented for a judge to do what Ito was
proposing now. Judge William Pounders, presiding over the
lengthy McMartin Preschool child molestation case, had
given a juror financial assistance to keep the panel intact and
prevent a mistrial. By week's end, Michael Viner, a book
publisher, as well as the Apartment Owners Association of
Southern California, offered to solve the problem without
using county funds. On September 14, a donation was made
anonymously. The problem went away.

On Wednesday, September 13, Marcia Clark called D.A.'s
office investigator Stephan Oppler, who had been present at
the recent videotaping of Thano Peratis, the nurse who drew
Simpson's reference sample. Before the grand jury in June
of 1994 and at the preliminary hearing the following month,
Peratis had testified under oath that he had drawn 8 cc of
blood from Simpson. The defense claimed that when the
amounts used for testing were subtracted from that total,
more than 1.8 cc of blood were unaccounted for. The
prosecution had no explanation other than that Peratis had
actually drawn less than the amount originally stated.

800

Weeks before, the prosecution had gone to Peratis's home, where he was recovering from open-heart surgery, to videotape him saying that he didn't draw 8 cc of blood but considerably less. He was not placed under oath and no one from the defense cross-examined him or was present.

I hope the jury sees how stupid this is, Chapman thought. She couldn't believe Ito would admit Peratis's unsworn statement into evidence, but he did.

Since Peter Neufeld couldn't cross-examine Peratis he attacked Clark's witness. Stephan Oppler's testimony established when and where the taping occurred. On cross, Neufeld accused Oppler of helping Peratis rehearse his answers to the questions that deputy D.A. Hank Goldberg would be asking. Neufeld made sure the jury understood that Simpson's representatives *weren't* at the taping.

Neufeld raised so many questions about Oppler's participation in the taping that Clark called one of the videographers to back Oppler's story. No one coached Peratis, the camerawoman said.

But once again, the defense had cast doubt on the D.A.'s good faith.

In the holding cell the next morning, Thursday, September 14, Simpson is melancholy.

"I want to go home," he says.

"That depends on how long the jury takes to cover five hundred exhibits," Kardashian tells him.

"Will they go over it all?"

"That's the question," Bob says.

"I think the Demon will point out some things," Simpson tells him, "but I can't see them being more than a week. They want to go home, too."

"You're looking at three more weeks in here," Kardashian says.

"Will they give me back my golf clubs right away?" Simpson wonders aloud. His clubs are now a trial exhibit.

"Not right away," Bob answers jokingly. "Vannatter is using them now."

* * *

In court the testimony is serious.

Marcia Clark has put Douglas Deedrick, the FBI expert on trace evidence and fabric impressions, on the stand again. His job today is to discredit Dr. Lee's second-shoe testimony. Clark starts with questions on the bloody "shoe imprints" that Lee saw on the envelope containing Judy Brown's glasses, on the uncollected piece of paper, and on Ron Goldman's shirt and jeans.

Deedrick testifies that he's now taken test impressions of the fabrics from Goldman's shirt and pants. The "parallel line" marks Lee identified as possible shoe prints were more likely impressions made by the ribbed fabric of Goldman's clothes during his struggle.

Prompted by Clark, Deedrick attacks Dr. Lee's procedures. Was the witness aware, Clark asked, that Lee made no test impressions of Goldman's clothes to support his observations? Deedrick wondered aloud "how you can make a statement like that without knowing the kind of pattern the shirt actually makes."

The best Barry Scheck could do on cross was to force Deedrick to admit he was not an expert on either blood-pattern analysis or crime-scene reconstruction.

At lunchtime Cochran received an urgent phone call. There had been a bomb threat at his office. It wasn't the first, but this one sounded real.

"I want somebody to guard my house," Johnnie told his secretary. He called his wife, Dale, who went to a friend's home; then he tried to reach his office again, but couldn't get through. Everyone had been evacuated while the bomb squad searched.

The bigger problem was publicity. When Johnnie finally reached Carl's assistant, Carmen, he said, "I don't want people to know what happened. Forget the press. We go back to work as usual. If someone wants to go home for the day, that's okay." Nevertheless, Cochran ordered private security guards through the night for his office and home.

* * *

That afternoon Clark recalled Bill Bodziak, the FBI shoe-print analyst. He was calm and solid on the stand, first identifying some of the parallel lines as "typical of imprints of fabric or material and not imprints of shoes." Then he landed hard on the trowel marks.

"With respect to the parallel lines that were pointed out during Dr. Lee's testimony . . ." Clark asked, indicating photographs of the walkway, "in your opinion, sir, is that an imprint?"

"No, it's not an imprint, nor is it a shoe print," Bodziak said.

"What is it?"

"It's a result of the making, the finishing, of the concrete tiles," Bodziak answered.

The FBI expert explained that the walkway was actually poured concrete, shaped by trowelwork to resemble a surface made of individual tiles.

Nothing on the walkway "looks like a shoe impression," Bodziak testified, "other than the ones that I previously testified to . . . which were the Bruno Magli design."

During Barry Scheck's angry cross the following Monday, Douglas noticed that several jurors seemed indifferent. They were *tired*. One woman gazed around the room; another examined her fingernails. A man in the front row swayed restlessly in his chair.

LEE SAYS HE'S SORRY HE GOT INVOLVED IN SIMPSON TRIAL

"It's time to move on, there's life after O.J.," Dr. Henry Lee said at a hastily called news conference Friday after a prosecution rebuttal witness challenged his findings.

FBI agent William Bodziak testified that imprints on the sidewalk near Nicole Brown Simpson's condominium actually were small bumps that had been embedded in the sidewalk when the concrete was poured years ago. They were not the shoe imprints of a second killer, as the defense has suggested, Bodziak said.

"I feel a little bit disappointed about the whole process," [Lee] said. "I'm sorry I ever got involved in the
whole thing. One time experience is enough."

He said he won't return to the trial even though
Simpson's attorneys have asked him several times to be
a defense rebuttal witness. And he definitely will not get
involved if there is a second trial.

—Strat Douthat, AP, September 16, 1995

37

ON SATURDAY, SEPTEMBER 16, THE DEFENSE'S FOCUS
group met in Santa Monica. Shapiro wanted the group,
twenty-four people in all, to help determine who should give
the closing arguments, but Johnnie had already decided the
speakers would be Scheck and himself. No discussion.

Jo-Ellan Dimitrius observed alone through the one-way
glass. None of the attorneys had time to come, except for
Bob Blasier, who gave the "prosecution's" closing argument, and Shawn Chapman, who spoke for the defense.
Blasier held the group's attention. When Shawn gave her
presentation, she was scared. She felt the audience wasn't
interested.

Then the focus group split into two groups of twelve.
Suddenly all the black people present started talking about
their own miserable encounters with the police. There
wasn't a word about O.J. Simpson. They discussed only
their own experiences, their own pain.

From the observation room, Shawn noticed that the white

jurors were listening carefully and seemed sympathetic to the blacks.

Then both groups voted.

Group one: Not guilty. Unanimous.

Group two: Not guilty. Ten to two. The person selected demographically to parallel the Demon voted Guilty.

Shawn didn't have to call Johnnie. He'd been doing this for thirty-three years. He would have expected these results. Shawn had known the defense would come off well, but not this well.

Then the groups answered the questions Jo-Ellan had prepared.

Q: In the O.J. Simpson trial, what has made the prosecution's case most believable?

A: The prosecution case is not believable to me because there was no violent behavior for a long period of time. Nicole was a very happy woman 95 percent of the time.

A: Blood samples, blood here and there, and the mix of two blood types.

A: Nothing.

A: To me the prosecution's case is unbelievable.

Q: What was the most convincing argument in the prosecution's presentation?

A: The hat with O.J.'s hair. Proving that O.J. can act differently. O.J. had gloves that Nicole bought; where are they?

A: The cut O.J. Simpson had on his finger. No blood on the glass in his hotel room.

A: The circumstantial evidence found at the crime scene, at O.J.'s home and in his car. Blood, hat, glove, etc.

A: Again the DNA and the facts about blood and places it was found. The rest is too vague and is wishful thinking. The case they have put together has more holes than a colander.

* * *

Q: What would you like to hear from the defense's side that you've not yet heard?

A: I heard it all. There is nothing else to hear.

A: Gloves, where are O.J.'s gloves? Can he produce his gloves to show his innocence?

A: To really prove that evidence has been tampered with.

A: They've done their job.

When the defense meets on the same day, Shawn gives her report. Everyone shares her initial reaction: They expected to do well, but not this well.

Then Johnnie speaks of a conference he had with Judge Ito and Bill Hodgman yesterday in chambers.

"I was given very confidential information," he says. "We can't divulge it in any way. Hodgman knows that Vannatter was lying on the issue of probable cause, going over the wall. The D.A.'s office knows we're going to recall Vannatter and impeach him."

Alan Dershowitz, on the phone from Boston, says, "You say confidential, but I saw it on TV."

Bailey heard about it in Miami.

Kardashian read it today in the *Los Angeles Times*.

"We're not going to have a happy judge," Cochran adds.

Johnnie explains that Vannatter was exposed by the Fiato brothers, two former Mafiosi now in the federal witness-protection program. "Last February, they're in California in a hotel with Vannatter and Lange on a separate murder case. Apparently Vannatter makes a statement about O.J. being a suspect from the beginning." That contradicted Vannatter's testimony concerning why he sent Fuhrman over the wall.

"Larry Fiato was on a landing smoking a cigarette, and heard Vannatter say these words," Carl Douglas adds. "And—Juice is going to love this—Craig Fiato had an affair with Denise Brown." Douglas points out that Vannatter does not deny the statement, although he says he had no specific recollection of it.

Uelmen wants to put Vannatter, and then the Fiato brothers, on the stand.

"These guys are tough," Johnnie objects. "Criminals. Not the best witnesses."

Neufeld says he wants the uglier one on the stand first.

A vote is taken. Vannatter and the Fiato brothers are on the witness list.

O.J. then calls in. He wants the team to know that there is a doorman at his apartment building in New York—named Fuhrman, if you can believe that—to whom O.J. gives his coats, mufflers, and gloves. "I give everything away, every year," he explains. "Michele, my old housekeeper, will tell you this.

"The argument to make is that none of the stuff that I'm wearing in those pictures, I still have," Simpson continues. "The cops went through my closet and they didn't see any of that shit there."

"When did you get rid of the stuff?" Neufeld asks.

"At the end of each year. When I'm moving back to L.A., I give all the stuff away."

"The problem with that argument is that Rubin says the gloves in the '90 photos are the same gloves in the '93 photos," Neufeld replies, "the same style."

Cochran then points out that O.J. never acknowledged having the gloves at all.

"But what will it look like?" Neufeld persists. "Your concierge comes out from New York to say you gave everything away. So why are your gloves that are pictured in '90 also pictured in '93?"

"I don't know," O.J. replies. Then he says good-bye and hangs up.

Then Carl addresses the subject of expert testimony. "We finished with the D.A.'s case; now we'll put Herb MacDonell on to deal with glove shrinkage, then for sure, Vannatter and the Fiato brothers."

"Basically we're out of here in three days," Johnnie says. But "What about Arnelle?" he wants to know. "Juice wants the world to know he never hit Nicole."

Everyone laughs. They've run the gamut of emotions on O.J.'s obsession with domestic violence. Now it's a weary joke.

"Now to the David Letterman list: 'Ten Reasons Why O.J.'s Not Guilty,'" Johnnie says. "Here's my list: "'No blood on the white carpet; Park never sees a guy come from around the side of the house; Park never heard the Bronco drive up, never heard a door close or saw any lights from the Bronco. More important: No motive, no trigger for the crimes. Vannatter carrying the blood twenty-five miles, incredible. O.J.'s blood open at the LAPD lab at the same time as the blood swatches were on the table. The real reason Vannatter goes over the wall. No bruises or marks on Juice. Nobody saw the blood on the socks for so long. The blood-transfer marks.''

Johnnie still isn't finished. His list goes on and on.

Bob Blasier ends the meeting with a new joke: "You know when it's springtime,'' he says, "because Mark Fuhrman's out planting gloves.''

38

THE LAW PROVIDES THAT THE DEFENSE MAY RESPOND TO any issue raised in the prosecution's rebuttal. On Monday, September 18, Herb MacDonell was the defense's first surrebuttal witness. The researcher said he drew his own blood to test the prosecutor's claim that blood on the crime-scene gloves shrank them so that Simpson could not pull them on in court. MacDonell described smearing leather gloves with his own blood and letting them sit overnight. What was the result? Peter Neufeld asked.

"I would have to say negligible,'' MacDonell answered. "I could detect no shrinkage.''

* * *

During the day, Ito ruled that the jury would not be allowed to hear Lucienne Coleman's statement about the prosecution's prior knowledge of possible misconduct by Mark Fuhrman. Ito had already denied an earlier defense request to hold a full-scale inquiry into the matter. The court wasn't interested.

The next day, Tuesday, September 19, the defense called Phil Vannatter as a hostile witness in surrebuttal to show that the detective considered Simpson a suspect when he first entered Rockingham before dawn on June 13, 1994. The defense would call three witnesses to show that Vannatter had lied in testifying that he went to Simpson's house only to notify O.J. that his ex-wife had been killed.

But Simpson didn't care about Vannatter. He wanted to attack Denise Brown. One of the mobsters, Craig Fiato, said he had an affair with her. Bring that up, he insisted to Shapiro. I want that *out*. She wants to tell stories to the world that I grabbed Nicole's crotch. Now we tell one about her.

First, Shapiro had to tackle Vannatter. "In sum and substance, did you convey to anybody in that room [the police witness room]," he asked the detective, "that the reason you went to the O.J. Simpson residence was because he was a suspect?"

Vannatter insisted he had not. "If something was taken out of context, or if something was said in jest, I can't answer to that."

We're getting Vannatter positioned as Fuhrman's collaborator, Kardashian thought.

Did Vannatter say the husband is always a suspect?

"Anybody that has a personal contact with a murder victim before they are eliminated is a potential suspect," Vannatter said.

The defense attorneys knew that their next witness, FBI agent Michael Wacks, just might support Vannatter. They decided to risk calling him because the FBI uses Mob guys to make cases; the Fiatos are certified as reliable informants. The defense then had two federal informants testifying *against* the prosecution. Would their FBI mentor now swear in open court that his informants, his own star witnesses, were untruthful?

Wacks told Cochran that Vannatter's comment was "something to the effect of not going up to the house to save victims and that [Simpson] was a suspect."

On cross-examination, prosecutor Brian Kelberg asked about "the tone you heard in Mr. Vannatter's voice." Wacks answered, "In my opinion, it was totally sarcastic."

Carl Douglas watched, fascinated. In all his years as a federal public defender, he had never before seen one law enforcement officer impeach another.

The U.S. Department of Justice requested that the cameras be turned off when the Fiato brothers testified, since they were in the witness-protection program. Kardashian had to laugh. If people thought *he* looked like a gangster, they should have seen *these* characters. Larry Fiato was bald on top, with an oily ponytail. He wore a shirt and vest, no suit. His brother, Craig, was taller and more muscular, with bushy silver hair. He was wearing shiny sharkskin slacks that shimmered in the courtroom lights.

Shapiro did what Simpson wanted. "Craig Fiato told Mr. Kelberg and Mr. Hodgman that he was having an affair with Denise Brown," he said during a televised argument before the jury came in, "and the district attorney's office was embarrassed by it." The allegation was now on the public record and on TV.

When Larry Fiato took the stand, Shapiro asked about the relationship.

"Did your brother ever discuss it with you?" Shapiro asked.

"He had mentioned it," Larry Fiato said. O.J. was smiling as Shapiro returned to the defense table. Fred Goldman was beside himself.

Carl drives Johnnie and Kardashian back to the office that night; Bob has something on his mind.

"Last night at the Palm for Barry's birthday," he says, "I

810

put out my hand to say hello to an old buddy and his girlfriend said, 'I wouldn't shake anybody's hand or talk to anyone who's defending O.J. He's guilty.'" Kardashian tells the story calmly enough, but he's clearly upset. "When my friend apologized to me, his girl left without him. I felt bad about what happened to both of us."

"Not good," Johnnie comments. "I've never had that happen, when someone won't shake your hand."

"I was shocked," Bob says.

"Not good," Johnnie repeats.

Nicole Brown Simpson's sister Denise Brown was never romantically involved with Craig Fiato, her attorney said. . . . Attorney Gloria Allred called for Shapiro to apologize for his "disgusting and outrageous statement."

—Associated Press, September 20, 1995

On Wednesday, September 20, Cochran, Scheck, Shapiro, Kardashian, Douglas, Chapman, and Uelmen are in O.J.'s holding cell. The defense believes this will be its last day to present witnesses. Scheck is reviewing his latest list of problems and concerns.

"Barry, you worry a lot," Johnnie says. "The prosecution could have won back when they started, but now they're going to lose."

"I think it's going to hang on closing arguments," Uelmen adds.

"It's Marcia that's going to lose," Kardashian says.

Cochran chuckles. "She'll have to go into therapy."

"Marcia has a book deal," Scheck tells them. "She's out of here."

"By the way, after closing arguments, all restrictions are off," Cochran announces. "You can talk to anybody, do all the shows."

"I think we should be very careful," Neufeld cautions. "If you go on TV, don't give your opinion as O.J's attorney."

Johnnie wonders what Shawn plans to do after the trial.

811

"I'm going to raise flowers," she says.

Gerry Uelmen has a question: "Who's going to do the fuckin' retrial?"

"Bobby will put together another team," Johnnie declares. "Just don't call us!"

When the team settles down, Johnnie again asks everyone for a list of reasons why they think O.J. is innocent.

"Or why he should be acquitted," Shapiro feels obliged to add.

39

ON THURSDAY, SEPTEMBER 21, THE DEFENSE HAS NO more evidence to present. Today Carl is driving: Johnnie has the front passenger seat and Kardashian is in the back.

Johnnie practices his closing argument: "He's not just the defendant, he's Mr. Orenthal J. Simpson, a human being. We the members of the defense are privileged and pleased to have had the opportunity to represent—" He stops abruptly. Then, as if replying to an unheard critical voice, he says, "I *am* going to say that. Fuck them!"

"Nothing wrong with that," Carl says.

"I'm going to talk a lot about truth," Cochran goes on. "The truth can be forever on the scaffold, like Christ was. Wrong can be on the throne."

"That's good," Kardashian says.

"This is not for the faint of heart. If you're young or old, rich, poor, black, white, brown, it doesn't matter." Cochran was gearing up to full oratorical speed. He rehearsed his speech for the entire half-hour drive.

"How come Allan Park didn't hear the Bronco pull up," he asked, "or see the lights of the car?"

"Well, O.J. could have shut the lights off," Kardashian points out, "but you'd still hear that motor."

When Kardashian arrives in the holding cell, Simpson is deep into his own rehearsal. ". . . And the fact that Marcia Clark has made these representations," he's saying, "which are not true."

"Why would he use a ski cap?" O.J. asks the imaginary jury. "He could put a ski cap on and if you saw O.J. from two blocks away, you'd still say, 'Look, it's O.J.' "

"What about your bruises?" Kardashian asks.

"The prosecution is trying to make you believe," O.J. continues, "that a person who is fighting for his life is not throwing punches."

"No screams, yells, nothing?" Kardashian finds himself holding invisible cue cards. He makes suggestions, and O.J. takes off. Time disappears.

Then Johnnie comes in.

"Ito knows that today you're going to make a brief statement waiving your right to testify," Cochran tells O.J. "Tell him, 'The case is over as far as the jury is concerned. I would love the opportunity to address some of the misrepresentations made about Nicole's and my relationship.' Tell Ito that."

"And I'm going to say," O.J. adds, " 'I'm lonely, Dad. When are you coming home, Dad?' "

Then the conversation turns to how O.J. will leave when he's acquitted.

"Here's what you have to do," he tells Kardashian. "I'm driven to a place in an underground parking garage where the helicopters can't follow, like a shopping mall. You're waiting in the same type of car, same color. I arrive, I jump out of my car and get into your car, and then both cars leave by different exits at the mall."

"The question, Juice," Kardashian tells him, "is where do you go?"

"Well, that's the question," Simpson says.

Before they know it, court has convened.

The state's appellate court ruled against the defense. The jury would not be told officially that Mark Fuhrman was "unavailable." Of course, they might get the word unofficially, from their visitors.

"My understanding is that the defense is going to rest today," Ito said after he took the bench. Had Cochran advised Simpson of his right to testify?

"Mr. Simpson would like to make a brief statement regarding the waiver, if the court pleases," Cochran added.

Ito agreed, but Marcia Clark realized what was happening.

"Your Honor, the people would object to the defendant making any statement in court other than a waiver," she said.

Ito didn't get it. The jury isn't here, he said.

Clark *knew*. "We are all aware of the realities of life in this case," she said anxiously. ". . . This is a very obvious attempt by the defense to again get material admitted through those conjugal visits and telephone calls that has not been admitted in court."

Reporters realized something was about to happen.

"Please don't do this, Your Honor," Clark finished. She seemed almost panicked. "I beg you. I beg you."

Cochran stepped quickly into the argument.

"There seems to be this great fear of the truth, of anybody speaking in this case," he exclaimed, like an angry preacher. "This is *still* America, and we can talk. We can speak. Nobody can stop us."

Between the lines, Cochran had broadened the issue from procedural rules to Simpson's First Amendment rights.

"He has a right to speak with regard to the waiver, and they can't stop him," Cochran said. "That's what it boils down to, Your Honor."

"It also boils down to [the fact that] the court can control the orderly process," Ito remarked.

Everyone at the defense table sat up a little straighter. He hadn't ruled against the speech. Again, Cochran said Simpson wished to "respond" to the court.

Marcia Clark slumped in her chair. Ito turned toward Simpson.

"Mr. Simpson. Good morning, sir."

Simpson stood up. "Good morning, Your Honor."

O.J. did nothing obviously theatrical. He didn't square his shoulders or raise his eyes. He talked quickly, head down. He seemed humble. The speech he had rehearsed for weeks looked impromptu.

"As much as I would like to address some of the misrepresentations made about myself and Nicole concerning our life together," Simpson said, "I am mindful of the mood and stamina of this jury.

"I have confidence—a lot more, it seems, than Miss Clark has—of their integrity, and that they will find, as the record stands now, that I did not, could not, and would not have committed this crime.

"I have four kids, two kids I haven't seen in a year. They ask me every week, 'Dad, how much longer?' I want this trial over."

Always end with your strongest point. Kardashian smiled to himself.

"Thank you," Simpson concluded.

Marcia Clark had been right. Everyone in the courtroom, including the judge, now knew it. Vaguely sheepish, Ito asked the formal question.

"Mr. Simpson, do you understand your right to testify as a witness?"

"Yes, I do."

"And you choose to rest your case at this point?"

"I choose," Simpson replied.

"Thank you very much, sir," Ito concluded.

Several minutes passed before Marcia Clark fired a final shot.

"May I also ask, Your Honor, for the court to [make an] inquiry of Mr. Simpson?" she asked angrily. ". . . Since he would like to make these statements to the court, I would like the opportunity to examine him about them."

Clark glared at the defense team.

"May he take a seat in the blue [witness] chair, and we will have a discussion?"

Ito thanked the angry prosecutor and moved on immediately.

40

ON SATURDAY AFTERNOON, SEPTEMBER 23, THE DEFENSE hears a preview of Scheck's closing arguments. He plans to start with the LAPD "Black Hole" diagram from his opening statement.

"If the LAPD hadn't fucked up," he says, "O.J. Simpson wouldn't be in this courtroom now." Then Scheck reviews a jury instruction that Ito plans to use. "Each factor is essential to complete a set of circumstances necessary to establish the defendant's guilt, which must be proved beyond a reasonable doubt. If any factor or event is susceptible to two reasonable interpretations, one which points to guilt, the other to innocence, you have to adopt the explanation pointing to innocence."

"You must emphasize that over and over," Alan Dershowitz says on the speakerphone.

Scheck moves to the heart of his statement: corruption and contamination.

"Johnnie is going to lay out the time line, the demeanor, the basics beyond a reasonable doubt," Scheck says. "I deal with the fact that Peratis was available and healthy during their case, and they didn't call him. I'm going to hit them with the missing blood at the beginning, because that's where it all started."

Scheck turns to a DNA problem that he's not sure how to handle.

"There's a small amount of DNA, some very, very small amounts of Goldman's and Nicole's DNA, on the Bronco console. The amounts are consistent with somebody wiping the glove across the console." The important question: Was the glove wet or dry when it was wiped? If it was wet, then O.J.'s blood already on the glove would also have been wet; some of that, too, would have been transferred. If the glove was dry, it wouldn't get anybody's blood on the console. If the glove was used, there should be stains combining Nicole's, Ron's, and O.J.'s blood on the console, or none at all. The glove theory doesn't work.

"It does if the glove had been kept in a bag, still wet," someone says.

"No, if it's wet, we should have more of O.J.'s blood on the glove," Scheck points out. "All we have on the glove is this tiny, tiny little bit of O.J.'s DNA next to the wrist vent."

"Then we're back to sloppy Yamauchi," Neufeld says.

"The only answer is that the glove was smeared by Fuhrman," Scheck says, electing to ignore the problem of O.J.'s blood on the glove.

Scheck talks for almost two hours; then Dershowitz offers Johnnie a suggestion:

"Don't make any objections to the first part of Marcia's closing argument," he says. "Be very polite. Then make our objections within your closing argument."

But, Alan says, "when Marcia comes back for the last word, then I save all my impoliteness for the very end of her closing argument. Stand up and object. The worst Ito can do is shut you up. It's important to keep interrupting her final summation because she's going to throw everything in the book at us when we can't respond any longer."

"I plan to give her, in my close," Johnnie says, "ten questions she must answer in her final argument. Questions that she really can't answer. That's the way to play the game."

* * *

817

For three hours the defense continues the discussion, sometimes rambling, sometimes tightly focused. Then Johnnie closes out the night.

"Today—and I mention it for the first time today—after listening to everything here today, it occurs to me that we may win," he says. "Now, if we win this case, everyone has to do what he thinks is right. But I think for those of us with families and those who live out here, get your families that day and leave town. I've ordered extra security for everyone here. And if you want, my guys can be back in New York, too. I want all of you to be all right."

Everyone becomes quiet.

As the group is leaving, Shapiro says to Kardashian, "I want to tell you I'm totally indebted to you. I will remember for life that you had confidence in me; I will never forget it."

"Thanks, Bob." That was all Kardashian said.

41

ON SUNDAY, SEPTEMBER 24, JOHNNIE STARTS THE DE-
fense meeting by outlining a possible start for his closing argument. Dershowitz is in Boston and Uelmen is in Santa Clara, both on the speakerphone at different times.

"Maybe I'll say, 'That's not really important. Let me tell you what *is* important in this case.' I want to make the jury's job a lot easier. We need to lead right off into what we perceive as our strongest points."

Johnnie stresses that he must show them that the D.A.'s version of what happened on June 12 doesn't make sense. The defense must present its time line, O.J.'s demeanor. For nearly an hour Cochran reviews the topics to be covered. Hit hard on Fuhrman.

"Remember, Marcia never mentioned Fuhrman in her opening statement," Barry Scheck says.

Charles Lindner, a popular criminal defense lawyer who has joined the team to work with Johnnie on closing arguments, speaks up. "Keep in mind what corrupt cops represent. We're going to put the LAPD on trial," he tells them. "Put the LAPD, *and* the power structure which allowed it to run amok, on trial before the jury."

"I can summarize it," Scheck says. "Something is wrong. They can't be trusted. They lack integrity."

"Are we going to say that Fuhrman planted the glove?" Johnnie asks. "I mean, are we all saying the same thing?"

"Fuhrman denied he planted the glove," Scheck replies. "He's a perjurer, he's a racist, and he denied planting it."

"Number one, don't convey the impression that we have to prove he planted it," Uelmen suggests.

"*They* have to *disprove* beyond a reasonable doubt that Fuhrman planted the glove," Neufeld adds. "Then we want to put them in a position where they also have to disprove beyond a reasonable doubt that he didn't go into the Bronco."

"But we have four jurors," Neufeld reminds them, "who won't acquit because they accept the scientific evidence. Barry has to dismantle the scientific evidence brick by brick for those jurors."

"We have to go after the ones we think will hold out," Carl says. Jo-Ellan agrees that Scheck needs to keep those four jurors in mind, without being too technical for the others.

"Keep it entertaining," Douglas suggests. "Take the mountain of evidence they've been talking about for nine months and turn it into a molehill that collapses under an avalanche of lies. Let's boil our case down to one day."

"I agree with Barry," Shapiro says. "If we don't discuss all the facts, we're going to get killed."

"At the eleventh hour, Johnnie," Bailey comments,

"don't inundate yourselves with so much. Forget the paper-work."

"By the way, Johnnie, if you want to do some Bible-thumping," Gerry Uelmen adds, "Jesus Christ himself says that if someone is dishonest in small things, he's dishonest in big things. That's in Luke, chapter sixteen, verse ten." Uelmen has already been to mass today, and Kardashian wonders if Gerry knows his New Testament cold, or if he heard that passage in church.

Johnnie, who missed church today, has his Bible in the conference room. He finds the verse. Cochran's translation is slightly different from Gerry's.

"Chuck," Johnnie says to Lindner, "you pick the version and put it into the outline." Lindner chuckles aloud. Here's a Catholic citing Scripture to a Baptist, and a Jew deciding which translation of the New Testament the country will hear.

Then the discussion moves to Dr. Lee's cockroaches-in-the-spaghetti analogy to the LAPD mistakes.

"Henry Lee says, 'You see one cockroach, then two in a bowl of spaghetti,'" Uelmen quotes, "'you don't have to go through the whole plate of spaghetti to see if there's more cockroaches present or absent.' We have to use that."

"This jury won't understand that," Johnnie points out. "To them a cockroach is something you step on. I'm not endorsing using that." Scheck argues that he needs the analogy. Finally Johnnie says he can use it.

"Listen to this," Bob Blasier says. "The killer was soaked in blood: He had to get rid of his clothes. You can't get into your car with bloody clothes and not get the upholstery soaked. That means O.J. gets into his car wearing his socks and one glove."

"Like Michael Jackson," Kardashian adds.

"He now drives home," Blasier continues, "climbs over the fence with a bleeding hand, drops the glove, and leaves his sock in the bedroom. Now, I'm willing to accept that the man driving home is naked except for one glove. Then he goes into his house, but he's lost the one thing that's on his hand, which is one bloody glove. Is that good enough, Johnnie?''

"Not bad, not bad. Now, *that's* an argument," Johnnie agrees.

Dershowitz, who's been with them on the phone, now excuses himself. It's late afternoon in Boston, today is Rosh Hashanah, and he's late for synagogue. "Here's my pager number if you need me," he says.

Lindner is upset. The meeting, in his opinion, hasn't gone well. A lot of tension and cross talk, ideas thrown out at random. He walks into Johnnie's office to check both of Johnnie's Bibles. A minute later Cochran joins him.

Chuck remarks that on Rosh Hashanah, he'd normally be at services. He tells Johnnie that his mother was raised in Munich and saw the SA, Hitler's private army, marching through the streets. Peddler's carts overturned, buildings burned, lives destroyed. "Nobody took these men seriously until it was too late," Lindner says. His grandmother sent the young girl who would be his mother to safety. That girl was the only member of her family to survive the Holocaust.

Johnnie has visited Yad Vashem, the Holocaust memorial in Israel; he is a member of the Coalition of Christians and Jews. They talk about the way Jews were treated and the way blacks are so often treated. "Genocide" is the word they both use. They understand the Holocaust as a warning to all humanity. "Hitler was a man born outside of his time and place"—so Lindner saw it. "Fuhrman is like those SA officers" were Lindner's last words to Johnnie that night.

When Robert Shapiro left the meeting he went to the Stephen S. Wise Temple. The Jewish community strongly identified with the Goldman family, more as victims than as fellow Jews. Sympathy was equally strong for the Browns and for Simpson's children. Now, when the Torah was passed to Shapiro, members of the congregation hissed as he held it.

42

On Tuesday, September 26, Marcia Clark and Chris Darden would give the first of their closing arguments.

At Johnnie's office building, that same morning, members of the Fruit of Islam, the security arm of the Nation of Islam, were waiting for the defense team. A light drizzle fell over the city. To Shawn Chapman it looked as if there were suddenly about eighty trillion brothers all over their building. For the last nine months there had been hate mail and threatening phone calls. Nothing out of the ordinary for a case like this. As the trial wore on, the intensity of these threats increased. The bomb threats started at the courthouse; now Cochran's offices were constantly being evacuated. Some team members received threatening calls at home. And there was the day when someone brushed up against Johnnie in a crowd and said, "You're going to get hurt, boy." If a President of the United States could be shot, something could certainly happen to the defense attorneys.

Shaheed Ali, one of Johnnie's former clients, was now a member of the Nation of Islam. Johnnie normally employed his own bodyguard, Henry Grayson, an ex-police officer. But security was no longer a one-man job. Shaheed volunteered his Fruit of Islam brothers. Shawn Chapman disagreed sharply with Louis Farrakhan's attitudes toward Jews and women. But she had to respect the Nation of Islam's goal of uplifting the black race. These Fruit of Islam brothers were positive gentlemen doing the right thing, Shawn believed.

The night before, Shawn's bodyguards were in their car in

front of her house. When Chapman had gone to her gym that day, they'd gone too—right into her aerobics class. Carl felt guilty that these guys were going to camp outside his house all night: He knew Johnnie was in danger, but didn't think he himself was. Shapiro wanted nothing to do with the Nation of Islam. Scheck and his colleagues at the hotel decided the Bel Age security was sufficient.

On September 26, the defense arrived at court with six members of the Fruit of Islam in their trademark dark suits and bow ties. They carried walkie-talkies but no guns. When Johnnie went into the men's room, one followed.

The jurors were all decked out today. One had a handkerchief in his suit pocket, another a sweater vest. Chris Darden wore a red AIDS-awareness ribbon on behalf of his brother, who was dying. Everyone seemed energized.

At lunchtime Johnnie was walking through the courthouse cafeteria when an elderly black woman asked him to sign a copy of Simpson's book.

To Henry Weinstein of the *Los Angeles Times,* Johnnie looked like a candidate in the thick of a campaign. Henry put his hand on Cochran's back. "Are you running for office?" he joked.

Cochran's guards grabbed Weinstein and firmly shoved him away. Cochran didn't realize what had happened. Later when Johnnie was eating lunch, still surrounded by the guards, Weinstein tried to approach him again. The bodyguards sent him away.

When Johnnie heard what had happened, he left the table, told his security to stay behind, and walked across the room to Weinstein. Even if Henry hadn't been a member of the press, what had happened was unacceptable. "It was wrong," Johnnie told him. "It shouldn't have happened." His charm in high gear, Johnnie apologized again. Henry cooled down. His paper decided not to run a story about the incident.

Today was the day the prosecution's closing arguments would start. Marcia Clark would lead off and Chris Darden would follow. Then the defense would present its closing.

Two attorneys may speak for both the prosecution and the defense. Since the burden of proof lay with the prosecution, it was allowed a final presentation to the jury after the defense concluded.

The focus-group results showed that the prosecution's closing arguments would make little difference: These jurors had heard evidence for nine months and had probably made up their minds. Douglas was skeptical about that; it was too easy. Like Shapiro, he didn't want to be tripped up by something they had overlooked. Scheck wasn't sure how the jury was voting. He'd never had much faith in focus groups. He prepared, even overprepared. Then, in the courtroom, he usually followed his instincts.

Marcia Clark walked to the podium.

Simpson despised her. She's always changing her theory of how it happened, he said endlessly.

"Good morning." Marcia smiled to the jurors. For the first time in nearly a year, she was warm, almost gentle. Her eyes were ringed with dark circles. Clearly, she was exhausted and tense. The jury returned her greeting, and she held their eyes with a forced but radiant smile. "Finally," she said, letting the word float in the air. "I feel like it has been forever since I talked to you."

At the defense table, it was a nervous moment. Kardashian hadn't slept well. Neither had Simpson. "I feel bad," O.J. had told Kardashian that morning. Cochran's opener nine months earlier had given Clark weapons—notably, the witnesses he made so much of but never called. Douglas and Chapman worried that she would start right *there*, asking: What happened to Mary Anne Gerchas, who saw those four men? Where is Rosa Lopez?

Clark surprised them immediately. She apologized for Mark Fuhrman. Douglas hadn't expected this to come so soon. They knew Clark would distance herself from the detective, but from the moment she mentioned Fuhrman, the defense knew the prosecution's edge was gone. Clark was responding to their case, not making her own.

Did Fuhrman lie when he said he hadn't used the "N-word'' in ten years? Clark asked, and answered her own question. ''Yes.

''Is he the worst the LAPD has to offer?

''Yes,'' she answered again.

''Should such a person be a police officer?

''No. In fact, do we wish there were no such person on the planet?'' She paused. ''Yes,'' she said.

A dignified yet oddly apologetic summary of the issues followed. Mark Fuhrman's racism and perjury ''[do not] mean we haven't proven the defendant guilty beyond a reasonable doubt,'' she said. Moreover, the defense had raised questions: Did the LAPD have ''bad police officers''? Were there ''sloppy criminalists'' in its lab? Were there ''sloppy coroners''?

''The answer to all these questions is sure, yes,'' Clark said softly. Quality control should be examined; things should be better. ''We are not here to vote on that today.''

But we are, Kardashian thought.

Clark warmed to her attack. The defense case is ''all questions and issues that were raised as a distraction,'' she charged. ''But even after all their tireless efforts, the evidence stands strong and powerful to prove to you the defendant's guilt.''

The defense was surprised at how low-key Clark was. Maybe she'd heard what the focus groups were saying: She was too edgy, too tough. But was she going too far the other way?

Clark moved through the time line, using a huge blue chart with white lettering and bold red colors. Douglas watched the jurors. They were attentive, but few took notes. One closed his eyes from time to time. Another yawned. The presentation was good, Douglas thought: tight, detailed, strong. The problem was atmospheric, he decided. Marcia was so quiet. Did the prosecutors already feel beaten? Nobody would consciously admit that, Carl thought. Probably they just felt stressed as hell.

* * *

That morning, Henry Weinstein of the *Los Angeles Times* had stepped onto the elevator with Marcia Clark, on her way to court. As usual, she carried an armload of green loose-leaf notebooks. "Do you think the jurors are interested in what I have to say?" she asked the writer. Yes, he answered. "If you do, you are in the minority among the press," Clark replied. The elevator doors opened before anything else could be said. Weinstein thought the prosecutor, as always, seemed more confident about the evidence against Simpson than about how it was playing with the jury.

The top of the chart contained a large blue space titled "Defendant's Whereabouts Unknown." At one side of the empty area was the time, 9:36 P.M., with the notation, "Defendant and Kato return to Rockingham."

Clark took jurors through limousine driver Allan Park's experiences. She invited them to draw the "obvious conclusion" that the man he saw walking up the driveway was the defendant.

"But what is significant," Clark explained, "is that he [Simpson] lied." Park testified that Simpson said over the intercom that he'd overslept and was just emerging from the shower. "Why was it important for him to make Allan Park believe that he had been at home?" she argued. "I think we all know the answer to that question. . . . Because he had just come back from Nicole's.

"The defendant came back from Bundy in a hurry," Clark went on. "Ron Goldman upset his plans and things took a little longer than anticipated. He ran back behind the house . . . thinking he could get rid of the glove . . ."

What about climbing the fence to get there? Kardashian was smiling. The jury had seen the overgrown trees. There were no broken branches, no blood, no sign that someone had ever been there. Carl Douglas realized that Clark was omitting any discussion of how Simpson reentered his property.

"In his haste he ran right into that air conditioner that was hanging over that south pathway, and [that] caused him to fall against the wall, making the wall of Kato's room shake.

"Simple logic tells you that the thumping, the glove, and the defendant's appearance on the driveway almost immediately thereafter are all part of one set of events," Clark explained, "all connected in time and space. You don't need science to tell you that. You just need reason and logic."

In the afternoon Clark asked the jury to think of a jigsaw puzzle. "It helps to talk about reasonable doubt in this frame," she explained. To get beyond such doubt, you must find the missing pieces. They didn't all have to be perfectly in place. In a jigsaw puzzle, "if you're missing a couple of pieces of the sky, you still have the picture."

The time line was one piece of the puzzle. Simpson's strange mix of stories about his cut fingers was another, his behavior after the murders still another.

Clark then addressed the physical evidence and DNA.

The defense has offered "some of the most bizarre and far-fetched notions I think I have ever heard," she argued. "They hint that the blood was planted. . . . Somehow all the contamination only occurred where it would consistently prove the defendant was guilty.

"If you had one blood drop in this case, ladies and gentlemen," she continued, you might be concerned with "all of these possibilities they have raised." But "you've got five blood drops leading away from the bodies of the victims out to the driveway, and you've got blood on the rear gate."

Clark attempted to neutralize the conspiracy theories concerning that back-gate drop. Patrolman Terrazas shined his flashlight to show the drop to his partner, Robert Riske, she said. A supervisor, Sergeant Rossi, saw it. Detective Phillips observed it.

"Dennis Fung, who you can see is not the model of efficiency, forgot to collect it," Clark said, sacrificing Fung to the point.

"First of all," Clark said challengingly, in tight, staccato phrases, "I want to hear Mr. Cochran actually stand up in front of you and tell you he believes the blood was planted. I want to hear that. Because that is incredible. That is absolutely incredible."

All she can do is say it's smoke and mirrors, Kardashian thought. Thanks to those imbeciles on the LAPD, she can't say much else.

"So they took you through all this tortured and twisted road one moment saying that the police are all a bunch of bumbling idiots," Clark charged. "The next moment they are clever conspirators."

And then she did say it: "Is it smoke and mirrors? Is it all just smoke to cloud everything, cloud all the issues, distract you?"

The defense knew Clark had good arguments on the disastrous glove try-on: The latex gloves underneath were the real problem. The bloody gloves had shrunk. And if they were so tight, remember "how quickly he snapped them off."

"I will tell you something else that really struck me," Clark said, clasping her hands, speaking intensely. "If I were asked to put on the gloves, the bloody gloves, that were used to murder the *father* of my children, I would not be laughing," she said indignantly, "I would not be mugging. I would not be playing games. I wouldn't think it was funny at all."

Cochran objected. Ito told Clark to "move on."

She moved on to the murder scene.

As pictures of the Bundy courtyard appeared on the screen, Carl Douglas saw the jurors come to attention.

Clark offered a long discussion of stab wounds, blood flow, and shoe prints.

"This is not the mark of a professional killer," she told the jury. "These are not efficient murders. These are murders that are really slaughters, that are *personal*."

Kardashian knew Clark was scoring points.

Then the court took a mid-afternoon break.

Clark closed the first of her arguments with a nice visual, the defense had to admit. The projection screen flashed a picture of a nearly empty jigsaw puzzle of fourteen pieces.

"Let me summarize for you what we have proven," Clark

began. "One piece of the puzzle: We've proven the opportunity to kill. We've given the time window [when] his whereabouts were unaccounted for during the time the murders were occurring."

A section of the projected puzzle filled itself in. It was obvious now that the completed picture would be a portrait of Simpson.

"We have the hand injuries that were suffered on the night of his wife's murder to the left hand; as we know, the killer was injured on his left hand," she went on. "We have the post-homicidal conduct that I told you about . . ."

Another piece of the puzzle flashed into place.

"We have the manner of killings, killings that indicate that it was a rage killing, that it was a fury killing, that it was not a professional hit . . ."

Clark paused and waited for the screen to change. Good solid theater, Shawn Chapman thought.

"We have the knit cap at Bundy. We have the evidence on Ron Goldman's shirt of the blue-black cotton fibers, the defendant's hair . . ."

Another piece of Simpson's picture appeared.

"We have the Bundy blood trail: his blood to the left of the bloody shoe prints. We have the blood in the Bronco, his and Ron Goldman's. We have the Rockingham blood trail . . .

"We have the Rockingham glove with all of the evidence on it . . . We have the socks and we have the blue-black cotton fibers on the socks and we have Nicole Brown's blood on the socks."

Simpson's full face filled the puzzle. He was scowling. Clark smiled slightly. "There he is."

The defense was not pleased with the graphic, but was delighted that Clark had spent most of her time responding to their charges rather than presenting her own case.

43

CLARK HADN'T SETTLED INTO HER SEAT BEFORE JUDGE ITO addressed Chris Darden. The day was nearly over.

"Mr. Darden, are you ready to proceed?"

"Well, there's no better time than right now, Your Honor," he answered.

Darden was primed. Carl Douglas could see it.

We're in the danger zone now, he thought. For eight months, the defense had counted on Darden's lack of focus. He meandered through testimony and sat sullenly through much of the trial. He glared. He sulked. If the defense needed a sideshow, they pushed his fabled buttons. The race button. The manhood button. Darden was known to have joked sadly to reporters that Cochran had put his name on billboards in the black community: Traitor. Turncoat.

"This case is really a simple case," Darden began. "All you have to do is utilize the tools God gave you . . . utilize your common sense."

Darden was there, they knew, to resurrect the prosecution's domestic violence case. It had died abruptly after ex-jurors told talk-show hosts that Simpson's violence didn't impress them. An abusive husband isn't necessarily a killer, they said. Darden's witnesses were cut back. People who could have made a stronger case that O.J. stalked Nicole didn't appear.

Darden might have been stalling when he paused to echo Marcia's apology for Mark Fuhrman. Except, Douglas saw, he made no apology.

"The case of Mark Fuhrman, if there's to be a case, that's a case for another forum . . . another jury perhaps," Chris

Darden declared. "This case is about this defendant, O.J. Simpson, and the 'M-word,' murder. Not about Mark Fuhrman and the 'N-word.'"

Shawn Chapman understood that they were vulnerable today. As the prosecution's domestic violence case had evaporated, the defense had scratched most of its rebuttal witnesses on this issue.

Some witnesses were just too risky, Chapman knew. Dr. Lenore Walker, the battered-woman-syndrome expert, would testify that Simpson was no lethal abuser. But if asked, she would also say that he was a batterer.

Chapman recalled the aftermath of Walker's sessions with Simpson months earlier. On a speakerphone in a defense meeting, O.J. admitted his problems with violence. He asked for a therapist. Chapman was assigned to find one but never did; she had other urgent tasks. As weeks, then months, passed, she saw Simpson lose touch with whatever insights he'd gained. Soon he was denying again that he'd ever beaten Nicole, submerged once more in *his* self-created good-guy image.

To move the jury more quickly into deliberations, Judge Ito extended the court day into evening sessions.

On the second day of closing arguments, Darden told jurors that he and Clark believed the domestic violence evidence was "very important." Again he wore an AIDS ribbon in his lapel, a message to his brother. He said the jurors had to understand "the nature of this man's relationship with one of the victims in this case."

Darden predicted that Simpson's lawyers would argue that violence in this marriage "didn't mean anything." But "he hit her . . . he slapped her and threw her out of the house and kicked her and punched her," he said with tight, focused anger. "You ought to know about it."

That violent history, Darden charged, points to Simpson as the murderer. He extended his arm and pointed his finger at the defendant.

"*I'm* not afraid to point to him," Darden told them. "Nobody pointed him out and said he did it. I'll point to him. Why not? The evidence all points to him."

Douglas realized that Darden was *baiting* Simpson. The prosecutor had a second task now: to rehabilitate himself. He'd arrived in this case with a terrible burden, a black man representing the white-dominated justice system against a likable black sports hero. Johnnie had never let Darden forget it. It had worked. Under Cochran's attacks, Darden became sullen, distracted. Juries don't support prosecutors they don't respect. Today Darden had to change all that.

Darden said Simpson and Nicole's violent history was "like a fuse, a bomb with a long fuse."

Douglas saw that Darden was hard-edged, solid.

Taking a baseball bat to Nicole's windshield in 1985 "lit" the fuse, Darden said. He played the 911 tape from 1989. Nicole ran out shouting, "He's going to kill me!" When the cop asked who she meant, Nicole cried "O.J., O.J., O.J. Simpson!"

Linda Deutsch was impressed. Days earlier, he'd seemed almost fragmented. Now his delivery was tight and powerful, from his heart. He truly believed Simpson was guilty.

Chapman and the others had assumed Darden would wander through his presentation while Clark carried the flaming sword. But Clark had seemed a bit disorganized. Darden had the fire.

Shapiro and Douglas admitted they had been impressed. Cochran brushed it aside. He had to focus on his own speech, only hours away.

Darden pictured the murder night for the jury.

"Imagine the defendant in his Bronco," the prosecutor said. "He is full of anger and he is full of rage and it is nighttime and he is driving that Bronco . . . and the focus of his anger is Nicole."

Simpson began shifting in his seat.

"He is driving as fast as he can toward Nicole's house, and it is about ten o'clock," Darden continued. "He is out of control, folks."

In a few minutes, Darden told the jurors, he would be playing the 1993 Gretna Green tape.

People questioned, the prosecutor went on, how Simpson could commit murder when his children were in the house. But the children were at home for the 1989 beating, Darden told them. In 1993, "you will hear Nicole on the telephone say, 'The kids are upstairs.' The fact that the kids are in the house," Darden said firmly, "means nothing to this man."

Darden detoured to shove Lenore Walker down the team's throat. He read from the transcript of Cochran's opening statement:

"'There is an expert in the U.S. whose name is Dr. Lenore Walker and she is by all accounts the number one expert in America on the field of domestic violence.'" Cochran said Walker had "'interviewed and tested the defendant,'" Darden charged.

Cochran was stone-faced. Simpson doodled on his yellow pad.

"Why didn't they call Dr. Walker, who could have put all this in perspective for you?" he asked pointedly. ". . . They are a group of very, very fine lawyers. They called some of the most expensive experts money could buy. But we didn't see Dr. Walker."

Darden returned to the burning fuse. Simpson had lost Nicole, he said. "He is upset and angry that the relationship was terminated by her . . . and I just wish Dr. Walker had been here to help explain this to you. I'm sure she could have done a better job of it than me."

The prosecutor moved back to the murder night. "He can't find Paula. He is having a problem with Nicole. He is about to lose both the women in his life, and the fuse is getting shorter, folks . . . The anger is building."

Chris Darden's personal rage at months of ill-treatment from the defense, the long hours and months of frustration, the defeats and harassment he had endured in and out of court—all converged now. Shawn Chapman felt sure of it. The prosecutor was using his fury in service of his case.

"He is using a knife because he is there to settle a personal score, a personal vendetta," Darden said with mounting anger. "He stabs this woman in the neck. He is right there. It is one-on-one. And the rage that he has, the anger, the hate that he has for her that night at that time . . . it flows out of him and into the knife and from the knife into her.''

Kardashian saw Simpson's facial muscles tightening.

''With each thrust of that knife into her body and into Ron's body, there is a release, a small release . . . and he stabs and he cuts and he slices until the rage is gone,'' Darden continues, his voice rising, ''until these people are dead.''

The courtroom was hushed.

''He is a murderer,'' he said slowly. ''He was also one hell of a great football player. But he is still a murderer.''

''I assert,'' Darden concluded, ''that the defense case is a bunch of smoke and mirrors, all about distracting you from the real evidence in this case. So imagine the smoke and imagine a burning house.'' You hear a crying baby inside, Darden told the jury. ''Now, that baby is justice.

''And so you start to wade through that smoke trying to get to that baby,'' he concluded. If you ''happen to run into a couple of defense attorneys along the way, just ask them to politely step aside and let you find your way through the smoke.''

Darden looks hard at the jury.

''Because the smoke isn't over, okay? The smoke is going to get heavier because they are about to talk to you.''

44

DARDEN FINISHES ON WEDNESDAY MORNING, SEPTEMBER 27. During the lunch break the defense team goes to the attorneys' room beside the holding cell to see O.J. This afternoon, Johnnie will present the first of their closing arguments.

Simpson is emotional about any number of things Clark and Darden have said. As usual, he talks about himself in the third person. He's upset at Kato Kaelin. He's upset at Allan Park. He's upset about everything.

"First I broke the glass," Simpson says, referring to the glass in his Chicago hotel room. "I broke it on the counter. Not in the sink."

"They never talked about that," Kardashian says.

"If I had no visible cut going to Chicago," O.J. asks, "why would I intentionally inflict a bigger, more visible cut that no one can miss when I'm coming back?"

Now O.J. gives his version of Johnnie's argument. Today he's handcuffed to his chair, and can't pace. But he makes his points with passion, gestures with a yellow legal pad, with his glasses as he addresses the imaginary jury. He looks straight at the wall. Not at Kardashian, not at Johnnie. The wall is the jury.

"Let's talk about facts," he begins. "If there's one thing you've heard about Nicole from all her friends, this was not a weak woman. Nicole told O.J. on January 6 that she wanted to split, not divorce, but split. She lived in the house with him for the next month and half. She's not a woman who's afraid.

"They got divorced. She was dating people, he was dating Paula. You didn't hear one person come in here and say that they had arguments about anything that the other one was doing."

Now Simpson moves further into the role of defense attorney.

"He was talking about sex acts in the open with his kids there. He was raging about what anybody in this room would rage about. Listen to the 911 tapes! He is venting. You hear him talking about the sex act performed in the open in *his* house with *his* kids there. And let me tell you something else, ladies and gentlemen . . ."

Simpson went on and on: the shoes; the gloves; his life with Nicole. Then he turns to Johnnie.

"When Darden says something that is factually untrue, an exaggeration or misrepresentation, you should just stick it to him," he says. "Remind the jury that he was misrepresenting the facts."

After lunch it was Johnnie Cochran's turn to speak. Barry Scheck would follow him.

Today Johnnie would speak from the podium, which was now facing the jury. Cochran was your well-dressed neighbor. He wore a charcoal suit and a multicolored abstract tie. His lapel pin, a silver cross, was in place. He wished jurors a cordial good afternoon. They returned the greeting.

"The defendant, Mr. Orenthal James Simpson, is now afforded an opportunity to argue the case," Cochran began somewhat stiffly.

Johnnie wasn't going to *argue* with them. He'd discuss "the reasonable inferences which I feel can be drawn from this evidence." He'd lean on the podium as if it were the fence between your yard and his. His manner was comforting, yet a little larger than life.

He started with a few quotes from Abraham Lincoln and Frederick Douglass, then some social theory. Cochran was going to radicalize these jurors and empower them to look beyond mere evidence to the larger picture. He quoted Douglass as saying that all Americans must share "common citizenship, equal rights, and a common destiny."

"We haven't reached this goal yet," Johnnie said. But "in this great country of ours, maybe a jury such as this" can.

Reporter Linda Deutsch had already written about the likelihood of a "jury nullification" argument, in which Cochran would urge the jurors to correct some terrible social injustice with their verdict, regardless of the evidence. Deutsch knew he'd do it, but doubted Cochran would do only that.

"This is not a case for the timid or the weak of heart," Cochran now said. "This is not a case for the naive. This is a case for courageous citizens who believe in the Constitution.

"Your verdict in this case will go far beyond the walls" of this courtroom, he said, his voice rising. It will be about "justice in America," about "the police and whether they've been above the law."

Cochran's cadences moved more slowly. "They allowed this . . . investigation to be . . . *infected* by a . . . *dishonest* and corrupt . . . *detective*.

"They never, *ever* looked for . . . anyone else. We think if they *had* done their job, as we have done, Mr. Simpson would have been eliminated early on."

Cochran moved to the defense version of the time line.

"You look back and see what Miss Clark promised you a year ago," he said mockingly. "Ten-fifteen. Ten-fifteen was all they talked about."

What about Ellen Aaronson and Danny Mandel walking by at 10:20, seeing nothing and hearing no barking dogs? And Robert Heidstra, who heard a voice yelling "Hey, hey, hey!" at 10:40 P.M.? These people weren't sleeping, like the prosecution witnesses. They were out in the neighborhood; Heidstra was walking his two elderly dogs.

"He knows this neighborhood," Cochran declared. "He's been doing this for more than fourteen years . . . They didn't call him. You know why? Because it doesn't fit in their time line."

The start was a little slow, Kardashian thought, but Johnnie is flying now. Simpson was scribbling nonstop. At the first break, he ticked off all the points he thought Cochran had missed and demanded that Cochran put them in.

After the break, Cochran discussed the glove at Rockingham.

"When that glove is picked up, [do you] remember seeing any blood on the ground?" Cochran demanded. "No blood on that shrubbery, no blood on anything there. Where's the blood?"

Clark said that Simpson had the knife, the bloody clothes, and the shoes when he went into the house. Cochran made it into a prime theatrical moment, leaning over the podium, punching each phrase.

"If he went . . . *in that house* . . . with bloody shoes . . . *with bloody clothes* . . . with his bloody hands, as they say . . . where's the blood on the doorknob? Where's the blood on the banister? *Where's the blood on the carpet?*"

Cochran said he'd been thinking last night about how Simpson would have disguised himself. Shawn Chapman sat nearby with a knit cap. She handed it to Johnnie at the right moment and he pulled it on.

"You've seen me for a year," he stated. "If I put this knit cap on, who am I? I'm still Johnnie Cochran with a knit cap!"

Still wearing the wool cap with his expensive suit, Cochran pointed dramatically to his client.

"O.J. Simpson in a knit cap from two blocks away is still O.J. Simpson," he declared. "It's no disguise. It's no disguise. It makes no sense. It doesn't fit. If it doesn't fit, you must acquit."

That was Gerry Uelmen's line.

After a short break, Cochran returned to the gloves.

"Perhaps the single most defining moment in this trial is the day they thought they would conduct this experiment on these gloves," Cochran gloated.

Darden sat expressionless behind Cochran. Johnnie draped his hands over the podium like a hometown preacher.

"I suppose . . . that vision is *indelibly* imprinted in each . . . and every . . . one of your minds . . . of how Mr. Simpson . . . walked over here . . . and stood before you . . . and said *four simple words:* 'The gloves don't fit.'" Cochran paused dramatically. "And all their strategy started changing after that.

"The gloves didn't fit Mr. Simpson because he is not the killer."

Cochran worked his way through spousal abuse issues. He insisted that the 1993 episode when Simpson kicked in Nicole's door was nonviolent.

Johnnie then showed jurors the video, taken after Sydney's recital, in which Simpson embraced the Browns and Justin. He turned to a huge display picture of Simpson posing happily with Sydney after the program.

"Let's look at this photograph for a minute," Cochran said, "if you want to see how he looks while he is in this murderous rage . . ."

After the dinner break, Cochran dealt with the socks found in Simpson's bedroom.

"I asked [the LAPD videographer], 'Well, where are the socks, Mr. Ford?'" He reminds the jurors that Ford didn't see any socks. Yet the police logs show that Dennis Fung and Andrea Mazzola collected them about fifteen minutes later.

"Mr. Darden said something very interesting today," Cochran continued. "He said, 'I'm just the messenger.'"

How often had they heard that? Cochran asked angrily. "'Don't blame me. I'm just doing my job.'" Darden wasn't just *any* messenger, Cochran insisted. "He's a prosecutor with all the power of the State of California in this case. We are not going to let them get their way! We are not going to turn the Constitution on its head in this case.

"If you can't trust the messengers, watch out for their messages!"

Cochran went on to Vannatter and Fuhrman. "Vannatter, the man who carries the blood. Fuhrman, the man who finds the glove. Remember those two phrases!"

Now Carl Douglas brought out additional display boards. One was headlined "Vannatter's Big Lies." The veteran detective is pilloried for denying that he considered Simpson a suspect immediately, for writing a dubious search warrant, for carrying Simpson's reference blood to Rockingham.

Next Cochran outlined a conspiracy for the jury to consider. Vannatter lied to a judge, saying Simpson left town "unexpectedly," in order to get his search warrant.

"But," said Johnnie, "Vannatter comes in, says, 'Yes, Fuhrman told me about the thumps on the wall.' . . . If you cannot trust the messenger, you can't trust the message that they are trying to give you.

"Male officers get together to cover up for each other, don't tell the truth, hide, turn their heads, cover. You can't trust this evidence. You can't trust the messenger. You can't trust this message."

Johnnie ended the day with Mark Fuhrman.

"His misdeeds go far beyond this case because he speaks of a culture that's not tolerable in America."

Clark and Darden "knew about Mark Fuhrman, and they weren't going to tell you." Marcia made him "a choirboy" on the stand, all the while knowing he was "a liar and a racist."

Douglas felt the intensity. Johnnie might as well have been holding a Bible, proclaiming the word of God.

"There's something about good versus evil," Cochran trumpeted. "There's something about truth. The truth crushed to earth will rise again. You can always count on that."

Kardashian realized that Simpson was crying. He'd cried briefly when Cochran mentioned Arnelle's emotional behavior on the morning of Nicole's death. Now, at the talk of Mark Fuhrman, he wept again.

"Take deep breaths, O.J.," Bob whispered. "We've only got ten minutes left. Don't look at the camera."

Simpson pulled himself together.

*　*　*

Cochran pointed at a picture of Mark Fuhrman. "This man cannot be *trusted!*" he thundered. "He is *central* to the prosecution. And for them to say he's not important is untrue, and you should not fall for it. Because, as guardians of justice here, *we can't let it happen!*"

Afterward, everyone on the team glowed, deeply relieved. After Darden's fine presentation, the defense had worried that Cochran might be in trouble. But Johnnie held the jury in his hands. Today he was a storm, a cleansing force.

Simpson, however, was still working on the list of points he wanted Johnnie to make tomorrow. Stop dogging Johnnie, Kardashian told him. He had endured a long day with Shapiro on one side, telling him what Cochran was doing wrong, and O.J. on the other, whispering about what Johnnie was missing.

Barry Scheck was nervous. "How am I going to follow this act?" he asked Carl Douglas.

45

The next morning, September 28, Cochran, Douglas, Chapman, and Kardashian drive to the courthouse together.

"I'm going to talk like Barry Scheck today," Cochran tells them. "I'm linking Vannatter and Fuhrman. I'm going to call them twins of deception. Batman and Robin, the twins of deception. Just like that, they represent the messengers of evil in this case."

Kardashian wants to know how he's going to end his statement.

"I got twenty minutes more, half an hour," Johnnie says. "And O.J. wants me to cover domestic violence."

They chuckle, although there's an edgy fatigue in their voices. Kardashian knows Simpson has been pestering Johnnie.

"I told him yesterday, Stay away from me. I was jumping on him. I said, You know, O.J., look, you've never been clear about the cuts, the blood, the various cuts. You remember every detail of everything else. But about the cuts you say, 'I don't know exactly when I got them.' "

For nine months, Cochran has been frustrated by O.J.'s vagueness about his cuts. Today, for the first time since he took the case, Johnnie's professional mask has slipped. He was just plain pissed. Kardashian can't help but think that Cochran has his doubts about O.J.

"And O.J. says, 'I'm paying you guys,' " Johnnie continues. " 'You guys listen to me, listen to me.' " There's no holding Johnnie back.

Douglas jumps in, contempt mixing with his anger. "He has to pay me for my theories. *That's* why you're paying me,' I tell him. 'Because you put faith in what I know.' "

"Carl, can you go and talk to him?" Johnnie asks.

"I'm not going back in there anymore," Carl answers.

"He scared me, Carl," Cochran says. "It's a good thing I didn't have blond hair."

Never trash the client—everyone in the car knows that rule. Johnnie changes the mood fast.

"Man, Juice has the greatest endurance and patience in the history of the world," Cochran says. "Successful in his own right. Great lover, beautiful children." At the mention of O.J.'s kids, there is a sadness in the car. They all know that whatever happens, when the trial is over there will still be problems that no amount of lawyering can ever fix.

"And Lee," Johnnie continues almost wistfully. "He started off so brilliant, but couldn't hear at the end."

"He needed a hearing aid," Carl says, ever the pragmatist.

"Wait till *you* get to a certain age," Cochran tells Douglas.

The mood is somber. Cochran decides to do something about it.

"Here's a funny thing," he says. "Carmelita told my wife, Dale, last night—they've gotten close through all this—'Don't have any sex with him. Let him come back lean and mean tomorrow.' Dale is cracking up, telling me this."

Then he turns to Shawn.

"Ms. Chapman, this is not too steamy for you?" Johnnie asks. "Today I'm going to tell Carmelita, 'Thanks, I'm *mean*.'"

Everyone now laughs.

That morning, Johnnie began by positioning Phil Vannatter alongside Mark Fuhrman.

During rebuttal testimony, Johnnie reminded the jurors, Vannatter denied targeting Simpson. O.J. was "no more a suspect" than Bob Shapiro, the detective said under oath.

"The Book of Luke talks about that," Cochran told them. "If you are *untruthful in small things,* you should be *disbelieved* in big things!"

Johnnie was in his pulpit.

"This man with his big lies—and then we have *Fuhrman* coming right on the heels . . . the *twins of deception.* Fuhrman and Vannatter, twins of deception who bring you a message that you cannot trust, *that you cannot trust!"*

Johnnie's style echoed Malcolm X and Louis Farrakhan. The term "twins of deception" was intended to invoke the devil. In the jargon of the Nation of Islam, "devil" meant white. Vannatter and Fuhrman were twin *devils* of deception. White devils.

Cochran moved to LAPD photographer Rolf Rokahr, who photographed Fuhrman pointing to the gloves. Fuhrman testified that the picture was taken at about seven A.M., but Rokahr testified that it was taken before sunrise, at about 4:30.

"This man, this perjurer, this racist, this genocidal racist" had an opportunity "to get to the glove or to get access to anything," Cochran declared.

Then he read Kathleen Bell's entire letter, emphasizing Fuhrman's willingness to find "a reason" to arrest interracial couples, his wish that black people be burned.

At home, watching TV, Charles Lindner had his laptop booted up. He scrolled through the outline he had helped write for Cochran. Where Johnnie neared the final attack on Fuhrman, Lindner's outline read: "Have fun. Enjoy yourself."

"There was another man not long ago in the world who had these same views, who wanted to burn people . . ." Cochran said, leaning forward on the podium. "People said he was just crazy. He was just a half-baked painter. They didn't do anything about it."

Cochran was solemn.

"This man, this scourge, became one of the worst people in the history of this world, Adolf Hitler, because people didn't care, or didn't try to stop him."

Four jurors leaning forward suddenly moved back into their seats. To Jo-Ellan Dimitrius it seemed that the force of Cochran's image pushed these jurors back as if he'd struck them.

Lindner smiled and closed his computer. For Johnnie to move from Hitler burning Jews to Fuhrman wanting to burn blacks was a stroke of genius, he thought.

"And so Fuhrman wants to take all black people now and burn them or bomb them," Cochran thundered on, scowling fiercely. "That is genocidal racism . . . Do you think he talked to his partners about it? Do you think his commanders knew about it? Do you think everybody knew about it and turned their heads?"

Now all of Johnnie's cards were on the table.

"Maybe this is one of the reasons we are all gathered together this day," Cochran suggested. ". . . Maybe this is why you were selected. There is something in your background, in your character, that helps you understand this is wrong! Maybe you are the right people at the right time at the right place to say, *no more, we are not going to have this!*"

FAMILIES' ANGER ERUPTS
OUTSIDE THE COURTROOM

When Johnnie Cochran compared Mark Fuhrman to Adolf Hitler, Fred Goldman clenched his fists, twisted in his seat, and began to mutter angrily and audibly in the courtroom where the only sound had been the passionate final argument of O.J. Simpson's lead attorney.

"Cochran . . . is a disgusting human being" who "ought to be put away . . . He compares racism of its worst kind in this world to what's going on in this case."

Modern America is a complicated place and what it witnessed Thursday was not so much just another angry outburst in our ongoing national quarrel over race, but the collision between two strains of what is perhaps our most communal powerful force—victimhood. The only unchallenged moral authority in contemporary American society is the moral authority of victims. Thursday, both sides—Cochran, the indefatigable opponent of racism, and Goldman, the father of a murdered son—spoke in the righteous confidence all victims now enjoy. And this being America, people around them started choosing sides.

"We feel sorry for the Goldman family, because I see his family in court daily, and I know they hurt," Simpson's sister Shirley said as she stood with her sister Carmelita Durio, their mother Eunice Simpson, and Simpson's adult children, Jason and Arnelle.

Former Dist. Atty. Robert Philibosian was even more pointed. "Attorneys argue what they want in closing argument," he said, "but I've never heard anything as outlandish or as outrageous as a comparison between Mark Fuhrman—no matter how bad he is—and a man who carried out the systematic genocide of an entire people. The word overkill does not even come close to describing this portion of Mr. Cochran's argument. I do not blame Mr. Goldman at all for his emotional response."

—Tim Rutten and Andrea Ford,
Los Angeles Times, September 29, 1995

46

IN THE HOLDING CELL, SIMPSON WAS STILL WORKING WITH total concentration on his closing arguments, which would never be heard. He hadn't anticipated the public reaction to Johnnie's remarks on Hitler. None of Cochran's colleagues had.

"This shows you a man who for twenty years has been respected in America, who treated people right," O.J. was saying of himself. "Matter of fact, he was famous for how he treated people. And they have, for a year now, focused on what? Three incidents in his life where he wasn't perfect. One instance that had physical abuse where this man wrote three letters apologizing.

"Let me ask you a question: Do you think if John F. Kennedy, or the President of these United States today, if his background was investigated the way they investigated this man's background, are there going to be three or four things that he's not going to be proud of? Does that make you a killer? Does that make you a bad person? Those three things—do you want your life defined by them?"

When Barry Scheck stood up to present his closing argument, Linda Deutsch steeled herself. He could be tedious.

846

Scheck wore a gray suit, a white shirt, and a dull tie—a far cry from Cochran's resplendent plumage.

The choice of Scheck had surprised Deutsch. She'd expected Bob Shapiro, who'd connected well with jurors during voir dire. She wondered, however, whether anyone—especially Scheck—could follow Johnnie Cochran.

Deutsch was amazed again when Scheck revealed his own theatrical skills. He smiled often—half-shy, engaging; in the next moment he was aggressive, outraged, sneering, chopping the air with one hand.

Linda Deutsch settled back. It would be a good show after all.

Scheck put up his "Black Hole" slide. "All the testing—if it is contaminated, compromised, or corrupted here, it doesn't matter what the results are by these other testing agencies."

He railed against the lack of security in the LAPD's storage and handling of case evidence. "There is plenty of access, if you want to tamper with evidence, if you are authorized personnel, if you are a lead detective . . ."

Kardashian remembered Simpson's orders earlier in the week: "Make sure Barry speaks English." Now Simpson was pleased. He wasn't writing much.

"They [the prosecution] argue that the defense has to prove *how*, exactly *where*, exactly *when* tampering occurred with any of this evidence," Scheck told them.

"That is not our burden. They have to prove that this evidence *wasn't* tampered with beyond a reasonable doubt.

"I'm going to confront each and every one of these essential pieces of evidence in this case," he promised, "and raise a reasonable doubt about it."

As Barry Scheck saw it, demonstrating reasonable doubt was the heart of his job. Unlike Johnnie Cochran, he had never enjoyed the luxury of unwavering faith in Simpson's innocence. But, he felt, that was irrelevant. The defense had no burden of proof—not in this case, not in any case. Scheck's job was to show the jury where the prosecution had failed to meet *its* burden of proof. Early on, Scheck had suspected the blood evidence was seriously flawed—carelessly handled, tampered with, manufactured, planted. His subsequent investigations turned his suspicions into solid conviction. Today he had one final chance to convince the jury that the D.A.'s scientific evidence was worthless.

"Let's start with the sock."

Dennis Fung collected it on June 13. If the "big stain" was there, Scheck asked, why didn't Fung and others see blood? Prosecutors argued that bad lighting was the problem. "Please," he sneered in his best Brooklynese, "where I come from, that don't pass the laugh test.

"Then, suddenly, on August 4 . . . for the first time they find the stain on the ankle."

Scheck recapped Herb MacDonell's analysis of the bloodstain on the "third surface" of the sock. "The most *likely* and *probable* inference is the one that is *not* for the timid or the faint of heart," he said furiously. "Somebody"—he paused dramatically—"*played with this evidence,* and there is no doubt about it!"

For the rest of the morning and after lunch, Barry Scheck outlined the miraculously appearing back-gate blood drop, the EDTA issue, the missing blood from Simpson's reference sample. He summarized Dr. Lee's second-shoe-print and wet-transfer theories and Dr. Baden's conclusion that Ron Goldman died only after a lengthy struggle. He reminded the jury forcefully that the defense had demonstrated that the LAPD lab was a "cesspool of contamination," accessible to the likes of Mark Fuhrman.

The jurors were transfixed. Scheck's righteous indignation was irresistible. They showed little emotion, but were listening hard.

In mid-afternoon, Scheck began his final summary for the jury. Leaning forward on the podium not unlike Johnnie Cochran, furious at this terrible injustice, he shook his head slowly.

"So *much* of the essential facts in this case are just *shot through* with reasonable doubt," he said. "There *is* something wrong. There is something *terribly* wrong about this evidence. Somebody manufactured evidence in this case. There is missing blood. There is EDTA. There are questions, serious, deeply troubling questions."

He paused for effect. Then, softly, seriously, he said:

"You *must* distrust it. You *have* to distrust it. You *cannot* render a verdict in this case *beyond* a reasonable doubt on this kind of evidence. Because if you do, *no one* is safe, no one."

Then Johnnie Cochran spoke the final words for the defense. Cochran gave the prosecution fifteen questions it would find nearly impossible to answer. Some had come from his sister, others from the various defense attorneys.

Conviction is a prosecutor's burden, Cochran told the jury. Thus, "it is Miss Clark's duty to answer for you as best she can any legitimate questions, arising from the evidence, which we believe cast doubt upon Mr. Simpson's guilt."

Cochran consulted the black binder containing his questions. The first group probed Mark Fuhrman's racism, his movements the night of the murder, and the suspicious positioning and condition of the bloody glove. He used Rolf Rokahr's recent testimony to good effect: Why had the prosecution not called anyone from the LAPD to rebut the photographer's statements?

In his seventh question Cochran aimed at the next major LAPD target: "For what purpose was Vannatter carrying Mr. Simpson's blood in his pocket for three hours and a distance of twenty-five miles instead of booking it down the hall at Parker Center?"

Cochran had his geography wrong: The LAPD lab was several blocks away from Parker Center. And Vannatter had carried the blood in an envelope. But the prosecutors didn't object.

Johnnie then questioned the missing reference blood, the unsworn video interview with Peratis, the absence of blood-stains inside Rockingham, and the "less than seven tenths of a drop" of Goldman's blood in the Bronco. His eleventh question addressed the absence of bruises and marks on Simpson after the murders.

So far Johnnie's questions had been complex paragraphs. Now he started moving to his conclusion with sharp, short inquiries: "Number twelve. Why do the bloodstains with the most DNA not show up until weeks after the murder?

"Number thirteen: Why did Mark Fuhrman lie to us?

"Why did Phil Vannatter lie to us?"

Cochran, rushing a bit, had forgotten to say, "Number fourteen."

"And finally, fifteen: Given Professor MacDonell's testimony that the gloves would not have shrunk no matter how much blood was smeared on them . . . how come the gloves *just don't fit?*"

At the defense table the lawyers smiled. A very nice summation. Johnnie had reminded the jury of the trial's strongest moment. Simpson, however, continued to scribble on his yellow pad.

In conclusion, Cochran quoted the historian Thomas Carlyle that "No lie can live forever." He turned to Proverbs for thoughts about "false witnesses." He quoted James Russell Lowell: "Truth is forever on the scaffold, Wrong forever on the throne."

"Yet that scaffold sways the future," Cochran recited to the courtroom, voice rising, finger pointing high, "and beyond the dim unknown, standeth God within the shadows, keeping watch above His own.

"You walk with that every day," Cochran thundered. "You carry that *with you* and things will come *to you* and you will be able to reveal people who come to you in *uniforms* and *high positions* who lie and are corrupt.

"Don't be part of this continuing cover-up," Cochran boomed. "Do the right thing, remembering that if it doesn't fit, you must acquit. That if these messengers have lied to you, *you can't trust their message,* that this has been a *search for truth.*"

Cochran thanked the jury. He stopped momentarily, then added one last thought.

"God bless you."

47

On Friday morning, September 29, Chris Darden and Marcia Clark had the last word.

Darden went first. He told jurors of his record of prosecuting abusive cops. The jury couldn't "send a message" to the LAPD or "eradicate racism" by delivering a verdict of not guilty, he insisted. Not when it is clear "and you know in your heart. . . ."

Darden paused. "Everybody knows it. Everybody knows he killed—"

Cochran jumped up. Before the day was over, he and Barry Scheck, following Alan Dershowitz's suggestion, would object to almost everything the prosecutors said. Between them, they would object more than sixty times.

Ito overruled Cochran, but Darden didn't finish his sentence. "Everybody *knows*," he said, leaving it.

Darden tilted his head at the defense table. "You heard all the speaking and the fiery rhetoric and the quotes from Proverbs and the like. . . . You just need to calm down, take that common sense God gave you, go back in the jury room. Don't let these people get you all riled up and all fired up because Fuhrman is a racist."

Darden hooked a thumb at Simpson. "It is true that Mark Fuhrman is a racist," he told them. "It is also true that *this* man killed two people."

Now it was Marcia Clark's final turn. Today she looked no less exhausted. But she had fire in her dark, tired eyes.

Barry Scheck was ready for her.

Linda Deutsch was amazed at his endless objections. In decades of reporting, she'd seen nothing like it. In the pressroom afterward, everyone agreed that Scheck's behavior today was ugly. No other word for it.

Scheck objected so often that before long Ito furiously warned him to stop. During an argument over Marcia's use of personal references while the jury was absent, Scheck objected out of turn.

"Sit down!" Ito shouted, livid, pointing his finger at the attorney.

Scheck was almost daring the judge to cite him for contempt. Peter Neufeld was delighted. All along, he'd hoped *somebody* would go to jail in this trial. Maybe Barry would make it. A grand civil liberties tradition.

Carl Douglas cared nothing about this ivory tower civil liberties stuff. The important issue was the jury. He knew black audiences loved to see authority challenged. Scheck was now a hero. The jury loved him. Douglas saw it in their faces.

Clark eventually worked out a rhythm to counter Scheck's interruptions. Since Ito was overruling him, she didn't wait for the judge. She simply kept talking without breaking her cadence. She refused to be upstaged. Exhausted, determined, she doggedly made point after point. Then came her final exhibit board.

"This exhibit is entitled 'Unrefuted Evidence,'" she said.

She'd just handed Johnnie Cochran a loud "Fuck you." Cochran's fifteen questions yesterday had been a masterstroke. But Clark was ignoring them. Two aides brought out a huge magnetic board showing a large pyramid.

"This is the unrefuted evidence," Clark announced. "This is evidence which has not been contested by any contradictory evidence. That's *all* that's on this board."

Clark started with the bottom, the broad base, peeling back the lower section of the pyramid's outer wall to show jurors the first piece.

"First of all, opportunity. Opportunity deals with the time. . . ." For each level of evidence, Clark pulled back a strip of outer covering. Underneath were rows of boxes with accompanying artwork. Time-line evidence featured clocks. Physical evidence was illustrated by photos of hair, bloody gloves, the knit cap. The blood-smeared Bronco seat. The Bloomingdale's receipt for Aris Isotoner Light gloves.

Row by row, Clark covered the time line, the gloves, the hair and fiber evidence. This is powerful, Linda Deutsch decided. The pyramid was huge, the squares of evidence underneath detailed and easy to read. Marcia moved along the rows.

After an hour of talking through constant objections, Clark neared the top of the pyramid:

"Full circle. Spousal abuse, domestic violence against Nicole Brown. Unrefuted. You can see, ladies and gentlemen, this is just what hasn't been contested . . ." Her voice now carried an obvious note of triumph. "It is truly overwhelming."

The defense attorneys were motionless. Simpson still wrote notes.

After a moment, Marcia Clark continued:

"None of us wanted to believe that O.J. Simpson could commit murder," she said quietly. "We all wanted to believe that our image of him was right." It was hard to believe, she conceded, "that the man we saw in the movies and commercials could do this."

Clark stopped still.

"But he did."

She seemed sad now. "And the fact that he did doesn't mean that he wasn't a great football player. It doesn't mean he never did a good thing in his life. Nothing takes that away. . . . It will always be here."

She paused.

"But so will the fact that he committed these murders."

The courtroom was silent. Clark had them.

She leaned forward with her hands clasped behind her back. Her voice could hardly be heard.

"Usually I feel like I'm the only one left to speak for the victims," she said calmly, swaying slightly on her feet. "But in this case, Ron and Nicole are speaking to you. . . . Nicole started before she ever died. Remember back in 1989, she cried to Detective Edwards, 'He's going to kill me! He's going to kill me!' ''

She had one last exhibit.

In 1990, Nicole ''put photographs of her beaten face and her haunted look in a safe-deposit box along with a will. She was only thirty years old. How many thirty-year-olds do you know [who] do that, a will, a safe-deposit box? . . .''

Clark recalled the 911 tape from 1993. ''The children were there. He was screaming. She was crying and she was frightened. I think the thing that perhaps was so chilling about her voice is that sound of resignation . . . inevitability. She knew she was going to die.''

The courtroom was completely hushed. More than one spectator was fighting tears.

''And Ron, he speaks to you . . . struggling so valiantly. He forced his murderer to leave the evidence behind that you might not ordinarily have found. And they both are telling you who did it—with their hair, their clothes, their bodies, their blood. They tell you he did it. He did it. Mr. Simpson, Orenthal James Simpson, he did it.''

Clark signaled to an aide.

''I want to play something for you, ladies and gentlemen, that puts it all together.''

She explained that jurors would now hear ''a compilation of the 1989 tape, 911 call, the 1993 911 call.'' On the screen, they would see photographs from Nicole's safe-deposit box.

Cochran rose quickly. ''I object to that without further explanation, Your Honor.''

Ito ruled that the combined tape could be played.

Nicole's pain was wrenching and eerie, as if it truly came from the grave. Kardashian watched Simpson's shoulders tremble. Bob knew nothing would ever be the same for him again, whatever the jury decided.

''I don't have to say anything else,'' Clark told them. ''Ladies and gentlemen, on behalf of the people of the State of California, because we have proven beyond a reasonable doubt, far beyond a reasonable doubt, that the defendant committed these murders, we ask you to find the defendant guilty of murder in the first degree of Ronald Goldman and Nicole Brown.''

After the closing arguments, after all the trash talk, after all the representations and misrepresentations that had occupied the court for almost a year, Judge Ito was ready to instruct the jury. The jury, now nine blacks, two whites, and one Latino, had been sequestered since January 11. Ten jurors had been dismissed. The remaining twelve jurors and two alternates now had before them 1,105 pieces of evidence and 45,000 pages of trial transcript from 133 witnesses, which they could have read back to them on request.

The judge's instructions were brief; the jury retired to deliberate at 4:12 P.M. Within minutes they notified the court they had picked a foreperson. Ito said it was a good sign: They had agreed on *something* quickly. At 4:30 P.M. deliberations ended for the weekend. The jury would return on Monday morning at nine.

48

ON SUNDAY, OCTOBER 1, O.J. WAS NO LONGER ALLOWED to receive visitors in the special attorney's room. He was no longer on trial. Now he was simply another inmate, whose visitors stood in line and talked to him over telephones through thick glass.

Skip Taft visited Simpson to discuss several business matters. There was an offer to buy exclusive photographs of him and his family if and when he was released. Taft considered it very speculative. Larry Schiller, who had been a professional photographer, advised Taft and would shoot some of the pictures himself. Simpson had some reservations about the deal, but agreed to it. He needed the money.

Nicole Pulvers visited him. They had been together for almost fifteen months, and by now Simpson trusted her almost more than he did his attorneys. He'd never once asked her to leave, no matter what he was discussing or with whom. Now she had to say good-bye. He smiled at her; she couldn't look at him head on. As she left with his last visitor on Sunday afternoon, her eyes filled. She would wait for the verdict at his home.

Each day of the jury deliberations, an attorney from the defense was assigned to be in court. Scheck and Neufeld had returned to New York. Johnnie had to travel north of the city. Blasier took a few days off. Nobody could guess how long the jury would be out.

Carl Douglas had the court assignment on Monday, October 2. The jury began deliberations at 9:16 A.M. Douglas knew that nothing ever happens on the first day. Ito had already told both sides that whenever the verdict came down, the court would wait until the next day to announce it.

At eleven o'clock, the jury sends a note to the judge requesting a readback of Allan Park's testimony. The court reporter, Janet Moxham, doesn't want to go through the whole thing. "Let's find out what part they want read." The bailiff is sent in with the court reporter's query. Douglas goes into the holding cell to see Simpson. Nothing unusual, he tells him. It means the jury is working.

But Simpson is agitated. Why didn't we ask Park about this? Why didn't we ask about that?

"Goddammit," Simpson screams, "I told you to ask him again about the two cars! I *told* Johnnie!"

Douglas knows better than to say a word. After twenty minutes he leaves. In the courtroom he finds Moxham. Now she's smiling.

"They only want to hear about the description of the shadowy figure going back into the house," she tells him. This part of the testimony is the prosecution's point. Now Carl wants the entire testimony read: all the inconsistencies, all the defense points, should be heard again.

Douglas, Darden, and Hodgman meet in Judge Ito's chambers. Carl talks first.

"I think this entire testimony should be read," he tells the judge, "because it's piecemeal, it's disjointed. It wouldn't be fair to do otherwise."

"If they only want certain parts read," Hodgman says, "just read the part they want."

Ito agrees with Douglas. Janet Moxham is unhappy. Ito says he will put his ruling on the record at one o'clock, after lunch, and then have the entire transcript read to the jury.

About fifteen spectators, including a few reporters, watch the jury come in. As usual, the twelve familiar faces are impassive.

At 1:07 P.M. Janet Moxham starts reading Marcia's direct and Park's answers. After an hour, the jury seems frustrated. Ito notices the discomfort and orders a break.

Bill Dinwiddie, the bailiff, escorts the jury back to the jury room. "Wow, are they mad," he tells Moxham and Ito's clerk, Deirdre Robertson, when he returns. "They didn't want to hear all this."

Carl sits at the defense table, listening.

Robertson suggests to the bailiff that the jury write a note to Ito saying what they do want to hear. Carl checks his watch. It's about two o'clock.

At 2:08 the bailiff returns with a note and tells Deirdre, "They say they heard enough. No more read-back necessary."

Douglas is pretty sure the part they wanted to hear, the shadowy figure, wasn't read.

At 2:20 the bailiff brings another note: "We've reached a decision. Would you please send us the instructions."

Ito calls all the attorneys present—Douglas, Hodgman, and Darden—to a sidebar.

"Look at this, Carl." The judge is pale.

Nobody understands what the note means. The jury instructions are in the jury room. Ito asks Deirdre what papers they might be missing. She checks her desk. "Maybe that's what they're asking for." She's pointing to a manila folder holding the verdict forms. It's the only necessary paperwork they don't have. They should have been given to the jury this morning.

"Holy shit," Carl says softly. "They're saying they want the verdict forms."

"Let's give them the forms and sit tight," Ito says.

The blood leaves Hodgman's face. He looks out at the empty courtroom.

"Damn, Bill," Carl says to Hodgman, "you look like I feel."

"How do I get by the press?" Hodgman asks Douglas. Can't help there, Douglas says. Then Carl calls his office and tells Jan: "Call Johnnie. Tell him we have a Stage One emergency." That was their code for a verdict. Then he heads for the holding cell.

"Listen, Juice, this can't be a conviction!" he shouts.

Simpson isn't listening. He's still carrying on about Park. Douglas tries to talk calmly, but soon he's yelling at Simpson.

"Damn it, Juice," he says, "this is a nine-month trial. It doesn't turn on three questions. Give me a break." He walks out on Simpson.

Just as he's about to open the door to the courtroom, he hears three buzzes far in the distance. That's supposed to be the jury's signal that they have a verdict. In the courtroom Carl finds Deirdre talking to Chandra Trower, a bailiff. Yes, it's three buzzes and the buzzes came at 2:28. Douglas asks Deirdre to write the time down.

The verdict forms contained five questions that had to be answered if the vote was for conviction: First- or second-degree murder for Goldman and Nicole? Use of a dangerous weapon on Goldman and Nicole? Finally a long question in legalese about special circumstances. But the jury would only have to vote "Not guilty" on the first two questions for an acquittal.

Carl tried to figure the time it would take to garner five "Guilty" votes for a conviction. He counted the seconds, the minutes, in his mind. How long to pass out the papers, take one vote, tally it, take a second vote, tally it, take all five votes, and write the note to the judge? Douglas is sure the jury couldn't have done all that in eight minutes. That meant acquittal.

He runs back to Simpson.

"Juice, they have a verdict," Carl says. "And it's not a guilty one." He tells Simpson how he reached his conclusion. O.J. is not convinced. He's still preoccupied with Park's testimony.

"I have had gang-bangers and drive-bys with eyewitnesses," Carl tells O.J., "and a conviction took more than three hours."

Then Johnnie calls the courtroom. Carl tells him it's an acquittal.

Linda Deutsch goes upstairs to the pressroom to get a notebook, then waits for the elevator down. As the doors open, she runs into Darden and Hodgman.

"Is this it?" she asks Hodgman. "Is this a verdict?"

Hodgman just shrugs, looks at the ceiling, says nothing. Once downstairs, Deutsch runs to the pay phone. "This sounds incredible," she tells her office. "I think it may be a verdict."

At 2:49 Ito asks Simpson to come into the courtroom. The jury comes in at 2:51.

Douglas feels stunned. His hands are clasped tightly. He sits alone with Simpson.

"Ladies and gentlemen," Ito said, "while we were taking our brief recess Mrs. Robertson advised me that you buzzed three times and indicated that after receiving the verdict forms, you have reached a verdict in this case. Is that correct, Madam Foreman?"

The juror sitting in Seat 1 rises.

"Yes."

O.J. doesn't look at the jury. Douglas tries to look calm, knowing the TV camera is on him. Then he looks over at the jury, searching for a clue. None of the jurors looks toward the defense table. Douglas starts to worry.

Ito asks if the forms are signed and dated, if they have been placed in an envelope and sealed. Yes to everything. But the envelope has been left in the jury room. Not a good place, Ito says gently. Deputy Browning escorts the forewoman to retrieve the sealed envelope.

Browning opens the door to the jury room. There on the table sits the verdict. The forewoman, still nervous, picks it up and gives it to Deputy Trower.

Ito asks the jury to return the next morning at ten o'clock to announce their verdict. It is now 2:55 P.M.

As the jury leaves, Douglas scrutinizes the jurors the defense always thought were on Simpson's side. He gets no vibes. With an acquittal, you get some vibes. But then it hits him: This is a *professional* jury. They've been at it for nine months now, always mindful of the eyes watching them. No *way* will they look at anyone yet.

O.J. is returned to the county jail.

At the chichi spa Beverly Hills Hot Springs, Shawn Chapman has a massage, a long-overdue treat. This is her first day off in six months. While she dresses, a woman is using a pay phone nearby.

"I'd like Richard Dreyfuss," Shawn hears the woman say. *The* Richard Dreyfuss? Shawn eavesdrops for the fun of it.

"Hey, Richard, how ya doin'—*What, they have a verdict?*"

Shawn thinks it must be about some other case. Then the woman says, "How could they have a verdict that quick?" Chapman's heart stops. That's impossible, she tells herself. She digs her pager out of her locker. A billion messages from the office. Kardashian, Johnnie. Once she's in her car, Douglas calls on her cell phone.

"Hi, what are you doing?" Carl says, and then gives her his analysis of the eight minutes.

"How can you say that?" Shawn asks. She's afraid to believe.

"No way Juror 2179 is going to convict Juice," he tells

her. "She could never go back to her Compton neighborhood and face people who knew she voted for conviction in *that* amount of time."

Shawn can't take this in. All she can think is that she finally gets a day off and now she can't concentrate on her shopping.

Peter Neufeld had returned to New York with Scheck. He is strolling on the Brooklyn Bridge, looking at the sunset over Manhattan, when someone with a Walkman stops him and says there is a verdict.

Gerry Uelman immediately booked a flight to L.A. from his home in Santa Clara in northern California.

At the San Francisco airport, Johnnie is mobbed by the press. His arrival even gets live TV coverage. Seeing Cochran bathed in TV lights, Shawn jokes to her mother, "As black as Johnnie is, today he was white. Completely white."

When Carl arrives home, almost every member of the defense calls, even some of the experts. He gives his theory about the eight minutes over and over. When he finally turns out the lights, he realizes that Bob Shapiro hasn't called.

Late that afternoon, Kardashian is at a PR firm when someone says there is a verdict in the Simpson case. Kardashian excuses himself and drives to the jail.

Kardashian has been assuming he has a few weeks to make arrangements for a possible acquittal. He feels strongly that Simpson should get out of the country for six months or so. Straight from the courthouse to an airport. Always, O.J.'s answer has been "Let's wait."

Kardashian sits opposite Simpson in the attorneys' room. They need a plan *now*.

"I haven't touched, hugged Sydney or Justin in over a year," O.J. says quietly. "I want to sleep in my own bed, in my own home."

"I think you're crazy," Kardashian tells him. "Somebody can take a shot at you."

"I'm not going to go." O.J. is adamant.

The two friends never discuss the possibility of a guilty verdict.

A sheriff comes in and tells O.J. he'll have to finish soon; they want him to pack his things.

O.J. and Bob grin at each other. Not a beaming grin like "We won." Just "Maybe we're getting out of here."

After O.J. left, Kardashian met with various jail officials.

"We want him out of the country," Pat Devany, the Sheriff's Department area commander, told him. "We don't want him going to Rockingham."

"He's going home," Kardashian said.

"If he leaves the country, we will escort him to an airport or fly him by chopper," the officer continued. "But if you're saying he's going to Rockingham, the freeway is down the street from here and that's as far as we go."

"Can we get an escort to his home?" Kardashian asked.

"No." A polite no. "He's a private citizen. You arrange your own security from this door."

Kardashian went back to Simpson and delivered the message: The sheriff's *really* concerned. Someone can get you.

"I don't care," O.J. said. "I'm going home to sleep in my own bed."

Months ago, O.J. had hired Tom Gleason to provide security at the house. Now Gleason and Kardashian stood outside, by the Rockingham gate. Larry Schiller was already there, taking some photographs. A few newspeople drove by. No one stopped.

"We need a couple of vans," Bob told Tom. "One for security, and one for us." It was okay with Simpson for Schiller to be around, anyplace he wanted.

"We need a motorcycle escort," Bob said. "We can't drive on the freeway with all the choppers following. Traffic will stop. We'll be pinned down. Something is bound to happen." The three men were lost for a second. Kardashian tried calling mortuaries and movie studios. They always use escorts. No luck after several calls, and it was now after eleven P.M.

Kardashian then turned to Tom. "Screw it," he said. "Let's just punt."

Everyone was nervous.

49

AT SEVEN A.M. ON TUESDAY, OCTOBER 3, TWO WHITE vans with tinted windows drive up to the back entrance of the Los Angeles County Jail. Simpson's security and bodyguards have arrived. They are met by Mark Squiers, head of the Sheriff's Custody Division, and shown where they can wait.

Johnnie Cochran had asked the defense team to assemble in the parking lot of his office building at Highland and Wilshire. The Fruit of Islam bodyguards are out in full force. Everyone will ride to court in security vans. Cochran, Douglas, Bailey, Uelmen, Chapman, Blasier and his wife, Charlotte, and Kardashian stand around making small talk. Everyone seems edgy, except Cochran. Johnnie is his normal upbeat self. It's been 474 days since Simpson's arrest.

The defense team's vans pull out. The courtroom is seven miles away. For Shawn it is the worst drive she's ever taken. Nobody says a word. Well—actually, she realizes, someone is talking a little bullshit, but it barely registers. Suddenly they are in the underground garage, avoiding the thousands of spectators and reporters all along Broadway and Temple. They go immediately to the ninth floor and enter Judge Ito's courtroom, Department 103. Shapiro has just come from seeing Simpson.

Chris Darden sits at the prosecution table. Marcia Clark is pacing wearily; she seems exhausted but restless. The time is 9:15. Then Judge Ito, not robed, walks into the courtroom and stands in the well area where the court reporters work. He wants to talk to the attorneys informally and off the record.

"I'm going to come out at ten," he tells them. "There should be no shows of emotion today. And if your client is acquitted," he says to Johnnie, "I will not release him here. Mr. Kardashian has made arrangements. If he's convicted, I'm going to put over sentencing. Either way, I'm going to tell the jurors that, if they want, they can talk to you on this floor."

The next forty-five minutes are painful for most of the defense team. Johnnie and Kardashian visit Simpson in the holding cell. Shapiro follows. Shawn starts to cry. Jo-Ellan hugs her. Carl Douglas tells the two women they're acting ridiculous. "It's a not guilty," he says. "What's wrong with both of you?"

All the worry, all the work, all the long hours and late nights seven days a week are catching up with each member of the defense.

In the holding cell Cochran and Kardashian find Simpson pacing. Even Johnnie shows a little anxiety. Kardashian suggests they say a prayer. O.J. stands behind the wire mesh of the cell and holds the Bible Kardashian gave him the day after his arrest. The three men put their hands on the wire and touch fingers.

"Our Lord, your will be done," Kardashian starts. "Only you know if this man did it or not. Let your justice be done."

Kardashian tries to act positive, but he feels horrible.

At 9:50 the deputies allow the spectators and media into the courtroom. There are extra chairs in the back row. The single TV camera points to the seal of the State of California, where it always rests until Judge Ito takes the bench. The Goldman family comes in first: Fred Goldman, his wife, Patty, his daughter, Kim, and their youngest child, Lauren. The little girl is already sobbing. Writers Joe McGinnis, Kathy Braidhill, Jeffrey Toobin, Dominick Dunne, Joe Bosco, Larry Schiller, and Linda Deutsch take their places, as do other members of the media. Then the Browns, Juditha and Lou, arrive with their daughters, Denise, Tanya, and Dominique. Johnnie's wife, Dale, sits in the second row with Ron Goldman's mother, Sharon Rufo, beside her. Reporters David Margolick, James Willwerth, Michelle Caruso, Michael Fleeman, Shirley Perlman, Kardashian's ex-fiancée, Denice, and Dan Whitcomb watch from the pressroom on the eleventh floor.

Then Eunice Simpson is wheeled into the courtroom. She holds her Bible. Jason's sobs can be heard throughout the courtroom. Arnelle seems ready to break down. Their mother, Marquerite Simpson Thomas, sits between them. The rest of Simpson's family hang on to their composure. The sound of crying becomes noticeable. Before long, it seems as if everyone present in the packed room is in tears.

Then Cochran and Kardashian walk out of the holding cell. Neither looks at the audience or shows emotion.

As happy as this day may yet be for Shawn, these minutes are terrible. Carl keeps telling her to stop crying. She can't.

Then Douglas, Chapman, Jo-Ellan, Howard Harris, Uelmen, and Detectives Vannatter and Lange take seats at the rail. At the defense table, Shapiro and Cochran sit on the left of Simpson's place. Kardashian, Bailey, and Blasier take their seats to the right. Johnnie smiles at Lee, who has been faithful to the end. Cochran feels the unspoken bond.

A moment later, Simpson is escorted from the holding cell to his seat at the defense table. He stands between Cochran and Kardashian, waiting for court to begin.

Linda Deutsch thinks Simpson looks as if he's been up all night.

Simpson turns to Kardashian as Judge Ito comes through the door. "Well, Robert, this is it," he says.

"Juice, the Lord is with us," Kardashian replies.

Impassive, Judge Ito climbs the two steps to the bench as the TV camera pans down. Marguerite places both arms around Arnelle. Jason buries his head in his mother's shoulder. Carmelita and Shirley are motionless.

"Good morning, counsel," Ito says, looking down at the attorneys.

The judge then makes a series of statements for the record: He's met with the attorneys at 9:15. The jury has now requested that their privacy be protected. The jurors do not wish to speak to anybody after the verdict is read.

"Deputy Trower, let's have the jurors, please," Ito then says.

Slowly the jury walks in and sits down. Ito asks Deirdre Robertson if she has the sealed verdict forms. She does. He asks that they be given to Deputy Trower, who will give them back to Juror 1, the forewoman.

For the first time since the votes were taken and the envelope sealed, the envelope is opened. The forms are in the same condition, the forewoman says, as they were when sealed up the day before. Then the envelope, now open, is handed back to Deputy Trower.

Shawn Chapman turns and looks at Juror 6. The juror looks straight back at her. For the first time Shawn thinks she sees a sign of acquittal. It's the way he's looking at me, she thinks, the look in his eyes says, "Not guilty." Then the same juror looks at Carl and nods. Kardashian doesn't notice any of the jurors looking at anyone. Deutsch finds them expressionless. Bailey sits with a small smile on his face, arms folded across his chest, and looks straight ahead.

As Deirdre takes the envelope, Shapiro leans across Johnnie and says directly to O.J.: "I think it's going to be bad news."

"Fuck *no*, Bob, we're going to win," Johnnie says. His voice is sharp with disdain.

Deirdre reads aloud as 95 million Americans watch their TV sets. "Superior Court of California, County of Los Angeles, in the matter of the State of California versus Orenthal James Simpson, case number BA097211. We the jury, in the above-entitled action, find the defendant, Orenthal James Simpson, not guilty of the crime of murder . . .''

It takes almost two seconds for Simpson to understand the verdict. He bites his lips. Johnnie, standing behind O.J., immediately puts his right hand on Simpson's right shoulder, then places his head on his client's left shoulder. He hugs O.J. It's a formal gesture, almost stylized. Simpson jabs Kardashian in the back. Bailey, still with arms folded, now looks over his shoulder at Simpson. O.J.'s expression finds its way to a smile, his fists tightly clenched at his sides. Chapman and Dimitrius are weeping. Kardashian feels his heart coming through his chest. Douglas is limp with relief.

"Thank you, Lord," O.J. says softly.

Now the courtroom erupts. Dominick Dunne, covering the trial for *Vanity Fair,* looks as if he's been hit. His mouth drops open. "What happened?" he asks Shoreen Maghame of City News Service, who sits beside him. It looks to her as if Dunne has lost a moment of time. She even worries that he might be having a heart attack. Then she notices that Linda Deutsch remains cool.

Eunice Simpson's hands fly up in the air as she thanks God over and over. The Simpson family is crying, yelling, and praying. Patty Goldman buries her head in Fred's shoulder, as Kim, his older daughter, wails aloud for the first time. Their younger child is now hysterical. Fred Goldman stares off in the distance, muttering, "Murderer, murderer." Lou and Judy Brown are immobile, impassive, in shock.

At Simpson's home, Al Cowlings has been watching the proceedings on TV. He's sitting on the couch in O.J.'s den. His head is buried in his left hand, his right fist clenched between his legs. Cathy Randa, Nicole Pulvers, and Gary Randa sit beside him. O.J.'s housekeeper, Gigi, and her newborn baby sit on the floor.

As the words "Not guilty" are spoken, and register, A.C. recoils. He yells at the top of his voice, "Not guilty!" and falls to the floor, sobbing uncontrollably.

* * *

Back in Ito's courtroom, a sheriff's deputy walks up to Kardashian and pulls him away from the group. Bob is whisked into the hallway adjacent to Ito's private office, where he watches the rest of the proceedings through an open door. The second and third counts are read. Not guilty. Not guilty. Then Sheriff Block and six of his deputies take Kardashian to an elevator. He never sees the official end of the trial.

Simpson smiles tightly. He mouths, "Thank you," to the jury. His fists are clenched and they rise higher and higher as each juror is asked to confirm the verdict. Johnnie looks past Simpson's shoulder to get a better view of the jury. Bailey's smile has widened. Shapiro walks away from the team.

Ito thanks the jury and formally excuses them.

As they walk out, Juror 6, Lionel Cryer, gives a black-power salute. The defense and prosecution have known from the beginning that Cryer is a former Black Panther, but the media and public haven't. The members of the defense team start hugging each other.

Simpson is taken back to the holding cell.

Ito clears the courtroom except for the two legal teams. Chapman notices that Robert Shapiro stands apart. Then something strange: He walks over to the fax machine and sends a fax. He doesn't say a word to anyone; he seems emotionless and distant.

As Johnnie heads for the holding cell, he says to Shawn, "Call Georgia's. It's a victory party."

Then Bob Shapiro walks up to Johnnie. A few days ago, he praised Cochran's closing arguments. Now he says: "I'm going to say something on TV about my beliefs in this case. I want you to know." That's all he says. His tone is polite and professional. Cochran takes it as a warning. Shapiro then leaves to meet Barbara Walters at her hotel.

No one on the team was aware of the public reaction to the verdict. In a black beauty salon in New York, everyone flew out of their seats, cheering and shouting. There were both cheers and silence from a mixed group of students in

Illinois. In a shopping mall in Orange County, California, the white employees were shocked, silent, and stunned. Outside the courthouse, the black-power salute was everywhere.

50

SHERIFF BLOCK, HIS DEPUTIES, AND KARDASHIAN ARRIVE at the bowels of the parking garage, an underground level Bob had never seen before. They wait for Simpson. Instead, the jury emerges to board a bus to their hotel. Most of them are crying.

"O.J. thanks you," Kardashian says to each of them as they pass. One juror comes over to Kardashian and hugs him. As the jurors' bus pulls away, Simpson emerges through the same door.

Kardashian is taken aback. Something is wrong: Simpson is still handcuffed and shackled.

"He's still our prisoner," the deputy explains to Kardashian. Then they all board the sheriff's huge Greyhound bus. Apparently the little van that always brought O.J. to and from court won't do today. Simpson is locked in a small cage within the bus. Here's this monster bus with all these empty seats, Kardashian thinks, and O.J. is caged. Kardashian sits beside the cage.

As the bus pulls out of the underground parking lot, led and followed by police cars, the crowds of black supporters near the courthouse cheer. As they leave Broadway, Kardashian notices that the streets are empty, as if the city has been evacuated, as if time has stopped. As they move toward the jail a mile away, the cheering of the crowds at the courthouse echoes throughout the streets.

When the bus arrives at the back entrance of the jail, Simpson is let out of the cage, his handcuffs and shackles removed. Kardashian is told he still can't touch O.J., who is, technically, still in custody.

To the right of the bus are the two white vans ready to take O.J. home. Simpson is told to enter the jail's discharge area. A loud cheer goes up as he comes in. The county employees have been waiting for the Juice. Simpson looks around, says thank you. They hand him a paper. He signs without glancing at it. It all takes less than a minute.

With Kardashian at Simpson's side, Tom Gleason leads them to his van. Dave Sevik is driving; Gleason takes the passenger seat. The second van, with additional security, sits waiting, engine running.

Then the police escort Simpson's two vehicles the half mile to the freeway entrance. As the vans enter the freeway, they are immediately caught in L.A.'s downtown gridlock. Simpson says nothing. From the 101, they inch their way to the Harbor Freeway South. Sevik almost rear-ends two cars trying to get out of the mess. The motorists beside them don't notice Simpson behind the tinted windows.

Simpson takes Gleason's cell phone and calls Paula Barbieri in Florida.

"I'm out, I'm on my way," he says. He's finally starting to sound excited. "I'm on the freeway. I never thought I would enjoy being on the freeway as much as I am now."

Once on the Harbor Freeway, Sevik races toward the Santa Monica Freeway. "Slow down," Kardashian tells him. "This is not the way I want to die."

Now cars traveling beside the van start honking. The helicopters circling above alert other drivers to the white vans. The ride home is being covered on live TV. As Simpson's caravan moves west, cars race to keep up. People cheer, mostly blacks. They are hanging out of their windows, taking pictures, holding their hands high in the air with black-power salutes.

O.J., with his Bible on his lap, makes a second, a third phone call. Kardashian thinks O.J. is starting to get his bearings.

51

FROM THE SANTA MONICA FREEWAY, THE VANS TRAVEL TO the 405 North, then up the off ramp to Sunset Boulevard going west toward Rockingham. Simpson is off the phone now and looking out the window. The last time O.J. drove down this street, A.C. was driving the white Bronco and he had a gun to his head. That day the public's hopes and prayers were with him.

Simpson looks out the window. The cheering from the freeway is far behind them. Now people line the street in silence. His white neighbors hold signs: "Murderer." "Go Home, Murderer."

Kardashian understands that the times have changed. Simpson seems taken aback.

As the vans drive down Rockingham, Simpson's neighbors are outside chanting, "Murderer, murderer." The press is already photographing the protesters.

The few people inside Simpson's home are watching TV as the white vans come down Sunset, up Bristol Circle, and down Rockingham. By the time Simpson's gates open, Cathy Randa and her son Gary wait in the driveway. The van carrying O.J. comes to a stop. The door opens.

A.C. runs from the house. He engulfs Simpson. Both

men are weeping and laughing. Simpson is almost lost in Cowling's arms. Then Gleason guides them inside. Kardashian follows.

Simpson dances down his foyer, holding Kardashian's Bible high in the air. "Hallelujah!" he declares, "Hallelujah!" Kathy Amerman, a photographer, snaps pictures. Nicole Pulvers cries as she hugs Simpson.

Then Simpson walks into his den with the three TV sets on the white multimedia wall. A.C. follows him; Kardashian is by O.J.'s side. Amerman is still shooting as Simpson takes off his coat. Skip Taft arrives. Someone gives O.J. a glass of water.

Then Simpson notices a face on the TV, a live broadcast from the courthouse. Gil Garcetti is holding a press conference.

There, in close-up on the thirty-eight-inch TV, Garcetti gets Simpson's complete attention. The D.A. is saying that his office has no plans to look for other killers. O.J. is the man who murdered Nicole Brown Simpson and Ronald Goldman.

"We stand in front of you," Garcetti says, "with the belief that the evidence was there. This was not, in our opinion, a close case."

"Garcetti!" Simpson shouts. *Fuck you!*"

"In our professional judgment," the D.A. says, "it was overwhelming evidence. We still believe in the evidence in the case."

"He wouldn't even give me that!" O.J. yells. "Why doesn't that guy give me something? Just say he'll look into it?" Simpson points at the screen. "Fuck you!"

Kardashian watches Simpson and Garcetti. The old O.J. is back again. Bob can sympathize with Simpson's anger at the self-righteousness of a corrupt establishment, but he is troubled as well. Nothing in Simpson has changed over the last fifteen months. Bob wonders if O.J. learned anything at all from his ordeal.

Bob's own relationship to Simpson is a bigger problem. Now he knows that for years O.J. lied to him—at least by omission—about his troubled life, his abuse of Nicole. How

872

can there be real friendship if you don't let your friend know who you are? Friendships are almost more about the bad times than the good, Bob knows.

Standing there, watching O.J. shout at the TV set, Bob realizes that if Simpson has withheld and hidden and disguised so much of himself for so many years, he must be hiding still more now. Bob started out believing in O.J.'s innocence. But over the months, he has begun to doubt— quietly at first, then more insistently. In public he has never wavered. He has kept his private thoughts private. Now the jury has spoken, and, as Kardashian has feared for a long time, it has settled nothing. Kardashian knows his doubts will never leave him, his friendship with O.J. will never be the same. He has learned a great deal. He wonders if Simpson has.

Within minutes, O.J. went upstairs to his bedroom. For a moment he was alone. He knelt and prayed. Then he phoned Sydney and Justin. He turned on the TV and watched a replay of the verdict. Then Jason came into the bedroom and hugged his father for the first time in over a year. He had a gift for O.J.: an eight-week-old Great Dane puppy.

Outside, the helicopters hovered as hundreds of reporters and photographers perched on ladders to get a view inside Rockingham. There were dozens of satellite trucks with microwave towers. The mounted police arrived. The press would camp out for a week before the police sent them away.

By one o'clock the house had filled up. Simpson's family arrived from their press conference. Almost every friend and relative of O.J.'s came by to savor the victory. Before long, Gigi discovered there was no food in the house. Jason and a friend went out for health food. Cathy Randa ordered ham and turkey. A guest came with a festive bouquet of balloons. No one had planned for this day.

F. Lee Bailey, Bob Blasier, Gerry Uelmen, Robert Shapiro, Johnnie Cochran, Pat McKenna, Howard Harris, Carl Douglas, and Shawn Chapman visited O.J. in his bedroom, where he stayed for the next seven hours. He telephoned Barry Scheck and Peter Neufeld and thanked them for their work.

O.J.'s mother was helped up the stairs to her son's bedroom, where she sat with him. Marquerite Simpson Thomas joined them. She kissed O.J. and noticed he had some gray hairs. His first, they decided.

Soon the house was uncomfortably hot. O.J. stood out on his balcony, having his picture taken with family and friends. The photographer asked a guest of O.J.'s to move closer to Simpson for a snap. Instead, he moved away. Others quietly avoided being photographed with Simpson.

In the garage, between Simpson's Ferrari and his gym equipment, were some 70,000 letters to him, still unopened. There were boxes containing the hundreds of Bibles he'd received, which O.J. planned to donate to churches.

After dark O.J. came downstairs and posed for a family picture. Johnnie Cochran was singing "Amazing Grace." O.J. joined in.

> *Amazing grace, how sweet the sound*
> *That saved a wretch like me!*
> *I once was lost, but now am found,*
> *Was blind, but now I see . . .*

PART SEVEN

Less Is More

1

THAT SAME MORNING, TUESDAY, OCTOBER 3, MARK
Fuhrman was back in his new home in Sand Pointe, Idaho.
He had slept late instead of making his usual early start on
remodeling the house. He wanted to watch the verdict.

As all the networks go live, Fuhrman turns on his TV in
the family room. His wife, Caroline, walks in and stands at
his side. The jury has come back so quickly that Fuhrman
expects to hear "Guilty."

The verdict registers slowly. "How could they ignore so
much evidence?" Fuhrman finally whispers. He feels that it
must have been decided along racial lines.

His wife looks at him. "They're going to blame all this on
you," she says

Fuhrman doesn't respond. He just stands there. Can't
believe any twelve people can be so dumb. There is nothing
to say, nothing else he can do. He goes back to working on
his house.

Fuhrman couldn't get the sickening images of the crime
scene out of his mind as the weeks passed. Some law
enforcement officers have their private rituals for closing the
book. Ronald Campise, a police photographer who joined
the force at about the time Fuhrman retired, always washes
his hands and the soles of his shoes when he finishes a case.
It washes the horror away.

Daniel Petrocelli, an obscure corporate attorney, stayed
home from work to catch the verdict on TV. He hadn't
followed the trial closely but had watched all the closing

arguments. He had always been a Simpson fan, and followed his broadcasting career. The blood evidence indicated O.J.'s likely guilt, but Petrocelli found it unthinkable that Simpson could have committed the crimes. He was curious to see what would happen.

When the verdict was read Petrocelli had an empty feeling in his stomach.

The defense had done a better job in closing arguments, he knew. Not brilliant, just a better job of organizing their material and presenting their story points. The prosecution had looked weary and disorganized to Petrocelli. They'd never really told their story, he thought, the way stories should be told.

On Thursday, October 5, Petrocelli is on the 405 freeway heading to his office in West Los Angeles when his car phone rings. It is Bob Briskin, a friend and fellow attorney, who tells Dan that his friend, Phyllis Harvey, has attended a luncheon with some wealthy women friends. They are all outraged over Simpson's acquittal and want to help Fred Goldman. Someone has mentioned Dan's name and Phyllis asked Bob to get in touch. "What do you think?" Briskin asks. "Can you help?"

"I'd like to meet Goldman," Petrocelli responds.

On Saturday, October 7, Petrocelli drives to the Goldman home in Agoura, California. He is nervous. Always is when he's meeting someone for the first time. When Goldman opens the door, Petrocelli is struck by his host's suffering. In the first moments, he sees real pain and grief, something he'd never felt watching Goldman on TV. Petrocelli realizes that Fred Goldman has suffered a profound loss.

Tonight there is no talk of a business deal or litigating over lost profits. For the first time in his life he is sitting with clients in mourning—Fred, his wife, Patti, and their daughter, Kim, talking about the murder of a promising young man. The depth of the Goldmans' pain has real meaning for Petrocelli.

By the time Dan leaves Fred Goldman's home, late that

night, he knows if he is asked to take the case he'll accept. For justice to be done, however belatedly, Ron Goldman has to be brought back to life for a jury. Driving home, Petrocelli doesn't think of Simpson, never thinks of the day he might confront him in court, doesn't consider the legal issues. He thinks only of Goldman's pain. He knows he wants the case. He wants his own small share of legal history: Fred Goldman's wrongful death suit against O.J. Simpson.

Within days Fred Goldman called him. Petrocelli met with the executive committee of his firm, Mitchell, Silberberg and Knupp. Money was not the object here. Many of the firm's clients were expressing their own outrage at the verdict. There were institutional reasons for taking the case.

The Ronald Goldman Justice Fund would be set up and administered by the Marciano brothers of Guess Jeans, who were Petrocelli's clients. The Fund would raise enough, they hoped, to cover legal costs. The firm committed the resources to assemble the necessary litigation team. They took the case on a standard one-third contingency fee basis.

A few days later, Ed Medvene, a senior member at Petrocelli's firm, was having breakfast with his son at Junior's on Westwood Blvd. He had just turned sixty-six. Petrocelli was across the room with a client. As Medvene left, Petrocelli came over to him. "I've been asked to get involved in Goldman's civil case against Simpson," Dan said. Medvene considered it a kind of invitation. It was. Ed was the first lawyer Petrocelli asked.

Medvene had a good deal of criminal experience, both in the U.S. Attorney's Office, and in representing death row inmates. Marlon Brando had hired him to defend his son Christian in the wrongful death case brought against him. Though Robert Shapiro had defended Christian in his criminal case, Medvene had never met him.

Medvene always considered himself sympathetic to the accused, but in thinking of Simpson that day after Dan spoke to him, he had a sense that O.J. was guilty. Even though he didn't know the case in detail, something about the blood, the hair and fiber evidence impressed him. Unlike his usual feelings for defendants, Medvene felt no connection to Simpson at all. Maybe it was the way O.J. conducted himself now.

Medvene felt the race issue had been artificially—and unjustifiably—introduced into the criminal case by the Simpson defense. He knew it could ultimately hurt other defendants with legitimate reason to use it.

Peter Gelblum had worked with Petrocelli and Medvene for years. He'd even gone to night school at Southwestern Law while Dan was studying there. Petrocelli was number one in his class and a year later so was Gelblum. During the Simpson trial they joked that Marcia Clark had been about in the middle of Dan's class. Right out of law school Peter joined Mitchell, Silberberg and Knupp and had been there ever since.

When Peter heard that Petrocelli was representing Fred Goldman he phoned him to say he'd like to work on the case. "I've followed the criminal case closely."

Petrocelli said "Great."

To Peter this case was simple compared to some of his anti-trust cases. He'd had researched the workings of entire industries. But jury trials are where the action is for Peter. Simpson's case would have a jury.

John Kelly enjoyed doing the gavel-to-gavel commentary on the Simpson criminal case for New York City's Fox Television. He'd tried lots of felony cases in New York since becoming an attorney in 1981 and enjoyed real trials before real juries much more than the commercial or contractual work he was now doing.

Back during the criminal case, Kelly had received a call from Lou Brown, who said he'd been referred to Kelly. Lou Brown asked if Kelly was familiar with his situation. That was all—nothing about the civil case.

A month later Lou Brown was in New York and the two men met. Lou talked about the Browns' foundation for battered women and its work. Kelly liked the man. He was a very down-to-earth, friendly guy, quiet, articulate, and a real gentleman.

On Thursday, June 8, 1995, Kelly received another call from Lou Brown. Lou wanted to retain Kelly to file a civil action against O.J. Simpson. The statute of limitation would expire in four days.

That Sunday Kelly flew to California. He thought Simpson would be found guilty and there would never be a civil trial. Once a conviction was in, Simpson's case would automatically move to the liability stage. Hardly much of a trial. That's how Kelly saw it.

2

DURING THE SECOND WEEK OF OCTOBER, DAN PETROCELLI turned on his TV and saw Simpson's new attorney, Robert Baker, a defense attorney who handled many medical malpractice cases. He had been recommended to O.J. by Johnnie Cochran. His co-counsels would be his son Phil Baker, Robert Blasier and Dan Leonard, one of F. Lee Bailey's partners.

Baker read a prepared statement and took no questions from the reporters. Petrocelli had never heard of him.

That second week Petrocelli formally took over the case from Robert Tourtelot, Goldman's original attorney, who also represented Mark Fuhrman before the McKinny tapes came to light. Within days Petrocelli refiled Fred Goldman's wrongful death complaint against Simpson and a week later subpoenaed the criminal case evidence and files from the D.A., the L.A.P.D., and the courts. Time was of the essence.

A first-stage war room was set up at Mitchell, Silberberg and Knupp to receive the D.A.'s and police files, the defense discovery, the entire trial transcript. The firm would install the most intricate cross-indexing system available, so that every word in every document could conceivably be referenced.

The problem facing the attorneys was how to present the same case to a jury and walk away with a different verdict. Petrocelli assumed the crimes had been fully investigated. But as he read interviews, police statements, the D.A.'s reports, and met his first witnesses, he realized the full story had never been covered.

Petrocelli knows he is on unfamiliar ground. None of the team has ever tried a wrongful death lawsuit before: in fact, such suits are almost unheard of against people accused of murder.

Deputy D.A. Bill Hodgman, sidelined in the criminal trial, tells Petrocelli that he feels Simpson is obsessed with control. He knows Petrocelli will have to reveal the real man behind the nice-guy persona. Hodgman feels Clark and Darden's case had lacked soul. Their story didn't ring true. But now, Simpson will have to testify in the civil case. He has been acquitted of criminal charges and can no longer hide behind constitutional rights against self-incrimination.

Hodgman came to admire Petrocelli's ability to assemble, coordinate, and synthesize a large body of information. They talked at length about where Hodgman felt the D.A.'s case had fallen short. How to streamline the DNA evidence. How to highlight the domestic violence. More important, how to push the human side. "Tell the Simpson story. Forget about the knives," he told Petrocelli.

Petrocelli felt the D.A.'s case had been spread out among too many lawyers. Every witness should have fit neatly into an overall story. In hindsight Petrocelli saw the mistakes, but he discovered he also had the burden of dealing with lots of things that shouldn't have happened. Carrying the baggage from the criminal trial.

Petrocelli knew he had to know Simpson's whole life before the murders. Everything there was to know about O.J.'s seventeen-year relationship with Nicole.

Peter Gelblum first sees the case as a typical domestic violence homicide, even though Simpson hasn't hit Nicole in the last five years. Domestic violence, he feels, is still the key, even though the criminal jury felt differently.

Petrocelli assigns Gelblum behavioral sciences, all the domestic violence experts. Dan takes motive and opportunity. Medvene will take the police and crime scene experts. Tom Lambert, 50, a senior lawyer with the firm who specialized in intellectual property and securities litigation, will take the sciences and present the blood and DNA. Lambert knows he has a lot to learn.

Dan worried about having too many lawyers spread around the courtroom. Ron Goldman's mother, Sharon Rufo, had filed her own suit against Simpson within a month of the murders and had retained Michael Brewer, who was about to take his first depositions. John Kelly, now working for the Browns, had recruited Michael Piuze, a well-known personal injury attorney.

Petrocelli was certain the court didn't want three new Simpson trials on the same issues. But Fred Goldman wanted his own day in court. Michael Brewer had a problem with his client. Rufo hadn't even seen her son in recent years. Brewer understood that combining his case with Fred Goldman's, who had a better public image, would be an advantage. Brewer agreed to take a back seat to Petrocelli.

During the last week in October, 1995, John Kelly met Dan Petrocelli for the first time. Like Brewer, he wanted the cases consolidated. But Kelly also knew that his co-counsel Piuze and Petrocelli were both first-rank lawyers. Stars. Each would want to be the lead attorney. That could be resolved later. Kelly agreed with Petrocelli that the Brown Foundation would pay the expenses of Kelly's witnesses, including depositions, transcripts, and travel if the court ordered the cases consolidated. The deal was done.

* * *

Before long Ed Medvene's corner office is crowded with defense and prosecution discovery, police and D.A. interviews, trial transcripts and evidence. The black binders are piled so high he can hardly see his view of the Santa Monica Mountains.

Medvene feels that Simpson's guilt is obvious, but the question remains: how to present the evidence and get a liability verdict. Should they use the same witnesses or find new ones?

As Medvene reviews coroner Lakshmanan Sathyavagiswaran's nine days on the witness stand, it is obvious that his past testimony is open to cross examination by O.J.'s civil attorneys and a liability to their side. Why hand Simpson's attorneys all that ammunition? Still, the autopsy evidence has to be presented. But how?

Reading the trial testimony of pathologist Michael Baden, Medvene understands he doesn't have the science background to examine an expert in forensic medicine. At the same time, he keeps coming across a certain Dr. Werner Spitz, a world renowned forensic pathologist constantly quoted and cited in the criminal case. An expert Baden admires. Spitz can examine the same evidence Baden has, Medvene thinks. Time to drop the coroner and find a new pathologist to explore how Nicole Brown Simpson and Ron Goldman died. It is Medvene's first preemptive strike.

By mid-November the entire team was working long hours. Petrocelli was living and breathing the case. Everywhere he went he had a transcript to read. His other clients were on hold, or passed to other lawyers in the firm. Petrocelli was absorbing Simpson's life, trying to be a fly on the wall during O.J.'s every moment.

Every night Petrocelli called Fred Goldman, Patti, or whoever was at home, to review the day's progress. Since Goldman was back at work in sales and marketing, he wasn't available for meetings. Goldman never spoke Simpson's name—he was always "the killer." It was Fred's detachment, his ability to analyze the evidence, no matter how devastating, that impressed Petrocelli the most. No matter how harrowing the details of Ron's death, Fred was able to control himself.

On November 15, Judge Alan Haber consolidated the cases. The next day the court set a trial date of April 2, 1996. Petrocelli did not object. This would allow the plaintiffs to take Simpson's deposition immediately. Moreover, an early trial date was in the firm's interest. The case would be cost effective.

What was clear very early was that Simpson would have to testify if called. But at first the team tried to de-emphasize Simpson. The defense would depend heavily on their client and count on his giving a remarkable performance on the stand. Could the plaintiffs present their case without calling Simpson? What if he became unavailable? The team wanted to try the case without regard to Simpson's star quality and wondered if the blood and DNA evidence alone could convict him.

Lambert wouldn't be involved in the pre-trial discovery. Most of the early depositions were in Petrocelli's area. After reading the trial transcripts, Lambert went on the road to interview the experts who had worked for the prosecution on the criminal case. He traveled from city to city, reading the technical literature, gaining the confidence of Drs. Robin Cotton and Gary Sims. In Los Angeles he consulted with Woody Clarke, Rockne Harmon, Lisa Kahn and Hank Goldberg.

By now, Petrocelli had hired Decision Quest as jury consultants. Lambert wanted to know what potential jurors already knew about the science of DNA and how much information they needed to understand terms like DQ Alpha or RFLP. How much would you have to teach a jury during the trial?

3

On December 14 Petrocelli deposed Paula Barbieri in Los Angeles as Simpson watched attentively. This was the first time Simpson's attorney Robert Baker and his son Philip saw Petrocelli and Company in action. Petrocelli was no less eager to see the Bakers at work. The lawyers already knew that Paula had split with Simpson, but the questions were *when,* and *why.*

Paula was quiet. She looked down most of the time. Simpson hardly spoke to her.

"Did you and Mr. Simpson have a fight or an argument about something on the evening of June 10 or the morning of June 11?" Petrocelli asks her.

"No."

"Did you call Mr. Simpson up and tell him that you wanted to end the relationship?"

"Yes."

"Where did you reach him?"

"I didn't, I left a message."

"Where did you leave that message?" Petrocelli asks.

"I think it was his car phone."

"There is an answering machine on his car phone?"

"Yes," Paula answers in a quiet voice.

"When did you leave that message?"

"Approximately 7 o'clock in the morning," Paula says, just above a whisper.

"On Sunday morning, June 12?"

"Yes, if I recall correctly."

"What was your message?" Petrocelli asks.

"I can't remember exactly, but between work, the kids,

golf, my schedule, it was just too difficult to work things out. Something to that effect.''

Petrocelli knows that Paula broke up with Simpson the day of the murders. But could this have triggered the crimes? Had Simpson picked up her message?

"Did you receive any messages back from him at any time on June 12?'' Petrocelli asks.

"Yes,'' she answers.

"What were the messages that you picked up? What did they say?''

"I can't remember what . . .'' She pauses. "Something about we were talking the night before about filling the house with babies and what was wrong now. Sort of what was wrong now,'' Paula replies.

"Did you understand that Mr. Simpson had already picked up your message that you left on the Bentley phone?''

Philip Baker interrupts, objecting that it calls for speculation.

"You can answer,'' Petrocelli adds.

"Yes, I assumed,'' Paula says.

"In other words, from the content of the messages he left, you understood that *he* had already received your message. Is that right?''

"Yes,'' Paula responds. This is a major point to get on the record. However, Petrocelli knows he still has to prove Simpson had picked up Paula's message.

In the third week of December, John Kelly calls Petrocelli from New York. "I'm having difficulties with Mike,'' he says. He is referring to his associate Michael Piuze. Petrocelli can't wait to find out what is happening. Is the two lead attorney problem fading away? When Dan flies east for the holidays, he and Kelly discuss the idea of Piuze stepping down and Kelly working directly with Petrocelli. Kelly says Piuze is unwilling to defer his fees and invest financially in the case. From Petrocelli's point of view Kelly's position makes sense in light of the courtroom demands Piuze will probably make. Control of the case is now within Petrocelli's grasp. After his meeting with

Kelly, he considers it a fait accompli: he will be lead counsel.

Kelly is realistic about his own role. Petrocelli is already living in Simpson's mind. Nobody on the team knows the O.J. story better than Petrocelli, and that story Petrocelli is sure will be the centerpiece of the trial. Kelly isn't about to give up the spotlight completely, but he knows there would be nothing worse than re-crossing O.J. on the same topics once Petrocelli has finished. Kelly wants something in return for dropping Piuze and letting Petrocelli examine Simpson. "I'll find an area that you won't be covering," he tells Dan. "I want to be sure I'll have some time with Simpson." Petrocelli agrees. John Kelly is now co-counsel in the case he never thought would go to trial. He will share examining the star witness. He will be in front of the TV cameras again. Exactly where he wants to be.

4

In January, after Petrocelli returned to California, he knew the first priority was to take Simpson's deposition. With Paula's sworn statement that she had broken up with Simpson the morning of the murders, Dan had promising territory to explore.

By mid-January Petrocelli had learned enough about the blood and physical evidence that he absolutely believed Simpson was guilty of the crimes. Petrocelli had never taken a deposition before where he was so certain the defendant would lie to him.

Petrocelli intended to treat Simpson's deposition like any

other. Good old-fashioned discovery. He'd been doing that for years. Forget the media furor. Don't even think this deposition would break the case. Just get everything Simpson has in his mind on the record. Nail him down on all the crucial issues. Make sure he can't change his story during trial. Petrocelli's goal was to commit Simpson irrevocably to whatever lies he would tell.

The deposition started on January 22 at Petrocelli's offices and continued over nine non-consecutive days. The court had approved videotaping all depositions; the tapes could be used at trial. The plaintiffs' entire team was present: Petrocelli, Gelblum, Medvene, Kelly, Brewer, and Arthur Groman, a senior partner with the firm. Simpson was represented by Robert Baker, Robert Blasier, and Dan Leonard.

Fred Goldman sits a few seats from his attorney, looking straight at Simpson. Staring across the table as close as he has ever been. There is tension in the room.

Petrocelli feels well prepared to tackle Simpson. He works slowly and meticulously. In the third session, Petrocelli gets to Paula Barbieri's June 12 phone message. Just one item on a lengthy list.

"Now, when did you pick up Miss Barbieri's message left for you at 7:06 A.M., [that] eight-minute message?"

"I don't believe I ever did," Simpson responds.

"Not the whole day?"

"I don't believe so. No," Simpson repeats.

"You never checked your messages that whole day?"

". . . I don't believe I ever checked my message."

Petrocelli confronts Simpson with Paula's deposition.

"Now, when you left that message, you were acknowledging her prior message that she was splitting up with you. Right?" Petrocelli asks.

"No, that's not correct."

"You were at her deposition when I took it. Right?" Petrocelli asks next.

"Yes."

"And you heard her testify that she left you a message early in the morning saying that she was breaking up with you. Right?"

"Yes," Simpson answers again.

"Did you ever pick up that message of hers?"

"I don't believe so," Simpson insists. ". . . I've never heard the message that she said she was splitting up with me, no."

"Never?"

"Never," O.J. repeats.

Simpson has locked himself into a "Never." Dan hadn't expected that. Petrocelli is surprised that Baker is letting his client paint himself into corners. Baker isn't even tying to get Dan off track by interrupting him. Petrocelli expected at least that much from defense counsel.

During a break, Simpson tries to engage Medvene in a conversation. Tries a little small talk. When that doesn't work, he smiles at Ed. Medvene, like the other plaintiffs' attorneys, make it a point not to talk to Simpson, not to look at him, not to be familiar with him in any way. Medvene wants O.J. on a playing field where the other team are not his friends.

Later in the day Petrocelli gets to the cuts on Simpson's fingers.

"And you don't know one way or the other whether you had three or four cuts on your left hand before you went to Chicago. Correct?" Petrocelli begins.

"I didn't see them," O.J. answers.

"Are you saying you did *not* have those cuts on your hand?"

"I'm saying I didn't see any cuts on my hand."

Petrocelli tries a slightly different question. "So you are not saying that you didn't have the cuts on your left hand. Correct?"

"I'm saying I did not see any cuts on my hand."

"You cannot say that you did not have the cuts on your left hand. Correct?" Petrocelli asks.

"I can say I did not see any cuts on my hand," Simpson repeats.

"Did you look closely at your left hand sufficient to know whether or not you would have had such cuts?"

"I looked at my hand to see if there was a cut because I thought I was bleeding, and did not see any cuts."

When the questioning moves to the cuts he got in Chicago, O.J. says he received only one cut on his left hand when he broke a glass in his hotel room. As the day goes on, Simpson becomes so confused about the cuts he asks for a break and leaves the conference room. He tries to make casual conversation with Petrocelli about baseball, one of Dan's favorite sports. Petrocelli can only think, that's O.J. Simpson.

Petrocelli is puzzled at Simpson's lack of a coherent scenario. Simpson has delivered on all the hard questions so far. He has answers for everything, and he's stuck to them doggedly. But when it comes to the cuts on his hands, Simpson has no cogent explanation.

On the fifth day, Petrocelli introduces the Bruno Magli shoes that apparently left bloody prints at the Bundy crime scene.

"There are shoes that you wore prior to Nicole's death that you did not know the name of the manufacturer or the brand name," Petrocelli begins.

"Yes, correct," Simpson says.

"So you would not know whether such shoes . . . were Bruno Magli. Correct?"

"Yes."

"No one but you bought shoes for yourself. Is that what you're saying?"

"Yes."

"Did you ever buy shoes that you knew were Bruno Magli shoes?"

"No."

"How do you know that?"

"Because I know, if Bruno Magli makes shoes that look like the shoes they had in court that's involved in this case, I would have never owned those ugly-ass shoes."

"You thought they were ugly-ass shoes?"

"Yes," Simpson says, smiling.

Petrocelli follows up by asking Simpson "Why were they ugly-ass shoes? What about them was ugly, Mr. Simpson?" O.J. keeps elaborating. Again Dan knows by the time they get to trial Simpson can't budge from his statement. By the end of the deposition, O.J. has committed himself to not owning the shoes.

What really surprised Petrocelli was that Simpson was not a very good witness. Definitely not prepared as well as he could have been. Although he was certainly smart enough to keep track of all his lies. Petrocelli could see Simpson had done a masterful job of learning all the discovery. Plenty of time for that while he sat in jail. But he was overconfident. O.J. probably thought he knew the material better than anyone else. Petrocelli knew he didn't.

He felt sure O.J. was tailoring his story to fit what he thought other witnesses would be saying. That meant there might be room to surprise him.

Mark Fuhrman checked his computer every night to see if Simpson's deposition was on the Internet. When it finally showed up, Fuhrman spent night after night downloading it. He'd sit up past midnight reading, then get up at five A.M. and continue.

"I worked for a company that made knives," Simpson said.

"What is the name of that company?" Petrocelli asked.

"Forschner."

"And what kind of knives does Forschner make?"

". . . Swiss Army knife, basically."

Fuhrman could see Petrocelli was on track. Fuhrman was writing his own book on the case in which he explored the Forschner/O.J. connection.

Reading the depositions days after they were taken, Fuhrman could picture Petrocelli questioning Simpson. He could see Petrocelli asking himself, "How do I connect this to Rockingham?"

"Where are these knives?"

"I have no idea," Simpson responded.

"What was their purpose in your having them?"

"We went camping a lot . . ."

"Where were those [knives] kept?"

"Wherever. Downstairs in drawers. I give them out as gifts, so they're all over the place," O.J. answered.

"Were they in boxes?"

"Most of them, yes."

Later in the day, Petrocelli asked, "You attended a board meeting at Forschner. Right?"

"Yes."

"And you were driven from Connecticut to Long Island?"

"Correct."

"By a limo driver. Right?"

Simpson confirmed it.

"Did you bring back with you any knives?"

"I believe so, yes," was O.J.'s answer.

Those knives, the limo driver's statement that Simpson waved an open knife and made stabbing gestures, and the empty Swiss Army knife box Fuhrman saw in Simpson's house on June 13 was Fuhrman's key to the killings. His partner also knew about the empty knife box. Petrocelli didn't seem to.

Fuhrman sat in front of a bright computer screen day after day, reading and rereading Simpson's deposition. Over a thousand pages when printed. He saw connections and evasions nobody else could spot. He could see Simpson distancing himself from those Swiss army knives, distancing himself from that open knife box Fuhrman had seen.

The words on paper were low key, but to Fuhrman they crackled with drama. There were stretches of Q&A where he could see Petrocelli getting a lock on Simpson's throat and not letting go.

When Petrocelli finished those nine days of deposition, he was struck by the fact Simpson was low on energy. Not at all charismatic. Not even very persuasive. Despite the video camera on him all the time, O.J. didn't make eye contact. He looked down and breathed heavily. Not exactly the knockout performance everyone had expected.

Petrocelli now had the confidence he could beat Simpson on the witness stand. He knew he would never have to read that deposition from cover to cover. It was all inside his head. And there was no rush in deciding whether or not to call Simpson.

893

5

By the end of February, Petrocelli's concern was presenting the story of Simpson's relationship with Nicole so O.J.-as-murderer would make sense to the jury. His single greatest fear was that the jury would overlook the physical evidence because Simpson didn't seem capable of such slaughter. Worse, he seemed to have no motive.

No rational motive, perhaps, but Petrocelli knew Simpson's motivation grew from the dark side of his life. The challenge was to show the jury that Simpson *was* capable of violence, even murder, when things went wrong in his relationships with women. That was clear to him from Simpson's deposition.

On February 28 all the parties attended a status conference with Presiding Judge David Perez. Petrocelli said he was not ready to go in April. He asked for mid-July. Over the objections of the plaintiffs a new trial date of September 9, 1996 was set.

Marcia Clark's barking dog time line had been central to the prosecution's case, but the defense had turned it to their own advantage. Robert Heidstra ended up being Simpson's star witness.

Gelblum, Medvene, Lambert, and Petrocelli meet to discuss what time line should be adopted: Clark's wailing dog at 10:15, or Heidstra's "Hey, hey, hey," at 10:35. Lots of debate on this point.

Everyone kicks the subject around. They want to be sure

nobody gets isolated in his own area of the case and loses the overview.

First Gelblum and Medvene want to keep it vague, not commit to any one position. But Petrocelli believes Heidstra's 10:35 is the time of death. He feels the "Hey, hey, hey" Heidstra had heard was Ron's final outcry and will have more impact on a jury than a wailing dog. He is prepared to take his chances with the truth. So is Fred Goldman.

"If it's the truth, then it should play," Petrocelli says. Goldman emphasizes that everything is based on Heidstra's time estimates and the witness had never looked at his watch. Maybe the murders took five minutes and Simpson had ten minutes after that to get home. Or the victims could have died five minutes earlier, giving Simpson even more time. Finally Peter comes around to Dan's point of view.

But Petrocelli's time line presents problems. Dr. Baden has testified that the deaths took some fifteen minutes, maybe more. Medvene knows he has to challenge Baden's estimate. Ron Goldman's murder had to have happened quickly. Thirty stab wounds in a couple of minutes. If they can't demonstrate that, they might lose the case, no matter how much forensic evidence they have. The team needs their own expert who believes the murders only took one to three minutes.

Medvene makes his phone call to Dr. Spitz, who says he had followed the case closely because he was a good friend of Michael Baden's. Medvene knows that in Spitz they have an expert whose credentials Baden will readily acknowledge. Ed knows if Dr. Spitz will say the murders took place in less than three minutes, he has solved Petrocelli's time line problems.

On March 14, Medvene meets with Dr. Spitz at the Wyndham Hotel, near the Los Angeles International Airport. The two men review the crime scene and autopsy photographs. The doctor feels Goldman's aorta had been cut very early in his struggle with the killer. In his opinion Ron Goldman had suffered massive internal bleeding which would have caused unconsciousness quickly. Spitz feels Goldman might have been out of action in the first minute. Quite different from Baden's protracted struggle. If Spitz is right, Petrocelli's time line and Heidstra's "Hey, hey, hey" gave Simpson ample time to commit the murders and get home.

Then Medvene gets a bonus. "Look at these pictures of Simpson's fingers," Spitz says. "Look at these marks. The cause of these marks: somebody scratching with her nails." It is the first time Ed has heard the possibility that the cuts on Simpson fingers could have been caused by Nicole's fingernails. Spitz has a microscope with him and shows Medvene how he'd reached this conclusion. He has even written a chapter on fingernail scratches in his own book on forensic pathology. Now Medvene has a new, graphic image for the jury. And he knows he can challenge Baden successfully.

Between February and the end of April, the plaintiffs took over two dozen depositions from non-expert witnesses. As they amassed information the role of each attorney became more clearly defined. Each became absorbed in his own minutiae, all details so necessary for the trial. But it was Petrocelli who knew his command of all the information would ultimately give him the expertise and confidence to lead the case.

Fuhrman lost himself in each deposition he read. He followed each motion as it was filed. He looked for clues to what people were thinking or doing. He even considered entering the case. He felt he had information to contribute.

Now, writing his own book, he felt the police and investigative work was seriously flawed. "Shoddy" was the description he often used. Following the civil case meant the subject was foremost in his thoughts every waking moment. He remembered the fact that Vannatter hadn't even bothered to read his crime scene notes for a long period after the murders. The veteran detective had missed the bloody fingerprint on the back gate.* Lange and Vannatter had overlooked other evidence at Rockingham. The open knife box, for one thing. Then they tried to go back on June 28 to

---

*In an interview for this book John Kelly said the fingerprint Fuhrman was referring to was removed when a locksmith, on June 14, 1994, changed the lock on the back gate at the direction of Lou Brown.

cover their tracks. No escaping it: it was poor police work. That's how Fuhrman saw it.

He also remembered that Ron Phillips and Brad Roberts were there for him when the McKinny tapes made headlines. To his friends in the L.A.P.D., it was his work that got Simpson arrested.

Bill Hodgman thought Fuhrman was the most professional detective involved in the case. His crime scene work had been excellent. He considered Fuhrman the only intuitive cop on the scene, always asking questions, probing, taking nothing for granted. Maybe the glove would not have been found that day if it was not for Fuhrman, Hodgman thought.

Of course, Hodgman also knew Fuhrman had not been forthright with the D.A.'s office. If he had been candid about his dark side, they could have quietly introduced his past racist bravado, defused the whole "n-word" issue. Judge Lance Ito wouldn't have allowed Fuhrman's ten-year-old statements to Kathleen Bell and the McKinney tapes to overwhelm the case if the prosecution had presented the matter properly.

6

ON APRIL 15, JOHN KELLY IS IN HIS OFFICE IN NEW YORK when he receives a phone call from Michael Conner, an attorney in Buffalo. Conner says he has important information on the Simpson case.

"I have a client who took a photograph of O.J. Simpson," he says. "And Simpson is wearing Bruno Magli shoes.'' The attorney says the photograph has been independently verified by the Rochester Institute of Technology. Has been sent to London, and a few days ago sold to the *National Enquirer*. Kelly goes from delight to depression. He knows he is walking an emotional tightrope; he likes what he heard. But he hasn't seen the photo. This description is coming from a stranger. Harry Scull is the photographer; he is willing to come forward. Kelly ends the conversation quietly: "I'd like to see the photograph.''

The next day a large color print arrives at Kelly's office. It shows Simpson at a football game on September 26, 1993, almost nine months before the murders. This photograph has not been processed by the L.A.P.D. and therefore Simpson's defense can't label it contaminated or corrupted.

Kelly remembers how he'd badgered the Browns for full-length snapshots of Simpson. He knew that O.J. was photographed so frequently that somewhere there had to be a picture of him in those shoes. Juditha took out every photo from every box and album that anyone in the family had ever taken. No luck. Kelly never expected the picture he wanted would surface in Buffalo.

Kelly immediately walks over to Bruno Magli on Fifth Avenue and shows the salesman the photo. Points out the shoes. ''Absolutely,'' the man says. ''Bruno Magli.''

When Petrocelli heard from Kelly that he had a photograph of Simpson wearing Bruno Maglis and it had been sold to the *National Enquirer,* the tabloid was already being shipped to the supermarkets. Petrocelli's first reaction was to dismiss the whole idea. He'd been inundated from day one with not hundreds but thousands of tips and crazy calls. Minutes later a copy of the *Enquirer* was dropped on his desk. Petrocelli couldn't identify the shoes one way or another. He assumed they weren't Bruno Maglis.

However, Petrocelli had Medvene send the photograph to their shoe expert, Bill Bodziak of the FBI.

The next day Petrocelli heard Medvene's voice on his speaker phone. Can you come up? he began. Bodziak called. Said the shoe in the photo was a Bruno.

"Holy shit!" Dan exclaims. For the first time in the case Petrocelli gets excited.

Ed is happy but not jumping for joy. Take it in stride. See how it plays out, he says. Next step is to make sure the photograph is authentic. Bodziak recommends Jerry Richards, an ex-FBI photo expert, look at the negative and print. Within a few days Richards is on a plane to Buffalo with his own microscope. He soon reports back that the photograph is the real McCoy.

Fred Goldman has his own list of questions. Can we determine the weather conditions on the day of the football game to see if they match the photo? Are there other photographers in the Scull shots? Maybe they have photos of Scull taking that picture or Simpson wearing the shoes? He wants Scull's credentials as an Associated Press photographer confirmed. Fred Goldman is becoming a lawyer. The fifth member of the team.

When Simpson hears about the Scull photo he simply says to his colleagues: "It's a forgery." He stands by his statement: he had never owned those "ugly ass shoes."

On April 29 the defense went to Idaho to depose Mark Fuhrman. Robert Baker, Dan Leonard and Ed Medvene made the trip.

Fuhrman was eager to help. He and Medvene hit it off immediately. But he was under investigation on perjury charges in the criminal case. There were also federal and state investigations in progress. The L.A.P.D. Internal Affairs division was still looking into all his cases. Everyone understood Fuhrman would take the Fifth in his deposition.

"Is it your belief, Detective Fuhrman," Medvene asked, "that even if you did nothing improper in your investigation of the double murder of Nicole Brown and Ronald Goldman, it is still necessary for you, on advice of counsel, to claim the Fifth Amendment?"

"Yes," Fuhrman answered.

For a moment, Simpson's team thought he might be waiving his Fifth Amendment rights and took a break to consult. But when they resumed, Fuhrman took the Fifth on the next question.

A couple of weeks later, however, Fuhrman called Ed Medvene. "Get hold of my partner Brad Roberts," he said. "Roberts knows a lot about this case." Medvene could see that Fuhrman wanted to aid the plaintiffs. Just couldn't do it directly.

By now the plaintiffs were interviewing the police and other prosecution witnesses and getting all the help they needed. Ron Phillips told them about the tape of Lange's conversation with Simpson during the slow-speed Bronco chase. But that tape and many others never showed up in the material from the D.A.'s office. For months Gelblum had been trying to gather everything related to the investigation.

There were hundreds of audiotapes, many of them unmarked. Gelblum started listening to them in every spare moment. No time to wait for the transcriptions. He had twenty minutes every night as he drove home. Another twenty minutes in the morning when he took his fourteen-year-old daughter to school. "Emily, you have to listen to this thing I heard last night," he'd say, "this is amazing."

One morning Peter puts in a tape in the cassette deck and there is Tom Lange talking to Simpson during the Bronco chase.

> LANGE: Man, just throw it out the window [referring to the gun Simpson had to his head].
> SIMPSON: Ah—
> LANGE: And nobody's going to get hurt.
> SIMPSON: I'm the only one that deserves it.
> LANGE: No, you don't deserve that.
> SIMPSON: I'm going to get hurt.
> LANGE: You do not deserve to get hurt.

Simpson is clearly in intense pain. It sounds genuine. Gelblum believes immediately that Simpson is suicidal. And Lange is trying to keep him alive.

Gelblum is almost in tears. This is the guy the defense has been accusing of framing O.J.? Lange, the bad guy? Peter can hear Lange's professionalism. When Simpson trails off, the detective talks about O.J.'s kids, his mother. Anything to bring him back, keep Simpson in touch.

Gelblum remembers the suicide note Kardashian had read to the media. That had never impressed him. It showed no real pain.

Gelblum knows Simpson's statement to Lange is truly extraordinary. Once in his office, he writes a memo to the whole team saying they have to hear it for themselves. Everyone takes it home. The verdict is unanimous: they will use it. Petrocelli feels if Simpson is innocent, he would have been outraged during the Bronco chase; he would have been screaming at Lange to go find the real killer. But he wasn't.

Strategically, there were several ways of handling the tape. Gelblum wanted the tape played in court. He went on a campaign to convince the team that Simpson's intense suicidal pain was undeniable. To Gelblum, Simpson's "I'm the only one who deserves it" was a confession: there was no other explanation for those words. And he felt suicidal intent was inconsistent with innocence.

But would Simpson's pain arouse sympathy, make him an object of pity rather than a brutal murderer? That was a tough judgment call. Petrocelli finally decided he would use only a transcript of the tape.

Tom Lambert couldn't figure out why Simpson's defense team wasn't doing a more thorough investigation. Why they didn't try to discover who'd really committed the murders. Lambert felt the answer to that one might lie in what Simpson's attorneys really thought about their client's guilt or innocence. If he were defending the client, Lambert knew he would be revisiting every single thing, just as they were doing now for Goldman.

7

On July 26, Judge Perez appointed Judge Hiroshi Fujisaki to try the case in Santa Monica. Neither side objected.

Fujisaki's first move was to impose a gag order. None of the attorneys or their witnesses could discuss the case publicly. There would be no radio, no still or television cameras in the courtroom. The media appealed.

To Petrocelli, the gag order is a huge asset to the plaintiffs. He knows keeping the cameras out would confine the case to the issues. Petrocelli has wanted an old-fashioned case and he is now getting it.

Fred Goldman is disappointed with the ruling. He wants the entire country to see all the evidence. He wants the whole world to see O.J. testify.

The defense doesn't like the gag order either. It stops all the media spin that they'd used so effectively in the criminal case. Petrocelli knows the defense welcomes any distraction they can get. Chaos. A media circus.

Simpson's defense had been reviewing all the depositions. Bob Blasier was going to handle the scientific evidence, and Dan Leonard would work under Robert Baker. Blasier and Leonard now lived at Simpson's home to save costs. Of course, it was also convenient for working with O.J. Baker's son, Phil, liked Simpson. The two men started to bond. The defense learned from the expert depositions about Spitz's opinion on the length of the death struggle, and Richards' and Bodziak's confirmation of the Scull photograph. Simpson's many public statements, his book, his video, and his deposition set O.J.'s position in concrete on all the major points. There was little, if any, room for Baker to maneuver. Baker decided not to depose many witnesses. Lange and Vannatter lasted only about two hours. Robert Riske, the first officer at Bundy, wasn't even interviewed.

But when it came to the bottom line for Baker, down to crossing the t's and dotting the i's, the blueprint already existed. It was all there in the criminal case. Nobody wanted to deviate from it. O.J. agreed.

Simultaneously, Simpson was preparing his case to regain custody of his two young children, Sydney and Justin, who were living with the Browns in Dana Point. Had been since the day of his arrest. When John Kelly arrived in Los Angeles he brought with him another New York attorney, Paul Callan, whose first assignment was to go to Orange County and observe what was happening. To Lou and Juditha Brown, custody of the children was every bit as important as the civil case. Indeed, the civil claim was important because of the custody issue. They feared that if Simpson won the civil suit, it would put him in a much better position to take Nicole's children away from them. Keeping Sydney and Justin with them was the Browns' paramount concern.

Simpson was concerned he might lose custody permanently. O.J. kept saying that he didn't like the way the kids were changing under the Browns' guardianship. They were losing one part of their heritage. Custody of his children became his most important concern. By now he had accepted the fact that the majority of America considered him guilty. When all was said and done, the civil case was only about money. He decided to give the lion's share of his time to the custody battle.

In the months preceding the custody trial, Simpson worked hard creating a stable environment for his children. His sister Shirley and her husband moved in to help out. O.J. was a master at creating homelike surroundings. Sydney's and Justin's friends roamed the house and sleep-over parties were common. They played with all their old friends, including Cora Fishman's kids. The hardest part for Simpson was when the children were being interviewed by the court-appointed evaluator at his home. He had to stay out of it. And he knew kids are kids. Never can predict what'll pop out of their mouths. During the visit, Sydney didn't like the brand of pasta that had been ordered and threw a temper tantrum. "Let's cook what we have," Simpson said, "and if you don't like it we'll get another." Sydney wound up loving it.

Of course, O.J. wasn't ignoring financial considerations. Those working on the civil case with O.J. didn't have tunnel vision. They knew their client had a second agenda for the custody case. They fought the battle for the kids to lay a foundation in case Simpson's civil verdict went against him. If Simpson had custody of his children and lost the civil case, he could still win. The Browns were suing, after all, on behalf of Nicole's estate, i.e., Sydney and Justin. O.J.'s plan was to give everything to his kids. Not a dime to anyone else.

Petrocelli thought Simpson had delayed his custody claim to coincide with the civil trial. Simpson could have filed for custody much earlier and had it out of the way by now. Petrocelli knew if a decision came during the civil trial it would affect the case. One way or the other. There was no way to protect a jury from exposure to any custody ruling.

8

ON AUGUST 20, SIMPSON'S CUSTODY TRIAL STARTED IN Department 605 of the Betty Lou Lamoreaux Justice Center in Orange County. Simpson was there with his attorney Bernard Leckie. Marjorie Fuller represented the children, and Natasha Roit and Saul Gelbart were counsel for the Browns.

Domestic violence was the major issue the Browns would use against O.J. This was a father who abused his children's mother. The Browns had witnesses who would say O.J. had slapped and hit Nicole. And Simpson would have to take the stand.

Simpson went on an all-out campaign to neutralize the domestic violence witnesses. A limo driver. Someone walking on the beach. Simpson started to investigate the Browns and presented evidence on how they had profited financially by their daughter's death.

On August 26, the plaintiffs filed a number of motions with Judge Fujisaki. Petrocelli and his associates wanted to bar the defense's claims of evidence planting, and all discussion of Fuhrman's racism including his invoking the Fifth Amendment. The plaintiffs wanted Fuhrman out of the case. In an effort to protect Nicole's reputation, they asked the court to exclude testimony about Faye Resnick's drug use, Simpson's financial assistance to the Brown family, and the sales of Nicole's property to the media by members of the Brown family.

That same day, the defense filed their own motions asking the court to bar introduction of Nicole's journal entries and therapist's notes, evidence of O.J.'s infidelity, Simpson's drug use, and Nicole's statements to the police. They wanted all evidence of domestic discord between Nicole and Simpson barred.

On August 28, Peter Gelblum takes Dr. Lenore Walker's deposition in Los Angeles. Walker is the psychologist who had pioneered the theory of battered woman syndrome and interviewed Simpson several times in January, 1995 for the criminal defense team. Now her findings might be used by the Simpson defense, and Gelblum wants to know what Simpson might have told her.

Gelblum asks Walker if she has any notes with her. Just a standard lawyer's question he'd asked countless times of expert witnesses. Surprisingly, Walker says yes.

"Do I need to produce these?" she asks Dan Leonard, who is representing her.

"Yes," Peter says, answering her question before Leonard can say a word. Not entirely sure he is entitled to the notes, Gelblum bluffs. Leonard says nothing and Walker turns over a five-inch-high stack of handwritten notes along with an unedited typed copy. Simpson's own defense team has never seen the material.

The deposition is continued so Gelblum can review the notes. By evening, Gelblum knows he has a gold mine.

What emerges from the notes is the possibility Simpson has been rehearsing an alibi with Walker.

Petrocelli and Gelblum start piecing Simpson's story together from Walker's notes. The two attorneys are shocked by Walker's dialogue with O.J. It seems she is prompting Simpson to explain his activities innocently. Could she have been helping him with his alibi? She's supposed to be Simpson's domestic violence therapist? Gelblum says to himself.

Walker had written down that O.J. had gone to his Bentley to get his golf shoes. But Dan knows that O.J. had sworn in his deposition that he had gone only as far as the benches outside his front door.

Gelblum looks again at Walker's notes. Are they seeing the evolution of Simpson's lies? They know that by the time Walker interviewed Simpson, the limo driver, Alan Park, has testified at the preliminary hearing and drawn an "X" in the middle of Simpson's driveway, between the Bentley and the front door. At that "X" Park had seen a dark figure walking. Prior to the criminal trial Simpson talked to Walker and had an explanation. He told the doctor that he went out to the Bentley to check his golf shoes and was walking back when Park saw him. Gelblum is sure Simpson never expected Walker's notes to surface.

Then, in the criminal trial, Alan Park had put his "X" closer to the house than to the Bentley. Gelblum can see Simpson saying to himself: "If I have to testify, I don't have to be out that far in the driveway. Okay, I only went out to the benches." Simpson has changed his story from the Bentley to the benches. Petrocelli has no doubt that that is exactly what had happened in Simpson's mind. He consciously figured out his story.

They catch Simpson in another lie. Walker's notes has O.J. telling her that he had picked up Paula's phone message on June 12, that he had called her from outside, at the Bronco, and not from the driveway, as he had said in his deposition. Petrocelli has been right. Simpson is creating another alibi that will be consistent with the body of knowledge existing at the time. But nobody can plan for every contingency. And Petrocelli knows the unexpected is happening.

Gelblum had hit pay dirt with Dr. Walker. The deposition continued in Denver, Colorado, where Walker practices. Now Peter explored her detective work. She discussed a nightclub owner named Brett Cantor who had been stabbed to death, and how the defense was trying to tie it to Ron Goldman. Gelblum found it startling that Walker had investigated the matter on her own. Had Walker fallen under Simpson's spell, become his advocate rather than an impartial professional?

9

ON SEPTEMBER 1, PETROCELLI AND HIS TEAM MOVED FROM their offices in West Los Angeles into the Doubletree Hotel just fifty yards from the Santa Monica courthouse. Within walking distance of the beach. Not that the team expected much time for R & R. Petrocelli vowed he would not return to his old office until the case was over. Distractions were something he didn't need.

Petrocelli's war room was not his first. He'd had one during Armand Hammer's last litigation, but this one was by far his most extensive. Petrocelli considered this case fact-intensive. Very few legal issues of any complexity. The computers in Suite 205 and its adjoining rooms were linked with the mainframe back at his law offices. A complex alarm system was installed with motion detectors that activated automatically when the last authorized person left the suite. Paper shredders were plentiful.

Now Petrocelli's team had to plan their presentation. Use evidence that only points to Simpson's guilt. Stay away from anything that suggests there was another killer. The attorneys agreed a bare bones case would best serve their purposes. No courtroom endurance contests that would exhaust the jury. They believed in the integrity of the evidence. Less had to be more.

Medvene knew the challenge was covering all the essentials without repetitions, contradictions, or inconsistencies. The team decided to have Tom Lange tell the overall story of the police investigation. Lange would neutralize criticism of Vannatter who would only explain his most controversial action, taking Simpson's reference blood sample to Rockingham. Kelly, who would be presenting Vannatter, felt that by focusing on the reference blood issue, the whole police conspiracy theory could be diffused. Kelly knew if one of the lead detectives testified first about everything, the jury would understand why Vannatter was discussing only the blood sample.

Other officers would take the stand to cover specific areas where the defense would blame Fuhrman. Medvene knew they had to keep Fuhrman out of the case as much as possible. The disgraced detective was the cornerstone of the defense's conspiracy theories. Separate him from the critical evidence, and the conspiracy theories become flimsy. If every piece of evidence at Bundy was found by other officers hours before Fuhrman had even arrived, the story could be told without mentioning Fuhrman's name. That was Medvene's plan.

By now Petrocelli knew where all the pieces fit. He could see the big picture.

Paul Callan considered Dan to be within that one percent of lawyers who are born with courtroom smarts. However, Callan saw the team as a collection of enormous egos each wanting to play an important role. Luckily for all of them, Petrocelli was adept at involving everyone in strategy decisions. No one felt slighted or excluded. Petrocelli would wind up with few witnesses.

On September 7, Ed Medvene deposed Dr. Henry Lee in Hartford, Connecticut.

All during Medvene's preparation, he remembered Dr. Lee's words in the criminal case, "Something wrong here."

Now Medvene wonders if Lee, like Mark Fuhrman, can contaminate their case. Fuhrman is safely offstage by now, but Dr. Lee will testify either in person or on videotape. Medvene knows it is imperative to limit Lee's impact on this jury.

He studies Barry Scheck's closing arguments and admires the masterful way Scheck has spread Lee's doubts over the entire scientific case. Lee, a charming man with impeccable police credentials, is able to make complicated science downright entertaining. Medvene has to make sure Baker doesn't use the Scheck/Lee refrain of "Something wrong here" in his closing arguments.

In preparing for Lee's deposition, Medvene has Dick Fox, a criminalist, and Rod Engler, a former homicide policeman, reenact the murder. How long would it take to drop the glasses, the pager, splatter blood in seven different places? They give him a graphic demonstration of Dr. Spitz's proposed time line. After several run-throughs, Medvene feels confident it all could have happened in less than a minute.

First, Medvene questions Lee on the shoe prints at Bundy, the fabric print on Goldman's clothing, and the length of the death struggle. Then he has to get Henry Lee to support the plaintiffs' DNA case. By keeping his questions tightly focused, Medvene limits Lee's answers.

During the three-day deposition Lee admits "Something wrong" did not refer to the hair and fiber evidence. Then Medvene gets the DNA excluded from "Something wrong."

Medvene moves on to the bindles that held the blood swatches. Lee concedes that "Something wrong here" refers only to the wet blood transfers in the bindles.

Finally, Dr. Lee says that he can't state with any scientific certainty that the police had planted evidence or cheated in any way. That is it. Medvene has neutralized the defense's use of Dr. Lee. He is no longer Simpson's advocate. If they put him on, Medvene has excellent ammunition in the videotaped deposition.

Medvene went back to California wondering if he had handled Lee as well as he could have. He wasn't sure until two weeks before the end of the trial, when he learned Dr. Lee wasn't coming to California to testify. When Baker told him that, Medvene finally felt he'd won.

The defense had hired Robert Groden as their photographic expert to establish that the Scull photograph of O.J. in the Bruno Magli shoes was a forgery. The plaintiffs' expert, Jerry Richards, had already been deposed by the defense, and Simpson's team knew what they were up against, a photographic expert with impeccable credentials.

Ed Medvene planned to take Groden's deposition, since he was handling Bodziak, the FBI shoe expert. But at the last minute, Gelblum was assigned to depose Groden. Petrocelli wanted every attorney to have something important to do.

Gelblum considered his knowledge of photography just a little above average . . . nothing close to expertise. His plan was not to cross examine Groden or try to prove he was wrong, but simply determine his opinion. Peter knew that once he had all the facts in hand he would figure out how to knock Groden down.

Gelblum quickly saw that there might be a question as to whether Groden was qualified to testify. He could see Groden was an amateur by Peter's standards. Gelblum knew he'd be relatively easy to beat.

10

On September 16, the civil trial starts in Santa
Monica. The jury will have to decide if O.J. Simpson is
liable for the deaths of Nicole Brown Simpson and Ronald
Goldman. The media is ready for round two in the Simpson
courtroom battles. Across the street from the courthouse
"Camp O.J. by the Sea" is set up. Rows of trailers fill a
parking lot. The street is lined with television satellite
trucks, their dishes pointed into the sky. Members of the
media are already trampling the lawn that fronts the courthouse. Jurors from other cases can no longer sit out front
while they deliberate. The courthouse is now held hostage by
"O.J. II" and the inevitable media circus.

That same day, Judge Fujisaki ruled that the defense team
could not in their opening arguments portray Mark Fuhrman
as a racist who might have framed Simpson.

That evening Fuhrman checked the on-line trial coverage.
He wanted to read the rulings concerning his work, the
glove, and the McKinny tapes. Motion presented, motion
denied. The judge didn't want a shotgun approach from the
defense. If Fuhrman was to be part of this trial, the court
wanted chapter and verse.

As Fuhrman read the decisions on the 39 motions, he saw
the defense was allowed to challenge specific items of
evidence that might have been planted or contaminated, but
the judge would not allow the L.A.P.D. in general to be put
on trial. Although videotapes of Dr. Lee could be introduced, Fujisaki said he would not allow Lee to expound on
police mistakes.

For all practical purposes, Fuhrman was out of the case. The next day his phone started ringing. His friends in law enforcement were touching base. Brad Roberts. Ron Phillips.

Vannatter never called. He'd turned against Fuhrman.

Peter Gelblum never expected Judge Fujisaki to grant the defense's motions to prevent the plaintiffs from presenting psychologists in the trial. Gelblum, who had deposed the domestic violence experts, now found himself with no major witness to present. The court had ruled for the defense: most experts in the area of domestic violence were out. Peter didn't agree with the judge's legal reasoning, but he understood his intent. The ruling said, in effect, that the plaintiffs didn't need the experts; they had other evidence of motive.

Gelblum had always considered the case a typical domestic violence homicide, even though Petrocelli had decided to present Nicole's death as a jealousy/revenge murder. Peter knew domestic violence might not work with the jury; it hadn't in the criminal case. After all, they had no evidence that Simpson had hit Nicole in the last five years before her death. The experts the judge excluded would have explained the sporadic and episodic course lethal domestic violence can take.

Now the plaintiffs had to show a murder of this type didn't require a steadily escalating pattern of violence. The capacity for violence could be established earlier, and then, after a peaceful interlude, could surface again. Suddenly the victim is dead.

Fujisaki's pre-trial rulings made it obvious that this trial would not be a reprise of the criminal case. This judge would be tough at every opportunity. Unlike Judge Ito, Fujisaki was not enamored of the media attention. He had no interest in becoming a celebrity.

In contrast, his courtroom rules were very informal. His work style was almost casual, as if he didn't notice the gallery full of reporters. Cell phones could be used when court was not in session. Since nobody was under arrest, anyone could talk to anyone. In the aftermath of the media appeal, the state's appellate court had revised the gag order and freed the witnesses to speak.

After two days of motions and rulings, jury selection got under way. The jury pool was not overwhelmingly white, as had been expected, but forty percent black. It looked like O.J. had a chance for another "downtown" jury.

On the first day of jury selection, Petrocelli barely moves from the lectern. He's impaneled only two juries. He is following a detailed script.

This is not the attorney Paul Callan has expected to see in court. Petrocelli isn't getting the jurors to open up. His formal style is hurting him. That night the press criticizes him as stiff and wooden.

Medvene and Lambert know there is little margin for error. They've been here before. That night they analyze and over-analyze Petrocelli's performance. The discussion is candid but low key. No angry confrontations. Callan knows that if Petrocelli doesn't revamp his style overnight, they may lose the case.

Next day Petrocelli is walking around the courtroom and engaging the jurors as real people. The plaintiffs start gathering the information that enables them to shape the jury. The team handles jury selection like a capital murder case: individual voir dire, then group voir dire. Every question, every skirmish with the defense, is important. Lambert knows this is the most vital part of the trial. The right jury will be a fair jury.

The team uses a five number rating system. "One" is very favorable to the plaintiffs, "five" very favorable for the defense.

When the jury is finally seated, only one black juror has been impaneled. The plaintiffs wind up with a jury of nine whites, two Asians, and one black. On Lambert's list they were all threes.

During jury selection the plaintiffs subpoena Simpson's phone records from the D.A.'s office. Several bundles, each two feet high, finally arrive in court, and Erin Kenny, the judge's clerk, locks them up. The court order allows the attorneys on both sides to only examine the original records in court and then replace them in the locked cabinet. At lunch, Phil Baker and Melissa Bluestein from the defense leaf through one stack while Gelblum goes through another. These are printouts of raw data that is kept for a few weeks in phone company computers before being routinely purged. Rows and rows of fine print. Records of local phone calls never itemized on a phone bill.

There are calls to Nicole's condo and several other numbers from Simpson's phone. One with a 310, followed by seven digits. Another one marked 061294—June 12, 1994. Then Gelblum finds five calls that he knows aren't on Simpson's phone bill. Calls that have never been entered into evidence in the criminal trial.

Suddenly Gelblum sees a 999 number. What the hell is that? He tabs it. And tabs some other numbers at random just to throw the defense off when they check Peter's stack. Later Peter's office contacts the cellular phone company, to see if they can explain a 999 number.

999 turns out to be O.J. Simpson's message manager number, his cell phone voice mail. Now Gelblum has proof that Simpson has picked up Paula's telephone message on the day of the murders. He had been on the phone for five minutes listening to her message. And at the right time, too: just after the recital, and after Simpson said he had talked to Kato Kaelin. Simpson had known Paula was ending their relationship.

That night Gelblum shows a copy of the documents to Petrocelli. A telephone record buried in the D.A.'s files, lost in the criminal case. Dan is petrified that it isn't really what Peter thinks it is. Gelblum has to explain it to Dan over and over again. "Here's Simpson's phone number," Peter says, "here's the time, the date, and here's the duration of the call." A document Simpson didn't know existed. To Gelblum, a breakthrough. Proof of Simpson's perjury.

"If he denies it," Gelblum adds, "we can bring someone from the telephone company to verify it." The two attorneys sit picturing Simpson denying it. Petrocelli would say:

"You're saying the record is wrong. It shows you picked the message up. But you say the record is wrong."

That week, Paul Callan started preparing the police officers for their court appearances. He'd been Deputy Chief of Homicide in the Brooklyn D.A.'s office and had tried numerous murder cases and his share of wrongful death suits. Callan came from the old school of witness prep: you take the cop back to the scene of the crime and walk him through it.

Callan calls Riske, one of the first witnesses scheduled, and arranges to meet him at Bundy. "I testified in the criminal trial," he tells Callan, "and I was never prepped for my testimony."

"It's been a long time since you testified," Callan says. "You'll be much clearer if we review the crime scene."

Riske is waiting when Callan arrives with transcripts in hand. The empty condo is eerie. Callan asks Riske to show him where the blood trail was, and if the drops were fresh. Nobody in the criminal case had ever asked him that question.

"You know, those drops were absolutely fresh," Riske tells Callan. "I know what fresh blood drops look like." That is all Callan needs to counter the defense theory that the blood had been left there one of the many times Simpson visited his kids.

As they are leaving, the thought strikes Callan: what if Sydney or Justin had woken up that night? Would it have been another Jeffrey McDonald scenario? Would O.J. have killed his own children if they'd caught him in the act?

Callan is certain Simpson left those bodies, left the place wide open, and just took off. Never thought once about his kids.

The next day Paul Callan walks into Medvene's office. Paul is about to prep Tom Lange and wants to chat.

Medvene is sitting behind his desk, looking straight at two life-size dummies. One of Nicole. One of Ron. Trash bags over their heads. Marked with the locations of all their wounds. A strange scene. Spooky. Medvene is literally surrounded by tens of thousands of documents in hundreds of black binders. And now two department store dummies.

Medvene is trying to decide whether to use them in court or not. Paul and Ed kick the subject back and forth that day. The dummies never have their fifteen minutes of fame.

On October 2, Mark Fuhrman pled no contest to one count of perjury, a felony in the state of California. The federal government was finished with their inquiry, but the L.A.P.D. Internal Affairs investigation was still pending.

Fuhrman paid a two hundred dollar fine and was sentenced to three years' probation. He was stripped of his rights to vote, carry a gun, and work as a police officer. "Mark Fuhrman is now a convicted felon and will forever be branded a liar," California Attorney General Dan Lungren added.

It was almost a year to the day after Simpson's acquittal and Fuhrman still hadn't heard the McKinny tapes that had caused all that trouble. He never could, even now, attach any guilt to his involvement with that screenplay.

Fuhrman was still taken aback by the importance everybody had placed on his testimony in the criminal case, still felt embarrassed. Such a harmless project had exploded. He had known McKinny for many years. She knew his sense of humor, knew all the things that never got on the tapes, the raised eyebrow or rolled eyes. What he had done was simple and straightforward, given her police background for a screenplay with a female heroine, a Vietnam vet husband, a single mother, guys who laughed at the way their mustaches were curled and how they wore their glasses. He'd still like to see that film made someday.

11

ON OCTOBER 23, OPENING STATEMENTS ARE PRESENTED. For the first time all the plaintiffs were in court: Lou and Juditha Brown, Fred and Patti Goldman, and Ron's mother, Sharon Rufo.

Kelly has an agreement with Petrocelli that there will be no bickering in the courtroom. Kelly's client's interest outweighs his own desire for equal time. Petrocelli will carry the case before the jury. Kelly and Brewer will have some court time to represent their clients. But the jury will see clearly that Dan Petrocelli is the lead attorney.

Petrocelli stands before the twelve jurors and eight alternates. He just wants to present the facts. He introduces the 10:35 time line time with Heidstra's "Hey, hey, hey."

"Ron Goldman died with his eyes open," Petrocelli tells them. "The last person he saw through his open eyes was the man who ended his young life, the man who now sits in this courtroom, the defendant." Petrocelli's words become images he hopes the jury will never forget.

Petrocelli plans a low-key presentation. No videos or audio tapes. He tells the entire story of the two murders. His indictment of Simpson is factual and concise. None of the rhetorical flourishes that the attorneys had leaned on in the criminal case. His only visual aids are photos of the victims and maps of Simpson's estate and the Brentwood neighborhood. He reads from his notes in a flat monotone. At first the jury pays close attention, but by the end of Petrocelli's three-hour opening, many are fidgeting. Some members of the press consider it a shaky start. They say it lacks emotional impact.

John Kelly then presents the domestic abuse case. He feels the prosecution has never properly presented Nicole's murder as the culmination of years of domestic violence. This isn't a case of some stupid lout who occasionally slapped his wife around until one day he happened to hit her too hard. As far as Kelly is concerned, this has been a calculated murder.

John touches briefly on the overall evidence and reviews the entire history of violence between O.J. and Nicole. Kelly emphasizes that Simpson has demonstrated he is capable of losing control to the point where he could commit murder with his two children right in the house.

Michael Brewer wraps up the plaintiffs' opening by depicting Simpson as a self-centered, ego-driven star obsessed with his public image.

Simpson is outraged at the plaintiffs' attacks on him. He lets Baker know exactly what he wants said in their opening. O.J. wants it *his* way: he is paying the bill after all. His insurance liability policies are now covering much of Baker's fees.

Baker starts his opening argument by noting that Petrocelli's case "didn't pass the smell test." That his theories are preposterous and the seemingly incriminating testimony is just "character assassination."

It isn't long before Baker is doing his own character assassination—this time on Nicole.

"Nicole had been with O.J. since she was 18. . . . At this point in 1992, [she was] kind of exercising her wings. And she had many boyfriends . . . she became pregnant by one of her boyfriends. And she turned to O.J. Simpson for moral support . . . and she decided to terminate what was apparently an unwanted pregnancy.

". . . a fellow named Keith had been seeing Nicole, he was heavily into drugs and Nicole was hanging around with him . . . and he [O.J.] saw Nicole performing oral sex on this Keith. Lights on, draperies open, kids in the house. . . . Nicole was having parties, visiting people who were prostitutes, inviting drug users [into her home] . . .

918

you'll hear the name Heidi Fleiss, you'll hear [about] prostitutes, you'll hear drugs.''

Peter Gelblum never expected Baker to attack Nicole although Simpson had done so freely in his deposition.

Kelly lost respect for Baker when defense counsel even dragged Heidi Fleiss into his opening. Trashing a murder victim so crudely put Baker on the wrong side of a line Kelly felt no attorney should cross.

Baker's presentation that morning was disjointed. Paul Callan was sure he had prepared a well-crafted opening and had to wonder if Simpson's demands had thrown him off stride. In the afternoon, Baker was well organized and his argument effective.

Petrocelli could now see the real Baker at work for the first time. He was impressive, a legal Goliath. But Petrocelli had no doubt he was beatable.

''Mr. Simpson, through his attorneys,'' Baker says, ''offered the services of some forensic scientists, including Michael Baden and Barbara Wolf. It was refused. He offered to take a polygraph. It was refused.''

Petrocelli flashes back to Harvey Levin's report on KCBS early in the year. The TV journalist reported that Simpson might have taken a polygraph and failed it with worse than a minus six. Petrocelli has been told the report is accurate. The score is actually a minus twenty-two. Dan wonders if Baker knows his client has indeed taken a polygraph.

Since Baker has introduced the topic, Petrocelli can now question Simpson about the lie detector test.

Gelblum knows that the polygraph story Levin has reported is detailed in *American Tragedy,* a book about Simpson's criminal defense published just the week before. That night he reads the entire account of the hitherto secret polygraph. It is amazing stuff to Peter. The next day Gelblum moves to have the polygraph technician's records subpoenaed but nothing ever comes of it.

* * *

Petrocelli wonders how Baker will handle the Scull photograph that shows Simpson in those Bruno Magli shoes.

". . . you will hear that a photographer, Harry Scull," Baker says, "out of Buffalo, New York, produced a photograph that was not given to any police department; not given to any prosecutorial agency; it's not even given to Mr. Petrocelli. It's given to the *National Enquirer* for money.

"And you will hear that this photograph is a phony. It isn't real. It was doctored. . . . The photograph is a phony."

Paul Callan can't believe Baker is taking such a hard position on the photograph. He can see an enormous tactical error in the making. At the very least, Callan thinks Baker should say, "Listen carefully to the evidence and we'll prove to you what the plaintiffs are telling you about the shoes and the photograph are not true." Callan knows Baker should have left it open.

Kelly isn't surprised that Baker has taken a strong stand on the Scull photograph. He knows that no expert could ever say, with one hundred percent certainty, that the photograph has not been altered because Scull had lost custody of it. But to go that far still surprises John.

The minute opening arguments were over, Judge Fujisaki had the plaintiffs call their first witness. No time would be wasted in *his* courtroom.

In criminal cases, the prosecution is held to the most rigorous burden of proof under the law. Marcia Clark and her colleagues had had to prove Simpson's guilt beyond a reasonable doubt. In pursuing civil redress for his clients, Petrocelli had the easier job of proving that Simpson was liable for the wrongful deaths of Ron and Nicole by a preponderance of the evidence. Obviously, the more evidence of O.J.'s guilt Petrocelli mustered, the better, but in order to win, he did not have to answer every possible doubt. Weighting the scales on the side of Simpson's guilt would do it.

* * *

920

On Friday, October 25, Petrocelli presented his first witnesses, Karen Crawford followed by Stewart Tanner and Robert Heidstra. Each witness was given just enough time on the stand to tell that part of the story that would benefit the plaintiffs. Heidstra introduced the time line Petrocelli would use. Then it would be Medvene's job to prove that the murders could have taken place quickly, giving Simpson time enough to return home and meet his limo on schedule.

On Monday, October 28, the plaintiffs began their procession of police witnesses. Again less was more. In a single day, Officers Riske, Terrazas, and Rossi all completed their testimony. Riske had been the first officer on the scene. On cross examination he confirmed that he was the one who first said he believed Simpson might have been involved in the murders. The next day Ron Phillips and Donald Thompson continued the story.

Tom Lange, Vannatter's partner, spent the better part of two days on the stand. He spoke in a slow monotone and used impersonal jargon in describing the murder scene. He pinpointed the location of every piece of evidence. Petrocelli placed special emphasis on two key items: the left-hand leather glove and the dark blue knit cap.

During Baker's cross examination, conflicts between Lange's criminal trial testimony, his written reports, and his statements in pre-trial hearings were raised.

Baker tried to get Simpson's interview with Lange and Vannatter the day he returned from Chicago, introduced during cross examination. Fujisaki denied Baker's request. The defense wanted Simpson's demeanor on the record before he took the stand: this "fine" man, devastated by this tragedy, voluntarily sitting down with the police just hours after the murders, shedding whatever light he could on these traumatic and confusing events.

Petrocelli was delighted when the court ruled against Baker. He knew the spin any decent defense attorney would have given that interview.

Lange told the entire story of the police work at Bundy and Rockingham. There was very little ground left for Phil Vannatter to cover.

* * *

Kelly wanted Vannatter on the stand for fifteen minutes at the most. He remembered Judge Ito had ruled that Vannatter's search warrant to enter Rockingham displayed a "reckless disregard for the truth."

Baker had promised the jury, in his opening, that the defense would prove that Vannatter had planted Simpson's blood. The plaintiffs had to address that issue.

Kelly wanted Vannatter to discuss his actions with the reference blood. Nothing more. If the defense was going to undermine the evidence—and they would certainly make the attempt—Kelly had to make sure Vannatter's testimony would defuse the whole police conspiracy theory.

Lange had already outlined the overall investigation from the time the detectives arrived at Bundy, to going over the wall at Rockingham, to interviewing people the next day. It left no room for the defense to attack Vannatter on cross examination.

Under Kelly's examination, Vannatter made it clear he just took Simpson's blood sample to his desk, put it in an envelope, got in his car, and drove over to Rockingham, where a videotape showed him walking into Simpson's house with the envelope.

Petrocelli had expected to take a beating on Vannatter. But the defense couldn't budge the stolid detective from his account: he had planted nothing. Period. Vannatter was sick of the whole thing. He was glad to get out of the courtroom and return to his home in Indiana. At the end of Vannatter's testimony Petrocelli felt they'd done better than expected.

By Monday, November 4, the case was moving at lightning speed. The cross examinations weren't slowing things down at all. Tom Lambert could see immediately that Simpson's defense was not the offense it had been in the criminal trial. Petrocelli's team had taken away their weapons. Greg Matheson and Dennis Fung were next up. Fung was the only liability left in the plaintiffs' case.

In the criminal trial Fung was on the stand for nine days, as Barry Scheck hammered away at his long list of mistakes. Now Fung's direct and cross examination lasted only a day.

12

PETROCELLI IS IN THE COURTROOM EVERY DAY FOR THE first two weeks. He finds himself uncomfortable. He has only a few short direct examinations and knows he should be establishing his relationship with the jury. Petrocelli feels himself fading into the background, and starts to object more. Make it clear to the judge and jury who is really in charge.

Lambert knows the first weeks presenting the police witnesses will be the hardest. Once they get into the forensic science, it will be smooth sailing.

In the evenings, after the plaintiffs' team hold their wrap-up and strategy meeting in Suite 205 at the Doubletree, Petrocelli makes a habit of stopping at the bar on the second floor. The press has made it their hangout. Dan calls it "the gag free zone."

"How'd you think the day went?" Petrocelli asks one writer or another. Petrocelli soon finds out the reporters aren't afraid to speak up.

Kelly, Lambert, and Gelblum also visit the "zone." They socialize with the reporters, too, but it is only general small-talk. Lambert is surprised at how knowledgeable some of the writers are.

Petrocelli, however, is always focused on the case. Offering the writers useful off-the-record stuff. Always looking for feedback on the day's events. He becomes "the star" outside of the courtroom, as well as inside, whether he has witnesses to present or not.

* * *

On Wednesday, November 6, counsel for the plaintiffs called six witnesses. Today they would start to dress Simpson in the clothes the killer wore. Photographers Michael Romano, Mark Krueger, Bill Renken and Kevin Schott laid the foundation for the photographs they had taken of Simpson wearing the Aris Isotoner gloves. Later Richard Rubin would confirm that the gloves in the photos were the same style as those found at the crime scenes.

John Kelly does the direct on Rubin, the former vice president and general manager of Aris Isotoner. Kelly has reviewed Rubin's previous testimony, knows how the witness had enjoyed the limelight. Kelly is sure the defense will either have Simpson try on the gloves for this jury or play the videotape from the criminal trial. Maybe the gloves had shrunk from the blood or moisture. No matter. Kelly has to make sure that this time the gloves fit Simpson.

When Kelly gets Rubin on the stand, he has him put the actual gloves on his hands so he can make a proper comparison with the photographs that have just been introduced.

Kelly has Rubin work each glove carefully onto his hand as he testifies. First the left glove. Kelly wants the lining put properly into all five fingers and the gloves stretched out to their original size. Rubin does just that. He keeps the glove on for at least ten minutes as he manipulates it. Baker doesn't object.

At one point, Kelly pages through his notebook at some length as if he has lost his place. Then he walks over to Medvene at the table. "Ed, I have nothing to say to you. I'm just killing time while Rubin plays with those gloves."

Finally Baker catches on. He objects. The judge shrugs. Says the witness is just examining the gloves. Then Baker tries to call what is happening to the jury's attention. Gets nowhere and gives up. Fifteen, twenty minutes go by. Each finger, the base at the wrist, the top, the width, the whole glove is worked back to its original size, something that has never been done before. Now if anyone with similar hands were to try on the gloves, Kelly is sure they would fit.

Baker, seeing what Kelly has accomplished, will never let Simpson near the gloves. Instead, he will play the video tape from the criminal trial of Simpson unable to fit into the gloves.

At the end of the day, Harry Scull's videotaped testimony was entered. He confirmed that he took the full-length picture of Simpson wearing the Bruno Magli shoes in September, 1993.

Fuhrman logged on to the Internet again. He knew nobody had ever been able to link Simpson to those shoes. Only O.J. could put himself in the shoes, and he had done just that by insisting he'd never owned them. Fuhrman always considered the Bruno Maglis the weakest piece of evidence. In themselves, they're only shoes. Fuhrman knew you have to put the killer in them before they're relevant. Nobody had seen Simpson wearing them. They were never seen in his closet. There was no sales slip to show he'd purchased them.

Fuhrman was convinced that by lying, by insisting he didn't own the shoes, Simpson put his own feet in them on June 12. Because O.J. was guilty, he had to distance himself from all the evidence. There was no other reason to lie.

Lying about the cuts on his fingers, lying about hitting Nicole—O.J. was sealing his fate more firmly with every new lie, Fuhrman thought. If not for the jury, for the rest of the world.

Ed Medvene had been waiting to present Dr. Spitz, the forensic pathologist who would explain the murders of Nicole and Goldman. Medvene would cross examine Dr. Baden when he took the stand for the defense and knew Baden would acknowledge Spitz's reputation as a nationally renowned pathologist.

Medvene's job was to convince the jury that someone could kill two people in that tiny Bundy courtyard in less than three minutes. As the day neared for Dr. Spitz's testimony, Medvene was apprehensive. His prime concern was not to open any topics that Bob Blaiser could attack on cross. And everything Spitz said was open to dispute by Dr. Baden.

On Friday, November 8, Spitz is sworn in. The doctor gives his opinion that Nicole's death was caused by massive loss of blood from a large neck wound. The entire attack would have lasted only about fifteen seconds.

Then Medvene moves to the death of Ron Goldman. Everyone agreed that Goldman had put up a fierce struggle. But for how long?

Spitz says he is sure Goldman became unconscious within a minute. Probably in less than a minute, considering that the aorta had been cut almost in half very early in the struggle. The internal bleeding showed Goldman would have lost his ability to stand, his ability to think, very quickly. He considers Goldman's other injuries superficial.

Spontaneously Medvene asks Dr. Spitz just to sit there and measure off a minute by the clock. Medvene is sure Blaiser will object. Or the judge will interrupt. Nobody says a word. The entire courtroom sits in silence for a full minute. It is a long, powerful, sixty seconds. It makes the point that Ron Goldman could have been killed in a minute.

Doug Deedrick, an FBI Special Agent, would testify on the hair and fiber evidence. Medvene had prepared by tracing each item to its origin.

Perhaps the most damning evidence was the rarity of the Bronco carpet fibers. The prosecution could not introduce this information in the criminal trial because of a discovery rules violation. Medvene had gone to Pennsylvania to depose the person who had manufactured the unique fiber. Then he traced the fiber as it had become carpet, and the carpet to the car, then the car to the Department of Motor Vehicles. He learned how auto industry computers work and found out where individual cars are registered. He had traced an unusual synthetic fiber all the way to a small group of Broncos with that carpet that were distributed in California. Every piece of evidence Deedrick discussed, Medvene had investigated in similar depth.

On Tuesday, November 12, Special Agent Deedrick testified that the hair found on Ron Goldman's shirt had the same microscopic characteristics found in Simpson's reference hair sample. He said that the blue/black cotton fibers on Goldman's shirt matched fibers found on O.J.'s socks. And he confirmed that fibers from Simpson's Bronco matched fibers found on the glove discovered at Simpson's house.

Medvene had handled Deedrick so well that the defense accomplished nothing in their cross.

13

THAT SAME DAY SIMPSON STARTED HIS TESTIMONY IN THE custody case before Judge Nancy Wieben Stock. There was no jury; the judge would make a ruling when all the testimony had been heard.

Simpson is the first witness called in the case. Indeed, he is the case. His behavior, his history, and his attitude is the central issue. Natasha Roit, who represents the Browns, wants to get Simpson's denials of domestic violence on the record and then impeach him. And along the way, get him to lose his temper. Show the judge that when he's embarrassed, or crossed, or pressured, he's a violent man.

The key to Roit's case is the 1989 New Year's Eve domestic violence incident. Simpson says that in the immediate aftermath, Nicole was just sitting around smoking a cigarette.

"Did you see any injuries?" Roit asks.

"No," Simpson answers.

"Was she calm?"

"Yes."

"And at what point did she calm down?" Roit asks.

Simpson is vague. Roit persists.

"After she stopped shivering and screaming," Roit inquires, "as the police officers described her?"

During Simpson's three days on the stand, Roit is deliberately provocative. "Is it true you offered Nicole five thousand dollars to have sex with you?"

Roit knows that her question is especially insulting to a man like Simpson. Women chased him. So he sees it. But Roit, unmoved by the great O.J., has the temerity to suggest otherwise.

"How dare you ask me something like that?" Simpson bellows.

There is silence in the courtroom. Roit lets the silence play.

"Are you angry now, Mr. Simpson?"

"Yes, I am."

By the end of Simpson's testimony, Roit knows that if anyone was inclined to be won over by Simpson, he has succeeded in presenting himself as regretful about domestic abuse. If you want to believe him, Simpson has given you the wherewithal. The man has an answer for everything.

John Kelly is surprised Simpson maintained such a hardline position. He expected O.J. to give a little ground, at least offer something to explain the photos of a battered Nicole. Simpson had insisted in his deposition he'd never hit her. It is obvious O.J. is going to stick to his story. All those bumps, bruises, contusions, and cuts on Nicole's face? Simpson just doesn't know how they'd happened. It doesn't seem to shock the Browns. They have heard it before.

On November 14, Dr. Robin Cotton took the stand. She was Tom Lambert's lead-off witness. Cotton had wanted to give the jury a full blown DNA lesson, but Lambert had talked her out of it. Now he was able to condense Cotton's six days of testimony in the criminal case to just slightly over a day. No long lectures.

Lambert prepared Cotton for Blasier's cross examination. Instead of just answering with a yes, he suggested she say:

"Yes, but I didn't see any evidence of contamination."
Cotton became more combative.

On the stand Dr. Cotton reviewed all her test results. It was Simpson's blood that showed up in so many places. On cross examination she had to admit that her 1 in 170 million number was based on data from only 200 individuals and there were only two blacks among that 200.

Another important point was the question of Nicole's and Ron's reference blood sample that the defense said was used in planting evidence on the socks found in O.J.'s bedroom. These reference samples had also been in Vannatter's possession.

Lambert's questioning revealed that when Cotton reviewed the DNA strips of Nicole's and Ron's reference blood, she discovered that the blood contained far less DNA than the blood found on Simpson's socks. This important fact had never surfaced in the criminal case.

That same day Gary Sims, the DOJ's criminalist, started his testimony on the DQ Alpha DNA tests. His whole manner said "responsible scientist." Lambert knew Sims would exude credibility just by sitting in the witness chair.

Sims said the match to Nicole's blood on Simpson's socks was very significant, 1 in 7.7 billion and 1 in 41 billion. And it was 1 in 57 billion that the blood on the back gate came from someone other than Simpson.

Bob Blasier used Sims' cross examination to undermine Dr. Cotton. He cast doubt on Cotton's conclusion that DNA testing ruled out the possibility that Nicole's reference blood was planted on Simpson's socks. Sims became a defense witness when he said that different blood from the same test tube could show different quantities of DNA at different times.

The question of evidence planting was still open.

John Kelly and Paul Callan had been having strategic disagreements for weeks. They were miles apart on the role Callan should play in questioning witnesses. The bottom line for Callan was that Kelly had brought him in. Even though he had more trial experience than Kelly, his role in the trial was Kelly's call. Callan didn't like being treated like a subordinate. He hadn't signed on to be a bench-warmer in court. Before the Thanksgiving break he would leave.

On Tuesday, November 19, Kato Kaelin took the stand. The media was out in full cry. At his computer in Idaho, Fuhrman read every word of his testimony. Kato had been the first witness Fuhrman had interviewed in the early morning hours of June 13. Fuhrman saw his story had changed in significant details. Now Kato described the famous "three thumps" as someone falling back against the wall, something he'd never said during the criminal case.

Much more important was Kaelin's statement that Simpson had taken him aside the day after the murders and said, "You saw me go into the house," referring to when they'd returned from McDonald's the previous night. That created the distinct impression that Simpson had been trying to establish an alibi for the time of the murders.

Simpson is rarely in court these days. He is immersed in the custody battle in Orange County. But when he does attend, he is working the room, turning his charm on the reporters. Simpson knows the media wants his every word. He starts inviting selected reporters to his home for off-the-record conversations that go right to the edge of the gag order.

Petrocelli hangs out at the Doubletree bar more and more. He has to know how each of his witnesses are coming across. The "zone" is the place for straight answers. He works seven days a week, rarely goes home before 10 P.M. and always returns at 6:30 A.M. when the café opens.

Petrocelli is very sensitive to ongoing press coverage. If he reads something inaccurate, he calls the reporter. On one occasion he even called an editor at the *Los Angeles Times* to complain about a story. He thinks the media is exaggerating the defense gains, considers the reporting unbalanced. Petrocelli is constantly annoyed that Baker's argumentative questions are reported as if they have evidentiary significance. He wants any mistakes corrected.

* * *

Petrocelli and his colleagues finished with their time line by putting Allan Park, the limousine driver who'd taken Simpson to the airport, on the stand. This time he placed the ''X'' where he'd seen Simpson out in the driveway—further away from the house and closer to the Bentley.

One more of the little things that Petrocelli was looking for. All the facts that would impeach Simpson.

14

PETROCELLI FELT THE TIME WAS RIGHT TO CALL SIMPSON AS a witness. He was the key to winning the case. Everyone knew it, the defense, the plaintiffs, the judge, and the media. Petrocelli knew he'd have to put Simpson on the ropes from the first minute.

The timing of Simpson's appearance had been a big source of debate since jury selection. Paul Callan wanted to go for Simpson's throat, destroy his credibility immediately, then handle the details later. Medvene and Brewer sided with the conventional wisdom. Put Simpson on at the beginning. Nail him with all his prior statements. If he crumbles, the case becomes very easy. If he manages to be charismatic and compelling in spite of everything, at least he's out of the way, long forgotten before the evidence is presented to the jury.

But then there was another way to view the second possibility: if Simpson's on first and wins, the jury may discount all the physical evidence that follows.

Petrocelli knew that examining Simpson toward the end was the high-risk approach. He had to break him, show the jury he was lying, that he was a vicious killer. If Simpson connected with the jury, if he sold them the charming, engaging O.J. rather than the real man Dan knew was underneath, Petrocelli's presentation of the evidence would be undermined. Maybe destroyed altogether. The defense was counting on it playing out that way.

The physical evidence against Simpson was so compelling that Paul Callan knew if Petrocelli could destroy Simpson on the stand—if he was tough enough to do the job—Petrocelli's plan would work.

The plaintiffs wanted to get all the facts about the murder night on the record before Simpson was sworn in. That was now completed. Then get him on the stand and impeach him on all those facts. Then move along—get him committed on all the other issues: domestic violence, his life with Nicole, everything. When that's done, put on all his close friends like Al Cowlings and Paula Barbieri. Get their stories on the record and that will impeach him all over again. Impeach him before his performance on the stand. Impeach him again after.

Dan Leonard's job was to prepare O.J. to testify. F. Lee Bailey had always wanted to see Simpson on the stand. Now it was finally happening. But Simpson's mind was still on the custody case. He looked at his testimony in the civil case as merely a replay. Anticlimactic. Every day he waited for the custody ruling. Leonard could never get his full attention.

Just days before Simpson was to take the stand, a friend looked him in the eye and told him straight out, "It's not going to be good." Knew he wasn't getting through. Simpson was set in concrete on how to handle Petrocelli. Just as stubborn about that as he was on his definition of hitting Nicole. Hitting someone meant punching them. No room for discussion. No shades of meaning. "If I was to punch her," he said, "she wouldn't be able to get up. She'd be dead. And if I kicked her, she wouldn't have three ribs. So I didn't hit or kick her."

Simpson had been fixed on his answers since the first days after his arrest. When Simpson took a stand on Planet O.J.,

Population One, there was no talking to him. But his friend felt he had to try. Gave it his best shot. Hopeless. Just couldn't make Simpson see that he wasn't ready for the toughest questions of his life.

The sudden appearance of the Scull photograph wreaked havoc on the confidence of some of the defense attorneys. Their spirit was broken. Baker was having his problems. Phil, his son, stayed close to Simpson. He was like a college kid volunteering for his first political campaign. Idolizing the candidate.

The defense's only hope was Simpson. He had to pull it out. He had to get on that witness stand and make it happen. Robert Baker went on *Larry King Live* and said Simpson would do just that. Count on it.

Fred Goldman is scared that Simpson's charisma will carry the day. He just might win. He's always been worried about that. On the one hand, he has always wanted "the killer" on the stand. On the spot. Wanted Petrocelli in his face. Aggressive. He's been waiting for two and a half years for someone to confront Simpson.

Then Goldman starts pumping Petrocelli up. Pumping himself up at the same time.

"Yeah, go get the son-of-a-bitch," Goldman says. "You can do it. I know you can." He is Petrocelli's corner man.

Late in the evening of Thursday, November 21, Goldman calls Petrocelli at the hotel. "I know you're going to get him," he says again. "Go after the guy." Fred wants Petrocelli to know he isn't worried. He has total confidence in him. Then Patti gets on the phone, Kim as well. When the Goldman family hangs up, Petrocelli feels his corner man has given him the word.

On Friday, November 22, the lawn outside the courthouse is a mess. It has been raining off and on for days. Now the crush of reporters and technicians mixed with the surging throngs of hecklers have churned the area into a sea of mud. Barricades are up to protect Simpson, his attorneys, and the plaintiffs from the media crush. Helicopters are already hovering at Simpson's home ready to follow him to court. The courthouse itself is under siege. All the networks are ready to break into their regular programming when Simpson steps from his black Suburban. Two hundred and fifty spectators have lined up to get one of the sixteen public seats. Many have been there since 4 A.M.

Cries of "Murderer! Murderer" compete with "Right on, O.J." as Simpson leaves his car and enters the courthouse.

"We love you, Fred!" greets Goldman as all the plaintiffs walk those fifty yards from the Doubletree Hotel to the courthouse. And Larry Green, a persistent Simpson gadfly, well known to the principals by now, brings along a pair of Bruno Magli shoes.

The Browns and Nicole's sister Denise sit in the second row. Fred Goldman is inside the rail with his attorneys while Ron's stepmother, Patti, and his sister, Kim, sit in the first row. Sharon Rufo, Ron's mother, is in the third row.

On Simpson's side of the courtroom, O.J.'s sister, Shirley, her husband, Bennie, and their daughter, Teri, are in the first row.

Before the jury enters, Robert Blasier makes a motion on behalf of the defense to preclude the plaintiffs from using the contents of the book *American Tragedy* in the cross examination of Simpson. The defense is trying to make a preemptive strike. Simpson has been advised that the book contains information damaging to his case.

Fujisaki rejects the motion almost out of hand, telling Blasier, among other things, that he is too late.

"There was ample time to exercise that privilege," the judge says, "at the time the book was published. You should have filed a motion at that time." Blasier continues to argue. Fujisaki points out that Simpson has not taken legal steps to suppress its publication. He repeats his denial and calls for the jury.

Lambert, wanting Simpson to realize they have read the book and might question him on it, places a copy of *American Tragedy* on the plaintiffs' table, on its end, so that

Simpson and his attorneys can see all the Post-It notes protruding. Baker walks over and lays the book face down.

As Simpson walks to the witness stand he does not glance at anyone. He sits staring straight ahead. He is ready.

What Petrocelli fears at that moment is that Simpson on the stand might be a different person from the man he'd deposed months before. Would he be more energetic today? More charming? How would he play to the jury? O.J., after all, is a performer. Simpson might have seen the deposition as a kind of rehearsal, something he could phone in. But this is it. Showtime. Would this crucial audience of jurors bring all the old charisma back to life?

That is Petrocelli's biggest fear. Simpson is only four feet from juror number one. This larger-than-life witness is so close to the jury they can reach out and touch him.

Petrocelli's examination is a pure search for the truth. Nothing less. And O.J.'s answers, truthful or not, will still make the truth plain for all to see. Or so he hopes.

Petrocelli starts from the beginning of O.J.'s relationship with Nicole. He plans to cover all their years together right up to the murders by day's end. He wants the whole O.J.-Nicole story to emerge through Simpson's own words.

Simpson has to be kept on a short leash. Petrocelli knows he can't let him pontificate, or turn on the charm. The mystique has to be broken from the beginning.

Petrocelli works from a one-hundred-and-five-page outline. He has marked in a number of places where he wants photographs to appear on the large TV placed just beside the witness stand. The jury can see the witness and the screen simultaneously. Petrocelli plans to use the juxtaposition of the two images to maximum effect.

Ten minutes into the story of Simpson's life with Nicole, Petrocelli reaches the 1989 domestic violence incident. The photo of Nicole's battered face with its welts, bruises and cut lip now appears on the TV.

"And how many times, Mr. Simpson, in the course of these physical altercations did you hit Nicole?"

"Never."

"How many times did you strike Nicole?"

"Never."

"How many times did you slap Nicole?"

"Never."

Over and over again, as Nicole's bruised and cut face stares right at the jurors, Simpson denies everything. Petrocelli feels Simpson's credibility disintegrate.

"How many times did you kick her?"

"Never."

"How many times did you beat her, sir?"

"Never."

"And if Nicole said [in her diary that] you hit her, she would be lying; is that true?" Simpson is cornered. He can call this beautiful murdered woman a liar, or admit he is lying. He calls her a liar.

In the first ten minutes, Petrocelli sees he has Simpson on the ropes. With any luck, it will all be downhill from here.

Gelblum and Medvene are watching the jury closely. At the break they give Petrocelli their verdict: Simpson isn't connecting. Then and only then does Petrocelli dare to look at the jury. There are no nods, no signs of agreement with anything Simpson is saying.

Later in the day, Petrocelli moves to the night of the murders, and Simpson starts fumbling for words.

"This wasn't—it wasn't—I didn't have a date with Kato; I was going to get a burger," he says.

"I didn't ask you if you had a date."

"I didn't have a date with Kate," Simpson replies.

No one in the courtroom even smiles.

"You think this is funny?" Petrocelli asks.

"No. They laughed. Not me."

Petrocelli isn't going to drop it. "Do you think this is to make jokes?" he continues.

"No, I don't think any of this is funny. I wish I was anywhere but here."

Petrocelli sees the jury is getting the message. Simpson is coming across as a jealous and abusive husband.

Petrocelli points out that Simpson's rage and frustration

increased when Barbieri broke off their relationship in a telephone message early on the morning of June 12. Petrocelli asks Simpson if he'd picked up Barbieri's message.

"No, I never picked up a message," Simpson responds.

A minute later Petrocelli quotes the phone company records.

"Does that help you remember that at 6:56 from your home phone number, 476-4619, you called and picked up a five-minute message?"

"No," O.J. insists. "I didn't pick up any message."

"The records, then, are incorrect?" Petrocelli asks.

"I don't know about the records."

Paul Callan is amazed at how Petrocelli keeps producing a steady stream of the most minute details about Simpson. With each new bit of data, Simpson gives Petrocelli a sharp look as if to say, "How did you know *that?*" Callan can see Simpson's awe growing as his denials are neutralized. He is forced to be a person. The O.J. persona is gone. The case has turned a corner.

As the day wears on, Simpson starts to take longer pauses during his answers. His brow wrinkles frequently. At five P.M. Petrocelli goes for his weekend headline.

"And you confronted Nicole Brown Simpson and you killed her, didn't you?" Dan asks.

Simpson turns in his seat in a feigned gesture of looking at the jury.

"That's absolutely not true."

"And you killed Ronald Goldman, sir, did you or did you not?"

"That's absolutely not true."

Petrocelli knows Simpson's answers are thoroughly rehearsed. Insincere.

Medvene thinks Simpson is handling the final questions badly. Much better if he would say, "I didn't like Nicole's lifestyle. I was angry because of everything I had done for her and her parents. But God knows, I didn't kill her." Instead, as Medvene sees it, Simpson has said to the jury: "I'm in control here. I'm macho man."

* * *

937

Petrocelli, and his last question, was the lead story on all the evening news programs. One journalist on MSNBC repeated what everyone had been saying at day's end: "I think Simpson came off cocky. He came off with no credibility. He just wasn't believable."

Despite the great headlines, Petrocelli knew he had work to do. He wanted to rewrite Monday's outline. He hadn't covered the murders yet. Simpson's alibi was still a long way off.

That night he and Gelblum sat in the war room cranking out a new outline, Peter at the computer and Dan pacing. They debated constantly, tore apart every approach. Gelblum could see Dan working and reworking every possible implication of each and every question he might ask. They worked late Friday night and all day Saturday. Dan still wasn't happy. Finally on Sunday it started to come together.

On Monday, November 25, Petrocelli begins by revisiting the cell phone message that Simpson has denied picking up. Judge Fujisaki might stop him from reviewing the same topic, but Petrocelli knows it's worth a try.

". . . you checked your messages a second time from your house, by calling your message manager. True or untrue?" Petrocelli asks.

"I never picked up a message from Paula that night. No."

After confronting Simpson with Lenore Walker's notes on Paula's message, Petrocelli goes back to the telephone records. "And you see Exhibit 434 shows that you called your message manager at 6:56 for five minutes to pick up a message. Do you see that, sir, on your cell phone record?"

"I see—I don't see where it says pick up message. I do see it's message manager," O.J. responds.

"You do see '6:56, message manager,' true?"

"Yes."

"And you also see it again [at] 8:55, 'message manager,' true?"

"Yes." Simpson agrees.

Petrocelli continues through the time segments. Then he quotes Simpson's police interview to show where he has lied to the cops. On every detail Petrocelli demonstrates that Simpson has lied. His new outline is working.

Simpson is being impeached by his own phone calls.

After the deposition, Simpson must have expected tough questions on domestic abuse and Paula's phone message. But that afternoon, Petrocelli hits him with the unexpected. He begins with Simpson's thoughts after the murders, and Simpson responds by saying he'd made an offer to the D.A. to take a polygraph test. Petrocelli jumps at the opportunity.

"And you did take the test, and you failed it, didn't you?"

Baker objects. But Simpson answers before the judge can rule.

"That's not correct."

"You failed it, true?" Petrocelli snaps.

"No . . ."

Baker objects again. Again Simpson speaks before the judge responds. "That's not correct," he finishes.

"You got a minus 22?"

Baker asks to approach the bench. "This is an outrage," he begins. The judge asks the jury to step outside.

At the sidebar, Petrocelli points out that Simpson himself had just introduced the topic.

"That's exactly what Mr. Baker argued to the jury in his opening statement," Petrocelli goes on. ". . . [Baker] has absolutely opened the door on that issue, and I'm entitled to follow up, to demonstrate not only did he take it, but he failed it, Your Honor."

Baker angrily denies Simpson has ever taken or failed a lie detector test. He says Petrocelli's information is absolutely false. The two attorneys argue back and forth about the source of the information, the book *American Tragedy,* which has been on sale for a month. The conversation becomes so heated that Fujisaki warns them to lower their voices.

The judge notes once again that Simpson has never taken legal action to enjoin publication. Therefore, he will allow Petrocelli to question Simpson on the polygraph.

When court resumes, Simpson admits that before he made

the offer to the D.A.'s office, he did, in fact, visit Ed Gelb's office. He says, not to take a test, but to see how it worked. Simpson says Gelb's assistant gave him a demonstration.

Nice try, Petrocelli thinks. No matter what O.J. calls it, he has been hooked up to the machine and has answered questions. Petrocelli gets straight to the point.

". . . at the end of that process, you scored a minus 22, true?"

"I don't know what the score was."

"And you understand that was a polygraph test, right?"

"I understood that once I finished," Simpson says. "And I understood it, that I was willing to do one for the police."

Simpson's admission and the reported score echo throughout the courtroom and down the corridors of the courthouse. Polygraph results are not admissible in California and in many other states. Courts generally consider them unreliable.

Baker is certain Fujisaki has erred in allowing Petrocelli to pursue the subject. It will be a major point in any future appeal. But that is cold comfort now when Simpson's minus 22 is out there for all the world—and every juror—to ponder.

Petrocelli feels it is imperative to establish Simpson's link with the clothes he wore when he killed Nicole and Ron. Put him in those shoes: put the gloves on his hands; put him in his sweat suit: put the hat on his head. Petrocelli wants a full-length portrait of a killer before the jury.

Late in the day Petrocelli gets to the Scull photograph of O.J. wearing the Bruno Magli shoes.

"Now, after [your] deposition testimony," Petrocelli begins, "this picture of you appeared in the *National Enquirer,* right?"

"Yes."

The photo appears beside Simpson on the TV.

"Now, Mr. Simpson, you are wearing Bruno Magli shoes, size 12, in that photograph?"

"The photograph depicts that, but I don't—I wouldn't—wasn't wearing Bruno Magli shoes."

Simpson continues to deny ever owning or wearing those shoes.

"What you're saying to the jury is that picture is a fraud?"

"I believe so. Yes."

"What do you mean, you believe so? Is it, or is it not?"

"I would say it is."

"State your opinion. Is it, or is it not a fraud?"

"My opinion is that it is a fraud."

Medvene could see Simpson was calling all the shots on his defense. "I'm doing this my way," Medvene could almost hear him thinking, "I'm putting my head down and I'm going through the wall." He left his attorneys no room at all—no room to maneuver, no room for strategy, no room to be good lawyers. Medvene felt sorry for Baker.

When Petrocelli was finished, he was sure Simpson had lost the will to fight. He knew the truth had connected with the jury. Simpson hadn't.

Then Kelly and Brewer took their turns examining O.J. When they were done, Baker approached Petrocelli in the hallway. "In light of that," he said quietly, "I don't have to do my witness now. I don't have to question him." Petrocelli could see Baker's statement was born of desperation. He hadn't been at all prepared for the debacle on the witness stand. Petrocelli saw Baker's heart was no longer in it. His spirit was broken. He had gambled his whole case on Simpson. And he had lost.

Simpson struck Bill Hodgman as a supreme narcissist, someone who, no matter what he does, can always justify his behavior. He can do no wrong. Nothing is ever his fault. The people around him may abuse his generosity, but he himself is flawless.

After Hodgman read about Simpson's testimony, he knew O.J. wasn't delusional. He knew he'd committed the murders but felt entirely justified in doing so. Nicole had victimized him; she had to go: it was a kind of self-defense. Ron just got in the way—that was self-defense too.

15

DURING THE THANKSGIVING BREAK, KELLY contem-
plated all the media attention Petrocelli was getting as the
lead attorney. He could see his work with Simpson drew
little notice. Petrocelli had the spotlight while he was barely
onstage. If Kelly had known what an event Simpson's
testimony would become, he'd never have agreed to let
Petrocelli take the lead in handling Simpson.

After Thanksgiving, Petrocelli moves into part two of his
plan to impeach Simpson. Call Simpson's closest friends
before the defense can use them. Let them show the jury
more of O.J.'s lies.

John Kelly, who will examine Al Cowlings, considers
A.C. a decent man. His deposition had been taken very early
in the year and Simpson knew everything A.C. had said.

A week before Cowlings is scheduled to take the stand,
Kelly is crossing Third Street in a downpour, heading for
Shutters Hotel, where he is staying. Suddenly Kelly hears a
horn blasting and someone yelling at him. Cowlings has
stopped at a red light. Kelly runs over and shakes hands.

"I'll see you soon," Kelly says to him, laughing.

"Oh, fuck, you don't need me," Cowlings replies. He is
laughing, too. A.C. rolls his eyes. Kelly is certain he'll be a
truthful witness.

On December 3, Cowlings is sworn in. He tells Kelly
about the secret entrances that let Simpson come and go
from his estate unobtrusively. The out-of-the-way path was
nowhere near the front gates. The defense never challenges
A.C.'s statement.

Then Kelly asks about O.J. hitting Nicole. A.C. confirms that Nicole told him O.J. had struck her in 1989. Simpson has denied all of it just days before on this same witness stand. The jury sees that Cowlings is unable to repeat the lie Simpson is telling. Kelly understands, when forced to make a choice, Cowlings obviously loves Nicole more than he loves O.J.

That night Kelly and Petrocelli show up at the "zone." Kelly is all over everyone, pointing out how well he'd done with Cowlings. Tonight he wants to be the star.

Petrocelli no longer asks anyone's opinion. He is pointing out how well they are doing. If a reporter doesn't seem to get what had happened in court that day, Petrocelli makes sure he understands it from the plaintiffs' point of view.

On December 5, Paula Barbieri went on the trial record via her videotaped deposition. Petrocelli kept it short. He used only that portion where Barbieri confirmed that she'd left the telephone message for O.J. the day of the murders.

That same day Gelblum used the notes Lenore Walker had turned over. Her recollections of her interviews with O.J. confirmed once more that Simpson had lied about Paula's message. Petrocelli wanted the jury to consider one question: if O.J. wasn't guilty, why was he lying?

On December 6, Sharon Rufo and Juditha Brown testified briefly about their relationships with their children, a necessary formality to establish the basis for monetary damages.

As Juditha left the stand, it occurred to Petrocelli that he'd hardly seen her during the trial. He was, after all, fighting just as much for her daughter as for Fred Goldman's son. He'd expected to see the Browns in court every day they weren't needed at the custody hearings. Instead, they seemed oddly detached from the case.

On December 9, Fred Goldman, the plaintiffs' sixty-fifth and final witness, is sworn in. He has attended almost every day of the trial. Simpson sits solemnly behind Robert Baker. Never once looks at Goldman.

Petrocelli takes Goldman through his son's early years,

his ups and downs with school and numerous jobs. When Goldman weeps, Simpson shows no emotion.

Ron was no angel, Goldman says, turning toward the jury. He explains how Ron sank into debt and declared personal bankruptcy.

"Did you love your son?" Petrocelli asks carefully.

"Oh God, yes," Goldman replies. He is barely able to speak.

"Do you miss him?"

"More than you can imagine."

Petrocelli rests his case for the plaintiffs after just six weeks.

Tom Lambert can't get Simpson's courtroom conduct out of his head. The press always surrounding him, chatting, asking questions, absorbing some of the limelight. Celebrity status has trumped killer status.

Simpson is constantly playing petty games. He would stick his feet out in the aisle when Lambert approached the bench for sidebar. He'd have to step over him time and again. But then, he never has had to deal with a celebrity murderer before.

Ed Medvene has his own list of objections to Simpson's behavior in court. Many times he watched Simpson standing at the back during breaks, chatting about golf or something equally trivial, holding his arm across the door opening, so everyone who wanted to pass had to ask him to move. Far worse, there were many times Simpson seemed to be taunting Kim Goldman, deliberately trying to anger her. At least once it got so bad that it touched off a shouting match between Fred Goldman and Simpson. It energized Ed. He vowed not to ease up until he nailed Simpson absolutely and completely. O.J. might have some surface glamour, but to Medvene he is just one more mean guy.

That night when Petrocelli's team goes back to the Doubletree, Fred Goldman asks them all to join him in the little back room. He wants to express his deep gratitude for what they had done for him.

Goldman becomes surprisingly emotional. He even surprises himself. It moves all the lawyers. Goldman just wants to thank them, even though they are still a long way from the end of the trial.

Robert Baker started his defense case just minutes after Fred Goldman left the stand. His plan was to attack the police and the evidence. Then when Simpson took the stand in his own defense, he would cover domestic violence and the time line.

Philip Vannatter was Baker's first witness. Blood planting was number one on the defense hit list.

Baker intimated to Vannatter that there was no reason not to seal the envelope in which Vannatter carried Simpson reference blood unless he had wanted to take blood from the vial. Then the audiotape of the interview Simpson voluntary gave to Vannatter and Lange was played publicly for the first time. Finally Baker challenged the truthfulness of Vannatter's statements to a judge to obtain his search warrant to enter Rockingham.

The next day criminalist Andrea Mazzola responded to defense claims that she had handled the evidence carelessly. Thano Peratis testified via videotape in support of the defense assertion that he drew 7.9 to 8.1 cc's of O.J.'s blood. But, Peratis said on cross, when he heard that blood was missing from Simpson's vial, he conducted his own experiment to re-estimate how much blood he drew. He decided it might have been less than 7.9 cc's.

On Monday, December 16, the defense presented their "less is more" version of Michael Baden.

Baden challenged most of Dr. Spitz's conclusions. He explained why he felt the cuts on Simpson's fingers could not have been caused by fingernails. They were too deep and irregular, he said. They could only have been created by a piece of glass or a jagged knife.

Medvene was more concerned with the duration of the murders. When he crossed Baden, the doctor stated that Goldman might have been able to stand only five minutes. At least Medvene had gotten Baden down from his fifteen minute estimate, giving Petrocelli more support for the plaintiff's time line.

The defense then continued with an attack on the blood found in the Bronco. Gilbert Aguilar repeated his testimony that Simpson's fingerprints were not found at Bundy, and that there were unidentifiable prints at the crime scene.

On Wednesday, December 18, Dan Leonard calls Robert Groden, the defense's photographic expert. After Groden's credentials are established in a special hearing, the witness tells the jury that the original negative of Scull's photograph contains six major discrepancies. Groden uses photographic blowups to show that the negative is longer and offset when compared with other negatives on the same roll of film. He points out that the shot of Simpson wearing the Bruno Magli shoes does not have the same color balance as others on the roll. And from the knees down, the picture has a different tonal quality.

Petrocelli can see Groden is doing a good job of discrediting the photograph during the direct examination. He needs that picture to put the lie to Simpson's testimony more graphically than anything else. It is proof of perjury the jury can hold in their hands.

By now, Gelblum has investigated Groden and is prepared to attack his credentials. Groden has misrepresented his relationship with government agencies. On cross, Gelblum tries but is unable to get Groden to admit he has no facts to back up his conclusions and personal opinions. They have no scientific basis. Gelblum knows that to finish Groden off he will need their own expert, Jerry Richards. But Richards is being held in reserve for their rebuttal case.

The defense then asked the court to continue Groden's cross examination until after the holidays. Robert Blasier was scheduled for back surgery and Fredric Rieders, the defense's forensic toxicologist, had to be examined by Blasier. The plaintiffs agreed to hold Groden over until the first of the New Year.

Rieders testified about the EDTA content of the back-gate blood drops. Once again the defense stuck close to the criminal case strategy.

* * *

For the last week Kelly and Petrocelli had been nervous. They had learned that Judge Wieben Stock would announce her custody ruling by Friday. The law was in Simpson's favor. He was the natural father and had been acquitted of all criminal charges. The civil case had no legal standing in Family Court. The only issue to be settled was his fitness as a father.

Kelly felt the plaintiffs' case would be hurt if Simpson regained custody. He remembered his reaction last summer when Lou Brown called him and said they were going to drop the custody case because they "didn't have a chance."

"Have you lost your minds?" Kelly asked him. "How can you give the kids to a killer? What will the world think if you just hand the children back without a fight?"

Kelly understood only too well that winning custody would give Simpson's defense a big boost. Simpson himself might come off the ropes a different man when he took the stand again in the defense case.

Simpson was home waiting for the news. It seemed to his friends that his life was on hold until the custody issue was resolved, even though he had every indication the ruling would be favorable. He'd even invited a few members of the media, Star Jones of *American Journal,* Greta Van Susteren of CNN, and Linda Deutsch of the Associated Press, to be there when he got the news.

"The Brown family failed to show clear and convincing evidence that O.J. Simpson's custody of his children with Nicole Brown Simpson would be detrimental to the youngsters," Wieben Stock wrote. "The children share a relationship with their father that appears to be strong, positive, and healthy, with powerful psychological bonding," the ruling continued. "All experts who had the benefit of analyzing the children with all of their significant adults came to the same conclusion on this point."

That said it all. Simpson made a statement to the AP and the *Los Angeles Times* thanking the Browns for doing their best during a very difficult time.

Petrocelli knew the jury was bound to hear about it over the holidays. He could only pray he'd done a good enough job damaging Simpson's credibility.

16

GELBLUM HEADS FOR SAN FRANCISCO FOR A MUCH
needed vacation. Kelly goes back to New York. Petrocelli
stays in LA to work on the case.

On Friday, December 28, Kelly receives a phone call
from Scull's attorney, Michael Connor.

"Listen," Connor tells him, "there's this guy, Denny
Lynch, with the Bills, who's telling people there are other
photographs of Simpson in those shoes."

The last thing Kelly wants to do is to fly to Buffalo on New
Year's weekend. He tells Connor he'll get back to him. But
the call keeps nagging at Kelly. He knows the importance of
a photograph that will corroborate Scull's picture.

Monday Kelly boards a flight to Buffalo. At the Bills'
office the press is everywhere. The day before they had lost
their playoff game. Kelly becomes nervous with all the
media around, worried someone might recognize him.

Lynch says he'll look for the *Bills Report* where the
picture in question had first appeared. Kelly can't wait to
call Petrocelli at the Doubletree to update him. The good
news is that the picture had been published months before
the murders.

"Make sure nobody finds out about it," Petrocelli tells
Kelly, "and don't leave before you get me a copy."

Then Lynch walks in holding an old cardboard box.
Twenty copies of the newspaper containing the photo.
"Nobody has ever asked for this," Lynch says. "I was
never visited by the D.A.'s office or the cops." Kelly just
smiles.

The photographer is E. J. Flammer.

"Flammer is selling some of his photographs today," Lynch then tells Kelly. Kelly's smile fades.

Within hours Kelly, Flammer, and his attorney, Mark Kramer, meet for the first time. Kelly begs Flammer not to sell the photographs. Flammer says he'd be glad to help Fred Goldman, but he isn't about to let the money go out the window.

Kelly leaves with a selection of the photographs. The question left open is whether the photographs can be kept secret until Petrocelli confronts Simpson with them.

That night Petrocelli is watching television when there is a news story on ABC about the Flammer photos. He is angry. The entire element of surprise is lost.

When Gelblum gets the pictures from Kelly, he calls Petrocelli. "They're perfect, they're magnificent," he says, "they're just incredible."

Thirty eleven-by-fourteen photos of O.J. wearing the Bruno Maglis. Minutes later Petrocelli is looking at the photographs. He is awestruck. Gelblum knows this is even better than the Fuhrman tapes. Nothing slippery like attitude and motive. This is tangible physical evidence with a direct bearing on the case.

Petrocelli wanted to save the pictures for Simpson's testimony, but Gelblum wanted to use them immediately with Groden. Kelly wanted to introduce them through Flammer when the plaintiffs opened their rebuttal case. They all were afraid Fujisaki would say, "you've had these photos for a couple of weeks. You should have introduced them then." Finally they agreed to see how Groden's cross examination went.

On Monday, January 6, Groden is back on the stand. Gelblum gets Groden to admit "there was a greater than 90 percent possibility that either the pants [in the Scull photograph] and the shoes, or the pants alone were changed."

Gelblum has set up Groden for the kill. He glances over at Petrocelli. Dan nods.

"Sir, if there were other photographs of Mr. Simpson

taken on the same day, September 26, 1993, in the same stadium, at the same football game, with a different camera, by a different photographer, and Mr. Simpson had the same clothes on, same jacket, same tie, same shirt, same belt, same pants, same shoes, wouldn't that compel you to conclude that your testimony that these shoes have been [added to the photo] is wrong?''

''It wouldn't,'' Groden says.

Leonard jumps up to object. ''It's a total sandbag,'' he declares.

''That's usually what impeachment amounts to,'' Fujisaki replies. He lets Gelblum continue.

Gelblum takes eight of the Flammer photographs out of a large envelope. He hands them to the defense for review. Leonard, Phil Baker and Simpson examine the prints with a magnifying glass. Robert Baker just stays in his chair, his back to Simpson and the group.

''It would not change what [you] found in the [Scull] photograph?'' Gelblum asks. He brings the prints to Groden. Gelblum knows Groden couldn't label the Flammer photographs fakes.

''Do you see the shoes Mr. Simpson is wearing?''

''Yes,'' Groden answers.

''I ask you if that one changes your opinion, sir?'' Gelblum asks. He hands Groden another picture.

''Does not.''

''Okay.'' Gelblum, seeing that Groden is humiliated, asks the court's permission to pass all eight photos to the jury. For fifteen minutes the courtroom sits in silence. Reporters lean forward trying to see what the jury is being shown.

Would these photographs of Simpson wearing Bruno Magli ''. . . affect the conclusion you draw from your observations of the Scull photograph?'' Gelblum asks again.

''. . . If I could confirm that the photographs are legitimate, and if they can be proven that those were, in fact, Bruno Magli shoes in the photographs, I would say that it would affect my—my overall conclusion.''

Gelblum has what he wanted. ''No further questions,'' he says.

Petrocelli still considers confronting Simpson with Flammer's photos. It would be the ice cream atop the icing on the cake.

Within an hour Flammer and his attorney are selling publication rights to the photos for the evening news programs.

A friend of Simpson's could see that all the air went out of O.J.'s balloon that day. He had been shoved and knocked down, then trampled. He had no energy, no spark left in him. His friend could only hope that a defeat in the civil case would still leave Simpson resilient enough to bounce back. At least it would be over. He could go on with his life. But that day his friend saw a broken man.

Lambert knew something serious must have happened to Baker that day. Simpson had probably told him categorically: "I never wore those shoes, I never owned them, the Scull photograph is a fake." Then the Flammer photos showed up. Lambert knew that had to throw one giant monkey wrench into Baker's relationship with his client.

The defense spent the next four days presenting the rest of their witnesses. Kato Kaelin appeared again to discuss what Simpson had been wearing. His recollection of the color of Simpson's clothes did not match the fiber evidence.

Dennis Fung was called now as a defense witness. Lambert was startled when Fung was shown a new photograph of the glove found at Bundy. It looked like there was a hole in it. Fung agreed. The gloves produced in court had no holes.

The defense was trying to suggest the DA had produced the *wrong* pair of bloody gloves in court? It seemed like an act of desperation to Lambert. It would take Jerry Richards, the ex FBI photo expert, to clear up the mess. The "hole" was just a piece of debris lying on the glove.

Dr. Lee's videotaped deposition was shown and Simpson's demeanor witnesses told the same stories they had in the criminal case.

In an attempt to introduce further doubt into the case the

951

defense called Steve Merrin, an L.A.P.D. sergeant who received a call at 10:30 P.M. the night of the murders, from someone who said she was with Channel 4. The caller asked if the police were "sitting" on two bodies on the West Side. Merrin told the caller there was no knowledge of a double homicide on the West Side. The bodies of Nicole and Ron had not yet been discovered.

17

ON FRIDAY, JANUARY 10, SIMPSON TAKES THE STAND again. He looks rested and relaxed, his energy back.

Petrocelli takes a hard look at Simpson and thinks, Okay, O.J., we've got all the evidence against you. Now give us your best story. If we believe you, we'll overlook the evidence.

Robert Baker spends three hours taking O.J. through Simpson's version of his life with Nicole.

Simpson insists he wasn't vengeful. Certainly not a killer. He was a loving husband and father. He was always concerned for his ex-wife. He just didn't approve of her hanging out with prostitutes and living a questionable lifestyle.

Baker works hard at humanizing Simpson, attempting to restore his credibility.

Ed Medvene waits for Simpson to own up to at least some part of the domestic abuse problems. It never happens. Simpson just repeats that he had never hit Nicole. Medvene can see he isn't giving his attorneys much of anything to work with in their closing arguments.

* * *

On Monday, January 13, Simpson returns for his final day on the stand.

When Baker gets to the Bruno Magli shoes, Medvene expects Simpson to now say something like: "I'm really design conscious. I'd never wear unusual $150 shoes to kill my wife. Do you think I'm stupid? I'd wear the same kind of sneakers everyone owns." Nothing like that ever comes. All Simpson says is that he did not wear those shoes.

"On June 12, 1994, did you," Baker asks, "with your children in the house in their beds sleeping, murder your ex-wife, and leave her body where your kids could find it?"

"No," Simpson says firmly. "Absolutely not."

Baker finishes his direct examination. It is Petrocelli's turn.

Simpson is much more combative with Petrocelli this time. He seems to have learned his lesson: passivity doesn't pay. The judge makes it more difficult for Petrocelli as well.

Petrocelli has outlined a long cross examination, but as he begins working through it, he understood that Fujisaki isn't going to let him review ground already covered in Simpson's November testimony.

When Petrocelli gets to the 1989 New Year's Eve incident the judge cuts him off yet again. Petrocelli wants to show now that the fight hadn't been confined to their bedroom, that Simpson had followed Nicole downstairs, all the way across the house, then outside and into the housekeeper's room to confront Nicole again. He wants to show that Simpson was lying about the location and duration of the fight, that O.J. consistently changed and minimized the facts. With the judge's interruptions, it isn't working.

Petrocelli decides to shelve his entire outline and move right to the Flammer photographs.

"Mr. Simpson, when you testified last time . . . you did not know about the existence of these 30 photographs, correct?"

"No."

"And you told this jury that you were not wearing those shoes depicted in the Scull photograph, correct?"

"Correct."

"You lied to this jury?" Petrocelli asks.

"No," Simpson snapped.

"You lied to this jury." This time it was a statement. "Didn't you, sir?"

"No."

"It's still your testimony, sir, that you would never attempt to tell a lie, correct?"

"Not in a court of law, no."

"Or in anything important in your life, correct?"

"Certainly not nothing close to this important."

"By the way, did you contact anyone else [shown] in these pictures to discuss the shoes that you're wearing?"

"No."

"Did you call them to discuss what clothes they're wearing?" Petrocelli asks.

"No."

"Have you made any attempt—you, yourself, made any attempt to find out anything about these photographs?"

Baker objects. Petrocelli's statement is irrelevant. The judge sustains the objection.

Petrocelli had nothing further to ask Simpson.

At that moment, the photographs are everything. Kelly admires Petrocelli's final cross. He doesn't want to see another witness after the Flammer photos. Let the jury have that for their final impression. Kelly considers the case won.

Simpson is told he can step down.

Petrocelli wanted to do his rebuttal case in one day but actually it took two. The focus was on the blood, the EDTA, and O.J. Simpson's Bruno Magli shoes. Photo expert Jerry Richards would be Petrocelli's star witness.

On January 14, Peter Gelblum did the direct examination with the former head of the FBI photographic department. Richards started by refuting Robert Groden's opinions. "I could find no indication whatsoever . . ." he said, "of any sign of alteration to any portion of the [Scull] photograph." Richards said the photograph was authentic and hadn't been tampered with in any way.

Richards then went step by step through every one of Groden's accusations, showing the jury the mistakes Groden had made. Groden had even used an ordinary copier in a

Kinko's outlet to make the enlargements he used for his "accurate" measurements.

That afternoon, E. J. Flammer, the twenty-four-year-old photographer, testified that he'd shot his thirty photographs the same day the Scull photograph was taken. He could even produce the field press pass he had worn that day.

Brian Lysaght, a civil attorney in Santa Monica, was quoted by the press that night. "If the shoe photos hold up," he said, "nothing else matters."

On Thursday, January 16, Richards was back on the stand confirming that Flammer's photographs were authentic. Under cross examination he admitted that a motivated forger with time and good equipment could fake photographs. But, he insisted, Flammer's shots were no forgeries.

William Bodziak then testified that Simpson was wearing the Bruno Magli shoes in both Scull's and Flammer's photos. And the Bruno Maglis on Simpson were the same style as those worn by whoever had left bloody footprints at the Bundy crime scene.

Petrocelli rested their rebuttal case. The defense didn't call any additional witnesses.

As Medvene walked back to the Doubletree that day, he knew the plaintiffs had had two jobs to do. One was to present the case as effectively as they could. The second was to try it clean, minus the racial overtones that had muddied all the issues in the criminal case. If they had met both goals—and Medvene felt they had—they had reason to feel satisfied. A verdict of liability would be icing on the cake.

Prepare as hard as you can. Work as hard as you can. Hope you'll win. Medvene felt that was how any lawyer worth his fee handled a case. If you don't win, move on to the next battle.

Petrocelli, who had come down with the flu, asked the judge for a day's delay so he could be better prepared for closing arguments. Fujisaki looked at him with total incredulity. You've got to be kidding, his stare said. You want extra time just because you're sick? You could argue this case in your sleep. Judge Fujisaki turned him down.

18

ON TUESDAY, JANUARY 21, PETROCELLI IS FULL OF passion and energy as he starts his closing arguments.

His plan is to tell the story of Simpson's life with Nicole and establish the foundation for Tom Lambert's review of the physical evidence. The dull monotone of his opening statement is ancient history now. Never before in any case has he had such a total grasp of the facts, or deeper conviction of their truth. Petrocelli knows that the truth will be obvious to the jury.

He speaks of the many clues in Simpson's life that say O.J. had the character to kill, had the motive to kill, and finally *had* killed.

"These crucial bits of evidence are the voices of Ron and Nicole speaking to us from the grave, telling us, telling all of you, that there's a killer in this courtroom," he says. Then he points to Simpson, who looks up. "That is the man who attacked them, who confronted them, who killed them that Sunday in June. *That* man, the defendant, Orenthal Simpson."

Petrocelli looks straight at each juror. They are bonded now in a common cause. He knows they are all here to right a wrong. To bring some measure of justice to the deaths of Nicole Brown Simpson and Ron Goldman.

Petrocelli again presents the most dramatic evidence of the trial, the thirty photographs of O.J. wearing those Bruno Magli shoes. He hammers home the point that Simpson *still* denies wearing those shoes, denies it even when confronted with the evidence.

"If the photo is real, O.J. Simpson is the killer,"

Petrocelli shouts. "This is the kind of man . . . who has lied and lied and lied and *lied* to you about every important fact in this case. Every one of them."

The next day, January 22, Petrocelli continues reading from Simpson's deposition, from his police statement, and from Lenore Walker's notes to point out most of Simpson's lies.

Petrocelli ends the first part of his closing somberly. He quotes a sixteenth-century poet, Guillaume Du Bartas:

> *My lovely living boy,*
> *My hope, my happiness,*
> *My love, my life, my joy.*

"Fred Goldman's 'lovely, living boy,'" Petrocelli says quietly, "is no more."

Despite a bad cold, Baker comes out hitting hard on his client's behalf. Like Petrocelli, he covers Simpson's life, this time from O.J.'s point of view. With a raspy voice and a cough, Baker explains to the jury that Robert Blasier will present the defense response to the physical evidence and the facts that supported that evidence has been planted.

Then Baker attacks Fred Goldman. "This isn't a fight for justice," he insists. "It's a fight for money." He notes that Fred Goldman has sold his book rights for $450,000.

Then Baker's narrative becomes disjointed, wandering from subject to subject, getting the date of the murders wrong time and again.

Simpson's face hardens. He looks very disturbed. His distress seems to grow as the day wears on. At four in the afternoon, O.J. sends a note to Baker at the podium. He virtually jerks him away from the jury. Things aren't going the way Simpson wants. He demands a break to speak to Baker.

Baker needs to buy time. He needs a few days to get over his cold and resolve his differences with his client. More important, he has to determine the strongest points of their case and how to best deliver them. How to neutralize what they hope the jury would ignore. Baker and his team know if they are to have any chance at a hung jury, they have to do the job their way. It is long past time for Simpson to step aside. Baker needs until Monday. He will have Blasier and Leonard do their closing arguments to buy him that time.

On Thursday, January 23, Robert Blasier and Dan Leonard took over. Judge Fujisaki wasn't happy when Baker said he himself wouldn't be ready until Monday morning.

Blasier followed the broad outlines of the criminal case to attack the physical evidence. EDTA and wet swatches that transferred blood when they should have been dry. Evidence that showed up weeks, months, and even years after the murders, from the blood in the Bronco to the Flammer photographs. Blasier insisted that the blood and other physical evidence was contaminated, corrupted, compromised. Blasier was a compelling figure. He was still recovering from back surgery and had to address the jury from a wheelchair. Barry Scheck's voice echoed unheard behind him as he told the jury that the evidence was "garbage in, garbage out." There was "something wrong."

At the end of Blasier's four-hour summation, the battle of plaintiffs' objections became so fierce that both sides were sniping at each other in front of the jury.

Dan Leonard's job was to discredit all the photographs of Simpson wearing the Bruno Magli shoes. He attacked both photographers and their motives, questioning why the evidence had surfaced so late. He asked the jury to use their common sense in analyzing the evidence and the photographs.

On Monday, January 27, Robert Baker concludes his closing arguments on behalf of Simpson. He speaks just above a whisper to the jury.

"You can't give Ron Goldman's life back," Baker says, "but you can give Mr. Simpson his life back." He asks the jury to give a loving father back to Justin and Sydney.

Then Baker turns nasty, attacking Fred Goldman and even Ron himself. He chides Goldman senior for his "tough love" parenting and for not helping his son out of bankruptcy. "He'd be lucky to have a credit card [today]," Baker sneers. "Don't buy into these emotional ideas because it isn't reality." He ends by implying that Simpson was the true victim in the case.

In the afternoon Tom Lambert presented the first part of plaintiffs' rebuttal closing. As he rose to address the jury, he realized Baker hadn't presented a coherent narrative. He'd made isolated points, thrown things out at the jury, and hoped something would stick.

Lambert never considered what the term "preponderance of evidence" meant. The team had decided to prove its case one hundred percent. Show that one hundred percent of the physical evidence demonstrates that Simpson is the killer. Every bit of it points to him.

Lambert took the transcript of Blasier's closing. You know Mr. Blasier said this, but the expert said the contrary. Mr. Blasier says the expert said this, but the expert actually said something different. It was fun for Lambert. He could tell the jury was rolling right along with him. The evidence was on his side. He felt like he was rounding third coming home.

At 10:05 A.M., on Tuesday, January 28, Dan Petrocelli presents his final statement to the jury.

"I want you to think about this," he begins. "If O.J. Simpson was innocent, truly innocent . . . this young man [Ron Goldman] tried to save the life of the mother of his [Simpson's] children. He [would be] a hero to O.J. Simpson."

Then Petrocelli addresses Baker's closing on Monday. The lead defense counsel had tauntingly argued that the Goldmans' lawsuit could be filed by anyone with the two-hundred-dollar filing fee, whatever the evidence.

"My stomach turned when I heard that," Petrocelli says now, turning to face Simpson. He extends a fistful of cash to O.J. "You know, Mr. Simpson, here's two hundred dollars. You want it?" He pauses. The entire courtroom is frozen, silent. "Give me back my client's son." His words cut the air like a knife.

Simpson stares back, stolid, indifferent.

Baker's professional calm falls apart. "Give it up," Baker shouts to Petrocelli.

Petrocelli ignores him. He gives the hushed room a moment to ponder Baker's lapse. Then he continued: ". . . Two people lost their lives. They deserve their due . . ." He points to O.J. "And the man who took their lives should be held accountable."

Petrocelli ends with a quote from Daniel Webster, who, he said, over 150 years ago had been addressing a jury "just like this one in a case involving murder.

"'Absence of duty pursues us forever. If we take to ourselves the wings of the morning, and dwell in the uttermost parts of the sea, duty performed or duty violated is still with us, for our happiness, for our misery.'"

Petrocelli sits down. He has done all he can.

Arthur Groman was still in the courtroom as the jury was instructed and withdrew to begin deliberations. He was mentor to all the attorneys for the plaintiffs. A senior partner at the firm, almost a Supreme Court justice himself, he had represented Howard Hughes and was Armand Hammer's personal lawyer for over thirty years. He'd even questioned Eleanor Roosevelt on the witness stand.

Groman was the plaintiffs' secret weapon. He had watched almost the entire criminal trial on TV. Now, Petrocelli asked Groman to take second chair. It was Arthur who came up with the poem Dan used at the end of his closing. Groman read and reread all the outlines for opening and closing arguments. His insights were a priceless resource for the team throughout the trial. Sometimes Groman could find the one sentence, the one key phrase, that brought everything together for the team. A fine writer and orator himself, now in his eighties, he didn't need the spotlight. He had spent a lifetime there. Now he enjoyed leaving it to the younger lawyers in the firm.

19

No one was prepared for events outside the court-room. Overnight the media increased their numbers tenfold. The attorneys themselves couldn't get across the parking lot to the courthouse. Network anchors flew out from New York. The low-key O.J. II had suddenly become O.J. I.

Petrocelli found waiting for the verdict torture. The first day he couldn't make himself leave the courtroom. Then he went back to his "cocoon," as he was now calling the Doubletree. The plaintiffs huddled in two small rooms, fretting and worrying, trying to tease scraps of meaning from the readbacks the jury requested.

Simpson talked to his friends. He knew what was going to happen. It wasn't the end of the world for him.

One friend of his knew O.J. had become a person who didn't give a fuck about white America. Simpson knew America—the white majority, that is—would feast on a guilty verdict. Let them enjoy themselves. His friend knew Simpson would ignore them. Maybe now he could get on with his life.

On Tuesday, February 4, at about 3 P.M., the jury finishes hearing a readback of Al Cowlings' testimony. John Kelly is sitting in his room at Shutters, trying to figure out what it means. Cowlings had been his witness.

Kelly has just hung up with the war room at the Double-tree when the phone rings again. It is Erin Kenny, the judge's clerk. "John, I'm calling you . . ."

"There's a verdict," Kelly cuts in.

"Yeah, we have a verdict. And I haven't told anybody else yet. Don't mention it to anybody. Just get your clients up here for it."

John can't see how the jury could have found Simpson liable so quickly. They haven't had enough time since the readback to set compensatory damages. Kelly calls Lou Brown's foundation office where everyone is supposed to be on standby, sixty miles away in Laguna Beach. Lou had just stepped out to run errands. He'd waited all day and finally gave up. Juditha wasn't home. Their cell phones didn't answer. Kelly kept trying every five minutes.

At 4:30 P.M. Erin calls back. She wants to know how soon the Browns will be in court. Kelly explains what is happening. "You haven't even talked to them," she says. "I'll tell the judge."

A minute later she calls again. The verdict will be read at 5:30 with or without the clients. Kelly should be in court representing them. Finally the Browns call Kelly. They don't want to leave without Nicole's sister, Denise. Even if they started out immediately, there is no way they can be in Los Angeles before seven with rush hour traffic.

At 5:30 Erin calls Kelly to find out why he isn't in court. "The judge wants you over here now," she says. As Kelly listens he keeps one eye on his TV, and sees Petrocelli and the Goldmans arrive. He can hear the helicopters and see the spotlights from his window. Simpson's Suburban pulls up while Erin is still trying to convince Kelly to show up alone.

In Washington, President Clinton is about to make his State of the Union address. It is 6 P.M. California time. The President knows the Simpson verdict is due at just about the same time he will begin. The President asks to be kept apprised. If the verdict comes in at 9 P.M. in the East, Clinton can slow down his walk into Congress. He even considers referring to the verdict if it is announced before he starts, then decides not to.

At Shutters, Erin is calling yet again. "I'm not coming in without my clients," Kelly says. He knows the judge wouldn't take the verdict without someone present representing the Browns. By 6:30 the Browns still hadn't arrived. Hotel security is now guarding Kelly's room to keep the press away.

Again the phone rings. The front desk this time. "There are a couple of sheriffs here from the court," the clerk says. "Can they come up to your room?"

"No. Just tell them I'll be out shortly," Kelly says.

The judge has sent them to impress upon Kelly that he is wanted in court. Now.

When the Browns call and say they are minutes away, Kelly finally steps outside into the glare of lights. Four sheriffs' cars are waiting for him.

As Gelblum waits in the courtroom he looks over to where Simpson is seated. "This guy couldn't have done that deed," he thinks. "This handsome, charming guy sitting over there chatting so easily with the press—I can't see that man doing this."

Then reality hits. He is curious. What has O.J. done with the weapon and the clothes? Where did he get rid of them?

20

THEN EVERYONE IS SEATED. A PACKED COURTROOM. SHER-iffs everywhere. The room is stuffy. It is past closing time for the courthouse.

At 7:12 Judge Hiroshi Fujisaki takes the bench and asks for the jury.

Simpson is stone faced as he sits in front of the rail. He looks straight ahead as Phil Baker puts his arm around him and occasionally squeezes his neck. At the plaintiffs' table Petrocelli is apprehensive, Medvene nervous, Lambert calm as usual.

One by one the jury take their seats. One Latino, one Asian, one black/Asian, and nine whites. And the two surviving alternates. All of them dressed to go home, holding their notebooks. They look tired.

Not one of them looks at the Goldmans, at Rufo, or at the Browns. Simpson's jaw starts to quiver. Robert Baker stares at the jury. Dan Leonard leans far back in his chair.

The bailiff hands a slim manila envelope to the jury foreman, who opens the envelope and reviews its contents. He informs the judge they are the jury's findings. Then Fujisaki reads it silently and hands it to his clerk.

Erin Kenny reads the verdict. "Did you find by a preponderance of the evidence that defendant Simpson willfully and wrongfully caused the death of Ronald Goldman?" Erin reads. "Write the answer 'yes' or 'no' below." She pauses.

"Yes."

Simpson doesn't move. His jaw continues to quiver.

Cheers and gasps engulf the courtroom. "Oh, my God," Kim Goldman shouts, "you murderer!"

Goldman's attorneys echo, yes, yes, yes. Petrocelli loses track of everything. Fred Goldman starts crying, clutching his wife Patti's hand.

Petrocelli looks at the jury. Tears come to his eyes. For the first time in the entire trial a juror makes eye contact. Then another juror, in seat number eleven, just nods.

The judge quiets the courtroom so that his clerk can read the balance of the verdicts. Simpson is guilty of causing the death of his ex-wife Nicole Brown Simpson. The jury awards the plaintiffs $8.5 million in compensatory damages. Later they will be awarded another $25 million in punitive damages.

Finally Petrocelli looks at Simpson, who is staring vacantly up at the ceiling. "You're lucky to be a free man," he says to himself.

* * *

President Clinton had just finished his speech when the verdicts were read. Minutes before, stations throughout the country had gone to split-screen coverage of both events, showing both the President and the crowds outside the courthouse. As the President thanked the Congress and the nation and moved away from the podium, the first verdict was read. On most stations, Clinton wound up in the small box in the corner of the screen as Simpson left the courthouse.

Mark Fuhrman was at the Roxbury Capital Hotel in New York City getting ready to be interviewed by ABC's *Prime Time Live*. Brad Roberts, his partner, had joined him. When they heard the verdict was coming down, they ordered room service—a New York steak and beer—and turned on the TV.

When the first verdict was announced Fuhrman turned and looked at Roberts.

"*ALL RIGHT!*" Fuhrman shouted.

Fuhrman liked the fact that things would now be difficult for Simpson.

After the verdict, the jury spoke privately to the attorneys. They had, by and large, dealt first with the physical evidence. They seized on the blood trail at Bundy. They realized that there was no way it could all have been planted. They pretty much discounted the socks found in the bedroom and the glove. But the blood trail at Bundy had never been explained away. The photographs of O.J. in the Bruno Magli shoes were the strongest single piece of evidence.

When they finished with the physical evidence they looked at Simpson's credibility. Nobody on the jury believed that he'd never hit his ex-wife. They were equally sure he'd lied about not owning the Bruno Magli shoes.

Lambert knew what the jury was saying: the physical evidence proves he did it. Moreover, he seems to us not to be telling the truth. Once the jury settled those two points, it was over for Simpson.

21

A WEEK LATER, PETROCELLI IS FLYING TO NEW YORK to do some TV shows, and there, sitting just across the aisle, is Al Pacino. Petrocelli loved *The Godfather,* all the *Godfather* movies. He knows all the lines. Pacino is his favorite actor.

Then Pacino looks over at Petrocelli and Dan takes that as his cue to cross the aisle and introduce himself. "I know who you are," Pacino says. The two men chat.

Later, sitting alone again, Petrocelli realizes he has just met a *real* celebrity. He also knows his life has changed forever. He will always be identified with Simpson just as Pacino will always be linked with *The Godfather.*

Being the guy who beat Simpson, Petrocelli knows, is unquestionably an asset, but can he prevent it from defining the rest of his life?

Medvene decides to clean out his desk. He finds something he'd put there during another case, when he'd come back from San Quentin. He had just seen a client in the death row visiting room. He'd written a few paragraphs on the way home after his first or second trip there. It had had nothing to do with the details of the case. There was no need to file it. But he'd kept it for some reason, stuffed it in his desk years ago.

He'd watched the people in the death row visiting room. The wives and girlfriends, the family members, the kids at the vending machine. He'd been in the same room with men he'd read about, men whose notorious cases had made headlines. Yet there was no violence in that room. There were just people. Condemned men he could talk to, or might have had dinner with.

Medvene looks again at what he'd written. Reads it several times. There has to be a reason he keeps staring at the thoughts he'd jotted down so long ago. Then it hits him.

He knows he could never have feelings like those about Simpson, if he had been in that room. In the death row visiting room there was resignation, there was peace, there was an inescapable sense that no matter how antisocial the behavior, how horrendous the crime had been, there was humanity. No one in that room was the center of his own world. He saw growth in those convicted and condemned men.

Medvene had never seen any growth in O.J. No insight. No change. He sees no humanity in Simpson.

Simpson has so many defenses. Shields and walls, towers and battlements, a moat around it all, and the drawbridge always up. And inside the walls, behind the gates, O.J. is lord of the manor, master of all he surveys.

He is the center.

O.J. Simpson is a whole different kind of man from those guys in San Quentin.

EPILOGUE

BEFORE THE CIVIL TRIAL STARTED, ON SATURDAY, JUNE 29, 1996, O.J. Simpson hosted a black-tie fund-raiser for the Stop the Violence, Increase the Peace Foundation on the grounds of his Rockingham estate. Some three hundred guests paid from $100 to $1,000 to attend.

Late in the evening, when most of the guests had left, Linda Deutsch of the Associated Press and Mark Brown from KABC-TV sat with Simpson at his dining room table. This was the first time Deutsch had spoken to Simpson face to face. Two days later, her story was released by the Associated Press.

> . . . But sometimes at night, Simpson admits that he wanders the rooms and grounds of his elegant estate pondering his past and future.
>
> "I can get outside of it and try to be objective," Simpson said. "But I walk around the house some nights and I get angry. I get angry with Nicole.
>
> "I've been to the grave and I've just gone off at her," he said. Why is he angry at Nicole? Simpson seemed lost for words.
>
> "Nicole was a good person," he said after a pause. "Maybe a little lost in the last years of her life. But she was a good person . . . ."
>
> —Linda Deutsch, AP, July 1, 1996

ACKNOWLEDGMENTS

I AM ESPECIALLY GRATEFUL TO ROBERT KARDASHIAN, with whom I worked most closely and who has assisted me in the preparation of this book.

My own involvement in the Simpson defense presented me with a dilemma. Unlike most writers covering the case, I knew Robert Kardashian personally and spoke to him often. No journalist would have passed up the opportunity to meet Simpson in October and November 1994, while he awaited trial. But by assisting him in writing his book, *I Want to Tell You*, I was understandably viewed by many as a member of Simpson's team. As a friend of Kardashian's, I had access to some members of the defense team, and my relationships with them grew as the trial proceeded. An incidental event in which I participated in the case has been noted in the text.

During the course of the trial I was approached by many publications, including *The New York Times*, the *Los Angeles Times*, *The Washington Post*, *Time*, and *Newsweek*, to comment and provide information on the trial and related events. In all cases I responded to inquiries as appropriately as I could.

Inevitably, there came a day, after the verdict in the criminal trial, when I knew I had to step away from being on the inside and resume a normal journalistic stance, free to tell the inside story without obligation to Simpson or his defense. I knew my involvement with Simpson and *I Want to Tell You* would always cast some shadow on my work regardless of the verdict or of Simpson's guilt or innocence. That was the reality of the situation. I was and remain prepared to live with it. I told O.J. Simpson and his attorney

969

Skip Taft that I would work with Robert Kardashian on a book that would include Bob's story as well as the recollections of other members of the defense. They voiced no objection.

I decided to portray Simpson only through the eyes and ears of third parties. My private conversations with him would never be used in this book. I never asked him for an interview for this book and he never offered one. I do want to state for the record that nothing he said to me would have changed a word of this book. My agreement with Simpson makes clear that I am free to write a book of my own without any obligation to him. Indeed, neither Simpson nor any of the lawyers who argued in court had any approval over, and did not even review, any of the contents of this work.

During and after the criminal trial I had a number of conversations with Robert Shapiro and Johnnie Cochran, but no formal interviews were conducted. Nonetheless, I thank them for the insights and help they afforded me. In acknowledging this cooperation, I do not suggest that either Shapiro or Cochran has endorsed or approved this book.

During the last year I have come to respect the members of the defense team and, on the whole, their effort—notwithstanding a number of specific controversies along the way.

The name of Robert Kardashian's college friend has been omitted and identifying details changed to protect his privacy. In six places the names of third parties have been omitted at the request of the person providing the information. This book contains no fictitious names or events.

The "wildfire" epigraph that begins the book is excerpted from my interview with Al Cowlings.

I am grateful to the following who generously allowed me to interview them: Dr. Michael Baden, F. Lee Bailey, Dr. Ed Blake, Bob Blasier, Sara Caplan, Shawn Chapman, Al Cowlings, Robert Craig, Alan Dershowitz, Carl Douglas, Rosey Grier, Howard Harris, Robert Kardashian, Dr. Henry Lee, Charles Lindner, Pat McKenna, John McNally, Bill Pavelic, Barry Scheck, Gerry Spence, Dr. William Thompson, Gerry Uelmen, Dr. Barbara Wolf, and Dr. Bernard

Yudowitz. A special thanks to Gary Sims and George "Woody" Clarke for their help on the scientific issues.

Three journalists who covered the criminal trial were interviewed about events they reported. At their request, credit is given within the text. Three additional sources have asked to remain anonymous.

In addition I wish to thank Michael Brewer, Paul Callan, Mark Fuhrman, Peter Gelblum, John Kelly, Tom Lambert, Edward Medvene, Arthur Parra, Daniel Petrocelli, and Natasha Roit, who granted me interviews pertaining to the civil action brought against Mr. Simpson in Santa Monica, California.

James Willwerth, himself the author of four nonfiction books, shares credit for this book. In November 1995 I asked Jim to collaborate with me. He received a leave from *Time* magazine, for which he covered the trial, and shared the writing responsibility with me throughout the first draft of this book. We discussed, sometimes argued, and even fought about what a line from an interview might mean, or when some events took place. Jim went far beyond the call of duty, and his devotion to this work will long be remembered.

The contributions of Kathy Braidhill and Judith McNally were indispensable.

Judith McNally was my consultant from the first stages of this book until its completion. Her advice and suggestions have affected the book throughout; to say that Judith was an invaluable colleague would be an understatement.

Kathy Braidhill, a writer of nonfiction books, was first recommended to me by David Margolick of *The New York Times*. Kathy possesses a unique understanding of the case on many levels. She soon became my right hand, reviewing all my interviews and organizing the material for both Jim and me. Her expertise in various aspects of the case has helped shape this work.

Dan Whitcomb, a freelance journalist who covered the civil trial, analyzed my interviews and arranged my material for the section of this book that relates to the civil case. His unclouded view of the events was an enormous help to me.

Anne Garofalo and Brenda Williams aided Jim and me as editorial assistants, and their dedication helped make this book possible. David Barron, Dennis Litwin, and David Eck also made significant contributions.

A special acknowledgement is due to Sandy Lyon of Sandy and Company, who provided the office staff and who personally labored seven days a week on countless occasions.

I offer grateful appreciation and much admiration to Jason Epstein, whose critical insights on every aspect of this book guided me during this entire project. My thanks also go to Harry Evans, Joy de Menil, Andy Carpenter, Jolanta Benal, Benjamin Dreyer, Kathy Rosenbloom, and Walter Weintz at Random House, and to my son, Howard Schiller, for his design concepts.

A hearty thanks to John Taylor Williams, of Palmer and Dodge, who has assisted me on three book projects, and to Kelli Sager, of Davis Wright Tremaine, who reviewed the manuscript for me.

—LAWRENCE SCHILLER
April 26, 1997

INDEX

A

Aaron, Richard, 603–604
Aaronson, Ellen, 592, 641–42, 643, 837
Abrahamson, Alan, 765
Aguilar, Gil, 722–23
Alan (Grill maître d'), 113–14
Albaneze, Michael, 90
Ali, Shaheed, 822
Alibaruho, Gloria, 409
Allen, Kathryn, 124, 211, 303
Allen, Marcus, 14, 124, 211–12, 268, 302–303, 454, 632, 732, 770
Allred, Gloria, 120, 582, 811
American Journal, 159–60, 947
American Tragedy, 919, 934, 939
Amerman, Kathy, 872
"Anita" (witness), 171
Arguedas, Cristina, 594, 625–27, 632, 673
Associated Press, 947
Aston, Officer, 546
Austin, Alan, 124
Azoff, Irving, 4
Azoff, Shelli, 4, 5, 108

B

Baden, Michael, 42–43, 58, 59–60, 66–69, 76, 77, 90, 97, 125–27, 139, 142, 145–47, 168, 173–74, 178, 227, 236, 255–56, 284, 316, 353, 364, 380–81, 416, 435, 488–89, 517, 524, 561, 575, 591, 683, 697, 701–707, 735, 760, 884, 895, 919, 945
Baden, Sarah, 167
Bailey, F. Lee, 44–46, 50, 51, 81, 97–98, 109, 119–20, 154–55, 166–69, 173, 174–76, 183, 184, 187–88, 190, 193, 194–95, 201, 202, 210, 215, 220–21, 223, 256–57, 260, 285, 289, 292–93, 334, 345, 346, 353, 354–55, 356, 364, 367–68, 371, 380, 388, 398, 419, 422–25, 429, 438, 455, 466, 500, 504, 508, 519, 537–38, 556, 592, 594, 607, 634, 639, 641, 654, 660–61, 672, 684, 686, 687, 699, 708, 729, 741, 744, 752, 754, 756, 759, 762, 767–70, 772–73, 781, 783, 785, 806, 819–20, 873, 881, 932
blood evidence and, 236, 353, 368, 389, 415–16, 422

973

H

Haber, Alan, 885

Halicki, Denice Shakarian, 6, 31, 42, 48, 55, 61, 62, 65, 73, 98, 115, 152, 154, 162, 187, 212, 213, 232, 300, 635, 688

Hampton, Tracy, 562

Hannak, Carol, 537–38

Hard Copy, 118, 171, 185, 210

Harman, Francesca, 592, 643

Harmon, Rockne, 219–20, 397, 486, 489, 533–34, 571, 572, 573, 574, 583, 585, 659, 674, 693, 694, 695, 799, 894, 895

Harris, Art, 393

Harris, Howard, 195, 201, 228–29, 231–32, 257, 319, 379, 380, 391, 404, 426, 518, 524, 865, 873

Harris, Jeanette, 535–36, 539, 541, 554, 579–80

Harris, Robert Alton, 12

Harris, Wilmer J., 400

Hartl, Dan, 350

Hearst, Patty, 44, 183, 787

Heider, Bill, 129, 131–32

Heidstra, Robert, 205–206, 222–23, 277, 468, 562, 644–49, 650, 703, 837, 895, 917, 921

Heiser, Stephen, 653

Hertz, 14, 32, 165–66, 330, 357, 410, 411, 656

Hirsch, Richard, 162

Hitler, Adolf, 821, 844, 845, 846

Hodge, Roderic, 538, 592, 754, 756, 758–59, 773, 783–85

Hodgman, Janet, 485–86

Hodgman, William, 140–41, 157, 158, 202–203, 245, 256, 273, 275, 326–28, 329, 352, 426, 434–38, 446, 485–86, 553, 714, 715, 806, 810, 857, 858, 882, 897, 941

Hookstratten, Ed, 113–14, 211–12

Hostetler, Barry, 184

House of Blues, 29

Hudson, Dr. H. Range, 477

Hughes, David, 161, 177

Hughes, Wayne, 8–9, 51, 65, 84–85, 101, 112, 116–17, 124–25, 160–61, 176, 177–79, 190, 204, 211, 241, 246

Huizenga, Robert, 48, 49, 65, 67, 72, 77, 90, 589–90, 656–57, 658–59, 661–62

I

Innocence Project, 203

Inside Edition, 29, 159–60, 659

Ito, Lance A., 156–57, 194, 222, 234, 241, 242, 256, 267, 268–70, 278, 288–90, 296, 297, 316, 325, 329, 340, 347, 348, 350, 351–53, 358, 359–60, 361, 366, 369, 397–99, 414–15, 424–25, 427, 434–35, 438, 439–40, 446, 455, 458, 471, 473, 474, 479, 484, 485–86, 492–95, 507, 509, 513, 521, 529, 548, 557–58, 560–61, 568, 571, 583–84, 592, 596, 599, 600, 602–603, 607–608, 622, 623–24,

M

McAlary, Mike, 343, 395, 396–97
McCabe, Ed, 461
McCollum, Thomas C., III, 620–21, 633
MacDonell, Herbert, 591, 669, 670–71, 679–81, 688–89, 807, 808, 848, 850
McGinnis, Joe, 748, 865
Mack, John, 193
McKay, Patti Jo, 111
McKenna, Pat, 45, 50–51, 81, 83–84, 164–66, 167, 174, 182–89, 201, 202, 210–12, 215, 222, 223, 228–29, 230, 248, 249, 260, 277, 318, 344–45, 354, 364, 367–68, 379–80, 384, 391, 396–97, 403–404, 414–15, 416, 426, 439, 490–91, 493, 495, 497, 518, 592, 593, 603, 614–15, 616, 632, 641, 645, 646, 652–53, 665, 667, 682, 755, 760–61, 766, 772, 873
McKenzie, Al, 702
McKinny, Laura Hart, 652–53, 654, 659, 665, 671–72, 684–86, 700, 707–708, 723, 724, 725, 729, 741, 744–46, 754, 769, 775–83, 794, 795, 797
McKinny tapes, 881, 897, 911
McMorron, Brian, 172, 186
McNally, John, 45–46, 50, 174, 182–83, 185–86, 187, 202, 210–11, 215, 222–23, 228–30, 233, 245, 289–90, 318–19, 343, 368, 371–72, 395–96, 426, 603–604

Madden, Bob, 159–60
Maddox, Art, 520
Maghame, Shoreen, 603, 867
Magnera, Guy, 516–17, 559–60
Maltz, Bertram, 590
Mandel, Danny, 592, 641–43, 837
Margolick, David, 411, 865
Marks, Louis, 65, 124
Martinez, Carlos, 184–85
Martz, Roger, 571, 634, 675–77
Matheson, Greg, 179, 269, 287, 390, 563, 564, 922
Maxwell, Officer, 553
Mazzola, Andrea, 136–37, 138, 222, 234, 235, 288, 390, 484, 485, 526, 539, 540, 541–42, 547, 559, 560, 561, 666, 668, 738, 839, 883, 945
MCA, 719, 728
Medvene, Ed, 879, 880, 884, 889, 894, 895–96, 898, 908, 915–16, 921, 925, 926, 931, 937, 941, 944, 945, 952, 966–67
  crime scene experts, and, 883
  Henry Lee deposition, 909–10
  at trial, 925–26
"Men Against Women," 341, 342
Menendez, Eric, 102, 105
Menendez trial, 107
Mengers, Sue, 162
Menzione, Lori, 750
Meraz, John, 185, 664, 671
Merrill, Jim, 164, 165, 656
Merrin, Steve, 952
Meyer, Ron, 719
Mezzaluna, 31, 172, 183, 207, 224, 229, 289, 355, 466, 473, 480, 641, 642

989

Y

Z

ABOUT THE AUTHORS

LAWRENCE SCHILLER WAS BORN IN 1936 IN BROOKLYN, and grew up in San Diego. After graduating from Pepperdine College, he went to work for *Life* magazine and the *Saturday Evening Post* as a photojournalist. He published his first book, *LSD*, in 1966. Since then he has published eleven books, including W. Eugene Smith's *Minamata* and Norman Mailer's *Marilyn*. He collaborated with Albert Goldman on *Ladies and Gentleman, Lenny Bruce* and with Norman Mailer on *The Executioner's Song* and *Oswald's Tale*. He has directed seven motion pictures and miniseries for television; *The Executioner's Song* and *Peter the Great* won five Emmys.

JAMES WILLWERTH, who collaborated on this book, was born in 1943 and has published four books, including *Eye in the Last Storm,* a journal of the Vietnam War. After graduating from the University of California at Berkeley he joined *Time* magazine, where he has been a correspondent specializing in social and psychiatric issues for thirty years. His stories have received awards from the National Alliance for the Mentally Ill, the American Bar Association, and the American Speech-Language-Hearing Association.